Jenn Kwon
jkwon217@gmail.com
951.515.6862

W9-CPE-730

Environmental Justice

Environmental Justice

Law, Policy & Regulation

Second Edition

Clifford Rechtschaffen

PROFESSOR,
GOLDEN GATE UNIVERSITY SCHOOL OF LAW

Eileen Gauna

PROFESSOR,
UNIVERSITY OF NEW MEXICO SCHOOL OF LAW

Catherine A. O'Neill

ASSOCIATE PROFESSOR,
SEATTLE UNIVERSITY SCHOOL OF LAW

CAROLINA ACADEMIC PRESS
Durham, North Carolina

Copyright © 2009
Clifford Rechtschaffen
Eileen Gauna
Catherine A. O'Neill
All Rights Reserved

Library of Congress Cataloging-in-Publication Data

Rechtschaffen, Clifford, 1957-
   Environmental justice : law, policy & regulation / Clifford Rechtschaffen, Eileen
Gauna, Catherine A. O'Neill. -- 2nd ed.
      p. cm.
   Previouse ed. has subtitle: Law, policy, and regulation.
   Includes bibliographical references and index.
   ISBN 978-1-59460-595-6 (alk. paper)
   1. Environmental law--United States. 2. Environmental justice. I. Gauna, Eileen P.,
1953- II. O'Neill, Catherine A. III. Title.

   KF3775.R385 2009
   344.7304'6--dc22

                                   2009022323

Carolina Academic Press
700 Kent Street
Durham, North Carolina 27701
Telephone (919) 489-7486
Fax (919) 493-5668
www.cap-press.com

Printed in the United States of America

In Fond Memory of Luke Cole,
Center on Race, Poverty & the Environment
Clifford Rechtschaffen
Eileen Gauna
Catherine A. O'Neill

To my dad, for his great example
Clifford Rechtschaffen

In Memory of Jeanne Gauna,
SouthWest Organizing Project
Eileen Gauna

To Conor and Tiarnan
Catherine A. O'Neill

Summary of Contents

Preface   xxi

Acknowledgments   xxiii

Chapter 1 · Overview of the Environmental Justice Movement   3

Chapter 2 · The Evidence   35

Chapter 3 · Theories of Causation   73

Chapter 4 · American Indians and Environmental Justice   107

Chapter 5 · Regulation and the Administrative State   139

Chapter 6 · Risk and Health   175

Chapter 7 · Standard Setting   213

Chapter 8 · Permits and Public Enforcement   249

Chapter 9 · Contaminated Properties   285

Chapter 10 · Governmental Initiatives to Address Environmental Justice   317

Chapter 11 · Land Use Planning, Environmental Review, and Information
             Disclosure Laws   355

Chapter 12 · Responding to the Challenge of Climate Change   389

Chapter 13 · Litigation, Citizen Enforcement, and Common Law Remedies   433

Chapter 14 · Constitutional and Civil Rights Claims   471

Index   519

Contents

Preface   xxi

Acknowledgments   xxiii

Chapter 1 • Overview of the Environmental Justice Movement   3
  A. Introduction: History of the Movement   3
     Pathfinder on Environmental Justice Generally   5
  B. Fairness and Justice Considered   6
     Robert R. Kuehn, A Taxonomy of Environmental Justice   6
     Vicki Been, What's Fairness Got to Do With It? Environmental
       Justice and the Siting of Locally Undesirable Land Uses   13
     Notes and Questions   17
     Christopher H. Foreman, Jr., The Promise and Peril of
       Environmental Justice   17
     Notes and Questions   21
  C. "We Speak for Ourselves"   22
     Letter, Circa Earth Day 1990   22
     Principles of Environmental Justice, Proceedings, The First
       National People of Color Environmental Leadership Summit   24
     Letter, Circa Earth Day 2001   25
     Notes and Questions   27
  D. Environmental Justice Communities in Context   28
     Eric K. Yamamoto & Jen-L W. Lyman, Racializing Environmental
       Justice   28
     Notes and Questions   32

Chapter 2 • The Evidence   35
  A. Introduction   35
     Pathfinder on Race and Income Disparities   36
  B. Hazardous Waste Facilities   36
     Douglas L. Anderton, Andy B. Anderson, John Michael Oakes,
       Michael R. Fraser, Environmental Equity: The Demographics
       of Dumping   38
     Notes and Questions   39
     Vicki Been & Francis Gupta, Coming to the Nuisance or Going
       to the Barrios? A Longitudinal Analysis of Environmental
       Justice Claims   40
     Notes and Questions   42

Paul Mohai & Robin Saha, Racial Inequality in the Distribution
    of Hazardous Waste: A National-Level Reassessment   43
    Notes and Questions   45
C. Other Industrial Activities and Environmental Harms   46
    1. Background   46
       Notes and Questions   47
    2. Farmworker Exposure to Pesticides   47
       Ivette Perfecto & Baldemar Velásquez, Farm Workers: Among
          the Least Protected   47
       Notes and Questions   48
    3. Exposure to Contaminated Fish   49
       National Environmental Justice Advisory Council, Fish Consumption
          and Environmental Justice   49
       Notes and Questions   50
    4. Toxic Release Inventory (TRI) Facilities   51
       Evan J. Ringquist, Equity and the Distribution of Environmental Risk:
          The Case of TRI Facilities   51
       Notes and Questions   52
    5. Cumulative and Multiple Exposures   52
       a.   Air Toxics Exposures   52
       Rachel Morello-Frosch, Manuel Pastor, & James Sadd,
          Environmental Justice and Southern California's "Riskscape":
          The Distribution of Air Toxics Exposures and Health Risks
          among Diverse Communities   52
       Notes and Questions   53
       b.   Multiple Environmental Harms   54
       John A. Hird & Michael Reese, The Distribution of Environmental
          Quality: An Empirical Analysis   54
       Notes and Questions   55
    6. Disaster Vulnerability   56
       Manuel Pastor, Robert D. Bullard, James K. Boyce, Alice Fothergill,
          Rachel Morello-Frosch & Beverly Wright, In the Wake of the
          Storm: Environment, Disaster, and Race after Katrina   56
       Notes and Questions   57
D. Disparities in Environmental Benefits   58
    1. Transportation Benefits   58
       Robert D. Bullard, Glenn S. Johnson & Angel O. Torres, The Routes
          of American Apartheid   58
       Robert García, Mean Streets   60
       Notes and Questions   61
    2. Parks and Open Space   61
       Jennifer Wolch, John P. Wilson, and Jed Fehrenbach, Parks and Park
          Funding In Los Angeles: An Equity-Mapping Analysis   61
       Notes and Questions   63
    3. Environmental Enforcement and Cleanup   65
       Notes and Questions   67
    4. Emergency Response   68

Manuel Pastor, Robert D. Bullard, James K. Boyce, Alice Fothergill,
    Rachel Morello-Frosch, and Beverly Wright, In the Wake of the
    Storm: Environment, Disaster, and Race After Katrina   68
Notes and Questions   69

Chapter 3 • Theories of Causation   73
A. Introduction   73
B. Land Use Practices   73
    Yale Rabin, Expulsive Zoning: The Inequitable Legacy of Euclid   73
    Robert W. Collin, Environmental Equity: A Law and Planning
        Approach to Environmental Racism   75
    Craig Anthony Arnold, Planning Milagros: Environmental Justice
        and Land Use Regulation   77
    Notes and Questions   79
C. The Market   81
    1. Market Forces in Site Selection   81
        Robin Saha & Paul Mohai, Explaining Racial and Socioeconomic
            Disparities in the Location of Locally Unwanted Land Uses:
            A Conceptual Framework   81
        Luke Cole & Sheila Foster, From the Ground Up: Environmental
            Racism and the Rise of the Environmental Justice Movement   82
        Notes and Questions   84
        Lynn E. Blais, Environmental Racism Reconsidered   85
        Notes and Questions   88
    2. Post-Siting Changes   89
        Vicki Been, Locally Undesirable Land Uses in Minority
            Neighborhoods: Disproportionate Siting or Market Dynamics?   90
        Notes and Questions   92
D. Politics, Social Capital, and the Structure of Environmental Laws   93
        Manuel Pastor, Jr., Jim Sadd & John Hipp, Which Came First?
            Toxic Facilities, Minority Move-In, and Environmental Justice   94
        Notes and Questions   95
        Luke W. Cole, Empowerment as the Key to Environmental
            Protection: The Need for Environmental Poverty Law   97
        Richard J. Lazarus, Pursuing "Environmental Justice": The
            Distributional Effects of Environmental Protection   99
        Notes and Questions   101
E. Racial Discrimination   102
        Charles R. Lawrence III, The Id, the Ego, and Equal Protection:
            Reckoning with Unconscious Racism   102
        Notes and Questions   105

Chapter 4 • American Indians and Environmental Justice   107
A. Introduction   107
    1. An Introductory Note   107
        Pathfinder on American Indians and Environmental Justice 108
    2. Historical Background   108
        Judith V. Royster, Native American Law   109

3. Situating American Indian People within the Environmental
   Justice Movement   111
      Robert A. Williams, Jr., Large Binocular Telescopes, Red Squirrel
        Piñatas, and Apache Sacred Mountains: Decolonizing
        Environmental Law in a Multicultural World   111
      Notes and Questions   117
      Dean B. Suagee, The Indian Country Environmental Justice
        Clinic: From Vision to Reality   118
      Notes and Questions   119
   B. Tribes as Environmental Regulators   120
      Rebecca Tsosie, Tribal Environmental Policy in an Era of
        Self-Determination: The Role of Ethics, Economics and
        Traditional Ecological Knowledge   120
      Notes and Questions   125
      James M. Grijalva, Closing the Circle: Environmental Justice
        in Indian Country   126
      Darren J. Ranco, Models of Tribal Environmental Regulation:
        In Pursuit of a Culturally Relevant Form of Tribal Sovereignty   127
      Notes and Questions   130
   C. Protection of Resources and Rights   133
      Michael P. O'Connell, Indian Tribes and Project Development
        Outside Indian Reservations   135
      Notes and Questions   136

Chapter 5 · Regulation and the Administrative State   139
   A. Introduction   139
   B. Environmental Regulation: The Historical Context   139
      Richard J. Lazarus, The Tragedy of Distrust in the Implementation
        of Federal Environmental Law   140
      Notes and Questions   142
   C. "Stakeholder" Approaches to Decision-Making   144
      Eileen Gauna, The Environmental Justice Misfit: Public
        Participation and the Paradigm Paradox   144
      Jody Freeman, Collaborative Governance in the Administrative State   146
      Notes and Questions   149
      William Funk, Bargaining Toward the New Millennium: Regulatory
        Negotiation and the Subversion of the Public Interest   151
      Notes and Questions   152
   D. The Cost-Benefit Approach to Regulation, and Its Alternatives   153
     1. Cost-Benefit Analysis and Its Critics   153
      Robert W. Hahn & Cass R. Sunstein, A New Executive Order
        for Improving Federal Regulation? Deeper and Wider
        Cost-Benefit Analysis   153
      Frank Ackerman & Lisa Heinzerling, Pricing The Priceless:
        Cost-Benefit Analysis of Environmental Protection   155
      Notes and Questions   157
     2. A Pragmatic Alternative   161
      Sidney A. Shapiro & Christopher H. Schroeder, Beyond
        Cost-Benefit Analysis: A Pragmatic Reorientation   161

Notes and Questions   164
E. Federal/State Relationships   164
  1. Introduction   164
  2. Preemption   165
      Robert L. Glicksman & Richard E. Levy, A Collective Action
        Perspective on Ceiling Preemption by Federal Environmental
        Regulation: The Case of Global Climate Change   165
      Notes and Questions   169
  3. Devolution   170
      Rena I. Steinzor, Devolution and the Public Health   170
      Notes and Questions   172

Chapter 6 · Risk and Health   175
A. Introduction   175
      Pathfinder on Risk Assessment   176
B. Quantitative Risk Assessment   176
  1. An Introductory Note on Quantitative Risk Assessment   176
      The Carnegie Commission on Science, Technology, and
        Government, Risk and the Environment: Improving
        Regulatory Decision Making   177
      Notes and Questions   178
      Catherine A. O'Neill, Variable Justice: Environmental Standards,
        Contaminated Fish, and "Acceptable" Risk to Native Peoples   179
      Notes and Questions   180
  2. Criticisms of Quantitative Risk Assessment   180
      Robert R. Kuehn, The Environmental Justice Implications of
        Quantitative Risk Assessment   181
      Notes and Questions   184
      National Environmental Justice Advisory Council, Fish
        Consumption and Environmental Justice   185
      Notes and Questions   186
      Stephen Breyer, Breaking the Vicious Circle: Toward Effective
        Risk Regulation   186
      Notes and Questions   187
      Matthew D. Adler, Against "Individual Risk": A Sympathetic
        Critique of Risk Assessment   187
      Notes and Questions   188
  3. Risks to Children   190
      Philippe Grandjean et al., The Faroes Statement: Human
        Health Effects of Developmental Exposure to Chemicals
        in Our Environment   191
      Notes and Questions   191
  4. Risk Assessment in Context: The Example of American Indian Tribes   192
      Jamie Donatuto and Barbara L. Harper, Issues in Evaluating
        Fish Consumption Rates for Native American Tribes   193
      Notes and Questions   193
C. Cumulative Risk Assessment   195
  1. Introduction to Cumulative Risk Assessment   195

National Environmental Justice Advisory Council, Ensuring Risk
    Reduction in Communities with Multiple Stressors:
    Environmental Justice and Cumulative Risks/Impacts   197
        Notes and Questions   199
    2. Community-Based Participatory Research   200
        Gerald J. Keeler, J. Timothy Dvonch, Fuyuen Y. Yip, Edith A. Parker,
            Barbara A. Israel, Frank J. Marsik, Masako Morishita, James A.
            Barres, Thomas G. Robins, Wilma Brakefield-Caldwell and
            Mathew Sam, Assessment of Personal and Community-Level
            Exposures   201
        Notes and Questions   203
    D. Risk Avoidance   204
        Catherine A. O'Neill, No Mud Pies: Risk Avoidance as Risk Regulation 204
        Notes and Questions   207
    E. Comparative Risk Assessment   208
        Stephen Breyer, Breaking the Vicious Circle: Toward Effective
            Risk Regulation   209
        Notes and Questions   209

Chapter 7 · Standard Setting   213
    A. Introduction   213
        1. An Introductory Note on the Taxonomy of Standards   214
        2. Legal Sources of Authority   215
            Richard J. Lazarus & Stephanie Tai, Integrating Environmental
                Justice Into EPA Permitting Authority   215
            Notes and Questions   216
    B. The Case of National Ambient Air Quality Standards   217
            Rena I. Steinzor, Mother Earth and Uncle Sam: How Pollution
                and Hollow Government Hurt Our Kids   219
            Notes and Questions   221
    C. Standards under the Clean Water Act   223
        1. An Introductory Note on the Statute's Different Standards 223
        2. Water Quality Standards   225
            Catherine A. O'Neill, Variable Justice: Environmental Standards,
                Contaminated Fish, and "Acceptable" Risk to Native Peoples 225
            Notes and Questions   226
            City of Albuquerque v. Browner   228
            Notes and Questions   231
    D. Market-Based Approaches   232
        1. An Introduction to Market-Based Approaches to Regulation 232
            Pathfinder on Economic Incentives   232
            Stephen M. Johnson, Economics vs. Equity: Do Market-Based
                Environmental Reforms Exacerbate Environmental Injustice? 233
            Notes and Questions   236
        2. Emissions Trading   238
            Richard Toshiyuki Drury, Michael E. Belliveau, J. Scott Kuhn &
                Shipra Bansal, Pollution Trading and Environmental Injustice:
                Los Angeles' Failed Experiment in Air Quality Policy 238
            Notes and Questions   240

3. Mercury   242
    Catherine A. O'Neill, Environmental Justice in the Tribal Context:
        A Madness to EPA's Method   242
    Notes and Questions   245

Chapter 8 · Permits and Public Enforcement   249
A. Facility Permitting   249
    1. Introduction   249
    2. The Legal Hook: Potential Federal Sources of Authority to Address
       Environmental Justice and the Decisions of the EPA's Environmental
       Appeals Board   250
        Richard J. Lazarus & Stephanie Tai, Integrating Environmental
            Justice into EPA Permitting Authority   250
        Notes and Questions   251
        In re Chemical Waste Management of Indiana, Inc.   253
        Notes and Questions   258
    3. Environmental Justice Claims in State Permit Proceedings   259
        NAACP — Flint Chapter v. Engler   259
        Colonias Development Council v. Rhino Environmental Services
            Inc. & New Mexico Department of Environment   261
        Notes and Questions   265
    4. The Permit Applicant's Perspective   267
        Terry R. Bossert, The Permit Applicant's Perspective   268
        Notes and Questions   270
B. Enforcement of Environmental Pollution Control Laws by Public Officials 271
    1. Introduction   271
    2. Sources of Disparate Enforcement   272
        Robert R. Kuehn, Remedying the Unequal Enforcement of
            Environmental Laws   272
        Notes and Questions   272
        Clifford Rechtschaffen, Competing Visions: EPA and the States
            Battle for the Future of Environmental Enforcement   273
        Notes and Questions   276
    3. Strengthening Public Enforcement in Environmental Justice Communities 277
        a.   Enhanced Penalties and Penalty Return   278
        Alex Geisinger, Rethinking Environmental Justice Regulation:
            A Modest Proposal for Penalty Return   278
        Notes and Questions   281
        b.   Supplemental Environmental Projects   281
        Notes and Questions   283
        c.   Targeting Enforcement Resources   283
        Notes and Questions   284

Chapter 9 · Contaminated Properties   285
A. Introduction   285
    1. An Introduction to CERCLA Cleanups   285
        Rena Steinzor and Margaret Clune, The Toll of Superfund Neglect:
            Toxic Waste Dumps & Communities at Risk   287
        Notes and Questions   289

2. A Note on Relocation   291
    Notes and Questions   293
B. Brownfields   294
    Pathfinder on Brownfields and Environmental Justice   294
1. Brownfields Background   295
    Joel B. Eisen, Brownfields of Dreams?: Challenges and Limits of
        Voluntary Cleanup Programs and Incentives   295
    Notes and Questions   298
    Kirsten H. Engel, Brownfield Initiatives and Environmental Justice:
        Second-Class Cleanups or Market-Based Equity?   299
    Notes and Questions   301
    Andrea Ruiz-Esquide, The Uniform Environmental Covenants
        Act — An Environmental Justice Perspective   302
    Robert Hersh & Kris Wernstedt, Out of Site, Out of Mind:
        The Problem of Institutional Controls   304
    Notes and Questions   305
2. Evaluating Brownfields Redevelopment on the Ground   307
    Jessica Higgins, Evaluating the Chicago Brownfields Initiative:
        The Effects of City-Initiated Brownfield Redevelopment on
        Surrounding Communities   308
    Notes and Questions   313

Chapter 10 • Governmental Initiatives to Address Environmental Justice   317
A. Introduction   317
B. Environmental Justice at the International Level   317
    Human Rights and Environment   318
    Notes and Questions   319
    Barry E. Hill, Steve Wolfson & Nicholas Targ, Human Rights and
        the Environment: A Synopsis and Some Predictions   320
    Notes and Questions   323
    Tseming Yang, The International Significance of an Instance of
        Urban Environmental Inequity in Tijuana, Mexico   326
    Notes and Questions   327
C. Federal Initiatives   328
1. The Executive Order on Environmental Justice   328
    Executive Order 12,898: Federal Actions to Address Environmental
        Justice in Minority Populations and Low-Income Populations   328
    Notes and Questions   330
2. Limitations on Governmental Initiatives   333
    Grutter v. Bollinger   333
    Notes and Questions   335
D. State Initiatives   338
    Notes and Questions   339
E. Tribal Initiatives   340
    Dean B. Suagee & John P. Lowndes, Due Process and Public
        Participation in Tribal Environmental Programs   342
    Notes and Questions   344
F. Collaborative Approaches   345

Charles Lee, Submission to the National Environmental
        Policy Commission   346
    Notes and Questions   349

Chapter 11 · Land Use Planning, Environmental Review, and Information
        Disclosure Laws   355
A. Introduction   355
B. Planning, Land Use, and Compensated Siting Approaches   356
    1. Planning and Zoning Changes   356
        Craig Anthony Arnold, Planning Milagros: Environmental Justice
            and Land Use Regulation   356
        Notes and Questions   358
    2. Compensated Siting Proposals   361
        Vicki Been, Compensated Siting Proposals: Is it Time to Pay Attention? 361
        Notes and Questions   365
C. Environmental Review: The National Environmental Policy Act and State
    Environmental Policy Acts   366
    1. An Introductory Note on NEPA And SEPAs   366
        Pathfinder on NEPA   368
        Notes and Questions   369
    2. Agency NEPA Guidance   369
        Notes and Questions   371
    3. Judicial Review of NEPA   371
        In the Matter of Louisiana Energy Services, L.P.   371
        Notes and Questions   374
    4. Analysis of Social and Economic Impacts   377
        Bakersfield Citizens for Local Control v. City of Bakersfield 378
        Notes and Questions   379
    5. New Approaches: Health Impact Assessments   380
        Brian L. Cole, Michelle Wilhelm, Peter V. Long, Jonathan E. Fielding,
            Gerald Kominski, & Hal Morgenstern, Prospects for Health
            Impact Assessment in The United States: New and Improved
            Environmental Impact Assessment or Something Different? 380
        Notes and Questions   382
D. Right to Know and Information Disclosure Laws   383
        Bradley C. Karkkainen, Information as Environmental
            Regulation: TRI and Performance Benchmarking, Precursor
            to a New Paradigm?   384
        Notes and Questions   386

Chapter 12 · Responding to the Challenge of Climate Change   389
A. Introduction   389
B. Background on Climate Change   390
C. The Disproportionate Impacts of Climate Change   392
    1. The International Context   392
        M.L. Parry, O.F. Canziani, J.P. Palutikof, P.J. van der Linden &
            C.E. Hanson, eds, IPCC, 2007: Summary for Policymakers 393
        Kevin Watkins, United Nations Development Programme   394
        Notes and Questions   398

2. Impacts in the United States   398
    Congressional Black Caucus Foundation, African Americans and
        Climate Change: An Unequal Burden   398
    Notes and Questions   399
D. Climate Justice in the International Context   400
    1. International Responses to Date   400
        Notes and Questions   403
    2. Designing an International Response   403
        Eric A. Posner and Cass R. Sunstein, Climate Change Justice   404
        Daniel A. Farber, The Case for Climate Compensation: Justice for
            Climate Change Victims in a Complex World   409
        Notes and Questions   412
        Paul Baer, Tom Athanasiou, Sivan Kartha, & Eric Kemp-Benedict,
            The Greenhouse Rights Development Framework: The Right
            to Development in a Climate Constrained World   412
        Notes and Questions   417
E. The Food vs. Fuels Debate   417
    The Right to Food, Interim Report of the Special Rapporteur
        Jean Ziegler   418
    Notes and Questions   419
F. Climate Justice in the Domestic Context   421
    1. The Debate About Cap-and-Trade   421
        A. Denny Ellerman, Paul L. Joskow and David Harrison, Jr.,
            Emissions Trading in the U.S.: Experience, Lessons, and
            Considerations for Greenhouse Gases   421
        Alice Kaswan, Environmental Justice and Domestic Climate
            Change Policy   423
        Notes and Questions   427
G. Human Rights Based Approach   429
    Sara C. Aminzadeh, A Moral Imperative: The Human Rights
        Implications of Climate Change   429
    Notes and Questions   431

Chapter 13 · Litigation, Citizen Enforcement, and Common Law Remedies   433
A. The Role of the Lawyer and Litigation   433
    1. Environmental Justice Lawyering   434
        Francis Calpotura, Why the Law?   434
        Notes and Questions   434
        Luke W. Cole, Empowerment as the Key to Environmental
            Protection: The Need for Environmental Poverty Law   435
        Notes and Questions   439
    2. A Note on Environmental Law Clinics   441
        Notes and Questions   441
B. Private Enforcement — Citizen Suits   442
    1. Legal Requirements for Filing Suit   442
        Lujan v. Defenders of Wildlife   444
        Notes and Questions   448
        Friends of the Earth v. Laidlaw Environmental Services   449
        Notes and Questions   451

2. The Practicalities of Private Enforcement   453
    Eileen Gauna, Federal Environmental Citizen Provisions: Obstacles
        and Incentives on the Road to Environmental Justice   453
    Notes and Questions   456
3. Building Community Enforcement Capacity   459
    a.   Upwardly Adjusting Attorney's Fees   459
    b.   Technical Assistance to Communities   459
    Notes and Questions   461
C. Common Law Remedies   461
    Notes and Questions   462
    Richard T. Drury, Moving a Mountain: The Struggle for
        Environmental Justice in Southeast Los Angeles   464
    Notes and Questions   467
    United States District Court, Northern District of California,
        Native Village of Kivalina & City of Kivalina, Plaintiffs v.
        ExxonMobil Corporation, et al, Defendants   467
    Notes and Questions   469

Chapter 14 · Constitutional and Civil Rights Claims   471
A. Environmental Justice Framed as Constitutional Claims   471
1. The Free Exercise/Establishment Clause Cases   471
    Lyng v. Northwest Indian Cemetery Protective Association   472
    Notes and Questions   474
    Bear Lodge Multiple Use Association v. Babbitt   475
    Notes and Questions   477
2. The Equal Protection Cases   480
    Pathfinder on Equal Protection and Environmental Justice   480
    Dowdell v. City of Apopka   481
    Bean v. Southwestern Waste Management Corporation   482
    Notes and Questions   486
    R.I.S.E. v. Kay   487
    Notes and Questions   489
B. Enforcement of the Civil Rights Act   492
1. Introduction   492
    Pathfinder on Title VI and Environmental Justice   493
2. Administrative Complaints Grounded upon Disparate Impact Regulations   494
    The Select Steel Administrative Decision   494
    Notes and Questions   497
3. Private Right of Action for Claims Grounded upon "Disparate Impact"   500
    South Camden Citizens in Action v. New Jersey Department of
        Environmental Protection   501
    Notes and Questions   505
    Alexander v. Sandoval   506
    Notes and Questions   509
    Bradford C. Mank, Can Administrative Regulations Interpret
        Rights Enforceable under Section 1983?: Why Chevron
        Deference Survives Sandoval and Gonzaga   510
    Notes and Questions   516

Index   519

Preface

Environmental justice is one of the most important and dynamic developments in environmental law in the past two decades. Drawing on principles from environmental law, civil rights law, and broader movements for economic and social justice, the environmental justice movement has focused attention on the disparate environmental harms and benefits experienced by low-income communities and communities of color. Indeed, some of the claims presented by activists challenge some of the fundamental underpinnings of environmental law and policy. Environmental justice considerations arise in virtually all aspects of environmental law, including standard setting, program design, facility permitting, enforcement, contaminated site cleanup, and brownfield redevelopment. And the environmental justice movement has generated an explosion of scholarship.

This book is designed to provide students with a comprehensive introduction to environmental justice, whether or not they have prior background in environmental law. While its focus is oriented toward legal and regulatory issues, the book also draws considerably on non-legal disciplines; thus, it can be used in undergraduate or graduate courses as well. We have included frequent introductory notes to provide background for students unfamiliar with some of the environmental statutes and other materials. This book is designed for use in a single semester seminar course, and each of the 14 chapters roughly corresponds to a week's worth of reading. The book also can be easily used as a supplement in other environmental, land use, or civil rights classes in which the professor wishes to cover selected issues in environmental justice. The book also can serve as a reference for practitioners, government officials, and activists involved in environmental justice matters, as well as for students wishing to engage in more focused research on environmental justice. On key areas of interest, we have included pathfinders for students and others wishing to undertake further research on specific topics.

A note about the scope of the book's coverage. Environmental problems are far ranging, and environmental disparities implicate land use, public lands law, transportation, civil rights, labor issues, international law, American Indian law and other areas. A single course book of this nature cannot cover all of these disparate and intricate legal specialties in great depth. Primarily, we focus on domestic environmental regulation and related claims by environmental justice activists involving land use, constitutional or civil rights laws. In this second edition, we also have broadened our coverage to include some of the emerging international environmental justice claims, and added a chapter on environmental justice and climate change. We also have updated our discussion of the empirical evidence underlying claims of environmental justice to reflect new research in this area, and we cover significant new developments in regulatory areas that have environmental justice implications, in particular risk and health, cost-benefit analysis, permitting, market-based approaches, environmental review and health impact assessments, government enforcement, brownfields and contaminated sites, and state environmental justice legislation and other initiatives. In addition, we have broadened our coverage of

Native American issues and have updated our discussion of claims asserted by impacted communities, including environmental citizen suits, common law actions, and civil rights actions. We are delighted that Professor Catherine O'Neill has joined as a co-author for the second edition.

The editors of this book maintain the position that pursuing complete neutrality in these difficult and politically charged issues is unrealistic. Although we are sympathetic to environmental justice struggles, we recognize that the issues are complex and raise hard questions that often generate compelling arguments from all perspectives. We strive to bring that complexity to the surface by choosing a range of materials that present different viewpoints. To further tease out the clash of interests and viewpoints, our notes often contain intentionally provocative questions. Those with a perspective different than ours may take issue with the way that some of the issues are framed and discussed. In response, we can only invite alternative ways to frame the debates and similar disclosures of author's position.

A note on the editing conventions we use: In general, we have omitted footnotes, citations, and other references from excerpted materials. We have left in case citations that are directly discussed in a judicial opinion, or that we believe are important to understanding the excerpt. The few case footnotes that are included are numbered as they appear in the original opinions. We have indicated text that we omitted from the original sources with three ellipses without spaces, i.e., ... Text that was omitted in the original excerpts is indicated by three ellipses separated by a space, i.e., ...

We are deeply grateful to the following people who reviewed draft chapters of this second edition: Don Anton, John Applegate, Wil Burns, Carl Cranor, Sheila Foster, Jim Grijalva, Helen Kang, Alice Kaswan, Bob Kuehn, John LaVelle, Brad Mank, Paul Mohai, Jenny Moore, Nicholas Targ, and Rob Verchick. We are also deeply appreciative of the excellent research assistance provided by Golden Gate Law student Emily Keller, University of New Mexico Law students Melissa Kennelly and Tuesday Kaasch, and Seattle University Law students Mike Morita and Sarah Dawe. We appreciate as well the extraordinary administrative support provided by Lenora Santos of Seattle University, and the research assistance provided by Golden Gate law librarian Marisa Diehl and Seattle University law librarian Kerry FitzGerald. The authors also thank Golden Gate University School of Law, University of New Mexico School of Law, and Seattle University School of Law for financial support.

Finally, we dedicate this book to activists from the grassroots. Their insight, courage, tenacity and wit constantly inspire.

Acknowledgments

We gratefully acknowledge the permissions granted by the authors and publishers of the following works to reproduce excerpts in this book:

Frank Ackerman & Lisa Heinzerling, *Pricing The Priceless: Cost-Benefit Analysis of Environmental Protection*, 150 University of Pennsylvania Law Review 1553 (2002). Reprinted by permission of University of Pennsylvania Law Review.

Matthew D. Adler, *Against "Individual Risk": A Sympathetic Critique of Risk Assessment*, 153 University of Pennsylvania Law Review 1121 (2007). Reprinted by permission of University of Pennsylvania Law Review.

Sara C. Aminzadeh, *A Moral Imperative: The Human Rights Implications of Climate Change*, 30 Hastings International and Comparative Law Review 231 (2007). Reprinted by permission of University of California Hastings College of the Law.

Douglas Anderton et al., *Environmental Equity: The Demographics of Dumping*, 31 Demography 229 (May 1994). Reprinted by permission of the Population Association of America.

Donald K. Anton & Dinah Shelton, Human Rights & Environment (Donald K. Anton & Dinah Shelton eds., forthcoming 2009). Reprinted by permission of Cambridge University Press and the authors.

Craig Anthony Arnold, *Planning Milagros: Environmental Justice and Land Use Regulation*, 76 Denver University Law Review 1 (1998). Reprinted by permission of the Denver University Law Review.

Paul Baer, et. al, , *The Greenhouse Rights Development Framework: The Right to Development in a Climate Constrained World*, published by the Heinrich Böll Foundation, Christian Aid, EcoEquity, and the Stockholm Environment Institute (2d ed. Nov. 2008). Reprinted with permission.

Vicki Been, *What's Fairness Got To Do With It: Environmental Justice and the Siting of Locally Undesirable Land Uses*, 78 Cornell Law Review 1001 (1993). Reprinted by permission of the Cornell Law Review.

Vicki Been, *Locally Undesirable Land Uses in Minority Neighborhoods: Disproportionate Siting or Market Dynamics?*, 103 Yale Law Journal 1383 (1994). Reprinted by permission of the Yale Law Journal Company and William S. Hein Company.

Vicki Been, *Compensated Siting Proposals: Is it Time to Pay Attention?*, 21 Fordham Urban Law Journal 787 (1994). Reprinted by permission of the Fordham Urban Law Journal.

Vicki Been & Francis Gupta, *Coming to the Nuisance or Going to the Barrios? A Longitudinal Analysis of Environmental Justice Claims*, 24 Ecology Law Quarterly 1 (1997). Copyright © 1997 by the Regents of the University of California. Reprinted by permission of the University of California, Berkeley.

Lynn E. Blais, *Environmental Racism Reconsidered*, 75 North Carolina Law Review 75 (1996). Reprinted by permission of the North Carolina Law Review.

Stephen Breyer, Breaking the Vicious Circle: Toward Effective Risk Regluation (1993). Copyright © 1993 by the President and Fellows of Harvard College. Reprinted by permission of the publisher.

Robert Bullard et al., *The Routes of American Apartheid*, 15 Forum for Applied Research and Public Policy 66 (2000). Reprinted by permission of the Forum for Applied Research and Public Policy.

Francis Calpotura, *Why the Law?*, Third Force Magazine (May/June 1994). Reprinted by permission of the Center for Third World Organizing.

The Carnegie Commission on Science, Technology & Government, *Risk and the Environment: Improving Regulatory Decision Making* (1993). Reprinted with permission.

Brian Cole et al., *Prospects for Health Impact Assessment in the United States: New and Improved Environmental Impact Assessment or Something Different?*, 29 Journal of Health Politics, Policy and Law 1153 (2004). Copyright © 2004, Duke University Press. Reprinted by permission of the publisher.

Luke Cole, *Empowerment as the Key to Environmental Protection: The Need for Environmental Poverty Law*, 19 Ecology Law Quarterly 619 (1992). Copyright © 1992 by the Regents of the University of California. Reprinted by permission of the University of California, Berkeley.

Luke Cole & Sheila Foster, From the Ground Up: Environmental Racism and the Rise of the Environmental Justice Movement, 70–74 (2000). Reprinted by permission of New York University Press.

Robert Collin, *Environmental Equity: A Law and Planning Approach to Environmental Racism*, 11 Virginia Environmental Law Journal 495 (1992). Reprinted by permission of the Virginia Environmental Law Journal.

Jamie Donatuto & Barbara Harper, *Issues in Evaluating Fish Consumption Rates for Native American Tribes*, 28 Risk Analysis 1497 (2008). Reprinted with permission of the authors.

Richard Toshiyuki Drury et al., *Pollution Trading and Environmental Injustice: Los Angeles' Failed Experiment in Air Quality Policy*, 9 Duke Environmental Law and Policy Forum 231 (Spring 1999). Reprinted by permission of the Duke Environmental Law and Policy Forum.

Richard T. Drury, *Moving a Mountain: The Struggle for Environmental Justice in Southeast Los Angeles*, *in* Creative Common Law Strategies for Protecting the Environment 173 (Clifford Rechtschaffen & Denise Antolini eds., 2007). Reprinted by permission of the publisher, Environmental Law Institute.

Joel B. Eisen, *Brownfields of Dreams?: Challenges and Limits of Voluntary Cleanup Programs and Incentives*, 1996 University of Illinois Law Review 883 (1996). Copyright © 1996 by the Board of Trustees of the University of Illinois. Reprinted by permission of the University of Illinois Law Review and the Board of Trustees of the University of Illinois.

A. Denny Ellerman, Paul L. Joskow & David Harrison, Jr., *Emissions Trading in the U.S.: Experience, Lessons, and Considerations for Greenhouse Gases*, Pew Center on Global Climate Change (2003). Reprinted with permission.

Kirsten H. Engel, *Brownfield Initiatives and Environmental Justice: Second-class Cleanups or Market-based Equity?*, 13 Journal of Natural Resources and Environmental Law 317 (1998). Reprinted by permission of the Journal of Natural Resources and Environmental Law.

Daniel A. Farber, *The Case for Climate Compensation: Justice for Climate Change Victims in a Complex World*, 2008 Utah Law Review 377 (2008). Reprinted with permission.

Christopher H. Foreman, Jr., The Promise and the Peril of Environmental Justice (1998). Reprinted by permission of the Brookings Institution Press.

Sheila R. Foster, *Meeting the Environmental Justice Challenge: Evolving Norms in Environmental Decisionmaking*, 30 Environmental Law Reporter 10,992 (2000). Reprinted by permission of the Environmental Law Institute.

Jody Freeman, *Collaborative Governance in the Administrative State*, 45 University of California Law Review 1 (1997). Reprinted by permission of the University of California Law Review.

William Funk, *Bargaining Toward the New Millennium: Regulatory Negotiation and the Subversion of the Public Interest*, 46 Duke Law Journal 1351 (1997). Reprinted by permission of the author.

Robert Garcia, *Mean Streets*, 15 Forum for Applied Research and Public Policy 75 (2000). Reprinted by permission of the Forum for Applied Research and Public Policy and the author.

Eileen Gauna, *Federal Environmental Citizen Provisions: Obstacles and Incentives on the Road to Environmental Justice*, 22 Ecology Law Quarterly 1 (1995). © 1995 by the Regents of the University of California. Reprinted by permission of the University of California, Berkeley.

Eileen Gauna, *The Environmental Justice Misfit, Public Participation and the Paradigm Paradox*, 17 Stanford Environmental Law Journal 3 (1998). Reprinted by permission of the Stanford Environmental Law Journal.

Eileen Gauna, *EPA at Thirty: Fairness in Environmental Protection*, 31 Environmental Law Reporter 10,528 (2001). Reprinted by permission of the Environmental Law Institute.

Robert L. Glicksman & Richard E. Levy, *A Collective Action Perspective on Ceiling Preemption by Federal Environmental Regulation: The Case of Global Climate Change*, 103 Northwest University Law Review 579 (2008). Reprinted by special permission of Northwestern University School of Law, *Northwestern University Law Review*.

Philippe Grandjean et al., *The Faroes Statement: Human Health Effects of Developmental Exposure to Chemicals in our Environment*, 102 Basic & Clinical Pharmacology & Toxicology 73 (2007). Reprinted with permission.

Robert W. Hahn & Cass R. Sunstein, *A New Executive Order for Improving Federal Regulation? Deeper and Wider Cost-Benefit Analysis*, 150 University of Pennsylvania Law Review 1489 (2002). Reprinted by permission of University of Pennsylvania Law Review.

Robert Hersh & Kris Wernstedt, *Out of Site, Out of Mind: The Problem of Institutional Controls*, 8 Race, Poverty and the Environment 15 (Winter 2001). Reprinted by permission of Race, Poverty and the Environment.

Jessica Higgins, *Evaluating the Chicago Brownfield Initiative: The Effects of City-Initiated Brownfield Redevelopment on Surrounding Communities*, 3 Northwestern Journal of Law & Social Policy 240 (2008). Reprinted with permission.

Barry E. Hill, Steve Wolfson & Nicholas Targ, *Human Rights and the Environment: A Synopsis and Some Predictions*, 16 Georgetown International Environmental Law Review 359. Copyright © 2004. Reprinted with permission of the publisher, Georgetown International Environmental Law Review.

John A. Hird & Michael Reese, *The Distribution of Environmental Quality: An Empirical Analysis*, 79 Social Science Quarterly 693 (1998). Copyright © 1997 by Social Science Quarterly and Blackwell Publishers. Reprinted by permission.

Stephen M. Johnson, *Economics vs. Equity: Do Market-Based Environmental Reforms Exacerbate Environmental Injustice?*, 56 Washington and Lee Law Review 111 (Winter 1999). Reprinted by permission of the Washington and Lee Law Review.

Bradley C. Karkkainen, *Information as Environmental Regulation: TRI and Performance Benchmarking, Precursor to a New Paradigm?*, 89 Georgetown Law Journal 57 (2001). Reprinted by permission.

Alice Kaswan, *Environmental Laws: Grist for the Equal Protection Mill*, 70 University of Colorado Law Review 387 (1999). Reprinted by permission of the University of Colorado Law Review.

Alice Kaswan, *Environmental Justice and Domestic Climate Change Policy*, 38 Environmental Law Reporter 10,287 (2008). Reprinted with permission of the Environmental Law Institute.

Gerald J. Keeler et al., *Assessment of Personal and Community-Level Exposure to Particulate Matter Among Children with Asthma in Detroit, Michigan, as Part of Community Action Against Asthma* (CAAA), 110 Environmental Health Perspectives 173 (Supplement 2: Community, Research, and Environmental Justice, 2002). Reprinted by permission of Environmental Health Perspectives.

Robert Kuehn, *Remedying the Unequal Enforcement of Environmental Laws*, 9 St. John's Journal of Legal Commentary 625 (1994). Reprinted by permission of the St. John's Journal of Legal Commentary.

Robert Kuehn, *The Environmental Justice Implications of Quantitative Risk Assessment*, 1996 University of Illinois Law Review 103. Copyright © 1996 by the Board of Trustees of the University of Illinois. Reprinted by permission of the University of Illinois Law Review.

Robert Kuehn, *A Taxonomy of Environmental Justice*, 30 Environmental Law Reporter 10,681 (2000). Reprinted by permission of the Environmental Law Institute.

Charles R. Lawrence III, *The Id, the Ego, and Equal Protection: Reckoning with Unconscious Racism*, 39 Stanford Law Review 317 (1987). © 1987 by Stanford Law Review. Reproduced with permission of the Stanford Law Review.

Richard J. Lazarus, *The Tragedy of Distrust in the Implementation of Federal Environmental Law*, 54 Law & Contemporary Problems 311 (1991). Reprinted by permission of the Journal of Law and Contemporary Problems and the author.

Richard Lazarus, *Pursuing "Environmental Justice": The Distributional Effects of Environmental Protection*, 87 Northwestern University Law Review 787 (1993). Reprinted by special permission of Northwestern University School of Law, *Northwestern University Law Review*.

Richard J. Lazarus & Stephanie Tai, *Integrating Environmental Justice Into EPA Permitting Authority*, 26 Ecology Law Quarterly 617 (2000). © 1999 by the Regents of the University of California. Reprinted by permission of the University of California, Berkeley.

Bradford C. Mank, *Can Administrative Regulations Interpret Rights Enforceable Under Section 1983?: Why Chevron Deference Survives Sandoval and Gonzaga*, 32 Florida State University Law Review 843 (2005). Reprinted with permission.

Paul Mohai & Robin Saha, *Racial Inequality in the Distribution of Hazardous Waste: A National-Level Reassessment*, 54 Social Problems 343 (2007). Reprinted by permission of University of California Press-Journals.

Rachel Morello-Frosch et al., *Environmental Justice and Southern California's Riskscape: The Distribution of Air Toxics Exposure and Health Risks Among Diverse Communities*, 36

Urban Affairs Review 551 (2001). Copyright © 2001 by Sage Publications, Inc. Reprinted by permission.

Michael P. O'Connell, *Indian Tribes and Project Development Outside Indian Reservations*, 21 Natural Resources & Environment 3 (2007). Copyright © 2007 by the American Bar Association. Reprinted with permission.

Catherine A. O'Neill, *Variable Justice: Environmental Standards, Contaminated Fish, and "Acceptable" Risk to Native Peoples*, 19 Stanford Environmental Law Journal 3 (2000). Reprinted by permission of the Stanford Environmental Law Journal.

Catherine A. O'Neill, *No Mud Pies: Risk Avoidance as Risk Regulation*, 31 Vermont Law Review 273 (2007). Reprinted with permission of Vermont Law Review.

Catherine A. O'Neill, *Environmental Justice in the Tribal Context: A Madness to EPA's Method*, 38 Environmental Law 495 (2008). Reprinted with permission.

Manuel Pastor et al., *In the Wake of the Storm: Environment, Disaster, and Race After Katrina*, © 2006 Russell Sage Foundation. Reprinted with permission.

Eric A. Posner & Cass R. Sunstein, *Climate Change Justice*, 96 Georgetown Law Journal 1565 (2008). Reprinted by the permission of the authors.

Yale Rabin, *Expulsive Zoning: The Inequitable Legacy of Euclid*, *in* Zoning and the American Dream 101 (Charles M. Haar & Jerold S. Kayden eds., 1989). Reprinted by permission of the American Planning Association, Suite 1600, 122 S. Michigan Ave., Chicago, IL 60603-6107.

Darren Ranco, *Models of Tribal Environmental Regulation*, Vol. 56, No. 3, The Federal Lawyer, March/April 2009. Reprinted by permission of the author and the Federal Bar Association.

Clifford Rechtschaffen, *Competing Visions: EPA and the States' Battle for the Future of Environmental Enforcement*, 30 Environmental Law Reporter 10,803 (2000). Reprinted by permission of the Environmental Law Institute.

Evan J. Ringquist, *Equity and the Distribution of Environmental Risk: The Case of TRI Facilities*, 78 Social Science Quarterly 811 (1997). Copyright © 1997 by Social Science Quarterly and Blackwell Publishers. Reprinted by permission.

Sylvia Rodríguez, *Land, Water, and Ethnic Identity in Taos*, *in* Land, Water, and Culture: New Perspectives on Hispanic Land Grants 313 (Charles L. Briggs & John R. Van Ness eds., 1987). Reprinted by permission of the author.

Judith V. Royster, *Native American Law*, *in* The Law of Environmental Justice: Theories and Procedures to Address Disproportionate Risk (Michael B. Gerrard & Sheila R. Foster eds., 2d ed. 2008). © 2008 by the American Bar Association. Reprinted with permission.

Andrea Ruiz-Esquide, *The Uniform Environmental Covenant Act – An Environmental Justice Perspective*, 31 Ecology Law Quarterly 1007 (2004). Reprinted by permission of the Regents of the University of California.

Robin Saha & Paul Mohai, "Explaining Race and Income Disparities in the Location of Locally Unwanted Land Uses: A Conceptual Framework," Paper presented at the 1997 Annual Meeting of the Rural Sociological Society (Toronto, August 1997). Reprinted by permission of the authors.

Patricia Salkin & Amy Lavine, *Understanding Community Benefits Agreements: Equitable Development, Social Justice and Other Considerations for Developers, Municipalities and Community Organizations*, 26 UCLA Journal of Environmental Law and Policy 291 (2008). Reprinted by permission of UCLA School of Law.

Sidney A. Shapiro & Christopher H. Schroeder, *Beyond Cost-Benefit Analysis: A Pragmatic Reorientation*, 32 Harvard Environmental Law Review 433 (2008). Reprinted by permission of Harvard Environmental Law Review.

Rena Steinzor, *Devolution and the Public Health*, 24 Harvard Environmental Law Review 351 (2000). Copyright © 2000 by President and Fellows of Harvard College and the Harvard Environmental Law Review. Reprinted by permission.

Rena Steinzor & Margaret Clune, *The Toll of Superfund Neglect: Toxic Waste Dumps and Communities at Risk* (2006). This material was created by the Center for American Progress & the Center for Progressive Reform (www.americanprogress.org & www.progressivereform.org). Reprinted with permission.

Rena I. Steinzor, Mother Earth and Uncle Sam: How Pollution and Hollow Government Hurt Our Kids (2008). Copyright © 2008. Reprinted by permission of the University of Texas Press.

Dean B. Suagee, *Symposium: Environmental Justice: Mobilizing for the 21st Century: The Indian Country Environmental Justice Clinic: From Vision to Reality*, 23 Vermont Law Review 567 (1999). Copyright © 1999 by Vermont Law Review. Reprinted by permission of Vermont Law Review and the author.

Dean Suagee, *Dimensions of Environmental Justice in Indian Country and Native Alaska*, Second National People of Color Environmental Leadership Summit Resource Paper Series (2002). Reprinted by permission of Dean Suagee.

Nicholas Targ, *A Third Policy Avenue to Address Environmental Justice: Civil Rights and Environmental Quality and Relevance of Social Capital Policy*, 16 Tulane Environmental Law Journal 167 (2002). Reprinted with permission of the Tulane Environmental Law Journal.

Melissa Tofflon-Weiss & J. Timmons Roberts, *Toxic Torts, Public Interest Law, and Environmental Justice: Evidence from Louisiana*, 26 Law and Policy 259 (2004). Reprinted with permission.

Rebecca Tsosie, *Tribal Environmental Policy in an Era of Self-Determination: The Role of Ethics, Economics, and Traditional Ecological Knowledge*, 21 Vermont Law Review 225 (1996). Copyright © 1996 by Vermont Law Review. Reprinted by permission of Vermont Law Review and the author.

Kevin Watkins, *Fighting Climate Change: Human Solidarity in a Divided World*, Human Development Report 2007/2008. © United Nations Development Programme. Reprinted with permission.

Robert A. Williams, Jr., *Large Binocular Telescopes, Red Squirrel Piñatas, and Apache Sacred Mountains: Decolonizing Environmental Law in a Multicultural World*, 96 West Virginia Law Review 1133 (1994). Reprinted by permission of the author.

Jennifer Wolch, John P. Wilson & Jed Fehrenbach, *Parks and Park Funding in Los Angeles: An Equity-Mapping Analysis*, 26 Urban Geography 4 (2005). © Bellwether Publishing. Reprinted with permission of the publisher. All rights reserved.

Working Group II Contribution to the Fourth Assessment Report of the Intergovernmental Panel on Climate Change, Summary for Policymakers, *Climate Change 2007: Impacts, Adaptation and Vulnerability*. Cambridge University Press. Reprinted with permission.

Eric K. Yamamoto & Jen-L W. Lyman, *Racializing Environmental Justice*, 72 University of Colorado Law Review 311 (2001). Reprinted by permission of the University of Colorado Law Review and Eric Yamamoto.

Tseming Yang, *The International Significance of an Instance of Urban Environmental Inequity in Tijuana, Mexico*, 31 Fordham Urban Law Journal 1321 (2004). Reprinted by permission of the author.

Jean Ziegler, *The Right to Food*, Interim Report of the Special Rapporteur, United Nations General Assembly, Sixty-second session, Item 72(b) of the provisional agenda. © United Nations, August 12, 2007. Reproduced with permission.

Environmental Justice

Chapter 1

Overview of the Environmental Justice Movement

A. Introduction: History of the Movement

In the 1980s, communities of color alarmed conventional environmental organizations, regulators and industry stakeholders with allegations of "environmental racism." These charges reflected long-standing frustration on the part of such communities, and their view that people of color systematically receive disproportionately greater environmental risk while white communities systematically receive better environmental protection. Across the country, communities of color began to challenge the siting of hazardous waste facilities, landfills, industrial activities and other risk-producing land practices within their community. These efforts at the grassroots level soon coalesced into a national campaign referred to as the environmental justice movement. The roots of the movement lie in diverse political projects — the civil rights movement, the grassroots anti-toxics movement of the 1980s, organizing efforts of Native Americans and labor, and, to a lesser extent, the traditional environmental movement. *See generally* LUKE COLE & SHEILA FOSTER, FROM THE GROUND UP: ENVIRONMENTAL RACISM AND THE RISE OF THE ENVIRONMENTAL JUSTICE MOVEMENT (2001).

"Environmental Justice" soon came to mean more than skewed distributional consequences of environmental burdens to communities of color. Becoming multi-issue and multi-racial in scope, the movement began to address disparities borne by the poor as well as people of color, acknowledging the substantial overlap between the two demographic categories. Concerns about regulatory processes surfaced as well. Often, the communities most impacted by environmentally risky activities had been excluded from important decision-making proceedings, sometimes intentionally so and sometimes because of a lack of resources, specialized knowledge, and other structural impediments. Initially, environmental justice activists used direct action such as demonstrations as the primary means to raise public awareness of the issue.

Largely in response to this early activism, several investigations and studies were undertaken which lent support to charges of environmental injustice. For example, a 1983 report by the U.S. General Accounting Office found that in the Environmental Protection Agency's (EPA's) Region IV, three of four major offsite hazardous waste facilities were located in predominantly African American communities; in 1987, a national study by the United Church of Christ Commission for Racial Justice found a positive correlation between racial minorities and proximity to commercial hazardous waste facilities and uncontrolled waste sites. Significantly, the study found that race was a more statistically significant variable than income. This early activism also culminated in an extraordinary gathering of grassroots activists at the First National People of Color Environmental Leadership Summit in Washington, D.C. on October 24–27, 1991, where the Principles of Environmental Justice, which are reprinted below, were adopted.

In 1992, a National Law Journal investigation found that EPA enforcement under various federal statutes and cleanup under the Superfund law was inequitable by race and, to a less pronounced degree, income. Other national and regional studies, including a review of the evidence by an EPA-established workgroup, began to find the same patterns of disproportionate location of industrial facilities and waste sites, exposure to contaminants, and adverse health effects in poor areas and in communities of color, further galvanizing the movement. Some criticized the methodology of the early studies, and questioned the extent of disparities and whether they might have existed at the time of the initial siting of polluting facilities, thus leading to a round of subsequent studies. The later, more sophisticated studies confirmed many findings of the earlier studies.

In response to the earlier studies and to continuing pressure from communities of color, former President Clinton in 1994 signed an Executive Order on Environmental Justice requiring all federal agencies to make environmental justice part of their mission and establishing an interagency work group. (The Order is reproduced in Chapter 10). In 1992, EPA established what ultimately came to be called the Office of Environmental Justice. EPA also convened the National Environmental Justice Advisory Council (NEJAC), a diverse federal advisory group charged with making recommendations to the EPA concerning a broad range of environmental justice matters. The EPA also began to take steps to include environmental justice organizations and community residents in a variety of agency projects, such as the EPA-sponsored "Brownfield" initiatives, which involves the re-use of idle industrial sites that are contaminated or perceived to be contaminated. These actions in the name of environmental justice marked a new course for environmental regulation, as environmental regulators did not traditionally consider demographics and social context in the course of their regulatory activities.

Also in the 1980s and 1990s, heavily impacted communities continued to organize and began undertaking legal efforts to redress the inequitable environmental burdens that were apparent across the country. As explored in detail later in this book, legal challenges have met with mixed success. Claims alleging violations of the Equal Protection Clause of the U.S. Constitution have largely failed because of the difficulty of proving intentional discrimination. Other claims, some using traditional common law theories and environmental laws, have been somewhat more successful. Community groups have also filed numerous administrative complaints with EPA against state and regional environmental agencies alleging violations of Title VI of the Civil Rights Act of 1964. Title VI, which prohibits discrimination in programs or activities that receive federal financial assistance, had historically been applied in the education and employment context but not in the environmental context.

EPA was slow to develop a framework for investigating and deciding the Title VI cases, issuing Interim Guidance in 1998 and an expanded Draft Guidance in 2000. But the Agency has been even slower in taking any specific action on the complaints. Since 1993, it has decided only one case on the merits after an investigation; some other cases were settled, but the great majority of the complaints have been rejected or dismissed.

Under the Bush Administration, EPA took a different approach to environmental justice, redefining it to mean environmental protection for everyone, and de-emphasizing the need to focus special attention on minority and low-income populations (as described in Chapter 10). As a result, and because of the perception that the Administration generally was hostile to environmental justice claims, advocates largely shifted their attention to state and local governments to remedy environmental disparities. As this book goes to press in 2009, it remains to be seen whether the recent change in administrations portends a more robust level of attention by EPA and other federal agencies to environmental justice.

As noted, environmental disparities have been found in the siting, compliance and cleanup contexts. However, it also appears that environmental inequities can be caused in part because of the failure to consider environmental justice when regulatory standards are set and programs are designed. Accordingly, it is clear that environmental justice issues must be considered at the earliest stages of regulatory activity, not only at the permitting and enforcement stages, but particularly during the formation of policy, including the design of new programs—for example, programs tackling climate change.

Unfortunately, integrating environmental justice into environmental regulation in a manner that meaningfully responds to both the distributional and process issues has proven to be exceptionally complex. Environmental regulators are concerned with the scope of their authority to consider environmental justice under environmental statutes, with the extent of any legal duty to do so under the civil rights laws, as well as with the uncertainty and complexity such an undertaking might add to their regulatory programs. The regulated community is concerned about the potential for increased delay to their projects and about compliance costs. Environmental justice advocates continue to attempt to address concerns and participate in various proceedings under severe resource constraints, and in some areas still confront considerable hostility and resistance by government officials. In addition, participation by environmental justice advocates is hampered by the tendency among other stakeholders and governmental agencies to view environmental justice as a "special interest." Yet, environmental justice advocates stress that the relevant issues are not demands for special treatment, but are grounded upon precepts of basic fairness and equal environmental protection: that there should be a level playing field for all stakeholders and that environmental burdens and benefits should not fall in disproportionate patterns by race and income.

The thrust of this book is therefore twofold, first to examine the complexities presented by environmental inequity; and second, to explore the potential that exists within the current system to move environmental regulation forward in a responsible manner that makes good on a promise of a more just society and, ultimately, an ecologically sustainable environment.

Pathfinder on Environmental Justice Generally

Among the numerous books and articles about environmental justice are RACE AND THE INCIDENCE OF ENVIRONMENTAL HAZARDS: A TIME FOR DISCOURSE (Paul Mohai & Bunyan Bryant eds., 1992); CONFRONTING ENVIRONMENTAL RACISM: VOICES FROM THE GRASSROOTS (Robert D. Bullard ed., 1993) and UNEQUAL PROTECTION: ENVIRONMENTAL JUSTICE AND COMMUNITIES OF COLOR (Robert D. Bullard ed., 1994); BUNYAN BRYANT, ENVIRONMENTAL JUSTICE: ISSUES, POLICIES AND SOLUTIONS (1995); CHRISTOPHER FOREMAN, THE PROMISE AND PERIL OF ENVIRONMENTAL JUSTICE (1998); LUKE COLE & SHEILA FOSTER, FROM THE GROUND UP: ENVIRONMENTAL RACISM AND THE RISE OF THE ENVIRONMENTAL JUSTICE MOVEMENT (2001); Tseming Yang, *Melding Civil Rights and Environmentalism: Finding Environmental Justice's Place in Environmental Regulation*, 26 HARV.

ENVTL. L. REV. 1 (2002); POWER, JUSTICE, AND THE ENVIRONMENT: A CRITICAL APPRAISAL OF THE ENVIRONMENTAL JUSTICE MOVEMENT (David N. Pellow & Robert J. Brulle eds., 2005); Robert D. Bullard et al., *Toxic Wastes and Race at Twenty: Why Race Still Matters After All of These Years*, 38 ENVTL. L. 371 (2008); and THE LAW OF ENVIRONMENTAL JUSTICE: THEORIES AND PROCEDURES TO ADDRESS DISPROPORTIONATE RISKS (Michael B. Gerrard & Sheila R. Foster eds., 2d ed. 2008).

Urban Habitat publishes a (usually semi-annual) newsletter entitled *Race, Poverty & the Environment* that focuses on particular environmental justice issues. It can be found at: http://www.urbanhabitat.org/rpe. EPA's Office of Environmental Justice maintains a web page: http://www.epa.gov/compliance/environmentaljustice/index.html. Other very useful resources can be found on the web page of the Environmental Justice Resource Center at Clark Atlanta University, http://www.ejrc.cau.edu/. The Resource Center has published THE PEOPLE OF COLOR ENVIRONMENTAL GROUPS DIRECTORY 2000, which lists more than 400 people-of-color groups working on environmental justice. Professor Denis Binder has collected environmental justice cases in three articles, *Index of Environmental Justice Cases,* 27 URB. LAW. 163 (1995), *Environmental Justice Index II,* 3 CHAPMAN L. REV. 309 (2000), and *Environmental Justice Index III,* 35 ENVTL. L. REP. 10,606 (2005).

B. Fairness and Justice Considered

The fundamental question that presents itself when considering environmental justice is the working definition of "fairness" and "justice." Consider the views of these prominent environmental justice scholars. In the first excerpt, Professor Robert Kuehn explains that underlying the environmental justice movement are four concepts of justice: distributive, procedural, corrective, and social justice.

Robert R. Kuehn, A Taxonomy of Environmental Justice
30 Environmental Law Reporter 10,681 (2000)

Efforts to understand environmental justice are [ ] complicated by the term's international, national, and local scope; by its broad definition of the environment—where one lives, works, plays, and goes to school; and by its broad range of concerns—such as public health, natural resource conservation, and worker safety in both urban and rural environs. Disputes at the international level include allegations that governments and multinational corporations are exploiting indigenous peoples and the impoverished conditions of developing nations. At the national level, although an overwhelming number of studies show differences by race and income in exposures to environmental hazards, debate continues about the strength of that evidence and the appropriate political and legal response to such disparities. At the local level, many people of color and lower income communities believe that they have not been treated fairly regarding the distribution of the environmental benefits and burdens....

Shifting Perspectives and Uses of Terms

The U.S. Environmental Protection Agency (EPA) initially used the term "environmental equity," defined as the equitable distribution of environmental risks across population groups, to refer to the environmental justice phenomenon. Because this term implies the redistribution of risk across racial and economic groups rather than risk reduction and avoidance, it is no longer used by EPA, though it is still used by some states.

In some instances, the phrase "environmental racism," defined as "any policy, practice or directive that differentially affects or disadvantages (whether intended or unintended) individuals, groups, or communities based on race or color," is used to explain the differential treatment of populations on environmental issues. Commentators disagree over the proper usage of this term, particularly over whether an action having an unequal distributive outcome across racial groups would in itself be a sufficient basis to label an action environmental racism or whether the action must be the result of intentional racial animus. Today, many environmental justice advocates and scholars avoid the term "environmental racism," though the phrase continues to be employed and is useful in identifying the institutional causes of some environmental injustices. This shift is attributable to a desire to focus on solutions rather than mere identification of problems, as well as a desire to encompass class concerns and not to be limited by issues of intentional conduct....

In 1994, President Clinton issued Executive Order No. 12898 ... and adopted the phrase "environmental justice" to refer to "disproportionately high and adverse human health or environmental effects ... on minority populations and low-income populations." The Executive Order's use of the term "environmental justice" is significant in at least three respects. First, the Executive Order focuses not only on the disproportionate burdens addressed by the term environmental equity, but also on issues of enforcement of environmental laws and opportunities for public participation. Second, the Executive Order identifies not just minorities but also low-income populations as the groups who have been subject to, and entitled to relief from, unfair or unequal treatment. Finally, the Executive Order, and in particular the accompanying memorandum, refers to environmental justice as a goal or aspiration to be achieved, rather than as a problem or cause.

In 1998, EPA's Office of Environmental Justice set forth the Agency's "standard definition" of environmental justice:

> The fair treatment of people of all races, cultures, incomes, and educational levels with respect to the development and enforcement of environmental laws, regulations, and policies. Fair treatment implies that no population should be forced to shoulder a disproportionate share of exposure to the negative effects of pollution due to lack of political or economic strength.

Def.

Going beyond the issues of disproportionate exposures and participation in the development and enforcement of laws and policies, EPA further elaborated that environmental justice:

> is based on the premise that: 1) it is a basic right of all Americans to live and work in "safe, healthful, productive, and aesthetically and culturally pleasing surroundings;" 2) it is not only an environmental issue but a public health issue; 3) it is forward-looking and goal-oriented; and 4) it is also inclusive since it is based on the concept of fundamental fairness, which includes the concept of economic prejudices as well as racial prejudices.

Professor Bunyan Bryant defines environmental justice as referring "to those cultural norms and values, rules, regulations, behaviors, policies, and decisions to support sustainable communities, where people can interact with confidence that their environment is safe, nurturing, and protective." Some critics of environmental justice contend that these definitions of environmental justice by government agencies and environmental justice advocates are so broad and aspirational as not to state clearly the ends of environmental justice.

An alternative approach to defining environmental justice that does state its desired ends, albeit very ambitious ones, was developed by environmental justice leaders during the 1991 First People of Color Environmental Leadership Summit. Its "Principles of Environmental Justice" sets forth a 17-point paradigm [excerpted below]....

Dr. Robert Bullard has distilled the principles of environmental justice into a framework of five basic characteristics: (1) protect all persons from environmental degradation; (2) adopt a public health prevention of harm approach; (3) place the burden of proof on those who seek to pollute; (4) obviate the requirement to prove intent to discriminate; and (5) redress existing inequities by targeting action and resources. In his view, environmental justice seeks to make environmental protection more democratic and asks the fundamental ethical and political questions of "who gets what, why and how much." ...

Students and lawyers are often left without an understanding of unifying themes or common political, legal, or economic approaches to addressing allegations of injustice. The classification method set forth in this Article seeks to overcome this shortcoming and to advance the understanding of environmental justice by disassembling the term into the four traditional notions of "justice" that are implicated by allegations of environmental injustice....

Environmental Justice as Distributive Justice

... Distributive justice has been defined as "the right to equal treatment, that is, to the same distribution of goods and opportunities as anyone else has or is given." Aristotle is often credited with the first articulation of the concept and explained it as involving "the distribution of honour, wealth, and the other divisible assets of the community, which may be allotted among its members." The focus of this aspect of justice is on fairly distributed outcomes, rather than on the process for arriving at such outcomes.

In an environmental context, distributive justice involves the equitable distribution of the burdens resulting from environmentally threatening activities or of the environmental benefits of government and private-sector programs. More specifically, in an environmental justice context, distributive justice most commonly involves addressing the disproportionate public health and environmental risks borne by people of color and lower incomes....

Distributive justice in an environmental justice context does not mean redistributing pollution or risk. Instead, environmental justice advocates argue that it means equal protection for all and the elimination of environmental hazards and the need to place hazardous activities in any community. In other words, distributive justice is achieved through a lowering of risks, not a shifting or equalizing of existing risks.

With such a strong focus on the inequitable distribution by race and income of environmental hazards, an often overlooked aspect of distributive justice is that it also involves the distribution of the benefits of environmental programs and policies, such as parks and beaches, public transportation, safe drinking water, and sewerage and drainage....

Some of the best known local environmental justice disputes have involved dramatic evidence of distributive inequities.

In Chester Residents Concerned for Quality Living v. Seif [132 F.2d 925 (3rd Cir. 1997), vacated, 524 U.S. 974 (1998)], residents of Chester, Pennsylvania, alleged that the state's issuance of a permit for a new waste facility would create an unlawful disparate impact on African-American residents. As evidence, they noted that Chester, with a population of 42,000, 65% of which are African-American, had become the designated dumping grounds for the rest of Delaware County, with a population of 502,000, 91% of which are white. Though one-twelfth the size of the county, Chester already has five permitted waste facilities, while the rest of Delaware County has only two. All of Delaware County's municipal waste and sewage is processed in Chester, although only 7.5% of the county's population resides in the town. Most dramatically, the permitted capacity for the waste facilities in the much smaller city of Chester [is] 1,500 times greater than the permitted capacity for the remaining facilities in Delaware County (2.1 million tons vs. 1,400 tons), and the capacity per person for the waste facilities in the 65% African-American Chester area is almost 18,000 times greater than the capacity per person for the facilities in 91% white Delaware County.

The dispute over a proposal by Shintech to build a new polyvinyl chloride (PVC) plant in the lower income, 84% African-American community of Convent, Louisiana, also raised substantial distributive justice concerns. An analysis of toxic air emissions from the 10 existing petrochemical plants in the Convent area revealed that residents were already exposed to 251,179 pounds of toxic air pollution per square mile per year, and Shintech proposed to emit an additional three million pounds of air pollution per year, over 600,000 pounds of which would be toxic. This existing cumulative impact on the 84% African-American Convent-area residents is 67 times greater than the toxic air pollution burden for the rest of St. James Parish (the third most polluted parish in the state and 43.5% African American), 93 times greater than the average toxic air pollution exposure per square mile for the heavily polluted Louisiana Mississippi River industrial corridor (36.8% African American), 129 times greater than Louisiana's average exposure per square mile (the second most polluted state in the nation and 30.8% African American), and 658 times higher than the average toxic air pollution exposure per square mile in the United States (12% African American). EPA's disparate impact analysis, using its "relative emissions burden ratio" method, found that, were Shintech permitted to operate, African Americans in St. James Parish would experience a 71% to 242% greater toxic air pollution burden than non-African Americans in the parish....

Environmental Justice as Procedural Justice

Claims of procedural injustice also are common in environmental justice disputes, and it is not usual for people of color and low-income communities to complain about both the distributive and procedural aspects of an environmental policy or decision. Indeed, in many situations, a community's judgment about whether or not an outcome was distributively just will be significantly determined by the perceived fairness of the procedures leading to the outcome.

Procedural justice has been defined as "the right to treatment as an equal. That is the right, not to an equal distribution of some good or opportunity, but to equal concern and respect in the political decision about how these goods and opportunities are to be distributed." Aristotle referred to this as a status in which individuals have an "equal share in ruling and being ruled." It involves justice as a function of the manner in which a decision is made, and it requires a focus on the fairness of the decision-making process, rather than on its outcome....

The Executive Order on environmental justice has a strong focus on procedural justice, directing agencies to ensure greater public participation and access to information for minority and low-income populations. The Principles of Environmental Justice demand that public policy be based on mutual respect and justice for all peoples and free from bias or discrimination, affirm the fundamental right to self-determination, and insist on the right to participate as equal partners at every level of decision-making.

Environmental justice complaints raise both *ex ante* and *ex post* considerations of procedural fairness. Looking at the process in advance of its use (*ex ante*), they question whether the decision-making and public participation procedures are fair to all concerned or whether they favor one side over the other. Also, looking back (*ex post*), the complaints question whether the completed decision-making process did, in fact, treat all with equal concern and respect.

One way to judge procedural justice *ex ante* is to determine if those to be affected by the decision agree in advance on the process for making the decision. Thus, procedural justice requires looking not just to participation in a process but to whether the process is designed in a way to lead to a fair outcome. In this respect, environmental decision-making processes have been roundly criticized by commentators who have examined issues of environmental justice and public participation. One common observation is that the predominant expertise-oriented, interest-group model of environmental decision-making favors those with resources and political power over people of color and low-income communities. Even the [civic] republican process, which outwardly seeks to advance community interests over private interests, may obscure the true private interests at issue and the continuing disparities in resources, power, and influence. In general, to achieve procedural justice, observers advocate developing more deliberative models of decision-making, providing disadvantaged groups with greater legal and technical resources, and ensuring equal access to decision-makers and the decision-making process....

A common procedural justice complaint at the national level is that people of color and lower income communities [have] little influence on the decision-making processes of legislatures and environmental agencies.... Even where citizens are able to participate, environmental decision-makers are skeptical of the validity of citizen information and are biased in favor of the scientific data submitted by regulated industries.

Underrepresentation on the technical or scientific boards and commissions that make environmental decisions and recommendations is also a problem, particularly since the actions of these boards often reflect politics and personal values....

Another procedural justice aspect is the manner in which the government collects and analyzes data on environmental exposures and public health. In one case, EPA and the National Institutes of Health announced a $15 million, 10-year epidemiological study on the health of farmers and farmworkers that would omit Hispanics from the study, even though farmworkers are largely Hispanic. The justification for the omission? The difficulty of tracking the highly mobile Hispanic population....

In addition to the procedural justice issues arising from the manner in which the state handled the permitting process, the Shintech case illustrates the ex ante obstacles that people of color and lower income communities confront. Under the state permitting process, the permit applicant has an automatic right, if requested, to an adjudicatory hearing, yet local residents have no such right....

The county's handing of a permit to build a hazardous waste incinerator near the Hispanic community of Kettleman City, California, illustrates the procedural barriers often encountered by ethnic communities. Despite the repeated, strong interest expressed by [Spanish]-speaking residents to participate in the permitting process, environmental impact documents, meeting notices, and public hearing testimony were never provided in Spanish. The court in El Pueblo Para el Aire y Agua Limpio v. County of Kings [22 Envtl. L. Reptr. 20,357 (Cal. Super. Ct. 1991)] held that the meaningful involvement of local residents was effectively precluded by the failure to provide Spanish translations and set aside the local permit. When similar translation concerns were raised by Vietnamese-speaking residents regarding efforts to reopen the Marine Shale hazardous waste incinerator in Amelia, Louisiana, the state responded that it would take care of the inability of the Vietnamese community to participate in the public hearing process *after* the permit was issued....

An unresolved aspect of procedural justice is whether a fair process can negate a claim that a disproportionate outcome is unjust. Some argue that if the decision-maker has given impartial attention to and consideration of competing claims to different benefits, an outcome would not be unjust even if the result were to subordinate one group to another....

While environmental justice requires, at a minimum, a procedurally just process, the emphasis on disparate effects, rather than discriminatory intent, in the Executive Order, Principles of Environmental Justice, and Title VI's implementing regulations indicates that a fair process alone will not negate claims of distributive injustice....

Although there has been a great deal of discussion about the need to reform existing public participation models and although many government agencies now recognize their failure to ensure meaningful participation by disadvantaged populations, EPA's refusal to require that waste facilities and permitting agencies "make all reasonable efforts to ensure equal opportunity for the public to participate in the permitting process" [in EPA's Resource Conservation and Recovery Act's public participation regulations], the antagonistic attitudes of some state officials toward allegations of environmental justice, the hostility of environmental justice critics toward government grants to community groups for environmental education and outreach efforts, and the assertions by some regulated entities that increased public participation is not appropriate do not bode well for finding consensus on the format of a fair decision-making process or for avoiding future allegations of procedural injustice.

Environmental Justice as Corrective Justice

The third aspect of justice encompassed by the term environmental justice is "corrective justice," a notion of justice that is sometimes referred to by other names and may be subsumed within claims for distributive or procedural justice....

"Corrective justice" involves fairness in the way punishments for lawbreaking are assigned and damages inflicted on individuals and communities are addressed.... Corrective justice involves not only the just administration of punishment to those who break the law, but also a duty to repair the losses for which one is responsible....

Therefore, as reflected in claims made in the environmental justice context, corrective justice encompasses many aspects of wrongdoing and injury and includes the concepts of "retributive justice," "compensatory justice," "restorative justice," and "commutative justice." I adopt the term corrective justice here because environmental justice seeks more than just retribution or punishment of those who violate legal rules of conduct. Corrective justice is also preferred over the phrase compensatory justice because the latter term may imply that, provided compensation is paid, an otherwise unjust action is acceptable. It is also important to note that although some concepts of corrective justice view fault or wrongful gain as a necessary condition for liability, environmental justice principles impose responsibility for damages regardless of fault (e.g., the polluter-pays principle). Corrective justice, therefore, is not used in the narrow Aristotelian rectificatory sense but instead in a broader, applied sense that violators be caught and punished and not reap benefits for disregarding legal standards and that injuries caused by the acts of another, whether a violation of law or not, be remedied....

The theme of corrective justice ... figures prominently in the efforts of indigenous people to achieve environmental justice. Native Americans have long complained that the federal government and mining and oil companies have failed to take responsibility for and address contamination caused by their nuclear testing and resource development activities on Indian lands. In addition, hundreds of open dumps, many originally operated by the Indian Health Service, currently exist in Indian country and are in need of cleanup. The recent, expanded ability of tribes to obtain authority to implement federal environmental laws presents tribal governments with the opportunity to promote corrective justice by directly enforcing compliance with environmental statutes on tribal lands, rather than having to rely on federal agencies, yet finding the financial and technical resources to carry out that authority remains a problem.

Local efforts to achieve corrective justice are illustrated by community efforts to address contamination from lead smelters in West Dallas—"the classic example of government inaction and callous disregard for the law." [quoting Robert Bullard. Eds.] As early as 1972, Dallas officials were aware of significantly elevated lead levels in the blood of children living in a minority neighborhood near a lead smelter that had repeatedly violated the law. EPA's own study in 1981 confirmed the high lead concentrations in children living near the smelters. In spite of repeated complaints by local residents, government officials took no action; EPA even rejected a voluntary cleanup plan, preferring still further tests of local children and suggesting that spreading dirt and planting grass would be sufficient.... Finally, after 50 years of operation without necessary local permits and 20 years after government officials became aware of the public health problems caused by the illegally operated smelter, authorities closed the facility and started a comprehensive cleanup program....

Environmental Justice as Social Justice

The fourth and final aspect of justice implicated by the term environmental justice is "social justice," a far-reaching, and some say nebulous, goal of the environmental justice movement....

Social justice is "that branch of the virtue of justice that moves us to use our best efforts to bring about a more just ordering of society—one in which people's needs are more fully met." "The demands of social justice are ... first, that the members of every class have enough resources and enough power to live as befits human beings, and second, that the privileged classes, whoever they are, be accountable to the wider society for the way they use their advantages."

Environmental justice has been described as a "marriage of the movement for social justice with environmentalism" integrating environmental concerns into a broader agenda that emphasizes social, racial, and economic justice. Dr. Bullard refers to this aspect of environmental justice as "social equity: ... an assessment of the role of sociological factors (race, ethnicity, class, culture, lifestyles, political power, and so forth) in environmental decision-making."

Professor Sheila Foster has argued that a narrow focus on issues of distributive justice neglects the search for social structures and agents that are causing the environmental problems. A social justice perspective presents environmental justice as part of larger problems of racial, social, and economic justice and helps illustrate the influence of politics, race, and class on an area's quality of life. This broader social perspective contrasts with traditional environmentalism and its narrower focus on wilderness preservation and the technological aspects of environmental regulation.

Environmental justice's focus on social justice reflects reality. As one community organizer explained, oppressed people do not have compartmentalized problems—they do not separate the hazardous waste incinerator from the fact that their schools are underfunded, that they have no day care, no sidewalks or streetlights, or no jobs. The reason disadvantaged communities do not separate these problems is that their quality of life as a whole is suffering and the political, economic, and racial causes are likely interrelated....

Social justice influences can work in two ways. The same underlying racial, economic, and political factors that are responsible for the environmental threats to the community also likely play a significant role in why the area may suffer from other problems like inadequate housing, a lack of employment opportunities, poor schools, etc. In turn, the presence of undesirable land uses that threaten the health and well-being of local residents and provide few direct economic benefits negatively influences the quality of life, development potential, and attitudes of the community and may lead to further social and economic degradation.

Government officials are often hesitant to embrace the social justice aspects of environmental justice, reflecting a reluctance to take on the broader systemic causes of environmental injustice or to consider issues outside the narrow technical focus of the agency. Nonetheless, the President's Executive Order acknowledges the significance of social justice by directing each federal agency to consider the economic and social implications of an agency's environmental justice activities, and the memorandum accompanying the Executive Order requires analysis of the economic and social, not just environmental, effects of federal actions on minority and low-income communities....

[C]riticism of environmental justice as too myopic and a diversion of scarce resources away from other more important social and public health problems is not well-founded. Most often, environmental justice efforts do not wastefully divert a community's attention but instead bring residents together to focus on a broad array of social justice problems.... [G]overnment officials and firms seeking community acceptance for environmentally risky projects must as a practical, if not also moral, matter consider whether social justice is served by their projects. For if the environmental and other social burdens of a proposed project are imposed on the local community while the economic and other benefits flow elsewhere, "community opposition will be fierce and the chances for success lessened." ...

* * *

The following article presents various models of fairness in one important area of environmental justice, the siting of locally unwanted land uses (LULUs).

Vicki Been, What's Fairness Got to Do With It? Environmental Justice and the Siting of Locally Undesirable Land Uses
78 Cornell Law Review 1001 (1993)

The various legislative solutions to the problem of disproportionate siting reflect different conceptions about why disproportionate siting is wrong, and about what would constitute "fair" siting. The differences are not surprising. Calls for environmental justice are essentially calls for "equality" and, as Peter Westen has noted, "equality in the end is a rhetorical device that tends to persuade precisely by virtue of 'cloak[ing] strongly divergent ideas over which people do in fact disagree.'" Advocates of environmental justice have wisely chosen to advance general concepts of equality, rather than endanger their coalition by attempting to specify the precise content of "justice," "equity" or "fairness." ...

Fairness in the Pattern of Distribution

A broad conception of fairness in siting would require that a LULU's burdens be spread on a per capita or proportional basis over society as a whole....

There are strong and weak versions of the equal division conception of fairness. Under the strong version, fairness demands a proportional distribution of benefits....

A weaker version of the theory asserts that fairness requires a proportional distribution of burdens, even if benefits are not allocated proportionally. The United States embraces this view regarding societal burdens, such as jury duty and military service under a draft. This version of the theory assumes that an objective distinction can be drawn between burdens and the absence of benefits, and that the distinction mandates an equal division of burdens regardless of the distribution of benefits....

Several means of distribution are plausible under the proportional distribution of burden theory. One scheme would impose a physical proportional distribution: LULUs themselves would be distributed equally among neighborhoods. This distribution could be either equal *ex post* or equal *ex ante*. In an *ex post* scheme, the facilities and the harms that they pose would be distributed proportionately among neighborhoods. For example, if New York City requires facilities for 10,000 homeless individuals and has 100 neighborhoods, all holding some land suitable for a facility, each neighborhood would receive one facility housing 100 individuals. In an *ex ante* scheme, each neighborhood has an equal chance of being selected for the site through a lottery process. For example, if New York City requires a sewage sludge treatment plant, each of the 100 neighborhoods would have a 1/100 chance of being selected for the site. The *ex ante* physical distribution scheme is particularly well-suited to situations in which there are economies of scale in building and operating fewer but larger LULUs. Some types of hazardous waste, for example, are stored most efficiently in large, centralized facilities....

Instead of either *ex ante* or *ex post* physical equality, a distribution might seek "compensated" equality. In this distribution scheme, all individuals or communities that gain a net benefit from a particular LULU must compensate those who suffer a net loss. For example, if a sludge treatment plant imposed costs upon a neighborhood, each of the neighborhoods that benefitted from the plant, but did not suffer the detriment of close proximity, would have to pay a proportionate share of the costs....

Both the *ex ante* and *ex post* mechanisms for physically distributing LULU burdens face significant problems of definition and measurement....

First, what criteria should be used to compare the burdens of the LULUs to be distributed? Depending upon the basis of comparison, even the same type of facility may impose different types or levels of burden upon various communities. Two neighborhoods hosting identical hazardous waste treatment plants, for example, might bear different burdens if the basis of comparison is health risk, because the geology or transportation networks or composition of the workforce of one area could make one plant somewhat riskier than the other. Some criteria, such as health risk or loss in property value, are obvious grounds for comparison. But others, such as psychological harms or interference with social networks, are controversial.

When the LULUs being compared are different, such as a prison and a sludge treatment plant, comparisons will require agreement on how different criteria are to be weighted or reduced to some common metric such as dollar loss. Whether and how to translate burdens such as health risks to monetary terms is also a controversial issue....

Although environmental justice advocates have not been specific about the grounds for their assertion that compensation schemes are immoral, several arguments could be offered. One argument against compensation schemes would focus on the immorality of commodifying certain matters involving life, health and safety, or human dignity....

An additional argument could assert that compensation schemes take unfair advantage of the existing unequal distribution of wealth.... When a community suffers severe disadvantage from existing inequalities of wealth, the voluntariness of its agreement to host the LULU is questionable....

Compensatory schemes face a variety of pragmatic hurdles. The most important hurdle is the difficulty of translating the risks of a LULU into monetary terms. As a first step, the proponents of the facility, regulators, and those affected by the facility must reach some consensus about the probability and expected consequences of the hazards posed by the facility....

Compensation mechanisms also raise difficult questions about who should receive compensation: residents, property owners, the neighborhood itself, or some combination of the three. Residents would claim that they bear the most immediate risk and injury. Landlords, however, would assert that they absorb at least some, if not all, of the tenants' damages through lower rents. Moreover, if residents received compensation, the rights of future residents would have to be considered because they undoubtedly would bear part of the risks. For residents who benefit from the LULU (by obtaining employment at the facility, for example) difficult questions will arise about whether those benefits sufficiently offset any damages that those residents also incur. Additionally, compensation paid to the neighborhood itself would raise questions about how to define the affected neighborhood and whether to spend the money to mitigate the harms caused to individual residents....

One could argue that a fair distribution of LULUs would require advantaged neighborhoods to bear more of the burden that LULUs impose than poor and minority neighborhoods. Such a distribution could involve either a physical siting scheme in which advantaged neighborhoods receive a disproportionately greater number of LULUs or a compensated siting scheme in which advantaged neighborhoods pay a greater share of the cost of LULUs. One rationale for such "progressive" siting would be compensatory justice: advantaged neighborhoods should bear more of the LULU burden in order to redress or remedy past discrimination against poor and minority neighborhoods....

Fairness As Cost-Internalization

Many environmental justice advocates argue that fairness requires those who benefit from LULUs to bear the cost of the LULUs. Forcing the internalization of costs leads to greater fairness in two ways. First, it is fairer to hold individuals responsible for their actions than to let costs fall on innocent bystanders. Second, forcing the internalization of costs results in greater efficiency, and greater efficiency is likely to mean fewer LULUs. Purchasers of products that generate waste will reduce consumption once the prices of the products reflect the true cost of waste facilities. In turn, producers will develop more efficient means of production, given the cost of disposing the waste generated. The number of LULUs will thereby decrease to the socially optimal level—the level at which the marginal utility of the product necessitating the LULU equals its costs.

Such a "user pays" approach is not always possible because it requires a precise matching of benefit and burden. Additionally, some LULUs, such as homeless shelters, result more directly from political decisions about how to allocate society's resources than from personal consumption choices. In those circumstances, fairness as cost-internalization requires that the burdens be spread throughout society, so that all are forced to confront the costs of society's choices and to make better decisions....

The practical problems of calculating the full costs of a LULU and determining who should receive compensation also remain. The problem of ensuring that all costs are accounted for is especially troubling. Compensation set at a negotiated level, for example, would undermine the goal of full internalization unless negotiations were carefully structured to ensure that the community did not settle for insufficient compensation.... [T]he process by which the community negotiates a compensation package may undervalue the interests of a particular subgroup within the community. Protecting against such bargaining failures would be costly and difficult....

Fairness as Process

Rather than focusing on the distribution of burdens to determine whether the siting process is equitable, the fairness as process theory focuses on the procedures by which the burden is distributed. The most obvious theory of fairness as process would assert that a distribution is fair as long as it results from a process that was agreed upon in advance by all those potentially affected. Although there are examples of interstate siting compacts and regional intrastate siting agreements, in which all participants voluntarily agree to a particular siting process, most LULUs are sited in communities that had no opportunity to remove themselves from the selection process. Therefore, this Section focuses on theories of fairness as process that do not rest upon voluntary agreement for their legitimacy....

A siting decision motivated by hostility toward people of a particular race is unfair under almost any theory of justice, and would not be considered fair under the Constitution. Under the intentional discrimination theory, fairness requires that a decision to site a LULU be made without any intent to disadvantage people of color.

The first problem with an intentional discrimination theory is the difficulty of proving intent. Many in the environmental justice movement charge that developers and siting officials "deliberate[ly] target[] people of color communities for toxic waste facilities." Siting opponents have yet to prove that charge to the satisfaction of a court. Their efforts have been stymied, in part, by the general difficulty of proving the intent of a legislative or administrative body. That difficulty is compounded in the siting context because siting choices tend to involve a series of decisions by a variety of multi-member entities....

Even if discrimination is unintentional or based upon characteristics that do not trigger strict scrutiny under the Equal Protection Clause, disproportionate siting arguably would be inappropriate if it stemmed from a siting process that failed to treat people with "equal concern and respect," instead valuing certain people less than others. Under this theory, if a siting process is more attentive to the interests of wealthier or white neighborhoods than to the interests of poor or minority neighborhoods, that process illegitimately treats the poor and people of color as unequal....

The notion that fair siting requires treating all potential host communities as equals is extremely difficult to implement on a practical level. The most plausible way to ensure that decision makers accord equal concern to all communities is through an "impact statement" requirement. This would require decision makers to consider all of the effects that a siting might have on a neighborhood, including its impact on health, the environment, and the neighborhood's quality of life. Theoretically, by forcing decision makers to examine the possible effects of a siting, the process would ensure that the decision reflects equal consideration for both communities. In reality, impact statements may give only the illusion of neutrality in their analysis of a facility's potential effects. Further, decision-makers required to think about such effects may give only the illusion of consideration....

Burden shifting

Refer to CY 0220005125

ANTITRUST AND REGULATION IN THE EU AND US:
legal and economic perspectives.

Edited by Francois Leveque, Howard Shelanksi, Cheltenham, Edward Elgar Publishing Ltd., 2008. 264p. (New horizons in competition law and economics) ISBN 9781847207616. $125.00.   CLOTH.

Antitrust

-- United States; -- European Union

L.C. 2007047853.   K3850.

William S. Hein & Co., Inc. Buffalo, New York 14209
www.heingreenslips.com / mail@wshein.com / 800-828-7571

Like several other theories of fairness, the treatment as equals theory rests on the problematic premise that the costs and benefits that a LULU imposes upon communities are measurable, and that different costs and benefits can be reduced to a common metric. Even if that premise were true, impact statements detailing the potential effects of a siting still would not necessarily show equal concern for the interests of the poor and minorities....

* * *

Notes and Questions

1. The different models of fairness outlined by Professor Been can be summarized as follows: ① even apportionment of LULUs among all neighborhoods; ② compensation of communities hosting LULUs by other communities; ③ progressive siting—wealthier neighborhoods receive more LULUs; ④ cost internalization—those who benefit bear the cost; ⑤ the siting process involves no intentional discrimination; ⑥ the siting process shows "equal concern and respect" for all neighborhoods; and ⑦ [not included in the above excerpt] all communities receive an equal number of vetoes that can be used to exclude a LULU. What model of "fairness" do you favor?

In the following excerpt, Christopher Foreman critiques the environmental justice movement. In his remarks, does he reveal a preference for any particular conception of justice?

Christopher H. Foreman, Jr., The Promise and Peril of Environmental Justice
(1998)

Reducing and avoiding threats to health is a major, but often unproductive, theme of environmental justice advocacy. When activists call attention to alleged unfair environmental burdens, surreptitious mass poisoning is a primary (if sometimes implicit) fear. After all, why care about an inequity unless it makes a difference? And isn't the difference between life and death the biggest difference of all? Given the vehemently articulated community health anxieties evident in countless public forums, including the National Environmental Justice Advisory Council (NEJAC), one might mistakenly conclude that health is the main, or even sole, focus of environmental justice activism.

[P]olicymakers and activists alike have tended to concentrate on questions and mechanisms of community involvement, not community health. This is not surprising. One reason for this focus is that activists and policymakers alike possess a far better understanding of procedural inclusion, and of the tools that seem useful for producing it, than they do of ways to reduce risk and enhance health.... For activists, involvement offers outlets for advocacy, opportunities for dialogue and the casting of blame, and the promise of institutional accountability. Resourceful and well-timed advocacy may even lead to significant material benefits for a community. On the other hand, involvement mechanisms allow policymakers to exhibit responsiveness and deflect criticism. By comparison, channeling health anxieties effectively toward risk reductions and improved health prospects among low-income and minority persons is far more difficult.

It is not hard to understand why activists are inclined to think that what they do generally promotes healthy communities. An ability to exercise power, as when a neighborhood effectively mobilizes to block visible sources of perceived additional risk, strongly implies a protective capacity. People commonly attribute harm to things they intensely dislike or fear, such as dumps and pollution. While both can certainly cause harm, so can many other things not nearly so fearsome. Moreover, fighting polluters clearly requires collective action or governmental intervention; rugged individualism cannot suffice.... Finally, health, wealth, and political efficacy are clearly correlated; no one would deny that wealthy persons extract better health care, healthier surroundings, and greater overall solicitude from politicians than poor persons.

For these reasons it may appear obvious that successfully exercising power over environmental questions where health concerns have been raised is in fact to protect health.... But the victory may actually be hollow or insignificant, for the connection between successful activism and the advancement of public health is much less straightforward than it might appear. In fact environmental justice advocacy and policymaking might subtly impede efforts to improve and protect health among precisely those persons or advocates and policymakers desire to help. This can occur if mechanisms of mobilization and involvement draw citizen concern and protective effort away from important sources of risk (to less important sources) and away from preventable adverse effects (to unpreventable or unsubstantiated ones). Citizen energies thus displaced may complicate the task policymakers must face in allocating scarce resources to their most productive use....

The [environmental justice] movement's obsession with disproportionate adverse impact may obscure more important questions relating to the absolute size, scope and source of such impacts. Second, environmental justice proponents generally eschew personal behavior (and necessary changes in it) as a primary variable in the health of low-income and minority communities. Third, from among the vast array of issues raised to date under the environmental justice rubric, adherents have been incapable of fashioning a coherent agenda of substantive public health priorities. Instead the movement is drawn to an overall procedural priority of citizen involvement, an orientation that unrealistically envisions every issue as a substantive priority.

These limitations exist largely because environmental justice is not mainly a public health movement. It is instead a loose coalition of citizens and groups advocating greater grassroots democracy, usually with an eye fixed on broader social justice goals. Because its primary political aims are to bind residents together, to raise their collective profile in policy debates and decision-making, and to reallocate society's resources, environmental justice activism can ill afford an agenda driven solely by health impacts....

Hazards perceived to be imposed on residents by firms — especially by ones viewed as community intruders — or by governmental actors suspected of being distant, unaccountable, or racist are more suitable for this purpose. Under such circumstances, anger and suspicion easily overwhelm risk and health as driving forces. Hazards linked strongly to individual behavior (such as smoking and excessive alcohol consumption) generally have far larger implications for personal and collective health but do not easily resonate politically.... [R]eminding residents that they consume too many calories, or the wrong kinds of food, is likely to appear intrusive, insensitive, or simply beside the point.

Once their underlying democratizing aims are clearly understood it is not hard to make sense of the insistent emphasis by environmental justice activists and by grassroots environmentalists generally on relatively unlikely or weakly documented — but nevertheless profoundly fear-inducing — hazards, such as dioxin and Superfund sites. This democratizing imperative accounts for the deference regularly accorded intuitive (as opposed to scientific) perceptions of risk, as illustrated by the enduring folk myth of a so-called cancer alley in Louisiana.... Anemic mobilizing capacity (that is, low usefulness for generating collective outrage) helps explain why many well-established health hazards, including tobacco use, find no place in the litany of environmental justice concerns.

The political imperatives of the movement also explain why environmental justice lacks substantive health priorities. Real priorities would mean downgrading the concerns of at least some movement constituents, creating the great likelihood of conflict.... [Thus, environmental justice advocates] primarily advance general concepts of equality, not wishing to endanger their coalition by specifying the precise methods of achieving "justice," "fairness," or "equity." The egalitarian position that everyone should be heard and that no one should suffer maintains movement harmony, but at the cost of focus....

Conceptual Drawbacks of Environmental Justice

From a rationalizing perspective, a major problem with the environmental justice version of the democratizing critique is that, like ecopopulism more generally, it threatens to worsen the problem of environmental policy's mission priorities. As Walter Rosenbaum elaborates:

> Like the man who mounted his horse and galloped off in all directions, the EPA has no constant course. With responsibility for administering nine separate statutes and parts of four others, the EPA has no clearly mandated priorities, no way of allocating scarce resources among different statutes or among programs within a single law....

Environmental justice inevitably enlarges this challenge of missing priorities, and for similar reasons. As noted earlier, the movement is a delicate coalition of local and ethnic concerns unable to narrow its grievances for fear of a similar "political bloodletting." ... Real priority-setting runs contrary to radical egalitarian value premises and no one (perhaps least of all a strong democratizer) wants to be deemed a victimizer.

Therefore movement rhetoric argues that no community should be harmed and that all community concerns and grievances deserve redress. Scholar-activist Robert Bullard proposes that "the solution to unequal protection lies in the realm of environmental justice for all Americans. No community, rich or poor, black or white, should be allowed to become a 'sacrifice zone.'" When pressed about the need for environmental risk priorities, and about how to incorporate environmental justice into priority setting, Bullard's answer is a vague plea for nondiscrimination, along with a barely more specific call for a "federal 'fair environmental protection act'" that would transform "protection from a privilege to a right."

Bullard's position is fanciful and self-contradictory, but extremely telling. He argues essentially that the way to establish environmental priorities is precisely by guaranteeing that such priorities are impossible to implement. This is symptomatic of a movement for which untrammeled citizen voice and overall social equity are cardinal values. Bullard's position also epitomizes the desire of movement intellectuals to avoid speaking difficult truths (at least in public) to their allies and constituents.

Ironically, in matters of health and risk, environmental justice poses a potentially serious, if generally unrecognized, danger to the minority and low-income communities it aspires to help. By discouraging citizens from thinking in terms of health and risk priorities ... environmental justice can deflect attention from serious hazards to less serious or perhaps trivial ones....

From a health perspective, the [environmental justice] model's most serious drawback may be subtle opportunity costs. If one accepts that citizens inherently have limited time and energy to devote to their health, attention to distant or relatively minor health risks—

however politically compelling—very likely means less attention for some more sub-stantive health problems. And if one accepts that low-income citizens, in particular, have even fewer resources, and greater vulnerabilities, than more affluent citizens, then a focus on relatively low or unlikely risks could have a particularly insidious effect.

More frequent resort to a rationalizing, if not solely economic, perspective would en-courage minority and low-income citizens and community leaders to think more care-fully about priority-setting and myriad tradeoffs. Might widespread successes of NIMBY (not in my back yard) initiatives keep older and dirtier pollution sources active longer and thus adversely affect minority and low-income persons living adjacent to those sources? By the same token, does local insistence on full treatment at some Superfund sites (that is, the obsession with [Justice Stephen] Breyer's "last ten percent" [raised in his 1993 book, The Vicious Circle: Toward Effective Risk Regulation] mean that risks elsewhere might have been addressed under a more limited or flexible regime will not get attended to at all? ...

If conventional environmental justice advocacy cannot confront risk magnitudes hon-estly, it cannot help much in the assessment and management of tradeoffs, either of the risk/risk or risk/benefit varieties. The notion that attacking some risks may create others is largely foreign to environmental justice—beyond a fear that attacking the risk of poverty with industrial jobs may expose workers to hazardous conditions. A focus on community inclusion, although necessary to the ultimate acceptability of decisions, offers no auto-matic or painless way to sort through tradeoffs.

When confronted with choices posing both risks and benefits—such as a proposed hazardous waste treatment facility that would create jobs, and impose relatively low risks, in a needy area—environmental justice offers, along with disgust that such horrendous choices exist, mainly community engagement and participation. But because such situ-ations tend to stimulate multiple (and often harshly raised) local voices on both sides of the issue, activists are at pains to decide where (besides additional participation and de-liberation) the community's interest lies. Because an activist group will be in close touch with both the fear of toxics and the hunger for economic opportunity, the organization itself may be torn. The locally one-sided issue presents far preferable terrain for activists. It should surprise no one that activists are anxious to deemphasize community-level dis-agreement of this sort. Nor is it surprising to learn from the head of a prominent envi-ronmental justice organization that her group tries to avoid situations that pose precisely these locally polarizing tradeoffs....

A further problem pervading environmental justice discourse is that some analysts in-sist on viewing the issue primarily through the prism of race, as environmental racism, and this is probably a misplaced focus. Although Clinton's Executive Order 12898 presents environmental justice in terms of both race and class, many movement partisans un-hesitatingly assign race a dominant causal role leading to unfair outcomes. Environmental historian Martin Melosi explains this insistence on a starkly racial analysis:

> The core view that race is at the heart of environmental injustice is borne of an intellectual and emotional attachment to the civil rights heritage of the past sev-eral decades. Few would deny—including the EPA—that poor people of color are often disproportionately impacted by some forms of pollution. But the qual-ifiers are significant. Outside the movement, there has been serious question-ing: Is the issue really environmental racism or just poverty? Even within the movement there are those who cannot cleanly separate race and class in all cases.

One additional, and especially disturbing, potential pitfall stems from an unwarranted focus on race as a dominant cause. Such analyses may encourage the dishearteningly alienated frame of mind that leads substantial numbers of African Americans to embrace racial conspiracy explanations. If people of color have been deliberately targeted for environmental poisons, then it stands to reason that they were "set up" for AIDS and crack cocaine and other evils as well. Conversely, this conspiracy mindset doubtless contributes to the grassroots appeal of environmental racism rhetoric. America's legacy of slavery, segregation, and racism (epitomized in the health arena by the infamous Tuskegee syphilis study) has nurtured an understandable inclination among many African Americans to believe the worst of the system....

* * *

Notes and Questions

1. As Professor Kuehn noted, a prominent criticism of the environmental justice movement is that the terms "justice" and "fairness" are too vague to translate into coherent environmental policy. Do you agree? Can you think of other instances in environmental regulation where broad, aspirational concepts generate regulatory and legislative initiatives? In your view, what would be the best way to incorporate environmental justice goals into environmental policy and implementation?

2. The criticisms made by Foreman are premised upon three main assertions: (a) environmental justice advocates focus too much on involuntary (public) risks and not enough on voluntary (behavioral) risks; (b) environmental justice advocates refuse to prioritize risks; (c) environmental justice advocates focus too much on procedural reforms. How would you evaluate the criticisms made by Foreman? Are his criticisms premised upon a lack of theoretical consistency or political viability? Does it matter? If premised upon political viability—and assuming Foreman's empirical observations are correct—might there be good strategic reasons why advocates focus on public risks and procedural reforms while refusing to engage in a debate about priorities and tradeoffs? How would you evaluate the "opportunity costs" born by adopting environmental justice strategies as described by Foreman? In other words, if environmental justice advocates were to change their focus in response to Foreman's criticisms, how would you predict their chances of success?

Just as Foreman criticized the work of various scholars and researchers, Foreman has been subsequently criticized for his failure to acknowledge studies with better methodology that supported the (criticized) seminal studies of environmental inequities, his failure to acknowledge the work of environmental justice scholars who advocate reform (rather than abolition) of risk assessment, and his "indulging in a superficial psychological deconstruction of the movement." Alan Ramo, *Book Review, The Promise and Peril of Environmental Justice*, 40 SANTA CLARA L. REV. 941, 942 (2000). *See also* David Lewis Feldman, 9 L. & POL. BOOK REV. 66 (Feb. 1999) (acknowledging Foreman's contribution but questioning his reliance on risk-based studies that are inconclusive and also noting that use of the emotion-packed rhetoric with which activists have been attributed is commonly heard among a wide range of stakeholders).

3. As you proceed to consider the various environmental justice campaigns that are described throughout this book and the writings on various subjects, bear in mind the fundamental theoretical questions posed by the foregoing discussion of what it means, within the context of environmental protection, to be "fair and just." Consider, too, whether there is a possibility of an "objective," "neutral" or "value-free" analysis of environmental justice— or are all analyses necessarily colored by the ideological perspective of the author?

4. From a taxonomic perspective, how would you categorize each of the principles of environmental justice that are set forth in the next section? Does it matter whether any given claim is based upon distributive, procedural, corrective or social justice? Do some categories of justice naturally lend themselves to more successful regulatory reform efforts? If so, why? Given the principle that impacted communities should speak for themselves, is it appropriate for academics to attempt to situate environmental justice claims within broader theoretical frameworks? Why or why not?

C. "We Speak for Ourselves"

Environmental justice advocates have long observed that environmental laws have not prevented disproportionate environmental harms from occurring. The reasons for this are examined in Chapter 3. With few exceptions, environmental regulation focuses on improving overall ambient environmental conditions, and does not consider the distributional consequences of where pollution is occurring. Therefore, the relationship between environmental justice activists, on the one hand, and conventional environmental organizations, industry and government stakeholders, on the other, has been marked by suspicion and hobbled to some degree by a framework that did not envision the considerations that environmental justice advocates bring to the table. Yet individuals in each of these groups understand the pragmatic need to work collaboratively to address serious problems. The wariness felt by environmental justice leaders toward environmental regulators, environmental laws, and mainstream environmental organizations is reflected in a 1990 letter sent by environmental justice activists to the leaders of the ten largest environmental organizations. In addition, many activists were concerned that business interests, academics and others were misinterpreting their positions. Thus, in 1991 environmental justice activists gathered in a historic summit and proposed a set of principles to guide their efforts and clearly state their positions. A decade later, a group of activists again sent a letter, this time to then-President George W. Bush. These writings reflect the strongly held view by many activists, a view that people living in heavily impacted communities, who are on the forefront of political campaigns, "speak for themselves."

Letter, Circa Earth Day 1990

March 16, 1990

Addressed individually to Jay Hair, National Wildlife Federation; Michael Fisher and others from the Sierra Club; Frederick Sutherland, Sierra Club Legal Defense Fund; Peter Berle and others from the National Audubon Society; Frederick Krupp, Environmental Defense Fund; Mike Clark, Environmental Policy Institute/Friends of the Earth; Lack Lorenz and others, Izaak Walton League; George Frampton and others from the Wilderness Society; Paul Pritchard, National Parks and Conservation Association; John Adams, Natural Resources Defense Council:

Dear [Representative]:

We are writing this letter in the belief that through dialogue and mutual strategizing we can create a global environmental movement that protects us all.

We are artists, writers, academics, students, activists, representatives of churches, unions, and community organizations writing you to express our concerns about the role of your organization and other national environmental groups in communities of people of color in the Southwest.

For centuries, people of color in our region have been subjected to racist and genocidal practices including the theft of lands and water, the murder of innocent people, and degradation of our environment. Mining companies extract minerals leaving economically depressed communities and poisoned soil and water. The U.S. military takes lands for weapons production, testing and storage, contaminating surrounding communities and placing minority workers in the most highly radioactive and toxic worksites. Industrial and municipal dumps are intentionally placed in communities of color, disrupting our cultural lifestyle and threatening our communities' futures. Workers in the fields are dying and babies are born disfigured as a result of pesticide spraying.

Although environmental organizations calling themselves the "Group of Ten" often claim to represent our interests, in observing your activities it has become clear to us that your organizations play an equal role in the disruption of our communities. There is a clear lack of accountability by the Group of Ten environmental organizations towards Third World communities in the Southwest, in the United States as a whole, and internationally.

Your organizations continue to support and promote policies which emphasize the clean-up and preservation of the environment on the backs of working people in general and people of color in particular. In the name of eliminating environmental hazards at any cost, across the country industrial and other economic activities which employ us are being shut down, curtailed or prevented while our survival needs and cultures are ignored. We suffer from the end results of these actions, but are never full participants in the decision-making which leads to them.

[Selected examples from the letter follow. Eds]:

> Organizations such as the National Wildlife Federation have been involved in exchanges where Third World countries will sign over lands (debt-for-nature swaps) to conservation groups in exchange for creditors agreeing to erase a portion of that country's debt. In other cases the debt is purchased at reduced rates; the creditors can then write it off. This not only raises the specter of conservation groups now being "creditors" to Third World countries, but legitimizes the debt itself through the further expropriation of Third World resources. The question arises whether such deals are in the long term economic interests of both the countries involved and of the people living on the land.

> The lack of people of color in decision-making positions in your organizations such as executive staff and board positions is also reflective of your histories of racist and exclusionary practices. Racism is a root cause of your inaction around addressing environmental problems in our communities.

> Group of Ten organizations are being supported by corporations such as ARCO, British Petroleum, Chemical Bank, GTE, General Electric, Dupont, Dow Chemical, Exxon, IBM, Coca Cola, and Waste Management, Incorporated. Several of these companies are known polluters whose disregard for the safety and well-being of workers has resulted in the deaths of many people of color. It is impossible for you to represent us in issues of our own survival when you are accountable to these interests. Such accountability leads you to pursue a corporate strategy towards the resolution of the environmental crisis, when what is needed is a *people's strategy* which fully involves those who have historically been without power in this society.

Comments have been made by representatives of major national environmental organizations to the effect that only in the recent past have people of color begun to realize the impacts of environmental contamination. We have been involved in environmental struggles for many years and we have not needed the Group of Ten environmental organizations to tell us that these problems have existed.

We again call upon you to cease operations in communities of color within 60 days, until you have hired leaders from those communities to the extent that they make up between 35–40 percent of your entire staff. We are asking that Third World leaders be hired at all levels of your operations....

Sincerely,

/S/ 117 signatures of organizations and individuals.

* * *

Principles of Environmental Justice, Proceedings, The First National People of Color Environmental Leadership Summit
xiii (October 24–27, 1992)

WE THE PEOPLE OF COLOR, gathered together at this multinational *People of Color Environmental Leadership Summit,* to begin to build a national and international movement of all peoples of color to fight the destruction and taking of our lands and communities, do hereby re-establish our spiritual interdependence to the sacredness of our Mother Earth; to respect and celebrate each of our cultures, languages and beliefs about the natural world and our roles in healing ourselves; to insure environmental justice; to promote economic alternatives which would contribute to the development of environmentally safe livelihoods; and, to secure our political, economic and cultural liberation that has been denied for over 500 years of colonization and oppression, resulting in the poisoning of our communities and land and the genocide of our peoples, do affirm and adopt these Principles of Environmental Justice:

1. Environmental justice affirms the sacredness of Mother Earth, ecological unity and the interdependence of all species, and the right to be free from ecological destruction.

2. Environmental justice demands that public policy be based on mutual respect and justice for all peoples, free from any form of discrimination or bias.

3. Environmental justice mandates the right to ethical, balanced and responsible uses of land and renewable resources in the interest of a sustainable planet for humans and other living things.

4. Environmental justice calls for universal protection from nuclear testing, extraction, production and disposal of toxic/hazardous wastes and poisons and nuclear testing that threaten the fundamental right to clean air, land, water and food.

5. Environmental justice affirms the fundamental right to political, economic, cultural and environmental self-determination of all peoples.

6. Environmental justice demands the cessation of the production of all toxins, hazardous wastes, and radioactive materials, and that all past and current producers be held strictly accountable to the people for detoxification and the containment at the point of production.

7. Environmental justice demands the right to participate as equal partners at every level of decision-making including needs assessment, planning, implementation, enforcement and evaluation.

8. Environmental justice affirms the right of all workers to a safe and healthy work environment, without being forced to choose between an unsafe livelihood and unemployment. It also affirms the right of those who work at home to be free from environmental hazards.

9. Environmental justice protects the right of victims of environmental injustice to receive full compensation and reparations for damages as well as quality health care.

10. Environmental justice considers governmental acts of environmental injustice a violation of international law, the Universal Declaration On Human Rights, and the United Nations Convention on Genocide.

11. Environmental justice must recognize a special legal and natural relationship of Native Peoples to the U.S. government through treaties, agreements, compacts, and covenants affirming sovereignty and self-determination.

12. Environmental justice affirms the need for urban and rural ecological policies to clean up and rebuild our cities and rural areas in balance with nature, honoring the cultural integrity of all our communities, and providing fair access for all to the full range of resources.

13. Environmental justice calls for the strict enforcement of principles of informed consent, and a halt to the testing of experimental reproductive and medical procedures and vaccinations on people of color.

14. Environmental justice opposes the destructive operations of multinational corporations.

15. Environmental justice opposes military occupation, repression and exploitation of lands, peoples and cultures, and other life forms.

16. Environmental justice calls for the education of present and future generations which emphasizes social and environmental issues, based on our experience and an appreciation of our diverse cultural perspectives.

17. Environmental justice requires that we, as individuals, make personal and consumer choices to consume as little of Mother Earth's resources and to produce as little waste as possible; and make the conscious decision to challenge and reprioritize our lifestyles to insure the health of the natural world for present and future generations.

Adopted today, October 24, 1991, in Washington, D.C.

* * *

Letter, Circa Earth Day 2001

April 19, 2001

George W. Bush
President of the United States of America
The White House
1600 Pennsylvania Avenue NW
Washington, DC 20500
USA

Dear Mr. President,

We are writing you today to express our profound concern with your new climate change policies with respect to their impacts on poor people and people of color in the United States and around the world.

It is our firmly held belief that climate change is not only an ecological, economic or political question, but it is a moral issue with profound ramifications for all of the inhabitants of this planet Earth. It is a question of environmental justice and human rights. It is also an issue of equity between nations.

Particularly hard hit will be low-lying countries like Bangladesh and small island states whose very existence is threatened. The poor here in the United States — especially poor people of color — will also bear the brunt of climate change. Your policies will only intensify those impacts.

Given its potentially profound ramifications, climate change must be tackled with serious and vigorous leadership and international cooperation rather than a misguided isolationist approach that protects a handful of powerful fossil fuel corporations.

The United States, whose four percent of the world's population generates one-quarter of all man made carbon dioxide — the leading global warming gas — must take the lead in reversing its role as the main contributor to this looming global crisis.

Certainly, your predecessor's climate change policies came up well short of the measures we believe are necessary to address the problem. But your administration's response so far — your failure to follow through on campaign promises to reduce carbon dioxide emissions and your abandonment of the Kyoto Protocol — borders on nothing short of gross global negligence.

Your negation of the increasingly irrefutable scientific evidence on climate change is distressing. It is no longer a question of whether sea levels will rise, but rather of how many coastlines, people, communities, and entire island nations will be submerged.

Global warming is starting to make itself felt. The 1990s was the warmest decade and 1998 was the warmest year on record. The icecap atop Mount Kilimanjaro in Africa is melting away and will completely disappear in less than 15 years. It is an abuse of power to turn your back on this, the most serious environmental issue ever to confront humanity.

If it is not halted, climate change will probably result in increased frequency and severity of storms, floods and drought. And it will cause the spread of diseases, such as malaria. It will increase hunger and bring about displacement and mass migrations of people with ensuing social conflict.

Mr. President, you claim that you don't want to harm the American consumer, yet you're setting us all up to pay a huge price in the future. This is especially true for the poor. Earlier this year, the United Nations Intergovernmental Panel on Climate Change (IPCC) concluded that the impacts of global warming "are expected to fall disproportionately on the poor."

People who are highly dependent on farming, fishing or forestry, especially indigenous people, are most likely to see their livelihoods destroyed by climate change. Meanwhile, the urban poor — mostly people of color in the U.S. — will be most vulnerable to climate change-related heat waves, diseases and respiratory ailments.

Many of us come from or work with communities that are already directly affected by the oil industry. These are communities and workers that are suffering the social and environmental effects of oil exploration, production, transportation, refining, distribution and combustion. These communities are also some of those who will be hardest hit by climate change — whether they are in Nigeria's Niger Delta, in Arctic Village Alaska, or in Louisiana's "cancer alley." These communities face a "double whammy" suffering oil's acute toxic impacts first and then its long-term effects in the form of the harsh hand of global warming.

Rather than cater to the socially and ecologically destructive oil industry, Mr. President, you should severely curb U.S. carbon emissions and support the Kyoto Protocol. At home you should also support a just transition for fossil fuel industry workers and fenceline communities while investing the United States' resources in energy efficiency and renewable energy resources, such as solar, wind and biomass.

Mr. President, we urge you to reconsider your position on climate change before the United States becomes universally known as an environmental rogue state, and you go down in history as G.W. Bush, the Global Warming President.

Sincerely,

/S/ Nnimmo Bassey, Oilwatch Africa; Ricardo Carrere, World Rainforest Movement, Uruguay; Chee Yoke Ling, Third World Network, Malaysia; Oronto Douglas, Environmental Rights Action/Friends of the Earth, Nigeria; Tom Goldtooth, Indigenous Environmental Network, U.S.; Sarah James, Gwich'in Steering Committee, U.S.; Esperanza Martinez, Oilwatch International, Ecuador; Richard Moore, Southwest Network for Environmental and Economic Justice, U.S.; Ricardo Navarro, CESTA/Friends of the Earth, El Salvador; S. Bobby Peek, GroundWork, South Africa; Amit Srivastava/Joshua Karliner, CorpWatch, U.S.; Connie Tucker, Southern Organizing Committee for Economic and Social Justice, U.S.; Dr. Owens Wiwa, African Environmental and Human Development Agency, Nigeria

Cc: Christie Todd Whitman, Administrator, U.S. Environmental Protection Agency

Endorsed by: /S/ Tom Athanasiou, EcoEquity, U.S.; Dr. Lilian Corra, Asociacion Argentina de Medicos por el Medio Ambiente, Argentina; John Harrington, Harrington Investments, Inc., U.S.; Allan Hunt-Badiner, Rainforest Action Network, U.S.; Daniel Kammen, University of California, Berkeley, U.S.; Ansje Miller, Redefining Progress, U.S.; Aaron Rappaport, Ph.D., American Lands Alliance, U.S.; Satinath Sarangi, Bhopal Group for Information and Action, India; Karla Schoeters, Climate Network Europe, Belgium; Richard Sherman, Earthlife Africa, South Africa; Jon Sohn, Friends of the Earth, U.S.

* * *

Notes and Questions

1. The writing of environmental justice activists is both aspirational and hard-hitting. To many, it strikes a dissonant chord with the brand of technical jargon used both by regulators and academics, perhaps intentionally so. What are the implications of a "bottom-up" perspective for addressing environmental problems in fora that are dominated by formal professionalization? As you consider the various strategies—legal and technical— available to reduce environmental disparities, consider which of them are better equipped to work with and utilize a grassroots perspective. Also consider which strategies are likely to build capacity within impacted communities to continue to ward off environmental assaults after the campaign at issue has concluded.

2. Some people believe that environmental policies to protect communities of color and low-income communities from environmental hazards are needed, but many environmental justice advocates resist top-down government approaches, noting that the decisions of scientists, bureaucrats, lawyers, and judges are often paternalistic and disempower them. Is there an inherent tension between the movement's process-oriented goals of having greater voice and power, and the movement's morality-based goals of eliminating risk of environmental harm altogether? In other words, is it possible that greater participa-

tion would not lead to the policies environmental justice activists desire, and that the adoption of regulatory policies that environmental justice advocates desire would not lead to improved empowerment of these communities?

D. Environmental Justice Communities in Context

The readings in the previous section sketch the history of the environmental justice movement, in the process providing a sense of the efforts of multiple and diverse groups to articulate a common critique of mainstream environmental approaches. These readings also provide a glimpse of the fact that this movement and its claims are not static. Instead, with the passage of time, the movement has identified newly pressing issues, enlisted alternative legal and other tools, and, at times, refined earlier approaches and theories.

Thus, as the readings above suggest, environmental justice advocates have crafted an inclusive, multi-racial and multicultural coalition on the ground, and scholars have attempted to articulate a coherent theoretical framework for the common claims of this movement. But it is nonetheless important to recognize that each environmental justice campaign is rooted in its locale and unique combination of culture and history. And, while community-based groups have sought to learn from efforts of sister organizations, often forging effective coalitions and regional networks, it is important to consider how each group is different and how the context—historical, social, cultural, political—in which each group's effort takes place inevitably affects the relevant issues and claims. We will often use the term "environmental justice communities" or "environmental justice groups" throughout this book as a shorthand to refer to all of the various groups and subgroups that are affected by any particular issue. In doing so, we mean to embrace the inclusive posture of the environmental justice movement itself and to recognize common institutional and structural forces that generate environmental inequities. But, at the same time, we also mean to recognize that each group's circumstances are, in fact, unique and that each group's claims for justice can only properly be understood in context.

The following excerpt, written at a time when environmental justice advocates had had some success in bringing the issue of environmental injustice to the attention of the broader society, urges a refinement in framing and considering environmental injustices—namely, one that takes a contextual approach.

Eric K. Yamamoto & Jen-L W. Lyman,
Racializing Environmental Justice
72 University of Colorado Law Review 311 (2001)

"[Racial c]ommunities are not all created equal." Yet, the established environmental justice framework tends to treat racial minorities as interchangeable and to assume for all communities of color that health and distribution of environmental burdens are main concerns. For some racialized communities, however, environmental justice is not only, or even primarily, about immediate health concerns or burden distribution. Rather, for them, and particularly for some indigenous peoples, environmental justice is mainly about cultural and economic self-determination and belief systems that connect their history, spirituality, and livelihood to the natural environment....

The Established Environmental Justice Framework

... The roots of environmental injustice lie in what the Reverend Benjamin Chavis termed "environmental racism." Environmental racism is described as the "nationwide phenomenon" that occurs when "any policy, practice, or directive ... differentially impacts or disadvantages [whether intended or unintended] individuals, groups, or communities based on race or color." For most scholars, this "differential effect," measured against white communities, results in the unfair distribution of environmental hazards. The established environmental justice framework addresses this problem of environmental racism and seeks to achieve healthy and sustainable communities.

This vision of environmental justice has four general characteristics. First, it focuses on traditional environmental hazards such as waste facilities and resulting pollution.... Second, and closely related, the environmental justice framework focuses on the disproportionate distribution of hazardous facilities and on the re-siting of those facilities.... Third, the established environmental justice framework seeks to ensure that communities of color have equal representation in the administration of environmental laws and policies.... Fourth, the environmental justice framework emphasizes "a community-based movement to bring pressure on the person or agency with decision-making authority." ...

The established [environmental justice] framework sometimes furthers, and at times undermines, environmental justice. It furthers environmental justice when it provides racial and indigenous communities the concepts and language they need to advocate effectively for the siting and health outcomes they desire.

The framework, however, at times also undercuts environmental justice struggles by racial and indigenous communities because it tends to foster misassumptions about race, culture, sovereignty, and the importance of distributive justice....

The first misassumption is that for all racialized groups in all situations, a hazard-free physical environment is their main, if not only, concern.... Not all facility sitings that pose health risks, however, warrant full-scale opposition by host communities. Some communities, on balance, are willing to tolerate these facilities for the economic benefits they confer or in lieu of the cultural or social disruption that might accompany large-scale remedial efforts....

The established framework also assumes that fair distribution of physical burdens is the primary, if not sole, means of achieving environmental justice. Sheila Foster rejects this assumption as "monolithic" and "one-dimensional," focusing "too much on outcomes and not enough on the processes that produce those outcomes." According to Foster, by not addressing why racial communities are overexposed to pollution, hazardous waste sites, and poisoned fish stocks, agencies like the EPA fail to confront: "discriminatory housing and real estate policies and practices, residential segregation and limited residential choices influenced by such discrimination, discriminatory zoning regulations and ineffective land use policies, racial disparities in the availability of jobs and municipal services, imbalances in political access and power, and 'white flight.'" ...

Finally, the established framework tends to assume that all racial and indigenous groups, and therefore racial and indigenous group needs, are the same. In general, it assumes that in terms of cultural needs and political-legal remedies, one size fits all....

Courts usually forgo meaningful analysis of racial or cultural discrimination in considering environmental justice issues. In particular, when addressing claims of environmental racism, courts focus their equal protection inquiries on the disparate impact of a governmental decision and a search for racial animus by individual government actors.

Under this narrow approach, affected racial and indigenous communities need to establish that identified government decision-makers were motivated by some form of racial ill-will. This proof is not only difficult to muster, it focuses attention on government officials and tends to flatten racial and cultural distinctions into a monolithic "racial minority" victim. It does not call for participants to examine closely racial groups' cultural or economic connections to the environment or the ways in which those connections have been damaged or possibly enhanced.

This narrow judicial focus is illustrated by ... R.I.S.E. v. Kay [768 F. Supp. 1144 (E.D. Va. 1991), discussed in Chapter 14, Eds.]. [In this case,] the United States District Court for the Eastern District of Virginia rejected an equal protection challenge to the siting of a regional landfill near a historical African American church in an area populated primarily by African Americans. Three other landfills in the County were also sited in areas where the racial composition was ninety-five to one hundred percent African American.... The court found that the County's siting of landfills over the past twenty years did in fact have a disproportionate impact on black residents. It nevertheless held that plaintiffs failed to show that the siting was racially motivated, without examining what "racial motivation" might mean in this particular situation to the affected African American communities. The court, instead, simply declared that the "Equal Protection Clause does not impose an affirmative duty to equalize the impact of official decisions on different racial groups." ... Without thoughtfully discussing the African American community's spiritual and cultural concerns, which deeply animated its opposition to the siting decision, the court stated, as a seeming afterthought, that the Country had properly "balanced the economic, environmental, and cultural needs of the County in a responsible and conscientious manner." ...

[But] the court disregarded underlying social conditions ... The African American plaintiffs complained that the landfill would interfere with their community activities and their worship as African Americans in the Second Mt. Olive Church; they believed the landfill would desecrate the special significance of the historic church founded by freed slaves. The court discussed their claims without reference to history or context and was therefore able to conclude easily that the African American plaintiffs failed to state a claim of environmental racism.

For those African Americans, however, the church was historically and socially important to their existence as a racial community. Indeed the black residents had long been racialized and segregated and had been compelled by Southern racism to create their own African American institutions. Desecration of the church was, to that community, a racial act with profound social and cultural consequences. By summarily ignoring this historical context, the court undermined the black community's ability to call the local government to account for the potentially devastating social and cultural impacts of its decision....

So how can environmental justice scholars, commentators, activists, and decision makers grapple with important differences among groups while advancing concepts, language, and methods for addressing concrete problems? [William] Shutkin and [Charlie] Lord suggest that "the legal system has perpetuated environmental injustice by misreading or disregarding [a] community's history." These scholars urge "a more complete history that incorporates not only a view of the past, present, and future, but also the question of justice." ...

This suggested contextual approach moves closer to treating racial and indigenous groups and their relationships to the environment in light of cultural and social differences. The approach, however, needs both expansion and refinement in order to: (1) address explicitly how racial categories are constructed, racial identities forged, and racial meanings developed; (2) account for significant differences between groups traditionally described as racial minorities (African Americans, Asian Americans, Latinas/os, and indigenous peoples (including American Indians, Aleuts, Eskimos, Native Hawaiians)); and (3) recognize and deal more directly with the influences of whiteness in the formation and implementation of environmental law and policy. What is needed, then, is a framework that more subtly interrogates social, political, historical, cultural, and power interactions among whites and racial and indigenous groups.

Racializing Environmental Justice

Critical race theory offers communities and environmental justice proponents important critical tools for evaluating past experiences and present conditions. Beginning with a skepticism of legal impartiality common to all legal realists, critical race theory pays particular attention to the roles that race, racism, and nativism play in the formation of legal norms and the administration of justice....

"Racializing environmental justice," in part, is a method of inquiry and analysis that builds on critical race theory concepts of "differential racialization" and "differential empowerment." It recognizes that for traditional "racial minorities" and for America's indigenous peoples, "group and subgroup identities, political and socioeconomic goals, and 'available responses' may sometimes coincide and oftentimes differ." ...

Critical race theory challenges the very concept of "race" as "immutable" or biological, as something objective and largely devoid of social content or historical context. It moves analytical understandings of "race" beyond its conception as "an independent variable requiring little or no elaboration." ... This process of racialization extends "racial meaning to a previously racially unclassified relationship, social practice, or group." Racializing environmental justice thus entails interrogation into the ways evolving public perceptions and the particular struggles of a community have generated racial or cultural meanings for that community....

For example, for Asian Americans, different social forces lead to differential racialization of Asian American groups.... "The problems encountered by a rich entrepreneur from Hong Kong and a recently arrived Hmong refugee are obviously distinct. The sites and types of discriminatory acts each is likely to encounter, and the range of available responses to them, differ by class location." Differential racialization may exist even within subgroups, such as between a first generation Vietnamese American immigrant and a second generation Vietnamese American, or as between black descendants of Jamaica and Senegal....

The racialization process, furthermore, "fixes status and allocates power differentially among and within racial groups." So, for instance, more "'established' immigrant groups, with greater resources and access to political power may organize around mobility issues ('glass ceiling'), while recent immigrant groups may focus on 'survival issues' (funding for language classes and job-training programs)." As a result, differential racialization primarily pursues a framing of race that acknowledges that historical and contemporary social and cultural influences have important consequences for "individual identity and collective consciousness, and political organization."

For Native peoples, differential racialization fosters another kind of inquiry, one that addresses often substantial differences among immigrant racial populations in America, imported slaves, and conquered indigenous peoples. The inquiry focuses on the effects of land dispossession, culture destruction, loss of sovereignty, and, in turn, on claims to self-determination and nationhood (rather than to equality and integration).

To further refine the differential racialization analysis, "Jeff Chang suggests a notion of 'differential forms of disempowerment among communities of color.'" Differential disempowerment focuses on recognition of power differences among racial or Native groups and sees power in terms of status, locale, time, and economics....

For example, before Hawai'i became a state, "white oligarchical control, Asian immigration and Native Hawaiian separation from land and traditional cultural roots constructed differing racial group identities." Native Hawaiians, as the subjects of a conquered sovereign, and Asians, as first or second generation immigrants, were differentially racialized. The two groups were differently situated although they had experienced similar hardships. Unlike Asian Americans, Native Hawaiians underwent land dispossession resulting in large-scale cultural destruction, along with "death and dying and spiritual suffering." Moreover, "the rhetoric describing group characteristics, the market distribution of labor, the opportunities for education, housing and economic advancement towards the middle of the century lifted Asian Americans above Native Hawaiians in terms of socio-economic status."

Thus, although mainstream America sometimes treats "Native Hawaiian" as a race — for example, the U.S. census classifies Native Hawaiians as a racial group — many Native Hawaiians view themselves and their social-political situation in terms of nationhood. Their claims are not to racial equality but to sovereignty....

Differential racialization and disempowerment concepts reveal how history has "present effects on group identity and group claims" and thus provide a preliminary framework for inquiry into particulars of environmental racism in a given setting. That framework enables us to ask meaningful questions about the interplay between race and the environment because it focuses on ways in which history and culture are linked to what we call "the environment." Specifically, what emerges from this framework is this: environmental justice must recognize that each racial or Native group is differently situated and that differing contexts contribute to differing group goals, identities, and differential group power. This idea is important because it enables scholars, activists, and others to analyze particular kinds of harms to specific racial or Native communities and to fashion appropriately tailored remedies for those harms. When applied, this framework illuminates the underlying racialized character of environmental justice claims and treats each racial or Native community separately according to its specific socio-economic needs, cultural values, and group goals.

* * *

Notes and Questions

1. Professor Yamamoto and Ms. Lyman urge the environmental justice community to rethink what they suggest is an undue emphasis on the distributional aspects of traditional environmental hazards, an emphasis they argue may promote a misconception that facility siting and environmental hazards are of primary concern and that communities of color will always forgo economic development to resist the risks generated by these facilities. As noted above, however, the Principles of Environmental Justice reflect a much broader view by environmental justice activists, emphasizing fair process, self-determination, cultural and spiritual values, and sustainability. Is there a disjunction between the values as articulated in those principles and the various environmental justice campaigns undertaken throughout the United States and beyond? Some suggest there is, while others argue that the diversity of environmental justice campaigns and presence of sta-

ble coalitions among diverse environmental justice organizations suggests a much broader range of values is at play. If the latter is more accurate, the perception that environmental justice activists unduly emphasize siting challenges may be due to frequent media portrayals of environmental justice campaigns as single-mindedly anti-development and anti-siting. On the other hand, if the environmental justice movement is in fact too preoccupied with distributional issues and traditional pollution-generated risk, how can the broad group of community-based movements that comprises the environmental justice movement reorder its collective priorities or broaden its collective mission?

2. Yamamoto and Lyman advocate for the use of critical race theory to "racialize" environmental justice, meaning in part the process of using techniques such as outsider accounts to analyze the way in which different groups—variously situated historically, economically, culturally, and politically—are racialized, and how that process of racialization may generate different cultural meanings and political goals for different groups. In what ways might their approach be different from or similar to one of the stronger tenets that has emerged from the environmental justice movement: that impacted communities should "speak for themselves?" For example, one of the most effective political strategies used by environmental justice activists may be viewed as a variant of the "outsider account" described by critical race theorists. Community residents tell their own stories through compelling testimony, or at times by physically taking governmental officials and others to impacted areas. The experiential value of a site tour has proven a powerful counter-narrative to those that argue that the risk environmental justice communities are experiencing is negligible or that the impact is trivial. In a similar vein, Professor Robert Verchick has described how women of color in the environmental justice movement employ techniques long advanced by feminist theorists such as consciousness raising and unmasking. Robert R. M. Verchick, *In a Greener Voice: Feminist Theory and Environmental Justice,* 19 HARV. WOMEN'S L.J. 23, 73–74 (1996).

3. As you consider the materials in the chapters that follow, notice the ways in which the various groups' circumstances, values, and goals are similar and the ways in which, as Yamamoto and Lyman suggest, each group's "specific socio-economic needs, cultural values, and group goals" are unique.

Chapter 2

The Evidence

A. Introduction

A central building block of the environmental justice movement is empirical evidence about the unequal distribution of environmental benefits and burdens. Such evidence has played a key role in galvanizing public attention to the issue of environmental justice and has helped inform what the appropriate legal responses should be. Conversely, those who challenge the existence of environmental discrimination and the breadth of environmental justice claims have questioned how solid the evidence of environmental inequities is and whether seeming disparities are better explained by other demographic factors and life style choices. This chapter examines some of the most important evidence on this critical issue.

There long has been widespread anecdotal evidence that communities of color and low-income communities suffer disproportionate environmental burdens. This includes the alarming rates of lead poisoning among minority children; the high rates of pesticide-related illness among farm workers, a predominantly Latino work force; the high rates of Native Americans who mined uranium ore and suffer lung cancer and other exposure-related illnesses; the growing rates of childhood asthma in inner-city areas; and the proximity of communities of color to hazardous waste sites and polluting facilities in areas throughout the country. Charles Lee, Environmental Justice: Creating a Vision for Achieving Healthy and Sustainable Communities 8–9 (1996) (unpublished manuscript). Over the past two decades, however, especially since publication in 1987 of the United Church of Christ's study of the siting of toxic waste facilities (see below), academics and others have more systematically evaluated the distribution of environmental harms and benefits.

The remainder of this chapter is divided into three sections. Section B examines research about the location of hazardous waste facilities. Some of the most well-publicized and influential research has occurred in this area. Section C looks at studies involving a range of other environmental harms. Section D explores a topic that researchers have increasingly focused on in recent years—the unequal distribution of environmental benefits such as transportation funding, access to parks and open space, environmental enforcement, and emergency response efforts.

While most of the research concludes that there are racial and income disparities in various types of environmental harms and benefits, some of this research has been challenged on methodological grounds. The most well-developed methodological critique is that the choice of the appropriate geographic unit of analysis (census block vs. zip code area, for example) and the appropriate comparison population can significantly influence the results of research, with researchers debating which unit of analysis best captures the areas that suffer the greatest impacts. Other criticisms are that results can vary based on whether the studies are national, state, regional, or local in scope; that some early studies did not control for the independent effect of factors such as population density, economic activity, education, and other demographic factors; and that studies have only evaluated proximity to polluting facilities, not risk to host communities or actual health outcomes. We examine some of these methodological issues in the sections that follow, but consider these issues mainly in the context of hazardous waste facilities. The lessons and principles drawn from the hazardous waste siting context, however, can be applied to research about other environmental disparities. The major studies in the chapter are presented within each subsection chronologically, illustrating how the empirical research has become more sophisticated over time. The state of the empirical evidence, and debates concerning that evidence, has been closely linked with the development of the environmental justice movement over the last several decades.

Pathfinder on Race and Income Disparities

An annotated bibliography of studies about racial and income disparities in environmental harms can be found in LUKE COLE & SHEILA FOSTER, FROM THE GROUND UP: ENVIRONMENTAL RACISM AND THE RISE OF THE ENVIRONMENTAL JUSTICE MOVEMENT (2000). Three surveys of the empirical literature are Paul Mohai & Bunyan Bryant, *Environmental Racism: Reviewing the Evidence, in* RACE AND THE INCIDENCE OF ENVIRONMENTAL HAZARDS: A TIME FOR DISCOURSE (Bunyan Bryant & Paul Mohai eds., 1992); BENJAMIN GOLDMAN, NOT JUST PROSPERITY: ACHIEVING SUSTAINABILITY WITH ENVIRONMENTAL JUSTICE (1994); and JAMES P. LESTER, DAVID W. ALLEN & KELLY M. HILL, ENVIRONMENTAL INJUSTICE IN THE UNITED STATES (2000). MANUEL PASTOR ET AL., IN THE WAKE OF THE STORM: ENVIRONMENT, DISASTER, AND RACE AFTER KATRINA 14 (2006) contains a summary of some more recent research.

A number of articles discuss methodological issues involved in environmental justice research. These include Christopher Boerner & Thomas Lambert, *Environmental Injustice*, 118 PUB. INT. 61 (1995); Paul Mohai, *The Demographics of Dumping Revisited: Examining the Impact of Alternate Methodologies in Environmental Justice Research*, 14 VA. ENVTL L.J. 615 (1995); Vicki Been & Francis Gupta, *Coming to the Nuisance or Going to the Barrios? A Longitudinal Analysis of Environmental Justice Claims*, 24 ECOLOGY L.Q. 1 (1997); Liam Downey, *Environmental Injustice: Is Race or Income a Better Predictor?*, 79 SOC. SCI. Q. 766 (1998); Laura Pulido, *A Critical Review of the Methodology of Environmental Racism Research*, 28 ANTIPODE 142 (1996); Robin Saha & Paul Mohai, *Historical Context and Hazardous Waste Facility Siting: Understanding Temporal Patterns in Michigan*, 52 SOC. PROBS. 618 (2005); and Paul Mohai & Robin Saha, *Reassessing Racial and Socioeconomic Disparities in Environmental Justice Research*, 43 DEMOGRAPHY 383 (2006).

B. Hazardous Waste Facilities

One of the seminal events in the environmental justice movement occurred in 1982, when the siting of a polychlorinated biphenyl (PCB) landfill in predominately African

American Warren County, North Carolina sparked nonviolent demonstrations resulting in over 500 arrests. Against a well-publicized charge that the community was targeted for siting because the residents were predominantly African American, the General Accounting Office (GAO) (now the Government Accountability Office) undertook an investigation in the southern region (EPA Region IV) and found that three of the four major offsite hazardous waste facilities were in fact located in predominantly African American communities, even though African Americans comprised only about one-fifth of the region's population. U.S. GEN. ACCOUNTING OFFICE, SITING OF HAZARDOUS WASTE LANDFILLS AND THEIR CORRELATION WITH RACIAL AND ECONOMIC STATUS OF SURROUNDING COMMUNITIES, GAO/RCED 83–168 (1983). Other early research was conducted by Professor Robert Bullard, who found that twenty-one of Houston's twenty-five solid waste facilities were located in predominantly African American neighborhoods, even though African Americans made up only twenty-eight percent of the Houston population in 1980. Robert Bullard, *Solid Waste Sites and the Black Houston Community,* 53 SOC. INQUIRY 273, 275, 278–83 (1983).

In 1987, the United Church of Christ's Commission for Racial Justice (CRJ) released an influential national study that documented a significant relationship between the location of commercial hazardous waste facilities (often referred to as Treatment, Storage and Disposal Facilities, or TSDFs) and uncontrolled toxic waste sites and race. The study was based on a comparison of such facilities and demographics in zip code areas throughout the country. The CRJ reported the following conclusions:

• Race proved to be the most significant among variables tested in association with the location of commercial hazardous waste facilities. This represented a consistent national pattern.

• Communities with the greatest number of commercial hazardous waste facilities had the highest composition of racial and ethnic residents. In communities with two or more facilities or one of the nation's five largest landfills, the average minority percentage of the population was more than three times that of communities without facilities (38% vs. 12%).

• In communities with one commercial hazardous waste facility, the average minority percentage of the population was twice the average minority percentage of the population in communities without such facilities (24% vs. 12%).

• Although socio-economic status appeared to play an important role in the location of commercial hazardous waste facilities, race still proved to be more significant. This remained true after the study controlled for urbanization and regional differences. Incomes and home values were substantially lower when communities with commercial facilities were compared to communities in the surrounding counties without facilities.

The report also found that three out of every five blacks and Hispanics, and approximately half of all Asian/Pacific Islanders and American Indians lived in communities with uncontrolled toxic waste sites. COMMISSION FOR RACIAL JUSTICE, UNITED CHURCH OF CHRIST, TOXIC WASTES AND RACE IN THE UNITED STATES: A NATIONAL REPORT ON RACIAL AND SOCIO-ECONOMIC CHARACTERISTICS OF COMMUNITIES WITH HAZARDOUS WASTE SITES (1987).

In 1994, researchers at the Social and Demographic Research Institute (SADRI) of the University of Massachusetts released a study at odds with the conclusions of the CRJ report. They found that based on 1980 census data there was no statistically significant difference in the percentages of the population that were African American or Hispanic in census tracts hosting commercial hazardous waste facilities as opposed to non-host tracts. An excerpt from this report follows.

Douglas L. Anderton, Andy B. Anderson, John Michael Oakes, Michael R. Fraser, Environmental Equity: The Demographics of Dumping
31 Demography 229 (1994)

.... [This article reports] the results from a national analysis of the distribution of commercial hazardous waste facilities. This analysis is based on population data characterizing census tracts, areal units which are smaller and more refined than zip code areas.... Generally a census tract is a small statistical subdivision of a county with clearly identifiable boundaries and a relatively homogeneous population of about 4,000 persons. Tracts are the most commonly used geographic regions of analysis; as an additional advantage, they are delimited by local persons and thus "reflect the structure of the metropolis as viewed by those most familiar with it." ... [I]t seems appropriate to make a locally delimited area the basis for our analysis....

Our initial concern in this analysis is to determine how census tracts with TSDFs differ from those without TSDFs. We compared the tracts containing [TSDFs] to the tracts without TSDFs but within SMSAs [Standard Metropolitan Statistical Areas] that contain at least one facility inside their borders....

[The results show that] the percentage of black persons in census tracts with TSDFs is approximately the same (14.54%) as in tracts without TSDFs (15.2%).... [W]e found no significant difference in the median percentage Hispanic [in tracts with TSDFs, and] we found no significant difference in the mean percentage of families below the poverty line or of households receiving public assistance.... Both the mean and the median percentage of males in the civilian labor force who are employed are lower in tracts with TSDFs than in tracts without. In what are the most dramatic differences, both the mean and the median percentages of the population employed in precision manufacturing occupations are substantially greater in tracts containing TSDFs than in other tracts....

These findings based on census tracts differ substantially from prior studies based on zip code areas, which are larger....

[An] analysis of [areas surrounding a TSDF] suggests how [census] tract-level results may be reconciled with previous studies by using larger geographic units of analysis such as zip code areas. TSDFs appear to be located in census tracts characterized by industrial activities. Also, the tracts surrounding these industrialized areas appear to contain higher concentrations of minority and economically disadvantaged residents. If it is a general feature of the social character and structure of cities that such groups are more likely to live near industrial centers, then the use of larger geographic areas in an analysis might obscure local neighborhood differences and indicate (correctly) that this larger geographic unit contains both industrial enterprises, such as TSDFs, and a higher average percentage of minority and disadvantaged persons.... [When] TSDF tracts are combined with their surrounding-area tracts for comparison with the remaining tracts of the SMSAs[, the] larger unit of comparison ... produces findings more similar to prior studies based on larger geographic units of analysis....

[The results of regression analysis in which the authors controlled for the effects of various demographic factors confirmed that manufacturing employment and the apparent industrial nature of areas were important factors in determining the location of TSDFs, and that racial characteristics of an area were not.]

... [W]hen the areal unit of analysis is the metropolitan census tract, we find almost no support for the general claim of environmental inequity.... [O]ne variable is conspicuous for its strong, consistent association with TSDF location. The concentration of persons in manufacturing occupations is consistently higher in TSDF tracts for the nation as a whole and in nine of the 10 EPA regions....

* * *

Notes and Questions

1. The above article reports findings based on 1980 census tract data. The same research team reported similar results based on their study of 1990 census tract data, although in the latter study they also found that a significantly higher percentage of low-income families and families receiving public assistance lived in tracts where TSDFs are located. Andy B. Anderson et al., *Environmental Equity: Evaluating TSDF Siting Over the Past Two Decades,* Waste Age, July 1994 at 84. *See also* Pamela Davidson and Douglas L. Anderton, *Demographics Of Dumping II: A National Environmental Equity Survey and the Distribution Of Hazardous Materials Handlers,* 37 Demography 461 (2000) (study of facilities that included hazardous waste handlers as well as TSDFs found that these facilities are more likely to be sited in working-class neighborhoods with lower percentages of Hispanic and black residents).

2. The publication of the Anderton article (the SADRI study) led to a debate about the methodology underlying the empirical data. Differences between the CRJ and SADRI studies appear to stem from differences in the methodological designs of the studies. First, the SADRI study does not use the entire U.S. as its comparison group, but only metropolitan areas with commercial waste sites. The researchers so limited the study on the theory that areas without currently operating waste facilities are not feasible for TSDFs. Professor Paul Mohai criticizes this approach, arguing that being rural (or a metropolitan area without an existing waste site) does not necessarily disqualify an area from being considered for waste siting, and in fact the largest commercial hazardous waste landfill in the country, with twenty-three percent of the nation's hazardous waste landfill capacity, is located in the rural (predominantly African American) community of Emelle, Alabama. The effect of using the narrower control group is to increase significantly the percentage of people of color in the control areas, which reduces the likelihood of finding racial disparities. Mohai argues:

> In effect, the UCC [CRJ] study addresses the question of where hazardous waste facilities are most likely to be located, regardless of whether these areas are urban or rural. The UMass [SADRI] study, on the other hand, addresses the question of where within metropolitan areas currently containing a facility such facilities are likely to be located. Unlike the UCC study, the UMass study treats as unimportant the fact that metropolitan areas currently hosting hazardous waste facilities are places with simultaneously high concentrations of people of color.

Paul Mohai, *The Demographics of Dumping Revisited: Examining the Impact of Alternate Methodologies in Environmental Justice Research,* 14 Va. Envtl L.J. 615, 648 (1995).

Second, the SADRI study does not examine disparities for all people of color as a group, but rather only separately for blacks and Hispanics, which leaves out eleven percent of the people of color population in the U.S. Third, the SADRI study uses census tracts rather than zip code areas as its geographic unit of analysis. When the SADRI researchers combined census tracts to create larger local areas, they also found racial disparities. The question of the appropriate unit of analysis is explored in more detail below.

Professor Vicki Been and Dr. Francis Gupta subsequently conducted a national study to (a) examine where TSDFs are sited, and (b) test Been's "market dynamics" theory that areas hosting polluting facilities become more minority after the facilities are sited there. (*See* Chapter 3 for an excerpt of the article elaborating upon that theory.)

Vicki Been & Francis Gupta, Coming to the Nuisance or Going to the Barrios? A Longitudinal Analysis of Environmental Justice Claims
24 Ecology Law Quarterly 1 (1997)

[E]nvironmental justice advocates point to a score of studies that analyze the correlation between the location of LULUs [locally unwanted land uses] and the demographics of the neighborhoods.... I cautioned against making policy changes based on this evidence in early 1994, arguing that the research failed to examine whether the host communities were disproportionately poor or minority at the time the sites were selected, or whether they became so following the siting.... Instead, the research left open the possibility that the sites for the facilities originally were chosen in a manner that was neither intentionally discriminatory nor discriminatory in effect, but that market responses to the facilities led the host neighborhoods to become disproportionately populated by the poor, and by racial and ethnic minorities....

Determining whether siting processes, market dynamics, or some combination of the two were responsible for the disproportionate burden revealed by [prior studies] required an analysis of the demographics of host communities at the time their facilities were sited, and of subsequent changes in the demographics of those communities....

[M]y research team conducted a nationwide study of the demographics of the 544 communities that in 1994 hosted active commercial hazardous waste treatment storage and disposal facilities.... Our research focused on the same types of facilities that the CRJ and SADRI studied—commercial hazardous waste treatment storage and disposal facilities (TSDFs)....

The Geographic Area Analyzed

There is a great deal of controversy about whether census tracts, smaller census units like block groups, larger zip code areas, or concentric circles of various radii are the preferred unit of analysis for environmental justice studies. For our longitudinal analysis, census tracts were the only option.... Census tracts are preferable to zip codes for several other reasons as well. Census tracts are drawn up by local committees, and are intended to reflect the community's view of where one neighborhood ends and another begins....

We compared the demographics of host tracts to those of all non-host tracts [as opposed to comparing host tracts to just non-host tracts in metropolitan areas that contained at least one TSDF. Eds.]....

Were Host Communities Disproportionately Composed of Minorities or the Poor at the Time the Facility Was Sited?

... [W]e examined whether the areas selected to host facilities were disproportionately populated by minorities at the time the siting decisions were made....

[C]omparisons of the means and comparisons of the distributions of host and non-host tracts provide little evidence that between 1970 and 1990 TSDFs were sited in communities that had disproportionately high percentages of African Americans at the time of the siting. Both types of tests provide evidence, however, that at least those facilities sited in the 1970s were placed in communities that had higher than average percentages of Hispanics.

Both the comparisons of means and distributions focus only on one dimension of a neighborhood's demographic profile at a time. They leave open the possibility that although the mean percentage of African Americans is not significantly different in host and non-host tracts, other variables that are closely correlated with the percentage African Americans, such as mean family income, are hiding some of the relationship between race and the probability of a siting. To isolate the influence of each demographic variable if all other variables are held constant, multivariate techniques are necessary....

[Multivariate analysis] of the demographic characteristics of those tracts chosen to host facilities since 1970, as of the census conducted immediately before the site was selected, reveals scant evidence that the siting process has a disproportionate effect on African Americans.... The analysis also provides no support for the notion that neighborhoods with high percentages of poor are disproportionately chosen as sites. Indeed, in 1980, the percentage of poor in a tract was a negative and significant predictor of which tracts would be selected as hosts.

The analysis does support the claim that the siting process was affected, either intentionally or unintentionally, by the percentage of Hispanics in potential host communities. The comparison of means in 1970 reveals a significantly higher percentage of Hispanics in host tracts than in non-host tracts, and the [results of the multivariate analysis] for both 1970 and 1980 show that the percentage of Hispanics is positively and significantly correlated, at the ninety-nine percent confidence level, with the probability that a tract hosts a facility.

Did the Demographics of Host Tracts Change Significantly Following the Siting of a Facility?

The primary competing explanation of why facilities might be located in areas that are now disproportionately composed of African Americans and Hispanics blames the residential housing market for the problem. Under this theory, the presence of a TSDF makes the host neighborhood less desirable because of the nuisance and risks the facility poses. Property values therefore fall, and those who move into the neighborhood are likely to be less wealthy and have fewer housing choices than those who leave the neighborhood. The siting of the facility results, then, in a neighborhood with lower housing values, lower incomes, and higher percentages of those who face discrimination in the housing market—primarily racial and ethnic minorities—than the neighborhood had before the siting.

To test [the] market dynamics theory, we compared the demographic characteristics of host and non-host neighborhoods as of the decennial census before the siting and as of the 1990 census.... [T]he study does not support the argument that market dynamics following the siting of a TSDF change the racial, ethnic, or socioeconomic characteristics of host neighborhoods. The analysis suggests that the areas surrounding TSDFs sited in the 1970s and 1980s are growth areas: in host areas, the number of vacant housing units was lower than in sample areas, and the percentage of housing built in the prior decade was higher. Such growth suggests that the market for land in the host areas is active and should respond to any nuisance created by the TSDFs. It also may suggest that the burdens of the TSDF are being off-set by the benefits, such as increased employment opportunities....

The Current Demographics of Host Neighborhoods

.... We compared the means of various demographic variables for the 544 tracts hosting active TSDFs in 1994 to those of the approximately 60,000 non-host tracts, as of the 1990 census.... As the claims of the environmental justice movement suggest, the percentages of African Americans and Hispanics both are significant positive predictors of the presence of a facility. Contrary to the claim that host neighborhoods currently are disproportionately poor, the percentage of individuals with incomes below the poverty line is a significant but negative predictor: the higher the percentage of the poor, the lower the likelihood that the tract hosts a facility. Also contrary to expectations, median family income is positive and significant, and median housing value is positive, although not significant.

* * *

Notes and Questions

1. Professor Been and Dr. Gupta conclude that the poorest neighborhoods appear to repel, rather than attract, facilities, and that working class or lower middle class neighborhoods bear a disproportionate share of TSDFs. What factors might account for this? A study of the distribution of TSDFs in Los Angeles County also found that rising income has a positive, then negative effect on the probability of TSDF location. The study concluded that "some areas are too poor to have any economic activity, even a TSDF, while others are wealthy enough to resist TSDFs[] being sited nearby. In short, the most 'at-risk' and impacted communities are working class, heavily minority neighborhoods located near industrial activity...." J. Tom Boer et al., *Is There Environmental Racism? The Demographics of Hazardous Waste in Los Angeles County,* 78 Soc. Sci. Q. 793, 795 (1997).

2. Professor Been and Dr. Gupta report a seeming inconsistency: even though they found that the percentage of African Americans in a tract at the start of 1970 or 1980 did not lead to a greater likelihood that the tract would be selected to host a facility sometime in that decade, and even though they found no support for the thesis that host tracts become more heavily African American after a facility is sited there, as of 1990, there existed a positive correlation between the percentage of African Americans in a community and the likelihood that a TSDF was present there. They attribute this ongoing disparity in large part to the disproportionate siting of facilities in African American areas prior to 1970. *See* Been & Gupta, *supra,* at 32.

3. Support for the authors' hypothesis is found in a study of hazardous waste siting in Michigan from 1950 to 1990 conducted by Professors Saha and Mohai. They found that siting followed three distinct temporal patterns. Prior to 1970, when there was little public concern about hazardous waste, there were no racial or economic disparities in siting. In the 1970s, as troubling information about toxics came to light and the "NIMBY" (Not In My Backyard) syndrome developed, significant racial and economic disparities emerged. In the 1980s, following the highly publicized Love Canal incident (involving chemical dumping in a town near Niagara Falls) and when public opposition to siting of hazardous waste facilities became widespread, economic disparities widened even further, while racial disparities, although not increasing, remained significant. Professors Saha and Mohai argue that the changing historical context "increasingly encouraged hazardous waste facilities siting to follow the path of least (political) resistance and resulted in disparate siting in low-income and minority neighborhoods." Robin Saha & Paul Mohai, *Historical Context and Hazardous Waste Facility Siting: Understanding Temporal Patterns*

in Michigan, 52 Soc. Pros. 618, 618 (2005). (The authors also note that other empirical studies similarly have found that disparities did not exist in the pre-1970 period. *Id.* at 626–27.)

4. One study of high-capacity TSDFs in Los Angeles County found little support for the market dynamics theory, concluding that areas that attracted TSDFs were disproportionately minority but that siting of TSDFs did not encourage minority move-in. (Other studies on this question are summarized in Chapter 3.) An important additional insight of the Los Angeles study is the finding that whether an area was undergoing ethnic transition also was a significant predictor of siting. The authors posit that "such ethnic transitions may weaken the usual social bonds constituted by race and make an area more susceptible to siting." They describe this as a "social capital" effect, a concept explored in more detail in Chapter 3. Manuel Pastor Jr. et al., *Which Came First? Toxic Facilities, Minority Move-In, and Environmental Justice,* 23 J. URBAN AFFAIRS 1, 5 (2001).

5. Although most (but not all) studies over time have found significant racial and income disparities in the distribution of environmental harms, there has been considerable variation in the magnitude of the disparities. Professors Mohai and Saha argue that a principal reason for these differences is that the most commonly used methodology does not adequately account for the proximity of environmentally hazardous sites and nearby populations. In other words, a particular unit of analysis (such as a census tract) may actually omit certain areas that are impacted by a facility while including areas that are not impacted. Professors Mohai and Saha argue for using alternate "distance-based" approaches, and apply this methodology in the following study.

Paul Mohai & Robin Saha, Racial Inequality in the Distribution of Hazardous Waste: A National-Level Reassessment
54 Social Problems 343 (2007)

.... By far, the most frequently employed approach for conducting quantitative environmental inequality analyses has been to assess the proximity of hazardous sites to nearby populations [known as the "unit-hazard coincidence" methodology].... This approach involves selecting a pre-defined geographic unit (such as zip code areas or census tracts), determining which subset of the units is coincident with the hazard and which not, and then comparing the demographic characteristics of the two sets....

[T]he unit-hazard coincidence approach has been the most commonly used in conducting environmental inequality analyses, including by the most influential national studies [about the distribution of hazardous waste TSDFs].... However ... this approach fails to adequately control for proximity between environmentally hazardous sites and nearby residential populations in two principal ways. First, it does not take into account the precise geographic location of the hazardous site. It goes no further than determining whether the site is coincident with one of the geographic units of analysis. Not taken into account is the proximity of the site to its host unit's boundary or its proximity to adjacent and other nearby units. However, when the precise geographic locations of hazardous sites *are* taken into account, it is often found that they are located near the host units' boundaries and hence very close to adjacent and other nearby units....

Second, the unit-hazard coincidence method does not take into account the considerable variation in the size of the host units. It implicitly assumes that all the host units are of similar size and small enough to assure that the hazardous sites and residential populations within the units are in reasonably close proximity. However, examination of the census tracts hosting the nation's hazardous waste TSDFs reveals that this in fact is not the case. For example, we found that the smallest tract containing a hazardous waste TSDF is less than 0.1 square mile while the largest is over 7500 square miles, with all sizes in between. When a host unit is small, such as the former, it can be reasonably assumed that everyone living in it is close to the site. However, when the unit is large, such as the latter, it is uncertain how many people in the unit live close by....

In contrast to the studies employing the unit-hazard coincidence approach, a limited number of studies have used distance-based methods in which the precise locations of the environmental hazards or locally unwanted land uses under investigation are mapped and their distances to nearby populations are controlled. The demographics of all units, not just the host unit proper, within a specified distance of the hazardous sites are contrasted with the demographics of units further away....

By applying distance-based methods, we conduct a national level reassessment of racial inequality in the distribution of hazardous waste facilities and compare these results with the results of prior national level studies that have relied on the unit-hazard coincidence approach.... We found that on average the neighborhoods defined by ... [distance-based] methods, using 1.0, 2.0, and 3.0 mile radii [around the location of the TSDFs], were much smaller than the [census] host tracts proper. For example, we found the average area of the host tracts to be 58.41 square miles, while the average areas of the host neighborhoods defined by ... [the distance-based] methods were less than 3.25 square miles at the 1.0 mile radius....

We therefore wanted to determine whether by using distance-based methods we would find, nationally, larger proportions of poor people and people of color living near hazardous waste TSDFs than those living farther away and whether the differences found would be greater than what has been found in prior national studies using the unit-hazard coincidence method....

For purposes of providing a baseline comparison, we first examined nationally the results yielded by the unit-hazard coincidence method, i.e., we first contrasted the demographic characteristics of all host and non-host tracts in the country.... [F]or most characteristics the differences between host and non-host tracts are not very great....

We next examined the results obtained by employing the 50% areal containment method [one of the central distance-based methods]. These results reveal that, nationally, racial and socioeconomic disparities between neighborhoods that are within and those that are beyond the 1.0 and 3.0 mile distances are much more substantial than the disparities revealed by the unit-hazard coincidence method.... [I]n contrast to the unit-hazard coincidence method, controlling for proximity by using distance-based methods ... reveals substantial racial and socioeconomic disparities in the location of the nation's TSDFs. To further highlight the contrasting results obtained from using distance-based versus unit-hazard coincidence methods, we compared the above results with those obtained from the leading national studies that have analyzed the distribution of hazardous waste TSDFs by race and socioeconomic characteristics.... The disparities revealed are much less than those obtained by using distance-based methods. This is especially true regarding racial disparities. Indeed, [the SADRI study, *see* above, p. 38] found that the percentage of African Americans is actually slightly less in host than in non-host tracts....

Given that distance-based methods reveal greater racial disparities in the distribution of the nation's TSDFs than prior studies, does application of these methods also lead to different assessments about the possible underlying causes of these disparities? ... To determine whether application of distance-based methods leads to different assessments about the relative importance of economic and sociopolitical factors in accounting for racial disparities in the distribution of the nation's TSDFs, logistic regression analyses were performed.... Examination of the results ... reveals important differences obtained from applying unit-hazard coincidence and distance-based methods. For example, when applying the unit-hazard coincidence method, the African American and Hispanic percentages of the census tracts are not at all significant predictors of the location of TSDFs....

* * *

Notes and Questions

1. Professors Mohai and Saha and other colleagues subsequently employed the distance-based methodology using 2000 census data (the earlier studies used 1990 or earlier data) to assess the current extent of disparities in hazardous waste facility siting. They found that neighborhoods within 3 kilometers (1.8 miles) of TSDFs are 56% people of color whereas non-host areas are 30% people of color. Poverty rates in these neighborhoods are 1.5 times greater than non-host areas (18% vs. 12%), and mean annual incomes are 15% lower ($48,234 vs. $56, 912). Some of the results of the study are displayed in the table below. The study also found that race continues to be a significant predictor of where TSDFs are located, even after controlling for income, education, and other socioeconomic factors. ROBERT BULLARD, ET AL., TOXIC WASTES AND RACE AT TWENTY 1987–2007 at 52–53, 62 (2007).

Race/Socioeconomics	Host Neighborhoods	Non-Host Neighborhoods	Difference
Race/Ethnicity			
% People of Color	55.9%	30%	25.9%
% African American	20.0%	11.9%	8.0%
% Hispanic/Latino	27%	12.0%	15.0%
% Asian/Pacific Islander	6.7%	3.6%	3.0%
% Native American	0.7%	0.9%	−0.2%
Socioeconomics			
Poverty Rate	18.3%	12.2%	6.1%
Mean Household Income	$48,234	$56,912	−$8,678

2. As noted above, some scholars argue that proximity to polluting facilities should not be equated with actual exposure or elevated risk levels in host communities. For example, Christopher Boerner and Thomas Lambert maintain that:

> A ... flaw in the existing environmental-justice studies is that they imply rather than explicitly state the actual risk presented by commercial TSDFs. While the research attempts to disclose the prevalence of commercial-waste plants in poor and minority communities, there is no corresponding information about the dangers associated with living near such facilities. The regulatory requirements regarding the building and operation of industrial and waste facilities in the United States are among the most stringent of any industrialized country in the world. These requirements, along with the voluntary efforts of industry, significantly reduce the noxious emissions of commercial-waste plants and other facilities. Moreover, health risks are a function of actual exposure, not simply proximity to a waste facility. The environmental-justice advocates' claims of negative health effects are not substantiated by scientific studies.

Christopher Boerner & Thomas Lambert, *Environmental Injustice*, THE PUB. INT., Winter 1995 at 67. Do you agree? Should the adverse impacts of a facility on neighboring residents be defined by reference to their proximity to hazardous waste facilities? The health risk level they pose? What other adverse impacts on a community might be relevant? Studies that evaluate the disproportionate risk faced by communities from air emissions are discussed in Section C below.

C. Other Industrial Activities and Environmental Harms

1. Background

While some of the most highly publicized research about environmental justice concerns hazardous waste facilities, a substantial body of research has documented that low-income communities and communities of color also are disproportionately exposed to a wide range of other environmental harms. Some of the studies analyze distributions dating back to the early 1970s. For example, in 1992, Professors Paul Mohai and Bunyan Bryant published a review of fifteen studies that examined the distribution of various environmental hazards, many focusing on air pollution. With only a few exceptions, the studies found pollution to be inequitably distributed by income; and with only one exception, the studies found pollution to be inequitably distributed by race. Where the study analyzed distribution of pollution by income and race (and where it could weigh the relative importance of each), in most cases it found race to be more strongly related to the incidence of pollution. Paul Mohai & Bunyan Bryant, *Environmental Racism: Reviewing the Evidence, in* RACE AND THE INCIDENCE OF ENVIRONMENTAL HAZARDS: A TIME FOR DISCOURSE 163 (Bunyan Bryant & Paul Mohai eds., 1992). Professors Mohai and Bryant note that "[r]ather than being a recent discovery, documentation of environmental injustices stretches back two decades, almost to Earth Day—an event viewed by many as a major turning point in public awareness about environmental issues."

Based on its own review of the literature, EPA concluded in 1992 that racial minority and low-income populations experience higher than average exposures to certain air pollutants, hazardous waste facilities (and by implication, hazardous waste), contaminated fish, and agricultural pesticides. EPA further concluded, however, that there was insufficient data to determine whether these populations also suffer disparate health effects. The one exception was childhood lead poisoning. ENVTL. PROTECTION AGENCY, ENVIRONMENTAL EQUITY: REDUCING RISK FOR ALL COMMUNITIES, VOL. 2: SUPPORTING DOCUMENT 7–15 (1992). Indeed, there is unambiguous evidence that childhood lead poisoning—widely recognized as the most serious environmental health hazard facing young children—disproportionately affects low-income children and children of color. While blood lead levels of all children have been dropping nationwide, children from poor families are twice as likely to have elevated blood levels than those from higher income families, and African American children are three to thirteen times more likely (depending on the blood lead levels analyzed) to have elevated levels. Susan M. Bernard & Michael A. McGeehin, *Prevalence of Blood Lead Levels ≥ 5 µg/dL Among U.S. Children 1 to 5 Years of Age and Socioeconomic and Demographic Factors Associated With Blood of Lead Levels 5 to 10 µg/dL, Third National Health and Nutrition Examination Survey, 1988–1994*, 112 PEDIATRICS 1308 (2003).

* * *

Notes and Questions

1. Professors Mohai and Bryant's excerpt demonstrates that information about environmental inequities has been available for some time. Why has it taken so long for public awareness to catch up with this empirical evidence?

2. Two of the specific areas in which both EPA and Professors Mohai and Bryant found disparities are exposure to agricultural pesticides and contaminated fish. The next two excerpts explore these issues.

2. Farmworker Exposure to Pesticides

Ivette Perfecto & Baldemar Velásquez,
Farm Workers: Among the Least Protected
EPA Journal, March/April 1992 at 13

The United States is the largest single user of pesticides in the world. By EPA's own estimate, each year U.S. farmers use about 1.2 billion pounds of pesticides at an expenditure of $4.6 billion. More than 600 active ingredients are combined with other ingredients to form approximately 35,000 different commercial formulations. Yet, full evaluation of their hazards lags far behind the development of new products....

Those who suffer most directly from the chemical dependency of U.S. agriculture are farm workers, who are working in the fields while some of the most toxic substances known to humans are sprayed. The World Resources Institute has estimated that as many as 313,000 farm workers in the United States may suffer from pesticide-related illnesses each year. Another source estimates that 800 to 1,000 farm workers die each year as a direct consequence of pesticide exposure.

farm workers suffer most directly

Ninety percent of the approximately two million hired farm workers in the United States are people of color: The majority are Chicanos, followed by Puerto Ricans, Caribbean blacks, and African Americans. This primarily minority population has among the least protected jobs of all workers. Farm workers are intentionally excluded from the Occupational Safety and Health Act (OSHA), which governs health and safety standards in the workplace; from the Fair Labor Standards Act, which governs minimum wages and child labor; and most importantly, from the National Labor Relations Act, which guarantees the right to join a union and bargain collectively.

90% people of color

The exclusion of farm workers from OSHA regulations has particular relevance to the pesticide issue. Under OSHA's principles of environmental hygiene, when workers are exposed to a toxic substance in the workplace the priority course of action is to eliminate the substance from the workplace altogether or to replace it with a non-toxic or less toxic substitute. If this is impossible, the option next in priority is to separate the workers from the toxic substance. The last option usually involves provisioning workers with some protective measures (e.g., protective clothing, masks, glasses, etc.).

Not being covered by OSHA, and therefore not able to legally petition the Occupational Safety and Health Administration, farm workers are forced to petition EPA, which is the agency in charge of regulating pesticides. But such petitioning offers few formal legal remedies, leaving farm workers virtually unprotected against pesticide hazards....

Furthermore, evidence indicates that for some acutely toxic pesticides, extant protective measures are ineffective. A case in point is the deadly pesticide ethyl parathion, a leading cause of farm worker poisoning in the United States and worldwide....

Parathion is only one of many acutely toxic pesticides belonging to the organophosphate family. These pesticides came into wide use approximately 20 years ago, when environmental awareness called for limitations on persistent pesticides that were contaminating the environment and damaging wildlife. Many of the persistent pesticides belong to the organochloride family and have been associated with chronic health effects.... The organophosphates, on the other hand, degrade much faster and therefore reduced the risk for wildlife and for consumers.

However, for farm workers the switch from organochlorines to organophosphates meant exposure to more acutely toxic pesticides, since many of these rapidly degradable pesticides (parathion is one of them) are characterized by acute toxicity, which can cause dizziness; vomiting; irritation of the eye, upper respiratory tract, and skin; and death. There is an irony here that has not escaped the attention of farm workers: The new wave of environmental consciousness, which forced welcome changes in production technologies, may have actually made things more precarious for farm workers, substituting acute symptoms for chronic ones....

* * *

Notes and Questions

1. Does some form of racism (conscious, unconscious, institutional) explain the legal system's treatment of farmworkers who face some of the greatest occupational risks from environmental hazards? (*See* Chapter 3 for a discussion of various forms of racism.)

2. Outside the farmworker context, a number of studies show that workers of color and low-wage workers are more likely than the rest of the population to work in jobs with higher exposures to toxic chemicals and other hazardous conditions, and that they experience greater risks of occupational disease and injury. Some of these studies are discussed in George Friedman-Jiménez, *Achieving Environmental Justice: The Role of Occupational Health*, 21 FORDHAM URB. L.J. 604, 610–13 (1994). For example, Asian workers are disproportionately exposed to hazards in the high-tech industry, including exposure to solvents that cause reproductive harm and other chronic illnesses, and repetitive motion injuries. Employee exposures to toxics are typically far higher than those experienced by community residents who live near industrial facilities. In its 1990 comparative risk project, for example, EPA ranked occupational exposures as among the risks deserving greatest regulatory attention. Dr. Friedman-Jiménez notes that occupational diseases caused by exposure to toxic substances or hazardous conditions in the workplace are widespread: "The best available evidence indicates that 350,000 workers develop new onset occupational diseases and 50,000–70,000 active, disabled, or retired workers die of occupational diseases each year in the United States." *Id.* at 606. Why do you think workplace risks have received comparatively little attention from environmental groups in the past?

3. Social and economic factors add to the workplace risks faced by low-wage workers and workers of color. Because these employees are the most economically vulnerable, they may be less able than the general population to refuse or leave hazardous jobs, or to complain about unhealthy conditions. Recent immigrant workers fear retaliation not only in terms of potential job loss but also fear inquiry into to their immigration status. More-

over, "[l]imited English skills prevent them from grasping the scanty information on
health hazards that is available. Many times, as new immigrants unfamiliar with the American system, they are afraid and unaccustomed to speaking out, challenging their em-
ployer, and complaining about their illnesses and work environment." Flora Chu, *Asian
Workers at Risk*, Race, Poverty & Env't, Spring 1992 at 10, 12.

limited English skills

3. Exposure to Contaminated Fish

National Environmental Justice Advisory Council,
Fish Consumption and Environmental Justice
(2002)

.... Fish, aquatic plants, and wildlife are major dietary staples for some individuals, and
those who subsist chiefly or solely on fish, aquatic plants, and wildlife are more likely to
be people of color, low-income individuals, tribal members, or other indigenous people.
Thus, for example, a recent survey revealed that whereas 60% of "non-white" (primarily
African-American) fishers on the Detroit River fished there to meet their needs for food
or for a combination of food and recreation, only 21.7% of white fishers indicated that
they fished for reasons combining food and recreation, and none indicated that they
fished only to meet their needs for food. In Alaska, "[a]mong Yupiks of Gambell, over one-
half of their protein, iron, vitamin B-12, and omega-3 fatty acids come from subsistence
foods." ...

An African-American fisher on the Detroit River explains:

> I think that mostly black people fish on the river (due to lack of money); if they
> have the money they can go anywhere and fish—wherever they want. A lot of
> us don't have the boats or the cars to get to the good fish. We settle for the fish
> here but it's all good. I still get the fish. Some people fish because they have to
> fish. Fish is good food and it is cheap but river fish is the cheapest and I don't
> blame people for eating it....

Yin Ling Leung, Executive Director of Asians and Pacific Islanders for Reproductive Health,
California, summarizes:

> To our communities, being able to fish means being able to either put food on
> the table, or basically eat a much less nutritious meal. I think that's a non-choice.

... [F]or many communities of color, low-income communities, tribes, and other indigenous peoples, the nutritional, economic, and traditional or cultural aspects of fishing, preparing and eating fish are interrelated.... [Take, for example] the
Greenpoint/Williamsburg ("G/W") community in the Borough of Brooklyn in New York
City:

> In G/W, some anglers consume as many as two meals per day of fish caught in
> the East River, which forms the western boundary of G/W. Approximately 38
> percent of the G/W population lives below the poverty line, suggesting that many
> of the anglers fishing in this community may be urban subsistence anglers who
> rely on fish caught in the East River as a free source of nutrition. In addition,
> fishing is a way of life rooted in the cultural heritage for many of the black and
> Hispanic anglers observed fishing on the piers in G/W, many of whom come
> from Carribean [sic] fishing cultures....

38% below poverty line

Consumption and use of contaminated fish, aquatic plants, and wildlife is an especially pressing concern for many communities of color, low-income communities, tribes, and other indigenous peoples, whose members may ① consume fish, aquatic plants, and wildlife in greater quantities than does the general population; ② consume and use different fish, aquatic plants, and wildlife than does the general population; ③ employ different practices in consuming and using fish, aquatic plants, and wildlife than does the general population; (4) consume and use fish, aquatic plants, and wildlife in cultural, traditional, religious, historical, economic, and legal contexts that differ from those of the general population....

[margin note: However, Evidence of more consumption]

The EPA until quite recently based its environmental decisions on the assumption that humans eat just 6.5 grams of fish per day—*roughly one 8-ounce fish meal per month.* Yet there is abundant evidence that people of color, low-income individuals, tribal members, and other indigenous people eat far greater quantities of fish. For example, a recent study by the Columbia River Inter-Tribal Fish Commission of members of four Columbia River tribes registered a mean fish consumption rate of 58.7 grams/day and a maximum fish consumption rate of 972.0 grams/day—well over one hundred times the EPA value.... Similarly, studies of anglers in both Alabama and Michigan registered markedly higher fish consumption rates for low-income African-Americans—in Alabama, low-income African-Americans ate a mean of 63 grams/day; in Michigan, low-income African-Americans (together with other "minority fishers and off-reservation Native Americans") consumed a mean of 43.1 grams/day....

EPA also typically makes assumptions about the species and parts consumed and about the methods of preparation that reflect practices of the general population but often do not depict fully or accurately the practices of communities of color, low-income communities, tribes, or other indigenous peoples.... [T]he result in many cases is that when the fish are contaminated, those consuming in accordance with different practices will be exposed to greater quantities of the contaminants....

* * *

Notes and Questions

1. Other studies report similar results to those in the NEJAC report. For example, a survey in 1999 of ten Asian American and Pacific Islander (API) groups in King County, Washington (Cambodian, Chinese, Filipino, Hmong, Japanese, Korean, Laotian, Mien, Samoan, and Vietnamese) found that they consume fish at rates substantially greater than those of the general population or of recreational anglers. The consumption rate for even the 50th percentile of these API communities—89 grams per day—is more than five times the rate of the 90th percentile of the general population—17.5 grams per day. NEJAC report, *supra,* at 26–27, *citing* RUTH SECHENA, ET AL., ASIAN AND PACIFIC ISLANDER SEAFOOD CONSUMPTION STUDY IN KING COUNTY, WASHINGTON (1999).

2. As discussed in Chapter 7, many water bodies in the U.S. remain polluted to some degree, and fish consumption advisories cover close to 40% of the nation's lake acreage and 26% of the nation's river miles. Other studies confirm that contemporary fish consumption rates for Native Americans are significantly greater than comparable rates for the general population. These studies, and their implications for water quality standards set by environmental agencies, also are discussed in Chapter 7.

3. We now turn to industrial facilities that in the course of their production processes release a wide range of pollutants to the environment.

4. Toxic Release Inventory (TRI) Facilities

Evan J. Ringquist, Equity and the Distribution of Environmental Risk: The Case of TRI Facilities

78 Social Science Quarterly 811 (1997)

.... Are racial minorities and the poor exposed to greater environmental risk? [This study analyzes factors] accounting for the locational patterns of three underexamined elements of environmental risk; the distribution of Toxic Release Inventory (TRI) facilities, the density of TRI facilities, and the concentration of TRI pollutants....

Since 1987, the Environmental Protection Agency (EPA) has required over 75,000 industrial facilities to report their releases of some 200 toxic chemicals. [The number of chemicals subject to TRI reporting is now 654. Eds.] Together, this information makes up the Toxics Release Inventory (TRI)....

[The results of this study are as follows]: First, race clearly matters with respect to the distribution of TRI facilities.... TRI facilities are significantly more likely to be found in ZIP codes with large numbers of African American and Hispanic residents.... Second, class characteristics are associated with the distribution of TRI facilities.... [T]he probability that a residential area hosts a TRI facility is negatively associated with median household income. However, the probability that a residential ZIP code contains a TRI facility is also negatively associated with poverty rates and the percentage of adults who do not have a high school diploma. Thus, while TRI facilities are not prevalent in wealthy areas, neither are they disproportionately present in "underclass" neighborhoods. This suggests that these facilities, perhaps predictably, are located in working class residential areas....   *not prevalent in wealthy areas*

[T]he factors explaining the [density] of TRI facilities in a residential area are very similar to the factors explaining the probability that any residential area will have a TRI facility....

Proximity to these facilities, however, may not substantially increase one's exposure to environmental risk.... In order to do away with the assumption that proximity is a good proxy for risk, I obtained data on the total weight of TRI pollutants released in each residential ZIP code.... [The] results paint a picture of TRI pollutants being concentrated in urban working class neighborhoods.... However, once again race matters. All other things equal, residential areas with large concentrations of African Americans and Hispanics are exposed to substantially higher levels of TRI pollutants....

These results suggest three general conclusions regarding the distribution of risk from TRI facilities. First, there are racial biases in the distribution and density of TRI facilities and the concentration of TRI pollutants. Even when controlling for other factors, African American and Hispanic residential areas are more likely to be exposed to higher levels of these environmental risks. Second, certain class attributes also affect the likelihood that a residential area will host TRI facilities and high concentrations of TRI pollutants. The class results, however, are less predictable and consistent than many members of the environmental justice community might expect.... Finally, while racial and class biases in environmental risk should not be discounted, we have to remember that the general background characteristics of residential areas best account for the distribution of environmental risks from TRI facilities....

* * *

Notes and Questions

1. As Professor Ringquist notes, while up to this time most environmental justice research had examined the characteristics of hazardous waste facilities—and consequently made it a much more high profile issue—sources with TRI emissions are much more prevalent, outnumbering hazardous waste facilities by almost forty to one. *Id.* at 813.

2. A later study, using an EPA screening model, evaluated disparities in the health risks resulting from air toxic emissions from TRI facilities. The study also controlled for regional variations in patterns of existing development and base levels of environmental quality, which some researchers have suggested influence whether disparities are found. This study concluded that African Americans tend to live in more polluted cities than do whites, and also tend to live in more polluted neighborhoods within these cities. Hispanics tend to live in less polluted cities than do whites, but within these cities, they tend to live in more polluted neighborhoods. Michael Ash & T. Robert Fetter, *Who Lives on the Wrong Side of the Environmental Tracks? Evidence from the EPA's Risk-Screening Environmental Indicators Model,* 85 Soc. Sci. Q. 441 (2004). Air toxics are of particular concern because air emissions easily migrate beyond the boundary of a facility property line and into nearby communities.

5. Cumulative and Multiple Exposures

Thus far we have been discussing disparities in fairly specific contexts, such as proximity to one facility or type of facility (hazardous waste facilities or TRI sources), or exposure to a particular risk (pesticide exposure or consumption of contaminated fish). However, emissions of multiple pollutants and from multiple nearby sources can give rise to a problem of cumulative exposure and risk that is not captured in these single focus studies. In the study below, researchers begin to analyze disparities in potential health risks from cumulative exposures to air toxics.

Researchers also have begun to prepare studies that aggregate data about disparities that result from exposure to numerous different types of environmental hazards in different environmental medium. We examine some of these studies in subsection (b) below.

a. Air Toxics Exposures

Rachel Morello-Frosch, Manuel Pastor, & James Sadd, Environmental Justice and Southern California's "Riskscape": The Distribution of Air Toxics Exposures and Health Risks among Diverse Communities

36 Urban Affairs Review 551 (2001)

.... [Environmental justice researchers] have largely limited their inquiries to evaluating differences in the location of pollution sources between population groups while placing less emphasis on evaluating the distribution of exposures or, more important, potential health risks.... Of special concern has been the need to move beyond substance-by-substance analysis toward a cumulative exposure approach that accounts for the exposure realities of diverse populations....

We tackle this challenge.... We specifically study air pollution in the Southern California Air Basin looking at 148 air toxics, also known as hazardous air pollutants (HAPs) listed under the 1990 Clean Air Act Amendments. By combining modeled concentration estimates with cancer toxicity information, we derive estimates of lifetime cancer risks and examine their distribution among diverse communities in the region....

[The study shows that] [e]stimated lifetime cancer risks associated with outdoor air toxics exposures in the South Coast Air Basin are ubiquitously high, with a mean and median of 59 per 100,000 and a range from 6.8 to 591 per 100,000. Overall, cancer risks exceed the Clean Air Act goal of one in a million by between one and three orders of magnitude....

[To explore the correlation between race/ethnicity and lifetime cancer risks associated with outdoor air toxics exposures], we calculated PRIs [population risk indexes] for each racial and ethnic group. Results in Table 2 show that estimated lifetime cancer risks on average are high for each group, exceeding the Clean Air Act goal of one in one million by two orders of magnitude. Moreover, estimated cancer risks for people of color are higher than for Anglos and exceed the average PRI for all groups in the region, with Latinos experiencing the highest risk levels.

Table 2: Average Population Risk Index (Excess Lifetime Cancer Risk) by Race/Ethnicity for the South Coast Air Basin

Racial/Ethnic Group	PRI for Estimated Individual Lifetime Cancer Risk
African American	63/100,000
Latino	65/100,000
Asian American	63/100,000
Anglos	49/100,000
People of Color	64/100,000
Average Across all Groups	57/100,000

[These] racial/ethnic disparities in estimated cancer risks persist across household income strata.... [The] results suggest persistent racial differences in estimated cancer risks associated with ambient HAP exposures.... [T]he probability of a person of color in southern California living in a high cancer risk neighborhood is nearly one in three, but the probability for an Anglo resident is about one in seven....

[The results hold true] after controlling for well-known causes of pollution such as population density, income, land use, and a proxy for political power and assets (home ownership)....

* * *

Notes and Questions

1. As noted by Professor Morello-Frosch and her colleagues, an analysis of the cumulative risks reveals a much more comprehensive picture than risks posed by individual substances in isolation, or risks posed by one source in isolation. Relatively few studies have examined the distribution of cumulative risks, in part because of the lack of data about ambient environmental conditions in the U.S. (Indeed, some activists argue that historically fewer air monitoring stations have been placed in environmental justice communities). Recent developments in cumulative risk assessment are discussed in Chapter 6.

2. One of the surprising results of the Morello-Frosch study is that the concentration of hazardous air pollutants and their associated health risks in communities of color re-

sult mostly from smaller area and mobile sources, as opposed to large industrial facilities. As the authors of the study note, these sources are smaller, more widely dispersed and diverse in terms of their emissions and production characteristics than larger stationary sources, and have been subject to fewer regulatory controls. What special challenges do controlling such sources pose for policymakers? Does this suggest a greater need for examining land use and transportation policies?

3. Another study found a clear relationship between increasing levels of racial/ethnic residential segregation in metropolitan areas and increased cancer risk from air toxic exposures. The effect persists across all income categories, and racial disparities widen with increasing levels of segregation. Rachel Morello-Frosch & Bill M. Jesdale, *Separate and Unequal: Residential Segregation and Estimated Cancer Risks Associated with Ambient Air Toxics in U.S. Metropolitan Areas*, 114 ENVTL. HEALTH PERSP. 386 (2006).

4. Using EPA data that calculates a health risk score for areas throughout the U.S. based on exposure to toxic air emissions, an Associated Press study found that African Americans are 79% more likely than whites to live in areas with the highest risks. Poorer, less educated, and unemployed residents also faced higher risks. David Pace, *More Blacks Live with Pollution*, ASSOCIATED PRESS, Dec. 13, 2005.

b. Multiple Environmental Harms

The following is one of the first studies to look at disparities stemming from exposure to a wide range of environmental hazards.

John A. Hird & Michael Reese, The Distribution of Environmental Quality: An Empirical Analysis

79 Social Science Quarterly 693 (1998)

[This paper examines the relationship between demographic characteristics and the distribution of twenty-nine indicators of environmental quality throughout the nation, including industrial air emissions, industrial water discharges, water quality, air quality, and proximity to hazardous wastes. The results are reported as follows]:

Income. Somewhat surprisingly, in thirteen … of twenty-nine cases, income is positively and significantly related to pollution levels, and in only four cases … is higher income associated with less pollution at a statistically significant level. Therefore, the interpretation of the income variables is mixed.…

Poverty/Unemployment.. [W]hile there appears to be a strong positive relationship between the location of unemployed residents and increased pollution levels, the relationship is frequently negative between poverty rates and pollution levels. These confounding results do not allow us to confidently assert any clear relationship between pollution levels and counties with a large percentage of residents either unemployed or in poverty.

Race/Ethnicity. Even when numerous other potentially relevant variables are included in the analysis, race and ethnicity remain strongly associated with environmental quality, with both nonwhite and Hispanic populations experiencing disproportionately high pollution levels.…

Political Mobilization. There is a strong and generally consistent association in the analysis between the level of potential political mobilization and pollution levels. For many pollutants examined, a higher level of actual or potential political mobilization is associated with lower pollution levels. For owner-occupied housing [one of the factors used to measure levels of political mobilization], the relationship is particularly strong....

Manufacturing. As expected, the level of manufacturing activity, measured as the number of manufacturing establishments per square mile, is positively related to most pollution level indicators....

Population Density. One of the strongest empirical relationships is, not surprisingly, between population density and a wide variety of pollutants. Urban areas are subjected to far greater pollution than their rural counterparts, even accounting for differences in manufacturing, income, poverty, and unemployment....

The results of this study suggest that environmental quality is unevenly distributed, that nonwhites and Hispanics are significantly affected by that uneven distribution, and that this uneven distribution is a national rather than a regional phenomenon. Pollutants tend to be distributed in a way that disproportionately affects people of color, even across different model specifications, different pollutants, and when many other confounding characteristics are taken into account. This conclusion is all the more powerful because plausible alternative political and economic explanations are here modeled explicitly (e.g., the influences of income, urban locations, manufacturing activity). At the same time, the results show that a variety of other demographic variables play an important role in explaining the uneven distribution of environmental quality throughout the United States. For example, the negative relationship between indicators of political mobilization and pollution is one of the strongest, and the positive relationship between income and pollution appears to be an important factor explaining the distribution of some indicators of environmental quality, as does population density and manufacturing activity....

* * *

Notes and Questions

1. What factors might explain the somewhat surprising findings of the above study that for a number of environmental indicators, income is positively related to pollution levels, and poverty rates are negatively related?

2. More recently, Professor Evan Ringquist performed a "meta-analysis" of forty-nine studies examining disparities in environmental hazards (meta-analysis is a tool for aggregating the results of various research studies on a given topic into effectively one large study on the topic). The meta-analysis found that environmental inequities based on race are ubiquitous, and that while the magnitude of the disparities varies based on some factors in the design of the studies conducted, "protests claiming that these factors can explain away such inequities are empirically unsustainable." With respect to income, the evidence was more mixed: "while some environmental risks in some places may be concentrated in low-income areas, this result is not generalizable across areas and risk vectors.... [and] sources of environmental risk are less likely to be located in areas of hardcore poverty." Professor Ringquist also concluded that the magnitude of the race- and class-based environmental inequities that the studies found are "quite modest." Evan J. Ringquist, *Assessing Evidence of Environmental Inequities: A Meta-Analysis*, 24 J. POL'Y ANALYSIS & MGMT. 223, 241 (2005). Other scholars argue that Ringquist's conclusions that the racial disparities are small should be tempered, for two reasons: First, as Professsors Mohai and Saha discuss above, studies that use distance-based methods actually show large effects,

and second, the conclusion neglects cumulative impacts. MANUEL PASTOR, *ET AL.*, IN THE WAKE OF THE STORM: ENVIRONMENT, DISASTER, AND RACE AFTER KATRINA 14 (2006).

6. Disaster Vulnerability

Another type of risk that is often distributed inequitably is vulnerability to disasters. This was dramatically underscored by Hurricane Katrina, which swept through the Gulf Coast in August 2005, killing over 1,300 residents and displacing over one million more. As the excerpt below indicates, Katrina is a stark example of a pattern that has existed for many years.

Manuel Pastor, Robert D. Bullard, James K. Boyce, Alice Fothergill, Rachel Morello-Frosch & Beverly Wright, In the Wake of the Storm: Environment, Disaster, and Race after Katrina
(2006)

[One] ... illusion that Katrina swept away was the traditional belief that natural disasters are a sort of equal opportunity affair—acts of God that affect us all. But as the government's emergency rescue and recovery efforts floundered, particularly in beleaguered New Orleans, the country began to realize that this was not the case. It was a largely African American and often poor populace that had lived in the areas most vulnerable to the collapse of the levees, that proved unable to secure transportation to evacuate the city, and that was now scrambling in frightening conditions to secure scarce aid for their families, their friends, and themselves. Both the impacts of and response to disaster, it seemed, were heavily affected by income and race....

The areas most affected by Katrina were even blacker and poorer [than the overall area affected]. New Orleans was more than 67 percent black before Katrina [versus about 12 percent for the nation as a whole]. The coastal Mississippi counties where Katrina struck ranged from 25 percent to 87 percent black. Poverty was also a common characteristic. Some 28 percent of New Orleans residents lived below the poverty level and more than 80 percent of those were black. The poverty rate was 17.7 percent in Gulfport, Mississippi, and 21.2 percent in Mobile, Alabama, in 2000, versus 11.3 percent in the nation as a whole.

Of course, those most likely to be left behind as the flood waters rose in New Orleans were from neighborhoods that were even poorer and more African American.... Local, state, and federal emergency planners had known for years the risks facing New Orleans' transit-dependent residents.... More than 30 percent of African Americans in New Orleans do not own a car. Before Katrina, nearly 25 percent of New Orleans residents relied on public transportation. The city already knew that at least "100,000 New Orleans citizens do not have means of personal transportation" to evacuate in case of a major storm.

The city's emergency plan thus called for thousands of the city's most vulnerable population to be left behind in their homes, shelters, and hospitals. It also included the use of public buses to evacuate those without transportation: sixty-four buses and ten lift vans. The plan proved woefully inadequate, especially after nearly two hundred New Orleans Rapid Transit Authority (RTA) vehicles were lost to flooding....

The social dynamics that underlie the disproportionate environmental hazards faced by low-income communities and minorities also play out in the arena of disaster prevention, mitigation, and recovery.... Lack of wealth heightens the risks that individuals and communities face for three reasons. First, it translates into a lack of purchasing power to secure private alternatives to public provision of a clean and safe environment for all. Second, it translates into less ability to withstand shocks (such as health bills and property damage) that wealth would cushion. Third, it translates through the "shadow prices" of cost-benefit analysis into public policies that place a lower priority on protecting "less valuable" people and their assets....

Ninety-eight percent of the residents of the Lower Ninth Ward, the lowest-lying area of New Orleans that was most vulnerable to flooding, were African Americans (versus 67 percent in the city as a whole and 37 percent in the entire metropolitan area). As the hurricane drew near, many of the poor were unable to flee because they lacked private transportation. And, in the aftermath of the storm, a second disaster that involves disparities in recovery and reconstruction processes has started to unfold....

As we saw in the Hurricane Katrina disaster, contextually understanding the evacuation behavior of residents (especially the most vulnerable) following disaster warnings is critical. Some research indicates that race, ethnicity, and socioeconomic status have no effect, whereas other studies have found that the poor and minorities are less likely to evacuate or undertake protective action short of evacuation. This pattern of evacuation delay, even after warnings, may also reflect differences in wealth.... [T]he weight of home ownership in [one's] bundle of assets—which can include businesses, stocks, and other financial wealth—is much higher for African Americans [than whites]: home equity accounts for nearly 63 percent of black wealth but only about 43 percent for white. Home equity is also a disproportionately important component of Latino net worth. Thus the urge to stay behind and protect one's assets, especially if underinsured, may be understandable, albeit dangerous.

Nevertheless, evacuation delay is not primarily a matter of choice.... Before [Hurricane] Andrew hit [in 1992], blacks and those with low incomes in the evacuation zone were less likely to evacuate than other groups, most likely due to the lack of transportation and few affordable refuge options. There were also reports of public housing residents having to walk or hitchhike out of evacuation zones, and of poor women unable to leave because they did not have enough money for supplies or transportation....

What are the patterns of mortality, morbidity, and injury when disaster finally strikes? ... Research conducted in the 1970s concluded that disaster-connected deaths were disproportionately high among ethnic minorities, and research on loss from natural hazards in the United States from 1970 to 1980 further confirmed that lower income households experience higher rates of injuries in disasters such as floods, earthquakes, and fires than more affluent households. The pattern of differential impacts is often due to the quality of housing afforded those lower on the socioeconomic scale. The low quality construction of low-cost housing puts residents of such housing at greater risk....

* * *

Notes and Questions

1. Scholars have explained that a community's vulnerability to disasters is a function of both the character of the environment in a particular physical location, and a community's "social vulnerability;" i.e., social and economic characteristics such as education, gender, race, income level, the age and condition of housing stock, access to transportation and other "lifelines," and the percentage of special needs populations (very poor, elderly, mentally or physically challenged). Thus,

[p]opulations are not vulnerable simply because they are exposed [to physical hazards], but rather their plight "is a result of marginality that makes their life a 'permanent emergency.'" This marginality was laid bare along the Gulf Coast. For example, one of the main reasons for lower compliance with evacuation orders among the New Orleans poor was that Katrina struck on 29 August—two days before paychecks and welfare or disability checks would arrive—and they had no money to use for transportation.

Susan L. Cutter et al., *The Long Road Home: Race, Class and Recovery from Hurricane Katrina*, Env't, Mar. 2006, at 8, 11. To a considerable extent, these same factors are associated with a community's "resilience"—its ability to cope with disaster impacts and subsequently recover from them.

2. The factors discussed above also mean that poor and minority communities will be more vulnerable to the adverse impacts of climate change, which include more heat waves, floods, wildfires, hurricanes and other extreme weather events, and worse air pollution. The disproportionate impacts of climate change are discussed in detail in Chapter 12.

3. In addition to disaster vulnerability that arises from physical location and social factors combined, the overall impacts of natural disasters also depend on how government officials respond once disasters strike. Disparities in emergency response efforts are examined in Section D below.

D. Disparities in Environmental Benefits

Although less systematically than with respect to environmental hazards, researchers in recent years have begun to study the inequitable distribution of environmental goods or benefits. The following sections examine some studies from this emerging field.

1. Transportation Benefits

Robert D. Bullard, Glenn S. Johnson & Angel O. Torres, The Routes of American Apartheid

Forum for Applied Research and Public Policy, Fall 2000 at 66

The modern civil rights movement has its roots in transportation. In 1953, over half a century after *Plessy vs. Ferguson* relegated blacks to the back of the bus, African Americans in Baton Rouge, Louisiana, staged the nation's first successful bus boycott. Two years later, on December 1, 1955, Rosa Parks refused to give up her seat at the front of a Montgomery, Alabama, city bus to a white man. In so doing, Parks ignited the modern civil rights movement. By the early 1960s, young "freedom riders" risked death by riding Greyhound buses into the deep South. This was their way of fighting transportation apartheid and segregation in interstate travel.

Today, despite those heroic efforts, transportation remains a civil-rights and quality-of-life issue. All communities are still *not* created equal. Indeed, some communities accrue benefits from transportation development projects, while others bear a disproportionate burden in paying the costs. Generally, benefits are more widely dis-

persed among the many travelers who use new roads, while costs or burdens are more localized. Having a seven-lane freeway next door, for instance, is not a benefit to someone
who does not own a car.

Lest anyone dismiss transportation as a tangential racial issue, consider that Americans
spend more on transportation than any other household expense except housing. The
average American household spends a fifth of its income—or about $6,000 a year—for
each car it owns and operates. Americans also spend more than 2 billion hours a year in
their cars. According to the latest figures published in the Federal Highway Administration's *Highway Statistics*, total vehicle miles traveled in the United States increased by 59
percent from 1980 to 1995.

Federal tax dollars subsidized many of the roads, freeways, and public transit systems
in our nation. Many of these transportation projects had the unintended consequences
of dividing, isolating, and disrupting some communities while imposing inequitable economic, environmental, and health burdens on them....

Old War, New Battles....

Currently, only about 5.3 percent of all Americans use public transit to get to work. Most
American workers opt for private automobiles, which provide speed and convenience,
and most of them forgo car pooling. Indeed, nationally, 79.6 percent of commuters drive
alone to work. Generally, people who commute using public transit spend twice as much
time traveling as those who travel by car. Consider, for instance, that the average commute takes about 20 minutes in a car, 38 minutes on a bus, and 45 minutes on a train.
People of color are twice as likely as their white counterparts to use non-auto modes of
travel—public transit, walking, bicycles—to get to work....

[I]n Macon, Georgia, a city whose population is evenly divided between blacks and whites,
[over] 90 percent of the bus riders in Macon are African Americans, and more than 28
percent of Macon's African Americans do not own cars, compared with only 6 percent of
the city's whites.

A disproportionate share of transportation dollars in Macon and Bibb County, however, have gone to road construction and maintenance at the expense of the bus system.
In 1993, Macon and Bibb County devoted more than $33 million of federal, state, and
local funds for roads, streets, and highways, of which some $10 million came from fed-
eral funds. During the same year, local officials accepted no federal funds for the Macon-
Bibb County Transit Authority and budgeted only $1.4 million for public transportation.
Overall, the bulk of federal transportation monies received by Macon and Bibb County
have been accepted to support road construction in mostly white suburban areas outside
the reach of many African Americans....

[R]ace is at the heart of Atlanta's regional transportation dilemma.... The 10-county
Atlanta metropolitan area has a regional public transit system only in name. In the 1960s,
the Metropolitan Atlanta Rapid Transit Authority [MARTA] was hailed as the solution
to the region's growing traffic and pollution problems; but today, MARTA serves just two
counties, Fulton and DeKalb....

Between 1990 and 1997, Atlanta's northern suburbs reaped the lion's share of new jobs
and economic development. During that period, Atlanta's northern suburbs added 273,000
jobs. This accounted for 78.4 percent of all jobs added in the region. Another 70,500 jobs
or 20.3 percent were added in the southern part of the region. Only 4,500 jobs were added
in the region's central core of Atlanta, representing only 1.3 percent of all jobs created
during the height of the region's booming economy.

Clearly, Atlanta's people of color and the poor could benefit by having public transit extended into the job-rich suburbs. Public transit, however, does not go where most of the region's jobs are located....

* * *

Robert García, Mean Streets
Forum for Applied Research and Public Policy, Fall 2000 at 75

Martin Luther King Jr. recognized that urban transit systems in most American cities are a genuine civil rights issue. Today, close to half a century later, urban transit systems remain largely untouched by the reforms of the civil rights movement....

Consider the case of Kyle, a 26-year-old single Latina mother of two and a bus rider in Los Angeles. She works at a drug prevention program after having come off of welfare, which she describes as hell. Now she faces the new hell of her daily commute.

> At 6 a.m. Kyle is at the bus stop with her children. Fourteen-month-old Ishmael is asleep on her shoulder; five-year-old Mustafa holds her hand. Two buses later she drops off Mustafa at school in Inglewood. Then she rides two more buses to get Ishmael to his baby sitter in Watts. From there it is half an hour to work. Kyle arrives about 9 a.m., three hours and six buses after starting. "The boys and I read. We play games, we talk to other people, we spend the time however we can," she said. "In L.A. County, it's very difficult to live without a car."

Kyle's story is all too common. It illustrates the need for a national transportation equity agenda—one that provides choices to people who currently lack them.

The typical bus rider in Los Angeles is a Latina woman in her 20s with two children. Among riders, 69 percent have an annual household income of $15,000—which is below the federal poverty line—and no access to a car; 40 percent have household incomes under $7,500. Elsewhere in the United States, the statistics may change but the stories are similar....

Ruthie Walls, a single mother looking for affordable housing for her children, bought a house in Atlanta surrounded by freeways on three sides. Cleaner cars have not stopped the harm she and her neighbors still suffer from the air, water, and noise pollution of increased traffic congestion. Their children play in toxic brake and tire dust collected in the creek that often floods their homes with runoff from the roads. They breathe the diesel exhaust from dirty buses. But they pay higher taxes for storm water cleanup caused by roads that serve suburban commuters and truck drivers....

Equity into Action

.... The historic 1996 case *Labor/Community Strategy Center v. Los Angeles County Metropolitan Transportation Authority*, filed on behalf of low-income and minority bus riders [showed the following]:

• **Racial disparities.** While 80 percent of the people riding MTA's bus and rail lines were minorities, most of the minorities rode only buses. On the other hand, only 28 percent of riders on Metrolink—MTA's commuter rail line—were minorities. Thus, the percentage of minorities riding Metrolink varied by 173 standard deviations from the expected 80 percent. The likelihood that such a substantial departure from the expected value would occur by chance is infinitesimal.

• **Subsidy disparities.** While 94 percent of MTA's riders rode buses, MTA customarily spent 70 percent of its budget on rail. Data in 1992 revealed a $1.17 subsidy per boarding for an MTA bus rider. The subsidy for a Metrolink commuter rail rider was 18 times higher, however, or $21.02. For a suburban light-rail streetcar passenger, the subsidy was more than nine times higher, or $11.34; and for a subway passenger, it was two-and-a-half times higher, or $2.92.

For three years during the mid-1980s, MTA reduced the bus fare from 85 cents to 50 cents. Ridership increased 40 percent during the period, making this the most successful mass transit experiment in the post-war era. Despite this increase in demand, MTA subsequently raised bus fares and reduced its peak-hour bus fleet from 2,200 to 1,750 buses.

• **Security disparities.** While MTA spent only three cents for the security of each bus passenger in fiscal year 1993, it spent 43 times as much, or $1.29, for the security of each passenger on the Metrolink commuter rail and the light rail, and 19 times as much, or 57 cents, for each passenger on the subway.

• **Crowding disparities.** MTA customarily tolerated overcrowding levels of 140 percent of capacity on its buses. In contrast, there was no overcrowding for riders on Metrolink and MTA-operated rail lines. Metrolink was designed to have three passengers for every four seats so that passengers could ride comfortably and use the empty seat for their briefcases or laptop computers....

* * *

Notes and Questions

1. A study by community groups in the San Francisco Bay Area found similar disparities in how the local transportation agency distributes its $1 billion in public transportation funding, with much higher subsidies going to the regional subway system and commuter rail system, compared to urban bus service. The bus riders are overwhelmingly people of color and poor (ninety percent do not own cars), while higher percentages of the subway and rail riders are white. COMMUNITIES FOR A BETTER ENVIRONMENT, URBAN HABITAT, AND PUBLIC ADVOCATES, MTC, WHERE ARE OUR BUSES? CHALLENGING THE BAY AREA'S SEPARATE AND UNEQUAL TRANSIT SYSTEM (2006).

2. The lawsuit described in the *Mean Streets* article, which alleged that MTA's operations of its transit system violated Title VI of the Civil Rights Act, was settled, with MTA agreeing to invest over a billion dollars to improve its bus system. What other measures would you recommend to redress some of the transportation-related inequities detailed above? In 1998, the Southern California Association of Governments adopted a regional transportation plan that explicitly analyzes the impact of transportation proposals on low-income communities and communities of color.

2. Parks and Open Space

Jennifer Wolch, John P. Wilson, and Jed Fehrenbach, Parks and Park Funding In Los Angeles: An Equity-Mapping Analysis
26 URBAN GEOGRAPHY 4 (2005)

Parks and open space are fundamental to the livability of cities and their neighborhoods, and are often key to economic development. But in many U.S. cities, there exists a widely perceived deficit of parkland. This is especially true in older neighborhoods and communities of color, compared with newer suburbs.... In Los Angeles (LA), the challenge of equity in access to parks and open space is severe. The problem involves not only *inequality* of access across subgroups of the population to public parks and open space, but also *inequity* stemming from the physical and socioeconomic character of communities of color. Characterized by multifamily housing that typically lacks private yards for play and relaxation, their residents can seldom afford to frequent private recreational venues (such as golf, swim or tennis clubs, or gyms)....

At the turn of the century, urban parks were widely deemed to be representations of nature that would promote a better society by combating such social problems as poverty, crime, and poor health, and by providing major benefits such as better public health, social prosperity, social coherence, and democratic equality. Today, many of these same reasons for building parks are offered to justify parkland acquisition and facility construction. In addition, research reveals that outdoor play is critical to younger children's social and cognitive development, while for older children and youth, park-based activities have been shown as vital alternatives to passive pastimes such as computer games and television, as well as juvenile delinquency....

Past discrimination in housing and employment, ongoing environmental racism in the siting of industrial and other polluting facilities, and inequitable distribution of urban services, mean that low-income households and communities of color in Los Angeles are apt to be relegated to "park-poor" neighborhoods, while wealthier districts are more likely to boast plentiful parks and greenbelts provided by public funding. Since more parks and greenspace translate into higher property values, this inequality translates into growing wealth disparities.

On an everyday basis, however, children and youth relegated to concrete sidewalks for playgrounds are arguably the greatest victims of this type of environmental injustice. This deficit in parklands is particularly problematic for older, high-density, low-income communities where children tend to utilize park resources more intensively than kids in newer, suburban areas where most housing units have gardens and there are more recreational opportunities in the environment....

By the early 1990s, recognition was growing that the City of Los Angeles, with its rapid, moderate-to-low density growth pattern, had neglected to build an adequate number[] of parks and recreation facilities as its population expanded. At about 4 acres per 1,000 residents, provision of parklands falls far short of national standards, which range from 6.25 to 10.5 acres per 1,000 population....

[This study analyzes access to park space in Los Angeles. Eds.] The distribution of park resources is highly uneven across racial/ethnic communities of the city.... [T]hose areas with 75% or more Latino population have only 0.6 park acres per 1,000 population, and heavily African American dominated tracts have 1.7 park acres per 1,000 population. In comparison, heavily White dominated areas enjoy 31.8 park acres per 1,000 residents....

[In Latino dominated neighborhoods] less than a third of the population lives within a quarter-mile of parkland.... Almost 500,000 children — 73% — have no easy access to park facilities.... In [African American dominated] neighborhoods, less than a third of the population lives within a quarter-mile of parkland, and almost 50,000 children — 74% — have no easy access to park facilities.... In [Asian-Pacific Islander dominated] districts, less than 30% of the population lives within a quarter-mile of parkland....

Lower-income households have significantly inferior access to park resources when compared to those with higher incomes.... Only 30% of children [with household incomes below $20,000 per year] had easy access to parks.... On average, residents in such low-income neighborhoods enjoyed less than 0.5 park acres per 1,000 total population.... By contrast, neighborhoods where [] household incomes exceeded $40,000 ... boasted 21.2 park acres per 1,000 total population....

Summary Table

Basic Park Characteristics of Neighborhoods by Dominant Racial/Ethnic Group

Dominant group	Total population	Population density (people/sq. mi.)	Children younger than 18 (%)	Park acres per 1,000 population	Park acres per 1,000 children
White	1,296,671	7.2	18.2	17.4	95.7
Latino	2,071,044	19.7	32.0	1.6	5.0
African-American	233,986	19.3	27.8	0.8	2.9
Asian-Pacific Islander	97,944	22.1	19.0	1.2	6.3

Socioeconomic Status and Access to Parks

Socioeconomic status (1990 median household income)	Population within quarter-mile buffer (%)	Number of children outside quarter-mile buffer	Park acres/ 1,000 population	Park acres/ 1,000 population within quarter-mile buffer	Park acres/ 1,000 younger than 18 within quarter-mile buffer
>$40,000	20.8	136,595	21.2	102.9	517.0
$30–40,000	20.4	146,679	5.9	28.1	129.6
$20–30,000	27.7	195,991	1.4	5.0	17.7
<$20,000	29.9	160,353	0.5	1.6	5.2

[In 1996, voters in the city of LA passed a park-bond measure, Proposition K, to increase and enhance park and recreation space in the city. Proposition K generates $25 million per year for acquisition, improvement, construction, and maintenance of city parks and recreational facilities.]

[O]ur examination of funding patterns reveals that Proposition K was only moderately effective in redressing the maldistribution of park and open space resources in the city.... Proposition K funds do appear to have been targeted toward lower-income and poorer neighborhoods of the city. However, on a per child basis, spending was more evenly spread across poorer and more affluent areas.... [In terms of race,] [t]he most heavily Latino areas received $6.26 per capita ($18 per child younger than 18).... However ... in the "Whitest" areas, Proposition K spending rose to $45.13 per child, while in the moderately White-dominant areas, the rate per child was $26.64....

* * *

Notes and Questions

1. The authors above note that one problem with developing parks in urban areas is assembling the parcels needed for new facilities, since "in many park-poor areas, there exist no large tracts of land available for park development." They note, however, that such

areas often contain a variety of remnant lands that could be used for park development, including vacant lots, public or utility-owned property, and underutilized school sites. *Id.* at 32.

2. Robert Garcia and Aubrey White of the City Project in Los Angles point out that the lack of access to public parks contributes to childhood obesity, diabetes, and other diseases relating to inactivity. Numerous studies document that time spent outdoors is the most powerful correlate of physical activity. The City Project has spearheaded a sustained urban parks campaign in Los Angeles that has led to the creation of four new state parks in disproportionately minority areas, including the 32-acre "Cornfield," the last large remaining open space in downtown Los Angeles, and a two-square-mile park in the Baldwin Hills area that the authors note will be the largest urban park established in the U.S. in over a century. Robert Garcia & Aubrey White, *Warren County's Legacy for Healthy Parks, Schools and Communities: From the Cornfield to El Congreso and Beyond*, 1 GOLDEN GATE U. ENVTL. L.J. 127, 135–37 (2007).

3. In an examination of the parkland system managed by the East Bay Regional Park District in the San Francisco Bay Area (the largest metropolitan regional park system in the United States), Professor Paul Kibel found that the majority of park acreage is located in or near communities where the majority of residents are white and affluent, including many park acres in the East Bay's hillside communities. He cited survey data indicating that these hillside parks are in fact primarily used by white residents. Professor Kibel noted that a sizeable portion of residents and households in East Bay low-income minority neighborhoods do not have access to cars, and many East Bay Parks are not now conveniently accessible by public transit. He concluded that "[f]or these households and residents, hillside parklands ... may be just a gallon of gas away, but that may still be out of reach." Paul Stanton Kibel, *The People Down The Hill: Parks Equity In San Francisco's East Bay*, 1 GOLDEN GATE U. ENVTL. L.J. 331, 332 (2007).

4. Other studies have found that minority and poor residents access national parks at a much lower rate than other visitors. One observer argues that "[l]ow African-American visitation to the national parks qualifies as an environmental injustice.... When considered from [this] perspective, it is clear that there is more at stake than how one African-American family chooses to spend its vacation time. What is at stake is that a historically underprivileged group is not experiencing one of the most important communal environmental benefits in this country, a benefit that their tax dollars are helping to fund and that is supposed to be available to all." Andrea Waye, *An Environmental Justice Perspective on African-American Visitation to Grand Canyon and Yosemite National Parks*, 11 HASTINGS W.-NW. J. ENVTL. L. & POL'Y 125, 126 (2005). Do you agree that the disparity in visits to the national parks is an environmental justice issue?

5. Lawyer Samara Swanston found disparities in New York City in open space, access to the waterfront, and planting of trees. In particular, she pointed out that New York City has the lowest open space standards for its citizens of any metropolitan area in the country—only 2.5 acres of open space per 1000 residents. But despite that low standard, two thirds of the community planning districts (primarily communities of color) do not even meet that standard. She argued that the city's 578 miles of coastal waterfront are managed in a discriminatory manner; the least protective water quality goals set by the city for coastal areas are found in the poorest and most diverse communities; and that there are also fewer public access points and amenities such as marinas and greenways in communities of color. She also found that communities of color in the city have the lowest percentages of tree canopy and notes, "[t]his means that in the areas that have some of the highest rates of asthma morbidity and mortality in the nation, such as Community

Boards 1 and 2 in the Bronx, the City is missing the opportunity to improve environmental quality and environmental health by planting trees." Samara F. Swanston, *Environmental Justice and Environmental Quality Benefits: The Oldest, Most Pernicious Struggle and Hope for Burdened Communities*, 23 VERMONT L. REV. 545, 555–60 (1999).

6. Poor people and people of color have long faced barriers gaining access to public beaches. A classic example occurred in New York City in the 1930s and 1940s when master urban planner Robert Moses designed access roads to the city's suburban beaches with overpasses too low to accommodate buses with poorer city residents. The story of how localities in Connecticut and New Jersey excluded poor people and people of color from their beaches in the 1970s is told in Marc R. Poirier, *Environmental Justice and the Beach Access Movements of the 1970s in Connecticut and New Jersey: Stories of Property and Civil Rights*, 28 CONN. L. REV. 719 (1996).

7. Other Amenities. One recent study compared the availability of fruits and vegetables in the food outlets of two geographically similar communities in upstate New York—one predominantly white, the other predominantly African American. It found that the predominantly African American community had fewer varieties of fresh fruits and vegetables available to them and fewer stores—in particular supermarkets—offering larger varieties of fruits and vegetables. The authors argue that the lack of access to healthy food options contributes to the worsened health profile of African Americans compared to whites for a variety of diseases. They conclude that "[t]he free market is not working to get healthy foods into the neediest communities. Grocers understand that the money to be made is in the wealthier communities; therefore, they limit choice and selection in areas where they know they won't make as much money." Edith M. Williams, et al., *Where's the Kale? Environmental Availability of Fruits and Vegetables in Two Racially Dissimilar Communities*, 1 ENVTL. JUSTICE, 35, 42 (2008).

3. Environmental Enforcement and Cleanup

In 1992, the National Law Journal (NLJ) published a report analyzing whether EPA's enforcement of environmental laws was discriminatory. *See* Marianne Lavelle & Marcia Coyle, *Unequal Protection: The Racial Divide in Environmental Law*, NAT'L L.J., Sept. 21, 1992, at S1–S12. The report reviewed all civil judicial enforcement cases resolved by EPA from 1985 to 1991 (with minor exceptions). It also looked at EPA responses to abandoned toxic waste sites under the Superfund program (the Comprehensive Environmental Response, Compensation, and Liability Act, or CERCLA), specifically examining all sites listed on EPA's National Priority List (NPL) from 1980 to 1992 (again with minor exceptions). The study classified zip codes around the facilities and waste sites into four quartiles, ranging from those with the highest white population and highest income to those with the lowest white population and income. It then compared the quartile with the highest white population (which it termed the "white community") with the quartile with the lowest white population (referred to as the "minority community") and the quartile with the highest median income ("high income") with the lowest median income ("low income").

The study found that penalties for violations of federal environmental laws were substantially lower in minority communities than in white communities. (This does not include penalties assessed by states implementing federal environmental programs.) Specifically, average penalties imposed under the federal hazardous waste management law, the Resource Conservation & Recovery Act (RCRA) were 500% lower; under the Clean Water Act, 28% lower; the Clean Air Act, 8% lower; the Safe Drinking Water Act (SDWA), 15% lower; and in multi-media actions involving enforcement of several statutes, 306% lower. The overall average penalty for all environmental statutes was 46% lower in minority communities than white communities ($153,067 vs. $105,028).

With respect to the effect of a community's income on penalties, the picture was less clear. The report found that the average penalty for all violations was significantly lower in poor communities than in wealthy areas—$95,664 per case compared to $146,993. But this result varied considerably by individual statute. Penalties under four statutes—the Clean Air Act, SDWA, Superfund, and RCRA—were higher in poor areas, ranging from 3% (RCRA) to 63% (SDWA) greater than in wealthy areas. On the other hand, in Clean Water Act cases average penalties in low income communities were 91% lower than in upper income areas, and in multi-media cases, the average fine in high income areas was $315,000 compared to $18,000 in low-income communities. The study concluded that the pattern of penalties varied so markedly depending upon the particular law involved that income was not a reliable predictor of the size of penalties.

The study also found racial disparities in EPA's response to contaminated waste sites. In particular, it found that abandoned hazardous waste sites in minority areas take 20% longer to be placed on the national priority action list than those in white areas (5.6 years from the date of discovery until its listing on the NPL vs. 4.7 years). The report found that by the time cleanup commenced, this gap had narrowed and minority sites were only 4% behind white sites (10.4 years vs. 9.9 years), although in half of the EPA regions this difference was 12% to 42%. The study also found that EPA chose less protective cleanup remedies at minority sites, opting for "containment" (the capping or walling off of a waste site) 7% more frequently than permanent treatment methods that reduce or eliminate the volume or toxicity of hazardous substances (EPA is required by section 121(a) of CERCLA to give preference to such permanent remedies). At sites located in white communities, EPA ordered treatment 22% more often than containment.

Finally, the study found gaps between poor and wealthy communities in responses to waste sites, although less pronounced than that between white and minority areas. Sites took 10% longer to be listed on the NPL in poorer communities; moreover, EPA chose containment 18% more often than permanent treatment methods in low-income areas, and 35% more frequently in rich neighborhoods.

The NLJ study has been criticized on a number of methodological grounds. Critics have argued that the study's use of quartiles to divide cases into white and minority areas resulted in areas being classified as "minority" even though they were not in fact predominantly minority; that the disparities reported were not statistically significant; and that the NLJ study failed to control for other variables that might affect penalties.

Two subsequent studies of the cases reviewed by the NLJ study have questioned its conclusions. Professor Evan Ringquist found that the results varied depending on how one grouped the historical data. He first confirmed the study's findings that penalties from 1985 to 1991 were higher in white communities, but also found that penalties were higher in poor communities. Professor Ringquist also examined civil judicial enforcement actions filed by EPA dating back to 1974, and concluded that from 1974 to

1985, penalties were higher in minority and poor communities, and that during the entire period from 1974 to 1991, there was little difference in average fines between white and minority communities (and that penalties were higher in poor communities). After controlling for other factors that could influence penalties, Professor Ringquist concluded that "minorities are not disadvantaged by case outcomes in environmental protection, and the case for class bias in these outcomes is weak." Evan J. Ringquist, *A Question of Justice: Equity in Environmental Litigation, 1974–1991*, 60 J. Pol. 1148, 1162 (1998).

Researcher Mark Atlas also reevaluated the cases analyzed by the NLJ study using some different methodologies, such as geographic concentric rings around facility locations as the units of analysis (rather than facility zip codes), and correcting for mistakes in EPA's original enforcement database. Atlas found that the income level of an area had no meaningful effect on penalties, and that while a community's race affected penalties, it was in the opposite direction of what the NLJ study found, i.e. penalties *increased* as the proportion of minorities in a community increased. Atlas also concluded that factors which influenced penalties the most were the specific characteristics of the case, such as the types of violations, whether more than one facility location was involved in the violation, and how recently the case was resolved (also noting that many other factors likely to influence penalties, such as severity of the offense, past violations, recalcitrance by the defendant, etc. were not available in the database and could not be measured). Mark Atlas, Rush to Judgment: An Empirical Analysis of Environmental Equity in U.S. Environmental Protection Agency Enforcement Actions (unpublished manuscript).

There have been a number of additional studies examining bias in EPA's responses under Superfund. Professors James Hamilton and Kip Viscusi, for example, found that EPA Superfund cleanups were less stringent for sites in communities with a higher percentage of minority residents. While there was not much difference in the pace of cleanup, the race of the exposed community significantly affected the cleanup remedies chosen and the cost expended per cancer case averted. James T. Hamilton & W. Kip Viscusi, Calculating Risks: The Spatial and Political Dimensions of Hazardous Waste Policy 187–88 (1999). For a summary of other studies that have produced more mixed results, *see* Robert R. Kuehn, *A Taxonomy of Environmental Justice*, 30 Envtl. L. Rep. 10,681, 10,695 (2000).

In addition to these studies of federal enforcement practices, one state-level study found disparities in enforcement of environmental laws. The analysis concluded that air polluting facilities in New Jersey tended to concentrate in poor neighborhoods containing high minority concentrations, and that facilities in such areas had higher rates of significant violations than in other areas, but lower rates of state administrative orders issued and lower penalty amounts. Jeremy L. Mennis, *The Distribution and Enforcement of Air Polluting Facilities in New Jersey*, 57 Prof. Geographer 411 (2005).

* * *

Notes and Questions

1. What factors other than bias might explain unequal penalties in EPA's enforcement cases? Enforcement by public agencies is discussed in greater detail in Chapter 8.

4. Emergency Response

The following is a continuation of the report on Hurricane Katrina that was excerpted in Section C above.

Manuel Pastor, Robert D. Bullard, James K. Boyce, Alice Fothergill, Rachel Morello-Frosch, and Beverly Wright, In the Wake of the Storm: Environment, Disaster, and Race After Katrina

(2006)

.... The poor and minorities may also suffer disproportionately in terms of immediate disaster services.... Overall, the poor are one of the groups most likely to "fall through the cracks" during emergency relief operations. For example, after Hurricane Hugo hit Georgia and the Carolinas in 1989, service agencies found that providing assistance to the rural poor was complicated because of high illiteracy rates, physical isolation in rural communities, fear and distrust of government officials, and lack of electronic media for weeks following the storm....

Differences have also been found in post-disaster sheltering efforts.... In the United States..., those lower on the socioeconomic scale are more likely to use mass shelters. Language is often also an issue during the emergency response phase. Local, state, and federal emergency response agencies have either too few or no bilingual personnel for bilingual populations.... Complaints were ... numerous in the Katrina response about inadequate language capacities to deal with affected Latino residents, a rapidly growing population in the South.

Existing inequities are often played out in the interactions between relief workers and victims. For example, after the 1979 Hurricane Frederick in Alabama, black communities received less food, ice, shelter, and assistance than white communities, and white neighborhoods had their power restored first.... The inequities before and during a disaster are often played out further in the period after a disaster. Many minorities and the poor have had greater difficulties recovering from disasters due to less insurance, lower incomes, fewer savings, more unemployment, less access to communication channels and information, and the intensification of existing poverty....

Studies have also addressed racial, class, and ethnic differences in who receives disaster recovery assistance. [One study] concluded that the blacks, who had lower income than whites..., needed multiple aid sources to deal with large losses because they did not receive enough support from fewer sources. Blacks were also less likely than whites to receive Small Business Administration (SBA) loans, more likely to use interfaith disaster services, and tended to recover economically more slowly.... Upper middle-class victims in several disasters have been more likely to receive assistance than minorities and the poor because they knew how to navigate the relief system, fill out the forms, and work within the government bureaucracy. In addition, poorer victims had more trouble making trips to the disaster assistance centers following Hurricane Andrew because of transportation, child care, and work difficulties....

Housing continues to be a significant issue for low-income and minority disaster victims in the recovery period. Past research has found that housing assistance favors middle-class victims, particularly homeowners.... Renters are affected in several ways.

Higher-income evacuees often secure the surplus housing available in a community, leaving none for lower-income victims. In many disasters, rebuilding services are geared toward homeowners and legal tenants, and not toward multifamily and affordable housing units which are occupied by low-income tenants....

Reconstruction and Long-Term Effects

The long-term reconstruction after a disaster can simply continue the pattern of inequity and stress that has played out throughout the disaster itself. As with the stage of short-term recovery, the search for safe, affordable housing after a disaster is one of the most critical, and unsolved issues for lower-income families and minorities in the United States....

Numerous studies have found that problems of homelessness and low-income housing shortages become even more serious in the years after a disaster.... Several other studies have found that poor women have the most difficult time rebuilding homes, finding new places to live, and getting out of substandard temporary housing.

Members of racial and ethnic minorities and the poor are also less likely to qualify for and receive various types of aid for reconstruction, including SBA loans, and to have trouble with the housing process.... After the 1995 flooding in New Orleans, even though low-income elderly women were over-represented in the population applying to FEMA for low-interest loans, they were three times less likely than other elderly households to receive them.

A few studies show that some of the poorest victims may temporarily do better after a disaster.... But most of the empirical evidence shows that most victims—especially minority and low-income victims—are worse off in the years that follow the disaster. For example, residents of very low-income housing, such as single room occupancies (SROs), do not easily qualify for assistance programs. Many disasters have pushed the marginally homeless population into the category of permanently homeless. In general, disasters may also push many lower income and working class families into debt and financial insecurity, dashing hopes to buy houses, attend college, and so forth....

* * *

Notes and Questions

1. Professor Kathleen Tierney argues that

Katrina ... highlighted the vast differences that exist between better-off community residents who have wider options and poor disaster victims who lack such choices.... If a major earthquake were to strike majority communities on the west side of Los Angeles—communities such as Beverly Hills, Santa Monica, Brentwood, Bel Air, Westwood, and Pacific Palisades—and left tens of thousands homeless, it is inconceivable that the experiences of west Los Angeles residents would in any way resemble those of the poor African American residents of New Orleans. Not only would well-off Los Angeles residents have many more choices regarding how to find temporary shelter (such as second or third homes), and how to recover following the earthquake (for instance, by using savings, selling stocks, and drawing on generous insurance policies), but, owing to their political power, government agencies would be more responsive to their needs.

Kathleen Tierney, *Social Inequality, Hazards, and Disasters, in* ON RISK AND DISASTER: LESSONS FROM HURRICANE KATRINA (R.J. Daniels, D.F. Kettl & H. Kunreuther eds.) 109,

122 (2006). Do you agree with her conclusions? A survey of residents evacuated from Katrina and living in Houston found that 68% thought the federal government would have responded more quickly if people trapped in the floodwaters were "wealthier and white rather than poorer and black." U.S. House of Representatives, A Failure of Initiative: Final Report of the Select Bipartisan Committee to Investigate The Preparation For and Response to Hurricane Katrina 19 (2006).

2. Professor Tierney also contends that "assistance that is provided following disasters typically reinforces social inequities, rather than compensating for them." She notes, for example, that "of the two largest communities that were heavily damaged by Hurricane Andrew in 1992, one community, Homestead, had a white majority and was more affluent, while the other, Florida City, had a black majority and was significantly less well off. Disaster losses were proportionately greater in Florida City, but that community received less aid than Homestead and experienced greater problems recovering from Andrew." Tierney, *supra* at 123. Moreover, among those who filed insurance claims following Andrew, black and Hispanic households had significantly fewer of their resources covered. *Id* at 124. Professor Robert Bullard argues in an interview that this pattern has long historical roots: "over the past seven decades in the South, whether it's floods, droughts, hurricanes or accidents, government has responded to emergencies in ways that have endangered the health and welfare of African Americans." Gregory Dicum, *Here We Go Again*, Grist, Mar. 14, 2006, http://www.grist.org/news/maindish/2006/03/14/dicum/index1.html (quoting Professor Bullard).

3. Lessons Learned? In September 2008, a potentially devastating hurricane, Gustav, hit the Gulf Coast. In the end, Gustav produced far less damage than Katrina, but it nonetheless spurred charges that the poor were subjected to differential and substandard treatment in the evacuation process:

> Three years to the week after Hurricane Katrina's landfall, Louisiana executed a fundamentally unfair evacuation plan and did it badly. It relied on dividing the population into separate streams: People with their own cars were directed to shelters run by parishes, churches and the Red Cross.... All those without a car or a ride were taken on state buses to four state-run warehouses. It was in these shelters, including two abandoned stores, a Wal-Mart and a Sam's Club, that thousands of working-poor New Orleanians got a sickening reminder of Katrina.
>
> Evacuees said they had had no idea where they were going; bus drivers would not tell them. When they arrived, there were not enough portable toilets, and no showers. For five days there was no way to bathe, except with bottled water in filthy outdoor toilets. Privacy in the vast open space—1,000 people to a warehouse, shoulder-to-shoulder on cots—was nonexistent. The mood among evacuees was grim, surrounded as they were by police officers and the National Guard, with no visitors or reporters allowed.... Gustav ended up being no Katrina, and the week of suffering was not as severe as the deathly mayhem of three years ago. But residents had every right to expect far better treatment than they received....

Editorial, *"Never Again," Again*, N.Y. Times, Sept. 20, 2008, *available at* http://www.nytimes.com/2008/09/21/opinion/21sun2.html. Does this response suggest, as the editorial implies, that we have failed to learn important lessons about the disparate impacts of Katrina?

4. As discussed in this chapter, although it is not unmixed, the clear weight of empirical evidence supports claims that environmental harms, and to a lesser extent environmental benefits, are inequitably distributed in society. Moreover, racc is a more significant

factor in explaining cnvironmental disparities than any other single variable. These findings have persisted—in fact grown stronger—over time as research methodologies have become more sophisticated. In the next chapter, we explore various theories of why such disparities exist.

Chapter 3

Theories of Causation

A. Introduction

What is responsible for the disproportionate distribution of environmental burdens and amenities that has been documented by researchers and that is discussed in detail in Chapter 2? Explanatory theories offered are numerous and varied, drawing from economics, political science, urban planning, history, sociology, and other disciplines. Clearly, there are multiple, sometimes overlapping factors at work. This chapter outlines some of the major theories that have been advanced to explain the prevalence of environmental inequities. We begin with the explanation that the current disparities are to some degree the outgrowth of past land use practices, some of which were outright racist. Others posit that these disparities can be explained by more neutral market forces, both during the initial siting of polluting and risk-generating facilities and as the result of post-siting market dynamics. Alternative theories center on sociopolitical factors, such as a community's social capital, and how those factors interact within the structure of our environmental laws. Yet another explanation examines the unconscious and persistent forms of racial discrimination currently at play.

B. Land Use Practices

In part, the current distribution of environmental hazards is the result of land use and zoning practices that started over one hundred years ago. Restrictive racial covenants, exclusionary zoning practices like density and use restrictions, urban renewal policies that displaced thousands of residents, and other land use mechanisms all contributed to residential segregation and the prevalence of unwanted land uses in low-income communities and communities of color. In the following excerpt, Professor Yale Rabin describes one such long-standing zoning practice.

Yale Rabin, Expulsive Zoning: The Inequitable Legacy of Euclid
Zoning and the American Dream 101
(Charles M. Haar & Jerold S. Kayden eds., 1989)

... What follows sets forth the hypothesis that zoning, in addition to its well-recognized use as an exclusionary mechanism, also has been frequently employed in ways that have undermined the character, quality, and stability of black residential areas; that zoning not only has been used to erect barriers to escape from the concentrated confinement of the inner city, it has been used to permit — even promote — the intrusion into black neighborhoods of disruptive incompatible uses that have diminished the quality and undermined the stability of those neighborhoods. For reasons explained later, I refer to this practice as *expulsive zoning....*

[T]here is evidence to suggest that expulsive zoning practices have been relatively commonplace in black residential areas. The record, while admittedly fragmentary, indicates that in the years following the [Supreme] Court's rejection of racial zoning in 1917 and continuing through the thirties, and perhaps much later, a number of cities — mainly, but not exclusively, in the South — zoned some low-income residential areas occupied mainly, but not exclusively, by blacks for industrial or commercial use. These practices were sometimes carried out even in neighborhoods of single-family detached houses, thus undermining the quality of the very types of neighborhood housing which zoning ostensibly was intended to protect. To the extent that these practices were effective — that is, to the extent that residential uses were replaced by industrial or commercial uses, residents were displaced. Therefore, the term *expulsive zoning.* Because it appears that such areas were mainly black, and because whites who may have been similarly displaced were not subject to racially determined limitations in seeking alternative housing, the adverse impacts of expulsive zoning on blacks were far more severe and included, in addition to accelerated blight, increases in overcrowding and racial segregation....

[T]hese expulsive zoning practices are entirely consistent with the more general findings of my studies: that the land-use-related policies and practices of government at all levels, but particularly the decisions and initiatives of local government, have been and continue to be instrumental influences on both the creation and perpetuation of racial segregation. Expulsive zoning, as one of these practices, does not occur as an isolated or independent action, but as one element in a web-like pattern of interacting public practices that serve to reproduce and reinforce the disadvantages of blacks. Urban renewal, public housing site selection, school segregation, highway route selection, and code enforcement are a few of the other frequently encountered cords in the web....

Jackson, Tennessee

The most extensive and blighting effects of expulsive zoning that I have encountered have been in Jackson, Tennessee. Here expulsive zoning has been and continues to be a fundamental influence on other land-use-related policies and actions of the city which adversely affect the welfare of black residents....

South Jackson, a section of the city which until the mid-1960s housed approximately half of the city's black population, had been zoned industrial since the city first adopted zoning in 1928. The other half of the city's black population lived in northeast Jackson, in an area surrounding all-black Lane College. That area had been and continues to be zoned residential. Housing in the Lane College area, while modest, is, with the exception of a few scattered pockets of slum housing, sound and well maintained.

Although south Jackson is bounded along its southern edge by a number of labor-intensive, forestry- and agriculture-related industries, the area itself always has been overwhelming residential. The area's residents have been the city's lowest income blacks; the housing they occupied was of poor quality and what remains has become severely blighted as a direct consequence of city policies and actions.

Since the early 1960s the city has repeatedly and publicly made clear its intentions to redevelop much of south Jackson for industrial and commercial use and since that time has halted all code enforcement and municipal improvement in the area. At the time of my first visit in 1978, two urban renewal projects were underway. One, at the south-western edge of the city, was to provide land for industrial development, and in the other, in the center of south Jackson and adjacent to the central business district, a civic center was already under construction. By the city's own estimates, these two projects involved the displacement of approximately 940 black families including more than 2,600 people—about one-fifth of the city's black population. Between the two projects there remained an all-black-occupied public housing project and nearly 20 city blocks of black-occupied slum housing and unpaved streets....

By failing to require even minimal maintenance of housing and withholding mainte-nance of infrastructure, the city accelerated the deterioration of the housing in south Jackson and reduced the costs to the city of subsequent property acquisition. By failing to provide relocation resources they caused an increase in the level of racial segregation and overcrowding in the city, and prolonged the time during which south Jackson residents were subject to that area's deplorable living conditions....

Summary and Conclusions

The adverse impacts evident in these ... cases of expulsive zoning vary widely. They include environmentally blighting nuisances, displacement, and life threatening haz-ards.... [T]he evidence to date does appear to support three significant generalizations. First, illustrated most vividly by the case of Detroit, the magnitude and severity of adverse impacts are not necessarily proportional to the scale of intrusion or the extent of dis-placement. A single intrusive use can sometimes have disastrous effects. Second, the blighting and disruptive effects of expulsive zoning grow, rather than diminish, with the passage of time. Finally, expulsive zoning is not merely an historical remnant of a racially unenlightened past, but a current practice that continues to threaten, degrade, and desta-bilize black and other minority neighborhoods....

* * *

Picking up on the last point, Professor Robert Collin examines how past discrimina-tory land use practices have combined with more current land use dynamics—such as the "not in my back yard" syndrome in the site selection process—to exacerbate siting dis-parities.

Robert W. Collin, Environmental Equity:
A Law and Planning Approach to Environmental Racism
11 Virginia Environmental Law Journal 495 (1992)*

Zoning is the regulation of land use to control growth and development for the health, safety and welfare of the community.... Although approaches to land use control by zon-ing differ greatly by state and community, in general practice, the land use control frame-work determines where unwanted land uses are permitted.

Many early land use practices systematically excluded people on the basis of race, though today such an exclusionary practice is illegal.... Race-based exclusionary prac-tices, however, can take forms other than official zoning laws. For example, the enforce-ment of racially restrictive covenants, racially discriminatory site selection, tenant distribution procedures in public housing and the enactment of many urban renewal policies have also effectively excluded certain people from living in certain areas.

---

* Reprinted by permission of the Virginia Environmental Law Journal.

Zoning can be more than exclusionary; it can be expulsive. Expulsive zoning often designates black residential areas for industrial or commercial uses, a practice which results in the eventual displacement of blacks from these areas.... Expulsive zoning may have provided the original mechanism in land use law that has led to the current racially disproportionate distribution of environmentally hazardous land uses. It is possible that the roots of environmental inequity lie partially in these traditional race-based zoning practices. Before environmental regulation, many industrial and commercial facilities located in minority communities on account of zoning and may have disposed of waste either on-site or nearby because of the lower cost of doing so.

Many communities have excluded locally unwanted land uses (LULUs) from their neighborhoods by means of a well-documented process and philosophy that has been characterized as the "not-in-my-backyard" (NIMBY) syndrome. As a general proposition, a landfill is one of the most unwanted land uses, especially if that landfill will contain toxic and hazardous waste. Professor [Robert] Bullard maintains that these unwanted land uses are sited in politically and economically disenfranchised neighborhoods in a process he calls "PIBBY" or "place-in-blacks'-backyards."

As the need for new landfill sites increases, and as communities become aware of the potential hazards of landfills, the siting process becomes a decisive battleground. In general, the greater the known or suspected physical effects of an unwanted land use are, the greater the residential resistance will be. The concern over possible property devaluation deepens in communities with a higher ratio of homeowners to renters....

Hazardous Waste Site Selection: State Supervision, Local Resistance and Private Enterprise

Because the states are responsible for implementing the Resource Conservation and Recovery Act (RCRA) and other EPA regulations, they effectively control the siting of toxic and hazardous waste landfills. Unfortunately, state control of the siting process has not diminished the NIMBY problem. States generally take one of three broad approaches to site selection: super review; site designation; or local control.

Under the super review approach, the developer of the hazardous waste facility selects a possible site and applies for a land use permit from the state authorizing agency. The agency then reviews the application and evaluates the environmental impact. If the state decides to issue the permit, it then appoints a special administrative body to allow the public to participate in the site selection. These administrative bodies encourage public participation in order to decrease community resistance and to "minimize the issue of political expediency and emphasize environmental safety." All of the states that use this approach have preemption clauses that permit the siting despite community resistance.

Because private developers initiate the site selection process, the costs of acquiring the land and assembling the site influence decisions in the early phases of site selection. Unfortunately, low land cost and easy site assembly do not necessarily lead to the best site for waste transfer or disposal. Low-income and racial minority communities are often in areas with lower land values. With relatively few sites chosen in the initial phase of site selection, subsequent phases often place a final site in a minority neighborhood, due in large part to the lower community resistance that often accompanies minority sitings. The super review approach, then, probably does not alleviate inequitable distribution of waste disposal sites.

Under the site designation approach, the state, not a private developer, creates an inventory of possible sites. Techniques for developing the inventory vary from state to state. Because this approach lessens the cost incentive in site selection, it may lead to a more equitable distribution of waste sites. Furthermore, it provides the state with a statewide data gathering mechanism that can inform environmental decision-making in the future.

The third approach basically defers to local land use control. Here, the state does not exercise its right to preempt the authority of the locality to regulate toxic or hazardous wastes. This approach allows those communities that do not want a toxic or hazardous waste facility to simply prohibit that type of land use. As such, it does little but facilitate the NIMBY practice.

It is very difficult for any of these state siting approaches to overcome entrenched, well-funded community resistance. In wealthier communities, this resistance can take the form of protracted litigation. In site selection approaches that are developer-driven, the threat and reality of a lawsuit can increase the cost of the site and the site preparation process. Therefore, communities that cannot afford to litigate will be more vulnerable to site selection. Wealthier communities may also have better access to informal networks in the state government....

In addition to statutory site selection procedures, other environmental regulations governing land use, recycling and waste toxicity have made waste disposal sites more difficult to acquire and thus more likely to locate in minority communities....

* * *

Professor Tony Arnold also picks up on Professor Rabin's work and quantifies the current distribution of zoning patterns to demonstrate how, in several areas, low-income communities of color have a greater share of industrial and commercial zoning.

Craig Anthony Arnold, Planning Milagros: Environmental Justice and Land Use Regulation
76 Denver University Law Review 1 (1998)

The use of zoning and other land use regulatory mechanisms—requirements of large lots, minimum floor space, and significant setbacks; low-density zoning; and restrictions on multi-family housing—to exclude low-income people who cannot afford large single-family homes on large lots (exclusionary zoning) has been well documented.... Yale Rabin has focused scholarly attention on expulsive zoning, the practice of local governments rezoning neighborhoods of color to allow incompatible and noxious land uses.... However, Rabin's study did not attempt to quantify the distribution of zoning patterns in low-income neighborhoods of color and compare those distributions with zoning patterns of high-income white neighborhoods in the same cities. The distributional studies that have emerged in the environmental justice literature have focused on specific LULUs, not on land use regulatory patterns. This article documents land use regulatory patterns—the percentages of area designated for different land uses—in thirty-one census tracts in seven cities nationwide. Low-income, minority communities have a greater share not only of LULUs, but also of industrial and commercial zoning, than do high-income white communities.

Methodology

The study measures the percentages of area in census tracts that local zoning ordinances have designated for each type of land use. It contains data from thirty-one census tracts in seven cities: Anaheim, California; Costa Mesa, California; Orange, California; Pittsburgh, Pennsylvania; San Antonio, Texas; Santa Ana, California; and Wichita, Kansas....

Data and Analysis

... The data shows that low-income, high-minority neighborhoods in the cities studied are subjects of more intensive zoning, on the whole, than high-income, low-minority neighborhoods. This conclusion is supported by data from across the various types of cities studied, regardless of the cities' geographic features, spatial development, population, political characteristics, and the like. With respect to industrial zoning—the most intensive land use—thirteen out of nineteen low-income, high-minority census tracts had at least some industrial zoning, and in seven of those census tracts, the city had zoned more than 20% of the tract for industrial uses. In contrast, only one of the twelve high-income, low-minority census tracts contained any industrial zoning at all, only 2.84% of the tract....

The zoning of low-income neighborhoods of color for industrial uses places highly intensive activities near local residents' homes, creating the very sort of incompatibility of uses that zoning is designed to prevent. For example, among the "as of right" permitted uses in Pittsburgh tract #2808 are ammonia and chlorine manufacturing, automobile wrecking, blast furnace or coke oven, chemical manufacturing, iron and steel manufacturing and processing, airplane factory or hangar, brewery, poultry slaughter, and machine shop, and among the conditional uses are atomic reactors, garbage and dead animal reduction, rubbish incineration, radio and television transmission and receiving towers, and storage of explosives and inflammables....

Commercial uses are also located in greater concentrations in low-income, high-minority neighborhoods than in high-income, low-minority neighborhoods. In ten out of the nineteen low-income, high-minority census tracts, at least 10% of the area is zoned for commercial use, and in seven of those tracts, at least 20% of the area is zoned for commercial use. In contrast, only two of the twelve high-income, low-minority census tracts had at least 10% of the area zoned for commercial use, and none had more than 20% commercial zoning.

Although the term "commercial" conjures up images of office buildings and retail stores which may create parking and scale/shadow impacts on neighboring residences but generally do not pose health hazards, the cities studied allow in their various commercial districts uses that are far more intensive than offices and stores.... In about 30% of San Antonio tract #1307.85, permitted uses include electro-plating, brewery, chicken hatcheries, poultry slaughter and storage, machine shop, and certain kinds of manufacturing, such as ice cream, ice, brooms, mattresses, paper boxes, candy, cigars, and refrigeration.

... Over 75% of the area in each of six high-income, low-income tracts studied is zoned for single-family residences. If open space, a country club, and a private university (with significant open space) are included with single-family residential zoning, eleven of the twelve high-income, low-minority tracts have more than 75% of their respective areas zoned for these low-intensity land uses....

In contrast, the only low-income, high-minority census tract with more than 75% of the area zoned for single-family residential or open space uses is Pittsburgh census tract #2609.98— one tract out of nineteen. Although zoning for single-family residences or open space may preclude affordable housing needed by low-income people, the contrast in zoning patterns highlights the disparate impact of zoning designations on low-income people of color....

Caveats and the Call for Further Studies

... [T]his study does not establish a national pattern.... Perhaps most importantly, national trends are only marginally relevant to addressing overly intensive zoning (or expulsive zoning) of low-income communities of color. Instead, the existing patterns and the neighbors' concerns and land use goals are inherently local (indeed, specific to the neighborhood in question) and the regulatory authority is local. Changes will occur locality by locality, neighborhood by neighborhood, and not at a national level....

* * *

Notes and Questions

1. Professor Collin discusses three approaches to state siting of hazardous waste facilities—super review, site designation, and local control—and finds potentially serious problems with each of them. Does his article suggest that greater or lesser local control of the siting process is desirable?

2. Professor Arnold advocates greater use of land use planning tools to protect against disproportionate environmental sitings. Some of his suggestions are discussed in Chapter 11. Practices such as expulsive zoning and exclusionary zoning can have profound impacts on the character of communities and the land uses that are sited there.

3. Another potential threat to neighborhood stability in many urban areas is gentrification, a phenomenon that grew substantially throughout the 1990s. In response to skyrocketing housing costs, the high market demand for land, the growth in information technology-based companies, and other factors, urban neighborhoods, including low-income communities or communities of color that had long received little development attention, became much more attractive to investors. While increased economic development can bring important benefits to these areas, it also can make neighborhoods unaffordable and displace longtime residents. San Francisco's Mission District, for example, long an enclave for working class and recent immigrant Latino families, was targeted for development by many investors. This had the result of "squeezing out longtime tenants, small mom-and-pop stores, non-profits, artists and working class people of all colors." As noted by one environmental justice organization, such displacement is particularly devastating in San Francisco, where rental vacancies are scarce and 40% of renters pay more than a third of their incomes for housing. Antonio Diaz, People Organizing to Demand Environmental & Economic Rights (PODER), Race & Space: Dot-Colonization, Dislocation and Resistance en la Misíon de San Francisco (2001).

4. The legacy of urban renewal policies can persist for decades, as evidenced in this description of Boston's Chinatown, which engaged in a heated battle to preserve open space in the 1990s:

> Chinatowns are some of the most vibrant ethnic neighborhoods in America's landscape. Home to recent immigrants and old-timers alike, a city's Chinatown is the heart of many urban Asian American communities. But Chinatowns are often found in city centers and in crowded and polluted environments. Boston's Chinatown, the fourth largest in the United States, is no exception.

> What explains a Chinatown's location and circumstance? Is it pure chance? Unfortunately, no. At least not with Boston's Chinatown. Since the 1950s, urban planning has given Boston's Chinatown two massive highways, land-hungry medical institutions, and a red light district. Half a century of such policy came to a head in 1993, when the city of Boston tried to sell open land in the heart of Chinatown to build a mammoth garage. The proposed sale of this land, known as "Parcel C," sparked protest and organized resistance....

> Boston's Chinatown is a small but densely populated community ... For many, Chinatown is a purely commercial district of "exotic" shops, markets, and restaurants, which are toured on weekend excursions. However, Chinatown is also a residential community and home to more than 5,000 people.

The Chinese community was well settled and growing during the early and mid-twentieth century.... Starting in the 1950s, Chinatown became a victim of "urban renewal." Cities such as Boston adopted urban renewal strategies specifically to attract businesses and industries back into downtown, to refurbish its tax base, and to entice urban residents to remain in the area. Unfortunately, all communities did not equally share in the burdens and benefits of urban renewal. Certainly, Boston's Chinatown did not....

Chinatown has only 2.9 acres of open space. That means a mere 0.6-acre of open space per 1,000 residents—the least amount of open space per resident in the city. Although approximately twelve open spaces exist in and around Chinatown, three of them (city-owned) are unsafe.... [O]nly three are of the appropriate size to be actively used by the residents. The only open space with recreational facilities, such as volleyball and basketball courts, is adjacent to the Central Artery ramps, where thousands of cars enter and exit the highway daily....

Zenobia Lai, Andrew Leong & Chi Chi Wu, *The Lessons of the Parcel C Struggle: Reflections on Community Lawyering*, 6 Asian Pacific American Law Journal 1 (2000).

5. Some land use practices that may give rise to disparities go even further back than zoning, and this history has significant consequences to this day. Consider the following:

Control over land and water remains the primary bone of contention in the relations among Indian, Hispano, and Anglo populations in northern New Mexico. This multifaceted set of issues has evolved out of a historical context of successive conquest, land expropriation, and sociopolitical domination by one ethnic group over another.... The most fundamental contrasts between Pueblo Indian and Hispano cases of enclavement derive from the differences in their respective political and legal positions vis-à-vis the state. Trust status has meant, among other things, that Indians cannot alienate their land and do not pay taxes on it, and that legal defense of their land, water, and other tribal claims is the responsibility of the federal government.... Ironically, the immunities this nonetheless disastrously dependent status confers serve to preclude some of the very ways in which Hispanos have lost their land.... Today the land tenure situation of Taos Pueblo appears, at least superficially, far more favorable in comparison to that of rural and semi-rural Hispanos in the area, whose farmland is being expropriated at an escalating rate by the luxury tourism real estate boom....

Today these settlements are each struggling to protect their traditionally differentiated spheres of local land and water control, as always in competition or cooperation with one another, but also against the town's urban spread, and a corresponding escalation of Anglo in-migration and ubiquitous real estate development....

[C]ore elements in the Hispano niche have been occupation of contiguous village farmland and associated water rights ownership and management.... Both Indian and Hispano attachments to a land base are rooted in their traditional subsistence economies. Attachment to a land base remains intrinsic to the ethnic self-identities of both groups, even though neither subsists any longer by agriculture, pastoralism, or hunting....

Sylvia Rodríguez, *Land, Water, and Ethnic Identity in Taos, in* LAND, WATER, AND CULTURE: NEW PERSPECTIVES ON HISPANIC LAND GRANTS 313, 313–60 (Charles L. Briggs & John R. Van Ness eds., 1987). To what extent do you believe that the roots of current inequities may lie in very old land use practices? Tribal sovereignty issues and the trust obligation of the federal government to American Indians are discussed in greater detail in Chapter 4.

6. Given the long history of some land use practices, the intensely local nature of zoning, and, more currently, gentrification, and given the absence of a demonstrated national pattern of zoning practices, would federal or state preemption of local zoning matters be justified? If not, how should these causes of environmental injustice be remedied?

C. The Market

Many critics who challenge the salience of race and/or ethnicity in explaining environmental disparities argue that market forces best account for these differences. This section considers the debates surrounding two types of "market force" explanations — the first focusing on market forces in the site selection process, the second examining market-driven changes that occur after siting decisions are made.

1. Market Forces in Site Selection

Robin Saha & Paul Mohai, Explaining Racial and Socioeconomic Disparities in the Location of Locally Unwanted Land Uses: A Conceptual Framework

(Conference paper presented at the Annual Meeting of the Rural Sociological Society, Toronto, Canada, August 1997)

The economic explanation of disproportionate siting relies on classic economic theory and focuses on industry's site selection rationale, reducing it down to strictly economic criteria.... In calculating the feasibility of a particular location, a company evaluates the transaction costs associated with the siting process and anticipated operating costs which affect the competitiveness and profitability of the service that can be offered at a particular location.... The transaction costs are associated with site selection, design, permitting, and construction. These costs can be quite high, especially if public opposition results in long delays, court costs, large financial compensation packages, or other exactions....

It has been argued that disproportionate conditions arise coincidentally out of private site selection decisions concerning the transaction costs of acquiring land for proposed facilities. The sole purported basis of these decisions is to minimize property values costs. Disproportionate siting is said to occur because cost-efficient industrial areas with low property values are also likely to be nearby areas with low residential property values. These areas, in turn, typically suffer from depressed economic conditions relative to other areas. Thus, the reasonable presumption that areas with low property values coincide with areas with high proportions of persons of low socioeconomic status (SES) is used to explain disproportionate siting with respect to SES. In addition, the interaction between low SES and race has been used to explain racial siting disparities.

Another aspect of the economic explanation holds that the calculation of transaction costs stemming from potential public opposition may result in disproportionate siting. According to [Professor James] Hamilton:

A firm's anticipation of the price of public opposition from a given area can thus be thought of as an aggregation of the costs imposed on the firm by residents: the costs of participating in extensive regulatory proceedings and court battles ... and direct payments to the community in terms of corporate donations and taxes....

A rejected proposal is a costly matter for a sponsoring firm. Numerous activities are involved with putting forward a siting proposal such as securing finances and guarantees, conducting site assessments (e.g., geotechnical testing), developing business plans, negotiating and letting design contracts, and filing permit applications. These efforts represent "sunk costs" and are largely unrecoverable, since these investments of time, personnel, and money do not simply transfer to another proposal but must be carried out anew if a different location must be selected....

[I]t has been suggested that industry considers the potential costs of public opposition and selects a location where the probability of incurring such costs is minimized.... One way of avoiding the high costs of siting delays or defeats is to select communities where the likelihood of public opposition is reduced.... Evidence exists to support the claim that middle-income, affluent, and better educated communities are better equipped to wage effective opposition campaigns....

[A]s part of their transaction and operating costs firms are likely to consider the compensation costs that might be demanded in order for a community to accept a proposal.... Studies on class differences in the value placed on environmental quality suggest that communities with relatively well-educated and affluent residents are willing to pay more to preserve environmental amenities than communities with less educated and low-income residents. Even though these findings may reflect differences in ability to pay, they suggest that communities of lower SES would accept relatively smaller compensation packages in order to accept new facilities (disamenities).... More importantly, it appears that anticipated class differences in levels of acceptable compensation could be a factor firms consider, which, in turn, may contribute to disproportionate siting....

* * *

Attorney Luke Cole and Professor Sheila Foster question the assumption that race-neutral "market" forces are what drive siting decisions.

Luke Cole & Sheila Foster, From the Ground Up: Environmental Racism and the Rise of the Environmental Justice Movement
70–74 (2000)

Social Structure and the Siting Process

... Conventional industry wisdom counsels private companies to target sites that are in neighborhoods "least likely to express opposition"—those with poorly educated residents of low socioeconomic status. Not surprisingly, many communities that host toxic waste sites possess these characteristics. State permitting laws remain neutral, or blind, toward these inequalities; they therefore perpetuate, and indeed exacerbate, distributional inequalities.

In most states, the hazardous wastes siting process begins when the private sector chooses a site for the location of a proposed facility. Because the proposed location of a hazardous waste facility near, particularly, a neighborhood of white people of high socioeconomic status often faces strong public opposition, there is a limited supply of land on which to site such facilities. Inevitably, the siting process focuses on industrial, or rural, communities, many of which are populated predominantly by people of color. Because land values are lower in heavily industrial and rural communities than in white suburbs, these areas are attractive to industries that are seeking to reduce the cost of doing business. Furthermore, these communities are presumed to pose little threat of political resistance because of their subordinate socioeconomic, and often racial, status.

Rarely does a "smoking gun"—explicit racial criteria or motivation—exist behind the decision to locate a toxic waste facility in a community of color. The reasons frequently given by companies for siting facilities are that such communities have low-cost land, sparse populations, and desirable geological attributes. Notably, however, there is evidence that portions of the waste industry target neighborhoods that possess the attributes of many poor communities of color, using "race-neutral criteria." In 1984, the California Waste Management Board commissioned a study on how to site waste incinerators. The report, written by the political consulting firm Cerrell Associates of Los Angeles and entitled *Political Difficulties Facing Waste-to-Energy Conversion Plant Siting* (popularly known as the Cerrell Report), set out "to assist in selecting a site that offers the least potential of generating public opposition." The report acknowledged that "since the 1970s, political criteria have become every bit as important in determining the outcome of a project as engineering factors." The Cerrell Report suggests that companies target small, rural communities whose residents are low income, older people, or people with a high school education or less; communities with a high proportion of Catholic residents; and communities whose residents are engaged in resource extractive industries such as agriculture, mining, and forestry. Ideally, the report states, "officials and companies should look for lower socioeconomic neighborhoods that are also in a heavy industrial area with little, if any, commercial activity." ...

Likewise, even the "race-neutral" criteria used by government and industry for siting waste facilities—such as the presence of cheap land values, appropriate zoning, low population densities, proximity to transportation routes, and the absence of proximity to institutions such as hospitals and schools—turn out not to be "race neutral" after all, when seen in their social and historical context. Race potentially plays a factor in almost every "neutral" siting criterion used. "Cheap land values" is, understandably, a key siting criteria for the waste industry and other developers. However, because of historical segregation and racism, land values in the United States are integrally tied to race. In urban areas across the United States, this is starkly clear: an acre of land in the San Fernando Valley of Los Angeles has roughly the same physical characteristics as an acre of land in South Central Los Angeles, but people are willing to pay a premium to live in all-white neighborhoods. In rural areas, the pattern is similar: low land values tend to be found in poor areas, and people of color are overrepresented among the rural poverty population.

The land value cycle is vicious, too: once a neighborhood becomes host to industry, land values typically fall or do not increase as quickly as those in purely residential neighborhoods. Thus, a community that initially has low land values because it is home to people of color becomes a community that has low land values because it has a preponderance of industry, which in turn attracts more industry, creating a cumulative effect on land values.... [C]alling these changes "market driven" naturalizes the underlying racism in the valuation of the land....

Zoning is inextricably linked with race, as well.... Yale Rabin's studies of historical zoning decisions have documented numerous instances where stable African American residential communities were "down-zoned" to industrial status by biased decision makers.... [Such "expulsive zoning"] permanently alters the character of a neighborhood, often depressing property values and causing community blight. The lower property values and the zoning status are then easily invoked as "neutral" criteria upon which siting decisions are made....

Proximity to major transportation routes may also skew the siting process toward communities of color, as freeways appear to be disproportionately sited in such communities. Similarly, locational criteria — prohibitions against the siting of waste facilities near neighborhood amenities like hospitals and schools — skew the process toward underdeveloped communities of color, since such communities are less likely to have hospitals and schools. Hence, siting criteria that prohibit the siting of waste facilities close to such facilities perpetuate the historical lack of such amenities in these communities.

The sociologist Robert Bullard documented this underlying racial discrimination in an otherwise "neutral" siting process. Bullard's documentation was recognized in a 1997 decision by the Nuclear Regulatory Commission's Atomic Safety and Licensing Board, which overturned a facility's permit.... The race-neutral siting criteria — including the criteria of low population and the need to site the facility five miles from institutions such as schools, hospitals, and nursing homes — operated in conjunction with the current racial segregation and the resulting inferior infrastructure (e.g., lack of adequate schools, road paving, water supply) to ensure that the location selected would be a poor community of color.... [This case, *In the Matter of Louisiana Energy Services, L.P.*, is discussed in Chapter 11. Eds.]

* * *

Notes and Questions

1. The material above illustrates how difficult it can be to distinguish and categorize different but interrelated factors underlying siting decisions. How would you classify, for instance, a decision by a company to favor siting in areas with less-educated and lower-income residents because of a perception that these residents will accept smaller compensation packages in order to accept a new LULU? Are ethnically neutral criteria really employed when firms are counseled to look for communities with a high percentage of Catholic residents within a particular locale?

2. Businesses were quick to disavow use of the 1984 Cerrell Report, referenced above. What role do you think factors like those discussed in the report actually play in siting decisions? How should firms establish the factors upon which to base their siting decisions? Should they develop written policies, or other mechanisms to reduce the risk that siting decisions are grounded upon impermissible factors?

3. As Cole and Foster point out, rarely does a "smoking gun" document exist in which companies explicitly target low-income communities or communities of color for siting unwanted land use facilities. The few documents that candidly express such sentiments appeared relatively early, before environmental justice became a high profile issue. In addition to the 1984 Cerrell report, another example of such a document is a 1991 internal memo authored by Lawrence Summers (then chief economist of the World Bank, later U.S. Treasury Secretary and President of Harvard, and currently director of President Obama's National Economic Council). This memo advocated siting toxic waste facilities in the world's poorest countries because workers there had lower earnings. Summers queried: "Shouldn't the World Bank be encouraging more migration of the dirty industries to LDCs [Less Developed Countries]?" In his view, such targeting was appropriate because:

[t]he measurement of the costs of health impairing pollution depends upon the foregone earnings from increased morbidity and mortality. From this point of view a given amount of health impairing pollution should be done in the country with the lowest cost, which will be the country with the lowest wages. I think the economic logic behind dumping a load of toxic waste in the lowest wage country is impeccable and we should face up to that.

Memorandum from Lawrence Summers, Chief Economist, World Bank (Dec. 12, 1991), *quoted in* Robert Bullard, *Anatomy of Environmental Racism and the Environmental Justice Movement, in* CONFRONTING ENVIRONMENTAL RACISM: VOICES FROM THE GRASS-ROOTS 15, 19–20 (Robert Bullard ed., 1993). Summers also noted that there was likely to be less demand in developing countries for a clean and healthy environment. *Id.* When the memorandum was publicized, Summers issued a statement claiming that his remarks were intended as a "sardonic counter-point, an effort to sharpen the analysis." *World Bank Dumps on Third World Again,* RACE, POVERTY & THE ENV'T. Fall 1991/Winter 1992, at 12. His response is strikingly similar to the response of decision-makers in the wake of the Cerrell report. In both instances, the suggestion is that the expressed preference for siting polluting or risk-generating facilities in relatively more impoverished areas was in fact not acted upon. Implicit in these subsequent positions is that the "economic logic" was in fact ignored, presumably because of overriding ethical considerations. Should additional safeguards be put into place to guard against these economic impulses? If so, what safeguards might be appropriate?

4. If market forces are in fact primarily responsible for the current distribution of LULUs, or environmental "disamenities" (a term empirical researchers in this area often use), does this make the distribution less unfair and more acceptable? This issue is explored in the excerpt below.

Lynn E. Blais, Environmental Racism Reconsidered
75 North Carolina Law Review 75 (1996)

... Although the environmental racism movement conveys a simple story of discrimination, the reality of the siting of environmentally sensitive land uses is much more complex. At some point, and at some level, representatives of host communities make political and market-based determinations to permit the challenged sitings. In addition, the residents of these communities have made decisions either to remain in the community after the challenged use was sited, or, in many cases, to migrate to a community playing host to such a land use. In such circumstances, it is not clear why these preferences are more suspect than the myriad of others that emerge from the political and market system. Indeed, it is quite plausible that the communities and residents are better off, given the constrained positions from which they enter the market and/or the political process, with the challenged uses than they were without them.

... That more recent empirical evidence indicating that class influences (such as job status and income level) are more significant in the distribution of environmentally sensitive land uses than are racial factors should not be surprising. The market allocates according to ability to pay: the more money one has, the more of any particular good—including a clean environment—one can afford to purchase. Moreover, people tend to live near their jobs, those that depend on public transportation even more so than others. Thus, people employed in environmentally sensitive industries will be more likely to live in or near a community that hosts such industries. Finally, the political process responds to people who have the time, money, education, and inclination to participate.

The more one has of any or all of these, the more likely one is to have an effective voice in policy-making or enforcement decisions. Accordingly, we should ask ourselves the very difficult question whether the current distribution of environmentally sensitive land uses represents simply the revealed preferences of a society characterized by substantial and growing disparities in income and opportunities. As part of this new focus, we must be mindful that, in our society, class and race continue to interact in many disturbing ways. Thus, while the cries of environmental "racism" may be exaggerated, the plaint of inequity may not be. It may just be misdirected.

Private Preferences, Collective Judgments, and Choices

Our society relies on markets and the political process to allocate and distribute a vast array of society's goods and services, including many that are essential to health, welfare, and prosperity, and many that are risky or hazardous. In general, the market measures individual (or private) preferences through the very rough proxy of market choices and translates those preferences (choices) into allocative and distributive decisions. The political process responds to the community's preferences, or, if you will, its collective judgments. Measures designed to interfere with the preferences revealed through these institutions generally demand substantial justification.

... In a very limited set of circumstances, society has determined that particular decisions should be removed from the political process or the market system altogether. More commonly, we may consign the allocation and distribution of particular resources to these spheres, while at the same time adjusting those processes, or the preferences expressed through them, when demonstrated process failures undermine our confidence in the accuracy of the preferences they reveal. Additionally, society may reject even accurately measured private preferences. This generally occurs when society concludes that certain preferences are illegitimate or unacceptably harmful to self or others.... The task facing the environmental justice movement is to demonstrate that decisions resulting in the current distribution of environmentally sensitive land uses implicate one or more of the generally accepted justifications for rejecting choices expressed in the market or political arena.

Before we undertake that task, however, it seems that we should at least explore the possibility that these processes have functioned well, and that the distribution of environmentally sensitive land uses reflects the accurately measured, unobjectionable preferences of host and non-host communities.

Risk, Rewards, and Rational Preferences in the Siting of Environmentally Sensitive Land Uses

It is not difficult to construct a theoretical framework in which the choice to live in a community that hosts an environmentally sensitive land use is neither irrational nor otherwise objectionable.... Whether evaluated by a policy-making body or by individual residents of a proposed host community, the risk posed by a particular environmentally sensitive land use necessarily will fall along a continuum: At one end will be those environmentally sensitive land uses that have a low probability of a relatively minor adverse effect, at the other end will be those facilities that have a high probability of a catastrophic outcome. In between will be the entire range of facilities that have a measurable risk of some level of harm.

In contrast to the possible harms associated with residential proximity to environmentally sensitive land uses, many such uses offer benefits to residents of the host community. Such benefits may include increased job opportunities, increased property tax revenues, sharing of user fees, infusion of money into the local economy through increased demand for services, the building and maintenance of infrastructure, and even the environmental benefits of shifting from older to newer technology for industrial production or waste disposal....

Rational Preferences Revisited: Winners, Losers and Race

Citizens of affluent states and communities regularly exchange tax concessions and other benefits to serve as the location of new facilities for major enterprises, expecting to recoup their concessions through increased employment and tax revenues. For example, Austin and other central Texas communities routinely offer tax incentives to high-tech industrial enterprises to entice them to locate production facilities in central Texas instead of Silicon Valley.... For predominantly poor and/or minority communities, there may be no excess revenue to accommodate offers of tax breaks, or any other carrots to dangle before the desired industry. These communities can trade only what they have, and many have offered the willingness to accept risk. To be persuasive in their claims of inequity, environmental racism scholars must demonstrate why we should permit (and perhaps even encourage) the former exchange and prohibit the latter....

Siting Decisions in the Past: Sumter County, Alabama

A facility often held up as the leading example of discriminatory siting or environmental racism is Chemical Waste Management Corporation's Emelle hazardous waste treatment, storage, and land disposal facility in Sumter County, Alabama. African-Americans account for 69% of the residents of Sumter County, and for 90% of the residents who live in poverty. Environmental racism scholars allege that the facility was "foisted on the Emelle community without their input" because "[n]o blacks held public office or sat on governing bodies, including the state legislature, county commission, or industrial development board (an agency that promotes industrial operation in the county) from predominantly black Sumter County." ...

However, the story of Sumter County and Chemical Waste Management is much more complex. Formerly a rich farming and cotton-producing region (its heritage from the plantation system of slavery), for decades before the Emelle plant was built in 1978, Sumter County struggled against the decline of its agricultural economic base.... Between 1940 and 1980, the population of Sumter County declined more than 40%. Its remaining residents faced an extremely high incidence of poverty, alarming rates of illiteracy, and infant mortality rates that were among the highest in the state. With no hope that the agricultural economy could be revitalized, the opportunity to host an industry that would bring jobs and tax revenues may well have looked attractive to Sumter County residents.

... [I]t is unlikely that Sumter County was chosen as the location for the Emelle plant because its residents were poor and black. Prior to Chemical Waste Management's decision to purchase the Emelle site, the Environmental Protection Agency had identified it as one of the ten most protective sites in the nation for disposal of hazardous waste. The site's suitability was based on such factors as rural location and access to appropriate transportation systems. More important, the geologic conditions of Sumter county make it ideally suitable to the land disposal of hazardous wastes....

Moreover, it is not at all clear that the presence of the Emelle facility has been burdensome to its host community. While it may be true, as Professor Bullard claims, that "[t]he Emelle hazardous-waste site has not brought about an economic renaissance to this poor blackbelt community," the benefits are tangible. The facility employs over 400 people, 60% of whom live in Sumter County, and has an annual payroll of $10 million. State law provides that a portion of the hazardous waste excise tax collected at the Emelle facility be committed to Sumter County, with a minimum annual guarantee of $4.2 million. Since the landfill was opened in 1977, this increased tax revenue has been used to build infrastructure, enhance educational opportunities for the children of the county, and improve the deliverance of health care services. These services have reversed the percentages of illiteracy and infant mortality....

The economic transformation of Sumter County, from a declining agricultural community to a more stable industrial one, indicates that land uses which may be considered undesirable by some communities may in fact provide benefits to the host communities which outweigh their burdens. These benefits may be particularly attractive to those without jobs, social services, or adequate educational opportunities for their children....

* * *

Notes and Questions

1. Professor Blais assumes that most community residents have made a voluntary choice to live near LULUs. At the same time, she acknowledges that some people's choices are more constrained within our political and market system. Professor Sheila Foster and attorney Luke Cole explain the complicated ways in which race interacts with facially neutral criteria and decisions. In light of the ways that race might conceivably, if indirectly, constrain choices in this context, by what metric should voluntariness be measured? More broadly, to what extent are the preferences of individuals as revealed in the market or political process themselves shaped by non-market forces and social institutions, such as racial discrimination in housing and employment?

2. As Professor Blais notes, there are competing versions of the story behind the Emelle landfill:

> The initial move to establish the "Cadillac" of hazardous waste landfills in Sumter County was made by a small group of regional investors known as Resource Industries, Inc. In 1977, when they established the landfill, public hearings were not required.... The quiet manner in which the Emelle landfill was opened and operated in the late 1970s initially served to limit public opposition. "The thing was here in Sumter County before most people knew about it," remarked one local resident. Numerous rumors regarding the facility circulated at the time. Some people thought it was a brick factory; others, a cement kiln or fertilizer plant. A review of the weekly newspapers published in York and Livingston between 1978 and 1988 shows that the landfill attracted relatively little notice during its first ten years of operation....

> Many outsider observers assume that poor people are concerned first and foremost with improving their immediate economic condition. Poverty, the reasoning goes, makes poor people willing to accept certain risks that others would not. However, poor people did not bring [the] hazardous waste landfill to Sumter County: a white-controlled county commission did. Just as third world nations are pressured to accept loose environmental standards in order to attract foreign investment, many poor communities are presumed to be willing to trade an increased number of jobs for decreased environmental quality.... [O]n a daily basis, the people of Sumter County generally—black and white, rich and poor— face a complex set of problems stemming from their Deep South history and their economic and political marginality. Activists who focus on environmental issues without attending to the broader yet connected issues of economic and political justice are unlikely to succeed in fostering the natural alliances between those fighting for social justice and environmental quality ...

Conner Bailey, Charles E. Faupel & James H. Gundlach, *Environmental Politics in Alabama's Blackbelt, in* CONFRONTING ENVIRONMENTAL RACISM: VOICES FROM THE GRASSROOTS 107, 108–21 (Robert D. Bullard ed., 1993). This competing explanation involves the social capital of the community at the time of siting, as well as race, discussed in the sections below.

3. Professor Blais argues that siting prohibitions will harm poor and minority communities by preventing them from accepting facilities that will result in jobs and other net benefits. Environmental justice activists often dispute the claim that LULUs bring significant economic benefits to local residents in their communities. Professor Robert Kuehn gives the following examples:

> In the Shintech case [a proposed polyvinyl chloride plant in Convent, Louisiana], Louisiana offered Shintech, which was already realizing an annual $750,000 per-employee after-tax profit at its comparable PVC plant in Texas, a taxpayer-financed subsidy of almost $800,000 for each permanent job created.... [B]ecause of Shintech's need for employees with computer knowledge and the low educational level of most Convent residents, the staff director of the state agency promoting the plant admitted that "very few" of the permanent jobs created by the company would go to local residents.... Similarly, residents of West Harlem complain that although they are saddled with a disproportionate number of New York's sewage treatment plants, no minority contractors were hired to construct the most recent $1.1 billion plant; the few local minorities that were hired as plant workers were all gone within a year. In the Genesee Power Station case [in Genesee, Michigan], no minorities from the majority African-American area were hired to construct or were working at the $80 million plant, and the owners all resided outside the community. The judge found these facts "to be appalling" and opined that, in permitting industrial facilities, society ought to take into consideration that the people living in the polluted surrounding communities get no job benefits from the plants. Robbins, Illinois, stands as an example of a town that thought its support of a new waste incinerator would bring jobs and economic development but finds itself "arguably worse off than before" as the economic benefits never materialized and the town is now "saddled with a soaring, smoke-belching trash burner that shoos away commercial investment like a scarecrow guarding a cornfield."

Robert R. Kuehn, *A Taxonomy of Environmental Justice,* 30 ENVTL. L. REP. 10,681, 10,701 (2000). Which strikes you as the more correct view—that of Professor Blais or Professor Kuehn? Why? To what extent should demonstrated, tangible benefits to a host community be required to justify a siting?

2. Post-Siting Changes

One of the earlier arguments in environmental justice scholarship was that the prevalence of LULUs in low-income communities and communities of color resulted from market-driven changes that occurred in neighborhoods after an unwanted land use was located there. This thesis, called the "market dynamics" or "minority move-in" theory, was prominently developed by Professor Vicki Been, who also discusses why it is important to know which came first, the community or the unwanted land use.

Vicki Been, Locally Undesirable Land Uses in Minority Neighborhoods: Disproportionate Siting or Market Dynamics?
103 Yale Law Journal 1383 (1994)

The environmental justice movement contends that people of color and the poor are exposed to greater environmental risks than are whites and wealthier individuals. . . . [R]esearch does not, however, establish that [communities hosting LULUs] were disproportionately minority or poor at the time the sites were selected. Most of the studies compare the *current* socioeconomic characteristics of communities that host various LULUs to those of communities that do not host such LULUs. This approach leaves open the possibility that the sites for LULUs were chosen fairly, but that subsequent events produced the current disproportion in the distribution of LULUs. In other words, the research fails to prove environmental justice advocates' claim that the disproportionate burden poor and minority communities now bear in hosting LULUs is the result of racism and classism in the *siting process* itself.

In addition, the research fails to explore an alternative or additional explanation for the proven correlation between the current demographics of communities and the likelihood that they host LULUs. Regardless of whether the LULUs originally were sited fairly, it could well be that neighborhoods surrounding LULUs became poorer and became home to a greater percentage of people of color over the years following the sitings. Such factors as poverty, housing discrimination, and the location of jobs, transportation, and other public services may have led the poor and racial minorities to "come to the nuisance"—to move to neighborhoods that host LULUs—because those neighborhoods offered the cheapest available housing. . . .

Market Dynamics and the Distribution of LULUs

The residential housing market in the United States is extremely dynamic. Every year, approximately 17% to 20% of U.S. households move to a new home. Some of those people stay within the same neighborhood, but many move to different neighborhoods in the same city, or to different cities. Some people decide to move, at least in part, because they are dissatisfied with the quality of their current neighborhoods. Once a household decides to move, its choice of a new neighborhood usually depends somewhat on the cost of housing and the characteristics of the neighborhood. Those two factors are interrelated because the quality of the neighborhood affects the price of housing.

The siting of a LULU can influence the characteristics of the surrounding neighborhood in two ways. First, an undesirable land use may cause those who can afford to move to become dissatisfied and leave the neighborhood. Second, by making the neighborhood less desirable, the LULU may decrease the value of the neighborhood's property, making the housing more available to lower income households and less attractive to higher income households. The end result of both influences is likely to be that the neighborhood becomes poorer than it was before the siting of the LULU.

The neighborhood also is likely to become home to more people of color. Racial discrimination in the sale and rental of housing relegates people of color (especially African-Americans) to the least desirable neighborhoods, regardless of their income level. Moreover, once a neighborhood becomes a community of color, racial discrimination in the promulgation and enforcement of zoning and environmental protection laws, the provision of municipal services, and the lending practices of banks may cause neighborhood quality to decline further. That additional decline, in turn, will induce those who can leave the neighborhood—the least poor and those least subject to discrimination—to do so.

The dynamics of the housing market therefore are likely to cause the poor and people of color to move to or remain in the neighborhoods in which LULUs are located, regardless of the demographics of the communities when the LULUs were first sited....

If the siting process is primarily responsible for the correlation between the location of LULUs and the demographics of host neighborhoods, the process may be unjust under current constitutional doctrine, at least as to people of color....

On the other hand, if the disproportionate distribution of LULUs results from market forces which drive the poor, regardless of their race, to live in neighborhoods that offer cheaper housing because they host LULUs, then the fairness of the distribution becomes a question about the fairness of our market economy. Some might argue that the disproportionate burden is part and parcel of a free market economy that is, overall, fairer than alternative schemes, and that the costs of regulating the market to reduce the disproportionate burden outweigh the benefits of doing so. Others might argue that those moving to a host neighborhood are compensated through the market for the disproportionate burden they bear by lower housing costs, and therefore that the situation is just. Similarly, some might contend that while the poor suffer lower quality neighborhoods, they also suffer lower quality food, housing, and medical care, and that the systemic problem of poverty is better addressed through income redistribution programs than through changes in siting processes.

Even if decisionmakers were to agree that it is unfair to allow post-siting market dynamics to create disproportionate environmental risk for the poor or minorities, the remedy for that injustice would have to be much more fundamental than the remedy for unjust siting *decisions*. Indeed, if market forces are the primary cause of the correlation between the presence of LULUs and the current socioeconomic characteristics of a neighborhood, even a siting process radically revised to ensure that LULUs are distributed equally among all neighborhoods may have only a short-term effect. The areas surrounding LULUs distributed equitably will become less desirable neighborhoods, and thus may soon be left to people of color or the poor, recreating the pattern of inequitable siting....

The Evidence of Disproportionate Siting

Several recent studies have attempted to assess whether locally undesirable land uses are disproportionately located in neighborhoods that are populated by more people of color or are more poor than is normal.... [One of the] most frequently cited of those studies, which is often credited for first giving the issue of environmental justice visibility, was conducted by the United States General Accounting Office (GAO).... [The GAO found that in three of the four communities where hazardous waste landfills were sited in eight southeastern states, the population was disproportionately African American and poor. Eds.] Another frequently cited local study was conducted by sociologist Robert Bullard and formed important parts of his books, *Invisible Houston* and *Dumping in Dixie*. Professor Bullard found that although African-Americans made up only 28% of the Houston population in 1980, six of Houston's eight incinerators and mini-incinerators and fifteen of seventeen landfills were located in predominantly African-American neighborhoods.

[Professor Been then re-analyzed the GAO study and the Bullard study, looking at demographic characteristics of the host communities at the time of siting decisions and tracing subsequent changes in the demographics of these communities. She found mixed support for her thesis: of the four communities reviewed by the GAO, all were dispro-portionately African American at the siting, and in each case the percentage of African Americans decreased after siting decisions were made. For ten communities studied by Professor Bullard, she found 50% were sited in predominantly African American communities, and that the percentage of African Americans in all neighborhoods surrounding the landfills subsequently increased (as did the percentage of the population with incomes below the poverty level in all but two host neighborhoods.) Eds.]

* * *

Notes and Questions

1. The which-came-first question continued to be discussed and debated in subse-quent environmental justice literature. In 2006, a group of researchers summarized the state of the empirical evidence:

> Research on the temporal dimension—which came first, the minority com-munities or the hazards—has been the subject of a more limited range of quan-titative research, primarily because of the methodological challenges of such time-series analysis. The results have been mixed. In keeping with the work of Douglas Anderton and various colleagues (Anderton, Anderson, Rossi et al. 1994; Anderton, Anderson, Oakes, and Fraser 1994), John Oakes, Douglas An-derton, and Andy Anderson (1996) found little evidence of either contempo-rary disparity or historical patterns. Using an improved database, Vicki Been and Francis Gupta (1997) [in the previous excerpt] found no evidence for the move-in view but did find some that Latino communities were the subject of dispro-portionate siting. Sabina Shaikh and John Loomis (1999) found in a study of Denver that minority populations rose faster in areas without hazards, counter-ing the market dynamics view. James Mitchell, Deborah Thomas, and Susan Cutter (1999) find evidence of minority move-in for South Carolina. A study of the Los Angeles area by Manuel Pastor, James Sadd, and John Hipp (2001) [ex-cerpted below] found that siting was significantly disproportionate, and that the movement of minorities into affected neighborhoods was no faster than in the rest of the region.

MANUEL PASTOR ET AL., IN THE WAKE OF THE STORM: ENVIRONMENT, DISASTER, AND RACE AFTER KATRINA 14 (2006).

2. Some scholars have criticized the fact that while Professor Been identifies racial dis-crimination in housing as a factor in post-siting demographic change, she nonetheless includes this under the rubric of market forces.

> Housing choices among whites may be determined by the market, what is avail-able and affordable, individual preferences (of which the neighborhood racial mix may be one), and utility functions. In contrast, choices among minorities may be severely limited by various forms of institutionalized discrimination altogether separate from ability and willingness to pay. Been recognizes that market processes may result in a gradual downgrading in the economic status of residents of a host neighborhood and that housing discrimination may have a separate effect of concentrating minorities. Yet in combining both factors under the label of market dynamics, Been seems to negate the fact that demo-graphic change due to housing discrimination is a fundamentally different process.

Saha & Mohai, *supra*, at 19.

3. How does Professor Been's market dynamics theory square with Professor Rabin's and Professor Arnold's findings documenting expulsive zoning practices in communities of color? Is expulsive zoning an indication of a well-functioning market allocating risks and amenities efficiently, i.e., to those willing to pay the most for the resource in question (either an environmental good or the absence of an environmental risk)? Or, alternatively, is expulsive zoning evidence of a poorly functioning market?

4. While public opinion polls and research on risk perception and environmental attitudes support the notion that LULUs render host areas less desirable places to live, Professors Saha and Mohai caution that a mix of factors influences the decision of residents to leave a neighborhood. They argue, for example, that a neighborhood's pre-existing level of stability or change may be equally or more important than the impact of the LULU itself. Saha & Mohai, *supra*, at 21.

5. Some scholars seeking to explain disproportionate siting point to a complicated set of sociopolitical and legal factors. Their theories are examined in the following section.

D. Politics, Social Capital, and the Structure of Environmental Laws

As described above, companies may choose to site noxious facilities in low-income communities or communities of color because this represents the path of least political resistance. Minority and poor residents often have less political power than wealthier communities for a variety of reasons: lack of access to elected officials, lack of awareness of the appropriate officials to contact in order to express concerns about environmental conditions, and under-representation in local government. They are "likely to lack the know-how, the administrative, legal, and scientific expertise to participate effectively in administrative process of siting decisions." Saha & Mohai, *supra*, at 9, 11–13. Explanations that center upon these sociopolitical factors essentially posit that environmental burdens are shifted to groups that lack social capital.

> Social capital can be defined as resources embedded in a social structure that are accessed and/or mobilized in purposive actions. By this definition, the notion of social capital contains three ingredients: resources embedded in a social structure; accessibility to these social resources by individuals; and use or mobilization of them by individuals engaged in purposive action. Thus conceived, social capital contains both structural (accessibility) and action-oriented (mobilization or use) elements.... [S]ocial capital captures the extent to which individuals have differential accessibility to collective resources....
>
> [I]t is incumbent on a theory of social capital to delineate the patterns and determinants of the two ingredients of social capital or *the inequality of social capital* as accessible social resources and mobilized social resources....

Nan Lin et al., *The Position Generator: Measurement Techniques for Investigations of Social Capital*, in SOCIAL CAPITAL: THEORY AND RESEARCH 57, 58–59 (Nan Lin, Karen Cook & Ronald S. Burt eds., 2001). With this in mind, recall in Chapter 2 that researchers found that ethnic demographic shifts, a previously overlooked variable in the empirical data on disparities, significantly correlated with the siting of commercial hazardous waste facilities (called treatment, storage, and disposal facilities, or "TSDFs", under federal hazardous waste law). The excerpt below, describing this study, attempts to identify and measure the lack of social capital that explains some environmental disparities.

Manuel Pastor, Jr., Jim Sadd & John Hipp, Which Came First? Toxic Facilities, Minority Move-In, and Environmental Justice
23 Journal of Urban Affairs 1 (2001)

... Many have assumed that contemporary inequity is the result of discriminatory siting practices. The general argument is that low levels of political power in minority communities may induce polluters to locate hazards in these areas. Such a political argument is often implicitly based on notions of social capital and community efficacy: Where residents have more ability to organize and affect policy, perhaps because of their income or racial status in a stratified society, they will be more able to resist the placement of a hazardous facility. Of course, social capital may in fact be affected by other factors, such as the level of education of residents or the ability to bridge differences between minority groups, a topic we explore below....

[W]e focus on the effects of a new dimension of ethnic change. Previous work has stressed the percentage of minorities. But while a 40% increase in Latinos that is matched by a corresponding 40% decrease in African Americans may leave the percentage of minorities unchanged, the neighborhood will in fact be transformed. Such ethnic transitions may weaken the usual social bonds constituted by race and make an area more susceptible to siting. We investigate this "social capital" effect [] finding that it does indeed have an effect on the likelihood of receiving a TSDF....

Black to Brown shifts have been especially prevalent in South Los Angeles, an area laden with hazardous or toxic facilities and air pollution.... Such shifting neighborhood patterns can cause tensions between minority groups, weakening neighborhood social capital and increasing the area's vulnerability to siting locally undesirable land uses.... We label this measure of dynamics within a census tract "ethnic churning." ...

To see whether a change in the ethnic composition of an area—even if it remains minority—weakens social capital and makes areas more vulnerable to disproportionate siting, we re-estimated the model by using ethnic churning during the 1970s and 1980s and TSDF siting over the same period.... [The researchers then found that the churning variable is highly significant at predicting TSDF siting at the one-mile level; they also found that, controlling for other factors, minorities attract TSDFs but TSDFs do not generally attract minorities. Eds.]

This study offers a lesson consistent with the experience many environmental justice advocates: Demographics reflecting political weakness—including a higher presence of minorities, a lower presence of home owners, or a significant degree of ethnic churning—seem to be the real attractors of TSDFs. A special challenge is posed by the fact that areas undergoing transition and unable to lay claim to pre-existing racially based social capital may be especially vulnerable. If this is so, then the current strategy of most of the environmental justice movement—building social capital across ethnic lines by an explicit commitment to a people of color movement—may be an effective way to combat the environmental degradation often found in urban minority communities.

* * *

Notes and Questions

1. Two early campaigns illustrate the points made by Professors Pastor, Sadd, and Hipp, and underscore the potential of the environmental justice movement to promote social capital:

> Los Angeles, the nation's second largest city ... is one of the most culturally and ethnically diverse cities in the United States. People of color—Latino Americans, Asian Americans, Pacific Islanders, African Americans, and Native Americans—now constitute 63 percent of the city's population....

> The South Central Los Angeles neighborhoods suffer from a double whammy of poverty and pollution. [An] article in the *San Francisco Examiner* described the ZIP code in which South Central Los Angeles lies (90058) as the "dirtiest" in the state. The 1990 population in the ZIP code is 59 percent African American and 38 percent Latino American. Abandoned toxic-waste sites, freeways, smokestacks, and waste water pipes from polluting industries saturate the one-square-mile area....

> Why has South Central Los Angeles become the dumping ground of the city? Local government decisions are in part responsible. Trying to solve them, the city (under a contract with the EPA) developed a plan to build three waste-to-energy incinerators....

> After learning about the incinerator project ... residents organized themselves in a group called Concerned Citizens of South Central Los Angeles, most of whom were African American women. Local activists from Concerned Citizens were able to form alliances with several national and grass-roots environmental groups, as well as with public interest law groups to block the construction of the city-initiated municipal solid-waste incinerator....

> Just as Los Angeles's largest African American community was selected for the city's first state-of-the-art municipal solid waste incinerator, the state's first state-of-the-art hazardous-waste incinerator was slated to be built near East Los Angeles, the city's largest Latino community....

> Several East Los Angeles neighborhoods, made up mostly of Latino Americans, are located only a mile downwind from the proposed hazardous-waste incinerator site.... Residents of East Los Angeles questioned the selection of their community as host for the state's first hazardous-waste incinerator. Opponents of the incinerator saw the project as just another case of industry dumping on the Latino American community....

> Mothers of East Los Angeles (MELA) led the opposition to the ... incinerator. MELA consisted of Latino American women who had originally organized against the state's plan to locate a prison in East Los Angeles....

Robert D. Bullard, *Anatomy of Environmental Racism, in* TOXIC STRUGGLES: THE THEORY AND PRACTICE OF ENVIRONMENTAL JUSTICE 25, 30–32 (Richard Hofrichter ed., 1993)

2. Attorney Nicholas Targ, former general counsel to the U.S. EPA Office of Environmental Justice, describes ways in which social capital indicators correlate with environmental regulatory indicators:

> Using indicators, such as voter turn-out, as a measure of social capital, the following indicators strongly suggest the importance of community social capital in achieving the environmental policy and civil rights aspects of environmental justice:

• Communities that have high rates of voter turn-out in general elections (normalized for race, income, and education factors) have a higher rate of Toxic Release Inventory (TRI) chemical reduction than communities with lower voter turn-out;

• The level of clean-up and funds expended, on a risk of cancer basis, is greater in communities with higher voter turn-out. Researchers have found that the correlation between voter turn-out and level of clean-up was most significant at the least cost-effective site clean-ups and the lowest risk sites;

• A survey of 200 corporate counsels found that the overwhelming majority of attorneys said that they were more likely to recommend reducing their facilities' emissions if a community group could make a credible threat to take political or legal action against the facility;

• The best predictor for the location of new TRI facilities in Los Angeles is not race or income, but the rate of a community's ethnic change (ethnic churning), an indicator of social capital; and

• The occurrence of urban restoration projects (community gardens, reclamation of vacant lots, etc.) in New Haven, Connecticut, correlates with a sense of "being part of a solid community."

Community social capital is, therefore, a critical asset both for community-led efforts to halt unwanted projects and those community-led efforts that seek to work collaboratively with other stakeholders (e.g., government at all levels, industry, environmentalists, etc.) to achieve mutually consistent goals.

Nicholas Targ, *A Third Policy Avenue to Address Environmental Justice: Civil Rights and Environmental Quality and the Relevance of Social Capital Policy,* 16 Tul. Envtl. L. J. 167, 169–70 (2002). Mr. Targ recommends ways for governmental officials to enhance the social capital of communities by designing initiatives that will increase the capacity in environmental justice communities to identify and address community needs and goals. *Id.* at 171–72. (Governmental initiatives are examined in Chapter 10.)

3. Rather than stopping a facility, a group of residents may choose instead to negotiate with a facility sponsor to mitigate impacts from a new facility, or alternatively to provide community benefits. Scholars have implicitly examined a relationship between a community's social capital and the community's ability to form and maintain the coalitions necessary to undertake a successful negotiation, ultimately memorialized in a community benefits agreement, or CBA:

Usually framed as private agreements (with or without municipal involvement), CBAs may require a developer to mitigate potential impacts of the development. But often they go even farther, asking the developer to work with the community to improve housing, employment options, and recreational and cultural facilities. As a result, CBAs can empower communities to become active participants in the planning process.

… CBAs, which function best when the community base is large and where the developer needs community support in order to obtain subsidies, approvals, or regulatory variances (as is often the case in dense urban neighborhoods). As urban areas become more popular locations for large developments, residents are becoming increasingly empowered to demand that such developments "give back" to the community with benefits that improve urban quality of life.…

When developers do choose to engage in talks with community groups, they may persist in attempts to weaken the coalition's bargaining power. The "divide and conquer" techniques used by developers to balkanize coalitions require community groups to be united and to have coherent goals. Otherwise, a developer may attempt to appease some community groups without meeting others' needs— to "buy off" the minimum number of stakeholders to be able to spin the project as being community-supported. . . .

While developers may try to damage coalitions' reputations or seek to win over constituent groups, CBA coalitions have developed some tactics of their own to boost their bargaining power. From the start, coalitions must develop a language to frame the issues in their favor. This often involves emphasizing positive visions of the community's future, win-win solutions, inclusiveness, the grassroots character of the campaign and the nature of the CBA as fostering equitable development rather than preventing development altogether. These positions reflect strong social values, and they may draw more community members to the coalition and attract positive media attention. . . .

The costs of negotiating a CBA can be high. Organizing a coalition, holding meetings, conducting community research and preparing reports will all require funding. Coalitions that have no experience with CBAs, moreover, will likely need technical and legal assistance throughout the negotiation process. The funding required for all of this may inhibit the process. . . .

Patricia E. Salkin & Amy Lavine, *Understanding Community Benefits Agreements: Equitable Development, Social Justice and Other Considerations for Developers, Municipalities and Community Organizations*, 26 U.C.L.A. J. ENVTL. L. & POL'Y 291, 292–323 (2008). The excerpt above reveals a cyclical relationship. While community benefits agreements can promote social capital, to what extent must there be preexisting social capital to prompt formation of the coalition and avoid its disintegration? For example, would a community undergoing significant ethnic churning have enough social capital to form a coalition to either resist the siting or negotiate a favorable community benefit agreement?

4. In addition to a community's lack of social capital, some political explanations of disparities focus on the structure of environmental law and environmental policymaking (this also includes land use practices, discussed above). The following two excerpts explore this issue in greater detail.

Luke W. Cole, Empowerment as the Key to Environmental Protection: The Need for Environmental Poverty Law

19 Ecology Law Quarterly 619 (1992)

Environmental Law as the Problem, Not the Solution

Environmental laws are not designed by or for poor people. The theory and ideology behind environmental laws ignores the systemic genesis of pollution. Environmental statutes actually legitimate the pollution of low-income neighborhoods. Further, those with political and economic power have used environmental laws in ways which have resulted in poor people bearing a disproportionate share of environmental hazards.

Two Views of the Political Economy of Pollution

Mainstream and grassroots environmentalists generally have different views of the causes of pollution, and thus offer different solutions to the problem of pollution. The legal-scientific movement's law and policy in the past twenty-five years has largely been based on a "single bad actor" understanding of the causes of pollution. This "bad actor" theory holds that pollution occurs when a particular actor (such as a polluting corporation) acts outside societal norms; laws are thus written to punish particular violators of pollution standards....

[Grassroots activists] have acquired an "institutional" understanding of the political economy of pollution, which stands in contrast to the single bad actor theory. The institutional theory posits that the *normal operations* of some institutions (such as U.S. corporations) generate environmental hazards. People living in or near industrial communities know that law-abiding companies and law-breaking companies differ in degree only: both put pollutants out the smokestack, and both thus poison nearby communities. In contrast to the single bad actor model, which seeks to identify and punish individual bad actors, the institutional model identifies individual polluters "not as explanations themselves," but merely as part of an overall system centered on maximizing profit.

Mainstream environmentalists see pollution as the *failure* of government and industry—if the environmentalists could only shape up the few bad apples, our environment would be protected. But grassroots activists come to view pollution as the *success* of government and industry, success at industry's primary objective: maximizing profits by externalizing environmental costs. Pollution of our air, land, and water that is literally killing people is often not in violation of environmental laws. Grassroots environmentalists, realizing this, have a far more radical and systemic view of the changes needed to eliminate pollution....

Control v. Prevention

Because environmental laws were designed around the single bad actor model, they have failed to serve low-income communities. Traditional environmental law has focused on pollution *control:* on technologies to be placed on the end of the pipe to control or clean up the poisons coming out. This concept is the foundation for the complex regulatory scheme designed and honed by the mainstream environmental movement.

In contrast, grassroots activists have a different understanding and approach. Community activists have to live with the results of environmental groups' compromises with industry and the government ... [They] are pressing for the elimination of the chemicals themselves and arguing for a change in the processes that produce these chemicals in the first place....

Grassroots activists around the country, by stopping the siting of toxic waste disposal facilities in their communities, have begun to force industry to move from pollution *control* to pollution *prevention*. Put simply, because so few waste disposal sites exist, and because it is so difficult to establish new sites, the price of toxic waste disposal has risen to the point where companies are seriously working to replace toxic inputs to their manufacturing processes in order to minimize the production of toxic waste. By forcing companies to pay a cost closer to the true societal cost of toxic waste, grassroots activists have forced companies to begin to reduce toxic waste production.

NIMBY Works

... Environmental laws, and the siting of polluting facilities, are products of a political process which has historically excluded poor people, and in which poor people remain grossly under-represented. The importance of the political process is heightened by the procedural emphasis of many environmental laws. Lacking substantive standards, such statutes depend on the vigor of the political process for achieving environmental goals. In the end, it is those with political clout who win in the administrative process or siting decision. Because siting decisions are political decisions, the outcome—more facilities in poor communities—is neither surprising nor unpredictable. Thus, the decisions to place unwanted facilities in low-income neighborhoods are made not *in spite* of our system of laws, but *because* of our system of laws.

When middle-class neighborhoods say NIMBY (Not in My Back Yard) and use environmental laws to defeat proposed locally unwanted land uses (LULUs), such as toxic waste dumps or polluting industry, the developers usually go to a different neighborhood, where opposition is less organized and powerful. Thus, LULUs end up in poor neighborhoods and in communities of color. It is *because* the law works for white middle-class communities that it does not work for the poor, or for people of color....

* * *

Richard J. Lazarus, Pursuing "Environmental Justice": The Distributional Effects of Environmental Protection
87 Northwestern University Law Review 787 (1993)

Exacerbating Causes: The Structure of Environmental Policymaking

There exist ... factors more endemic to environmental law itself that may exacerbate distributional inequities likely present in the context of any public welfare law. These factors suggest more than the disturbing, yet somewhat irresistible thesis, that the distributional dimension of environmental protection policy likely suffers from the same inequities that persist generally in society. They suggest the far more troubling, and even less appealing, proposition that the problems of distributional inequity may in fact be more pervasive in the environmental protection arena than they are in other areas of traditional concern to civil rights organizations, such as education, employment, and housing.

Indeed, it is the absence of that minority involvement so prevalent in the more classic areas of civil rights concern that may render the distributional problem worse for environmental protection. Minority interests have traditionally had little voice in the various points of influence that strike the distributional balances necessary to get environmental protection laws enacted, regulations promulgated, and enforcement actions initiated. The interest groups historically active in the environmental protection area include a variety of mainstream environmental organizations representing a spectrum of interests (conservation, recreation, hunting, wildlife protection, resource protection, human health), as well as a variety of commercial and industrial concerns. Until very recently, if at all, the implications for racial minorities of environmental protection laws have not been a focal point of concern for any of these organizations.

Much of environmental protection lawmaking has also been highly centralized, with the geographic focus in Washington, D.C. The enactment of environmental statutes within that geo-political setting has required the expenditure of considerable political resources. As evidenced by the thirteen years required to amend the Clean Air Act, it is no easy task to obtain the attention of the numerous congressional committees, and to form the coalitions between competing interest groups, so necessary to secure a bill's passage.

Environmental legislation has ultimately been produced through intense and lengthy horse-trading among interest groups, a process necessary to secure a particular environmental law's passage. This process has often depended upon the forging of alliances between diverse interests both within the environmental public interest community and within government bureaucracy. Often, these unions have included so-called "unholy alliances" between environmentalists and commercial and industrial interests, where the latter have perceived an economic advantage to be gained (or disadvantage to be minimized) by their supporting an environmental protection law that allocates the benefits and burdens of environmental protection in a particular fashion....

It is not surprising, therefore, that those environmental laws enacted by Congress typically address some, but hardly all, environmental pollution problems. And, even with regard to those problems that are explicitly addressed, there are usually discrepancies and gaps within the statutory scheme. Which problems are confronted, and where the discrepancies and gaps occur, is quite naturally an expression of the priorities of those participants who wield the greatest influence and resources in the political process.

For this reason, much environmental legislation may not have focused on those pollution problems that are of greatest concern to many minority communities. For instance, air pollution control efforts typically have focused on general ambient air quality concerns for an entire metropolitan region rather than on toxic hot spots in any one particular area. Accordingly, while there has been much progress made in improving air quality as measured by a handful of national ambient air quality standards, there has been relatively less progress achieved over the last twenty years in the reduction of those toxic air emissions which tend to be of greater concern to persons, disproportionately minorities, who live in the immediate geographic vicinity of the toxic polluting source.... Likewise, and at the behest of mainstream environmental groups, substantial resources have also been directed to improving air and water quality in nonurban areas. Programs for the prevention of significant deteriorations in air quality, the reduction of "acid rain," and the protection of visibility in national parks and wilderness areas, all require significant financial expenditures. Substantial resources have similarly been expended on improving the quality of water resources that are not as readily accessible to many minorities because of their historical exclusion. Without meaning to suggest that these programs lack merit on their own terms (for the simple reason that they possess great merit), their return in terms of overall public health may be less than pollution control programs directed at improving the environmental quality of urban America's poorer neighborhoods, including many minority communities....

[R]acial minorities have had little influence on either the lawmaking or priority-setting processes at any of the legislative, regulatory, or local enforcement levels. They have not been well represented among the interest groups lobbying and litigating before governmental authorities on environmental protection issues. Nor have they been well represented, especially at the national level, within those governmental organizations actively involved in the relevant environmental processes. Their voices have not been heard in the mainstream environmental public interest organizations that participate in the policymaking debates and that, in the absence of governmental enforcement, are behind citizen suits filling the void. Traditional civil rights organizations have historically had little interest in, and have infrequently become involved with, environmental issues. At the same time, mainstream environmental organizations have historically included few minorities in policymaking positions. In 1990, this fact prompted several members of various civil rights organizations and minority groups to send a widely publicized letter to the national environmental public interest organizations charging them with being isolated from minority communities.... [An excerpt of this letter appears in Chapter 1. Eds.]

* * *

Notes and Questions

1. Since the date of Professor Lazarus' classic article on environmental justice, conventional environmental organizations have acted to better achieve diversity in their staffing, and have otherwise responded to environmental justice issues to varying degrees. A disturbing question remains, however: if environmental burdens are disproportionately distributed in society, why haven't environmental laws remedied the problem? As of 2009, there still is no federal environmental legislation explicitly addressing environmental justice. Although a few states have enacted such laws, these laws typically provide little more than enhanced procedures (governmental initiatives, including state laws addressing environmental justice concerns, are discussed in Chapter 10).

2. Does the current pattern of environmental inequities represent a failure of our environmental protection laws, or the *success* of these laws, as Luke Cole argues? In an article exploring connections between the history of land use, sociopolitical factors, economics, and the application of environmental laws in the Appalachian coal fields, Professor Patrick McGinley summarizes the challenges facing coal camp communities:

> The counties of southern West Virginia's so-called "billion dollar coalfields" contain enormously valuable coal reserves. Coal production from huge, highly efficient mountaintop removal and longwall mines has reached record levels, a fact that belies the dismal economic reality of the coalfield communities where coal production is greatest…. How is it that so many communities in the "billion dollar coalfields" are still mired in poverty and stagnant local economies continue to record some of the highest unemployment rates in the United States?
>
> … The coalfield struggle pitting communities against the oppressive coal industry forces that began in the coal camps of the nineteenth century continues today. Historians have documented a century of exploitation of coalfield communities…. In addition to the destruction of coalfield communities, conflicts between union and nonunion mine operators, poverty, high unemployment, underfunded schools, lack of community infrastructure, and the fear and intimidation generated by industry threats to close mines and layoff workers persist in the region….
>
> But the future of coalfield communities is not as bleak as it may seem. Modern communication technology, including the internet, allows people and organizations in remote and isolated coalfield venues to share information and work together toward the common goal of economic, environmental, and social justice. Across the coalfields people are coming together in grassroots organizations. In West Virginia, the West Virginia Organizing Project and Coal River Mountain Watch have made strides in drawing attention to conflicts between coalfield citizens and coal mining operations….
>
> Coalfield citizen activism and lawsuits, however, will not bring jobs to the region. Coal is the only game in town, so to speak, and it is not hiring….

Patrick C. McGinley, *From Pick and Shovel to Mountaintop Removal: Environmental Injustice in the Appalachian Coalfields*, 34 ENVTL. L. 21, 101–04 (2004). In the article, Professor McGinley discusses the reasons for the failure of a law that required commercial, residential, and industrial development as a condition for permitting radical alteration caused by mining. Part II of this book examines several ways that the implementation of environmental laws can generate inequities.

3. Given the decentralized nature of the environmental justice movement, and the limited resources available, what would be the most potentially useful points of inter-

vention? Direct action (e.g., demonstrations), litigation, collaborative projects, legislative lobbying, or pressure upon agencies? Can you think of other means? In which venues would lawyers likely be the most helpful? (Citizen responses to environmental justice concerns are examined in Part III of this book.)

E. Racial Discrimination

Another set of explanations for disproportionate environmental burdens and benefits involves racial discrimination. In part this refers to intentional racism, i.e. targeting communities of color based on pure racial bigotry. In today's society, such conduct is far less frequent than in the past, and given the prevailing societal opprobrium toward overt racial discrimination, far less likely to occur in the open. A softer, but related view of intentional discrimination posits that communities of color are targeted for unwanted land uses by those who believe they will be less likely to organize effective opposition than white communities, or by those who believe these communities to be more willing to trade off environmental risks for possible economic benefits.

A broader view of discrimination encompasses actions that are not grounded in intentional, conscious prejudice, but that, because of the structure or workings of social and political institutions, have discriminatory effects. For example, an all-white zoning board may render decisions with discriminatory effects because of unconscious racial prejudices, or because minority citizens, who do not live in the same neighborhoods and are not part of the same social networks as the board members, have less access to them, or because the white board members do not live in the area impacted by a proposed LULU, or because the decision-makers are less interested in the fate of minority residents for political reasons. In some respects, all of the above authors' insights point to specific mechanisms by which this form of "structural" or "institutional" racism works. For example, attorney Luke Cole and Professor Sheila Foster discuss instances where public officials employ seemingly technical criteria—such as that a facility should not be sited in proximity to schools, hospitals, or other sensitive institutions—that can discriminate against minority residents who because of past and present housing discrimination disproportionately live in areas without such facilities. In the following article, Professor Charles Lawrence adds to the general theory of structural racism. By using the insights of psychology, he articulates a theory of why racial discrimination may be far more prevalent than appears on the surface and, accordingly, more persistent throughout our society.

Charles R. Lawrence III, The Id, the Ego, and Equal Protection: Reckoning with Unconscious Racism
39 Stanford Law Review 317 (1987)

... Americans share a common historical and cultural heritage in which racism has played and still plays a dominant role. Because of this shared experience, we also inevitably share many ideas, attitudes, and beliefs that attach significance to an individual's race and induce negative feelings and opinions about nonwhites. To the extent that this cultural belief system has influenced all of us, we are all racists. At the same time, most of us are unaware of our racism. We do not recognize the ways in which our cultural experience has influenced our beliefs about race or the occasions on which those beliefs affect our actions. In other words, a large part of the behavior that produces racial discrimination is influenced by unconscious racial motivation....

Racism: A Public Health Problem

Not every student of the human mind has agreed with Sigmund Freud's description of the unconscious, but few today would quarrel with the assertion that there is an unconscious — that there are mental processes of which we have no awareness that affect our actions and the ideas of which we are aware. There is a considerable, and by now well respected, body of knowledge and empirical research concerning the workings of the human psyche and the unconscious. Common sense tells us that we all act unwittingly on occasion. We have experienced slips of the tongue and said things we fully intended not to say, and we have had dreams in which we experienced such feelings as fear, desire, and anger that we did not know we had.

... Racism is in large part a product of the unconscious. It is a set of beliefs whereby we irrationally attach significance to something called race. I do not mean to imply that racism does not have its origins in the rational and premeditated acts of those who sought and seek property and power. But racism in America is much more complex than either the conscious conspiracy of a power elite or the simple delusion of a few ignorant bigots. It is a part of our common historical experience and, therefore, a part of our culture. It arises from the assumptions we have learned to make about the world, ourselves, and others as well as from the patterns of our fundamental social activities.

... [H]ow is the unconscious involved when racial prejudice is less apparent — when racial bias is hidden from the prejudiced individual as well as from others? Increasingly, as our culture has rejected racism as immoral and unproductive, this hidden prejudice has become the more prevalent form of racism. The individual's Ego must adapt to a cultural order that views overly racist attitudes and behavior as unsophisticated, uninformed, and immoral. It must repress or disguise racist ideas when they seek expression.

Joel Kovel refers to the resulting personality type as the "aversive racist" and contrasts this type with the "dominative racist," the true bigot who openly seeks to keep blacks in a subordinate position and will resort to force to do so. The aversive racist believes in white superiority, but her conscience seeks to repudiate this belief, or, at least, to prevent her from acting on it. She often resolves this inner conflict by not acting at all. She tries to avoid the issue by ignoring the existence of blacks, avoiding contact with them, or at most being polite, correct, and cold whenever she must deal with them. Aversive racists range from individuals who lapse into demonstrative racism when threatened — as when blacks get "too close" — to those who consider themselves liberals and, despite their sense of aversion to blacks (of which they are often unaware), do their best within the confines of the existing societal structure to ameliorate blacks' condition....

A Cognitive Approach to Unconscious Racism

Cognitive psychologists offer a contrasting model for understanding the origin and unconscious nature of racial prejudice.... [T]hey view human behavior, including racial prejudice, as growing out of the individual's attempt to understand his relationship with the world (in this case, relations between groups) while at the same time preserving his personal integrity. But while the ultimate goal of the cognitive process is understanding or rationality, many of the critical elements of the process occur outside of the individual's awareness....

Cognitivists see the process of "categorization" as one common source of racial and other stereotypes. All humans tend to categorize in order to make sense of experience. Too many events occur daily for us to deal successfully with each one on an individual basis; we must categorize in order to cope. When a category—for example, the category of black person or white person—correlates with a continuous dimension—for example, the range of human intelligence or the propensity to violence—there is a tendency to exaggerate the differences between categories on that dimension and to minimize the differences within each category....

The content of the social categories to which people are assigned is generated over a long period of time within a culture and transmitted to individual members of society by a process cognitivists call "assimilation." Assimilation entails learning and internalizing preferences and evaluations. Individuals learn cultural attitudes and beliefs about race very early in life, at a time when it is difficult to separate the perceptions of one's teacher (usually a parent) from one's own. In other words, one learns about race at a time when one is highly sensitive to the social contexts in which one lives....

Furthermore, because children learn lessons about race at this early stage, most of the lessons are tacit rather than explicit. Children learn not so much through an intellectual understanding of what their parents tell them about race as through an emotional identification with who their parents are and what they see and feel their parents do. Small children will adopt their parents' beliefs because they experience them as their own. If we do learn lessons about race in this way, we are not likely to be aware that the lessons have even taken place. If we are unaware that we have been taught to be afraid of blacks or to think of them as lazy or stupid, then we may not be conscious of our internalization of those feelings and beliefs....

Case studies have demonstrated that an individual who holds stereotyped beliefs about a "target" will remember and interpret past events in the target's life history in ways that bolster and support his stereotyped beliefs and will perceive the target's actual behavior as reconfirming and validating the stereotyped beliefs. While the individual may be aware of the selectively perceived facts that support his categorization or simplified understanding, he will not be aware of the process that has caused him to deselect the facts that do not conform with his rationalization. Thus, racially prejudiced behavior that is actually the product of learned cultural preferences is experienced as a reflection of rational deduction from objective observation, which is nonprejudicial behavior. The decisionmaker who is unaware of the selective perception that has produced her stereotype will not view it as a stereotype. She will believe that her actions are motivated not by racial prejudice but by her attraction or aversion to the attributes she has "observed" in the groups she has favored or disfavored.

Unconscious Racism in Everyday Life

Whatever our preferred theoretical analysis, there is considerable commonsense evidence from our everyday experience to confirm that we all harbor prejudiced attitudes that are kept from our consciousness.

When, for example, a well-known sports broadcaster is carried away by the excitement of a brilliant play by an Afro-American professional football player and refers to the player as a "little monkey" during a nationally televised broadcast, we have witnessed the prototypical parapraxes, or unintentional slip of the tongue. This sportscaster views himself as progressive on issues of race. Many of his most important professional associates are black, and he would no doubt profess that more than a few are close friends. After the incident, he initially claimed no memory of it and then, when confronted with videotaped evidence, apologized and said that no racial slur was *intended*. There is no reason to doubt the sincerity of his assertion. Why would he intentionally risk antagonizing his audience and damaging his reputation and career? But his inadvertent slip of the tongue was not random. It is evidence of the continuing presence of a derogatory racial stereotype that he has repressed from consciousness and that has momentarily slipped past his Ego's censors. Likewise, when Nancy Reagan appeared before a public gathering of then-presidential-candidate Ronald Reagan's political supporters and said that she wished he could be there to "see all these beautiful white people," one can hardly imagine that it was her self-conscious intent to proclaim publicly her preference for the company of Caucasians.

Incidents of this kind are not uncommon, even if only the miscues of the powerful and famous are likely to come to the attention of the press. But because the unconscious also influences selective perceptions, whites are unlikely to hear many of the inadvertent racial slights that are made daily in their presence....

* * *

Notes and Questions

1. Under current jurisprudence, only acts of intentional discrimination are unconstitutional. Professor Lawrence argues that this view is unduly narrow and that "the law should be equally concerned when the mind's censor successfully disguises a socially repugnant wish like racism if that motive produces behavior that has a discriminatory result as injurious as if it flowed from a consciously held motive." *Id.* at 344. These issues are discussed further in Chapter 14.

2. How might unconscious racism play a role in a decision to site a hazardous waste facility or other unwanted land use? In *Bean v. Southwestern Waste Management Corp.*, 482 F. Supp. 673 (S.D. Tex. 1979), *aff'd without op.*, 782 F.2d 1038 (5th Cir. 1986), a case discussed in more detail in Chapter 14, plaintiffs alleged that the siting of a solid waste facility in a minority community in Houston was part of a pattern of racially discriminatory sitings by the Texas Department of Health (TDH). In rejecting plaintiffs' request for an injunction, the trial court noted:

> It simply does not make sense to put a solid waste site so close to a high school, particularly one with no air conditioning. Nor does it make sense to put the land site so close to a residential neighborhood. But I am not TDH and for all I know, TDH may regularly approve of solid waste sites located near schools and residential areas, as illogical as that may seem.... At this juncture, the decision of TDH seems to have been insensitive and illogical. Sitting as the hearing examiner for TDH, based upon the evidence adduced, this Court would have denied the permit. But this Court has a different role to play, and that is to determine whether the plaintiffs have established a substantial likelihood of proving that TDH's decision to issue the permit was motivated by purposeful discrimination.... [The Court found plaintiffs had not made this showing.]

Id. at 679–681. Do you think that TDH's decision, described by the judge as "insensitive and illogical," might have resulted from unconscious racism? Would it be appropriate for a judge to somehow take into consideration the phenomenon of unconscious racism?

3. One of the more highly charged issues surrounding the environmental justice movement is the claim that environmental racism underlies disproportionate environmental outcomes. The term environmental racism reportedly was coined by Rev. Dr. Benjamin Chavis in 1987, as he was preparing to publicly present the findings of the United Church

of Christ study on toxic waste sites and race (discussed in Chapter 2). Should the term be used to describe practices that unintentionally disadvantage groups based on race? Professor Richard Lazarus notes that Chavis' statement deliberately eschews the more neutral rhetoric of equity in favor of the far more volatile claim of racism, and that as a result "has had a transforming effect on environmental law. If environmental justice had not been so cast in terms of race, it is quite doubtful that the movement would have enjoyed such a strong political half-life." Richard J. Lazarus, *"Environmental Racism! That's What It Is."*, 2000 U. Ill. L. Rev. 255, 259 (2000). Do you agree?

4. All of the theories of causation described in this chapter are discussed and debated as competing—but also complementary—theories for the disparities examined in Chapter 2. For example, recall that empirical studies that control for both race and class have often found that race, not class, is the more significant predictor of location near a polluting or risk-producing activity. Given the above material, what do you think is the relative role in explaining disparities of the following: our discriminatory history of land use, the current structure of land use and environmental laws, market forces, economics, sociopolitical factors, and race?

Chapter 4

American Indians and Environmental Justice

A. Introduction

1. An Introductory Note

American Indian communities share many of the environmental burdens of other communities of color. However, environmental justice issues in Indian country take on a character special to Native American tribes. As attorney and Indian law scholar Dean Suagee explains:

> Many of the differences between tribes and other EJ communities can be seen as implications of the legal status of Indian tribes under federal law. Tribes have [a] legal right to be different. They have [a legal] right to be culturally distinct from the larger American society, and they have the collective right of tribal self-government within their reservations, as sovereigns that are distinct from the states. One of the basic lessons of the history of federal policies for relations with Indian tribes is that the right of tribal self-government is critical for the survival of tribes as distinct cultures....

> In addition to [the] differences resulting from their legal status, tribal communities also differ from other EJ communities in ways that reflect their cultural ties to the environment. Tribal cultural practices and religious beliefs are rooted in the Earth and woven into the web of life. Tribal members use wildlife and plants and other natural resources in ways that are different from other ethnic groups that exist within the American society. They use places in the natural world for religious and cultural activities, and their oral traditions include stories about these places. Like other cultures, tribal cultures are dynamic, and most Indian people do not live the way their ancestors did, but traditional cultural and religious beliefs and practices are still important components of the identities of contemporary Indian people.... While it is true that some immigrant minority populations have roots in similar cultural traditions from other parts of the world, it is also true that American Indian tribal cultures are indigenous to the United States with cultural roots in this land, and this is a significant difference from other minorities.

Dean B. Suagee, *Dimensions of Environmental Justice in Indian Country and Native Alaska,* Second National People of Color Environmental Leadership Summit Resource Paper Series (2002).

This chapter examines several important environmental justice issues in Indian country, although it is by no means exhaustive. The introductory section provides some background for considering these issues, highlighting the ways in which, as Mr. Suagee points out, environmental justice in the tribal context is "different." Section B considers the issues that arise when tribes exercise their governmental regulatory authority over lands and resources within their jurisdiction. Section C explores efforts by American Indian people to influence decisions that are made by non-tribal entities but that nonetheless often have a profound impact on Native peoples' rights, resources, and lifeways.

Pathfinder on American Indians and Environmental Justice

Comprehensive background on Indian law is provided in Felix S. Cohen's Handbook of Federal Indian Law (Nell Jessup Newton et al., eds., 2005). A discussion specific to some environmental issues can be found in the treatise William H. Rodgers, Jr., Environmental Law in Indian Country (2005). A concise discussion of governmental authority of Indian tribes to manage environmental matters within their jurisdiction can be found in Judith V. Royster, *Native American Law, in* The Law of Environmental Justice: Theories and Procedures to Address Disproportionate Risks 199 (Michael B. Gerrard & Sheila R. Foster, eds., 2d ed. 2008). A more comprehensive discussion of this authority and of tribal governments' role in securing environmental justice in Indian Country can be found in James M. Grijalva, Closing the Circle: Environmental Justice in Indian Country (2008). Some key federal documents include the Executive Order on Indian Sacred Sites, Exec. Order No. 13,007, 61 Fed. Reg. 26,771 (May 29, 1996); and the Executive Order on Consultation and Coordination With Indian Tribal Governments, Exec. Order No. 13,175, 65 Fed. Reg. 67,249 (Nov. 9, 2000).

In addition to the sources excerpted in this chapter, other articles on environmental justice in Indian country include Dean B. Suagee, *Turtle's War Party: An Indian Allegory on Environmental Justice,* 9 J. Envtl. L. & Litig. 461 (1994); John P. LaVelle, *Achieving Environmental Justice by Restoring the Great Grasslands and Returning the Sacred Black Hills to the Great Sioux Nation,* 5 Great Plains Nat. Resources J. 40 (2001); Jana L. Walker et al., *A Closer Look at Environmental Injustice in Indian Country,* 1 Seattle J. for Soc. Just. 379 (2002); and Michael S. Houdyshell, *Environmental Injustice: The Need for a New Vision of Indian Environmental Justice,* 10 Great Plains Nat. Resources J. 1 (2006). A host of information about environmental issues facing American Indians and local campaigns can be found on the website of the Indigenous Environmental Network, a national grassroots network of indigenous groups working on environmental issues *available at* http://www.ienearth.org/.

2. Historical Background

An understanding of environmental justice in the tribal context must begin with an appreciation of the historical background that has shaped the contemporary circumstances of indigenous peoples on this continent and given rise to tribes' unique political and legal status. To this end, Professor Judith Royster provides a primer on some of the foundational aspects of federal Indian law.

Judith V. Royster, Native American Law

The Law of Environmental Justice: Theories and Procedures to
Address Disproportionate Risks 199
(Michael B. Gerrard and Sheila R. Foster, eds., 2d ed. 2008)

Indian tribes are sovereign governments, exercising powers of self-government over both their citizens and their territories. Tribal sovereignty predates the U.S. Constitution and is not derived from the federal government or the states....

Nonetheless, Native American tribes do not have the full sovereignty accorded to nation-states at international law. Instead, tribes are "domestic dependent nations," subject to the authority and jurisdiction of the federal government.... Today, the U.S. Supreme Court maintains that congressional power over Indian tribes is plenary.

Congress thus *may* alter tribal sovereign powers, if it chooses to do so.... Under the Indian law canons of construction, [both treaties and] federal statutes should be liberally construed in favor of Indian tribes, all ambiguities should be resolved in tribes' favor, and the instruments should be construed to preserve tribal property rights and sovereignty absent clear congressional intent to the contrary. Accordingly, federal courts generally require either express language or clear expression of congressional intent before they will read statutes to abrogate Indian rights.

Moreover, congressional authority over Native American tribes is offset by the federal trust obligation. Commonly traced to Chief Justice John Marshall's guardian-ward analogy for federal-tribal relations, the trust doctrine likely evolved out of the protectorate status of tribes allied with the stronger United States. Although the trust doctrine was invoked as a source and justification of federal plenary power at the turn of the 20th century, by the 1970s the doctrine was instead a source of federal obligations to the Indian tribes. Today, Congress has the responsibility to protect Indian lands, funds, and resources that are held "in trust" by the federal government for the tribes or individual Indians. The trust obligation is not constitutionally based and therefore is not enforceable against the plenary power of Congress.... The trust relationship can, however, give rise to enforceable rights and duties on the part of the federal agencies....

* * *

The policy of the federal government vis-à-vis Indian tribes and their members has reflected quite different perspectives over the years, which have generally been divided by scholars into four eras. Up until the end of the 19th century, federal policy aimed to make way for European settlers and so focused on "removing" Indians to lands west of the Mississippi and establishing reservations in this territory. By the 1880s, however, the federal government worked along multiple fronts to break up the reservations, to destroy the tribes themselves, and to assimilate individual Indian people. In the early 1930s, the federal government briefly embraced a policy of supporting self-government, encouraging "reorganization" of tribal governments. This period lasted only about a decade, however; the federal government then reversed course again, and sought actively to "terminate" tribal governments and liquidate tribal assets. Finally, beginning in the 1970s, the federal government embarked on the current era, during which it has committed to promote tribal self-determination and observe a "government-to-government" relationship with tribes.

The federal government's relationship with Indians has also been significantly shaped by treaties signed with the United States. By means of these treaties, Indian peoples ceded vast amounts of their aboriginal lands to the U.S., but reserved certain lands and also certain rights on those lands outside the reservation borders, including rights to hunt, fish, and access water and other resources. These treaties also sometimes secured affirmative obligations from the U.S. government to provide various services or otherwise ensure the well-being of Indian people. In many instances, however, these treaty promises were quickly broken, as the U.S. looked to pave the way for the expansionist ambitions of its non-Native citizens. *See, e.g.,* LaVelle, *supra;* JOSEPH C. DUPRIS ET AL., THE SI'LAILO WAY: INDIANS, SALMON, AND LAW ON THE COLUMBIA RIVER (2006).

As tribes today work—in an exercise of self-determination—to protect their rights and resources, their labors must be viewed against this historical backdrop and within the resulting political and legal framework. And although the U.S. has now formally disclaimed its earlier policies, the years of efforts to address the "Indian problem" by terminating tribal governments and assimilating Indian people have left deep and lasting scars. Among the historical affronts with lasting impacts on tribes' current efforts to rehabilitate their lands and protect their culturally important resources are those stemming from the relentless political control exerted by the Bureau of Indian Affairs (BIA) over life on the reservations. Although tribes were theoretically recognized to be sovereign governments, all manner of decisions regarding the management of reservation lands and resources were, in practice, made by the BIA. As well, "the BIA and the churches ran a concerted campaign to suppress tribal religions and traditions and 'Christianize' Native Americans. Indian language, dress, and ceremonies all were labeled backward and uncivilized...." CHARLES WILKINSON, BLOOD STRUGGLE: THE RISE OF MODERN INDIAN NATIONS xii (2005). Tribes, however, worked to confront these multi-faceted assaults:

> Indian leaders responded and by the mid-1960s had set daunting goals: Reverse the termination policy; break the BIA's paternalistic hold and reestablish tribes as sovereign governments within reservation territory; enforce treaty rights to land, water, and hunting and fishing; and at once achieve economic progress and preserve ancient traditions in a technological age. This modern tribal sovereignty movement amounted to a last stand for Native people. As Vine Deloria, Jr., put it, "If we lose this one, there won't be another."

WILKINSON, *supra,* at xiii.

The legacy of the bleak times remains, however. As a result, many Native Americans suffer conditions of poverty, vulnerability and lack of capacity similar to those that exist in other environmental justice communities. For example, according to the most recent census data, approximately 1 out of every 4 American Indians and Alaska Natives (AI/ANs) lives below the poverty level (compared with about 1 of every 10 non-Hispanic Whites). U.S. CENSUS BUREAU, THE AMERICAN COMMUNITY—AMERICAN INDIANS AND ALASKA NATIVES: 2004, 3 (May, 2007). AI/ANs have a higher mortality rate than whites at every stage of life. HENRY J. KAISER FAMILY FOUNDATION, AMERICAN INDIANS AND ALASKA NATIVES: HEALTH COVERAGE AND ACCESS TO HEALTH CARE (Feb. 2004) . Cancer rates among AI/ANs have been increasing in the past twenty years. Notably, AI/ANs continue to have the poorest survival rate from "all cancers combined" of any other racial group. INTERCULTURAL CANCER COUNCIL, AMERICAN INDIANS/ALASKA NATIVES & CANCER 2 (undated report). A particular threat comes from diabetes. According to the Centers for Disease Control and Prevention, "[d]iabetes affects American Indians/Alaska Natives ... disproportionately compared with other racial/ethnic populations and has been increasing in prevalence in AI/AN populations during the last 16 years.... Overall, the age-specific prevalence of diagnosed diabetes was two to three times higher for AI/AN adults than for U.S. adults." Ctrs. for Disease Control and Prevention, *Health Disparities Experienced by American Indians and Alaska Natives,* 52 MORBIDITY & MORTALITY WEEKLY REPORT 702

(2003). The prevalence of diabetes, importantly, has been traced to the depletion, contamination, and lack of availability of traditional foods. *See, e.g.*, Kari Marie Norgaard, The Effects of Altered Diet on the Health of the Karuk People: A Preliminary Report (2004). Additionally, many in the AI/AN community lack adequate health care. "[M]ore than one-third (35%) of AI/ANs are uninsured and the problem is worse among low-income AI/AN people.... Although IHS [the Indian Health Service] is a resource for some of the AI/AN population, its reach is limited. Just under half of uninsured AI/ANs identify IHS as a source of coverage and care." Kaiser Family Foundation, *supra*, at 1.

While these metrics of health and well-being indicate disparities that are similar to those describing other communities of color or low-income populations, the dimensions of environmental justice for Native peoples may also include impacts that stem from their particular relationship to their traditional lands and resources. For example, Indians' "subsistence" use of resources refers not merely to a certain level of dietary intake but also an entire way of life that includes spiritual, social, and ceremonial components. As a consequence, when the resources on which Indian people depend are degraded, they will experience adverse impacts along multiple and inter-related axes — impacts that, in some cases, simply will not be felt by those who, for example, eat a lot of fish for purely economic reasons.

3. Situating American Indian People within the Environmental Justice Movement

How do American Indians' particular concerns, claims, and responses fit under the umbrella of "environmental justice?" As the next two excerpts illustrate, environmental justice in this context raises a unique set of issues.

Robert A. Williams, Jr., Large Binocular Telescopes, Red Squirrel Piñatas, and Apache Sacred Mountains: Decolonizing Environmental Law in a Multicultural World
96 West Virginia Law Review 1133 (1994)

Introduction

For two years, as Director of the Office of Indian Programs at the University of Arizona, I was involved on a near-daily basis with what has come to be known throughout the southwestern United States, and in other parts of the country and world, as the Mt. Graham controversy. The controversy centers around the efforts of the University of Arizona, together with a consortium of foreign astronomers from the Vatican, the Max Planck Institute in Germany, and Arcetri astrophysical observatory of Florence, Italy, to build an astronomical observatory on the peaks of Mt. Graham in southeastern Arizona. Because of my personal involvement, I cannot claim a detached neutrality in my recitation of the facts, or for my very tentative legal-cultural analysis of the controversy. But I do believe that as a minor bit-player in this multi-layered, multicultural drama involving large binocular telescopes, red squirrel piñatas, and Apache sacred mountains, I gained some valuable first-hand knowledge of how our environmental law has been colonized by a perverse system of values which is antithetical to achieving environmental justice for American Indian peoples....

One point which I want to develop in this essay is that any efforts aimed at decolonizing our environmental law must first identify and confront this perverse value system. As I attempt to illustrate, American Indian peoples possess their own unique visions of environmental justice which are capable of inaugurating this decolonization process. The values animating these American Indian visions are typically reinforced throughout tribal culture by myths and narratives which seek to invoke our imaginative capacities to see the social, physical, and spiritual worlds we inhabit as connected and interdependent....

As the Mt. Graham controversy demonstrates, however, the perverse system of values which has colonized our environmental law subjects these Indian visions of environmental justice to a political process, which presents these myths and narratives in a simplified and pejorative way. Indian resistance to the threats posed to our social, physical, and spiritual world by our environmental law are dismissed as attributable to "religious, magical, fanatical behavior." ...

A Layer Cake of Lifezones

... [T]he southernmost forest of spruce and fir in North America grows on Mt.Graham's peaks, and the ecological diversity of the mountain marks it as one of the truly unique environmental resources on the continent. It is reputed as the only mountain range to stack five of the seven major ecosystems of North America in one place.... But it is at Mt. Graham's summit, where you find a boreal zone of virgin spruce-fir forest standing yet untouched by the Forest Service's devouring lessees, that it becomes clear what makes this mountain worth fighting for. Wild nature still controls the desert sky-island at the top of Mt. Graham. Mountain lions and black bears roam freely atop the mountain's peaks. The Mexican Spotted Owl and goshawk, two gravely threatened species in the southwest, are found here as well....

The Universe is Expanding Constantly

... At least eighteen species and subspecies of plants and animals are reputed to be found nowhere else but on Mt. Graham's sky-island peaks. Among the creatures unique to the mountain is the appropriately named Mt. Graham Red Squirrel, a genetic variant of the North American red squirrel. This small, innocuous-seeming rodent occupies a crucial niche in the connective links that determine the health of the mountain's unique set of ecosystems....

In the mid-1980s, an international consortium led by the University of Arizona had first proposed construction of 13 telescopes, support facilities, and an access road on Mt. Graham's peaks. The proposal drew protests from a number of environmental groups, forcing the Forest Service in 1985 to begin the Environmental Impact Statement (EIS) process under the National Environmental Protection Act (NEPA) for the project.

The draft Environmental Impact Statement that the agency released the following year identified a "preferred alternative" in which only five telescopes would be constructed on High Peak, one of the various peaks of Mt. Graham. Meanwhile, in 1987, the U.S. Fish and Wildlife Service listed the Mt. Graham Red Squirrel as endangered. This action, not wholly unexpected, required the Forest Service to initiate "formal consultation" [under the Endangered Species Act, (ESA)] with the Fish and Wildlife Service regarding the suitability of an astrophysical complex on Mt. Graham given the endangered status of the red squirrel.... The Fish and Wildlife Service then issued a Biological Opinion in 1988, which found that "establishment of the seven telescope observatory on Emerald and High Peaks is likely to jeopardize the continued existence of the endangered red squirrel because this plan significantly increases the existing jeopardy status of this squirrel." ...

Given the language of Section 7 of the ESA that forbids federal agencies from taking action "likely to jeopardize" or endanger species, and a federal agency's biological opinion that the university's telescopes would "likely jeopardize the continued existence" of the Mt. Graham Red Squirrel, the university recognized that its project could be interminably delayed by legal and political challenges from environmentalists, and perhaps even killed....

A new strategy was developed to conquer Mt. Graham — simply exempt the entire project from NEPA and the Endangered Species Act. This stroke of brilliance was legislated into law in 1988, when Congress passed the Arizona-Idaho Conservation Act. In Section VI of the Act, Congress essentially assumed the role the Forest Service would ordinarily have played and [selected the alternative] that permitted construction on Emerald Peak, the most vital portion of the red squirrel's habitat....

Barometer Functions

Even up to this point in the story, the symbology generated by the Mt. Graham controversy is irresistible to the cultural critic. Like the Northern Spotted Owl, which has pitted environmentalists against the logging industry of the Pacific Northwest, endangered species like the Mt. Graham Red Squirrel perform a valuable "barometer function" in alerting humans to environmental threats. Our modern environmental law, however, as is evidenced by the Mt. Graham controversy, has generally done a poor job of explaining the basic importance to us, as human beings connected to our ecosystems, of protecting endangered species. Using an endangered species such as the Mt. Graham Red Squirrel or the Northern Spotted Owl as a symbol of the need for preserving biological diversity and respecting its importance translates poorly in the public imagination.... In the press and even on the campus, the environmentalists involved in the Mt. Graham controversy were caricatured as groups of slightly unbalanced tree-huggers and wildly unbalanced eco-terrorists of the Earth First! variety, who preferred saving a sub-species of an otherwise ubiquitous rodent, as opposed to constructing a multi-million dollar astronomical observatory devoted to the highest causes of science. Given this symbology, the Mt. Graham Red Squirrel never had a chance of surviving unmolested in its mountain habitat....

Imaginative Capacities

... One reason for this connected series of failures, I suggest, is that we have allowed our environmental law to be colonized by a perverse system of values which unquestioningly relegates certain vital issues of public policy to the vagaries and corrupting influences of the political process. According to the assumptions of this system of values, some issues, like free speech, religious liberty, or bodily integrity, are regarded as too intimately connected to who and what we are as persons to submit them to the processes of politics as usual. But beyond this select set of highly valued core "human rights" which are declared off limits to majoritarian processes and popular prejudice, we allow various interest groups to fight it out. In other words, those things which, according to this system of values, are not regarded as fundamentally connected to who and what we are as human beings, like a mountain and the biological diversity which it sustains, are subject to a process where all values are up for grabs. We allow large monied interests, influence peddlers, public relations campaigns, back-room deal-making, self-interest parading as high civil-mindedness, elected officials pandering to public fears and stereotypes, and bureaucrats advancing their ideological agendas under cover of the cold and sterile calculus of cost-benefit analysis to determine the importance of a place like Mt. Graham to us as humans. The perversity of this system is that it places the values of free speech and expression beyond politics as usual, but subjects environmental values, which may be every bit as intimately connected to who and what we are as human beings in the world, to the same sordid realm in which marginal tax rates for millionaires and pork barrel construction projects are determined according to the public will. It should come as no surprise, therefore, that with rare exception, when environmental statutes and regulations—the stuff of our environmental law—are debated in Washington, we rarely hear talk of the human values that are protected when we promote environmental values. That is because the political process to which we have subjected our environmental law is incapable of creating the imaginative capacity within us to see this absolutely vital connection.

The Gaans' Emergence

The first stage of the Mt. Graham controversy came to a close in October of 1989, when the university was given the go-ahead by a federal district court to cut an access road to the proposed telescope site on the mountain....

It was during this same period that the Mt. Graham controversy entered its second stage, with the appearance of a group called the Apache Survival Coalition. The Coalition claimed that Mt. Graham was sacred according to traditional Apache spiritual and ritual beliefs because it was the home of the Gaans. The Gaans, as members of the Coalition explained, represented the elemental forces of the Universe according to traditional Apache belief. The Gaans had emerged from Mt. Graham many ages ago to give the original medicine to an Apache medicine person. After performing this service for the Apaches, the Gaans had then gone back into Mt. Graham to rest. The university's telescopes, it was declared, would not only destroy the ability of traditional Apaches to worship on the mountain and give thanks to the Gaans, but if the Gaans were now disturbed by the university's digging and blasting on the top of the mountain, there would be a great cosmic disturbance in the universe.

University officials, to say the least, were skeptical about the Gaans resting on Mt. Graham. It was the first they had ever heard about any Apache religious interests in the mountain. They grew even more skeptical when it was discovered that the non-profit corporation calling itself the Apache Survival Coalition had on its board of directors several of the most prominent non-Indian environmentalists who had been fighting the telescope project since its inception.

It was at this point in the Mt. Graham controversy that university officials called on the office which I directed at the time, the Office of Indian Programs (OIP), for "advice." OIP had, as a primary function, liaison relations with all of Arizona's tribes, so it was not unusual for the university to look to OIP in this situation. While I was somewhat uncomfortable with my role as cultural mediator between the university and the Apaches, I took the time to talk with Apache members of the Coalition, whom I found to be sincere and entirely convincing in stating their belief that the university telescopes should not be built on Mt. Graham. I talked with the non-Indian members of the Coalition as well, all of them self-proclaimed environmentalists. I found them as a group to be quite cynical in their passionately professed concerns for Indian religious values that would be affected by the university's telescopes atop the mountain. I asked one of them what he would do if an Apache Gaan appeared to him in a dream and told him to ritually sacrifice all of the red squirrels that could be found on the mountain. All he could say was that he would not answer "trick questions."

In the course of OIP's efforts to gather information to gain a clearer understanding of the Apache's religious claims, the anthropologist who had worked for the office for nearly two decades, Gordon Krutz, took a walk over to the Arizona State Museum, which is a part of the university and located on the campus. The OIP had been given a lead on some old field notes collected among the Apaches at San Carlos by Grenville Goodwin, a noted University of Arizona anthropologist during the 1920s and 30s.

Anthropologists are the brunt of many jokes and much criticism in Indian country. There is an old joke one hears told among Indians in Arizona that captures the exasperated sense of exploitation Indian peoples have often felt at the hands of anthropologists—the traditional Indian family living in an Arizona reservation includes a grandmother, her daughters, their husbands, their children, and a University of Arizona anthropologist on research leave.

What goes around comes around, in a manner of speaking, and given that anthropologists collected reams and reams of information on Indians in the southwest, if any documentary evidence existed that would convince university officials of the bona fide nature of the claims of the Apache members of the coalition, it would be found among the dusty notebooks of some long dead anthropologist.

Sure enough, right there in the Goodwin field notes recorded half a century ago, we found several Apaches retelling the story of the emergence of the Gaans from Mt. Graham. There were songs and chants about Mt. Graham as well; a wonderful story about a sacred white horse that lived on the mountain and much more about age-old Apache beliefs and connections to Mt. Graham.

The Goodwin field notes confirmed, virtually verbatim, what the Apache members of the Apache Survival Coalition were claiming about Mt. Graham—that the mountain was a sacred site for the Apaches, or at least some of the Apaches who remembered the old stories about the Mountain. Obviously, that part of the oral tradition identified in the Goodwin field notes as it related to Mt. Graham had survived among those Apache families whose members belonged to the Coalition. If the telescopes were built on Mt. Graham, the Gaans would be disturbed, and this would cause tremendous strife in the world according to their Apache vision of environmental justice.

A Prayer to Mt. Graham

It should come as little surprise to find out that Indian values and belief systems are not reflected in or accepted by our environmental law. The point that I have learned from working and talking with many Indian people is that this is precisely what is wrong with our environmental law.

In many Indian belief systems, you will find an intimate relation between the spiritual world, the physical world, and the social world. These three dimensions of human experience are all closely integrated in most Indian belief systems, an integration which is totally alien to our environmental law. Indians have many ways to imagine and act upon this intimate relation between the spiritual, physical, and social worlds, but all of them basically boil down to a deep and abiding reverence for the land that sustains the interconnected worlds of the tribe. Without the land, in other words, there is no tribe. That is why tribal land is sacred land, because it has been given by the Creator to sustain the tribe. That is why tribal values seek to cultivate an attitude of respect for the land and the resources it yields.

Thus, in Indian visions of environmental justice, all land is sacred, but that does not mean that tribal land should never be used by the people. It is a question of attitude—an attitude of respect. Whether land should be used or developed in a certain way depends on the peoples' needs. If a hazardous waste dump on the reservation can be located in an area which is not being utilized by the tribe, then that option will be considered, along with its impact down to the seventh generation of the tribe yet to come. If it is decided by the tribe that the land can be used in this way, this decision, if made with respect and humility, will be blessed by the Creator because the land is providing for the tribe. If it can provide jobs for people in a reservation economy that has eighty percent unemployment, then you use that land for that hazardous waste dump or at least you consider it. But if the hazardous waste dump is going to be put in a place where important spiritual, social, or physical values of the tribe are implicated, then the tribe doesn't even think about it. It's just not done. There is an attitude of deep and abiding respect for the land and the resources it yields.

It is difficult for environmentalists to deal with tribal governments who seriously consider siting hazardous waste dumps in their reserves and for scientists to deal with a group of Indians opposed to siting a telescope on top of a mountain because neither group is capable of understanding the Indian vision of environmental justice which underlies all land use planning decisions in a tribal community—whether or not a particular use of land will be good for the people physically, socially, and spiritually. The tribe's determination will turn on the nature of the people's connection to that land resource; a connection which Indian people can more easily visualize through sacred stories and myths like the story of the Gaans …

… [A]ccording to this Indian way of looking at Mt. Graham, you protect what a modern environmentalist might call the biodiversity of the mountain because it is that biodiversity which physically sustains you and the members of your tribe. It is a source of food and other forms of sustaining nourishment. It provides herbs and healing medicines. The Gaan story teaches that not only does Mt. Graham sustain you physically, but socially as well, because the sacred story of the Gaans connects the tribal community around a set of cohesive values which define tribal social life. The tribal society is sustained by the mountain's life-giving forces. Protecting Mt. Graham fulfills our obligations to the future generations which will constitute the tribal society. And the Gaan story also illuminates how the mountain sustains us spiritually, because those values represented by the story connect us to a transcendent vision of our place in the world. Mt. Graham is a powerful representation of the life-sustaining forces provided by the Creator. Trouble for the people will ensue if the mountain is not treated properly with respect and humility. The spiritual, the physical, and the social worlds are all integrated under this overarching vision of the Gaans emerging from Mt. Graham to give the medicine to the Apaches and returning to rest within the mountain, to be respectfully worshiped by the Apaches.

Our environmental law is simply incapable of reflecting the types of connection that the story of the Gaans on Mt. Graham can teach us. According to this Indian vision of environmental justice, if the mountain is threatened, the people are threatened, and the Gaans will emerge to wreak havoc on the world. The Gaans help the Apaches imagine their connection to the mountain and the importance of protecting that connection because Mt. Graham is a very special place. It is sacred because it sustains the Apaches spiritually, socially, and physically.

"Who Protects the Law from the Humans Then?" The Grandfather Asked

I remember talking to an Indian elder once about our environmental law and how it sought to protect environmental values. I pointed to our National Wilderness Act and how it defines a wilderness "as an area where the earth and its community of life are untrammeled by man, where man himself is a visitor who does not remain." The elder laughed at this language; "Suppose there's deer there in that wilderness area?", he asked, "Can I hunt there?" I answered, "No, Grandfather, the law protects that area from humans." He then asked me, "Can that law be changed?" "Yes, Grandfather," I said. And so he asked me right back, "Who protects the law from humans then?"

In Indian visions of environmental justice the idea that "the earth and its community of life should be "untrammeled," thus disconnected from humans, is seen as an odd concept. There are sacred places, which should be approached with reverence, and in some instances, only by those properly trained in the rituals of respect for such places. Humans, however, are generally not viewed as mere visitors. What I think that elder was trying to tell me about our environmental law was that humans are connected to the land, and a law that fails to recognize that connection will not likely be respected for long by humans. I wonder, though, whether the best way to protect them is to legislate their separateness from us into law. It is hard to respect what we do not feel connected to, whether it be a parent, our Creator, or a mountain wilderness.

I am not saying that we should not protect our wilderness. The elder's insight into the sense of disconnection with our world that our environmental law fails to remedy, and in some cases actually reenforces, has helped me to better contrast between American Indian visions of environmental justice and the vision embodied in our environmental law....

Conclusion: Religious, Magical, Fanatical Behavior

... For Indians, stories and narratives like the Gaan creation myth invoke the imaginative capacity to visualize the connections between the physical environment, the social welfare of the community, and the spiritual values that create the consensus in Indian communities as to whether a particular use of the environment is beneficial or harmful to the human community. For non-Indians, there are no stories and myths which can help us imagine why preserving biodiversity is something deeply connected to who and what we are in the world—only science, economic analysis, vaguely stated appeals to aesthetic sensibility, and symbols generated by the Endangered Species Act such as the red squirrel. None of these has proven capable of generating consensus in our society about the importance of environmental values such as biodiversity to the human community.

Our technological society has lost its sense of reliance on nature for survival, and therefore, we have lost our sense of respect for the world we inhabit. We have thus lost those stories and myths which once must have helped us see our connections to our own world. And so our environmental law has been impoverished of such metaphors as the Gaans on Mt. Graham. Indian resistance to siting a telescope on Mt. Graham seems like "religious, magical, fanatical behavior." The price we pay for maintaining our dying colonialism is to dismiss the decolonizing potential of these Indian visions of environmental justice. And until we do decolonize our environmental law, we always risk the danger of the Gaans reemerging from Mt. Graham to wreak havoc upon our world.

* * *

Notes and Questions

1. What does Professor Williams mean by the term "colonized" and how does that term apply to environmental law? Williams cites two substantive environmental laws, the Endangered Species Act and the Wilderness Act. Both of these are viewed as among the most potent of the federal environmental statutes; the ESA, in particular, is considered to come down decisively on the side of protecting species and the habitats on which they depend. Yet, Williams suggests limitations to the approach taken by each of these statutes. In what ways do these environmental laws fail to protect biodiversity or ecosystems? To what does he attribute the failures of environmental law? How, if Professor Williams is right, does one begin to decolonize these and other environmental laws?

2. Professor Williams is as unsparing in his criticism of the environmentalists who opposed the Mt. Graham telescopes as he is of the scientists, university administrators and politicians who pushed it forward. In a similar vein, Dean Suagee notes that many Indians view environmental groups with some suspicion. The primary reason for this, he argues, is that "many environmentalists, like most people in the dominant American society, just do not know much about basic principles of federal Indian law, such as the doctrine of retained sovereignty." Suagee, *Turtle's War Party, supra,* at 463. Worse, some environmental groups have opted to challenge tribes' governmental status or otherwise undermine tribal sovereignty in pursuit of particular agendas. Professor James Grijalva recounts such an instance in the context of the Campo Band's decision to site a landfill on tribal lands (this decision is also discussed by Professor Rebecca Tsosie in the excerpt in Section B, below): The San Diego chapter of the Sierra Club "follow[ed] a ragtag organization Backcountry Against Dumps in challenging Campo sovereignty even though the Band's landfill standards were more stringent than California's requirements." GRIJALVA, *supra,* at 198. (The national organization, note, criticized its San Diego chapter for its actions and for potentially "jeopardizing long-term chances for a healthy alliance." *Id*)

Dean B. Suagee, The Indian Country Environmental Justice Clinic: From Vision to Reality
23 Vermont Law Review 567 (1999)

[In this essay, I] examine[] the concept of environmental justice as it might be applied to Indian country. In my view the concept holds great potential for protecting communities of Indian country from environmental degradation and for helping the people of these communities to bring about healing where Mother Earth has been injured. This potential will not be realized by simply taking the concept of environmental justice from the context in which it arose and assuming that it fits in Indian country. Indian country is different....

The Concept of Environmental Justice in Indian Country

... Civil rights laws generally prohibit discriminatory treatment based on race, color, religion, sex, or national origin. Most people probably think that at least some of these classifications include Indians. Not surprisingly, a handful of decisions by federal courts have ruled that discriminatory treatment against Indians is prohibited, although the reasoning has varied. But the Supreme Court has held that, at least for certain purposes, being an Indian is not a racial classification, but rather a political classification. Being an Indian is primarily defined by being a member of a tribe that is recognized by the federal government. Some individuals who are Indian by ancestry are not members of federally recognized tribes, and many tribal members have a high degree of non-Indian ancestry. It is because of the relationship between the federal government and the tribes that it is constitutionally permissible for Congress to enact laws that treat Indians differently from any other group of American citizens.

Regardless of whether Indians fit within a protected class, in the context of Indian country, I think that the concept of environmental justice is not very useful unless it is broader than just the intersection of civil rights and environmental law. Instead, I think that in Indian country a vision of environmental justice must also include the tribal right of self-government. Unless the larger American society honors the tribal right of self-government, the word "justice" as applied to Indian communities simply does not have much meaning. This means that tribal governments must be involved in performing the full range of functions that governments are expected to do in protecting the environment: making the law, implementing the law, and resolving disputes....

Environmental protection in Indian country does raise some challenging questions, and some of these questions are too important to ignore even if they do not have easy answers. For example, is it fair for a tribe whose members comprise less than half the population of its reservation to set water quality standards for all surface waters within its reservation? Answering this question requires an acknowledgment that opening the reservation to settlement by non-Indians in the late nineteenth or early twentieth century was accomplished over the objections of tribal leaders and in violation of the promises made in a treaty half a century earlier, and that these actions were done with the intent of destroying the tribe. If we are really concerned with fairness, then we must consider not only the rights of non-Indians to representative government, but also the right of the tribe to continue to exist as a distinct culture. And we must recognize that the tribe's identity as a distinct culture is inextricably interwoven into the portion of its homeland that it reserved to itself in its treaty (or that was otherwise set aside for it)....

* * *

Notes and Questions

1. As Mr. Suagee observes, one cannot simply import a concept of environmental justice framed in another context and assume that it is appropriate for Indian country. In particular, environmental justice claims here are not framed primarily in terms of securing "the same" treatment for American Indian people as for non-Indian Americans. In fact, as the Supreme Court has recognized, under the Constitution, it may be appropriate to treat American Indians differently, because of their membership in tribes — unique political bodies with long-standing relationships to the federal government. *See* Morton v. Mancari, 417 U.S. 535 (1974); *see also,* Matthew L.M. Fletcher, *The Original Understanding of the Political Status of Indian Tribes,* 82 St. John's L. Rev. 153 (2008). As Professor James Grijalva explains:

> The government-to-government and fiduciary relationships between tribes and the United States alters the constitutional concept of equal protection that underlies environmental justice; while American Indian citizens of the United States are entitled to fair treatment like other people of color, their dual citizenship in Indian tribes allows for different legal treatment, a sort of "measured separatism," reflected in an entire title in the United States Code of federal laws devoted specifically and exclusively to Indians and Indian country.

Grijalva, *supra,* at 8.

2. Mr. Suagee concedes that there will be challenging issues that arise as tribes seek to secure protection of their lands and resources by enacting and implementing environmental laws, particularly where a tribe's regulatory efforts impact non-tribal members, for example, those living within the boundaries of an Indian reservation. Tribes are not unmindful of these challenges and are working to address them; some of these tribal efforts are discussed in Chapter 10.

3. Mr. Suagee joins other scholars of environmental justice in Indian country in emphasizing that, while it is useful to see the commonalities as between American Indians and other environmental justice communities, it is also necessary to appreciate the differences in the sources of and remedies for environmental injustice from the perspectives of these different groups. (Relatedly, these perspectives may differ from tribe to tribe,

and, perhaps, within a given tribe, depending on how its members organize themselves—a point illustrated by Professor Williams' discussion of aspects of the Mt. Graham controversy not excerpted above). As you consider each of the various environmental problems confronting American Indian people, think about which legal tools and theories might be enlisted by individuals or by tribes and notice whether these are the same as or different from those available to other groups.

4. Professor Grijalva echoes Mr. Suagee's observations, in this excerpt and the excerpt with which this chapter began, about the ways in which environmental justice for American Indians is different. Grijalva goes on to suggest particular reasons for and solutions to the environmental harms that burden Indian country:

> Indian tribes' status as sovereign governments under federal law and their strong cultural and spiritual connections with the natural environment uniquely distinguishes them from every other minority and low-income group affected by environmental justice. To be sure, citizens of America's tribal nations often face a variety of disproportionately high health and environmental risks from multiple pollution sources just as members of other groups do. Yet, the existence of such risks may derive more from jurisdictional uncertainties hampering effective regulatory control than unfair program implementation [by federal and state agencies], and their solution may lie in tribes' inherent powers over their territories.

GRIJALVA, *supra*, at 4. The next section considers tribes' efforts, in their capacity as governmental regulators, to address environmental injustice in Indian country.

B. Tribes as Environmental Regulators

Indian tribes own approximately 56.6 million acres of land in the lower forty-eight states. Some of these lands are rich in hard rock minerals, timber, oil, natural gas, wildlife, and other natural resources. For instance, underlying Indian reservations is approximately half of all uranium deposits, one-third of all western low sulfur coal, and twenty percent of all known oil and natural gas reserves in the U.S. Mary Christina Wood, *Indian Land and the Promise of Native Sovereignty: The Trust Doctrine Revisited*, 1994 UTAH L. REV. 1471, 1481. The following excerpts consider the issues raised by tribes' status as governments, with management authority over tribal lands and resources.

Rebecca Tsosie, Tribal Environmental Policy in an Era of Self-Determination: The Role of Ethics, Economics and Traditional Ecological Knowledge
21 Vermont Law Review 225 (1996)

As Indian nations assume greater responsibility for managing tribal lands under the rubrics of tribal sovereignty and the federal self-determination policy, they are able to exercise more autonomy over environmental decision-making. That decision-making process, however, raises significant legal issues, ethical conflicts, and economic considerations.... [T]ribal environmental policy must be responsive to the interacting forces of traditional ecological knowledge, western science, economics, and tribal systems of ethics....

Tribal Environmental Authority in the Era of Self-Determination

... In 1970, President Richard Nixon called for a new federal policy of self-determination for American Indians. The self-determination policy represented a welcome change from the previous federal policy of "termination," which sought to abolish the federal trustee-ship over Indian tribes, dismantle the reservations, and end the Indian tribes' unique status as "domestic, dependent nations." The self-determination policy, intended to "strengthen the Indian's sense of autonomy without threatening his sense of community," encouraged tribes to assume control over many of the federal programs being administered on the reservation....

The federal policy of self-determination has also encouraged tribes to consolidate their land bases and exercise control over their natural resources, thereby reversing earlier federal policies that placed control over land and resources with the Bureau of Indian Affairs, often to the clear detriment of the tribes. These newer policies are significant because natural resource development has long been a predominant means of economic development on many reservations. In particular, the extractive industries, such as coal, uranium, oil, and gas, have played a major role in reservation economic development. Along with their fiscal contributions, however, the extractive industries have brought mining, milling, and smelting operations to Indian lands, causing pollution of reservation lands, waters, and air passages....

Environmental conditions on the reservation are therefore subject to a dual legal structure of federal and tribal law, providing added complexity to the notion of "environmental self-determination." Although tribal values and norms regarding environmental use should serve as the basis for tribal environmental policy under the principle of "self-determination," tribal policy is in fact heavily impacted by the values and norms of Anglo-American society, embodied in federal environmental law and policy....

The Role of Indigenous Land Ethics in Guiding Tribal Environmental Law and Policy

The diversity among American Indian people makes defining an "indigenous land ethic" somewhat difficult. Nevertheless, the similarities among indigenous world views regarding the environment cannot be discounted....

Traditional Indigenous Environmental Ethics: Finding the Common Ground

"[I]ndigenous" people ... generally refers to the "original inhabitants of traditional lands" who maintain their traditional values, culture, and way of life. Those collective values and ways of life are encompassed within the notion of "traditional ecological knowledge," which is "the culturally and spiritually based way in which indigenous peoples relate to their ecosystems." Thus, the concept of traditional ecological knowledge comprises both indigenous systems of environmental ethics and the group's scientific knowledge about environmental use that has resulted from generations of interaction.... Many of these principles, such as the concept of caring for the land for the benefit of future generations, have parallels among other Native American peoples throughout Canada and the United States. The similarities among American Indian environmental perspectives may stem from the fact that virtually all traditional Indian cultures had "land-based" rather than "industrial" or "market" economies.... A central feature of many indigenous world views is found in the spiritual relationship that Native American peoples appear to have with the environment....

Professor Ronald Trosper has drawn on several tribal traditions to construct a model of "traditional Indian world views" premised on four basic principles: "community," "connectedness," "the seventh generation," and "humility." ... Trosper's model of traditional world views, as affirmed by other scholarship, has several important aspects: a perception of the earth as an animate being; a belief that humans are in a kinship system with other living things; a perception of the land as essential to the identity of the people; and a concept of reciprocity and balance that extends to relationships among humans, including future generations, and between humans and the natural world.

The Role of Indigenous Ethics in Guiding Tribal Environmental Policy

The influence of traditional ethics and environmental knowledge on contemporary tribal policy cannot be underestimated. Indeed, there are many examples of successful implementation of traditional ethics in contemporary tribal environmental management. However, there are also many examples of tribal policy built on what appear to be Anglo-American norms, particularly in the case of industries such as mining and waste disposal, which also serve non-Indian interests....

Incorporation of Traditional Values into Environmental Policy

Notably, there are several examples of indigenous communities successfully applying traditional norms and values to community development projects. For example, the Zuni Pueblo instituted a comprehensive agricultural project that restores community control over food production and implements traditional methods consistent with the Zuni's unique environment such as "field rooting" and "dry farming." Jim Enote, the director of the Zuni Conservation Project, describes the goals of the project as being based on traditional Zuni knowledge: "Reaching a modern vision of Zuni sustainability requires developing full partnerships with the Zuni people and promoting the status of Zuni values, traditional knowledge, and resource management practices." ...

The Confederated Salish and Kootenai Tribes of the Flathead Reservation in Montana have developed a comprehensive environmental regulatory and land use management scheme that rests heavily on traditional values. For example, the Salish and Kootenai Natural Resources Department developed the "Mission Mountains Tribal Wilderness Management Plan" ("Wilderness Plan") to prescribe how the Tribe will manage natural resources and human uses within the Wilderness. In the Plan's statement of policy, the Tribal Council acknowledges that:

> Wilderness has played a paramount role in shaping the character of the people and the culture of the Salish and Kootenai Tribes; it is the essence of traditional Indian religion and has served the Indian people of these Tribes as a place to hunt, as a place to gather medicinal herbs and roots, as a vision-seeking ground, as a sanctuary, and in countless other ways for thousands of years.

An important part of the Wilderness Plan is the preservation of cultural and historical resources. The Flathead Culture Committee was given a critical role in determining specific policies and actions to govern specific sites. In some cases this has resulted in barring public access to certain ceremonial and religious sites. The Flathead Culture Committee explains the importance of the Mission Mountains:

> Our elders have many stories to tell about experiences in the mountains in hunting, berry picking and about Indian people seeking their powers in the mountains. They have become for us, the descendants of Indians, sacred grounds. Grounds that should not be disturbed or marred. We realize the importance of these mountains to our elders, to ourselves, and for the perpetuation of our Indian culture because of these stories. They are lands where our people walked and lived. Lands and landmarks carved through the minds of our ancestors through

Coyote stories and actual experiences. Lands, landmarks, trees, mountain tops, crevices that we should look up to with respect.

A central purpose of the Wilderness Plan is to preserve the wilderness for future generations. As one tribal Committee noted: "These mountains belong to our children, and when our children grow old they will belong to their children. In this way and for this reason these mountains are sacred." The mountains are thus preserved for future generations out of a "reverence for the land, its community of life, and what it means to the Indian culture more than out of a need to enjoy the benefits of direct use." Other documents developed by the Confederated Tribes to regulate environmental and land use on the reservation similarly speak to preservation of the tribal homeland and to ensure that natural resources on the reservation "survive and inure to the benefit of future generations."

The Northern Cheyenne Tribe is [an] example of an Indian nation that has applied traditional norms both to overcome the detrimental impacts of previous federal policies and to set a more positive direction for future policies. The Northern Cheyenne Reservation sits over the Fort Union coal formation, which stretches from northern Colorado to Canada, and houses an estimated 5 billion tons of coal worth approximately $400 billion. A significant number of the Northern Cheyenne Tribe are committed to maintaining traditional values and have resisted efforts to strip-mine the vast coal reserves, even though tribal unemployment rates continue to hover at 50%. During the 1970s, the Bureau of Indian Affairs leased more than half of the Cheyenne Reservation in Montana for coal mining. The leases provided for minimal lease royalties (17 cents per ton) and had no environmental safeguards. The Northern Cheyenne Tribe formed a committee to study ways to void the leases. After the Tribe brought its first lawsuit, federal legislation canceling the leases was enacted in 1980. The Northern Cheyenne Tribe's resistance to coal mining provides a sharp contrast to the neighboring Crow Tribe which is heavily engaged in coal mining and has opposed the Northern Cheyenne Tribe's attempts to secure enhanced protection for air quality.

The Northern Cheyenne Tribe was the first Indian nation to petition the EPA under regulations to the Clean Air Act to redesignate the reservation air quality as "Class I," a class reserved for near-pristine air quality. This was an important step in mitigating the air quality impacts of the two power plants directly north of the Reservation at Colstrip, Montana. The need for pristine air quality was a means of perpetuating the Northern Cheyenne commitment to the holistic preservation of the Cheyenne "environment, culture, and religion." ...

Tribal Environmental Policy That Departs from Traditional Norms

There are several categories of land use that appear to be inconsistent with the traditional environmental norms that we have explored, including coal strip-mining, uranium mining, and siting solid, hazardous, or nuclear waste repositories on tribal land. Both the mining industry and the waste industry carry the potential of severe environmental degradation and, as a result, would appear to be diametrically opposed to traditional indigenous land ethics. Yet both industries have found homes on some Indian reservations. Why?

[T]o a large extent, all Indian nations have been subjected to successive federal policies which encouraged the exploitation of mineral resources on Indian lands. In the late nineteenth century and early twentieth century, Indian treaty lands were often removed from Indian ownership and trust status to facilitate mineral exploitation. For example, the Crow Reservation once encompassed 39 million acres, including vast stores of coal, oil, and natural gas. After several land cessions, the Crow Reservation now encompasses only 2.2 million acres, although the Tribe has reserved mineral rights in certain of the ceded lands. Other lands remained in tribal ownership but were leased out for mineral development by BIA officials convinced, as was Commissioner of Indian Affairs Cato Sells, that it is "an economic and social crime ... to permit thousands of acres of fertile land belonging to the Indians and capable of great industrial development to lie in unproductive idleness." ...

Without direct policy control over mineral development, Indian nations were exploited financially and their lands and people were subjected to severe environmental contamination. By the 1970s, the beginning of the era of "self-determination," Indian nations could only hope to control the damage by renegotiating lease terms that practically gave away their mineral resources and by seeking remediation for the environmental degradation....

[M]any tribal members continue to protest mining operations on reservation lands, contending that such industry dries up precious water supplies, pollutes water, and endangers the health of people and livestock. The mining companies, however, point to the economic benefits they have offered to tribal communities, including increased funding for education. Given these competing claims, tribal decisions on mining policy are not clearly "right" or "wrong." Nor can tribal governments be faulted for trying to maximize the gain from on-going resource development by renegotiating lease agreements. In many cases, after nearly a century of mineral exploitation, there was no realistic opportunity to go back to a pristine natural world that would enable a traditional land based economy to flourish. The traditional land bases had been badly eroded, open mines and mineral tailings were located throughout many reservations, and many tribal members were dependent upon jobs with the local mines....

The "Not in My Backyard" movement among urban environmentalists and concerned citizens and increasingly stringent state environmental regulations have promoted the recent trend of waste disposal companies to approach tribal governments. The quasi-sovereign trust status of Indian lands has long exempted them from many types of state regulation, and the remote locations of many reservations appeal to the waste industry....

[N]ot all tribes agree that the waste business imperils Indian lands and communities. The Salt River Pima-Maricopa Community in Arizona has opened a second phase of its solid-waste landfill, established in the early 1980s. The Campo Band in California is proceeding with its landfill project after a heated battle with local non-Indians who opposed the project. Interestingly, by 1993, all members of the Campo Band supported the waste project and its only opposition has been from non-Indian residents of the adjacent community. Why was the sentiment at Campo different from Dilkon, Rosebud, or the Los Coyotes Reservation, also located in Southern California, where tribal members finally rescinded the Tribal Council's approval of a waste facility?

Poverty is obviously a factor in Campo's decision, but it is a factor that Campo shares with the tribes that have defeated such proposals. In 1987, when Campo first started considering the landfill proposal, the tribal unemployment rate was 79%, and more than half of those who were employed earned less than $7,000 per year.... Another factor in Campo's decision was that the Tribe's relatively small, remote, and arid reservation offered no other realistic opportunities for economic development. In the late 1800s, the Tribe was removed from its arable traditional lands to an area that one BIA official at the time described as "so nearly worthless that a living by farming is out of the question." ...

[Another factor,] tribal sovereignty, raises different issues: that is, whether opposition by non-Indians is seen as an attack on the tribe's ability to engage in self-determination as a sovereign government. In the Campo case, non-Indian activists pressured state legislators to introduce legislation that would extend state regulation to waste facilities on Indian land, constituting a blatant attempt to intrude on tribal sovereignty. [Daniel] McGovern, [a former EPA official who has written about the Campo project], suggests that if tribal members perceive a threat to their sovereignty, they tend to unite against the off-reservation forces, even if that means supporting a decision that may be contrary to certain traditional norms about appropriate land use. Thus, the value of maintaining tribal sovereignty may prevail over the value of protecting the integrity of the land. In fact, the Campo landfill represents some risk of permanent groundwater contamination, and thus, potential loss of the ability to even live on the reservation. However, the risk to sovereignty appears to have been perceived as the more immediate threat....

Concluding Thoughts

... Tribal governments who depart from traditional norms to engage in nontraditional economic development are responding to a complex history and set of realities. As the above cases demonstrate, these departures may be caused by a lengthy history of competing values imposed by federal policy, by values formulated as a protective response to ensure the continuation of tribal sovereignty, by values stemming from economic dependency on earlier development decisions, and by the cultural loss that has become endemic to many reservations as a result of loss of traditional lands, resources, and a certain measure of sovereignty....

* * *

Notes and Questions

1. Professor Rebecca Tsosie recognizes that the diversity among American Indian peoples makes any definition of an "indigenous land ethic" difficult; still, she points to several "similarities among indigenous world views regarding the environment." How, based on what you can discern from the readings, are these traditional norms reflected in the specific examples of contemporary tribal environmental policies she sketches? In what ways do these differ from the norms reflected in the mainstream environmental laws with which you are familiar?

2. When tribes choose among development projects, Professor Tsosie suggests that such decisions must be viewed in light of the fact that tribes are "responding to a complex history and set of realities." Among other things, these decisions may be premised in part upon a perceived threat to sovereignty and self-determination. What implications flow from these observations? What happens when such decisions have effects beyond the boundaries of tribal land? Does this mean that non-Indian residents adjacent to tribal land must sustain environmental impacts in part to support the self-determination and sovereignty of the tribe? By what (or whose) standards should we resolve these issues?

3. Professor Tsosie notes that in some instances it is no longer possible for Indian tribes to resume or revitalize a land-based economy, often because of environmental degradation caused by past extractive uses promoted by federal government agencies. What are possible remedies in such a situation?

4. Tribes, as sovereigns, make numerous decisions that shape the surrounding environment. Tribes have for generations acted as manager of these resources, regulating their use in accordance with their particular systems of law and custom. For example, attorneys Joseph Dupris and Kathleen Hill and Professor Bill Rodgers have detailed the extensive history of Indian management efforts respecting salmon and the Columbia River

Basin in JOSEPH C. DUPRIS ET AL, THE SI'LAILO WAY: INDIANS, SALMON, AND LAW ON THE COLUMBIA RIVER (2006). Tribal governments continue to do so today, as Professor Tsosie describes. In their capacity as environmental managers, tribes may also elect to enter into the "cooperative federalism" system created by the various federal environmental laws (*see* Chapter 5). Under this system, tribal governments may assume the relevant regulatory authority for certain programs (e.g., those governing water quality under the Clean Water Act) in areas over which they have jurisdiction. The following two excerpts explore this arrangement, by which tribes may apply to EPA to seek "treatment in the same manner as a state" (TAS) for purposes of administering these environmental programs. The first excerpt describes the history of the TAS provisions, which are now included in many (but not all) federal environmental laws. This excerpt highlights some of the advantages for tribes that avail themselves of TAS status. The second excerpt echoes this point, while raising some of the challenges faced by tribes seeking to design tribal environmental programs within the federal framework.

James M. Grijalva, Closing the Circle: Environmental Justice in Indian Country
(2008)

[Although by the 1970s, federal policy favored tribal self-determination as a general matter, the major environmental statutes enacted at this time were silent with respect to tribal management authority over tribal territories. Yet these environmental statutes—statutes such as the Clean Air Act and the Clean Water Act—embraced a model of cooperative federalism. That is, while the federal government was to set minimum or default national standards, it would be up to the states to implement these standards or to impose more stringent standards within their boundaries. "EPA's missing local partner[s] in Indian country," however, were the tribes.]

Nonetheless, EPA embraced tribal self-determination in two program-specific contexts in the mid-1970s. The first was a 1974 Clean Air Act program EPA created to prevent significant deterioration of existing good air quality by imposing on certain new sources of air pollution permit conditions whose stringency depended on the affected area's air quality classification. EPA initially designated nearly all areas of the country Class II, but provided for redesignation to the more stringent Class I or the less stringent Class III. EPA recognized such classifications implicated local (and highly political) considerations, so it offered redesignation authority to states, federal land managers, and on Indian reservations, to tribes. Once approved, the tribal redesignation begat federally enforceable conditions imposed by EPA via permits for air pollution sources within and adjacent to reservations.

The Agency's second self-determination action concerned local implementation of the 1972 federal pesticides law. The law prohibited commercial application of registered pesticides except by certified persons. Congress provided for state certification, but did not say whether a state certificate was required or applicable to reservation applicators. EPA's 1975 rules required applicators on Indian reservations [to] obtain certification from tribes. Commercial applications done without tribal certification violated the pesticides law, exposing the applicator to federal enforcement sanctions.

The tribal roles EPA proffered in the air and pesticides programs were identical to those played by state governments. Tribes were subject to the same eligibility and operation requirements, and once approved by EPA as meeting federal standards, carried the same potential to influence environmentally harmful activities. Significantly, the pesticide role offered tribes direct regulatory authority over non-Indian actors on reservations. The air quality role was indirect in that EPA and not the tribe translated the tribal air classification into facility-specific conditions. But it too was significant: the federally enforceable conditions derived from tribal value judgments, and could be imposed on facilities outside tribal territories and thus clearly beyond the reach of tribal sovereignty....

Congress validated EPA's view shortly thereafter, codifying EPA's tribal air program role in 1977 amendments to the Clean Air Act and adopting EPA's tribal pesticide program role in 1978 amendments to the federal pesticides law....

Congress' casual adoption of the treatment-as-a-state approach was remarkable in its own right, but especially so given an impending legal battle over the first exercise of the tribal air program role EPA created in 1974. While Congress debated the 1977 Clean Air Act amendments, EPA was considering the nation's first application for redesignation to the more stringent Class I air quality, submitted by the Northern Cheyenne Tribe for its reservation in south central Montana. The State of Montana did not object, but a host of off-reservation energy and coal mining companies (as well as the neighboring coal-rich Crow Tribe) saw the potential for increased compliance costs and urged EPA's disapproval.

The companies overlooked the opportunity to lobby Congress, but the Tribe did not. It proposed a tribal treatment-as-a-state provision, which [was] incorporated nearly verbatim....

Congress' affirmation of EPA's 1974 tribal experiment was clear. EPA approved the [Northern Cheyenne] Tribe's application just days before the 1977 amendments were signed into law. Several years later, after a federal court rejected the companies' and the Crow Tribe's legal challenges [in Nance v. Environmental Protection Agency, 645 F.2d 701 (9th Cir.), *cert. denied sub nom* Crow Tribe of Indians v. U.S. Environmental Protection Agency, 454 U.S. 1081 (1981). Eds.], the redesignation did impact off-reservation industry. EPA forced the Montana Power Company to redesign its proposed coal-fired energy facility in Colstrip, Montana in order to protect air quality on the Northern Cheyenne reservation thirteen miles away. And the Crow Tribe, whose own reservation was immediately upwind of the Northern Cheyenne reservation, abandoned plans for a similar facility when feasibility studies predicted a nearly $300 million pollution control cost increase attributable to the Northern Cheyenne redesignation. Illuminated by this hindsight, EPA's and Congress' treatment-as-a-state approach represented unparalleled respect for tribal value judgments on reservation environmental quality.

* * *

Darren J. Ranco, Models of Tribal Environmental Regulation: In Pursuit of a Culturally Relevant Form of Tribal Sovereignty
56 The Federal Lawyer 46 (March/April 2009)

... I am concerned that the approaches to regulation currently available to tribes—driven by federal mandates and notions of environmental management—not only are potentially vulnerable to challenge and erosion but also do not allow for tribes to fully address their cultural needs as sovereign nations. This article aims to call attention to what many tribal lawyers and environmental managers already know—that we must be diligent defenders not only of tribes' legal and juridical control over environmental regulations but also the forms of this control.

Most contemporary environmental law in the United States is carried out through "cooperative environmental federalism," in which the states play a prominent role. Much of the history of relations between Indian tribes and the federal government has been shaped by conflicts between states and tribes—conflicts in which the tribes usually rely on the federal government to keep states from intruding into tribal affairs. As a general rule, states have no authority over tribes and tribal members within reservations, and state authority over individuals who are not members of the tribe can be pre-empted by operation of federal law. Several major environmental statutes have been amended to authorize tribes to be treated the way states are when it comes to environmental regulations. These amendments, which were enacted between 1986 and 1990, typically use the phrase "treatment as States" (TAS); in response to comments from tribes during the rule-making process, the Environmental Protection Agency (EPA) has restated this approach, labeling it "treatment in the same manner as a State."

The TAS approach affords a significant measure of respect for the status of tribes as sovereign nations and also implicitly recognizes the importance of the natural environment for the survival of tribal cultures, which are rooted in the natural world. Treating tribes like states has not proven to be sufficient, however, primarily because of unmet funding needs for tribal programs. Just as important, when the interests of non-Indians are affected, tribal authority can be challenged under a number of decisions issued by the U.S. Supreme Court over the last quarter-century. To date, the lower federal courts have sustained the EPA in its support for tribal programs, but no case has yet been decided by the U.S. Supreme Court. This situation presents a paradox to tribes: the more closely a tribal program resembles a federal or state program, the more likely it is to survive litigation; but the more a tribe tries to build a program that reflects its own cultural values, the greater the risk to its own tribal sovereignty, especially if the tribal approach is different from the approach adopted by the state or states that surround the tribal land.

During the 1990s, a number of American Indian nations began to seek TAS status for various purposes under the federal environmental laws. As of March 1998, the EPA had approved TAS status for at least one program proposed by 146 tribes, although most of these approvals have been for financial assistance for planning and the development of regulatory programs rather than for administration of EPA-approved regulatory programs. The statute in which tribes seeking TAS status for regulatory programs have been most involved has been the Clean Water Act; the water program in which there are the most TAS approvals is the Water Quality Standards (WQS) Program, in which, as of October 2006, 30 tribes have EPA-approved WQS in place....

With varying success, tribes have begun to use these programs to control pollution within reservations and, by developing tribally based standards, the tribes are seeking to force polluters in neighboring jurisdictions to control pollution sources that affect Indian lands. The ability of a tribe to set its own standards is critical, because such standards can adopt ceremonial and other culturally specific uses of resources. Many consider the ability to incorporate standards that include culturally specific uses of resources an important aspect of self-determination, sovereignty, and therefore tribal survival....

... In *Albuquerque v. Browner* [excerpted in Chapter 7. Eds.] tribal involvement with the EPA produced a success for tribal sovereignty, because the EPA tried to set aside as many potential jurisdictional questions as possible and relied on scientific evidence put forth by the tribe related to the creation of water quality standards that could have an impact on the city of Albuquerque. In *Albuquerque,* the EPA ignored competing private interests and offered the tribes the authority to establish "what will count as truth in the policy process." In an article published shortly after the decision, Allison Dussias underscored the somewhat radical and impressive nature of the EPA's approval of the tribe's reliance on indigenous knowledge and interests in formulating regulations; the author pointed out that "this is a great departure from the efforts of earlier federal government officials to eradicate the nature-based religious beliefs and practices of Native Americans."

Thus, it appears that tribes might fare relatively well in the realm of agency control—in particular EPA control—and *Albuquerque* and later cases reaffirm this conclusion. However, the logic determining that tribes could benefit from such a relationship with the EPA rests on two rather dangerous assumptions: that agencies will always decide in favor of tribes (especially acknowledging that agency policy can change with the change of a presidential administration), and that reviewing courts will always defer to agencies' decisions. Accepting the provision of TAS status and subjecting themselves to agency control might, in some instances, be beneficial to tribes—as demonstrated in the case of *Albuquerque*—but if the agency or courts were to rule against a tribe, it would be left totally entangled within the federal government with few protections. If this were to occur, all the benefits cited above that safeguard tribes under agency control would then serve the opposite function: placing tribes in a restricted situation with few tools with which to reassert their tribal autonomy.

As we have seen, *Albuquerque v. Browner* and the cases like it can be viewed as a success not only for the reasons discussed above but also from an environmental perspective: the court upheld tribal rules that blocked the city of Albuquerque from polluting the Rio Grande River, which flows through tribal lands. But the case can also be viewed as an example of U.S. government efforts to limit tribal sovereignty and thus prevent tribes from making meaningful authoritative decisions. The case might be deemed a failure by the larger standards of tribal self-determination:

- The tribe obtained permission to adopt standards under a clean water law and system that the tribe did not devise and could not change.
- The tribe's standards were subject to review by a U.S. agency.
- Only the agency that reviewed the standards could enforce them.

By making these tools available to the tribe, was the U.S. government really making a fundamental change in U.S.-tribal relations and creating a new opportunity for tribal self-government? As Taiaiake Alfred, Mohawk scholar, notes, "From the perspective of the state, marginal losses of control are the trade-off for the ultimate preservation of the framework of dominance."

Before examining the potential cultural dilemmas that tribes face in the TAS process, it is important to point out some of the difficulties tribes face when they participate in the cooperative federalism involved in U.S. environmental law. The case of *Albuquerque v. Browner* demonstrated that in order to gain treatment as a state in programs that come under the Clean Water Act, for example, the Pueblo of Isleta—as well as other tribes—must apply to the EPA for such status and submit evidence that (1) it is a tribe, as recognized by the secretary of the interior; (2) it has a functioning tribal government; and (3) it has the authority and capability to create effective water quality standards. Thus, in order to gain any authority over its water quality standards, the tribe was required to go through a tedious procedure to gain the approval and recognition of the federal government. Thus, when one considers what TAS status actually signifies and who can obtain it, these stipulations for gaining TAS status have serious implications for understanding whether the TAS amendments to the Clean Water Act are even significant. For example, in a case concerning the Flathead WQS, attorney Daniel I.S.J. Rey-Bear pointed out that "the dispute is not really about the technical content of those WQS themselves. Rather, this dispute concerns the scope of the underlying federally recognized tribal authority to promulgate those standards under the CWA's section 518(e) TAS provisions." Therefore, TAS status is one of those ironic situations that *appears* to augment the authority of tribes but, in fact, diminishes tribal sovereignty.

It seems obvious that the regulatory approaches embedded in the TAS process are tied to America's environmental regulatory culture and do not emerge from tribal ideals regarding the environment. That said, in the *Albuquerque* case, the Pueblo of Isleta was able to set standards based on ceremonial uses of the Rio Grande—and that was no small victory. Still, there are some serious challenges in using the TAS regulatory approach in a way that not only protects but also reflects tribal cultures and also shows how they are different from the dominant culture.

As a point of departure, the meaning of "different" in this context should be clarified. In his discussion of tribal courts in *Braid of Feathers,* Frank Pommersheim discussed what he calls the "dilemma of difference" for tribal courts. He pointed out that the courts run by tribal communities "do not exist solely to reproduce or replicate the dominant canon appearing in state and federal courts. If they did, the process of colonization would be complete...." Pommersheim, like many others, is concerned about the possibility of maintaining tribal differences through the use of quasi-autonomous structures within the contours of the United States. Within the context of environmental regulation, these differences quickly become issues that affect the relative health not just of tribal cultures but also of Indians themselves, who often bear an inordinate amount of environmental risk.

In addition, the "dilemma of difference" in this sense is also a problem of recognition. In a system of unequal power, cultural differences and concepts like justice or environmental management have to be understood as features that occur in a system in which differences are not usually desired or communicated. According to Pommersheim, in the American federalist system, the "federal record *evinces* a tolerance of similarity rather than dissimilarity," and this makes it difficult for tribal courts and governments to define spaces for cultural differences. Therefore, to be protective of tribal cultural differences, tribal sovereignty cannot just mean that tribes are just another partner in the federal system, the dominant culture must also recognize that tribal governments can form the basis of a different civic community and a different sense of the public good. This idea can be seen as dangerous to members of the dominant culture when non-Indians are subject to this different sense of the public good; for example, the U.S. Supreme Court has repeatedly shown that it is not comfortable allowing tribal police powers over non-Indian residents within reservations because these individuals are not full participants in the political process that takes place on Indian reservations. Moreover, states often see tribal sovereignty claims as threats to their own territorial sovereignty, as demonstrated by the numerous challenges to the legality of environmental programs that tribes propose or conduct.

Therefore, the basic challenge for tribal governments is to maintain "separateness" by holding on to a difference that is recognizable and acceptable to the dominant culture and its institutions as well as to tribal citizens within the minority culture.

* * *

Notes and Questions

1. As a general matter, tribal environmental regulatory authority in Indian country stems from two sources. "First, Indian tribes possess inherent powers to govern their territories. Although those powers may be limited by federal law in certain respects, tribes nonetheless retain substantial authority over matters affecting tribal health and welfare." Cohen, *supra,* at 774. Within this realm, tribes may enact tribal environmental codes and provide for enforcement through tribal agency proceedings and in tribal court. "Sec-

ond, Indian tribes may exercise powers authorized by Congress. In the environmental context, Congress has authorized tribes to assume primary regulatory authority, or primacy, for administering most federal environmental programs in Indian country." *Id.* That is, Congress has authorized tribes, upon application to EPA, to obtain TAS status. Recall, however, that as a consequence of the allotment era, land ownership in Indian country is a complicated matter and many parcels of land within the exterior boundaries of Indian reservations are now owned in fee simple by individuals who are not members of the tribe whose reservation surrounds these parcels. In recent decades, the U.S. Supreme Court has been increasingly concerned about tribal assertions of civil jurisdiction over non-members or on non-Indian lands (e.g., land owned by non-members.)

In order fully to appreciate the position of tribal governments seeking to exercise their environmental regulatory authority, one would need much more background than we are able to cover here. *See, e.g.,* JUDITH V. ROYSTER & MICHAEL C. BLUMM, NATIVE AMERICAN NATURAL RESOURCES LAW: CASES AND MATERIALS 193–297 (2d ed. 2008).

2. The EPA, for its part, has as a matter of policy taken the position that tribes should have the primary role in protecting their environments and has supported tribal authority under various specific programs since the 1970s, as Professor Grijalva points out. And EPA approval of a tribe's TAS status confers an important advantage, should others wish to challenge the tribe's regulatory authority. As pointed out by the authors of the leading treatise on Federal Indian Law:

> [M]any tribes prefer to regulate environmental matters in Indian country by administering federal statutory programs and standards. Because tribal regulation under federal statutes generally requires the approval of EPA, any challenges are directed to the federal administrative action rather than the tribal plans and standards. As a result, most federal judicial decisions addressing matters of tribal environmental regulation are decisions reviewing the action of the administrative agency, and therefore implicate the *Chevron* principle of deference to the agency in cases of statutory gaps or ambiguities.

COHEN, *supra,* at 777.

In *Montana v. U.S. Environmental Protection Agency,* 137 F.3d 1135 (9th Cir. 1998), for example, the EPA had approved the TAS application by the Confederated Salish and Kootenai Tribes to promulgate water quality standards for all sources within the boundaries of the Flathead Indian Reservation, regardless whether those sources were on land owned by members or non-members of the Tribes. Citing the "unitary" nature of the water resource and the fact that the pollutants in surface water are mobile, such that it would be difficult to separate impairment on non-Indian fee land from impairment of the tribal portions of the reservation, the EPA found that "the activities of the nonmembers posed such serious and substantial threats to Tribal health and welfare that Tribal regulation was essential." *Id.* at 1141. State and municipal entities who owned fee interests in lands within the boundaries of the Flathead reservation challenged the EPA regulations on which it based its approval of the Tribes' TAS status. The district court and, ultimately, the Ninth Circuit upheld the EPA's determination.

In fact, tribes asserting environmental regulatory authority and seeking TAS status have regularly been challenged; as noted above, however, these challenges are generally directed at EPA's actions approving tribes' applications for TAS status, as was the case in *Montana v. EPA.* For example, a neighboring municipality challenged the Isleta Pueblo's water quality standards in *City of Albuquerque v. Browner,* 97 F.3d 415 (10th Cir. 1996); this case is excerpted and discussed in Chapter 7. *See also* Wisconsin v. U.S. Envtl. Prot.

Agency, 266 F.3d 741 (7th Cir. 2001) (rejecting a challenge to EPA's grant of TAS status to Mole Lake Band of Lake Superior Chippewa Indians). These and other cases are discussed in William H. Rodgers, Jr., *Treatment as Tribe, Treatment as State: The Penobscot Indians and the Clean Water Act*, 55 ALA. L. REV. 815 (2004).

3. The number of tribes that have obtained TAS status for one or more programs has grown, even since the time of the figures available to Professor Ranco in the article excerpted above. According to EPA, as of September, 2008, some 45 tribes had WQS that had been approved by EPA. U.S. ENVTL. PROT. AGENCY, INDIAN TRIBAL APPROVALS FOR THE WATER QUALITY STANDARDS PROGRAM. With respect to air quality authority, according to EPA, "30 tribes have received eligibility determinations (TAS) under the Tribal Authority Rule [and] two tribes have been approved to implement TIPs to address air quality issues on their reservations, with several more under development." U.S. Envtl. Prot. Agency, Tribal Air: Basic Information (2009). Still, tribal advocates have criticized EPA for its failure to provide clear guidance on the requisites for obtaining approval; for the dearth of technical and financial assistance to tribal environmental programs (especially when compared to the years of such assistance that states have received); and for the slow pace of its review of tribal applications for TAS status. The Government Accountability Office (GAO) in 2005 faulted the EPA for the numerous delays in processing tribes' TAS applications. U.S. GOV'T ACCOUNTABILITY OFFICE, INDIAN TRIBES: EPA SHOULD REDUCE THE REVIEW TIME FOR TRIBAL REQUESTS TO MANAGE ENVIRONMENTAL PROGRAMS. In response the EPA, with tribal input, in 2008 adopted a new strategy for its evaluation of tribes' TAS applications, which is meant to address the deficiencies in its previous approach. U.S. ENVTL. PROT. AGENCY, AMERICAN INDIAN TRIBAL PORTAL: TREATMENT IN THE SAME MANNER AS A STATE. Finally, it should be noted that the process of obtaining TAS status can be onerous. For a tribal perspective on this process, see, e.g., Jill Elise Grant, *The Navajo Nation EPA's Experience with "Treatment as a State" and Primacy*, 21 NAT. RES. & ENVT. 9 (Winter, 2007).

4. Professor Ranco points to a crucial paradox facing tribes as they contemplate seeking TAS status: "the more closely a tribal program resembles a federal or state program, the more likely it is to survive litigation; the more a tribe tries to build a program that reflects its own cultural values, the greater the risk to tribal sovereignty …." Ranco, *supra*, at 46. Professor James Grijalva similarly recognizes that "the racist and logically indefensible origins of federal Indian law cast indisputable questions on its contemporary legitimacy," and notes that, as a practical matter, "American Indian tribes self-determine their destinies only to the extent of and within the confines established by federal tolerance or indifference." GRIJALVA, *supra*, at 199. Still, he notes that the TAS approach "offers concrete practical benefits, in particular the prospect of limiting tribal health risks and environmental damage caused by harmful activities outside Indian country." *Id*. And, he offers: "[P]resumably tribes who elect [the TAS] path have either found it consistent with their traditional values or have developed means of making it consistent." *Id*. In your view, does the TAS model retain too much of its racist and colonialist underpinnings for it ever to provide a structure within which tribes can enact their own visions of environmental protection? To use Professor Williams' term, is there any hope for a "decolonized" environmental law? If a tribe makes the pragmatic decision to avail itself of the concrete benefits of the TAS structure that Professor Grijalva cites—consider, for example, that the Isleta Pueblo's water quality standards, which were set at a level stringent enough to protect its ceremonial uses of the Rio Grande river, were upheld within this structure—does it inevitably sacrifice a measure of self-determination? Is the answer to this question likely to be different for different tribes? How, if you were a tribal attorney, would you assist your client in navigating this fraught terrain?

5. When tribes act as environmental regulators, additional issues come to the surface. As Professor Ranco and Mr. Dean Suagee explain:

> A difficult challenge for tribal environmental programs is how to provide for the fair treatment of people subject to tribal regulatory authority who have no right to participate in tribal electoral and/or other political processes. If the United States lives up to its promise that tribes have a right to measured separatism, and if the United States acknowledges that the survival of tribes as distinct cultures depends on their being able to manage their environments, then tribes should generally be recognized as having environmental regulatory authority over all persons and all lands within their reservation boundaries. This, of course, means that many Americans will find themselves being governed, in some important ways, by American Indians. Will white America accept this? What, if anything, can tribal governments do to make this acceptable—what civic arrangements can be fashioned to enable peaceful coexistence within reservations among people who belong to tribal cultures and people of mainstream America?

Darren Ranco & Dean B. Suagee, *Tribal Sovereignty and the Problem of Difference in Environmental Regulation: Observations on "Measured Separatism" in Indian Country*, 39 ANTIPODE 691, 700 (2007). These questions are taken up at greater length in Chapter 10, which considers tribal governments' efforts to address non-members' claims for meaningful participation and other issues of procedural justice.

6. Many observers share the perspective that environmental justice for American Indian peoples cannot be fully realized so long as the vestiges of colonialism remain intact and these peoples cannot be the custodians of their lands and resources. As such, these observers have argued that efforts to increase tribal management of tribal homelands are the surest path toward environmental justice, even as these efforts are undertaken in the context of a legal and political system that is, at its root, colonialist. Given this current context, it is also the case that a host of decisions that affect Indian peoples' traditional homelands and culturally important resources are made by non-tribal governments. Tribes and non-governmental indigenous organizations have pointed out the adverse and unjust impacts of such decisions. The next section considers instances in which tribes and others have sought to influence the decisions of federal and other decision-makers that affect Indian resources and rights.

C. Protection of Resources and Rights

While tribal environmental managers exercise their authority over considerable lands and resources, the historical development of the United States means that many resources on which American Indian people historically depended—resources that remain important today—are managed primarily or entirely by non-tribal governments. In some cases, the rights to the relevant lands and resources were ceded to the U.S. via treaty or were transferred to the U.S. by other means. For example, the grasses and other plant materials that have traditionally been used by Indian basketweavers in what is now California may be located on non-tribally owned lands managed by the U.S. Forest Service or by the California Park Service. In other cases, the rights to the relevant resources were reserved by the tribes via treaty, even as the surrounding territory was ceded. For example, the tribes of the Pacific Northwest reserved the right to fish at their "usual and accustomed" places throughout the territory that they ceded to the U.S. by means of the Stevens treaties in 1855. These off-reservation places are today affected by the decisions of numerous federal and state agencies; in recent decades (and after judicial intervention), the fishery resource, at least in areas of the Pacific Northwest, is "co-managed" by the states and the tribes.

Additionally, since environmental contamination does not respect political boundaries, decisions made by non-tribal governments will nonetheless have impacts on reservation lands and resources. For example, a state may set water quality standards governing its lakes and rivers that are designed to ensure, among other things, that the fish these waters support are safe for human consumption. The state may, however, permit a level of contamination in the fish that presents an unacceptable risk to those tribal members who catch and consume (greater quantities of) fish from the same waters, e.g., downstream.

Indeed, the instances in which non-tribal governments' decisions may affect tribes' resources or rights are numerous. In addition to the example of state or federal water quality standards (discussed at greater length in Chapter 7), consider the federal air quality standards for mercury, which ultimately bioaccumulates in fish tissue, affecting the safety of fish caught both on- and off-reservation (also discussed in Chapter 7). Or consider federal decisions to license a hydroelectric dam that will imperil anadromous fish passage and survival and will cause upriver sacred sites to be flooded; or to approve a land swap that would enable a timber company to destroy an ancient tribal trail; or to prevent whale hunting in the name of conservation, irrespective of a tribe having reserved the right to whale by treaty. In each of these examples, American Indian people may be affected. The impacts, moreover, may not only be different in degree, but also different in kind, since they also mean a loss of traditional cultural practices. The Aroostook Band of Micmacs, for example, sought to make clear in its official comments to the EPA that a lenient rule governing mercury emissions from coal-fired utilities would mean unique losses to the tribe:

> Although many of our Tribal members continue to fish and consume fish despite [Maine's statewide] fish consumption advisory, there are many Tribal families that no longer engage in cultural practices associated with fishing, and are thus not passing these traditions on to new generations of Tribal members. The loss of our cultural ceremonies, language, and songs associated with fishing represents a significant impact on our Tribe, and results in permanent loss of the culture which defines our Tribe.

Letter from William W. Phillips, Tribal Chief, Aroostook Band of Micmacs, to U.S. Envtl. Prot. Agency (Apr. 30, 2004).

Given such stakes, tribes, as well as inter-tribal associations and non-governmental organizations of indigenous peoples, have sought to influence these non-tribal decisions by a variety of means. Tribes' governmental status, of course, places them in a unique position to affect such decisions, particularly those made by federal agencies. As mentioned above, the federal government is obligated to uphold the trust responsibility to tribes. Moreover, there are several executive orders that speak to federal agencies' obligations in this context. Among these is Executive Order 13,175, which commits federal agencies to interact with tribes in the context of a "government-to-government" relationship and directs these agencies to consult with tribes when their policies or regulations have tribal implications. Exec. Order No. 13,175, 65 Fed. Reg. 67,249 (Nov. 9, 2000). As in the case of other executive orders, however, Executive Order 13,175 explicitly states that it creates no enforceable rights. (Note that, as sovereign governments, tribes' claims to "consultation" are framed differently than the claim that might be advanced by a non-governmental entity, which is framed not in terms of "consultation" but, rather, "participation.") Additionally, several statutes provide a particular role for tribal governments to influence decisions made by non-tribal governments. The following excerpt, by a former tribal attorney and longtime practitioner in Indian country, canvasses some examples.

Michael P. O'Connell, Indian Tribes and Project Development Outside Indian Reservations
21 Natural Resources & Environment 54 (Winter 2007)

Indian tribes have become increasingly involved in project development outside Indian reservations....

NEPA

The National Environmental Policy Act (NEPA) promote[s] environmental quality by ensuring that federal agencies carefully consider information concerning significant environmental impacts of proposed actions before making decisions....

Proposed federal actions, including issuance of permits, for activities outside Indian reservations may affect human health and natural and cultural resources on Indian reservations. Federal actions may also affect tribal off-reservation treaty fishing, hunting, food gathering rights, and other tribal interests outside Indian reservations. As appropriate, the NEPA requires federal agencies to evaluate effects of proposed federal agency actions on such tribal interests. Correspondingly, the NEPA affords Indian tribes an opportunity to comment on proposed federal actions.

NHPA

The National Historic Preservation Act (NHPA) and implementing regulations adopted by the Advisory Council on Historic Preservation (Advisory Council) are binding on all federal agencies.... [Under Section 106,] the relevant agency official must consult on a government-to-government basis with any Indian tribe which attaches religious or cultural importance to a [traditional cultural property] TCP listed on, or eligible for, listing on the National Register that may be affected by an undertaking, regardless of location.

... The Advisory Council's regulations prescribe a rigorous consultation process. The responsible agency must make a reasonable good-faith effort to identify any Indian tribe that may attach religious or cultural importance to historic properties in the area of potential effects (APE) and invite such tribes to be consulting parties; gather information from such tribes which may assist in the identification of historic properties within the APE; notify such tribes of the agency's "no adverse effect" or "adverse effects" determination; consult with tribes on the assessment of potential adverse effects and measures to avoid, minimize, or mitigate any adverse effects; and notify consulting tribes, where applicable, of the action agency's decision to terminate the Section 106 process when there is a failure to resolve adverse effects.

A tribe's participation in these procedures is intended to, and can, have a powerful effect on an agency's decision whether and how to proceed with an "undertaking" outside an Indian reservation. In consideration of issues raised by a tribe, a federal agency could exercise discretion and impose conditions or other limitations on an undertaking not required by law.

A dramatic example of what can happen when these procedural steps are given short shrift is the Port Angeles Graving Dock Project, a major Washington State transportation project. Three years and more than $86 million into the Project, the Washington State Department of Transportation abandoned the Project site. By then, more than 300 Indian skeletal remains had been excavated and a world-class historic Indian village was being unearthed. An audit and legislative report prepared in the wake of this debacle found an inadequate and hurried site investigation and Section 106 consultation, compounded by decisions to move the Project footprint without reinitiating cultural resource surveys and the Section 106 consultation....

ESA

Section 7(a)(2) of the Endangered Species Act (ESA) directs each federal agency, in consultation with the U.S. Fish and Wildlife Service (FWS) or the National Marine Fisheries Service (NMFS), as appropriate, to ensure that any action authorized, funded, or carried out by that agency is not likely to jeopardize the continued existence of any listed endangered or threatened species or to destroy or adversely modify the critical habitat of such species.

In 1997, the Secretaries of the Interior and Commerce, on behalf of FWS and NMFS respectively, issued Secretarial Order 3206, American Indian Tribal Rights, Federal-Tribal Trust Responsibilities, and the Endangered Species Act (Secretarial Order). The purpose of the Secretarial Order was to clarify responsibilities of the Departments when their ESA actions "affect or may affect Indian land, trust resources, or the exercise of American Indian tribal rights." The Secretarial Order states that the Departments will carry out their ESA responsibilities in a manner that harmonizes the federal trust responsibility to tribes, tribal sovereignty, and statutory missions of the Departments and that strives to ensure that Indian tribes do not bear a disproportionate burden of the conservation of listed species....

CWA

The U.S. Army Corps of Engineers (Corps) issues permits for the discharge of dredged or fill material into navigable waters under Section 404 of the CWA and permits for obstruction of navigable waters under Section 10 of the 1899 Rivers and Harbors Act. Several cases illustrate the substantive effect that Indian treaty rights may have on the Corps's authority to issue permits for off-reservation projects.... [To take one example, in] *Northwest Sea Farms, Inc. v. United States Army Corps of Engineers*, [931 F. Supp. 1515 (W.D. Wash. 1996)], [the] federal district court upheld the Corps's decision to disapprove an application for a Section 10 permit to anchor a floating fish pen in Puget Sound after determining the fish pens would have interfered with Lummi Indian access to usual and accustomed fishing grounds or stations reserved by treaty....

* * *

Notes and Questions

1. Tribes have long recognized that tribal treaty rights, in particular, can pose a formidable obstacle to decisions that permit depletion or contamination of the relevant resources. *See, e.g.,* Catherine A. O'Neill, *Variable Justice: Environmental Standards, Contaminated Fish, and "Acceptable" Risk to Native Peoples,* 19 STAN. ENVTL. L.J. 3, 98 (2000) (observing that treaties between the U.S. and various Pacific Northwest tribes "support an interpretation that not only recognizes Indians' reservation of their right to take fish 'at all usual and accustomed grounds and stations,' but also includes some guarantee

that there be fish for taking (and consuming), that is, that the fishery habitat be protected from degradation or contamination."); Wenona T. Singel & Matthew L.M. Fletcher, *Indian Treaties and the Survival of the Great Lakes,* 2006 MICH. ST. L. REV. 1285 (arguing the relevance of tribes' treaty rights to efforts to restore health to the Great Lakes and advocating a greater place for tribes in the process). For an account of the Columbia River Basin tribes' sustained efforts to defend their treaty-secured rights to fish, including by "'going to law' to protect both the salmon and their own inherent right to harvest them," see DUPRIS ET AL., *supra,* at xxv and generally. For the most recent chapter in the litigation over treaty rights in the Pacific Northwest, see *United States v. Washington,* No. 9213RSM, slip op. at 11 (W.D. Wash. 2007) (finding, in the context of the state's duty to refrain from diminishing fish runs by constructing and maintaining culverts that block fish passage, that the treaty negotiators "specifically assured the Indians that they would have access to their normal food supplies now and in the future" and that "[t]hese assurances would only be meaningful if they carried the implied promise that neither the negotiators nor their successors would take actions that would significantly degrade the resource.").

2. Treaties are a legal instrument of significance to other groups' struggles for environmental justice as well. Professor Rebecca Tsosie discusses the continued significance of treaties for both American Indians and Mexican Americans affected by the 1848 Treaty of Guadalupe Hidalgo—which added to the United States territory that comprises all or part of the present states of Arizona, California, Colorado, Kansas, New Mexico, Nevada, New Mexico, Nevada, Oklahoma, Texas, Utah, and Wyoming.

> "[B]oth the Indian treaties and the Treaty of Guadalupe Hidalgo are being employed as instruments of intercultural justice, and claimants are seeking to establish the moral obligation of the United States to honor its promises to respect the land and the cultural rights of the distinct ethnic groups that were involuntarily incorporated through conquest."

Rebecca Tsosie, *Sacred Obligations: Intercultural Justice and the Discourse of Treaty Rights,* 47 UCLA L. REV. 1615, 1617 (2000). Treaties also figure prominently in the international environmental justice setting, discussed in Chapter 10.

3. Despite the existence of treaties and other laws designed to recognize and protect tribes' resources and rights, federal agencies have often taken actions adverse to tribal interests. As Mr. O'Connell observes:

> Despite the federal trust responsibility, federal agencies are not always aware on a project-by-project basis of either mandatory duties assumed by the United States under federal treaties, laws, and executive orders or the discretion they may exercise to fulfill tribal rights or to avoid, minimize, or mitigate adverse impacts of agency action on tribal interests.

O'Connell, *supra,* at 54. Why, in your view, is this likely to be so? Is this failure likely to be the result of a "blind spot" on the part of agency staff? Or are there larger, systemic issues in play? As you consider these questions, you might turn to Chapter 7, which details the EPA's proposal for regulating mercury emissions from coal-fired utilities. Although tribes repeatedly sought to remind EPA of its unique obligations to tribes and the fact that tribes' treaty-protected rights to fish were at stake, the EPA never grappled with this fact, mentioning the word "treaty" only once in the hundreds of pages that constituted its decision-making record for the rule, according to research by the National Congress of American Indians. *See* Catherine A. O'Neill, *Environmental Justice in the Tribal Context: A Madness to EPA's Method,* 38 ENVTL. L. 495 (2008).

4. Among the examples of provision for tribal consultation and influence mentioned in the O'Connell excerpt above are several that might be enlisted to ensure the protection of sacred sites and other "cultural property" found off-reservation. As these examples illustrate, many of the provisions make only procedural guarantees. That is, while tribes must be consulted, there are few substantive protections afforded and, in the end, tribes have no power to veto proposed actions that may adversely affect places or resources that are important for cultural or religious reasons. Tribes' efforts to invoke constitutional and statutory provisions to protect sacred sites are considered in Chapter 14.

Chapter 5

Regulation and the Administrative State

A. Introduction

In Part II, we turn to efforts by government agencies to respond to the environmental disparities identified in the prior chapters. In the next several chapters, we examine efforts by agencies to redress environmental disparities within their core mission and core functions, such as assessing risk, setting standards, issuing permits, enforcing permit requirements, and cleaning up contaminated properties. We conclude with a look at specific agency initiatives to address environmental justice concerns on the international, federal, state, and tribal levels and collaborative efforts among these levels of governance. We focus largely upon the U.S. Environmental Protection Agency because it is tasked with implementing many (but not all) federal statutes protecting the environment, largely through pollution control measures. Bear in mind, however, that the same dynamics typically apply in other agencies that undertake actions having significant environmental justice consequences, such as state agencies and other federal agencies within the Department of Transportation and Department of Interior.

Before examining these more specific agency actions, this chapter considers the regulatory process from a broader perspective. As environmental justice concerns are situated within this larger contextual view, a more complete picture of environmental inequities, and how they might be resolved, will emerge. This chapter begins with a discussion of the EPA at the time that environmental justice issues first garnered national attention, then proceeds to examine how environmental justice fares within administrative processes. In particular, we examine three high-profile issues in environmental regulation that have significant environmental justice implications: the stakeholder model of agency decision-making, the cost/benefit approach to regulation, and the federal/state relationship in environmental regulation.

B. Environmental Regulation: The Historical Context

Recall that the environmental justice movement first gained national recognition in the late 1980s. Considering the special challenges facing the EPA at that time helps to explain the ensuing tensions between environmental justice activists and other stakeholders. For reasons explained below, this was a time of instability at the EPA. Professor Richard Lazarus describes this period as a pathological cycle of distrust and agency failure that ultimately set the stage for EPA's movement in the 1990s away from traditional "command and control" regulation in favor of more flexible, market-oriented approaches to pollution control; away from federal control and in favor of greater autonomy for states; and away from top-down agency decision-making toward negotiation and consensus.

Richard J. Lazarus, The Tragedy of Distrust in the Implementation of Federal Environmental Law

Law and Contemporary Problems, Autumn 1991, at 311

In the dream, it works something like this: The huge hall of Environmental Control is lit from above. Operators below press controls and the translucent dome glows with the streams slashing the Upper Atmosphere, shaping the world's weather.... In and out of walls glide panels on which river basins shine with flood-crest warnings or change hue to show rise and fall of pollution.... Nearby, in the Surveillance Center of Environmental Health Services, pesticides, oxides, nitrates, adulterants, all 30,000 chemicals used by industry or everyday life are indexed, cross-referenced, computerized for interaction and contaminations.

Author Theodore White offered this fantastical description of a federal environmental agency just two weeks before President Nixon transmitted to Congress on July 9, 1970 his long-awaited executive order proposing the creation of the United States Environmental Protection Agency ("EPA"). Were EPA's performance now to be measured ... against that of the mythical agency in White's dream, many would consider EPA a colossal failure. Surely, however, no one would use such a yardstick to judge EPA. White's portrait was not intended to reflect reality.

Imagine nonetheless that Congress had [enacted] enabling legislation creating an EPA more akin to that fantasized by White. Also imagine that the statute mandated that the new EPA achieve that level and type of environmental control within six months.... The imagined scenario should seem highly improbable, if not absurd.... A review of EPA's last twenty years, however, suggests otherwise....

Congress has repeatedly demanded that the agency perform impossible tasks under unrealistic deadlines. Courts have rejected many of the agency's efforts to provide itself with more leeway in their implementation, while the White House, [Office of Management and Budget (OMB)], and congressional appropriation committees have simultaneously resisted subsequent agency efforts to comply with strict judicial mandates. The agency spends much of its limited resources defending its decisions in court, negotiating with OMB and the White House, and justifying its decisions to multiple congressional committees. A virtual state of siege and a crisis mentality have persisted at the agency for much of its existence as Congress has responded to each EPA failure by passing even more restrictive deadline legislation that the agency again fails to meet.... In short, a pathological cycle has emerged: agency distrust has begotten failure, breeding further distrust and further failure....

The cycle results from the way in which our governmental institutions have responded to persistent public schizophrenia concerning environmental protection policy. Public aspirations for environmental quality are relatively uniform and strongly held. But those aspirations contrast sharply with the public's understanding of their implications and its demonstrated unwillingness to take the steps necessary to have those aspirations realized.

... [T]hree variants of agency capture theory have predominated and strongly influenced EPA's institutional development. The first hypothesis ... concerns the tendency of administrative agencies to ally themselves, over time, with the community they regulate. At the time of EPA's creation, Ralph Nader's organization had published a series of books ... that accused various federal agencies ... of being in a state of agency capture.

The second thesis ... concerns the tendency of agency personnel to bargain away environmental values as part of the political process.... [A]gency officials are simply incapable of providing natural resources with long-term protection from persistent and influential economic interests. The constant demands on the bureaucracy for compromise are too great.

Finally, there are those who fear the agency's capture by its own bureaucracy. Unlike the other two theories, the primary proponents of this view are concerned with the agency paying too *little* attention to the needs of the regulated. The theory is premised on the reputedly liberal, pro-regulatory bias of the federal bureaucracy, particularly that in an agency rearrangement such as EPA with a social mission.

EPA's creation and the manner in which it was initially received within the executive branch, by Congress, and the courts can largely be traced to these three different capture theories....

The tug-of-war in which EPA found itself might have turned out to be nothing more than a benign, even healthy, application of the checks and balances necessary to realize this country's commitment to the separation of powers. After all, where important regulatory authority is at stake, the various branches will invariably vie for influence in fashioning national policy....

In the case of EPA, however, the effect has been neither benign nor healthy. The institutional forces set into motion by the various capture theories have repeatedly collided, breeding conflict, controversy, and ultimately a destructive pattern of regulatory failure. No one individual or institution is to blame for this phenomenon. Indeed, "blame" is an inappropriate characterization. Many of the problems that have arisen in the implementation of environmental law were likely the inevitable result of such a dramatic infusion of new values and priorities into the nation's laws.... [T]he country's spiritual environmental awakening in the 1970s occurred without much of an intellectual understanding of its implications. A strong national consensus in favor of environmental protection prompted the President to create EPA, Congress to pass sweeping environmental laws, and courts to open their doors to environmental plaintiffs. But both the public and those institutions were remarkably unsophisticated about the demands that they were placing upon themselves....

The federal environmental statutes of the early 1970s were dramatic, sweeping, and uncompromising, consistent with the nation's spiritual and moral resolution of the issue.... The statutes imposed hundreds of stringent deadlines on the agency and removed much of the agency's substantive discretion in accomplishing them. One-third of the deadlines were for six months or less. Sixty percent were for one year or less.... Congress and the courts had imposed 800 deadlines on the agency through 1989....

The result was a seemingly never-ending onslaught of impossible agency tasks.... EPA was "told to eliminate water pollution, and all risk from air pollution, prevent hazardous waste from reaching ground water, establish standards for all toxic drinking water contaminants, and register all pesticides." ...

These series of impossible tasks did more than guarantee repeated agency failure; they triggered a chain of events that profoundly influenced EPA's institutional development and the evolution of federal environmental law.... Forces within Congress were able to secure passage of various environmental statutes that reflected the nation's aspirations for environmental quality, but a very different set of institutional forces was responsible for appropriating funds for the implementation of those laws. Members of the appropriations committees typically did not share the environmental zeal of those on the committees who drafted the laws.... The skeptics may have been reluctant to voice publicly their opposition to passage of the statutes — because of the popular appeal of environmental protection — but they felt far more secure in undermining the statutory mandates in a less visible way through the appropriation process. Such congressional skeptics were joined in their efforts by those in the executive branch ... who shared their policy outlook and who, accordingly, routinely requested less funding for EPA than Congress ultimately provided. This coalition for modest EPA funding proved virtually unbeatable....

Partly to prevent agency capture, Congress encouraged judicial oversight of EPA by including citizen suit and judicial review provisions in each of the environmental statutes and by requiring EPA to follow decision making procedures more rigorous than those normally employed in informal notice and comment rulemaking.... [This] provided environmentalists with enormous leverage over EPA through litigation.... Environmentalists utilized the consent decree and the threat of contempt sanctions to control the agency's future actions. The filing of lawsuits also provided environmentalists with media events that provided publicity for their cause and incidentally aided fundraising efforts.

... Because the statutes demand the impossible of EPA and require EPA to demand the impossible, or at least very painful, from others, there has historically been plenty to fuel criticism [] within Congress. "EPA bashing" has been commonplace on Capitol Hill as legislators from both sides of the aisle have perceived its political advantages.... When EPA failed to meet statutory deadlines, members of Congress held hearings in which they chastised the agency for neglecting the public trust. Conversely, when EPA made politically unpopular decisions in an effort to comply with its statutory mandates, other members of Congress promptly joined in the public denunciation (including some who originally sponsored the strict environmental laws).

... Indeed, congressional oversight of EPA has periodically been so intense that the agency has been effectively paralyzed as a result. Ironically, therefore, much of the delay about which Congress complains may be the product of its own oversight of the agency.

Another adverse effect of excessive oversight of EPA is that it has caused the agency to go "underground" in its lawmaking. To avoid overseers, EPA has increasingly resorted to less formal means of announcing agency policy determinations. Instead of promulgating rules pursuant to the Administrative Procedure Act, EPA now frequently issues guidance memoranda and directives. Also, many important agency rulings are not reflected in generic rulemaking, but in individual permit decisions. OMB oversight is thereby avoided, and judicial review of agency action is limited....

* * *

Notes and Questions

1. Which capture theory identified in the article above do you consider most plausible? Why? Assuming each variant of agency capture theory has some legitimacy, how would each type of capture affect environmental justice concerns? Which form of capture would pose the greatest challenge?

2. Professor Lazarus suggests the crisis in regulation occurred largely because we were not prepared to pay the costs of our newfound environmental sensitivity, nor did we anticipate just how costly it would be. How might regulators resolve the inherent conflict between our values and cost? As you read this and following chapters on the subject, consider whether the existence of distributional inequity itself was the inevitable outcome of a conflict between lofty environmental values and an aversion to the high costs of risk abatement. Is it possible that environmental justice advocates are repeating the cycle, that is, making an ethical claim for distributional fairness without knowing how costly it will be to bring about that fairness, and whether society as a whole is willing to pay?

3. Consider Professor Lazarus's additional thoughts about EPA's regulatory history:

EPA's dilemma could nonetheless be viewed positively as a small price to pay in the United States' first effort to reshape its relationship with its natural environment. Certainly this nation's accomplishments in seeking to produce a legal regime for environmental protection have been extraordinary. In relatively few years, the nation's laws have been dramatically rewritten. Viewed from this perspective, repeated regulatory failure could be seen as the necessary cost of our attempt to address pressing environmental problems in the face of scientific uncertainty. There was not sufficient time to delay governmental action until its environmental objectives could have been fairly and accurately defined....

There is also some advantage to the public in the way environmental laws have evolved in response to repeated agency failure. The statutes allow for less agency discretion while arguably reflecting greater congressional assumption of responsibility for making public policy.... In the more prescriptive environmental statutes, Congress is now making many of the difficult policy determinations necessary to fashion environmental quality standards.

Finally, there is even a positive way to view public distrust of EPA. After all, "political distrust has been a recurrent and perhaps a permanent feature of the history of the republic." Effective democracy undoubtedly requires criticism of government based on mistrust of its institutions.

Lazarus, *supra*, at 348–50. Do you agree? Why or why not? From this brief but insightful history, do you see any parallels in the effort to achieve environmental justice? For example, in the abstract do we value fairness and equal environmental protection for all? If so, what actions do you anticipate we would have to take? Assuming that it will be very costly to remove environmental disparities, are we prepared to absorb that cost? For a detailed look at our attempt to protect health and our environment over the last three decades, see RICHARD J. LAZARUS, THE MAKING OF ENVIRONMENTAL LAW (2004).

4. Does the answer to the agency distrust and failure that Professor Lazarus describes lie in an agency insulating itself from conflicting political pressures, or, conversely, should an agency seek to encourage participation by all stakeholders? Beginning in the 1990s, while the EPA was caught in the dynamic described above, Congress was experiencing its own brand of paralysis in the environmental area, largely ceasing to enact environmental legislation but at the same time leaving the EPA with prescriptive statutes that, some argue, are ill-suited to respond to persistent environmental problems. This set of circumstances sparked a regulatory movement to reform environmental regulation. We discuss three of the key areas proposed for reform in the following sections.

C. "Stakeholder" Approaches to Decision-Making

This section examines agency decision-making through the lens of federal regulatory processes and uses negotiated rulemaking as an example. Although the dynamics may differ slightly, the same principles can be applied to state and local governments. Bear in mind that in a conventional rulemaking process, the agency typically develops a rule relying on internal staff, then publishes the proposed rule and accepts comment upon it from various "stakeholders" (agency parlance for public and private parties that might be affected by agency action, such as local governments, industry, agricultural concerns, environmental organizations, community-based groups, and others). At the end of this "notice and comment" period, the agency responds in general fashion to the comments and publishes a final rule, perhaps in a version that the agency changed from its proposed form due to comments it received. The various stakeholders do not directly interact with each other in the course of the rulemaking.

By contrast, negotiated rulemaking is a process in which the stakeholders come together to deliberate and ultimately reach consensus—at least a rough consensus—on a particular rule. This consensus is usually reflected in the initially proposed rule that the agency subsequently publishes for notice and comment. Some agencies have embraced this process because it reduces the likelihood that the final rule will be challenged in court. As you read the following materials about the theoretical underpinnings of the regulatory process, traditional notice and comment rulemaking, and negotiated rulemaking, think about how community-based environmental justice groups might fare when the agency is considering a rule that has significant environmental justice consequences.

Eileen Gauna, The Environmental Justice Misfit: Public Participation and the Paradigm Paradox
17 Stanford Environmental Law Journal 3 (1998)

Scholars have proposed several different models to prescribe the way in which administrative decisions should be made and the public's role within each model. The expertise model, a decision-making structure heavily reliant upon the regulatory ideal of formal expertise, ultimately rests upon empiricism and faith in the ability of science and technology to solve environmental problems. The pluralist model, with predominant regulatory ideals of interest group inclusion and agency neutrality, rests on a foundation of utilitarianism. The [] civic republican model rejects utilitarianism in favor of a belief in true civic virtue. Under this model, citizen inclusion is a regulatory ideal but is employed to achieve a form of deliberation focusing on true public good solutions rather than utility maximization. The form and efficacy of citizen participation may vary depending upon which model predominates in agency proceedings and the institutional mechanisms that might favor one approach over another.

The Ideal of Expertise and the Traditional Administrative System

One could look at agency decision-making as requiring no public input. Agency officials could regulate according to clear legislative mandate; in absence of such clarity, officials could use their expertise to fill in the detail. An extreme form of this view, supported by a strong belief in the ideal of formal expertise, could justify the rejection of public participation entirely....

Under this traditional view, the primary inquiry posed by legislation is the permissible extent of governmental intrusion into the sphere of private autonomy; it is the private interests that are at risk, not the public interest. Accordingly, there is no role for the general public in agency proceedings.... The regulated community's participation is allowed only to keep agency expertise within the consensual boundary of the legislation in question.

The Ideals of Pluralism and the Modern Administrative System

While agencies must be mindful of their non-representational footing and of their place in political theory, they also must perform their duties by implementing legislation. Viewed in this light, just as the regulated are protected from exuberant regulation, the public in general must be protected against inadequate regulation. The regulated community's entry into agency proceedings gave rise to a second concern: as they matured, regulatory agencies might develop a bias in favor of the organized interests of the regulated and might come to have a stake in the well-being of the industries they regulate. Consequently, agency officials might fail to discharge their respective mandates.

In order to protect against this new risk, the then-expertise-oriented traditional system had to change in order to accommodate interests other than the liberty and property interests of the regulated....

The interest representation model relies relatively less upon the regulatory ideal of expertise and more upon ideals associated with pluralism, although expertise is still important. This more recent view has been heavily influenced by the writings of theorists who posit that the behavior of regulators is influenced by inherent reward structures. Agency expertise alone is thus not likely to produce optimal regulation. A decision-making structure which accounts for and minimizes undue influence by the regulated is preferable....

A strong pluralist conception blurs the distinction between private and public interests, as public interests become mere aggregated private preferences. The public interest in very clean air, for example, would simply reflect the aggregated preferences for clean air by most people, a preference not inherently superior to an alternative aggregated preference for unfettered automobile use and industrial activity resulting in severely polluted air....

[A]n agency structure that accommodates pluralist ideals is one that is accessible to representatives of all legitimate interests and one that requires officials to maintain a relative neutrality towards the interest groups and legislatively expressed preferences. Under this conception, the agency is not a preference generator but a preference mediator. In the environmental context, the EPA's mission becomes less that of a "Protector of the Environment," and more a risk broker which manages risk within a legislatively expressed range of options....

This view supports the position that public participation in agency proceedings is necessary, not only to guard against agency bias toward the regulated, but also for the agency to get a clear grasp of the preferences of all interest groups and to successfully mediate among those preferences....

Although presently operating within a pluralistic paradigm, the environmental regulatory apparatus is not static.... The former view that environmental values were special has been replaced by the view that environmentalism is just another special interest. As environmental values are grounded in utility, environmental concerns are subsumed in an economic benefit-cost model on equal footing with other preferences. Finally, an earlier judicial enchantment with agency capture theories has been replaced by a confidence that agencies are competent to develop sound public policy....

The Ideals of Modern Civic Republicanism and the Proposed Administrative System

... Neorepublicanism rejects the belief that the public interest is merely aggregated self-interested utility. Rather, the public interest is an expression of a common good grounded in values people pursue not as individuals but as a community. This common good is the product of the deliberative process, not its discovery. This deliberative process does not involve utility-maximizing but instead requires participants to exercise civic virtue by putting aside their self-interested preferences to focus upon the greater, common good.... The product of a well-functioning deliberative process is not a set of aggregated preferences without intrinsic superiority to any other possible outcome; rather, the product is a universal common good which is substantively superior....

Pluralists are skeptical of the participants' ability to set aside personal preferences. From the pluralist vantage point, deliberation appears to yield under the legitimizing label of the transcendental "public good," a consensus that reflects aggregated preferences at best and "parochial perspectives in the guise of neutrality" at worst....

* * *

As you think about how environmental justice concerns are likely to be addressed under the three models described above (traditional, interest representation, and civic republican), consider the points in the following excerpt, where Professor Jody Freeman elaborates upon and examines assumptions underlying the pluralist (interest representation) model, and proposes an alternative collaborative framework.

Jody Freeman, Collaborative Governance in the Administrative State

45 University of California Los Angeles Law Review 1 (1997)

Interest Representation

... While the theory of interest representation first articulated by Richard Stewart ... might explain a great deal of interest-group behavior, failure to question its assumptions makes it difficult to imagine an alternative regulatory process built upon a different view of the parties' relationships and responsibilities. The assumptions of interest representation that often go unquestioned can be summarized in the following way:

1. Agency discretion should be constrained. Excessive and unchecked agency discretion creates a crisis of legitimacy in the administrative state. The best way to constrain discretion is to encourage competition among interest groups in rule making. Judicial review is critical to this regime: courts ensure that the relevant parties are represented in the rule making process by requiring agencies to take the parties' views into account in reasoned decision making. Through the threat of legal challenge, then, parties derive indirect bargaining rights.

2. Rules are bargains. Rules are transactions that require bargaining. Interest representation is motivated by a pluralist theory of politics.

3. Agency officials are insiders, whereas stakeholders are outsiders. Interested parties compete to influence agency decisions and have the right to challenge agency decisions in court, but they have no direct responsibility for devising or implementing solutions to regulatory problems.

4. Relationships are adversarial. Adversarialism drives interest representation. The goal for stakeholders is to maximize their interests by winning on important issues.

5. The agency is neutral and reactive. The agency is a neutral arbiter among stakeholders. It takes the relative power of interest groups as it finds it, and it seeks compromise in response to pressure from outsiders....

A Normative Model of Collaboration

... Collaborative governance seeks to respond to the litany of criticisms about the quality, implementability, and legitimacy of rule making by reorienting the regulatory enterprise around joint problem solving and away from controlling discretion. Collaborative governance is characterized by the following features.

1. A problem-solving orientation. The focus is on solving regulatory problems. This requires information sharing and deliberation among parties with the knowledge most relevant to devising and implementing creative solutions.

2. Participation by interested and affected parties in all stages of the decision-making process. Broad participation has an independent democratic value and may facilitate effective problem solving. It may take different forms in different contexts.

3. Provisional solutions. Rules are viewed as temporary and subject to revision. This requires a willingness to move forward under conditions of uncertainty. It also demands a willingness to devise solutions to regulatory problems without foreclosing a rethinking of both solutions and goals. To this end, continuous monitoring and evaluation are crucial.

4. Accountability that transcends traditional public and private roles in governance. Parties are interdependent and accountable to each other. New arrangements, networks, institutions, or allocations of authority may replace or supplement traditional oversight mechanisms. These might include self-monitoring and disclosure, community oversight, and third-party certification. In these arrangements, traditional roles and functions are open to question.

5. A flexible, engaged agency. The agency is a convenor and facilitator of multi-stakeholder negotiations. It provides incentives for broader participation, information sharing, and deliberation. It acts as a capacity builder of parties and institutions by providing technical resources, funding, and organizational support when needed. While the agency may set floors and ceilings and act as the ultimate decisionmaker, it views regulatory success as contingent on the contributions of other participants....

The collaborative claim that problem solving tends to produce higher-quality rules rests upon the belief that unanticipated or novel solutions are likely to emerge from face-to-face deliberative engagement among knowledgeable parties who would never otherwise share information or devise solutions together. A process conducive to the disclosure and debate of data is more likely to make better use of available information and expose information gaps than one that promotes secrecy and indirect communication. Moreover, parties have a difficult time insisting on arbitrary or indefensible positions when they are confronted with data or arguments that undermine their view. Problem-oriented deliberation is widely thought to be more conducive to creativity and innovation than either positional bargaining or indirect communication through a paper record.

... [A] flexible, adaptive system capable of responding to advances in science, technology, knowledge, and shifting human judgments will produce better rules that are more likely to accomplish legislative goals.... Provisionalism requires learning. In this sense, it is pragmatic.... Monitoring and information exchange are crucial to an effective implementation and compliance regime, as is the capacity to measure compliance. Rules are not one-time transactions, but rather, they are building blocks in a process, alternative hypotheses to be deployed and revised in light of experience....

In order to prevent well-resourced groups from dominating deliberative processes, the agency may provide technical assistance grants or other needed support to consumer or community groups. When collective action problems or differential power make balanced representation within a negotiating group impossible, the government itself will need to self-consciously represent the concerns of unrepresented interests. The critical difference here is the agency's posture toward outside groups: in traditional rule making, the agency reacts when groups exert pressure, as they are primarily viewed as a threat. In a collaborative model, the agency cultivates participation as part of its mission because outside groups are potential contributors....

The Limits of the New Processes

... Even if they wished to embrace collaboration, however, chronically understaffed public interest groups cannot afford to participate in multiple negotiations over multiple policy issues and at the same time continue to fight their traditional battles in courts and legislatures. Consensus-based processes, especially those that envision continued engagement and responsibility for oversight, require a tremendous commitment of resources. Public interest groups would [] need to diversify their skill base to engage effectively in deliberation. Very few organizations, and almost no community groups, have the requisite scientific and technical knowledge, as well as legal expertise. Even for those groups that can claim sufficient expertise, such as the [Natural Resources Defense Council], representatives resist sharing oversight responsibilities with the government. Rather, they view enforcement and oversight as the government's responsibility. As it turns out, then, public interest groups are as deeply committed to the public-private divide as any institution.

By contrast, industry groups suffer no lack of resources or technical knowledge. They may also have the strongest incentive to collaborate, given the possibility of reducing the expense, delay, and frustration associated with adversarial regulation. Still, front-end negotiations are very costly, forcing industry to underwrite much of the expense. The pressure to show short-term profit discourages executives from making large investments of company time and resources in uncertain processes that cannot guarantee results. It may be less costly, at least in the short term, to pursue a strategy of trench warfare. Indeed, it may not be in the industry's interest to collaborate when it can "win" battles over rules and permits in other fora. Industry groups have proven adept at exerting influence in legislatures and courts: they have successfully resisted enforcement of environmental regulation even when they could not defeat the legislation or persuade the agencies to weaken the rules. Fines are rarely so high that they cannot be efficiently internalized. Both corporate executives and their lawyers are skilled at adversarialism; indeed, the lawyers have a financial stake in it....

The least represented groups across EPA negotiations appear to be environmental organizations, particularly smaller, community-based environmental groups. While there is no empirical evidence suggesting that agencies attempt to "stack the deck" with parties that can be relied upon to achieve a predetermined result, there remains a danger that convenors will manipulate the convening process. One would expect, however, that such a practice would quickly and permanently undermine negotiated rule making. All the evidence suggests that convenors take considerable care in selecting parties so that a balance of interests is represented. Still, they appear to do so primarily to insulate the consensus rule from later challenge....

Given the substantial obstacles to broad participation and the degree to which it can delay and complicate already difficult negotiations, many would argue that, while desirable, broad participation should not be viewed as a necessary feature of collaborative governance. Indeed, some would argue that the degree of public participation in these processes already exceeds that which outsider groups currently enjoy in the traditional rule-making and permitting process. . . .

Unless one imagines a collaborative model that includes only agencies and industry (a system that would doubtless revitalize capture theory), agencies must view building the institutional capacity of communities—that is, their technical and financial ability to participate in the regulatory process—as part of their mission. Such a shift would radically depart from the defensive stance many agencies have adopted in the notice and comment process. Cultivating participation requires more than providing resources for technical experts. Agencies could build institutional capacity by promoting connections between universities and community groups or by investing directly in community organizations. Even if such steps go beyond what agencies can afford, or are legally entitled to do, they could take smaller steps, such as appointing a staff advocate or ombudsman for under-represented groups. . . .

In the end, despite their potential limitations and obvious shortcomings, initiatives such as negotiated rule making . . . provide glimmers of what a collaborative regime might look like. And yet, curiously, even the proponents of these new initiatives appear to minimize their potential to challenge the prevailing conceptual framework of administrative law. . . . [S]ome of the hesitancy to push these ideas further may be rooted in an unwillingness to grapple with the traditional model of the administrative process and the dominant conception of public and private roles in governance. Faced with having to envision a new decision-making regime, erect the legal structures necessary to support it, and defend its constitutionality, it is easier to insist that nothing really new is going on.

* * *

Notes and Questions

1. Professor Freeman maintains that the adversariness and disincentive to share information is premised upon an interest representational model that is essentially pluralist. Because of this, Freeman believes that stakeholder participation would be curtailed under a civic republican approach because of the risk of faction, i.e., that participants would pursue self-interest rather than public good. How do environmental justice advocates fit into this conceptual duality? Do they pursue utilitarian self-interests or do they pursue a greater public good?

2. How would environmental justice advocates fare under a predominantly pluralist (utilitarian) approach to agency decision-making? How would they fare under a civic republican approach? According to Professor Gauna,

> Environmental justice illuminates the conundrum inherent in environmental decision-making. The expertise approach is helpful to address scientific and technical questions, but it is inappropriate to resolve conflicting preferences and distributional issues in particular. Because of its focus on the public good, a [civic republican or neorepublican] approach might be helpful in resolving ethical conflicts, but it is not well-suited to resolve technical issues and, by definition, would not address conflicting utilitarian preferences. The pluralist model does address competing preferences, but when it contemplates an optimal distribution of en-

vironmental benefits and burdens, it breaks down. This occurs regardless of what one concludes is an "optimal" distribution. A fair distribution is not only difficult to value in economic terms, it is hard to legitimate using a short-term economic conception of rationality. An unfair distribution, although optimal in terms of economic efficiency, is an unethical preference. As a result, utilitarianism is unable to address the ethical dimension of distributional issues. This explains why the present approach of environmental regulation, which leans heavily towards utilitarian pluralism, is marked by persistent resistance to environmental justice claims.

Gauna, *supra*, at 51. If the central problem lies in the fact that environmental decision-making entails decisions about a range of matters that cannot be completely addressed by any one approach (expertise oriented, pluralist oriented, or civic republican oriented approach), can you see other alternatives? For further exploration on this theme, see, for example, Jonathan Poisner, *A Civic Republican Perspective on the National Environmental Policy Act's Process for Citizen Participation*, 26 Envtl. L. 53, 57 (1996); Rena Steinzor, *The Corruption of Civic Environmentalism*, 30 Envtl. L. Rep. 10,909 (2000).

3. Professor Freeman offers "collaborative governance" as an alternative to escape the perversities of pluralism and the utopianism of civic republicanism. Under a collaborative approach, the agency is not the neutral umpire of pluralism, nor the enlightened decision-maker of civic republicanism, but rather the agency is a facilitator and capacity builder. The success of this approach appears to depend upon the ability of the agency to define both the benefits and the measurement of those benefits, leaving to the stakeholders the task of deliberating about how to achieve them, presumably with an eye towards understanding the limitations and potential of various approaches. How does such an approach differ from the interest-representation (pluralist) model? Does the provisional nature of the enterprise, the fact that the participants must also devise a way to evaluate and reassess the agreements they come to, mark the point of departure? Would this provisionality inure to the benefit of environmental justice advocates? How? For an examination of collaborative governance theory in the land use context, see Alejandro Esteban Camacho, *Mustering the Missing Voices: A Collaborative Model for Fostering Equality, Community Involvement and Adaptive Planning in Land Use Decisions Installment I*, 24 Stan. Envtl. L. J. 3 (2005) and Alejandro Esteban Camacho, *Mustering the Missing Voices, a Collaborative Model for Fostering Equality, Community Involvement and Adaptive Planning in Land Use Decisions Installment II*, 24 Stan. Envtl. L. J. 269 (2005).

4. Under Professor Freeman's approach, the agency is not a neutral arbiter but rather self-consciously undertakes to make sure the playing field is level and assumes the role of representing unrepresented interests. Is this going to require a significant change in agency culture? If so, how might the EPA administrator facilitate this transformation?

5. Professor Freeman also sees a much larger oversight role by private citizens in the collaborative regime, while acknowledging that very few public interest organizations have the expertise for (or interest in) such a role. What mechanisms will be in place to keep the overseers accountable? Will regulated entities resist citizen oversight? If so, what incentives could agencies propose to further the acceptability of such oversight?

6. From a broader theory of government perspective, could a process characterized by capacity building, collaboration, provisionalism, and private oversight impede democratic values? How far should an agency venture from the realm of strict implementation of legislative mandates? Professor William Funk has a less optimistic view of this "new" environmental regulatory regime, specifically the practice of regulatory negotiation.

William Funk, Bargaining Toward the New Millennium: Regulatory Negotiation and the Subversion of the Public Interest

46 Duke Law Journal 1351 (1997)

Negotiated Rulemaking and the Perversion of the Administrative Process

The Rule of Law

First, consider the theory and principles of the [Administrative Procedure Act (APA), which governs the adoption of federal regulations. Eds]. Implicit in the APA is the notion of the rule of law. Agencies exist to carry out the law. Their statutory directions may be specific or general, but the agencies' actions are justified and legitimized by their service to those directions.... The statute is not just a brake or anchor on agency autonomy; it is the source and reason for the agency's actions.

Now consider regulatory negotiation. The law still exists, but the law is now merely a limitation on the range of bargaining.... The regulation that emerges from negotiated rulemaking is, as [Philip] Harter said, legitimized by the agreement of the parties.... [C]ourts should defer to an agreement of the parties that is not manifestly inconsistent with the purpose of the authorizing statute. Harter explains why:

> The parties are typically better able [than courts] to determine "what works" within the theory of the statute and hence what is the best way of achieving its overall goal. Or, a provision may be included in a statute to benefit a particular interest. If that interest does not insist on its full exercise as part of the agreement, ... [the fact] [t]hat they agreed indicates the interest achieved the protection sought in the statute.... In short, law becomes nothing more than the expression of private interests mediated through some governmental body....

The Agency as Responsible Actor

A second principle central to the APA is the role of the agency as the responsible actor. The agency is not a broker or mediation service.... Nor is the agency merely an enforcer of private agreements. Rather the agency is the authority responsible for and empowered to achieve the statutory design.

This is not, however, the role of the agency in regulatory negotiation....

[T]he formalities remain in place; the agency is titularly acting in a sovereign capacity. But the dynamics of the process all run in the opposite direction.... If [the agency] rejects or blocks consensus by invoking its "authority," it engenders bad will among those it has induced to come to the table; it largely negates any benefit of the negotiation and may have wasted valuable time and resources on a futile endeavor; and it is back to "square one" with its rulemaking. In short, the dynamics of "getting to yes" pervert the role of the agency as sovereign....

The Search for the Public Interest

... Many laws besides the Negotiated Rulemaking Act encourage and support methods to provide a voice for affected interests in developing rules that affect them.... Nevertheless, an inspection of all these laws rebuts any suggestion that these enhanced public participation requirements substitute for the agency's responsibility to engage in reasoned decisionmaking in search of the public interest. For example, environmental impact statement requirements are consistently described as intended to improve the agency's decisionmaking.... Thus, while modern rulemaking seeks full participation by interested persons, the agency still determines the public interest....

The effect on the culture and identification of the agency may outlive the particular negotiation. That is, when the negotiation is over, the consensus is obtained, and the rule is promulgated, where is the agency's interest in assuring compliance with the rule, in assuring that the rule continues to serve its purposes? The agency does not have the same sense of responsibility for the rule, because it does not reflect the agency's considered determination as serving the public interest; instead, it reflects the bargain of the parties. It is the parties' rule, not the agency's....

* * *

Notes and Questions

1. Professor Funk discusses various conceptions of the agency's traditional role on the one hand, such as that embodied in the Administrative Procedures Act, and the role required by negotiated regulation, on the other. He envisions yet another role for the agency, one that self-consciously advocates for the interests of unrepresented or inadequately represented stakeholder groups. Each role varies in the degree of "neutrality" that agency officials can appropriately maintain. Are there potential environmental justice pitfalls to the agency's role under this approach? For example, in the course of rulemaking, can the agency seek to protect the interests of disempowered communities potentially impacted by the proposed rule while also remaining loyal to the statutory design as the agency envisions it? Does the agency still, within that role, have to maintain the "neutrality" presumably necessary as ultimate arbiter of multiple conflicting interests? Are these various roles inherently inconsistent, or is there a way for an agency to successfully navigate within this nuanced terrain?

2. All things considered, how might environmental justice advocates fare in an implementation process that leans toward the following:

a. An expertise-oriented approach where the agency official makes a decision—based upon the "best science" or technology—with little or no prior stakeholder participation.

b. A pluralist (interest representation) approach where there is full stakeholder participation and the agency attempts in some fashion to make tradeoffs that accommodate the interests of all groups. This approach would rely heavily upon consensus.

c. A civic republican approach where the agency—with or without stakeholder participation—attempts to come to a decision that will capture the public interest or public good embodied in the environmental legislation.

d. A collaborative approach where the agency focuses upon building capacity of stakeholder groups and attempts to put mechanisms in place that continually reevaluate and refine the decision. This approach would also rely heavily upon consensus.

3. Another issue that has been of central importance in regulatory debates since the 1990s and that has profound implications for achieving environmental justice is the role of cost in environmental regulation. No one argues that cost considerations should be irrelevant. But several questions arise that are vigorously debated, including when cost should be compared against benefits; whether surviving a cost-benefit analysis should be the central criterion for decision-making; and how the valuation of benefits should be undertaken.

D. The Cost-Benefit Approach to Regulation, and Its Alternatives

1. Cost-Benefit Analysis and Its Critics

Very few federal environmental statutes mandate that agencies carry out a cost-benefit analysis (CBA) when adopting rules, and only two of the twenty-two major federal environmental, health, and safety statutes rely on a cost-benefit test as the statutory standard. Nonetheless, every president since President Nixon has sought to ensure a measure of oversight of the considerable number of rules issued by regulatory agencies, and beginning in the Reagan administration, each major rule has been subject to a regulatory impact analysis, the focus of which is a cost-benefit analysis. The Reagan administration argued that this approach would imbue federal rulemaking with comprehensive rationality and would increase the economic efficiency of government while providing regulatory relief to business interests. Although successive administrations have altered Executive Order 12,866, its core requirement that a cost-benefit analysis accompany each major rule has remained intact. Executive Order 12,866, in relevant part provides:

> In deciding whether and how to regulate, agencies should assess all costs and benefits of the available regulatory alternatives, including the alternative of not regulating.... Further, in choosing among alternative regulatory approaches, agencies should select those approaches that maximize net benefits (including potential economic, environmental, public health and safety, and other advantages; distributive impacts; and equity), unless a statute requires another regulatory approach.

Exec. Order No. 12,866, 58 Fed. Reg. 51,735 (Sept. 30, 1993). Shortly after assuming office, President Obama directed the Office of Management and Budget (OMB) to develop recommendations for a new Executive Order on federal regulatory review that will include suggestions on the role of cost-benefit analysis in the regulatory process, as well as how to address distributional considerations, fairness, and concern for the interests of future generations, and to identify methods of ensuring that regulatory review does not produce undue delay. *See* Memorandum for the Heads of Executive Departments and Agencies, Regulatory Review, 74 Fed. Reg. 5977 (Feb. 3, 2009). While the specifics of the new order may change aspects of how and when agencies carry out CBA, the basic contours of the debate about the practice are likely to continue. These are explored in the excerpts below, beginning with the proponents' view of CBA and continuing with a contrary, more critical view.

Robert W. Hahn & Cass R. Sunstein,
A New Executive Order for Improving Federal Regulation?
Deeper and Wider Cost-Benefit Analysis
150 University of Pennsylvania Law Review 1489 (2002)

What Is Cost-Benefit Analysis?

... [I]t is important to clarify our basic understanding of cost-benefit analysis. We mean to use the term in a modest, nonsectarian way, seeing cost-benefit analysis as a tool and a procedure, rather than as a rigid formula to govern outcomes. Thus understood, cost-benefit analysis requires a full accounting of the consequences of an action, in both quantitative and qualitative terms. Officials should have this accounting before them when they make decisions.

We do not insist that regulators should be bound by the 'bottom-line' numbers; qualitative considerations, and a sense of distributive impacts (not themselves considered 'benefits' in the analysis), are permitted to influence public officials. But if regulators are to proceed, they should be prepared to explain either how the benefits exceed the costs, or if they do not, why it is nonetheless worthwhile to go forward. When the benefits do not exceed the costs, it would make sense to adopt a presumption against proceeding—a presumption that might be rebutted by showing, for example, that children would be the principal beneficiaries of the regulation, or that poor people would be disproportionately benefited. We therefore understand cost-benefit analysis to require a certain *procedure*: A quantitative and qualitative accounting of the effects of regulation, together with a duty to explain the grounds for action unless the benefits exceed the costs. On this view, the antonym to regulation guided by cost-benefit analysis is regulation undertaken without anything like a clear sense of the likely consequences—or regulation that amounts to a stab in the dark.

... Regulation should ordinarily promote social welfare, and while social welfare might be promoted by regulations that fail cost-benefit analysis, cost-benefit analysis is an imperfect but useful and administrable proxy for the inquiry into the social welfare question. At the very least, it seems clear that regulation is unlikely to promote social welfare when its costs are very high and its benefits are very low—especially when we consider the fact that high costs are likely to be translated into some combination of higher prices, lower wages, and lower returns to capital....

Of course, it is possible that in practice, quantitative cost-benefit analysis will have excessive influence on government decisions, drowning out 'soft variables.' Since the numbers are not all that matters, any such effect would be a point against cost-benefit analysis.... [I]n appropriate cases, distributional considerations should also count. The risk that cost-benefit analysis will drown out relevant variables is not a reason to abandon the analysis, but to take steps to ensure against any such effect.

... One goal of cost-benefit analysis is to overcome cognitive limitations by ensuring that people have a full, rather than limited, sense of what is at stake. People often miss the systemic effects of risk regulation; cost-benefit analysis is a way of putting those effects squarely on-screen. At the same time, cost-benefit analysis helps overcome the problems created by cognitive heuristics that can lead people to misunderstand the magnitude of risks, by allowing an accounting of the actual consequences of current hazards and of the effects of reducing them. To the extent that people's emotions are getting the better of them, by producing massive concern about small risks, cost-benefit analysis should help put things in perspective, and at the same time might help to calm popular fears. And if people are indifferent to a risk that is actually quite large, cost-benefit analysis will help to stir them out of their torpor. The result should be to help with cognitive distortions and to produce sensible priority-setting.

There are democratic advantages as well. Interest groups often manipulate policy in their preferred directions, sometimes by exaggerating risks, sometimes by minimizing them, and sometimes by mobilizing public sentiment in their preferred directions. An effort to produce a fair accounting of actual dangers should help to diminish the danger of interest-group manipulation. More generally, cost-benefit analysis should increase the likelihood that citizens generally, and officials in particular, will be informed of what is actually at stake....

Of course, interest groups will also try to manipulate the numbers in their preferred directions. Industry will tend to exaggerate the costs and minimize the risks. Public interest groups will do the opposite. A government that attempts to produce cost-benefit analysis will face a formidable task; it is possible that government will lack the information necessary to do this task well. But if there is a degree of accuracy, and if ranges are specified where there is uncertainty, cost-benefit analysis can be seen, not as some anti-democratic effort to tyrannize people with numbers, but instead as an indispensable tool of democratic self-government.

... Prospective estimates of both costs and benefits often turn out to be wrong. This is not merely because of interest-group pressures. One reason is that officials lack the extensive information that would permit them to make accurate predictions; indeed, the informational demand on agencies is overwhelming, especially because technologies change over time. An enduring problem for regulatory policy is the absence of precise information on the cost or benefit sides. This point should be taken, not as a criticism of cost-benefit analysis as such, but as a reason for continuous monitoring and updating....

Requiring Explanation When Benefits Do Not Exceed Costs

We believe that agencies should generally act only when the benefits exceed the costs. To be sure, this is not meant as a rigid requirement. Agencies should be permitted, in unusual circumstances, to act even when the numbers do not support their action. But in such cases, we ask an agency that chooses to proceed with a regulation that does not pass a cost-benefit test to provide a rationale for doing so. By 'does not pass' a benefit-cost test, we mean that the expected quantifiable costs are likely to exceed the quantifiable expected benefits, before taking distributional effects and any other relevant factors into account. Of course there are typically large uncertainties in developing the relevant estimates, and hence a large number of discretionary judgments must be made before generating the numbers....

The agency head should be allowed to consider other relevant factors in her decision making, including distributional effects. These factors should be quantified to the extent possible, even if they are not included in the cost-benefit analysis itself. The purpose of the quantification is to make the analysis more transparent. We also believe that factors that cannot easily be quantified should be factored into the analysis where relevant. In providing the rationale for proceeding, the agency head has an opportunity (and in our view, a duty) to provide a well-reasoned analytical justification for the decision reached. Requiring a rationale for proceeding when expected net benefits are negative will give the regulatory process more legitimacy, and should also lend legitimacy to the use of cost-benefit analysis as a tool for decision making....

* * *

Professors Frank Ackerman and Lisa Heinzerling examine CBA to determine whether its methodology might contain systematic biases.

Frank Ackerman & Lisa Heinzerling, Pricing The Priceless: Cost-Benefit Analysis of Environmental Protection
150 University of Pennsylvania Law Review 1553 (2002)

Estimating Costs

The first step in a cost-benefit analysis is to calculate the costs of a public policy. For example, the government may require a certain kind of pollution control equipment, for which businesses must pay. Even if a regulation is less detailed and only sets a ceiling on emissions, it results in costs that can be at least roughly estimated through research into available technologies and business strategies for compliance.

The costs of protecting human health and the environment through the use of pollution control devices and other approaches are, by their very nature, measured in dollars. Thus, at least in theory, the cost side of cost-benefit analysis is relatively straightforward. In practice ... it is not quite that simple....

Monetizing Benefits

Since there are no natural prices for a healthy environment, cost-benefit analysis requires the creation of artificial ones. This is the hardest part of the process. Economists create artificial prices for health and environmental benefits by studying what people would be willing to pay for them. One popular method, called "contingent valuation," is essentially a form of opinion poll. Researchers ask a cross section of the affected population how much they would be willing to pay to preserve or protect something that can't be bought in a store.

Many surveys of this sort have been done, producing prices for things that appear to be priceless. For example, the average American household is supposedly willing to pay $257 to prevent the extinction of bald eagles, $208 to protect humpback whales, and $80 to protect gray wolves. These numbers are quite large: since there are about 100 million households in the country, the nation's total willingness to pay for the preservation of bald eagles alone is ostensibly more than $25 billion.

An alternative method of attaching prices to unpriced things infers what people are willing to pay from observation of their behavior in other markets. To assign a dollar value to risks to human life, for example, economists usually calculate the extra wage — or "wage premium" — that is paid to workers who accept riskier jobs. Suppose that two jobs are comparable, except that one is more dangerous and better paid. If workers understand the risk and voluntarily accept the more dangerous job, then they are implicitly setting a price on risk by accepting the increased risk of death in exchange for increased wages.

What does this indirect inference about wages say about the value of a life? A common estimate in recent cost-benefit analyses is that avoiding a risk that would lead, on average, to one death is worth roughly $6.3 million. This number, in particular, is of great importance in cost-benefit analyses because avoided deaths are the most thoroughly studied benefits of environmental regulations.

Discounting the Future

One final step in this quick sketch of cost-benefit analysis requires explanation. Costs and benefits of a policy frequently occur at different times. Often, costs are incurred today, or in the near future, to prevent harm in the more remote future. When the analysis spans a number of years, future costs and benefits are *discounted*, or treated as equivalent to smaller amounts of money in today's dollars.

Discounting is a procedure developed by economists in order to evaluate investments that produce future income. The case for discounting begins with the observation that $100 received today is worth more than $100 received next year, even in the absence of inflation. For one thing, you could put your money in the bank today and earn interest by next year. Suppose that your bank account earns 3% interest per year. In that case, if you received the $100 today rather than next year, you would earn $3 in interest, giving you a total of $103 next year. Likewise, in order to get $100 next year you only need to deposit

$97 today. So, at a 3% *discount rate*, economists would say that $100 next year has a *present value* of $97 in today's dollars.

For longer periods of time, the effect is magnified: at a 3% discount rate, $100 twenty years from now has a present value of only $55. The larger the discount rate, and/or the longer the time intervals involved, the smaller the present value: at a 5% discount rate, for example, $100 twenty years from now has a present value of only $38.

Cost-benefit analysis routinely uses the present value of future benefits; that is, it compares current costs, not to the *actual* dollar value of future benefits, but to the smaller amount you would have to put into a hypothetical savings account today to obtain those benefits in the future. This application of discounting is essential, and indeed commonplace, for many practical financial decisions. If offered a choice of investment opportunities with payoffs at different times in the future, you can (and should) discount the future payoffs to the present in order to compare them to each other. The important issue for environmental policy ... is whether this logic also applies to outcomes far in the future, and to opportunities—like long life and good health—that are not naturally stated in dollar terms....

* * *

Notes and Questions

1. Professors Ackerman and Heinzerling further explain how efforts to monetize the benefits of environmental, health, and safety regulation can lead to strange results:

> Randall Lutter, a frequent regulatory critic and a scholar at the AEI-Brookings Joint Center for Regulatory Studies, argues that the way to value the damage lead causes in children is to look at how much parents of affected children spend on chelation therapy, a chemical treatment that is supposed to cause excretion of lead from the body. Parental spending on chelation supports an estimated valuation of only about $1,500 per IQ point lost due to lead poisoning. Previous economic analyses by EPA based on the children's loss of expected future earnings, have estimated the value to be much higher—up to $9,000 per IQ point. Based on his lower figure, Lutter claims to have discovered that too much effort is going into controlling lead: *Hazard standards that protect children far more than their parents think is appropriate may make little sense. The agencies should consider relaxing their lead standards ...*
>
> For sheer analytical audacity, Lutter's study faces some stiff competition from another study concerning children—this one concerning the value, not of children's health, but of their lives. In this second study, researchers examined mothers' carseat [sic] fastening practices. They calculated the difference between the time required to fasten the seats correctly and the time mothers actually spent fastening their children into their seats. Then they assigned a monetary value to this interval of time based on the mothers' hourly wage rate (or, in the case of non-working moms, based on a guess at the wages they might have earned). When mothers saved time—and, by hypothesis, money—by fastening their children's car seats incorrectly, they were, according to the researchers implicitly placing a finite monetary value on the life-threatening risks to their children posed by car accidents.
>
> Building on this calculation, the researchers were able to answer the vexing question of how much a statistical child's life is worth to its mother. (As the mother

of a statistical child, she is naturally adept at complex calculations comparing the value of saving a few seconds versus the slightly increased risk to her child!) The answer parallels Lutter's finding that we are valuing our children too highly: in car-seat-land, a child's life is worth only $500,000 ...

Lisa Heinzerling & Frank Ackerman, Georgetown Envtl. Law & Pol'y Inst., Pricing the Priceless: Cost Benefit Analysis of Environmental Protection 30 (2002) (emphasis in original). They conclude that:

> The basic problem with the narrow economic analysis of health and environmental protection is that human life, health, and nature cannot be described meaningfully in monetary terms; they are priceless.... There are hard questions to be answered about protection of human health and the environment, and there are many useful insights about these questions from the field of economics. But there is no reason to think that the right answers will emerge from the strange process of assigning dollar values to human life, human health, and nature itself, and then crunching the numbers. Indeed, in pursuing this approach, formal cost-benefit analysis often hurts more than it helps: it muddies rather than clarifies fundamental clashes about values.

Frank Ackerman & Lisa Heinzerling, Priceless: On Knowing the Price of Everything and the Value of Nothing (2004). *See also* Mark Sagoff, Price, Principle, and the Environment (2004).

2. Professors Ackerman and Heinzerling also argue that the efficiency criterion is completely insensitive to questions of distributive justice. Because cost-benefit analysis compares costs and benefits in the aggregate, a decision that makes the rich richer and the poor poorer may nonetheless be "efficient" if it maximizes the net societal gains. *Id.* at 31–35. Professors Hahn and Sunstein agree that CBA is insensitive to distributional concerns; however, they suggest that such concerns can be meaningfully discussed after a CBA is performed, as a departure from the efficiency criterion, but the agency would have to make a case that the unusual circumstances warranted such a departure. Are you persuaded that Hahn and Sunstein's proposal would adequately account for distributive considerations?

3. Business interests and others seeking "regulatory relief" have been strong proponents of cost-benefit analysis. In a similar vein, Professor Shi-Ling Hsu argues for less of an emphasis on fairness in environmental regulation and more emphasis on efficiency:

> [A] fairness orientation inevitably biases environmental policymaking against the environmental side. The costs of pollution control measures fall on *identifiable* persons—identifiable coal miners, loggers, and factory workers who will ostensibly lose their jobs because of pollution control measures. These sacrifices are difficult to make, especially when the benefits of pollution control measures inure to the benefit of *unidentifiable* persons—future generations, persons sickened by pollution or persons whose illnesses would be aided or cured by as-yet undiscovered natural medicines....
>
> The process of conducting cost-benefit analysis [] forces policymakers to identify and catalog all of the consequences of pollution, and bundle them together under the category of "benefits of regulation." The momentous task of performing cost-benefit analyses under the Clean Air Act has caused researchers to inventory the numerous ways in which air pollution imposes costs upon society.... While this cataloging of effects could certainly occur without cost-benefit analysis, the bringing together of all of these effects highlights the manifold ways in

which air pollution harms us, and combines them into a single number. It might seem distasteful to express all of the human pains and losses as a number. Some take issue with the accuracy with which these pains and losses are quantified. But how else are we to aggregate all of the different harms from pollution? Monetization may not be ideal, but it provides a metric that can be applied to a variety of valued goods....

Shi-Ling Hsu, *Fairness Versus Efficiency in Environmental Law*, 31 Ecology L. Q. 303, 333, 344 (2004). Do you agree that cost-benefit analysis forces us to reckon with all of the consequences of pollution? That monetization provides a valuable metric?

4. Is there reason to believe, in the abstract, that cost-benefit analysis will systematically lead to less rather than more regulation? For an article finding that, in practice, this is indeed the case, see David M. Driesen, *Is Cost-Benefit Analysis Neutral?*, 77 U. Colo. L. Rev. 335 (2006). It may be worth noting that cost-benefit analyses have in some cases affirmed the wisdom of regulatory action. For example, looking at the first twenty years of the Clean Air Act, EPA has valued the total monetized health benefits achieved by regulation through 1990 at $22.2 trillion and the total compliance costs over the same years at $0.5 trillion. *See* U.S. EPA, The Benefits and Costs of the Clean Air Act 1990 to 2010 (1999).

5. As mentioned above, many environmental and health statutes do not explicitly mandate a CBA and some have been interpreted to preclude such an analysis. Some scholars argue that by alleviating some risks we tend in various ways to generate ancillary risks. As such, we should not only compare costs against benefits, but also compare risk reduced against other potential risk. Professors Samuel Rascoff and Richard Revesz explain this analytic method — sometimes referred to as "risk tradeoff analysis" — and what the analysis attempts to capture:

> "Risk-risk analysis," also referred to as "risk tradeoff analysis" and "health-health analysis," is transforming the practice of regulation....
>
> The guiding idea behind risk tradeoff analysis is simple and intuitively appealing: Regulations undertaken to minimize or eliminate certain health risks often have the perverse effect of promoting other risks. A serious analysis of a regulation should therefore pay attention not only to the regulation's primary effects in reducing the so-called target risk, but also to the secondary effects of the regulation in calling forth "countervailing" or "ancillary" risks. In this way, risk tradeoff analysis promises a more rational technique for the evaluation of regulation....
>
> *Direct Risk Tradeoffs*
>
> What we refer to as direct risk tradeoffs embrace a range of phenomena in which the very act of regulating the target risk itself brings about ancillary risks....
>
> The pattern of well-intentioned actions or decisions bringing about negative side effects is also familiar in health, safety, and environmental regulations. For example, the health risks posed by white asbestos (prevalent in schools and other public buildings) are minimal, while its removal "stirs up and sends into the air white asbestos fibers that would otherwise remain in place, thus threatening removal workers" — with the result that "removal is likely more dangerous than doing nothing." ...

Substitution Effects

Sometimes a regulation will bring about a risk tradeoff when it effects a shift from one product or process to another, which in turn gives rise to risks of its own. For instance, banning artificial sweeteners called cyclamates because of their carcinogenic properties led consumers to turn to saccharin, which itself was shown to cause cancer. Regulations aimed at making nuclear power generation safer might, by imposing large costs, encourage reliance on other risky methods of energy production....

Lulling Effects

The chain of events mediating between the regulatory intervention and the ancillary harm need not take the form of a substitution effect.... The introduction of a safety measure [] can have the effect of "produc[ing] misperceptions that lead consumers to reduce their safety precautions because they overestimate the product's safety." Thus, a regulation requiring that drugs be dispensed in child-safe packages gives rise to a mediated risk tradeoff when the rule has the effect of lulling parents into thinking that they no longer need to take precautions about storing medications outside the reach of their young children....

Health-Health Tradeoffs

Although certain authors regard health-health tradeoffs as a distinct analytic phenomenon, they are best thought of as instances of risk tradeoffs in which the chains of events mediating between regulatory intervention and ancillary harm take a distinctive form—namely a reduction in overall social wealth, which is thought to lead to a reduction in overall social health. Proponents of this methodology begin with the premise that wealthier people and societies are also healthier. They argue that because environmental and health-and-safety regulations impose large economic costs on society, they have negative health consequences. This negative effect must be weighed against the benefits of reducing target risks. "[R]egulatory expenditures represent opportunity costs to society that divert resources from other uses. These funds could have provided for greater healthcare, food, housing, and other goods and services that promote individual longevity."

Ralph L. Keeney, a prominent proponent of health-health tradeoff analysis, has argued that each $7.25 million of costs of regulation may induce one statistical fatality....

> More regulation means some combination of reduced value of firms, higher product prices, fewer jobs in the regulated industry, and lower cash wages. All the latter three stretch workers' budgets tighter (as does the first to the extent that the firms' stock is held in workers' pension trusts). And larger incomes enable people to lead safer lives....

Samuel J. Rascoff & Richard L. Revesz, *The Biases of Risk Tradeoff Analysis: Towards Parity in Environmental and Health-and-Safety Regulation*, 69 U. Chicago L. Rev. 1763, 1763–80 (2002). In their article Professors Rascoff and Revesz argue that risk tradeoff analysis, as currently executed, focuses on the negative secondary effects of risk regulation, i.e., "ancillary risks," while ignoring "ancillary benefits," the reductions in risk that take place in addition to—and as a direct or indirect result of—reductions in the target risk. They argue that this bias in favor of noticing ancillary risks but not ancillary benefits might occur, in part, because risk tradeoff analysis began as a tool of deregulation, to be used particularly in instances where CBA was prohibited by law. *See id.* at 1793. Should risk tradeoff analysis be used, either in addition to or in lieu of a CBA? Would this approach tend to cast environmental disparities in a different light?

6. Commentators who believe that cost-benefit analysis is a flawed process, not transparent, and subject to manipulation, often propose—particularly in areas where there is significant scientific uncertainty—that it is better to regulate to a level that is feasible. They propose that a focus on feasibility, without an elaborate and inevitably imprecise monetization of benefits, will allow us to better respond to environmental problems. Professors Sidney Shapiro and Chris Schroeder, who also find numerous deficiencies in an approach to decision-making that uses cost-benefit analysis as its touchstone, propose a process-oriented alternative grounded upon pragmatism. In the excerpt below, they critique the philosophical underpinnings of CBA and elaborate upon its methodological deficiencies.

2. A Pragmatic Alternative

Sidney A. Shapiro & Christopher H. Schroeder, Beyond Cost-Benefit Analysis: A Pragmatic Reorientation

32 HARVARD ENVIRONMENTAL LAW REVIEW 433 (2008)

CBA has become a one-size-fits-all technique applied to policy problems as varied as regulating mercury emissions from power plants to the roof strength standard for new automobiles. Its foundation rests on a positivist approach to knowledge....

Policy Science

Positivists share an epistemology that holds that knowledge is an objective phenomenon discoverable by empirical falsification of rigorously formulated causal generalizations. Positivism supports the separation of facts and values because knowledge accumulation should occur independently of the researcher's preferences or expectations....

Post-empiricists challenge the belief that science produces an objective description of reality on the ground that all knowledge is ultimately socially constructed.... Science, like all other forms of knowledge, is couched in language, and language reflects the meanings that people use to construct their social worlds.... Other post-empiricists contend it is more accurate to understand science as a mix of "discovery and construction of reality." Even though a well-proven theory may turn out subsequently to be false, these post-empiricists find it sufficient that we can identify theories that show "long-term survival prospects."

... [P]ost-empiricists object to the evaluation of public policy without explicit discussion of policy values.... [T]he role of an analyst is not to take a position over what constitutes the appropriate conception of society, but to "reveal and clarify" the value disputes that underlie public policy disputes.

Post-empiricists fulfill this mission by using a methodology that is multidisciplinary, deliberative, and reliant on practical reason.... Unlike positivism, there is no assumption that this outcome corresponds to some reality. The goal is to produce the outcome that best "coheres" to the evidence, arguments, and perspectives that have been considered....

Because post-empiricist policy scholars consider the range and scope of relevant interpretative standpoints, quantitative research "loses its privileged claim among methods of inquiry." ...

A significant number of scholars in different policy areas have adopted this post-empiricist perspective....

Regulatory Impact Analysis

The regulatory analysis methodology used by the federal government since the 1980s pretends that the evolution in policy science never happened....

The inability of CBA to measure regulatory costs and benefits accurately in many situations is well known....

First, the accuracy of a monetization depends on the reliability of scientific information about the risks posed by a chemical or some other hazard, but the risk information available to analysts is often not sufficiently definitive to permit a useful starting point for an estimation of the monetary value of regulatory benefits.... A related problem is that estimates often end up monetizing only some benefits of a health or environmental regulation because of the inability to monetize all of the risks it reduces. This means that CBA "in practice frequently turns out to be 'complete cost-incomplete benefit analysis.'" Since cost estimates are relatively complete, and overstated, but benefit estimates are substantially incomplete, the practice is "guaranteed to understate true benefits."

Second, the accuracy of a monetization depends on the reliability of "wage premiums." ... This methodology, however, assumes that workers have accurate information about the risks they face and that they are able to obtain wage premiums that fully compensate them for such risks but there are strong reasons to doubt both assumptions.... Another contextual problem arises from the difference in the valuation of voluntarily and involuntarily incurred risks. Research indicates that people are more adverse to risks that are thrust upon them than risks that they voluntarily take....

An additional contextual problem arises from the fact that wage premium studies are unrepresentative of the way in which many individuals value reductions in risk. The calculations, for example, ignore those outside the workforce, including persons, like the elderly, the disabled, children, and pregnant and nursing mothers, who are particularly vulnerable to environmental hazards. In addition, the wage premium studies primarily reflect how much money *men* demand for risky work, but academic studies indicate that women are much more risk-averse than men. Finally, reliance on the wage premium studies conflates market preferences with civic preferences....

Yet another problem arises from the use of willingness-to-pay ("WTP") to monetize health and safety risks. Since WTP is a function of a person's wealth, a person's wealth will limit how much money she or he can pay to be safer....

CBA supporters ... argue that, despite its lack of precision, the methodology is still useful in flagging proposed rules that are potentially highly inefficient.... [T]his information will alert an agency that some options might not produce significant benefits for the public. Second, supporters argue that CBA brings some useful information to the table, and that if agencies did not use CBA we would be left with no method to assess and discuss the rationality of proposed regulations.

... [However, t]he results of CBA are not only inaccurate, they are often biased by the analyst's policy preferences or the value judgments that are implicit in rational choice methodologies.... [A]n analyst must choose between methodological alternatives to reach an outcome, but there is no clear agreement in the discipline which choice to make....

The failure to include post-empiricism in the debate over CBA makes it easier for CBA's defenders to insist that there can be no competing rational methodology for the evaluation of regulatory policy because other methodologies mix facts and values. This attempt to privilege CBA as uniquely "rational" draws a false distinction between CBA as a "scientific" approach and other methodologies as "subjective" or value-laden approaches. As a problem-solving practice, CBA is no less value-laden than any other approach to public policy problems....

Despite the dominance of CBA logic in policy-making discussions within the Beltway, no government official will stand before a public gathering and announce something like "a tougher regulation could have saved more lives—in fact we have a risk assessment saying it would save sixteen more lives in the next five years—but our cost-benefit study showed that these lives were just not worth the costs that would have been imposed on industry by the regulation." ...

A Pragmatic Alternative

The pragmatist rejects the idea that the rationality of a belief can be established by reference to a metaphysical concept. Instead, an idea is rational if it "leads us into more useful relations with the world." ... The goal of pragmatism is to clarify and mediate ideas generated from [] different traditions, perspectives, and orientations.... [N]o particular discipline or culture has a privileged view of knowledge or truth. This does not mean that pragmatists do not value science. For pragmatists, science's value stems from its contributions to improving society and humanity.... A pragmatic approach to RIA [Regulatory Impact Analysis] would focus on the specific problem at issue and deploy whatever tools are proper, based on the statute under which the issue is addressed....

A pragmatic regulatory analysis would explicitly recognize the central role of social values in regulatory and social policy decisions ... to find solutions "that accommodate conflicting values to the greatest extent possible." Distributional considerations such as environmental justice, the loss of jobs, or the differential impact of general rules on different geographical locations and groups all deserve a place in a deliberation where they are neither reduced to a matter of dollars and cents nor treated as features extraneous to clear-eyed CBA analysis. Social values deserve a place in the mix of decisionmaking considerations, rather than being treated as improper deviations from a "best result" indicated by CBA....

Discursive analysis involves an open-ended qualitative evaluation of policy options that relies on discussion and logic to vet empirical information and to develop social ends and values.... [I]t requires analysts to give sufficient reasons to justify an option as improving society and the environment.... [F]our basic elements of discursive policy analysis [are identified]. First, the adequacy of the methods used to produce data is judged by the standards used in the discipline from which they come. Second, since "perfection of data is impossible," whether the data is sufficiently reliable to be used for policy purposes is "based on craft judgments on what is good enough for the functions that data perform in a particular problem." Third, "arguments" are used to connect "data and information" with the conclusions of the analysis. The validity of arguments depends on their cogency, persuasiveness, and clarity. Finally, the conclusion reached by analysts has to be evaluated for its "[p]lausibility, feasibility, [and] acceptability." ... [B]oth discursive policy analysis and legal analysis can be considered as forms of "practical reason." ...

Pragmatism expects regulatory analysis to be transparent and usable not only by government officials, but also by citizens. Pragmatists ... expect scientists and other experts to "bring their intelligence and their findings into the *public realm*."

… Written by economists for economists, a CBA report is technical and jargon-laden. A pragmatic report centers on statutory priorities and the identification of reasons why particular policy options are preferable. This means that a pragmatic approach has a "continuity with ordinary discourse and hence with real communities, real values, and real politics." Finally, unlike CBA, values and ideologies in a pragmatic approach are not "hidden behind the comfortable skirts of objectivity." A discursive approach therefore permits citizens to understand what is at stake in a regulatory issue.…

A pragmatic approach to RIA does not propose to dispense with the technical contributions inevitably involved in health, safety, and environmental regulations, and so it will not eliminate all the advantages that better financed and staffed participants in the regulatory process have over those less well funded and staffed. But it does promise to open up space in an RIA for recognizing the limits of technical expertise and for providing a richer description and consideration of the human values, norms, and understandings implicated by health and safety decisions.…

[O]ne does not have to monetize pros and cons to weigh them. Individuals make many decisions (perhaps even very important ones), without conducting formal CBA. A person might face a choice of jobs, one paying less in a city with a better climate and nearer to her parents, the other paying more and with better schools for children she does not yet have. Individuals can deliberate seriously over choices like this without performing CBA.…

* * *

Notes and Questions

1. Professors Shapiro and Schroeder point out that a pragmatic approach considers costs, but within the context of a wider range of values, including fairness concerns. To what extent would this approach depend upon employing an interest representation or collaborative model of decision-making?

2. How do you respond to Professors Shapiro and Schroeder's observation that their alternative, "pragmatic" approach has some of the same limitations as the present cost-benefit approach, for example, that it does not level the playing field among all stakeholders? Is there a way to mitigate this disadvantage? All things considered, which approach do you prefer?

3. Another central debate in environmental regulation over the past two decades has been the proper allocation of authority among various levels of government. As you read the next section, consider whether the federal, state, or local government is relatively better suited to address environmental justice concerns.

E. Federal/State Relationships

1. Introduction

The level of governance most appropriate to address environmental problems has rightly been the subject of much scholarly attention. While the Supremacy Clause of the United States Constitution allows the federal government to assume authority in a wide range of matters, there are also important principles of state sovereignty at stake, especially in areas of regulation traditionally occupied by the states, such as local land use matters. In the environmental arena, a "cooperative federalism" model has emerged, based upon the view that the federal and state governments should work together to provide optimal environmental regulation. For example, many federal environmental statutes set a minimum level of protection but allow the states to enact and implement more stringent standards if they choose. This idea is beguilingly simple, however, and there are significant tensions between states and the federal government as to which level of governance is most appropriate. In the following excerpts, scholars discuss when it is necessary and appropriate for the federal government to assume primacy, and when it is more appropriate for the states, which arguably have a better sense of local conditions, to have the primary regulatory authority.

Aside from issues concerning which level of governance is optimal as a policy matter, there are political considerations that inform the debate. When environmental justice campaigns began to coalesce as a national movement, many advocates initially turned to the federal government because of their view that on a more local level, concentrated political and economic forces acted to shift environmental burdens to their communities. In short, there was a sense that at the local and state level, the deck was stacked against them. As a result, there was (and remains) a concern that if too much federal authority is shifted to the state and local level (called devolution), impacted communities would not receive the attention and environmental protection that is necessary. Conversely, in more recent years, there emerged a growing concern that the EPA under the George W. Bush administration capitulated to the White House's anti-regulatory ideology and pressure to weaken environmental regulations, including the desire to preempt more protective state laws through administrative regulation. Because of this concern, at least in part, the focus of environmental justice advocacy shifted to regional and local regulation. As a result, states and localities began to fashion initiatives to attempt to address environmental justice concerns.

2. Preemption

The following article focuses on examining a preemption framework in the context of climate change initiatives. Consider, however, how the authors' insights might inform initiatives to address environmental justice.

Robert L. Glicksman & Richard E. Levy,
A Collective Action Perspective on Ceiling Preemption by Federal Environmental Regulation: The Case of Global Climate Change
102 Northwestern University Law Review 579 (2008)

... The development of a framework for thinking about preemption issues is especially important in light of recent trends in the regulatory state. From the New Deal through the "Great Society," the dominant political and academic mentality assumed that government regulation was necessary to prevent abuse of economic power, protect public health and safety, and preserve the environment. Over time, however, critics emerged to challenge these assumptions. Academics extolled the virtues of free markets and argued that most regulation is the product of rent-seeking by special interests (cloaked in public interest rhetoric). [Rent seeking is generally the attempt to extract economic value without making any contribution to productivity, as distinguished from profit seeking. Eds.]. Politicians blamed a variety of economic and social ills on excessive regulation, which they contended stifled economic growth while producing few, if any, measurable benefits. In light of this sustained challenge to the administrative state, we live in an era of regulatory skepticism.

Even though the opponents of regulation have not succeeded in dismantling the modern regulatory state, they have had a significant impact on the political and legal landscape. Deregulation or market-based approaches to regulation have been implemented in various areas.... [I]n the era of regulatory skepticism, the creation of new regulatory programs is difficult and the implementation of existing programs is often less robust; proponents of regulation bear a heavier burden of justification to persuade policymakers and must overcome a variety of new legal hurdles.

These forces are particularly apparent in the field of environmental law.... Congress has weakened procedural requirements designed to make it more difficult for federal agencies to engage in, or authorize others to engage in, environmentally damaging activities. It has also removed or weakened some of the substantive constraints applicable to activities that are potentially harmful to public health or the environment. The executive branch, through the issuance of executive orders and agency regulations, has embarked upon a similar path, although the antiregulatory thrust has been stronger under some administrations than others. Finally, the federal courts have restricted the scope and watered down the content of federal environmental law through their interpretation and application of both constitutional and statutory doctrines.

Due to an unreceptive federal government, environmentalists have increasingly turned to state and local regulatory bodies, many of which have been far more sympathetic to their regulatory agenda. Some of these state and local entities have adopted environmental regulations that are more protective of the environment than their federal counterparts, only to encounter federal obstructions.... [T]his flurry of state regulatory activity represents something of a role reversal.

State regulatory efforts in response to federal inaction and deregulation increasingly present a new kind of preemption question: when does federal environmental law preempt state laws that are more protective of the environment? To use terminology employed by William Buzbee, we will distinguish between "floor" and "ceiling" preemption. When the federal government sets more stringent standards than those adopted at the state or local level, it establishes a floor of federal environmental protection that state law cannot lower but leaves the states free to raise the floor by enacting more protective laws. When federal law preempts more stringent or environmentally protective state regulations, it establishes a ceiling above which states cannot go, although the law might leave the states free to enact less restrictive regulations. And when federal law completely preempts the field, it displaces state authority and establishes both a floor and a ceiling.

... [C]eiling preemption ... presents the more difficult and important questions.... Of course, no federal statute is intended to achieve environmental protection at all costs, and limiting regulatory burdens is always a countervailing concern, but those concerns may not justify ceiling preemption....

Preemption Doctrine

... The Supreme Court has constructed a well-established doctrinal approach to preemption. Under this doctrine, the Court distinguishes among three kinds of preemption: "express" preemption, occupation of the field by federal law ("field" or "complete" preemption), and preemption because of a conflict between federal and state law ("conflict" preemption). Field preemption and conflict preemption are often grouped together under the general rubric "implied" preemption. Ultimately, the underlying purpose of federal regulation is important for all three kinds of preemption.

... [E]xpress preemption arises as a result of the explicit language of a federal statute....

Field preemption is a form of implied preemption under which federal law completely displaces any state law in a given area—even if there is no apparent inconsistency between federal and state law. The idea is that federal law so completely occupies the field that there is no room for any state involvement; in effect, federal law is the exclusive law in that field....

The final category of preemption, conflict preemption, arises in two ways. The first is when it is impossible to comply with both federal and state law.... It is important to note that the existence of state standards that differ from federal standards does not always implicate impossibility of compliance, if the regulated party can physically comply with both standards. The second type of conflict preemption occurs when state law is an obstacle to the object and purpose of the federal law....

An essential principle of federalism is that states retain broad sovereign authority to regulate for the well-being of their people, even if the Constitution contemplates that state power will be restricted in some ways and that federal law will be supreme in cases of conflict. Displacement of this state authority is strong medicine and should not be undertaken lightly. When Congress displaces state regulatory authority it should have powerful and carefully considered justifications for doing so. By the same token, courts should not lightly infer a congressional intent to displace state regulatory authority. These principles underlie the presumption against preemption....

The Purposes of Federal Regulation

... The tragedy of the commons explains why environmental regulation may be necessary, but the question for federalism purposes is whether that regulation is best undertaken at the federal or state (or even local) level.... The traditional justifications for federal environmental regulation reflect commonly understood collective action problems, including negative environmental externalities, resource pooling, the "race to the bottom," uniform standards, and the "NIMBY" (not in my back yard) phenomenon.

... The most obvious and broadly accepted justification for federal environmental regulation is that state and local governments can externalize (or allow private entities operating within their jurisdiction to externalize) environmental harms, particularly air and water pollution.... [S]tate and local governments in upwind and upstream states may enjoy the economic and tax benefits of pollution-causing activities while exporting the burdens to other states, creating incentives to permit pollution-causing activities that result in a net loss to the United States as a whole....

One advantage of collective action is the pooling of resources, which can be especially advantageous to the collective if there are economies of scale or synergistic effects.

... One recent example in which the federal government's resource superiority has provided a rationale for federal regulatory implementation and enforcement relates to the Superfund law. Individual states may not have adequate resources to conduct remediation of "mega-sites" contaminated with hazardous substances or to finance litigation to recover their cleanup costs. The federal government is better equipped to do so.

... Another rationale for federal environmental regulation is the so-called "race to the bottom." A race to the bottom assumes that competition for business and industry will create a prisoner's dilemma in which states are driven to relax their environmental standards in order to gain the economic benefits and tax revenues that the business or industry brings [prisoner's dilemma is a game theory problem that illustrates how persons acting as individuals (two prisoners) are forced to take actions that are less advantageous than cooperative actions. Eds.] ...

Congress has relied on the race to bottom as a rationale for federal action, explicitly adverting to the fear that states would lower environmental standards to compete for industry.... A House Report on the 1977 amendments to the Clean Air Act warned that "[i]f there is no Federal policy, States may find themselves forced into a bidding war to attract new industry by reducing pollution standards." ...

A fourth justification for federal environmental regulation emphasizes the need for uniform standards....

A 1965 Senate committee report explained that federal regulation of automotive emissions was warranted because "it would be more desirable to have national standards rather than for each State to have a variation in standards and requirements which could result in chaos insofar as manufacturers, dealers, and users are concerned." ...

The NIMBY phenomenon arises when there is some undesirable but necessary activity or facility that must be located somewhere: people want one to exist, but "not in my back yard." In the environmental arena, states typically want to avoid becoming the location of a necessary but environmentally damaging activity. In such cases, states may impose regulatory burdens intended to drive the activity into other states....

Perhaps the best example of the adoption of federal environmental regulation as a response to the NIMBY problem concerns the location of radioactive waste disposal facilities. The efforts of both federal and state governments "to force hated facilities on terrified communities" spawned "a genuine political crisis—hundreds of battles have raged around the country, some dethroning elected officials, and some verging on violence." ...

A similar pattern has manifested itself with respect to other kinds of facilities, including hazardous, solid, and biomedical waste management facilities, and other kinds of potentially dangerous activities, such as hazardous waste transportation....

Collective Action Problems and Preemption

... When federal regulation is premised upon negative interstate externalities, superior federal resources, or the race to the bottom, the collective action problems that call for action at the federal level can be expected to result in inadequate or insufficient regulation at the state level.... Thus, federal environmental regulation to combat these kinds of collective action problems might support floor preemption, but ordinarily would not support ceiling preemption....

When a state imposes stricter environmental protection measures, moreover, it ordinarily does not create a corresponding negative regulatory externality. If a state regulates pollution-causing activities within the state, both the economic burdens and the environmental benefits are felt within the state, and the political process safeguards the weighing of regulatory costs and benefits.... Thus, negative externalities might justify floor preemption, but they would not justify ceiling preemption....

Like externalities and resource pooling, the race-to-the-bottom rationale posits a concern that states have incentives to underregulate in the field of environmental protection. Thus, this rationale might support floor preemption to the extent that concurrent state regulation impairs the effectiveness of federal law. But it does not support ceiling preemption. If, for example, a state adopted coal mining reclamation standards more stringent than the national standards under the Surface Mining Control and Reclamation Act, the congressional purpose of combating a race to the bottom would not support ceiling preemption because the race to the bottom provides no incentive to overregulate.

It is conceivable that some states or localities might engage in a "race to the top," competing to be the most environmentally friendly so as to attract some preferred group of citizens or businesses (for example, wealthy taxpayers). In extreme cases where states or local governments have such incentives, the problem merges with the NIMBY phenomenon.... To date, however, there is little evidence that there is a systematic prisoner's dilemma in which states are forced to overregulate in order to compete successfully with other states....

On the other hand, if the purpose of federal regulation is to ensure uniformity of standards or combat a NIMBY problem, then federal purposes may well support ceiling preemption....

Similarly, ceiling preemption makes sense when federal environmental regulation responds to a NIMBY problem because stringent state regulation may have the purpose and effect of forcing environmentally damaging activities to locate somewhere else.... [N]o state should be allowed to adopt a siting regime that effectively precludes any disposal facility from locating and operating a facility within the state. Accordingly, preemption of a state's siting law when it is more stringent than federal requirements would be consistent with the underlying justification for the federal regulatory program.

... Congress should, as a general matter, refrain from express ceiling preemption unless there are strong justifications, in collective action terms, for displacing state authority to adopt more protective environmental regulations....

In resolving ambiguities concerning the scope of an express preemption provision, courts should pay close attention to the extent to which ceiling preemption is, in a doubtful case, necessary to overcome collective action problems that would support it, such as the need for uniform standards or combating a NIMBY problem.

... In general terms, statutory purposes that reflect a desire to combat negative externalities, take advantage of superior federal resources, or preclude a race to the bottom would not support implied ceiling preemption of state environmental regulation because more protective state regulation is not inconsistent with those purposes. The need for uniformity or a NIMBY rationale may support ceiling preemption, but courts should be reluctant to infer ceiling preemption unless these purposes are primary statutory purposes or central to the success of the federal regime....

* * *

Notes and Questions

1. Siting is generally a local land use matter, although the federal government has preempted local siting laws in rare instances. Should the federal government enact a federal siting law that prohibits the siting of major polluting facilities in highly impacted communities? Would this be consistent with the approach discussed by Professors Glicksman and Levy? Would it depend upon what kind of facility is at issue? Consider the above justifications put forward for preemption for the following: nuclear power plants, hazardous

waste facilities, refineries, liquefied natural gas import facilities, hog farms, wind electricity turbines, biofuel production facilities, and chemical plants.

2. What if instead, states enacted laws making it exceedingly difficult (through stringent requirements) to site these types of facilities on the reasoning that many areas in the state have unacceptable cumulative impacts? A few state and local governments have enacted "fair share" siting laws that attempt to more equitably distribute facilities, such as solid or hazardous waste facilities that have adverse environmental impacts. Is there a sound rationale for the federal government to preempt these types of laws?

3. Tribal governments do not consider themselves to be "subfederal governments" in the same vein as state or local governments. Should a different preemption framework apply to tribal regulation?

4. Consider the flip side of the coin. Instead of preempting state and local actions, when would it be a good idea—even if not legally required—to devolve federal authority to the state or local level? Just like preemption, devolution has advantages and disadvantages and is highly dependent upon context. The next section takes a closer look at implementation of federal environmental laws by the states, and how devolution might affect environmental justice communities.

3. Devolution

Under the cooperative federalism model referenced above, many of the major federal environmental laws, including the Clean Water Act, the Clean Air Act, and the Resource Conservation and Recovery Act (RCRA), reserve a significant implementation role for the states. These statutes require EPA to establish minimum national standards, while authorizing delegation of authority to implement the programs, including issuing permits, monitoring compliance, and taking enforcement actions, to states that meet minimum federal requirements. (If a state chooses not to assume responsibility for administering a federal program, EPA operates and administers the program directly.) Once a state receives program authorization, EPA oversees the state's activities to ensure that they continue to meet federal standards. State agencies now administer approximately three-quarters of the major environmental programs that can be delegated to them. In recent years the states (and others) have pressed for greater autonomy in administering federal requirements. They contend that it is appropriate for them to assume a more prominent role in environmental regulation and that federal involvement should be reduced. Some of the implications of devolving greater authority to the states are explored in the excerpt below.

Rena I. Steinzor, Devolution and the Public Health
24 Harvard Environmental Law Review 351 (2000)

Races-to-the-Bottom and the Realities of Interstate Commerce

... If states are willing to sacrifice their authority to develop more stringent local laws, they are also more likely to weaken state regulation when federal standards are devolved....

Applying public choice theory, [scholars] argue that moving decision-making authority to the level of government closest to the people ensures that democratic and economically efficient decisions are made about the level of protection people are willing to finance and the level of pollution they are willing to tolerate [Public choice theory uses economic tools—such as game theory, utility maximization, and other behavioral models—to explain how laws tend to benefit small, cohesive special interest groups at the expense of the public. Eds.]....

One response to such theories is that the economic inefficiency of reinventing scientific and technical knowledge at the state level more than counterbalances the supposed advantages of moving the standard-setting aspects of such decision-making closer to the people.

Another response is that the exercise of free public choice depends on good, readily accessible information about the implications of available alternatives. However, when people exercise public choice in this context, they do not understand the ramifications of a state hitting the bottom because information about the states' actual environmental performance is so poor.

Perhaps the most compelling evidence that races-to-the-bottom will produce unacceptably lax regulation is the business community's strong interest in avoiding a "patchwork" of state regulatory requirements. This concern was a major motivation for the enactment of federal environmental laws, with congressional proponents arguing that maintenance of the free floor of interstate commerce requires a consistent system of uniform regulatory requirements. Because a patchwork of aggressive state regulatory programs would prove anathema to large corporations, the only plausible explanation for industry's tolerance of devolution is the belief that state regulatory activism will be foreclosed, rolling back federal regulation without allowing newly strengthened state regulatory programs to take its place....

Expired permits

Permits are the primary method used to achieve pollution control under the Clean Air and Clean Water Acts. Permits prescribe the efforts industrial facilities must make to control, reduce, and prevent pollution and serve as the vehicle for policing lapses in those efforts. Permit periods typically run for five years, with the clear expectation that the responsible federal or state agency will tighten their terms and conditions as necessary. If some states revise their permits and others do not, disparate levels of protection affect the communities near industrial facilities as well as the facilities' competitors.

Permit renewals are especially critical under the Clean Water Act because they are the opportunity to apply regulatory standards issued since the original permit was drafted. Because EPA's development of water quality standards has been so slow, lengthy delays in renewing permits written in the 1980s means that, as a practical matter, these new standards are never implemented....

[T]he senior officials responsible for permitting policy at EPA's headquarters admitted that the backlog of expired permits was increasing in twenty-five states. Only fifteen states would reduce their backlogs to ten percent by December 2001. The backlog had climbed to twenty-eight percent overall, with 26.2% of permits expired in state-run programs and forty-four percent in EPA-run programs. Nearly half of the facilities with expired permits discharge into waters classified as impaired under section 303(d) of the Clean Water Act.

This breakdown is significant because it suggests that the regulatory infrastructure is aging and weakened, a circumstance that does not bode well for unrestricted devolution. If EPA and the states lack the resources—or the willpower—to maintain the current regulatory foundation, unrestricted devolution could threaten the progress made in safeguarding public health without ever achieving the beneficial reforms that devolutionists have promised....

Indicia of Economic Health

[I]t is worth noting the paradox that states with large, low income populations and corresponding large social welfare "burdens" may have to spend more than comparatively wealthy states to achieve comparable levels of public health protection. Poor diet and lack of access to medical care can compound the harm caused by exposure to pollution because people in poorer condition physically are less likely to be able to resist adverse health effects....

There are troubling indications that [states] are falling behind in accomplishing the most basic functions, from writing permits to enforcing the law. Unable to keep pace with respect to traditional first-generation environmental problems [i.e., pollution caused by large identifiable point sources], many states are in no position to tackle second-generation problems [pollution from numerous diverse sources and land management practices] by innovative methods or otherwise.

The states appear to make decisions regarding the resources they commit to environmental protection for reasons unrelated to their environmental challenges. There are no obvious reasons to predict that more devolution of regulatory authority will result in improvement of this faltering performance. To truly stabilize environmental regulation in order to provide a baseline of protection for public health, devolution should proceed more slowly. States should have to demonstrate that they are prepared to manage additional responsibilities successfully....

* * *

Notes and Questions

1. Professor Steinzor provided information on the then-recent backlog of Clean Water Act Permits. In a 2005 report, the Office of the Inspector General (OIG) noted that "[a]s of June 2003 ... the backlog [of expired NPDES permits] was reported as consisting of 1,120 major, 9,386 individual minor, and 6,512 general minor nonstormwater facilities." OFFICE OF INSPECTOR GEN., EVALUATION REPORT: EFFORTS TO MANAGE BACKLOG OF WATER DISCHARGE PERMITS NEED TO BE ACCOMPANIED BY GREATER PROGRAM IMPLEMENTATION 5 (2005). Because 45 of the states have NPDES permitting authority, a substantial number of the expired permits are likely to be state-issued permits. While the issue is a complicated one, the EPA concurred with the OIG's assessment that resource constraints hamper a permitting authority's ability to meet permitting goals. EPA said that declining state resources is one of the most problematic issues facing permitting authorities. *Id.* at 16.

2. If different states implement federal environmental laws with relatively greater or weaker vigor, is there in reality a uniform "federal floor," i.e., a minimal level of environmental protection that citizens in all states can enjoy? If not, and if devolution of authority is one of the causal factors for uneven implementation of federal law generally, does this mean that devolution to sub-federal levels is always a bad thing? Consider Professor Sheila Foster's views on devolution and its effect on environmental justice communities:

> There is, notably, a shift underway to decentralize environmental decisionmaking and devolve more degree of influence to the "community" or local level. The shift is most discernable in a number of recent initiatives by EPA, particularly its Community-Based Environmental Protection (CBEP) initiative. If the last wave of environmental decisionmaking was marked by a "command-and-control" approach, the CBEP suggests that the next wave will be marked by the empower-

ment of those individuals who physically live in the communities most impacted by environmental decisions.

Community-based environmental decisionmaking promises, in theory, enhanced dialogue and shared power between governmental decisionmakers and ordinary citizens (public-private), as well as between citizens differently situated vis-á-vis particular environmental decisions (private-private). The promise of more egalitarian and meaningful public-private and private-private relations follows, in part, from the devolution of varying degrees of decisionmaking responsibility and influence to the local or "community" level. The CBEP recognizes, at least implicitly, that risk-bearing communities provide an important type of expertise in, and are more effectively able to bring forth public/community values into, the decisionmaking process.

How much the move toward community-based environmental decisionmaking will address the challenges of incorporating "justice" into environmental law remains to be seen. In many ways, such an approach mimics ongoing efforts to employ alternative dispute resolution processes in siting and other environmental decisions. Like those efforts, there may still be unresolved problems of representation, resource inequality (due to differences in education and training), and capture by more powerful interests in the deliberation process. Unfortunately, not enough research has been conducted on whether informal dispute resolution processes are necessarily the most appropriate or effective method of resolving conflicts with traditionally disempowered groups of people, such as racial minorities and the poor. Nevertheless, the movement toward more decentralized environmental decisionmaking is encouraging for its embrace of the importance of moving away from a narrow, technocratic decisionmaking and its effort to provide all communities with more meaningful participation with regard to the environmental and health risks they bear.

Sheila R. Foster, *Meeting the Environmental Justice Challenge: Evolving Norms in Environmental Decisionmaking*, 30 ENVTL. L. REP. 10,992, 11,005 (2000). From an environmental justice perspective, what are the benefits and risks of devolution to the states or to local authorities? What about devolution of authority over a particular resource to local groups? Is there a way to decentralize environmental decision-making while imposing safeguards for vulnerable communities? *See* Sheila R. Foster, *Environmental Justice in an Era of Devolved Collaboration*, 26 HARV. ENVTL. L. REV. 459 (2002).

3. Recall that the environmental justice movement itself is largely decentralized, with few resources to participate in national fora. Does this fact suggest that devolution, in some contexts at least, might be more advantageous? Does the fact that there can be powerful political and economic interests concentrated at the local level cut against this optimistic assessment? In your view, what would be an optimal mix of federal, state, and local regulatory authority? How would tribal regulatory authority fit into the mix?

4. In the following chapters, we will take a closer look at core agency functions, such as assessing risk, standard setting, permitting, enforcement, and cleanup of contaminated properties. As you consider these regulatory functions in greater detail, consider what kinds of decision-making models might be best, the optimal role of economic tools and the level of governance that would be best suited to address environmental justice con-

Chapter 6

Risk and Health

A. Introduction

From the perspectives of affected communities, the harms of environmental contamination are many and interrelated. These harms include adverse impacts to ecological health and to humans' physical, psychological, social, cultural, and spiritual health. In many instances, these harms represent an affront not only to an individual, but also to a group.

These harms, as environmental justice advocates have pointed out, are the result of multiple contributing "stressors." For example, in order to understand fully the adverse human health impacts of an individual's exposure to a chemical stressor such as mercury (which is now present in fish that live in contaminated aquatic environments), one needs to account for her circumstances of susceptibility and exposure (e.g., was she exposed *in utero*? to how much mercury?); appreciate the potential for the chemical stressor's interaction with other chemical stressors, such as PCBs, that may also be present in the fish; and consider the impact of social and economic stressors, such as a lack of access to adequate health care, a deficient diet, or a community fabric frayed by poverty and other pressures.

When health and environmental agencies evaluate and respond to the harms of environmental contamination, however, they frequently consider the problem in terms of risk to human health—understood in the narrow, individual physiological sense of the term. Agencies for the most part proceed chemical by chemical and consider whether human contact with that chemical is expected to result in an increased likelihood of various human health "endpoints" such as neurological damage or cancer. Agencies make this determination by means of risk assessment, an analytical tool that produces a quantitative prediction of this increase for given levels of environmental contamination.

Quantitative risk assessment enjoyed a striking ascendancy during the 1980s, when it was increasingly employed by health, environmental, and safety agencies to set human health-based standards. Although the use of risk assessment in this regulatory context has been criticized from numerous quarters, the method appears to be here to stay. In view of risk assessment's prominent role in environmental decision-making, it is important to understand the particulars of the method as well as the paradigm within which it operates.

Section B of this chapter begins by outlining the four steps of the risk assessment method and highlighting some of the limitations of the method. This section next canvasses the criticisms of risk assessment that have been raised from an environmental justice perspective, as well as from other perspectives. Finally, this section considers issues

175

with risk assessment that are particular to children and, then, to other identifiable groups, including tribal populations. Section C discusses one of the major criticisms leveled by environmental justice advocates in greater depth, elaborating the issues involved in cumulative risk assessment. Section D takes up a set of more recent agency responses to risk that can be gathered under the umbrella of "risk avoidance." Section E considers issues raised by arguments that agencies' assessment of and responses to risk ought to proceed by means of comparative risk assessment. The organization of this chapter thus roughly tracks the conventional distinction between "risk assessment" (Sections B and C) and "risk management" (Sections D and E). Generally, risk regulation is thought to involve a separation between risk assessment, which is the measurement of risk according to objective, scientific principles, and risk management, which involves subjective, value-laden policy judgments. As will become apparent, however, a strict separation of these two components of agencies' responses to risk may not be possible (or advisable) in practice.

Pathfinder on Risk Assessment

The seminal discussion of the risk assessment process in the regulatory context is the NATIONAL RESEARCH COUNCIL, RISK ASSESSMENT IN THE FEDERAL GOVERNMENT: MANAGING THE PROCESS (1983) (known as the "Redbook"). Three more recent reports of similar national significance are NATIONAL RESEARCH COUNCIL, ISSUES IN RISK ASSESSMENT (1993); NATIONAL RESEARCH COUNCIL, SCIENCE AND JUDGMENT IN RISK ASSESSMENT (1994); and NATIONAL RESEARCH COUNCIL, SCIENCE AND DECISIONS: ADVANCING RISK ASSESSMENT (2008). In addition to the materials discussed in this chapter, other pieces that examine risk assessment and environmental justice include Brian Israel, *An Environmental Justice Critique of Risk Assessment*, 3 N.Y.U. ENVTL. L. J. 469 (1995); Ashley C. Schannauer, *Science and Policy in Risk Assessments: The Need for Effective Public Participation*, 24 VT. L. REV. 31 (1999); and Carl F. Cranor, *Risk Assessment, Susceptible Subpopulations, and Environmental Justice*, *in* THE LAW OF ENVIRONMENTAL JUSTICE: THEORIES AND PROCEDURES TO ADDRESS DISPROPORTIONATE RISKS 341 (Michael B. Gerrard & Sheila R. Foster, eds., 2d ed. 2008).

↑ (Burden)

B. Quantitative Risk Assessment

1. An Introductory Note on Quantitative Risk Assessment

Although "risk" is not inherently or necessarily a quantitative concept, environmental agencies' formalized assessments of the harm that can be expected to result from exposure to toxic contamination start from the assumption that risk can be estimated and expressed in numerical terms. Today, the dominant paradigm for considering risk from environmental hazards entails a quantitative description of the likelihood and severity of adverse effects. Of course, contamination may adversely affect both human and non-human components of ecosystems, and agencies may need to consider both sorts of effects. However, the assessment methods that have evolved for each are somewhat different, with assessments of the impacts on humans termed "human health risk assessments" and assessments of the broader environmental impacts termed "ecological risk assessments." Throughout this chapter, we will be concerned primarily with efforts in the former category.

The quantitative risk assessment method is explained in the following excerpt.

The Carnegie Commission on Science,
Technology, and Government, Risk and the Environment:
Improving Regulatory Decision Making
(1993)

...Risk assessment is a composite of established disciplines, including toxicology, bio-statistics, epidemiology, economics, and demography. The goals of risk assessment are to characterize the nature of the adverse effects and to produce quantitative estimates of one or both of the following fundamental quantities: (1) the *probability* that an individual (a hypothetical or identified person) will suffer disease or death as a result of a specified exposure to a pollutant or pollutants; and (2) the *consequences* of such an exposure to an entire population (i.e., the number of cases of disease or death).

Risk assessment can either be generic (e.g., an estimate of the number of excess annual cancers caused by all 189 hazardous air pollutants identified in the 1990 Clean Air Act Amendments) or site- and/or chemical-specific (e.g., the probability that a specified child will suffer neurological impairment as a result of exposure to lead in his household drinking water).

The regulatory process is generally thought to encompass two elements, risk assessment and risk management. The distinction between the two components is important, though controversial. Risk assessment is usually conceived as the "objective" part of the process, and risk management the subjective part. In risk assessment the analyst decides how big the problem is, while in risk management political decision makers decide what to do about the problem. The "conventional wisdom" (which some believe needs rethinking) stresses that risk management must not influence the processes and assumptions made in risk assessment, so the two functions must be kept conceptually and administratively separate.

Numerical estimates derived from risk assessment serve as inputs to several very different kinds of decisions, including (1) "acceptable risk" determinations (wherein action is taken if the risk exceeds some "bright line," which can be zero); (2) "cost-benefit" determinations, where the risks reduced by a proposed action are translated into benefits (e.g., lives saved, life-years extended), expressed in dollar amounts, and compared to the estimated costs of implementing the action and some rule of thumb regarding how much cost it is wise to incur to achieve a given level of benefit (e.g., $10 million to save one additional life); and (3) "cost-effectiveness" determinations, where the action that maximizes the amount of risk reduction (not necessarily expressed in dollar terms) per unit cost is favored.

Since at least 1983 (with the publication of the National Research Council's "Redbook"), the dominant paradigm for risk assessment has been a sequential, four-step process:

• *Hazard Identification*—in which a qualitative determination is made of what kinds of adverse health or ecological effects a substance can cause. Typically, agencies have focused on cancer as the effect that drives further analysis and regulation. So, for example, a typical hazard identification for vinyl chloride released from industrial facilities would involve the collection and critical analysis of short-term test-tube assays (for mutagenicity, etc.), of long-term animal assays (typically—two-year rodent carcinogenicity tests), and of human epidemiologic data—either cohort studies (in which populations exposed to vinyl chloride are followed to assess whether their rates of any disease were significantly greater than those of unexposed or less-exposed populations) or case-control studies (which focus on victims of a particular disease to see whether they were significantly more likely to have been exposed to vinyl chloride than similar but disease-free individuals).

• *Exposure assessment*—in which a determination is made of the amounts of a substance to which a hypothetical person (usually the "maximally exposed individual") and/or the total population are exposed. To return to the vinyl chloride example, this part of risk assessment would bring to bear techniques of emissions characterization (how much vinyl chloride leaves the plant in a given time?), fate-and-transport analysis (how is the chemical dispersed in the atmosphere and transformed into other compounds?), uptake analysis (how much air do people breathe, both outdoors and indoors?), and demographic analysis (how many hours per day do people spend in various locations near the plant, and how long do they reside in one locale before moving away?).

• *Dose-response assessment*—in which an estimate is made of the probability or extent of injury at the exposure levels determined above, by quantifying the "potency" of the chemical in question. For vinyl chloride again, scientists would determine its carcinogenic potency by fitting the bioassay data (number of tumors produced at different exposure levels) to a mathematical model (usually one that is linear at low doses), and then transforming the resultant potency estimate for rodents into a human potency estimate through the use of a "scaling factor" (usually, a ratio of the body surface areas of the two species). Additionally, human epidemiologic data could be used to validate or supplant the animal-based potency estimate.

• *Risk characterization*—in which the results of the above steps are integrated to describe the nature of the adverse effects and the strength of the evidence and to present one or more "risk numbers." For example, EPA might say, "This vinyl chloride plant is estimated to produce up to 3 excess cases of liver cancer every 70 years among the 100,000 people living within 1 mile of the facility" or "the maximally exposed individuals faces an excess lifetime liver cancer risk of 5.4×10^{-4}."

Risk assessment is essentially a tool for extrapolating from scientific data to a risk number. The tool is made up of a host of assumptions, which are an admixture of science and policy. Sometimes either science or policy predominates, but it is often difficult to get a broad consensus that this is so....

* * *

Notes and Questions

1. In your view, does this description of the risk assessment method convey a sense of scientific precision? If so, consider that, in practice, the process entails numerous subjective judgment calls. The National Research Council (NRC) of the National Academy of Sciences has emphasized that "completion of the four steps rests on many judgments for which a scientific consensus has not been established. Risk assessors might be faced with several scientifically plausible approaches (e.g., choosing the most reliable dose-response model for extrapolation beyond the range of observable effects) with no definitive basis for distinguishing among them." NATIONAL RESEARCH COUNCIL, SCIENCE & JUDGMENT, *supra*, at 27. The selection of any one approach under these circumstances involves what the NRC terms a "science-policy" choice—to be distinguished from determinations that are more purely a matter of science. For a critique of the notion that quantitative risk assessment is an objective, precise scientific enterprise, see Wendy E. Wagner, *The Science Charade in Toxic Risk Regulation*, 95 COLUM. L. REV. 1613 (1995).

2. Professor Catherine O'Neill, in an article examining chemical contamination in fish, explains how the occasions for subjective judgment in quantitative risk assessment are many and stem from both uncertainty and variability in the requisite data.

Catherine A. O'Neill, Variable Justice: Environmental Standards, Contaminated Fish, and "Acceptable" Risk to Native Peoples
19 Stanford Environmental Law Journal 3 (2000)

[Quantitative risk assessment (QRA)] in practice is exceedingly malleable. Risk assessors must make subjective judgments at numerous junctures in the risk assessment process. Some of these judgments are necessitated by the present lack of the data on which QRA depends for its claimed value as a useful arbiter. And, even in cases where data exist— for example, where the value for some parameter in the risk assessment equation is known, but known to vary—current practice leaves it to risk assessors to choose among a range of true values. These occasions for judgment in QRA are termed "uncertainty" (incomplete data) and "variability" (known, but [several] values)....

Each nontrivial parameter considered in the risk assessment equation may be characterized by uncertainty; some parameters may also be variable. If risk assessors in health and environmental agencies select a single value for a parameter that is characterized by uncertainty or by variability, their resulting assessment of risk will be inaccurate in some measure. The nature of the error, however, is quite different in cases of uncertainty and cases of variability....

Uncertainty

Uncertainty, in general terms, is the lack of precise, complete knowledge of the true answer to a question.... Although scientists concede that uncertainty exists in any quest for "truth," and even science's more certain understandings are constantly subject to revision, the [NRC] has called the gaps in the data necessary for quantitative health risk assessment "uniquely large." ...

Variability

Variability refers to the fact that there is no single, correct answer to a question.... Rather, a range of values comprises the true answer. Importantly, these different values *each* describe an *actual, known* answer to the question. The true value for a parameter that is variable may thus be represented by a distribution (as opposed to a single point)....

Interindividual variability refers to differences between individuals. Two sorts of interindividual variability are relevant to predicting risk to humans from environmental hazards: variability in *susceptibility*, that is, differences among individuals in the biologically effective dose per unit exposure to a hazardous substance; and variability in *exposure*, that is, differences among individuals' contact with a hazardous substance at some nonzero concentration....

Different considerations inform agency responses to uncertainty and variability

In instances of uncertainty, where agencies lack knowledge of the true value of some parameter necessary to predict risk, the choice of any value for that parameter will be in error. A conservative response reflects a choice between errors: it is better to overestimate risk than to underestimate risk. This approach is a familiar response in private as well as public decision making, and is captured in common aphorisms, for example, "it is best to err on the side of caution," and "better safe than sorry." A non-conservative response chooses the opposite error....

In instances of variability, on the other hand, agencies know that there is a range of actual values for some parameter necessary to predict risk. An agency response does not require a conservative or non-conservative choice among errors: the values are not uncertain; they simply vary. In cases of interindividual variability, where agencies are aware of differences among individual exposures or susceptibilities, the response chosen instead reflects a determination about who merits protection. Should we seek to protect individuals at the median of the distribution that describes the variability? Individuals at the 90th percentile? The maximally exposed individual?

* * *

Notes and Questions

1. The fact that risk assessors must make so many judgment calls can have an extraordinary impact on the outcome of a particular risk assessment. The National Research Council has identified 50 quantitative risk assessment "components," each with "inference options," requiring the risk assessor to select between different plausible scientific judgments about uncertain data or theoretical connections. At each point, the consequences of selecting one assumption over another may be substantial. NATIONAL RESEARCH COUNCIL, RISK ASSESSMENT IN THE FEDERAL GOVERNMENT, *supra*, at 28–33. In fact, a risk assessment's "bottom line"—its numerical estimate of risk—can differ by several orders of magnitude, depending on whether the risk assessor has chosen a more or a less conservative response in the face of uncertainty and on whether she has chosen a more or less protective response to the presence of interindividual variability. In your view, is the choice to use a conservative input (where the true value is not known, i.e., in the face of uncertainty) or to chose a protective input (where the true value is known to vary, i.e., in the presence of variability) a matter of science, or a matter of policy? Can the two be completely separated in the applied context of risk regulation?

2. Although quantitative risk assessment appears now to be a staple of environmental decision-making, it remains controversial. The next section considers criticisms leveled by environmental justice advocates, who tend to be skeptical of both the method and its premises, as well as by others, who see the need to refine what is otherwise a useful analytic tool.

2. Criticisms of Quantitative Risk Assessment

Many of the criticisms of quantitative risk assessment are related to environmental justice. In some instances, the criticisms have been raised by environmental justice advocates and may be unique to environmental justice communities. In other instances, the criticisms are more general in origin, but may apply with particular force to environmental justice communities, given their greater "vulnerability" to the harms of environmental contamination—a comprehensive term that has emerged to describe an affected individual's susceptibility or sensitivity to the contaminant(s) in question; her circumstances of exposure to the contaminant(s); and her ability to prepare for and recover from the effects of contact with the contaminant(s), given the various other chemical and non-chemical stressors (for example, physical, social, cultural) that affect that individual. The risk assessment process also has been criticized for instating a highly technical process reserved to a cadre of "experts," one that ignores the expertise of those most affected and tends to diminish opportunities for public participation. Professor Robert Kuehn discusses some of these points in one of the first critiques of risk assessment from the perspective of environmental justice.

Robert R. Kuehn, The Environmental Justice Implications of Quantitative Risk Assessment
1996 University of Illinois Law Review 103

Methodological Limitations of Quantitative Risk Assessment and Their Impact on Environmental Justice

Quantitative risk assessment is frequently described as merely a tool to aid decision makers, not a process that dictates certain risk management results. The methodology, however, raises serious environmental justice concerns, because the results of risk assessments often are not representative of the risks borne by all segments of the population and the aspects of risk that risk assessment seeks to measure do not capture the concerns of all members of the public.

1 + 1 Does Not Always Equal 2

On a daily basis, people are exposed to numerous pollutants from a variety of different sources. The National Academy of Sciences estimated in 1984 that there were more than 64,000 different chemicals currently produced, with over 12,000 manufactured in substantial amounts. In 1989 alone, almost six trillion pounds of chemicals were produced in the United States.... The effects of such multiple exposures and mixing, however, are a matter of dispute and a problem for risk assessment.

Quantitative risk assessment has problems addressing the aggregation of risks, which include multiple exposure, cumulative exposures, and existing exposures. Multiple exposures occur when a person is exposed to a combination of two or more different chemicals or pollutants, while cumulative exposures result when an individual is exposed to one or more chemicals or pollutants from different media or over time. Existing or "background" exposures or risks are those exposures that a person presently experiences, before the addition of any new exposures or risks. Risk assessments generally address the risks posed by one chemical or one source, and a regulatory decision of what is an "acceptable" risk customarily focuses on the risk posed by that single chemical or source. The total risk that a person faces, however, is an aggregate of these many, many risks, each of which individually may be deemed acceptable but in the aggregate may be quite substantial. If a person already has a significant level of existing or background exposure or risk, then the addition of even a small exposure or risk may have a greater effect on that person than on another person who is not already above or near some threshold of safety.... Because minorities and low-income communities face greater exposures to environmental contaminants, it is reasonable to conclude that the failure of risk assessment to account for multiple and cumulative exposures impacts these subpopulations more adversely than other population groups....

Synergistic effects among pollutants that mix also pose a methodological problem for quantitative risk assessment. Possible effects when pollutants mix include "additivity," "synergism," and "antagonism." "Additivity," the simplest effect, occurs when chemicals or pollutants mix and result in an exact combination of all the individual effects. "Synergists" are chemicals or pollutants that, when combined, result in a greater than additive effect. "Antagonism" occurs when the mixture results in diminished toxicity....

The phenomenon of synergism may be widespread among pollutants. Approximately 5% of chemicals exhibit effects that are more or less than additive. Although this percentage may seem relatively small, because there are so many chemicals, synergistic possibilities are huge. For example, if there were 12,000 chemicals in commerce today, and 2.5% reacted synergistically, almost 1.8 million pairs of chemicals would act synergistically.

Despite the propensity for chemicals to react synergistically and increase in toxicity, risk assessments rarely take synergism into account....

A 70 kg, White Male Complex

... There is a high degree of variability in the response of humans to different levels of pollution. Age, lifestyle, genetic background, sex, ethnicity, and race may all play an important role in enhancing the susceptibility of persons to environmentally related disease. Studies have shown human variability of more than 1000-fold in drug metabolism and between 3 and 150-fold in the carcinogenic metabolism of various chemicals.

Variability in susceptibility may not only be large, but also wide-spread. Five percent of humans may be as much as twenty-five times less or more susceptible to cancer than the average person; one percent may be more than 100 times more susceptible....

The National Academy of Sciences found that interindividual variability is not generally considered in the EPA's cancer risk assessment.... The default assumption usually employed in a risk assessment is that humans on average have the same susceptibility as persons in epidemiologic studies or as the most sensitive of the few animal species tested. Most epidemiology studies used in risk assessments are based on studies of health[y] white male workers.... [C]ertain genetic traits that increase susceptibility to environmental pollutants are more prevalent in racial minorities. In addition, biological differences may make certain diseases such as hypertension, chronic liver disease, chronic respiratory disease, and sickle-cell anemia more prevalent among minority populations and increase their risk of adverse outcomes to environmental exposures.

Lifestyle and socio-demographic factors also place minority populations at higher risk. Alcohol, tobacco, and drug use are more frequent in minority populations and result in impaired respiratory, cardiovascular, and metabolic processes, and in reduced ability to metabolize or eliminate toxic substances. Most minority populations also have a higher proportion of young persons and women of childbearing age. Because fetuses, neonates, infants, children, and pregnant women are more susceptible to the adverse effects of pollution, minority groups are more severely impacted by pollution because a higher proportion of these susceptible individuals are found in minority populations. Inadequate diets due to poverty and high risk diets due to cultural or historical reasons also may be more prevalent in minority communities and increase susceptibility; lack of access to health care or poorer quality care may increase the adverse effects of environmental exposures on poorer minority and ethnic communities....

[R]isk assessment most accurately portrays the risks of a particular subgroup—the healthy, seventy-kilogram, white male. Risk assessments use a seventy-kilogram male with the general biology of a Caucasian, as a so-called reference man, in developing dose-response predictions and assume that this reference man is an appropriate surrogate for minorities, as well as women and children. In addition, the dose-response models used to extrapolate from high-dose animal studies to lower-dose human exposures are based on the assumption that the exposed population is of uniform susceptibility. The result of relying on this reference man is a risk assessment characterization that fits far less than half the nation's population, because the majority are women, children, the elderly, sick, or people of color....

Just the Probabilities and Nothing but the Probabilities

... The distribution of risks has not been a focus of risk assessment, at least to date. The social aspects of risk, which concern not only environmental justice advocates but also the public in general, are simply not part of the risk assessment calculus. In addition, the almost obsessive nature of risk discussions that revolve around the difference between risks of one in 100,000 and two in 100,000 undoubtedly ignore equally important questions such as who are these persons who are at risk; what benefits will those who must bear the risk receive from this increased risk; what benefits will those who produce the risk enjoy; and is it really necessary to impose the risks on these or any other people....

The Effect of Quantitative Risk Assessment on the Democratic Principles of Environmental Justice

Environmental justice is not just about distributional equity; it is also about procedural equity.... Under an ideal democratic model, citizens would participate fully and equally in the risk assessment process, along with agency officials and representatives of those who create environmental risks. Quantitative risk assessment, however, is a highly specialized decision-making tool that few can use or fully understand. To prepare, or even critique, a risk assessment takes a sophisticated understanding of complex issues of animal and human toxicology and physiology, mathematical modeling, and exposure measurements and predictions....

Risk assessment is also information intensive. Toxicological data must be generated through studies or tests, or, at the very least, such data must be located and interpreted, and information on exposure must be gathered or predicted. Thus, preparing, critiquing, or even understanding a risk assessment requires substantial expertise and resources. Few people possess such expertise; only a few organizations have the resources to hire such expertise and to gather or generate needed information. Given their resource limitations, people of color and lower-income communities rarely, if ever, are in a position to participate meaningfully in the risk assessment process....

Thus, quantitative risk assessment appears to reinforce, if not enhance, the special access and influence that powerful interest groups have on environmental agency decision making....

Quantitative risk assessment is extraordinarily information and resource intensive. Often little is known about how chemicals react in test animals and humans, or about the fate and transport of pollutants and the amounts that actually get to a target organ.... The cost of obtaining this necessary data is substantial. More than $1 million may be needed for an assessment of a single chemical.... Reliance on risk assessment not only results in fewer environmental hazards being addressed, but where regulatory action is taken, it is often subject to interminable delays....

Putting Quantitative Risk Assessment in Its Proper Place

Quantitative risk assessment provides the justification for a risk management paradigm that is hard to reconcile with the principles of environmental justice. Environmental justice is not about probabilities, statistical lives, acceptable levels of exposure to cancer-causing chemicals, substituting science for democratic decision making, or putting the opinions of experts before the wants and needs of citizens. "It is not about tinkering with risk analysis, risk assessment, risk management. It is about a new paradigm shift that emphasizes prevention and intervention." [Quoting Professor Robert Bullard. Eds.] Instead of measuring and defining an acceptable level of risk from a hazard, environmental justice adopts the public health approach of seeking to prevent the threat before it occurs and of remedying problems that already exist. In addition, the distribution of societal benefits and burdens and the justifications for actions that result in harm are as important as the science-based characterizations of environmental hazards.

* * *

Notes and Questions

1. Professor Kuehn, noting that "some form of risk assessment is not just here to stay, but … is likely to increase in use," advances numerous suggestions for reforming the risk assessment process. For example, he proposes that distributional information (the demographic characteristics of the populations at risk) and information on multiple and cumulative exposures be included in all risk assessments. Another suggestion is to provide for meaningful public participation at all stages of the risk assessment process, including its design, data collection, and analysis. He also recommends that risk assessors should inform the public about the pervasive uncertainties underlying the risk assessment process, suggesting that "[w]hen these unknown factors and assumptions are revealed, the public may see the lack of confidence in the estimates and may well question the reliability and relevance of risk assessment in resolving questions about environmental exposures." *Id.* at 150–153, 158–166. The latter suggestion is essentially a call for greater transparency in the risk assessment enterprise. How do you think industry stakeholders and government regulators are likely to react to these proposals?

2. Among the issues that Professor Kuehn raises are those stemming from variability in *susceptibility*. As he explains, two people may be exposed to the same amount of a contaminant in the environment, for the same period of time, yet have markedly different responses. These differences in susceptibility may stem from a variety of factors, including gender, lifestage, and genetic predisposition. For example, because methylmercury is a neurodevelopmental toxin, humans are more susceptible to this adverse effect during periods of neurological development, i.e., from prenatal through childhood lifestages. Moreover, as Professor Kuehn observes, "certain genetic traits that increase susceptibility to environmental pollutants are more prevalent in racial minorities." *Id.* Given these considerations, how should variability in susceptibility be taken into account in assessing risk? Professor Jamie Grodsky observes that advances in toxicogenetics and toxicogenomics will some day permit "personalized genetic screening for environmental susceptibility." *See* Jamie A. Grodsky, *Genetics and Environmental Law: Redefining Public Health*, 93 CAL L. REV. 171, 196 (2005). What are some of the implications of this promise?

3. Variability in *exposure* has also emerged as a basis for criticism of risk assessment from the perspective of environmental justice. A group or subpopulation may be more vulnerable to a given level of environmental contamination because its members' circumstances and lifeways leave them more exposed to the contaminants than members of the general population. As described in more detail in Chapter 2, these people might live nearer to the fence line of industrial facilities that emit multiple toxic air pollutants; they might live in older, deteriorated housing that harbors lead dust; they might depend to a greater extent on fish that has become contaminated with PCBs and other pollutants. The National Environmental Justice Advisory Council (NEJAC), an advisory body to the EPA representing multiple stakeholders and convened under the auspices of the Federal Advisory Committee Act, discusses the issue of variability in exposure to contamination in fish and other aquatic resources in the following excerpt.

National Environmental Justice Advisory Council, Fish Consumption and Environmental Justice

(2001)

[C]ommunities of color, low-income communities, tribes, and other indigenous peoples *depend* on healthy aquatic ecosystems and the fish, aquatic plants, and wildlife that these ecosystems support. While there are important differences among these various affected groups, their members generally depend on the fish, aquatic plants, and wildlife to a greater extent and in different ways than does the general population. These resources are consumed and used to meet nutritional and economic needs. For some groups, they are also consumed or used for cultural, traditional, or religious purposes. For members of these groups, the conventional understandings of the "health benefits" or "economic benefits" of catching, harvesting, preparing, and eating fish, aquatic plants, and wildlife do not adequately capture the significant value these practices have in their lives and the life of their culture. The harms caused by degradation of aquatic habitats and depletion of fisheries, moreover, do not only affect the present generation. They take their toll on future generations and on the transfer of knowledge from one generation to the next (e.g., ecological knowledge, customs and traditions surrounding harvest, preparation and consumption of aquatic resources).

Many of the rivers, streams, bayous, bays, lakes, wetlands, and estuaries that support these resources on which communities and tribes depend have become contaminated and depleted. Contamination is causing the communities' and tribes' everyday practices—their ways of living—to serve as a source of exposure to a host of substances toxic to humans and other living things. The depletion of aquatic environments and resources also threatens these groups' subsistence, economic, cultural, traditional, and religious practices. Aquatic ecosystems are contaminated with mercury, PCBs, dioxins, DDT and other pesticides, lead and other metals, sediments, fecal coliform and other bacterial and viral contaminants—in short, a host of toxins, most of which are particularly troubling because they *persist* in the environment for great lengths of time and because they *bioaccumulate* in the tissues of fish, aquatic plants, and wildlife, existing in greater quantities higher up the food chain.

For many communities of color, low-income communities, tribes, and other indigenous peoples, there are no real alternatives to eating and using fish, aquatic plants, and wildlife. For many members of these groups it is entirely impractical to "switch" to "substitutes" when the fish and other resources on which they rely have become contaminated. There are numerous and often insurmountable obstacles to seeking alternatives (e.g., fishing "elsewhere," throwing back "undesirable" species of fish, adopting different preparation methods, or substituting beef, chicken or tofu). For some, not fishing and not eating fish are unimaginable for cultural, traditional, or religious reasons. For the fishing peoples of the Pacific Northwest, for example, fish and fishing are necessary for survival as a people—they are vital as a matter of cultural flourishing and self-determination.

When health and environmental agencies respond to contamination and its impacts, they typically ... rely on assumptions about fish consumption rates, practices, and needs that reflect the circumstances of the general population, but often are not reflective enough of the circumstances of affected communities and tribes. Agencies' approaches to risk assessment, risk management, and risk communication similarly fall short of taking into account that affected groups consume and use fish, aquatic plants, and wildlife in different cultural, traditional, religious, historical, economic, and legal contexts than the "average American."

* * *

Notes and Questions

1. How should variability in exposure be taken into account in assessing risk? What if agencies were simply to assess the risk to the maximally exposed individual and then establish regulatory protections accordingly? Are there drawbacks to this protective response to variability in exposure?

2. Risk assessment has also come under criticism from those who believe that, as currently practiced by environmental agencies, risk assessment leads to overestimates of risk and, consequently, an overinvestment by society in regulations requiring risk reduction. Those who offer this perspective tend to be proponents of risk assessment and other quantitative methods of analysis (e.g., cost-benefit analysis, discussed in Chapter 5). While supportive of QRA as a general matter, they contend nonetheless that agencies' methods ought to be refined in several ways. Two influential sources espousing this view are: CASS R. SUNSTEIN, RISK AND REASON: SAFETY, LAW, AND THE ENVIRONMENT (2002); and STEPHEN BREYER, BREAKING THE VICIOUS CIRCLE: TOWARD EFFECTIVE RISK REGULATION (1993).

3. Among the arguments raised are two with particular import for environmental justice: arguments favoring the use of "central estimates" of risk and arguments favoring a focus on "population risk" in lieu of individual risk. First, critics have argued that environmental agencies inappropriately respond to both uncertainty and variability when they undertake a risk assessment, producing high-end estimates of risk. They cite the fact that EPA currently uses conservative responses to each instance of uncertainty, choosing, for example, an assumption about the mechanism of carcinogenesis that yields a much higher estimate of a chemical's potency than would competing assumptions. Additionally, they claim that EPA selects protective responses to each instance of variability, focusing on the highly exposed individuals represented by the 90th or 95th percentile of the distribution for the total population. While each of these assumptions might be plausible in isolation, they argue, taken together, they produce an effect of "cascading conservatism" such that the resulting estimate of risk is likely to be unrealistically high and to reflect no one's actual circumstances of exposure. Justice Breyer, prior to his appointment to the U.S. Supreme Court, presented this argument in the following excerpt.

Stephen Breyer, Breaking the Vicious Circle: Toward Effective Risk Regulation

(1993)

EPA sometimes makes a strictly mechanical assumption that the individual is exposed to emissions at a point 200 meters from the factory, all day, every day, for 70 years. OSHA assumes a factory worker exposed 8 hours per day, 5 days a week, 50 weeks per year, for 45 years. Other agencies use such "conservative" assumptions as that householders spend 70 years in the same house (they spend 9, on average); that adults drink 2 liters of water per day (they drink 1.4 liters of all liquids); that half of all houses near toxic waste dumps contain children ... and so forth.

If an agency uses these assumptions when calculating the risks run by individuals who are *maximally* exposed, they may be realistic; if it uses them to estimate effects on typical workers or citizens across the nation, they may be unrealistically conservative; if it uses them as "presumptions"—asking industry to come forward with proof of the contrary—they may, in practice, come to resemble the latter use. OMB argues that the agencies apply these assumptions too conservatively; it concludes that, taken together, they "often" overstate risks by factors of a thousand or even a million or more.

* * *

Notes and Questions

1. In the excerpt above, Professor O'Neill argues that, for clarity, agencies' responses to uncertainty ought to be viewed as more or less "conservative," whereas agencies' responses to variability ought to be viewed as more or less "protective." Commentators on various sides of the debate have not always maintained this distinction, however, as this excerpt from Justice Breyer illustrates. In particular, critics have decried agencies' "conservatism" in selecting 90th percentile values for each parameter contributing to exposure (e.g., those outlined by Justice Breyer, above). Professor O'Neill argues that, instead, this criticism ought to be understood as speaking to agencies' choice of whom to protect, that is, whether to protect the most exposed. She goes on to respond to these critics' claim that the composite of high-end or maximum values does not reflect anyone's actual circumstances of exposure:

> In the context of exposure via fish ingestion, this argument may have merit when applied to "the typical U.S. consumer eating fish in moderation from a variety of sources." But it fails when applied to many Native Americans of the Pacific Northwest. For many Native Americans in this region, actual individuals' exposures *are* described by a composite of the maxima. Actual individuals *do* live in the same place, and fish from the same spots, and consume relatively large quantities of fish per day for a whole lifetime. Indeed, many feel that they could not do otherwise.

O'Neill, *Variable Justice* at 79–80. Is her response likely to hold true for other situations in which environmental justice communities are among those exposed?

2. The solution, from the perspective of those who raise the argument advanced here by Justice Breyer, is for agencies to conduct risk assessments that focus on a central estimate of risk. This would counsel agencies to choose a "best" or "plausible" assumption in the face of uncertainty—as opposed to a conservative assumption; and to select a mean or average value from the distribution of values where there is variability.

Critics have also argued that environmental agencies' focus on "individual risk" is misplaced, again leading to the overregulation of risks and to a misallocation of resources toward risks to which very few people are actually exposed. Professor Matthew Adler makes this point in the excerpt that follows.

Matthew D. Adler, Against "Individual Risk": A Sympathetic Critique of Risk Assessment
153 University of Pennsylvania Law Review 1121 (2005)

EPA's rule for cleanups under the Superfund statute is ... risk-based: toxic waste dumps are to be remedied so that the lifetime fatality risk to the "maximally exposed individual" from carcinogens in the dump is within the range of 1 in 10,000 to 1 in 1 million....

What accounts for this regulatory focus on "individual risk"? One answer is tempting, but wrong. The temptation is to say that regulatory agencies inevitably take the maximal level of "individual risk" as the test of safety, at least for substances and activities that cannot be removed from our lives without massive cost.... How else to determine which toxic exposures merit a regulatory response except by setting an "individual risk" threshold which seems very low—say, 1 in 1 million to the maximally exposed individual—and taking that as the trigger for regulatory intervention? But this response overlooks a crucial deficit in "individual risk" tests of this kind: their insensitivity to population size. Compare an isolated toxic waste dump that (under worst-case modeling) leaches contaminants to a radius of ten miles, affecting a population of 10,000; a workplace toxin employed in certain industries, to which one million workers are exposed; and a chemical in drinking water that is consumed by 100 million. For simplicity, assume that in each case every person in the exposed population incurs a 1 in 1 million risk of dying from the hazard. Then in the waste-dump case it is overwhelmingly likely that the hazard will cause no fatalities; in the workplace case it is reasonably likely that the hazard will cause one or more fatalities, with one incremental death the expected outcome; and in the drinking water case it is overwhelmingly likely that the hazard will cause one or more fatalities, with 100 incremental deaths the expected outcome.

Risk assessors typically distinguish between "individual risk"—the risk of death borne by a particular individual, either a named person or someone identified by her exposure characteristics—and "population risk." "Population risk" (also sometimes called "societal risk") is the total number of fatalities resulting from a toxin, a hazardous activity, or some other threat to human life....

Whether regulators should intervene to abate some hazard depends, morally, on the number of persons at risk from the hazard.

* * *

Notes and Questions

1. According to these critics, if regulatory agencies were to reform risk assessment in the two ways urged above, agencies' estimates of the risks that attend environmental contamination would decrease, and the case for regulating the sources of risk would, correspondingly, be weakened. Professors Jim Hamilton and Kip Viscusi conclude that their survey of EPA's assessment of the risks associated with 150 Superfund sites bears out this point. They argue that, due to "conservative biases" in EPA's method, "[e]ven though actual risk exposures are usually low, individual lifetime cancer rates estimated to arise at sites under EPA's risk assessment methodology are extremely high.... Many of these risk estimates drop to levels deemed acceptable in EPA's remediation guidelines, however, if one uses more realistic parameter values [i.e., central estimates] in the risk assessment process.... Our analysis reveals that once individual risk levels are combined with data on exposed populations, the magnitude of apparent cancer risks diminishes...." JAMES T. HAMILTON & W. KIP VISCUSI, CALCULATING RISKS? THE SPATIAL AND POLITICAL DIMENSIONS OF HAZARDOUS WASTE POLICY 108 (1999).

2. Agencies already take the size of the affected populations into account in a number of ways in deciding how to respond to risks. For example, as elaborated in Chapter 9, when prioritizing contaminated sites for cleanup under the Comprehensive Environmental Response, Compensation, and Liability Act (CERCLA), EPA considers sites that impact greater numbers of people to be a higher priority than sites affecting

fewer people. But don't Professors Adler, Hamilton, and Viscusi contemplate something more? What do Professors Hamilton and Viscusi mean by their statement that,
if agencies combine individual risk levels with data on exposed populations, "the magnitude of *apparent* cancer risks diminishes?" Is the risk faced by an individual who in
fact lives at the fenceline of a polluting factory for his entire life lessened by the fact
that few others also live in the vicinity? How should regulatory agencies frame the relevant questions?

3. In 2006, the Office of Management and Budget, then highly sympathetic to calls
for curbing health, safety, and environmental regulation, issued its Proposed Risk Assessment Bulletin. OFFICE OF MGMT. & BUDGET, PROPOSED RISK ASSESSMENT BULLETIN
(Jan. 9, 2006). According to OMB, the Bulletin was designed to "improve the quality, objectivity, utility, and integrity of information disseminated by the federal government." The
Bulletin incorporated many of the reforms suggested over the years by regulated industries and those in academia and think tanks who favored "rationalizing" risk regulation.
Notably, the Bulletin adopted both of the suggestions discussed above, namely, that risk
assessments feature "central estimates" and consider "population risks." If you were to
write comments to OMB on the Bulletin's adoption of these arguments, what environmental justice points would you make? The National Research Council reviewed the controversial proposal and determined it to be "fundamentally flawed" on a number of scores.
NATIONAL RESEARCH COUNCIL, SCIENTIFIC REVIEW OF THE PROPOSED RISK ASSESSMENT
BULLETIN FROM THE OFFICE OF MANAGEMENT AND BUDGET (2007). Ultimately, OMB
withdrew the proposed Bulletin. For an excellent discussion of these events, see Sidney
A. Shapiro, *OMB and the Politicization of Risk Assessment,* 37 ENVTL. L. 1083 (2007).

4. Some commentators have responded to the charge that risk assessment is too conservative in the face of uncertainty by contending that it is prudent to continue to use
conservative assumptions given the fact that historically some toxic substances turned
out to be much more harmful than once believed. For example, the recognized level for
lead toxicity in the U.S. has been lowered dramatically over the past 30 years, from 60 to
10 micrograms of lead per deciliter of blood (Some recent studies found children with blood
lead levels as low as 5 micrograms experience learning problems, and many experts believe there is no safe level of lead exposure). Others have argued that any overestimates
of risk due to conservative assumptions are surely offset by the considerable underestimate of risk that results from the fact that risk assessment, at present, largely fails to account for the cumulative impacts of the multiple chemicals to which people are exposed.
(Developments in cumulative risk assessment are taken up in the next section.) What are
the pros and cons of using conservative assumptions in this manner to compensate for
other deficiencies in the risk assessment process?

5. Because of the many uncertainties and data gaps in the risk assessment process, the
outcome reflects discretionary decisions by risk assessors. Mary O'Brien argues that the
economic interests of risk-producing entities inevitably influence how these subjective
decisions are made:

> [M]ost risk assessments are prepared when permission is sought by a business,
> an agency, or a corporation to initiate or continue a hazardous activity or to
> use a poison. That is, a risk-management decision that will have consequences
> for a business or an agency is already on the horizon. The risk assessor is gen-
> erally hired by private industry or by the government to do a risk assessment
> of a value-laden and sometimes highly controversial situation. Most risk as-
> sessors do not stay clear of risk-management considerations during the process
> of estimating risk. Since there is a wide choice of which numbers will be plugged

into a risk assessment, and since no one usually knows for sure what is the "right" number to use, the pressure on a risk assessor to use numbers that will fulfill the wishes of the company or agency by which she or he is employed becomes tremendous. The bottom line in most (if not all) risk assessments is that if someone wants to continue some activity or to get a permit or approval for some activity, and if the outcome of the risk assessment will get in the way of that activity, there will be pressure to use optimistic numbers in the risk assessment....

... An industry or an agency wanting to defend its activities would be more likely to hire a risk assessor known for seeing "less" risk rather than "more" risk in various activities.

Mary O'Brien, MAKING BETTER ENVIRONMENTAL DECISIONS: AN ALTERNATIVE TO RISK ASSESSMENT 27, 37 (2000). Is there a solution to the problem O'Brien identifies? Is there any way to prevent risk assessors from being influenced by the financial stakes at issue for their employers?

3. Risks to Children

Risk assessment practice is starting to change to take into account the disproportionate risks faced by children. Children are especially vulnerable to environmental hazards because their systems are still developing, because they eat proportionately more food, drink more fluids, and breathe more air than adults, and because their behavior patterns, such as playing close to the ground and hand-to-mouth activity, increase their exposure to hazards. In 1995, EPA adopted a policy requiring that the environmental health risks of children be evaluated in risk assessments. EPA also pledged that it would set new regulatory standards at levels protective enough to address the potentially heightened risks faced by children and that it would re-evaluate a number of existing regulations to see if they met this standard. In 1997, President Clinton issued an executive order requiring that each agency make it a high priority to identify and assess environmental health and safety risks that may disproportionately affect children, and ensure that its actions address these disproportionate risks. Protection of Children from Environmental Health Risks and Safety Risks, Exec. Order No. 13,045, 62 Fed. Reg. 19,885 (April 23, 1997). The 1996 Food Quality Protection Act also explicitly requires EPA to address the special risks to infants and children when setting pesticide tolerances, the levels of chemical pesticide residues permissible on foods. If EPA does not have complete or reliable data to assess risks to children or infants, it can require an additional tenfold safety factor. 21 U.S.C. § 346a(b)(2)(C). In the Fall of 2008, EPA published a handbook setting forth the different factors that describe children's circumstances of exposure. U.S. ENVTL. PROT. AGENCY, CHILD-SPECIFIC EXPOSURE FACTORS HANDBOOK (2008). While EPA had previously provided some guidance as to how risk assessors ought to account for children's unique circumstances, this was the first time in which EPA issued comprehensive guidance exclusively devoted to children.

In May of 2007, a large group of scientists from various disciplines gathered at the International Conference on Fetal Programming and Developmental Toxicity, held in the Faroes Islands. These scientists published a joint statement, known as the "Faroes Statement," that summarized the most recent data regarding childhood exposure to environmental contamination. The following excerpt describes some of their conclusions.

Philippe Grandjean et al., The Faroes Statement: Human Health Effects of Developmental Exposure to Chemicals in Our Environment

102 Basic & Clinical Pharmacology & Toxicology 73 (2007)

The periods of embryonic, foetal and infant development are remarkably susceptible to environmental hazards. Toxic exposures to chemical pollutants during these windows of increased susceptibility can cause disease and disability in infants, children and across the entire span of human life. Among the effects of toxic exposures recognized in the past have been spontaneous abortion, congenital malformations, lowered birthweight and other adverse effects. These outcomes may be readily apparent. However, even subtle changes caused by chemical exposures during early development may lead to important functional deficits and increased risks of disease later in life. The timing of exposure during early life has therefore become a crucial factor to be considered in toxicological assessments....

Three aspects of children's health are important in conjunction with developmental toxicity risks. First, the mother's chemical body burden will be shared with her foetus or neonate, and the child may, in some instances, be exposed to larger doses relative to the body weight. Second, susceptibility to a wide range of adverse effects is increased during development, from preconception through adolescence, depending on the organ system. Third, developmental exposures to environmental chemicals can lead to life-long functional deficits and disease. Research into the environmental influence on developmental programming of health and disease has, therefore, led to a new paradigm of toxicologic understanding. The old paradigm, developed over four centuries ago by Paracelsus, was that 'the dose makes the poison'. However, for exposures sustained during early development, another critical, but largely ignored, issue is that 'the timing makes the poison'. This extended paradigm deserves wide attention to protect the foetus and child against preventable hazards.

* * *

Notes and Questions

1. The insight that "the timing makes the poison" could have considerable implications for the way agencies assess and respond to risks from those contaminants with developmental toxicity. How should attention to these crucial "windows of increased susceptibility" alter agencies' approach?

2. The most recent research continues to underscore the concerns articulated by the Faroes Statement, suggesting that the problem of these windows of susceptibility during embryonic, fetal, and neonatal development are more serious than previously understood. Professor Carl Cranor discusses the implications of this research, along with emerging data from biomonitoring efforts showing that the bodies of U.S. citizens—including women of childbearing age—harbor some 270 manmade chemicals in measurable quantities. See Carl F. Cranor, *Do You Want to Bet Your Children's Health on Post-Market Harm Principles? An Argument for a Trespass or Permission Model for Regulating Toxicants,* 19 VILL. ENVTL. L. J. 251 (2008). Professor Cranor recognizes that "[t]he presence of manmade industrial chemicals in citizens' bodies does not necessarily mean that they pose risks or are harmful." Nonetheless, "[t]heir mere presence is wrong on a trespass model," which would view these invasions as problematic in and of themselves. *Id.* at 255. He

proposes a shift to an understanding along the lines of this trespass model, and a regulatory approach that requires those seeking to introduce chemicals into commerce to provide data, subject to government certification, that the chemicals will not pose significant risks or harm to developing children or adults.

3. In a sustained critique, Professor Rena Steinzor examines how agencies' use of risk assessment, cost-benefit analysis, and other such analytic tools in a highly politicized climate has left children, in particular, underprotected from environmental harms. See Rena I. Steinzor, Mother Earth and Uncle Sam: How Pollution and Hollow Government Hurt Our Kids (2008).

4. Environmental justice advocates have joined other critics of quantitative risk assessment in noting that the method is insensitive to context, that is, to the circumstances of the particular group(s) affected by agencies' risk assessment methods and risk management decisions. The next section considers one such group, American Indians, by way of example.

4. Risk Assessment in Context: The Example of American Indian Tribes

Tribes have often taken issue with the entire paradigm within which risk assessment operates. Nonetheless, tribes, like other environmental justice communities, have recognized the immediate necessity of engaging the method and its implications, given its current favored place among federal and state environmental agencies' analytic tools. Some— but by no means all— of the issues raised by tribes are sketched below.

When American Indian tribes and their members are among those affected by contamination, a number of particular considerations come into play. Tribes are unique among highly-exposed or vulnerable groups in that they are sovereign nations, with unique political and legal status and rights. In this regard, as tribes have argued, when agencies assess and respond to risk, tribes cannot be viewed as simply another "subpopulation," nor as merely the "high-end tail" of a distribution of the general population.

When environmental agencies undertake a risk assessment, they typically rely on a snapshot of contemporary exposure. This focus on contemporary consumption is problematic for a number of reasons. Chief among these, as tribes have argued, is the fact that tribes are entitled to their traditional uses of natural resources. Tribes have inherent, aboriginal rights—secured in many instances by treaties or other forms of legal recognition—to continue to rely on their traditional resources, as they had prior to European contact. Moreover, as sovereign governments engaged in political and cultural self-determination, tribes' vision for the future anticipates members' ability to rely on their traditional resources and continue their lifeways. When agencies look only at contemporary consumption and resource use to assess risk and set human-health based standards (e.g., for water quality or cleanup of contaminated sediments), they will permit a larger amount of contaminants to be released to or to remain in the environment than would be permissible were agencies to account for tribes' traditional lifeways and the exposures these entail. For example, contemporary fish consumption rates—even those generated by studies aimed specifically at tribal members—need to be understood in light of what researchers have termed "suppression effects."

A 'suppression effect' occurs when a fish consumption rate (FCR) for a given population, group, or tribe reflects a current level of consumption that is artificially diminished from an appropriate baseline level of consumption for that population, group, or tribe. The more robust baseline level of consumption is suppressed, inasmuch as it does not get captured by the FCR."

NAT'L ENVTL. JUSTICE ADVISORY COUNCIL, FISH CONSUMPTION AND ENVIRONMENTAL JUSTICE, *supra*, at 43. Tribal researchers Jamie Donatuto and Barbara Harper elaborate.

Jamie Donatuto and Barbara L. Harper, Issues in Evaluating Fish Consumption Rates for Native American Tribes
28 Risk Analysis 1497 (2008)

Even though average contemporary tribal fish consumption rates are much higher than those of the average American, current average tribal rates are nevertheless lower than [historical or] heritage rates.... Many Native people have been forced to reduce their intake below original subsistence levels, in essence *suppressing* their fish consumption rate. There are several reasons for this suppression.

1. Treaty and aboriginal rights to access and harvest traditional foods are still hotly contested, with battles being fought across the country for recognition and protection of those rights. Many federal, state, local, and commercial entities still aggressively seek to diminish or extinguish tribal rights and culture.

2. People have less access to general and specifically inherited harvest sites due to loss of ownership, theft of land, and poorly scripted federal policies.

3. Fewer people have enough time to catch fully subsistent levels of seafood because they have been forced to assimilate into the dominant society's workforce and to share its economic beliefs. In many cases this assimilation is the unhappy result of decades of federal policies that deliberately tried to eradicate traditional tribal lifestyles, using such agents as missionaries and boarding schools, to obliterate native languages, religion, cultural practices, and connections to the land.

4. Tribal people are still harassed while participating in the harvest of traditional foods via verbal, physical, and legal threats by private citizens and public law enforcement authorities, and their gear is still being vandalized, stolen, or seized.

5. Aquatic species populations have been decimated or destroyed by dams and other development projects, commercial overfishing, invasive species, habitat fragmentation and loss, and many other causes.

6. Knowledge of contamination in areas traditionally harvested—learned through anecdotal, first-hand or visual data, and fish advisories—have influenced some native people to eat less subsistence seafood. Despite these obstacles, many tribal people continue to rely on subsistence foods with seafood being a primary source, although they may not always mirror levels of historic consumption.

* * *

Notes and Questions

1. Note that suppression effects may infect attempts to assess consumption practices for various subpopulations or for the general population as well—for example, consumption surveys of women of childbearing age may reflect a current level of consumption that is diminished from levels that women in this group would consume, but for the existence of fish consumption advisories due to mercury contamination. However, when

tribes are affected, there are two important differences. First, conceptually the "appropriate baseline level of consumption" is often clear for tribes, whereas it may be subject to debate for other groups. Only tribes have legally protected rights to a certain historical baseline level of consumption. Second, the causes of suppression have exerted pressure on tribes for a longer period, and in more numerous ways, than on the general population. Whereas, e.g., those the general population may have begun to reduce their intake of fish in response to consumption advisories once these became more prevalent in the 1970s and thereafter, those in the tribes have been excluded from their fisheries, harassed and imprisoned, for well over a century (in the Pacific Northwest, for example, litigation by tribes to enforce treaty rights began in 1884, not even three decades after the treaties were signed). An understanding of tribes' historical lifeways, then, becomes important to questions of environmental protection, cleanup, and restoration of the relevant resources.

2. Note, too, the potential for a continuing "downward spiral:" if agencies use a risk assessment that assumes fish consumption at contemporary, suppressed rates, the resulting water quality standards will permit a relatively greater level of pollution to be discharged into the water; agencies will then issue fish consumption advisories warning against fish intake above these rates; when agencies next conduct consumption surveys, these can be expected to generate even lower consumption rates, as some people reduce their fish consumption in compliance with advisories; in turn, agencies' will use these new, lower fish consumption rates in their risk assessments and set water quality standards that are gauged to protect only this further diminished level of consumption; and so on. Nat'l Envtl. Justice Advisory Council, Fish Consumption and Environmental Justice, *supra,* at 45. The potential for such a downward spiral might present particular concerns from the perspective of various environmental justice groups, for example, the fishing tribes or Southeast Asian-American communities in the Great Lakes states. How, if you were representing one of these groups, might you bring these concerns to the attention of agency risk assessors and risk managers?

3. Drs. Donatuto and Harper point out that contemporary consumption rates are not only suppressed from original or "heritage" rates, but also tend not to reflect "subsistence rates eaten by a subset of tribal members even now." The impact of this second failure can be profound, as they illustrate:

> For example, the average [value from a survey by the Columbia River Inter-Tribal Fish Commission (CRITFC)] contemporary consumption rate is 63.2 [grams per day (gpd)] and the 95th percentile is 170 gpd, as measured using conventional survey methods. However, within the Confederated Umatilla Tribes, one of the CRITFC member tribes, a subset of traditional consumers who adhere more closely to traditional subsistence practices such as harvesting and preparing their own food currently consume an average of approximately 540 gpd, illustrating that the reality of consumption is not captured by conventional survey methods.

Id. at 1500. Drs. Donatuto and Harper go on to enumerate a number of flaws with the conventional methods of data gathering and analysis—methods that were designed for the general population but that are often inappropriate to the tribal context. As they point out, the application of these conventional methods will often lead to results that are inaccurate and, frequently, that bias downward the resulting FCRs.

4. Agencies' risk assessments also tend to make assumptions about species consumed, parts used, and preparation methods employed that reflect the practices of the general population but fail to capture the practices of particular groups. For example, as the NEJAC recounts:

[A]ccording to a survey of first- and second-generation Asian and Pacific Islanders [(API)] in King County, Washington—including members of Cambodian, Chinese, Filipino, Hmong, Japanese, Korean, Laotian, Mien, Samoan, and Vietnamese ethnic groups ... API community members appear to eat shellfish parts that are thought to contain higher concentrations of chemical contamination, e.g., clam stomachs or the hepatopancreas of crabs. Bivalve shellfish were consumed whole by 24% (geoduck) to 89% (mussels) of the respondents depending on the species. The 'butter' as well as the meat of crabs were consumed 43% of the time....

NAT'L ENVTL. JUSTICE ADVISORY COUNCIL, FISH CONSUMPTION, *supra*, at 34, 38. As a consequence, agencies are likely to underestimate risk to members of API groups.

5. Ultimately, as Drs. Donatuto and Harper point out, although the development and use of more appropriate tools for analysis will address some of issues presented by the tribal context, the paradigm within which risk assessment operates is at odds with tribal understandings of health, which, among other things, include the interrelated aspects of individual and group health. "Rather, a public health approach that includes all facets of health—physical, mental, environmental, cultural—comes closer to truly meeting the needs of Native communities." Donatuto & Harper, *supra*, at 1505. For related efforts to address the shortcomings in current approaches and to envision alternative approaches more appropriate to the tribal context, see Stuart G. Harris & Barbara L. Harper, *Using Eco-Cultural Dependency Webs in Risk Assessment and Characterization of Risks to Tribal Health and Cultures*, 2 ENVTL. SCI. & POLLUTION RES. 91 (2000); Mary Arquette et al., *Holistic Risk-Based Environmental Decision Making: A Native Perspective*, 110 ENVTL. HEALTH PERSP. 259 (Supp. 2, 2002).

C. Cumulative Risk Assessment

1. Introduction to Cumulative Risk Assessment

Environmental justice advocates have long argued that risk assessment, as currently practiced, grossly understates the risks actually faced by those in tribes, communities of color, and low-income communities. This is so because agencies typically focus on a single chemical or source (for example, "a risk assessment for dioxin," or "an assessment of risk from TCE in the groundwater at a particular contaminated site") in isolation. But, as affected communities have pointed out, people are not exposed to only one chemical contaminant; rather, they are often exposed to multiple chemicals present in their environment. To the extent that agencies account for the cumulative effects of these multiple exposures, as noted above, they tend to treat the consequences as merely additive. However, as noted by Professor Kuehn, there are often synergistic interactions among the various chemicals to which humans are exposed, such that the actual consequences are multiplicative—as Professor Kuehn puts it: "1 + 1 does not always equal 2." While this failure to account for cumulative exposures and synergistic effects is a shortcoming of risk assessment that affects all those at risk, its import is amplified for environmental justice communities, who are often among the most exposed to the mixtures of chemical contaminants present in their environments—the urban toxic soup or the rural pesticide slurry.

Moreover, environmental justice advocates have pointed out, agencies' narrow focus on chemical stressors fails to account for the fact that the actual health consequences for those exposed can only be understood if one accounts for the complete roster of contributing stressors that affect human health. Thus, the same amount of a contaminant present in the environment can result in widely differing health consequences for members of two different communities or subpopulations, depending on the extent to which these other non-chemical (e.g., physical, social, cultural) stressors are also present. Environmental justice communities are often historically overburdened with contamination, disadvantaged in terms of services that would permit members to withstand or recover from environmental insults, and isolated or lacking in political influence. Agencies' failure to account for multiple stressors in their assessments of risk, therefore, is likely again to lead to especially large understatements of risk to these communities.

Wilma Subra, a chemist and environmental justice activist with the Louisiana Environmental Action Network, developed the following matrix of the myriad factors that are relevant to a complete understanding of the risk faced by those in the Mississippi River Industrial Corridor—also known as "Cancer Alley"—the 2,000 square-mile area between Baton Rouge and New Orleans, Louisiana:

Demographics	Pollution Sources	Existing Health Problems & Conditions	Unique Exposure Pathways	Social/ Cultural Conditions	Community Capacity & Infrastructure/ Social Capital
African American: 63% Caucasian: 35% Asian: 3%	Petrochemical facilities Refineries Wastewater treatment facilities not meeting permit limits and bypassing raw sewage due to under capacity Drinking water taken from Mississippi River • Toxic organics, pesticides and heavy metals in drinking water • Atrazine from Midwest agricultural fields present year-round in raw and finished water Pesticides, herbicides, and fertilizers applied to sugar cane crops, aerial and tractor application drifts on to adjacent residential areas and school yards Burning sugar cane during fall harvest season results in particulate matter and pesticides being dispersed into the air for a third of the year.	Asthma Respiratory distress Skin rashes High rate of a large variety of cancers Lack of access to health care Lack of trained environmental health physicians	Air • Industrial facilities: semi-volatile and volatile organics, dioxins, pesticides and herbicides • Toxic heavy metals, and smoke from sugar cane burning Water: • Drinking water contaminated • Surface water contaminated with industrial and agricultural chemicals and partially treated waste water • Contaminated crops, contaminated terrestrial game species • Seafood contaminated with pesticides, industrial chemicals, mercury from chlor-alkali facilities by way of air deposition.	Very poor/minority communities Live off land and gardens contaminated with air-deposited chemicals Hunting and fishing of contaminated organisms Generations have lived off the land and not profited by industrial development in the area.	Good infrastructure in areas of low-income communities of color with respect to roads and rail; the industry needs these items. Poor infrastructure within the communities: • poor road conditions • improper drainage • waste water collection and treatment system inadequate • very little to no social capital: education system very minimal • the area was impacted by white flight: primarily African Americans attend the public schools.

Ms. Subra's matrix was reprinted and cited by the NEJAC as an example of the multiple considerations that ought to bear on agencies' assessments of the risks faced by environmental justice communities. NAT'L ENVTL. JUSTICE ADVISORY COUNCIL, ENSURING RISK REDUCTION IN COMMUNITIES WITH MULTIPLE STRESSORS: ENVIRONMENTAL JUSTICE AND CUMULATIVE RISKS/IMPACTS 5 (2004).

Environmental agencies, for their part, have long been aware of the limitations of risk assessment's chemical-by-chemical approach. EPA nonetheless continues to employ the "additivity assumption" to address cumulative risks because in most cases, EPA simply does

not have the scientific data on which to base more accurate assessments of the risk from simultaneous or sequential exposure to multiple chemical or other agents. Still, prompted by
a variety of sources (e.g., criticism from scientific advisory boards and the public; statutory requirements, such as the Food Quality Protection Act of 1996) and enabled by developments in research, the EPA has made strides in accounting for cumulative risk. In
particular, in May of 2003, it published its *Framework for Cumulative Risk Assessment,* which
sets forth the principles and features of cumulative risk assessment. The Framework remains somewhat aspirational, however, given that it sets forth a process that relies on methods and data that may not currently exist. Michael A. Callahan & Ken Sexton, *If Cumulative
Risk Assessment is the Answer, What Is the Question?,* 115 ENVTL. HEALTH PERSP. 799 (2007).

The National Environmental Justice Advisory Council applauded the EPA's Framework as an important advance in addressing environmental justice advocates' concerns.
The NEJAC cited with approval the Framework's adoption of the term "vulnerability,"
which usefully clarified the terms of the discussion (concerns in this regard had sometimes
been discussed by reference to "co-risk" factors or other terms). As well, the Framework's
process envisioned a different orientation to the problem—one that situates risk assessment in context and envisions a more prominent role for the affected community.

National Environmental Justice Advisory Council, Ensuring Risk Reduction in Communities with Multiple Stressors: Environmental Justice and Cumulative Risks/Impacts

(2004)

Vulnerability

The concept of vulnerability goes to the heart of the meaning of environmental justice. Vulnerability recognizes that disadvantaged, underserved, and overburdened communities come to the table with pre-existing deficits of both a physical and social nature
that make the effects of environmental pollution more, and in some cases unacceptably,
burdensome. As such, the concept of vulnerability fundamentally differentiates disadvantaged, underserved, and overburdened communities from healthy and sustainable
communities. Moreover, it provides the added dimension of considering the nature of
the receptor population when defining disproportionate risks or impacts.

The Framework includes a definition of vulnerability that can serve as a starting point
for discussing this concept. According to the Framework, a subpopulation is vulnerable
if it is more likely to be adversely affected by a stressor than the general population. There
are four basic ways in which a population can be vulnerable: susceptibility/sensitivity,
differential exposure, differential preparedness, and differential ability to recover. Each of
these types of vulnerabilities is discussed below.

Susceptibility/Sensitivity: A subpopulation may be susceptible or sensitive to a stressor if
it faces an increased likelihood of sustaining an adverse effect due to a life state (e.g., pregnant, young, old), an impaired immune system, or a pre-existing condition, such as asthma.
A subpopulation could have been previously sensitized to a compound, or have prior disease or damage. In some cases, susceptibility also could arise because of genetic polymor-
phisms, which are genetic differences in a portion of a population. For example, a community
with a large subpopulation of young children could be more susceptible to the effects of
lead poisoning. A community with many elderly residents could be more vulnerable to a
stressor such as a heat wave. And a community with a high number of asthmatics will be
more susceptible to air pollution. The environmental justice implications of this phenom-

enon are significant. For example, given the fact that children are considered to be a highly susceptible subpopulation, then children in low-income and people of color communities must be considered an even more susceptible group within that subpopulation.

Differential Exposure: A subpopulation can be more vulnerable because it is living or working near a source of pollution and is therefore exposed to a higher level of the pollutant than the general population. Children living in older, deteriorated housing are more likely to receive greater exposure to lead paint dust, and their breathing zone is closer to the ground where such dust is more likely to be found. Communities situated close to the fence line of a facility that is emitting air pollutants, or living near a major roadway, will most likely experience higher levels of air pollution. Due to contaminated fish or wildlife, subpopulations, such as Native Americans, that are dependent on subsistence consumption represent another example of differential exposure.

In reviewing differential exposure, it is important to take into consideration what is sometimes referred to as background exposure or historical exposure. It is particularly important to recognize historical exposures in communities and tribes suffering environmental injustice. In some cases, community members were exposed to pollutants for many years in the past from facilities that are no longer functioning or in business. These past exposures could act to increase the body burden of a subpopulation so that vulnerable individuals start off at a higher dose....

Differential Preparedness: Differential preparedness refers to subpopulations which are less able withstand an environmental insult. This is linked to what kind of coping systems an individual, population, or community has: the more prepared, the less vulnerable. Examples of lessened ability to withstand insult include lack of actions to prepare for a stressor (vaccination, for example, to ward off disease) or poor access to preventive health care (which has the potential to improve community response to stressors). Poverty, poor nutrition, or psycho-social stress may affect the strength of one's coping system. Preparedness against many stressors also can depend on the general state of social and cultural health of a subpopulation.... [P]reparedness in [American Indian] communities often will be linked directly to the balance between emotional, physical, spiritual, and mental health.

Differential Ability to Recover: Differential preparedness and differential ability to recover are closely related categories of vulnerability. Some subpopulations are more able to recover from an insult or stressor because they have more information about environmental risks, health, and disease; ready access to better medical and health care; early diagnosis of disease; or better nutrition.

Clearly, social factors, including but not limited to income, employment status, access to insurance, discrimination in the health care system, language ability, and the existence of social capital, can play an important role in determining the ability to prevent, withstand, or recover from environmental insults. Last, isolation, whether economic, racial, linguistic, or otherwise, leads to less connections, less access to information or influence, and, thus, less ability to prevent, withstand, or recover from environmental stressors. Indices which measure such isolation, such as dissimilarity indexes, may be useful in this area. Once again, this may point to the relationship of health disparities to all four categories of vulnerability....

[More generally, the EPA's Framework] is key to ensuring the goal of environmental justice for all communities because of the following features:

• *It takes a broad view of risk.* The Framework explicitly states that the formulation of risk can include areas outside EPA's regulatory authority, and poses questions for which a quantitative method or answer does not yet exist.

• *It utilizes a population-based and place-based analysis.* Conventional human health risk assessments usually focus on the source or stressor ("a risk assessment for benzene, an industrial plant, etc.") and follow the stressor to various populations affected. Cumulative risk assessment, like many ecological assessments, will be done with the focus on a population or place, and consideration of various stressors affecting them ("a cumulative risk assessment for a community, etc.").

• *It promotes a comprehensive and integrated assessment of risk.* Although combining human health and ecological concerns has been a challenge for risk assessors for decades, the possible interaction between ecological and health risks makes this even more important in cumulative assessments than it has been in conventional risk assessment.

• *It involves multiple stressors (chemical and non-chemical).* While past risk assessments have often addressed a number of chemical stressors individually, the Framework for Cumulative Risk Assessment requires the consideration of how these multiple stressors act together. It also discusses broadly considering not only chemical stressors, but also other stressors such as biological, physical, or even cultural, and how they affect the cumulative risk.

• *It posits an expanded definition of vulnerability to include biological and social factors.* Using the definition of vulnerability from the Framework, "vulnerability" is broader than just another word for biological susceptibility or sensitivity. The Framework adopts a social science view of vulnerability which allows consideration of any number of types of stressors that result in a widely different effect for two populations who suffer the same intensity of insult.

• *It places a premium on community involvements and partnerships.* Cumulative risk assessment will largely play out in geographically or population-based settings. Because of this, the Framework puts heavy emphasis on making use of local expertise of various sorts available within the areas studied.

• *It emphasizes the importance of planning, scoping, and problem-formulation.* Cumulative risk assessment has the potential to be much more complex than conventional risk assessment. It is essential that the questions to be answered be clearly identified and articulated, and that the participants have clear agreement on what is to be done and the limitations of the potential results of the assessments.

• *It links risk assessment to risk management within the context of community health goals.* Because of its potentially broad scope, including many different types of stressors, cumulative risk assessment has a high potential for bringing attention to a variety of sources of risk. Managing these risks may require a wide variety of approaches (not all regulatory) discussed jointly among the participants.

* * *

Notes and Questions

1. Although the NEJAC was generally supportive of the EPA's Framework, it nonetheless flagged some concerns:

As important an advance as the Agency's Cumulative Risk Framework is, the NEJAC Work Group fears that … it can be used to slow down progress if it causes

> analysis of risk to be more complicated and time consuming in order to reach
> the answers needed for action to take place. In fact, the increased complexity
> can easily become an excuse for never taking action.

Id. at 16. In light of this concern—and given the considerable gaps in the data needed to conduct a cumulative risk assessment in most cases—how would you advise a community seeking cleanup of a nearby contaminated site (say a stretch of river contaminated with mercury and PCBs, or an aquifer contaminated with TCE) to proceed? Should they seek a full-blown cumulative risk assessment or should they advocate a more traditional quantitative risk assessment? Are there other approaches beyond this "either/or" formulation?

2. Does the NEJAC understand the terms "population-based analysis" to have the same meaning as the "population-based assessment" of risk advocated by Professors Adler, Hamilton, and Viscusi, above?

3. According to those familiar with the process, one of the major ways in which EPA's Framework differs from the traditional human health risk assessment is that "cumulative risk assessment does not necessarily have to be quantitative; a qualitative analysis may be appropriate depending on the circumstances." Callahan & Sexton, *supra*, at 801. What challenges do you anticipate in those instances in which a cumulative risk assessment produces a qualitative description of the risk posed, when the outcome of a traditional risk assessment is ordinarily a quantitative assessment? Keep this question in mind when you consider the materials in the next chapter, which discusses how agencies use the results of a risk assessment as an input into the equation that determines the numerical standards for, e.g., quantities of pollutants to be emitted to the air or released to the water or allowed to remain in the soil.

2. Community-Based Participatory Research

The NEJAC also emphasized the importance of implementing EPA's Framework for Cumulative Risk Assessment within a collaborative context, i.e., one that envisions the equitable involvement of the affected communities. To this end, they called upon agencies to enlist community-based participatory research (CBPR), a model that recognizes the considerable expertise possessed by community members. The journal *Environmental Health Perspectives* recently devoted an entire supplemental issue to CBPR; in the preface to that issue, longtime environmental justice activist Peggy Shepard and her co-authors outline the tenets of CBPR:

> [Community-based participatory research (CPBR) is] a model rooted physically
> and conceptually in community. In CBPR, scientists work in close collaboration
> with community partners involved in all phases of the research, from the in-
> ception of the research questions and study design, to the collection of the data,
> monitoring of ethical concerns, and interpretation of the study results. Impor-
> tantly, in CBPR, the research findings are communicated to the broader com-
> munity—including residents, the media, and policymakers—so they may be
> utilized to effect needed changes in environmental and health policy to improve
> existing conditions. Building upon existing strengths and resources, CBPR seeks
> to build capacity and resources in communities and ensure that government
> agencies and academic institutions are better able to understand and incorporate
> community concerns into their research agendas.

Peggy M. Shepard, Mary E. Northridge, Swati Prakesh & Gabriel Stover, *Preface: Advancing Environmental Justice Through Community-Based Participatory Research,* 110 ENVTL. HEALTH PERSP. 139 (Supp. 2, 2002).

The following excerpt describes one example of an effort to assess exposure among children in Detroit, Michigan, that employed CBPR.

Gerald J. Keeler, J. Timothy Dvonch, Fuyuen Y. Yip, Edith A. Parker, Barbara A. Israel, Frank J. Marsik, Masako Morishita, James A. Barres, Thomas G. Robins, Wilma Brakefield-Caldwell and Mathew Sam, Assessment of Personal and Community-Level Exposures to Particulate Matter among Children with Asthma in Detroit, Michigan, as Part of Community Action Against Asthma (CAAA)

110 Environmental Health Perspectives 173 (Supplement 2, 2002)

Background on Asthma Prevalence, Causation, and Aggravation

Asthma is the most common chronic disease of childhood in the developed world, affecting approximately 5 million children under 18 years of age in the United States. From 1982 to 1994, the prevalence rate of pediatric asthma (under age 18) in the United States increased by 61%. The mortality rate from asthma for persons 19 years of age and under increased by 78% from 1980 to 1993. Asthma is particularly prevalent among urban populations and minority populations. The national trends in the increase in asthma are visible in Detroit, where a 1993–1994 study found that 17.4% of the 230 children in the sample had a physician diagnosis of asthma and where pediatric hospital admissions for asthma among African American children has escalated (from 11.6% of pediatric hospital admissions in 1986 to 17.5% in 1989). Data from the Michigan Department of Community Health show childhood asthma hospitalization rates in Detroit were more than twice the statewide average during the period from 1991 to 1996....

Furthermore, pediatric asthma hospitalization rates, while stable throughout the rest of Michigan, continue to rise in Detroit....

The causation and aggravation of pediatric asthma is complex and multifactorial and includes genetic disposition, demographic variables, psychosocial stressors, and environmental exposures. Considerable research evidence suggests that both indoor and outdoor environmental exposures may be involved in the worldwide increase in asthma....

Air quality fluctuates considerably in the city of Detroit. Given that areas of Wayne County, including portions of Detroit, have been designated as nonattainment areas under the [National Ambient Air Quality Standard] NAAQS for PM10 as recently as 1995, there is reason to believe that residents of these communities may be exposed to levels of respirable particulates that can exacerbate respiratory illnesses. Although the Wayne County area was redesignated as being in attainment for the PM10 (particulate matter with a mass median aerodynamic diameter less than 10 μm) standard in October 1996, more recent data suggest that local levels of PM2.5 (particulate matter with a mass median aerodynamic diameter less than 2.5 μm) may exceed the proposed 1997 U.S. Environmental Protection Agency (U.S. EPA) standards for PM of that size....

Environmental Exposure Assessment: Community Action Against Asthma

All exposure assessment data collection for this project takes place through Community Action Against Asthma (CAAA), a field-based CBPR project. The overall goal of CAAA is to gain an increased understanding of the environmental and psychosocial triggers for asthma in children's homes and neighborhoods and to reduce those triggers through household- and neighborhood-level interventions. CAAA conducts research ... on the effects of environmental exposures among the residents of Detroit through a participatory process that engages participants from the affected communities in all aspects of the design and conduct of the research; disseminates the results to all parties involved; and uses the research results to design, in collaboration with all partners, interventions to reduce the identified environmental exposures. To ensure this happens, all strategies and plans for data collection and intervention activities are carried out in accordance with the principles of CBPR and are thus formulated and approved by the CAAA Steering Committee....

The CAAA project is being conducted in neighborhoods on the east side and in the southwest portion of Detroit. The two areas were selected initially as part of the Detroit Community-Academic Urban Research Center, with which the MCECH is affiliated, on the basis of statistics highly relevant to general child and family health (e.g., high infant mortality rates, high proportion of households living below the poverty level); evidence of community strengths and efforts to address health problems; and preexisting relationships among some of the partners involved. The east side of Detroit is predominantly African American (more than 90%), has a large number of single-family dwellings, and contains a major interstate highway and some manufacturing plants. Southwest Detroit is the part of the city where the largest percentage of Latinos reside [approximately 40% Latino, 50% African American, and 10% White] and has historically contained most of the industrial facilities of Detroit.... In addition, southwest Detroit experiences heavy car and truck traffic because of both the presence of two major interstates and the entrance/exit of the Ambassador Bridge, the international border crossing that connects Detroit to Windsor, Canada....

Methods

... The CAAA project includes participation of 300 children, 7–11 years of age, who were diagnosed with moderate to severe asthma through a mailed screening questionnaire. These families reside in one of two Detroit communities, eastside or southwest. As part of a community-level environmental exposure assessment, air quality measurements are performed at fixed monitoring locations within each of the communities. Four times each year, a 2-week seasonal field intensive data collection is conducted so that investigators can assess both levels of exposure as well as asthma health status of all 300 participants.... During the seasonal assessments, daily measures of PM2.5, PM10, and ozone are made at each of the two community locations on the rooftops of two elementary schools. In addition, daily measures of PM2.5 and PM10 are also made indoors in school classrooms to characterize indoor penetration of outdoor pollutants.

Indoor levels of PM2.5 and PM10 are also monitored daily in the homes of 20 study participants during each seasonal assessment....

In addition to indoor measurements in their home, these children also wear a personal exposure monitor (PEM) each day for characterization of their exposure to PM10. The rationale for this seasonal measurement approach considered the expected daily variability in PM exposure as well as issues related to retention and participation of families....

Discussion and Future Work

The first year results suggest that the levels of fine PM in the two Detroit communities will exceed the proposed annual NAAQS for PM2.5 of 15 µg/m3. The influence of local sources on both PM2.5 and PM10 was clearly observed in the year 1 data. Outdoor levels of PM in both size fractions were found to be significantly greater in the southwest community than in the eastside community and also appear to drive the indoor PM levels in both the schools and homes to be higher as well. The increased levels in southwest Detroit, where the coarse particle fraction (PM2.5-10) makes up nearly 40% of the total PM10, are likely due to the proximity of the southwest community to the heavy industry on and around Zug Island, as well as the proximity to interstate motorways and the entrance to the Ambassador Bridge leading to Windsor, Canada. The bridge from Detroit to Windsor is the most traveled international border crossing between the two countries. Because of local traffic patterns, truck routes take all bridge-bound traffic through the southwest Detroit community. This results in a continuous queue of diesel truck traffic through the community.

Preliminary analysis of data collected during the summer of 2000 at Maybury Elementary School suggests that traffic contributes a significant fraction of the PM measured at this site with a majority of the measured PM in the submicron size range. While outdoor PM levels across the city may not meet the new NAAQS for PM2.5, indoor levels of PM in nonsmoking homes are typically 1.5–2 times higher than the outdoor PM levels. Smoking continues to be a major contributor to the PM levels measured indoors, as well as contributing to the personal PM exposures of children with asthma. Whereas a child's exposure to secondhand smoke can voluntarily be reduced through education and intervention, exposure to such things as diesel emissions and other industrial emissions can only be remedied through effective policy decisions and through emissions control programs. Previous studies have attempted to find associations of higher incidences of asthma with specific sources such as traffic patterns and density. One study found evidence that children with asthma living near busy roads may have an increased risk of repeated medical care visits, compared with children with asthma living near lower traffic densities. Thus, identifying the sources of the PM exposure must be a high priority for children living in industrialized urban areas like Detroit....

There is considerable research evidence indicating an association between indoor and outdoor environmental exposures and childhood asthma and that such exposures are particularly concentrated in urban, low-income communities of color. The results presented here are consistent with these findings and point to the need to better understand and address the sources of both indoor and outdoor pollutants.... [T]he CAAA project is involving community partners in collecting, analyzing, interpreting, and disseminating the results of this research as well as in developing, implementing, and evaluating household-, community-, and policy-level strategies aimed at reducing these exposures and improving the health of children and their families in Detroit.

* * *

Notes and Questions

1. What do you imagine to be the strengths and weaknesses of CBPR? Are there facets of the risk assessment process for which you think CBPR is likely to be more or less well suited?

2. For an extended account of CBPR in action in a low-income community of color in the Greenpoint/Williamsburg neighborhood of Brooklyn, New York, see JASON CORBURN, STREET SCIENCE: COMMUNITY KNOWLEDGE AND ENVIRONMENTAL HEALTH JUSTICE (2005).

D. Risk Avoidance

Another set of concerns implicated by the current risk-based paradigm are those that are raised by agencies' reliance on "risk avoidance." That is, in responding to or "managing" risks, our environmental laws generally reflect a collective commitment to reducing those risks by addressing the sources of contamination. However, agencies have recently shifted in many instances from risk reduction to risk avoidance. Although risk avoidance strategies have only recently been categorized under this name, these measures — fish consumption advisories, ozone alerts, pesticide contact warnings, and the like — have increasingly become familiar aspects of the regulatory landscape. Professor Catherine O'Neill sketches some of the perils of a shift to risk avoidance in the excerpt that follows.

Catherine A. O'Neill,
No Mud Pies: Risk Avoidance as Risk Regulation
31 Vermont Law Review 273 (2007)

The Killarney Lake Recreation Site, in the Lower Coeur d'Alene River Basin, is a popular place for families to camp overnight or to spend the day picnicking, fishing, launching boats, and playing along the shore. This stretch of the basin, however, is heavily contaminated with lead and other metals — a legacy of mining and smelting operations conducted with scant attention to the consequences for human and environmental health. Although the parking lot at Killarney Lake has been paved to cap the contaminated material underneath and clean topsoil has been spread to help establish a grassy swale between the parking lot and the lake, no further cleanup has been undertaken at the site. The surrounding soils and the lake sediments continue to harbor high levels of lead and other metals. These contaminants continue to pose a risk to the health of humans and wildlife that use the site. So health and environmental agencies have posted a large sign urging people to take steps to protect themselves. The sign notes that small children and pregnant women are at particular risk from exposure. The sign directs people to wash their hands, faces, toys, and pacifiers if these have been in contact with the soil or dust; to avoid picnicking on the ground; to remove soil from clothing, camping equipment, and pets before leaving the area; and to ensure that their children: "Play Clean! Children should play in grassy areas and avoid loose soil, dust, and muddy areas. *No mud pies.*"

The government decision makers charged with cleaning up the Coeur d'Alene River Basin have opted for a form of risk avoidance — a regulatory approach that addresses environmental risks by asking those whose practices or lifeways expose them to contaminants to alter their ways in order to avoid exposure. Other examples of risk avoidance measures include fish and wildlife consumption advisories; use-restricted cleanups and institutional controls; ozone alerts; pesticide and herbicide contact warnings; beach advisories and closures; and boil-water notices. Risk avoidance stands in contrast to risk reduction, which addresses environmental risks by requiring contaminants to be prevented, reduced, or cleaned up at the source. Risk avoidance leaves contamination unabated, in whole or in part. It places responsibility on those exposed to avoid the fish, water, soils, or air left polluted.

According to proponents, this shift from risk reduction to risk avoidance promises large cost savings. Although the magnitude of the potential savings is a matter of some dispute, it is likely that erecting a fence, posting a warning sign, or maintaining a website entails modest sums—whereas the price tag for prevention, reduction, or cleanup can run into the millions. Other advantages, too, might be cited in favor of risk avoidance.

But a move to risk avoidance introduces a raft of perils....

Risk Avoidance is Myopic

Risk avoidance is myopic: it narrows the focus of environmental regulation. Risk avoidance targets only human health effects and considers only specific, direct threats to human health. Risk avoidance measures seek to break the chain connecting contamination with adverse human health effects by focusing on a link late in the chain—the point of human exposure. These measures therefore leave unaddressed the myriad other effects of contamination.

Risk avoidance declines entirely to address adverse effects on any non-human components of ecosystems. Signs erected along the South Fork of the Coeur d'Alene River warning of lead-contaminated sediments do not reach the mergansers and other waterfowl that live in the river.... Even if one's concern is chiefly with human health, however, risk avoidance may ultimately fail to address many direct and indirect effects on humans. Thus, whereas a risk avoidance measure may target a particular contaminant's direct effects on human health, e.g., its toxicity to humans, the measure may neglect its indirect effects, e.g., its capacity to deplete resources on which humans depend.... [For example,] EPA has issued a Worker Protection Standard that requires farmworkers to observe a certain waiting period or "restricted-entry interval" before reentering fields that have been sprayed with pesticides. Yet these pesticides or their breakdown products eventually enter the watercourses that support fish and other aquatic life. There is evidence that numerous pesticides impair several crucial physiological functions in both Pacific and Atlantic salmon, ultimately contributing to diminished reproduction and decreased populations of these species. Human health is thus indirectly impacted to the extent that humans rely on salmon for food and, in some cases, for economic, cultural, and spiritual well-being....

Risk Avoidance May Be Off Target

Risk avoidance efforts may be underinclusive or off target. Because risk avoidance focuses on the point of human exposure, it depends on a complete understanding of the human health endpoints involved and the pathways and circumstances of human exposure. Where such understandings are less than complete, warnings will miss their mark and institutional controls will be misconceived. For example, current risk avoidance measures for methylmercury focus on its neurodevelopmental effects. Thus, fish consumption advisories are aimed primarily at women of childbearing age and children. Yet the most recent studies reveal that methylmercury also adversely affects the cardiovascular system in adult males. This health endpoint and subpopulation at risk are largely missed by advisories.... Consumption advisories may also fail to mention particular parts, preparation methods, or uses of contaminated species—such as the bones, or internal organs of fish used by Russian immigrant communities along the Spokane River to make soup, or the clams used by Suquamish tribal members to alleviate their children's teething pain—perhaps because health and environmental agencies are unaware of such practices....

Risk Avoidance is Often Ineffective

Risk avoidance is often ineffective. In order for risk avoidance to work, advisories must be received and understood, restrictions must be monitored and enforced, and, ultimately, human behaviors must be changed. Even proponents of risk avoidance concede the considerable hurdles in each of these respects.

There is ample evidence that advisories and warnings often do not reach their intended audience. For example, a recent study showed that half of those consuming fish caught on the Great Lakes were unaware of the relevant fish consumption advisories. Similarly, another study found that only 45% of those fishing the Newark Bay Complex were aware of the relevant fish and crab consumption advisories. Notably, people of color, people with limited English proficiency, people with limited formal education, and low-income people tend to evidence the least awareness....

Even if risk avoidance measures ... reach and are understood by their intended audiences ... it is notoriously difficult to effect behavioral changes in people.... According to one recent survey, of the 48.5% of respondents who were aware of the relevant fish consumption advisories for the San Francisco Bay, only 60.3% reported reducing their fish intake as a result.... Similarly, people frequently do not comply with ozone alerts.... For example, only 56% of participants who voluntarily signed up to receive personal electronic notices of ozone alerts from the South Coast Air Quality Management District in the Los Angeles metropolitan area altered their behavior in accordance with the alerts they received.

These hurdles, moreover, loom larger and may become insurmountable when those affected do not speak the language in which advisories are dispensed, do not have the economic wherewithal to alter their practices, or do not share the culture of the dominant population. Those who do not speak English may be missed entirely by warning signs posted only in English. Those with modest economic means may have few options for risk avoidance: it may be wholly impractical to fish "elsewhere" if all of the rivers, lakes, and bayous nearby are contaminated and one does not own a car or have the money for gas; it may be unrealistic to stay inside on "ozone alert" days if one's livelihood depends on working outdoors. And those for whom fish consumption includes spiritual, traditional, or cultural dimensions may be deeply resistant to altering their practices.... [This is] likely the case for members of the fishing tribes in the Pacific Northwest. As the Columbia River Inter-Tribal Fish Commission explains: "Salmon and the rivers they use are a part of our sense of place. The Creator put us here where the salmon return. We are obliged to remain and to protect this place." Moreover, various tribes' aboriginal and treaty-based claims to the fish and other resources are tied to specific places; the legal protections that flow from these claims cannot simply be re-established somewhere else. As well, the particularized skills and ecological knowledge that these peoples have developed over generations are place-specific and, therefore, not transferable to other locations.

Risk Avoidance Has Finite Possibilities

Risk avoidance is an approach with diminishing and, ultimately, finite possibilities. Once contaminants are introduced or permitted to remain in the environment, there may be few options—perhaps even no options—for avoiding contact with them. The options that do exist, moreover, are likely to diminish over time, as uncontaminated environments are permitted one by one to become and remain degraded. Ultimately, heavy reliance on risk avoidance in lieu of risk reduction would leave no healthful alternatives....

Risk Avoidance May Itself Introduce Risks

Risk avoidance may itself introduce risks. If those exposed change their ways in order to avoid risks posed by contamination, they may adopt practices that subject them to a different set of risks. To the extent that asthmatic children heed warnings to avoid sports and other activities outdoors on "ozone alert" days, for example, they may face an increased risk of obesity and other ills that attend a more sedentary lifestyle. To the extent that those affected "comply" with fish consumption advisories, [they must forego the] nutritional benefits of frequent fish consumption, [which] are well known.... In addition, for people who consume fish as part of a traditional diet ... regular consumption of fish and other traditional foods may promote health and combat diabetes. Diabetes is a particular concern for tribes given that the incidence of diabetes is "two to three times as high among [American Indians and Alaska Natives] than among all racial/ethnic populations combined." ...

Risk Avoidance Discourages Diversity of Lifeways

Risk avoidance may discourage plural and diverse lifeways. Risk avoidance measures may call upon risk-bearers to forego an array of practices or pursuits—from frying fish caught in the Detroit River, to breastfeeding their infants, to spearing walleye, to allowing their children to play outdoors in the summer, to giving their babies clams on which to teethe.... Over time, the practices may fall into disuse, the lifeways may die out....

Risk Avoidance is Unjust

... [R]isk avoidance measures are likely to be evaluated by reference to the understandings and commitments of the dominant society and adopted only where avoidance is thought not to occasion great costs or profound loss. Yet, the understandings and commitments of those who will be faced with altering their practices and lifeways may be quite different than those of the dominant society. This will often be the case where Native peoples are prominent among the risk bearers, and may also be the case when other non-dominant groups are at risk. Thus, environmental injustice here arises not only from distributive inequities but also from cultural discrimination.

... [F]or example, a woman in the general population who habitually consumes two meals of fish per week might, when faced with fish consumption advisories for mercury, look to substitute food sources with relatively modest accommodations to palate and pocketbook. A woman in the Mille Lacs Band, however, might view such risk avoidance measures as *impossible*, given the affront this would mean to her tribe's very identity, to what it means to *be* Ojibweg....

* * *

Notes and Questions

1. Agencies charged with communicating fish consumption advisories have recognized at least some of the limitations in terms of advisories' effectiveness, and have made some progress here, typically by translating advisories into multiple languages. According to the National Environmental Justice Advisory Council, however, agencies' efforts have been uneven. NEJAC cites, for example, the Laotian Organizing Project's reaction to state advisory signs posted at a popular fishing site in Richmond, California in English, Spanish, and Vietnamese: "The Vietnamese language translation is useless to a predominantly Laotian population." NAT'L ENVTL. JUSTICE ADVISORY COUNCIL, FISH CONSUMPTION, *supra*, at 115. NEJAC counsels greater attention to the fact that multiple groups and subgroups may be among those affected and observes that "the composition of the affected groups may be changing rapidly in some areas such as cities that are ports of entry for immigrant and refugee groups or rural and other areas where particular groups have settled." *Id.* at 115–16. How might agencies better address these concerns with advisories' effectiveness?

2. As Professor O'Neill observes, the chief appeal of risk avoidance strategies is that they appear relatively cheap—at least in the short term. Can you think of other arguments in favor of greater recourse to risk avoidance strategies?

3. Professor O'Neill nonetheless concedes a limited role for risk avoidance:

> Given that it takes time to reduce or cleanup contamination, risk avoidance might appropriately be undertaken as an interim measure, designed to inform those exposed and to mitigate the human health impacts—while risk reduction is pursued in earnest. In the case of methylmercury contamination, for example, even serious efforts to reduce mercury emissions would take anywhere from a few months to a few years to net results in the form of reduced methylmercury in aquatic environments and, ultimately, in fish tissue. And in the case of a handful of pollution problems—mainly stemming from large-scale past releases of contaminants, such as the dispersal of PCBs over many miles of the Hudson River or the broadcast of arsenic throughout the southern Puget Sound as a result of copper smelting at the ASARCO facility in Tacoma, Washington—reduction efforts will likely reasonably take decades. In the meantime, it is vital that those exposed be made aware of the nature and extent of the contamination, the consequences for human and ecological health, the possibilities for avoidance, and, ideally, any opportunities to facilitate reduction.

O'Neill, *No Mud Pies, supra*, at 352–53. In this vein, the NEJAC similarly recognizes that fish consumption advisories are likely a necessary measure, at least in the short term, to inform affected communities and honor their "right to know." To this end, NEJAC devoted an entire chapter of their report to improving fish consumption advisories. NAT'L ENVTL. JUSTICE ADVISORY COUNCIL, FISH CONSUMPTION AND ENVIRONMENTAL JUSTICE, *supra*, at 90–127.

E. Comparative Risk Assessment

Comparative risk assessment is a tool that is used to rank environmental problems by their seriousness or relative risk (as opposed to quantitative risk assessment, an enterprise that merely quantifies any given risk). Advocates of comparative risk assessment believe that it can be the basis for redirecting regulatory efforts toward the most serious environmental risks. Prominent proponents include John Graham, director of the Office of Information & Regulatory Affairs within OMB during the George W. Bush administration, and Supreme Court Justice Stephen Breyer. Prior to his appointment, Justice Breyer, for example, decried the inconsistencies that plague federal agencies' efforts to address health and safety, observing that "the values that regulators implicitly attach to the saving of a statistical life vary widely from one program or agency to another" and citing "variations ranging from space heater regulations that save lives at a cost of $100,000 per life saved to bans on DES in cattle feed that require an expenditure of $125 million per statistical life." BREYER, *supra*, at 22. Justice Breyer further argued that EPA and other federal agencies spend too much time and resources regulating small risks and that there are "many concrete possibilities for obtaining increased health, safety, and environmental benefits through reallocation of regulatory resources." BREYER, *supra*, at 23. Two well publicized comparative risk reports by EPA likewise concluded that the agency's regulatory efforts were not targeted toward the environmental risks that experts believed were the most serious (and that they were instead more closely aligned with the public's ranking of risks). U.S. ENVTL. PROT. AGENCY, UNFINISHED BUSINESS: A COMPARATIVE ASSESSMENT OF ENVIRONMENTAL PROBLEMS (1987); SCIENCE ADVISORY BD., U.S. ENVTL. PROT. AGENCY, REDUCING RISK: SETTING PRIORITIES AND STRATEGIES FOR ENVIRONMENTAL PROTECTION (1990). Justice Breyer's argument is sketched below.

Stephen Breyer, Breaking the Vicious Circle: Toward Effective Risk Regulation
(1993)

[There is] a serious problem with the creation of regulatory agendas and with the establishment of rational priorities among the items that are included in those agendas.... [R]egulators will normally act against a major risk that comes to the public's attention.... Some critics point out that, of the more than sixty thousand chemical substances potentially subject to regulation, only a few thousand have undergone more than crude toxicity testing.... [Yet the EPA] has no particular strategy for determining which of these many chemicals are likely to need testing and which are not.... Other critics complain of a regulatory overemphasis on cancer risks compared with other, possibly greater, say, occupational, risks, such as the risk of neurotoxicity, causing potential brain damage....

More significant, in my view, is EPA's own, now famous, 1987 report called "Unfinished Business." In that report EPA managers provided their own views of proper program priority rankings and compared them with existing priorities. Subjects that risk managers ranked low, such as hazardous waste cleanup, had high funding priorities; subjects that they ranked high, such as indoor air pollution and global warming, had low funding priorities. In 1990 EPA's Science Advisory Board conducted a similar exercise and, after careful study, confirmed the risk managers' views. The general public's ranking of safety priorities is very different from these experts' views. Agency priorities and agendas may more closely reflect public rankings, politics, history, or even chance than the kind of priority list that environmental experts would deliberately create. To a degree, that is inevitable. But one cannot find any detailed federal governmental list that prioritizes health or safety risk problems so as to create a rational, overall agenda—an agenda that would seek to maximize attainable safety or to minimize health-related harms.

* * *

Notes and Questions

1. Justice Breyer's proposed solution to the misplaced regulatory priorities he describes above is to create a small, centralized, politically insulated, "blue ribbon" committee of health and environmental experts (a sort of super civil service), charged with developing coherent risk priorities for the federal agencies that regulate risk, including EPA. The committee would have authority to reallocate resources among agencies (e.g., shifting money from cleaning up toxic waste sites to vaccination or prenatal care), to decide on uniform assumptions to employ in the risk assessment process, and so forth. *See* Breyer, *supra*, at 55–81. Underlying Justice Breyer's proposal is the belief that insulating risk decisions from the current political and regulatory processes will produce superior results. Do you agree? Assuming it will, is it worth the trade off in terms of reduced opportunities for public participation?

2. By contrast, Professor Donald Hornstein questions the version of rationality upon which Justice Breyer's and others' reforms of risk assessment are premised. See Donald T. Hornstein, *Reclaiming Environmental Law: A Normative Critique of Comparative Risk Analysis,* 92 Colum. L. Rev. 562 (1992). As Professor Hornstein explains, a major criticism of risk assessment and comparative risk assessment is that they present risk as a single numeric estimate—the number of expected deaths or diseases in a given population. The public, however, evaluates risk based on a range of social, psychological, moral and emotional factors other than the probability of a hazard occurring. These include whether the risks

are involuntary, familiar, preventable, evoke dreaded consequences, are within a person's control, impact children or future generations, and whether those at risk from an activity are those that gain its benefits. Professor Vincent Covello notes further that "people perceive many types of risk in an absolute sense. An involuntary exposure that increases the risk of cancer or birth defects is perceived as a physical and moral insult regardless of whether the increase is small or whether the increase is smaller than risks from other exposures." *See, e.g.,* Vincent T. Covello, *Communicating Right-to-Know Information on Chemical Risks,* 23 ENVTL. SCI. & TECH. 1444, 1448 (1989). Moreover, perceptions of risk tend to differ by gender and race. One survey, for example, found that nonwhites perceived greater risks from most hazards than whites did, and that women perceived greater risks from most hazards than men did. When race and gender were considered together, white males as a group differed from everyone else, perceiving risks as much smaller and much more acceptable than did other people. James Flynn et al., *Gender, Race, and Perception of Environmental Health Risks,* 14 RISK ANALYSIS 1101, 1102–06 (1994). As Professor Kuehn notes, white males are "most likely to be the risk assessors, officials with companies who are risk producers, and government decision makers," Kuehn, *supra,* at 156. In your view, should risk regulation be rationalized so that we give priority to addressing those risks that are worst in an actuarial sense? Or should our regulatory priorities be permitted to reflect the various other bases on which humans evaluate risk?

    3. This debate continues. For recent contributions, see CASS R. SUNSTEIN, LAWS OF FEAR: BEYOND THE PRECAUTIONARY PRINCIPLE (2005); Dan M. Kahan et al., *Fear of Democracy: A Cultural Evaluation of Sunstein on Risk,* 119 HARV. L. REV. 1071 (2006); Cass R. Sunstein, *Misfearing: A Reply,* 119 HARV L. REV. 1110 (2006); Dan M. Kahan & Paul Slovic, *Cultural Evaluations of Risk: "Values" or "Blunders"?,* 119 HARV. L. REV. F. 166 (2006); Dan M. Kahan, *Two Conceptions of Emotion in Risk Regulation,* 156 U. PA. L. REV. 741 (2008); Peter H. Huang, *Diverse Conceptions of Emotions in Risk Regulation,* 156 U. PA. L. REV. PENNUMBRA 435 (2008). Professor Sunstein, for example, points to the problem of "bounded rationality," observing that when humans process information, they rely on a host of heuristics or rules of thumb that can produce errors in their assessments. He cites the "availability heuristic" as one example, by which humans assess the probability of an event (say, a "100-year flood") in light of their ability to recall actual, similar instances in which the risk materialized and the event came to pass. Professor Sunstein argues, "[a]s a result of various forms of bounded rationality, human beings are prone to 'misfearing': they fear things that are not dangerous, and they do not fear things that impose serious risks." Sunstein, *Misfearing, supra,* at 1110. He observes that, much of the time, these private fears get translated into public action. This is troubling, from his perspective: "No one doubts that democratic nations should respond to the public will, but there is reason for real concern if small problems receive significant attention and resources, and if large problems receive little or none." *Id.* at 1110–11. Note that both Justice Breyer and Professor Sunstein propose comparative risk assessment among the correctives for what they term "cognitive blunders" made by ordinary citizens in assessing risk. They hope that by looking to "objective" measures of the benefits and costs of risk regulation, we can make better regulatory choices. The related tool of cost-benefit analysis is discussed in Chapter 5. Professors Kahan and Slovic counter that disagreements between experts' and lay persons' assessments of risks originate in important part in conflicts over values: "We take the position that cultural worldviews pervade popular (not to mention expert) risk assessments and that a genuine commitment to democracy forbids simply dismissing such perceptions as products of 'bounded rationality.'" Kahan & Slovic, *supra,* at 166.

4. Overall, how would you evaluate our present regulatory approach to measuring, evaluating and responding to risk? If you were tasked to design a comprehensive framework for addressing risk, what would it look like? The implications of this framework are significant. As we will see, risk analysis and management features prominently in a wide range of regulatory contexts, such as standard setting, permitting and the cleanup of contaminated properties, to name a few. These are subjects explored in the following chapters.

Chapter 7

Standard Setting

A. Introduction

Environmental agencies are generally charged with preventing, reducing, or cleaning up environmental contamination. Agencies enlist an array of regulatory tools in their effort to protect human and environmental health. The choice of tool is often specified by Congress in one of the various environmental statutes (e.g., the Clean Air Act, the Clean Water Act) that direct agencies' efforts, but sometimes this choice is left to the agencies. In either event, environmental agencies are responsible for shaping the contours of the relevant regulatory measure—for example, determining what concentration of sulfur dioxide (SO2) in the ambient air is adequately protective of human health; deciding what level of mercury emissions reductions is technologically feasible; or devising an emissions trading regime for the contaminants that contribute to smog. When agencies undertake these varied tasks—discussed in this chapter under the umbrella of "standard-setting"—their orientation is general. That is, they typically set standards that apply broadly, to an entire geographic region (e.g., national air quality standards) or an entire category of industrial sources (e.g., coal-fired utilities). These standards are also typically fashioned with an eye toward protecting the "average American," although there are important instances in which agencies are directed to ensure that more sensitive or vulnerable individuals are also protected. Agencies then translate these generic standards into more local, source-specific requirements when they issue permits to individual polluting facilities, a topic that is taken up in Chapter 8.

While the permitting process has long been recognized as raising issues of environmental justice, agencies' prior efforts to set the standards that will be incorporated into these permits also have implications for environmental justice. What happens when a standard ensures that the ambient air in a given region is healthy, but permits localized "hot spots"—areas of concentrated pollution—that coincide with environmental justice communities? What happens when a national standard governing mercury emissions is designed to protect those who consume an average quantity of the fish that harbor mercury, but those in particular groups (e.g., Asian-Americans, Native Americans) consume much greater quantities of such fish? This chapter takes up these questions of environmental justice in standard-setting. The first section provides an overview of some of the most commonly employed regulatory tools and the statutory authorities for these tools. The next two sections consider examples from agencies' efforts to set standards to address, respectively, air and water pollution. The final section discusses a relatively new addition to agencies' regulatory toolkit: market-based approaches, focusing in particular on the environmental justice issues raised by emissions trading.

1. An Introductory Note on the Taxonomy of Standards

Environmental standards are the foundation upon which all regulatory requirements rest. Broadly speaking, there are three approaches that comprise the mainstay of agencies' standard-setting efforts. Some standards are made by reference to what is a safe level for humans and the environment. These are called "health-based" or "risk-based" standards and are often expressed by the ambient amount of a pollutant that is safe. For example, EPA may announce that if the air contains over X amount of sulfur dioxide per cubic meter over an 8-hour period, the air will be deemed unhealthy. If there are too many exceedances of this standard, then the airshed will be deemed to be in "nonattainment" with the national ambient air quality standard ("NAAQS" or "NAAQ standard"). "Technology-based" standards, on the other hand, are set by reference to what is currently technologically feasible to achieve, regardless of whether this standard results in a healthy environment. For example, EPA may announce that new facilities emitting sulfur dioxide in nonattainment areas must control their air emissions to the level of the "lowest achievable emissions reductions" possible, and "LAER" becomes the standard. It may be that achieving LAER will still result in troubling ambient conditions; conversely, it may be that achieving LAER will require emissions reductions beyond those necessary to reach healthful conditions. A third type of standard is termed "technology-forcing" because it is made by reference to technology not yet available, but is intended to force the development of such cleaner technologies. For example, in 1990 the Congress mandated that manufacturers of automobiles must find a way to reduce tail pipe emissions by 10% below 1990 emissions by 2004. The auto industry was then in a position of having to develop the technology to achieve these reductions (also called "rollbacks") in order to have vehicles certified for sale by that date. When promulgated, this was a technology-forcing standard because in 1990 the technology to achieve this level of reduction had yet to be developed.

The standards that appear to most concern environmental justice advocates are health-based standards. Some claim that these standards are often insufficiently protective because they are made by reference to their effect upon healthy adult males. In addition, many such standards are developed in isolation, a "chemical by chemical approach" that does not factor in the possibility that the exposed individual may use the resource more than the average citizen, may be subject to a range of other pollutants, may be vulnerable because of certain genetic predispositions or health conditions, or may have fewer preventive and health care resources available. Thus, they claim that ambient health-based standards should be tightened.

But technology-based standards also may raise environmental justice issues. While these standards may require fairly significant reductions in emissions or discharges from each source — for example, a 90% reduction in mercury emissions at each coal-fired power plant — they say nothing about how many such sources may be permitted to operate in a given area. It is entirely possible that the effect of multiple sources, each having reduced its emissions by the required 90%, will be a level of mercury that is unhealthful for those exposed. Given that, as discussed in Chapter 2, polluting sources are often concentrated in environmental justice communities, even the most stringent technology-based standards may leave unaddressed the question of community members' health.

Regardless of which type of standard they employ, current federal environmental laws do not directly address environmental justice issues. As advocates and scholars have argued, however, there nonetheless are opportunities within these statutes for integrating environmental justice concerns into agencies' substantive standard-setting efforts. The next section canvasses several of the major environmental statutes and highlights the sources of legal authority that might be tapped to enable agencies to consider and address environmental justice concerns.

2. Legal Sources of Authority

Richard J. Lazarus & Stephanie Tai,
Integrating Environmental Justice Into EPA Permitting Authority
26 Ecology Law Quarterly 617 (1999)

Clean Air Act

The Clean Air Act (CAA) presents EPA with more opportunities to integrate environmental justice concerns into the Act's substantive standards than the Agency has utilized. The national ambient air quality standards (NAAQS) that serve as the Act's cornerstone are illustrative. Pursuant to the CAA, EPA administrators must promulgate NAAQS to protect "public health" with an adequate margin of safety. It is well settled that Congress intended for EPA to consider especially sensitive subpopulations in determining what pollutant levels would meet the "public health" standard. Pollutant levels that pose no health hazard to average healthy individuals may nonetheless present significant hazards to some individuals who, because of preexisting physical conditions, have heightened vulnerabilities. The Act, accordingly, instructs EPA in developing the "air quality criteria" upon which the NAAQS are based to include information on "those variable factors . . . which of themselves or in combination with other factors may alter the effects on public health or welfare." . . .

EPA's statutory authority in this respect is also of a continuing nature. It does not end once a NAAQS is first promulgated. Pursuant to CAA Section 109(d), EPA is required to revise air quality criteria and standards at a minimum of every five years or as needed to ensure their adequacy in light of new information and changing circumstances. . . .

Section 112 [dealing with controls for hazardous air pollutants] also includes two other subsections relevant to environmental justice priorities. Section 112(c)(3) and Section 112(k) both authorize EPA to consider the aggregate effects of multiple sources of hazardous air pollutants, especially those emitted in urban areas. . . .

Clean Water Act

. . . The water quality standard provisions of the [Clean Water Act (CWA)] offer another opportunity for EPA to exercise its authority to consider and address environmental justice concerns. Under the CWA, states must establish water quality standards applicable to waters within the states' borders. Unlike the CAA's NAAQS, which are nationally uniform, these state water quality standards may not only vary between states, but need not be uniformly applied to all water bodies within any one state. A state may legitimately apply different levels of water quality protection to different water bodies depending on the specific uses (for example, recreation, transportation, or industry) the state designates for each body of water. EPA oversees a state's promulgation of water quality standards primarily to ensure that the standards are consistent with the state's "designated uses" but also to ensure compliance with EPA's nondegradation policy, which guards against unwarranted degradation of existing uses of water and associated water quality. CWA permits must ensure compliance not only with the Act's various technology-based effluent limitations, but also with the state water quality standards. The latter aspect of the Act requires the federal (or state) agency responsible for permitting, first, to determine the total maximum daily loads (TMDLs) of pollutants consistent with the water quality standard applicable to each body of water and, second, to allocate those loads among all the sources contributing pollutants to the water body....

The water quality program is especially relevant to environmental justice because it involves EPA and the states making a series of judgments with clearly distributional consequences. For instance, EPA's nondegradation policy, which protects "existing uses" of water, should provide protection to such existing uses by environmental justice communities, including those that are economically or culturally dependent on the subsistence use of water. TMDL planning, however, is even more relevant. EPA can ensure, through its oversight of state TMDL determinations, that the resulting allocations do not unfairly burden low-income communities or communities of color....

Federal Insecticide, Fungicide, and Rodenticide Act

The Federal Insecticide, Fungicide, and Rodenticide Act (FIFRA) confers substantial authority on the EPA Administrator to address environmental justice concerns. EPA's principal responsibility in administering FIFRA is its registration of pesticides to guard against "unreasonable adverse effects on the environment." Environmental justice advocates are interested in FIFRA's administration for many reasons, one of which is the substantial threat to the health of farmworkers posed by the unreasonably dangerous use of pesticides. FIFRA provides EPA with significant authority to eliminate these unreasonable risks through tactics as varied as use restrictions, disposal restrictions, labeling requirements, registration denials, and conditional registrations....

* * *

Notes and Questions

1. If EPA's authority under the federal environmental statutes is as broad and discretionary as Professors Lazarus and Tai suggest, why has the agency arguably failed to promulgate standards that are protective enough to address cumulative impacts and synergistic risks? As you read the materials in this chapter, consider whether these failures stem from a lack of legal authority, from an incomplete scientific understanding or insufficient engineering capability, or from a lack of political will.

2. A quick review of environmental cases can lead one to the conclusion that EPA will frequently get sued regardless of the standard promulgated, i.e., either the industrial stakeholders or environmental stakeholders will be dissatisfied, or possibly both. Those wishing to uphold EPA's decision will point to case law affording the agency great deference in technical matters. Those wishing to defeat the agency's decision will use a variety of arguments generally premised upon the failure of the agency to follow its legislative mandate, thus acting outside of the relevant statute's scope. It is likely that the ultimate success of these arguments will depend upon the inclination of the courts to be deferential to EPA. In reviewing the materials in the next section, in addition to judicial deference, also consider the importance of the NAAQS from the standpoint of public health and how much is at stake with the establishment or revision of these standards.

B. The Case of National Ambient Air Quality Standards

As noted by Professors Lazarus and Tai, two important standard-setting provisions allowing for integration of environmental justice concerns are sections 108 and 109 of the Clean Air Act, under which EPA is authorized to establish and periodically revise NAAQS for certain air pollutants, called "criteria" pollutants. As stated above, ambient standards refer to the amount of pollutant in an environmental medium (like an airshed or waterbody) over a period of time. Presently, only a handful of pollutants are regulated under this section, as opposed to the extensive list of hazardous air pollutants regulated under another section of the Clean Air Act (Section 112). Despite the relatively fewer number of NAAQS, regulation of these pollutants is the heart and soul of the Clean Air Act because these pollutants are both serious in their health implications and are difficult to regulate because they come from numerous and diverse sources. NAAQS presently cover six pollutants—particulate matter, sulfur dioxide (SO2), ozone, nitrogen oxides, carbon monoxide and lead. However, since ozone is formed as a result of a photochemical reaction in the air, pollutants that are precursors to ozone are directly regulated as surrogates; they include nitrogen oxides, volatile organic compounds, nonmethane organic gases and hydrocarbons. *See, generally,* Robert V. Percival et al., Environmental Regulation: Law, Science, and Policy, 475–562 (5th ed. 2006).

One of the most controversial features of setting the NAAQS is that the endeavor is supposed to be entirely "cost blind," meaning that the EPA cannot consider how costly it will be to achieve the national standards. Theoretically, NAAQS are supposed to reflect allowable concentrations of these pollutants in the outdoor air that are protective of public health "allowing an adequate margin of safety," even if achieving such levels will shut down entire industries and cause significant economic harm. 42 U.S.C. §7409(b)(1). These standards are not as draconian as they appear, however, because economic considerations can play a significant role in how the standards are implemented. States and tribes have several opportunities to consider economics and costs in developing their state implementation plans (SIPs) or tribal implementations plans (TIPs), which are plans submitted to EPA demonstrating how the state or tribe proposes to come into attainment with NAAQS within a given time frame.

Many regions in the U.S. do not meet the NAAQS. This failure has significant health and environmental justice implications. Environmental attorney Curtis Moore explains some of the harmful health impacts of particulate matter and ozone, pollutants for which the NAAQS were recently tightened:

> A large body of compelling evidence demonstrates that particulate matter is associated with early and unnecessary deaths, aggravation of heart and lung diseases, reduction in the ability to breathe normally, and increases in respiratory illnesses, leading to school and work absences. As particulate levels rise, so do runny or stuffy noses, sinusitis, sore throat, wet cough, head colds, hayfever, burning or red eyes, wheezing, dry cough, phlegm, shortness of breath, and chest discomfort or pain, as well as hospital admissions for asthma and bronchitis. Studies have shown that chronic cough, asthma, and emphysema rise among nonsmok[ers] … ; bronchitis and chronic cough increase in school children as do emergency room and hospital admissions…. In plain terms, at levels commonly encountered, particulate pollution kills and disables Americans, especially children, the elderly, and those who are ill….

[I]t is clear that the impacts of ozone exposure are grave. The body of evidence that ozone causes chronic, pathologic lung damage is overwhelming. At levels routinely encountered in most American cities, ozone burns through cell walls in lungs and airways, tissues redden and swell, cellular fluid seeps into the lungs, and over time their elasticity drops. Macrophage cells rush to the lung's defense, but they too are stunned by the ozone. Susceptibility to bacterial infections increases, possibly because ciliated cells that normally expel foreign particles and organisms have been killed and replaced by thicker, stiffer, nonciliated cells. Scars and lesions form in the airways....

As ozone levels rise, hospital admissions and emergency department visits do the same. In some laboratory animals, cancers appear. Children at summer camp lose the ability to breathe normally as ozone levels rise, even when the air is clean by reference to the former federal standard, and these losses continue for up to a week....

Curtis Moore, *The Impracticality and Immorality of Cost-Benefit Analysis in Setting Health-Related Standards,* 11 Tulane Envtl. L.J. 187, 195–198 (1998). Sulfur dioxide also can present significant health effects. As noted in a widely adopted environmental law casebook, asthmatics experience measurable changes in respiratory functions when exposed to sulfur dioxide (SO2) concentration "spikes" or "peaks" for periods as brief as five minutes. According to an EPA estimate in 1994, some "68,000 to 166,000 asthmatics could be exposed to at least one peak SO2 concentration while exercising outdoors" and "total [annual] exposure events could range from 180,000 to 395,000." Percival et al., *supra*, at 483–84.

In fact, childhood asthma rates have soared in the last decades. "The [Centers for Disease Control and Prevention (CDC)] estimates that self-reported asthma cases increased by 75 percent from 1980 to 1994 and that the largest increases in prevalence occurred in children." Rena I. Steinzor, Mother Earth and Uncle Sam: How Pollution and Hollow Government Hurt Our Kids 150 (2008). According to the most recent CDC estimates, in 2006, some 9.9 million children in the United States—14 percent of all children—have been diagnosed with asthma. Ctrs. for Disease Control and Prevention, Summary Health Statistics for U.S. Children: National Health Interview Survey, 2006 5 (2007).

The health effects, in turn, appear disproportionately to affect people of color and the poor. The CDC reports that children in poor families are more likely to have been diagnosed with asthma than those in families that are not poor: whereas 18 percent of children in poor families have been diagnosed with asthma, only 13 percent of their counterparts in wealthy families have been so diagnosed. Ctrs. for Disease Control and Prevention, *supra*, at 6. For more detail about the disparate impacts of air pollution on African Americans, Hispanics and Latinos in the United States, see Black Leadership Forum et al., Air of Injustice: African Americans & Power Plant Pollution 3 (2002) and League of United Latin American Citizens, Air of Injustice: How Air Pollution Affects the Health of Hispanics and Latinos 3–4 (2004). See also the sources discussed in Chapter 2.

Once EPA determines that a pollutant may endanger public health, it is required to promulgate air quality criteria and a NAAQS for the pollutant. However, because of the scientific uncertainty involved in determining the precise magnitude and duration of exposure that may trigger harmful health effects, EPA has substantial discretion in deciding whether or not to adopt standards for new pollutants. In fact, lead is the only new criteria pollutant EPA has added to the initial statutory list, and it did so only because of a successful citizen suit under a previous iteration of Section 108.

The EPA Administrator also exercises substantial discretion in decisions involving revisions to the NAAQS, although not without judicial scrutiny. The Clean Air Act directs EPA to review the air quality criteria every five years and to revise the NAAQS "as may be appropriate." 42 U.S.C. § 7409(d). EPA at various times has declined to revise the existing NAAQS for SO2, carbon monoxide, nitrogen oxides and particulate matter, despite new evidence indicating that levels of exposure below the then-current standards might be harmful. For example, EPA declined to issue a new short-term exposure NAAQS for SO2 (even though the longer averaging times under the existing standard allowed harmful SO2 spikes to occur), a decision the D.C. Circuit Court of Appeals remanded because of the agency's failure to explain "[w]hy is the fact that thousands of asthmatics can be expected to suffer atypical physical effects from repeated five-minute bursts of high-level sulfur dioxide not a public health problem?" *American Lung Association v. EPA*, 134 F.3d 388, 392 (D.C. Cir. 1998).

When EPA does seek to revise a NAAQS, its decision often generates controversy and, frequently, opportunities for judicial review. EPA's recent revisions to the ozone and particulate standards illustrate the interplay of science, economics, law, and politics that attend EPA's work in this context. In 1997, EPA lowered the ozone standard from 0.12 parts per million (ppm) over a one-hour average to 0.08 ppm over an eight-hour average and added a new standard for particulate matter of 2.5 microns or less. These more stringent standards (in addition to saving thousands of lives) are anticipated to shift many regions into nonattainment status, necessitate the revision of numerous state implementation plans, and consequently have a significant affect on the activities of the regulated community. The following excerpt from a book by Professor Rena Steinzor provides useful background for understanding the controversy surrounding the revisions to the ozone NAAQS and the courts' role in overseeing these revisions.

Rena I. Steinzor, Mother Earth and Uncle Sam: How Pollution and Hollow Government Hurt Our Kids
(2008)

Congress had the foresight to provide a built-in framework for scientific peer review of NAAQS revisions, creating the Clean Air Science Advisory Committee (CASAC) in 1977 amendments to the [Clean Air Act]. CASAC is organized and funded by EPA, but prides itself on its scientific candor and independence. The statute mandates that the NAAQS process depends upon close collaboration between CASAC scientists and EPA staff. The EPA administrator initiates a five-step process when a NAAQS revision is necessary:

1. EPA staff prepares a "criteria document" summarizing the scientific research available on the pollutant and submits it to a CASAC panel for review. Staff and CASAC members then debate the contents of the draft until they develop a revised document that reflects their consensus interpretation of the research.

2. On the basis of the revised criteria document, EPA prepares a "staff paper" summarizing both the science and the policy options for the administrator and submits it to CASAC for review, triggering a new round of collaboration and negotiation.

3. CASAC sends a "letter of closure" advising the administrator on the scientific soundness of the staff documents and offering any advice it chooses to on the policy options.

4. The administrator proposes a new NAAQS and puts the proposal out for [public] comment.

5. The administrator considers all of the above information, including public comments received by the Agency, and determines the final standard.

The statutory language states clearly that the final NAAQS shall be the number that "*in the judgment* of the Administrator" protects public health, making it clear that the person appointed by the president and confirmed by the Senate has full authority to make a final decision....

As it embarked on its consideration of a new ozone standard, CASAC was unanimous on one point: EPA needed to switch from the existing "one-hour standard" designed to address short-term ozone spikes and immediate health effects to an "eight-hour standard" designed to protect against long-term adverse health effects....

While CASAC endorsed the eight-hour metric, the panel differed on what number of parts per million (ppm) of ozone in ambient (outdoor) air should be tolerated; members of the group argued in favor of numbers from 0.08 to 0.12 ppm. After some heated debates, the panel issued the required letter of closure certifying the quality of the staff paper's analysis and allowing EPA Administrator Carol Browner to make a final decision on a new and more stringent NAAQS. She chose 0.08 ppm of ozone measured over eight hours and averaged over three years.

* * *

In reviewing the standards, the D.C. Circuit admonished the EPA by invoking the long-dormant "non-delegation" doctrine (a doctrine that prohibits unduly broad grants of authority from Congress to the Executive Branch), a legal rationale that provoked vigorous critique by academics. According to the D.C. Circuit, the EPA's interpretation (rather than the statute itself) violated the nondelegation doctrine by not articulating an intelligible principle upon which the standards were based. Ultimately, the U.S. Supreme Court rejected the view of the D.C. Circuit, reversing the latter's call for a reinterpretation that would avoid the supposed delegation of legislative power. The Supreme Court did, however, remand to the EPA for another reason, that is, a better interpretation of the implementation provisions at issue for the ozone NAAQS. *Whitman v. American Trucking Ass'ns,* 531 U.S. 457 (2001).

In March, 2008, after considering the results of more than 1,700 new scientific studies of ozone's adverse health effects, EPA again tightened the NAAQS for ozone, to 0.075 ppm. U.S. Envtl. Prot. Agency, National Ambient Air Quality Standards for Ozone, 73 Fed. Reg. 16,436 (March 27, 2008). According to EPA, among the benefits of this revision is an estimated annual prevention (in 2020) of between 420 and 2,300 premature deaths. U.S. ENVTL. PROT. AGENCY, FACT SHEET: FINAL REVISIONS TO THE NATIONAL AMBIENT AIR QUALITY STANDARDS FOR OZONE 3 (2008). Also among the benefits is an estimated annual reduction (in 2020) of 320 cases of chronic bronchitis, 890 nonfatal heart attacks, 1,900 hospital and emergency room visits, 1,000 cases of acute bronchitis, 11,600 cases of upper and lower respiratory symptoms, 6,100 cases of aggravated asthma, 243,000 days when people miss work or school, and 750,000 days when people must restrict their activities because of ozone-related illnesses. *Id.* EPA estimated that the total monetized ozone-related benefits of the new standard would be between $4 and $17 billion per year, while the costs of implementing the new standard would be between $7.6 and $8.8 billion. *Id.*

These most recent revisions also generated controversy, with EPA again being criticized by both industry and environmentalists. Among the criticisms were those leveled by the American Lung Association, which charged that EPA—then in the hands of the George W. Bush Administration—improperly selected the relatively more lenient 0.075 ppm standard despite the fact that the CASAC had recommended a more stringent standard, specifically, a standard between 0.060 ppm and 0.070 ppm. They argued that "[t]wo to three times as many people could have been protected from an early death from their exposure to ozone if EPA had followed the scientists' recommendations, according to the EPA's own estimates." AMERICAN LUNG ASSOCIATION, NEW OZONE STANDARDS DON'T PROVIDE ADEQUATE PROTECTION (2008).

Notes and Questions

1. For each NAAQS, there is typically a range of potential standards that are plausibly protective given the scientific information available at the time the standard is being considered. For example, in *American Trucking,* the D.C. Circuit questioned why EPA chose an 0.08 ppm level for ozone but not a level of 0.07 or 0.09 ppm, presumably standards that would have been sufficiently protective as well. How is EPA supposed to choose which standard is best without considering costs? Should the distributional aspects of adverse health effects play a role in choosing among several plausible options? It seems that asthma sufferers are a particularly sensitive subpopulation and the EPA likely considered this group in arriving at various NAAQS in the past. Should EPA also consider that asthma is increasingly common among the poor and non-white? If, for example, EPA were to find that racial and ethnic minorities are disproportionately affected by its decision to set the ozone standard at 0.08 instead of 0.07 (a more stringent standard), should the agency reconsider its decision?

2. Similarly, if EPA were to find that the poor suffer disproportionately from SO2 spikes, should it reconsider its decision not to issue a short-term SO2 NAAQS, especially because this group is less able to afford medications that can help prevent bronchoconstriction during peak episodes? What are the advantages and disadvantages to letting an environmental justice analysis help guide the agency to a more precise national standard? According to Professors Lazarus and Tai, "[t]he D.C. Circuit's ruling [in *American Lung Association*] suggests more than that EPA possesses statutory authority to consider the special sensitivities of environmental justice communities when establishing air quality standards under the CAA. The CAA may, in this respect, provide an instance in which the federal law mandates such consideration." Lazarus & Tai, *supra,* at 632.

3. Professor Steinzor relays an argument that has tended to be raised by industry and others who are generally opposed to more stringent regulation, but that nonetheless raises a concern relevant to those seeking social justice:

> [A] discussion of the costs and benefits of clean air would not be complete without a visit to the far right end of the spectrum, where some argue that implementation of the [CAA] actually kills people. The theory behind this remarkable claim is that the costs of regulation are passed directly on to the consumer in the form of higher electricity prices and more expensive consumer goods. These costs must be absorbed by families and will have an especially devastating impact on people with low incomes because the money lost will not be able to pay for essentials that make people healthier.... The researchers say these "economically transmitted impacts" of the [1997] ozone and particulate matter NAAQS could kill between 2,201 people (for $10 billion in annual regulatory costs) and 22,589 people (for $100 billion in annual costs). Families with incomes below $15,000 in 1994 dollars will pay by far the highest price, accounting for some 40

percent of lives lost at all levels of cost. In a particularly harsh twist, the researchers estimate that 25 percent of the fatalities will occur in African-American households.

Steinzor, *supra*, at 168. Professor Steinzor goes on to identify the "string of questionable assumptions" that underlies these claims. Can you think of what some of these might be? Even if you agree with Professor Steinzor that these claims rest on faulty premises, it is surely the case that the benefits of more protective standards come at some cost. How would you structure agencies' decision-making processes to ensure that they consider the appropriate questions in this regard?

4. The debate over the ozone NAAQS provides another illustration of agencies' quiet turn to "risk avoidance" strategies in lieu of "risk reduction." (See discussion of risk avoidance as a regulatory strategy in Chapter 6). Here the risk avoidance measure employed is a warning, commonly called an "ozone alert" or "Code Red day," that people, especially asthmatics and others with respiratory issues, remain indoors or restrict their level of exertion if they must go outside. As Professor Steinzor observes:

> The Clean Air Act does not allow EPA to even consider the alternative of telling people to stay inside when air quality is bad. Instead, the solution of putting the burden on the victim to avoid the risk has become the default reality as a direct result of the powerful combination of a dysfunctional legal framework and hollow government. For the many parents who live in cities afflicted by Code Red days and who bring their children's asthma inhaler every time they venture from home, all of these elaborate, convoluted calculations, research projections and public policy quarrels seem bizarre. To be sure, we drive cars, we depend on a stable supply of electricity, and we value the vast array of products that are available to American consumers. But would we really choose to impose smog on our and other people's children so that some of us have the option of buying the largest SUV on the market? Is it fair to expect the youngest among us to shoulder so much of the burden of allowing pollution to rise to levels that cause clear health problems, even if the economists tell us that such incidents are only worth a few dollars?

Steinzor, *supra*, at 168–69. How would you propose to resolve the problems Professor Steinzor identifies, i.e., can you imagine a system for asking and answering the value-laden questions that she highlights?

5. Pursuant to the Executive Order on Environment Justice 12,898 (exerpted in Chapter 10) EPA considered the implications for environmental justice of its most recent revision to the ozone NAAQS in 2008:

> Executive Order 12,898 establishes Federal executive policy on environmental justice. Its main provision directs Federal agencies, to the greatest extent practicable and permitted by law, to make environmental justice part of their mission by identifying and addressing, as appropriate, disproportionately high and adverse human health or environmental effects of their programs, policies, and activities on minority populations and low-income populations in the United States.
>
> EPA has determined that this final rule will not have disproportionately high and adverse human health or environmental effects on minority or low-income populations because it increases the level of environmental protection for all affected populations without having any disproportionately high and adverse human health or environmental effects on any population, including any mi-

nority or low-income population. This final rule will establish uniform national standards for O3 [ozone] air pollution.

U.S. Envtl. Prot. Agency, National Ambient Air Quality Standards for Ozone, 73 Fed. Reg. 16,436, 16,507 (March 27, 2008). Has EPA asked the right question? Are there alternative ways in which EPA might frame an inquiry into whether its "programs, policies, and activities" "address[] ... disproportionately high and adverse human health or environmental effects ... on minority and low-income populations?" Exec. Order No. 12,898, 59 Fed. Reg. 7629 (February 11, 1994).

6. The National Conference of Black Mayors, representing more than 600 officials, opposed EPA's 2008 revision to the ozone NAAQS. Citing the fact that many cities and counties in the South would violate the new, tighter standard, the Conference worried about the "stigma of being designated nonattainment" making it difficult to attract new industry, to expand existing businesses, and, ultimately to ensure "good jobs, economic growth and the quality of life that goes with it." This position was sharply criticized by longtime environmental justice advocate Beverly Wright, Director of Dillard University's Deep South Center for Environmental Justice, who called it "abominable," citing the higher risk faced by African Americans from ozone pollution, and suggesting that the Conference was "evidently not speaking for the people they represent." Daniel Cusick, *EPA Smog Proposal Sparks Debate Over Environmental Justice*, Earth News (Sept. 6, 2007). In an independent review, the Government Accountability Office gave the EPA poor marks overall for its attempts to consider and address environmental justice in developing rules under the CAA. *See*, Gov't Accountability Office, EPA Should Devote More Attention to Environmental Justice When Developing Clean Air Rules (July 2005).

C. Standards under the Clean Water Act

1. An Introductory Note on the Statute's Different Standards

This section will look at the environmental justice implications of standards though the lens of the Clean Water Act where, like many of the environmental statutes, there is an interplay between health-based and technology-based standards. In this statute, the standards that have been most vigorously implemented are the technology-based standards, generally under the National Pollutant Discharge Elimination System (NPDES) program. In this permitting program, a "point source" must acquire a permit before it discharges effluent that contains certain contaminants into a water body. State or tribal governments may obtain authority from the EPA to carry out the NPDES permit program but the EPA retains oversight authority, including the ability to veto state- or tribally-issued permits. NPDES permits typically require the installation of technology-based standards, such as "best available technology" (BAT) for dischargers of toxics, or "best conventional technology" for so-called conventional pollutants such as biological oxygen demanding chemicals, fecal coliform, suspended solids and pH. BAT is promulgated by reference to industrial sectors under the assumption that all facilities that produce certain products have similar production processes. Municipally owned waste water treatment facilities are also required to obtain NPDES permits and have their own sets of technology-based requirements. *See, generally,* Percival et al., *supra,* at 616–60.

It may occur to you that if there are too many point sources discharging pollutants into a small water body, the water resource could be severely degraded despite the installation of BAT. This has in fact been the case in many instances. But the Clean Water Act has provisions designed to prevent this from occurring. The Act envisions a safety net of health-based standards, called water quality standards.

Ideally, a water quality standard should be designed so that if the water body meets the standard, it should be safe for certain designated uses. The baseline use is determined by the EPA to be "fishable/swimable" waters. This means that for the majority of water bodies, water quality standards should be sufficient to protect persons who swim in and consume fish caught from the water body. Beyond this default standard, states and tribes are free to establish other designated uses for each water segment within their respective jurisdictions. If a water body does not meet the applicable water quality standards it may be categorized as "water quality limited" and point source dischargers (typically industrial and publicly owned treatment facilities) might have to undertake limitations to their processes above the normally required technology-based standards.

Implementation of the safety net of health-based standards involves a difficult procedure. State and tribal agencies must determine how much of a pollutant loading a given water body can take before it exceeds the applicable water quality standards. Once this "total maximum daily load" (TMDL) is established, the agency essentially rations the amount each contributor can discharge, resulting in the possibility that some point source dischargers will have their NPDES permits limited further with "waste load allocations." However, the section of the Clean Water Act that mandates such action had gone largely unimplemented until recent years. Whereas only 403 TMDLs were completed and approved in 1998, this number jumped to 9,129 in 2008. U.S. ENVTL. PROT. AGENCY, WATERSHED ASSESSMENT, TRACKING & ENVIRONMENTAL RESULTS: NATIONAL SUMMARY OF STATE INFORMATION (2008).

Thus far, we have been discussing only point source dischargers, but runoff from streets, agricultural activities, logging and other "non-point" activities are, in fact, now the primary contributors to degraded water quality. The CWA does not mandate technology-based standards or other direct mechanisms of controlling pollution from these sources, instead relying on states and tribes to enlist land use, planning and other measures to address non-point sources. As a consequence, non-point pollution had gone largely unregulated or underregulated. However, EPA recently took the position that TMDL plans should control non-point pollution as well, a controversial position that was challenged by agricultural and logging interests, among others. In a case involving the Garcia River in California, for which the relevant TMDL required a 60% reduction in sediment loadings, the Ninth Circuit upheld EPA's reading of the CWA, enabling agencies to establish and implement TMDLs even for those waters impaired only by non-point sources of pollution. *Prosolino v. Nastri*, 291 F.3d 1123 (9th Cir. 2002).

Although water quality throughout the nation has improved under the Clean Water Act, many water bodies still fail to support their designated uses. According the EPA's most recent data, 47% of assessed river and stream miles, 59% of assessed lake, reservoir and pond acres, and 40% of assessed bays and estuaries are impaired. The picture for the Great Lakes is especially bleak: 95% of assessed shoreline miles and 98% of assessed open waters are impaired. U.S. ENVTL. PROT. AGENCY, WATERSHED ASSESSMENT, TRACKING & ENVIRONMENTAL RESULTS: NATIONAL SUMMARY OF STATE INFORMATION (2006); U.S. ENVTL. PROT. AGENCY, WATERSHED ASSESSMENT, TRACKING & ENVIRONMENTAL RESULTS: NATIONAL SUMMARY OF STATE INFORMATION (2008). The proliferation of fish consumption advisories provides another measure of our failure to attain healthful waters. According to the most recent tally, twenty-two states and the District of Columbia have placed the entirety of their waters under advisory for one or more contaminants. Fish consumption advisories—warning mainly of contamination from mercury, PCBs, chlordane, dioxins, and DDT—currently cover 38% of the nation's total lake acreage, 26% of the nation's total river miles, and, additionally, 100% of the Great Lakes and their connecting waters. U.S. ENVTL. PROT. AGENCY, FACT SHEET: 2005/2006 NATIONAL LISTING OF FISH ADVISORIES (July, 2007).

From an environmental justice perspective, the present state of implementation of the Clean Water Act raises several important issues. First, the promulgation of the default "fishable/swimable" water quality standards requires an estimate of how much fish people typically eat. As noted in Chapters 2 and 6, however, individuals' fish consumption practices vary considerably, with members of certain environmental justice communities consuming fish at much higher rates than the "average American." Agencies' assumptions about the fish consumption rates of those affected by its water quality standards can mean the difference between a standard that is adequately protective and one that is likely to result in significant disparities in protection, as discussed in the first excerpt, below. Second, tribes may obtain authority to administer various programs under the Clean Water Act. (See Chapter 4, which discusses environmental justice for American Indians at greater length). Tribes that run their own water quality programs have been able to address these and other environmental justice concerns, at least to some degree. When tribes exercise their regulatory authority—presenting the unique situation of an "environmental justice community" as regulator—they face a new set of challenges, some of which are illustrated by *City of Albuquerque v. Browner*, the case that comprises the second excerpt, below.

2. Water Quality Standards

Catherine A. O'Neill, Variable Justice: Environmental Standards, Contaminated Fish, and "Acceptable" Risk to Native Peoples
19 Stanford Environmental Law Journal 3 (2000)

... EPA currently assumes a fish consumption rate (FCR) of 6.5 grams/day [when setting water quality standards]. This amounts to approximately one fish meal per month. The 6.5 grams/day value is derived from a diet recall study conducted in the mid-1970s of the general population of the United States, fish consumers and non-consumers alike....

Various studies of fish consumption rates in Puget Sound and the Columbia River Basin ... indicate marked differences among Native American subpopulations and the general population.... According to a 1994 diet recall study conducted by and of the Nez Perce, Umatilla, Yakama, and Warm Springs tribes fishing along the Columbia River, the 50th percentile or median fish consumption rate for tribal members is between 29 and 32 grams per day; the arithmetic mean is 58.7 grams per day; the 90th percentile is between 97.2 and 130 grams per day; the 95th percentile is 170 grams per day; and the 99th percentile is 389 grams per day. The maximum consumption rate is 972 grams per day.

In *Dioxin/Organochlorine Center*, the EPA employed its default assumption for the FCR, 6.5 g/day. Relying on this standard assumption about exposure, EPA derived a water quality standard, the TMDL for dioxin, by solving the risk equation for concentration with cancer risk held at 1(10-6). If a particular environmental standard is set, assuming the exposure of the "average American," to result in risk of no more than 1 in 1,000,000, that same standard will result in greater risk to a more highly exposed subpopulation. In

Dioxin/Organochlorine Center, this greater risk was estimated to be 23 in 1,000,000 or 2.3 in 100,000.

The Ninth Circuit accepted the EPA's choice of an FCR of 6.5 g/day by asserting that the resulting standards would provide "lower yet adequate protection" to higher-consuming Native American subpopulations.... [T]he court held that even if these subpopulations consume 150 g/day of fish and would therefore be subject to excess risk of 2.3(10-5), "this level of risk protection is within levels historically approved by the EPA and upheld by courts." The court endorsed EPA's argument that "the one-in-a-million risk level mandated by the state water quality standards for the general population does not necessarily reflect state legislative intent to provide the highest level of protection for all subpopulations but could reasonably be construed to allow for lower yet adequate protection for specific subpopulations." ...

* * *

Notes and Questions

1. What is your view of the merits of the "lower but adequate protection" rationale relied upon by the Ninth Circuit?

2. At what point (if any) should agencies be permitted to set standards that are protective of the majority of the population but not similarly protective of "outliers"—members of the population whose susceptibilities and circumstances of exposure place them at the extreme in a population distribution? What if it could be shown that it would be enormously costly to protect these highly susceptible or highly exposed individuals, and that they comprise only a small fraction of the population? How is your response affected if these individuals were revealed to be members of various groups (e.g., various indigenous peoples, various Asian American communities, African American communities), each of which might have quite different group-based environmental justice claims? Once the identity of the populations at greater risk is clearly known, is it unethical to ignore the heightened risks they face? What difficulties in accommodating the varied and complex histories of different groups might you imagine from the perspective of an environmental agency engaged in standard setting? Professor O'Neill argues:

> The mere fact that highly exposed subgroups exist in a context where the stakes are high necessitates differential treatment by health and environmental agencies.... The more significant the differences in the circumstances of exposure or susceptibility between the subpopulation and the general population, the more suspect an agency decision that fails to disaggregate these groups for differential treatment....

> [O]f the identifiable subgroups that are candidates for differential treatment, some may require agency attention because of their particular *identity*. Here, various moral and legal commitments may come into play. Agencies must address the intersection of variability and the fact that a particular identifiable subpopulation—Native Americans—occupies the high end of a variable exposure distribution.... [But, to date,] agencies have inadequately considered the relevant normative commitments respecting cultural integrity, equality [in the sense of freedom from both exclusionary and cultural discrimination], and process, and have not registered the applicable legal obligations arising from [inter alia] treaties [and] the federal trust responsibility.

O'Neill, *supra* at 75–76, 81. Do you agree?

3. EPA has since revised its default fish consumption rate, and now recommends a more subtle approach that includes a default rate of 17.5 grams/day for both the general

population and recreational fishers and a default rate of 142.4 grams/day for subsistence fishers. EPA employs these default values whenever it is in the position of setting standards and considers them as a baseline when it reviews water quality standards set by states or tribes. EPA further recommends a four-part hierarchy for determining the FCR on which water quality standards will be based, by which EPA encourages states and tribes, in order of preference, to "(1) use local data; (2) use data reflecting similar geography/population groups; (3) use data from national surveys; and (4) use EPA's default fish consumption rates." U.S. ENVTL. PROT. AGENCY, METHODOLOGY FOR DERIVING AMBIENT WATER QUALITY CRITERIA FOR THE PROTECTION OF HUMAN HEALTH 4–25 (Oct, 2000).

The states, especially, have been exceedingly slow to update their water quality standards, despite the CWA's requirement that states and tribes review and revise their water quality standards every three years (known as a "triennial review.") Washington's water quality standards, for example, still reflect the old 6.5 grams/day default fish consumption rate as this book goes to press, although studies quantifying the greater rates of consumption by local tribal members and recreational fishers have been available for at least a decade.

The fact that a state undertakes revisions to its water quality standards, of course, is no guarantee that the new standards will be adequately protective of affected tribes and other environmental justice communities. First, because agencies typically rely on quantitative risk assessment to set these health-based standards, they require quantitative evidence of the consumption practices of highly-exposed groups, and such studies are few and far between (and, as noted in Chapter 6, may not accurately capture even contemporary consumption practices, especially for tribal members). Second, given the considerable costs that may attend a more protective standard, regulated industries generally oppose more protective revisions. Federal and state agencies, moreover, have often been sympathetic to this concern about costs. Oregon's recent efforts to revise its water quality standards provide a case in point.

> The Oregon Environmental Quality Commission recently adopted revisions to its water quality standards. Oregon, of course, had local data, including the CRITFC survey and the Harris and Harper data [documenting consumption practices of tribal elders, traditional members, and subsistence fishing families in the Umatilla tribe and finding the average rate for this population to be 540 grams/day], and so was in the position to adhere to EPA's first preference. In fact, the Oregon Department of Environmental Quality (ODEQ) had constituted a Technical Advisory Committee, which endorsed the use of the values from the CRITFC survey. Specifically, the Technical Advisory Committee formally recommended that ODEQ assign values to the various regulated waters in Oregon depending on the intensity of fishing activity in those waters: it recommended an FCR for low-intensity use at 17.5 grams/day—the EPA's default for the general population; an FCR for intermediate-intensity use at 142.4 grams/day—the EPA's default for subsistence fishers; and an FCR for high-intensity use at 389 grams/day—the 99th percentile value from the CRITFC survey.
>
> The ODEQ, however, rejected the recommendations of its own Technical Advisory Committee. Instead, it opted for the least protective—and least preferred—option, a statewide FCR at the EPA's national default of 17.5 grams/day.... Oregon finalized its revised standards in May of 2004.

Catherine A. O'Neill, *Protecting the Tribal Harvest: The Right to Catch and Consume Fish*, 22 J. ENVTL. L. & LITIGATION 131, 141–42 (2007). Can you think of why a state might opt for less stringent standards? Although EPA is required under the CWA to approve or disapprove a state's water quality standards within 90 days, as of August, 2006, EPA had still declined to take action on Oregon's controversial standards. Both Oregon's decision and EPA's inaction were sharply criticized by the affected tribes. Finally, Oregon and EPA joined with the Confederated Tribes of the Umatilla Indian Reservation in an effort to revisit the standards that would be led by the three governments. After numerous public workshops, the Oregon Environmental Quality Commission in October, 2008, adopted a new fish consumption rate of 175 grams/day and directed the ODEQ to revise its water quality standards accordingly. The revisions are expected in fall of 2009. *See* OR. DEP'T OF ENVTL. QUALITY, OREGON FISH CONSUMPTION RATE PROJECT (2008). In your view, did EPA fully exercise the authority available to it under the CWA to address environmental justice issues?

4. Recall that EPA can delegate authority to tribes as well as states to administer programs under the CWA and other statutes. Given tribal members' higher fish consumption rates and ceremonial uses of water bodies, tribes might be more inclined to set more stringent water quality standards. The following case illustrates the political and legal difficulties involved when Isleta Pueblo, a federally-recognized American Indian tribe situated in New Mexico, took up the challenge to promulgate strict water quality standards.

City of Albuquerque v. Browner
97 F. 3d 415 (10th Cir. 1996)

McKay, Circuit Judge:

... This case involves the first challenge to water quality standards adopted by an Indian tribe under the Clean Water Act amendment.

The Rio Grande River flows south through New Mexico before turning southeast to form the border between Texas and Mexico. Plaintiff City of Albuquerque operates a waste treatment facility which dumps into the river approximately five miles north of the Isleta Pueblo Indian Reservation. The EPA recognized Isleta Pueblo as a state for purposes of the Clean Water Act on October 12, 1992. The Isleta Pueblo adopted water quality standards for Rio Grande water flowing through the tribal reservation, which were approved by the EPA on December 24, 1992. The Isleta Pueblo's water quality standards are more stringent than the State of New Mexico's standards.

The Albuquerque waste treatment facility discharges into the Rio Grande under a National Pollution Discharge Elimination System [NPDES] permit issued by the EPA. The EPA sets permit discharge limits for waste treatment facilities so they meet state water quality standards. Albuquerque filed this action as the EPA was in the process of revising Albuquerque's NPDES permit to meet the Isleta Pueblo's water quality standards....

Albuquerque argues that § 1377 does not expressly permit Indian tribes to enforce effluent limitations or standards under § 1311 to upstream point source dischargers outside of tribal boundaries.... Under the statutory and regulatory scheme, tribes are not applying or enforcing their water quality standards beyond reservation boundaries. Instead, it is the EPA which is exercising its own authority in issuing NPDES permits in compliance with downstream state and tribal water quality standards. In regard to this question, therefore, the 1987 amendment to the Clean Water Act clearly and unambiguously provides tribes the authority to establish NPDES programs in conjunction with the EPA.... [T]he EPA has the authority to require upstream NPDES dischargers, such as Albuquerque, to comply with downstream tribal standards.

... Under the water quality standards provisions of the Clean Water Act, it is the states and tribes which conduct rulemaking proceedings. This is in accord with Congress's intent to preserve a primary role for the states and tribes in eliminating water pollution. The results of state and tribal rulemaking proceedings are then presented to the EPA for approval. The Fourth Circuit has explained the EPA's limited role in reviewing water quality standards proposed by states, stating:

> EPA sits in a reviewing capacity of the state-implemented standards, with approval and rejection powers only....
>
> [S]tates have the primary role, under § 303 of the CWA (33 U.S.C. § 1313), in establishing water quality standards. EPA's sole function, in this respect, is to review those standards for approval....

Albuquerque also claims that the EPA's approval of the Isleta Pueblo standards was unsupported by a rational basis on the record and was therefore arbitrary and capricious. Albuquerque argues that the EPA was required to reject the Isleta Pueblo's water quality standards unless the EPA had established its own record based on a sound scientific rationale for each particular provision.

The EPA, however, reviews proposed water quality standards only to determine whether they are stringent enough to comply with the EPA's recommended standards and criteria. If the proposed standards are more stringent than necessary to comply with the Clean Water Act's requirements, the EPA may approve the standards without reviewing the scientific support for the standards. Whether the more stringent standard is attainable is a matter for the EPA to consider in its discretion; sections 1341 and 1342 of the Clean Water Act permit the EPA and states to force technological advancement to attain higher water quality. The EPA's letter approving the Isleta Pueblo standards explains that it is approving the standards, despite their departure from the EPA's guidelines, based on the Tribe's authority to adopt standards more stringent than the minimum requirements of the Clean Water Act.

The EPA considered Isleta Pueblo's rationale for each of the standards challenged by Albuquerque, and the tribe's record contains detailed responses to all of the criticisms expressed by the EPA and Albuquerque. The record contains a detailed explanation of the Isleta Pueblo's scientific, technical, and policy reasons for choosing to establish more stringent standards. For example, the Isleta Pueblo stated that stringent standards are justified because of prevailing drought conditions and the need to protect sensitive subpopulations. The EPA concluded that the standards were consistent with the Clean Water Act's requirements and should therefore be approved. The arbitrary and capricious review standard is very deferential; "an agency ruling is 'arbitrary and capricious if the agency has ... entirely failed to consider an important aspect of the problem.'" Albuquerque has not shown that the EPA failed to consider an important aspect of the Isleta Pueblo's water quality standards....

In its next claim, Albuquerque argues that the Isleta Pueblo criteria approved by the EPA are not stringent enough to protect the Tribe's designated use standard described as primary contact ceremonial use. The Tribe describes primary contact ceremonial use as involving the "immersion and intentional or incidental ingestion of water." Albuquerque argues that this requires the river water quality to meet the standards of the Safe Drinking Water Act, 42 U.S.C. § 300f, and the Isleta Pueblo's water quality criteria approved by the EPA fail to protect water used under the ceremonial use standard.

As the district court stated:

> This argument seems far-fetched. The primary contact ceremonial use appears to resemble a fishable/swimmable standard, which assumes the ingestion of some

water, more than it resembles a safe drinking water standard, which assumes the ingestion of a volume of water daily.

Albuquerque [v. Browner, 865 F.Supp. 733, 740 (D.N.M. 1993)]. The federal drinking water standards apply only to a "public water system," which is defined as a system supplying piped water for human consumption serving at least twenty-five persons or having at least fifteen service connections. 42 U.S.C. § 300f(4). The Isleta Pueblo's ceremonial use standard does not convert the Rio Grande River into a public water system. The EPA considered and approved this aspect of the Isleta Pueblo water quality standards. We decline to second-guess the EPA's technical determination, which is entitled to substantial deference, that the Isleta Pueblo's water quality criteria adequately protect its ceremonial designated use standard....

Albuquerque next claims that the EPA's approval of the Pueblo's ceremonial use designation offends the Establishment Clause of the First Amendment. The First Amendment provides in relevant part: "Congress shall make no law respecting an establishment of religion...." U.S. Const. amend. I. Government action does not violate the Establishment Clause if "[t]he challenged governmental action has a secular purpose, does not have the principal or primary effect of advancing or inhibiting religion, and does not foster an excessive entanglement with religion."

The EPA approved Isleta Pueblo's promulgation of "Primary Contact Ceremonial Use" as a designated use of the Rio Grande River within the boundaries of the Indian reservation. The tribe defines "Primary Contact Ceremonial Use" as "the use of a stream, reach, lake, or impoundment for religious or traditional purposes by members of the PUEBLO OF ISLETA; such use involves immersion and intentional or incidental ingestion of water." Albuquerque argues that the EPA's approval of this standard violates all three aspects of the Establishment Clause under Lemon [v. Kurtzman, 403 U.S. 602 (1971)].

First, Albuquerque argues that the reason for the designated use is explicitly sectarian. The secular purpose requirement does not mean that a law's purpose must be unrelated to religion because that would require "'that the government show a callous indifference to religious groups,' ... and the Establishment Clause has never been so interpreted." The EPA's approval of the primary contact ceremonial use designation serves a clear secular purpose: promotion of the goals of the Clean Water Act. The EPA's purpose in approving the designated use is unrelated to the Isleta Pueblo's religious reason for establishing it. The Isleta Pueblo's designation of a ceremonial use does not invalidate the EPA's overall secular goal.

Second, Albuquerque claims that the EPA's action has a primary effect of advancing religion. We disagree. The EPA is not advancing religion through its own actions, and it is not promoting the Isleta Pueblo's religion. The primary effect of the EPA's action is to advance the goals of the Clean Water Act.

Third, Albuquerque asserts the designated use results in excessive governmental entanglement with religion because the Pueblo and the EPA must inquire on an ongoing basis whether the standards adequately protect religious uses of the river water. This argument is meritless. "There is no genuine nexus between" the EPA's approval of the ceremonial use standard "and establishment of religion," and the EPA's approval of the standard provides only an incidental benefit to religion. The EPA's approval of the ceremonial use standard does not require any governmental involvement in the Isleta Pueblo's religious practices. Excessive governmental entanglement will not result when the EPA incorporates the Isleta Pueblo's water quality standards in issuing future NPDES permits....

* * *

Notes and Questions

1. Professor Denise Fort published an article on the dispute shortly before the above opinion was issued. In the article, she discusses a variety of important factual questions that this controversy raised:

> ... [I]n any dispute over water quality standards, the underlying factual questions are likely to be persuasive in how one views the merits of the dispute. For example, are tribal standards unreasonably strict, or are the state's unreasonably lax? How expensive will it be for upstream dischargers to comply with the standards? Should a tribe be allowed to continue its historic use of a river for ceremonial purposes, involving drinking from the river, when alternative water supplies are available, and if the answer is affirmative, should upstream taxpayers bear the cost of making a river safe for those practices? Should upstream polluters be allowed to endanger those who depend on a river, and, is it relevant that those uses predate the upstream discharge? One's views of the legal merits may vary with the answers to these questions. It is noteworthy that a state's standards provide the lens through which these questions are viewed; if tribes were to adopt standards identical to those of the surrounding states, dischargers would have no grounds to object. The Pueblo of Isleta's standards were at issue in the Browner case, not the standards set by the State of New Mexico.

Denise D. Fort, *State and Tribal Water Quality Standards Under the Clean Water Act: A Case Study,* 35 NAT. RESOURCES J. 771, 775–76 (1995). As with the issues concerning water quality standards and fish consumption discussed above, the legal issues in this dispute were framed with reference to the dominant population. Does framing environmental justice issues as deviations from an existing norm affect the analysis? If so, why did the tribe prevail in this case? In what ways is the case helpful to resolving environmental justice disputes outside the context of tribal sovereignty?

2. For a detailed discussion of tribal implementation of the water quality standards programs under the CWA, *see* Dean Suagee & James H. Havard, *Tribal Governments and the Protection of Watersheds and Wetlands in Indian Country,* 13 ST. THOMAS L. REV. 35 (2000); *see also, Wisconsin v. E.P.A.,* 266 F.3d 741, 748 (7th Cir. 2001) (upholding, over challenge by Wisconsin, EPA's decision to grant Sokaogon Chippewa Community "treatment as state" status for purpose of adopting water quality standards, and noting that once a tribe is given such status, "it has the power to require upstream off-reservation dischargers ... to make sure that their activities do not result in contamination of the downstream on-reservation waters"). Anna Fleder and Professor Darren Ranco observe that *Albuquerque v. Browner* highlights tribes' difficult position in their quest for environmental justice. This case

> illustrates [a] potentially paternalistic relationship, because it reinforces strong checks on tribal sovereignty by the American government and paves the way for future environmental regulation by tribes that is limited and contestable. At the same time, the case serves as a remarkable example of committed attempts by the federal government to promote tribal autonomy and decision-making.

Anna Fleder and Darren J. Ranco, *Tribal Environmental Sovereignty: Culturally Appropriate Protection or Paternalism?,* 19 J. NAT. RESOURCES & ENVTL. L. 35 (2004–05). American Indian tribes' unique circumstances are discussed in Chapter 4.

D. Market-Based Approaches

1. An Introduction to Market-Based Approaches to Regulation

The previous sections of this chapter focused on health-based standards in the context of air and water quality regulation. To a lesser extent, these sections considered technology-based and technology-forcing standards, and recognized the role that these standards play in agencies' efforts to meet ambient, health-based standards. Critics have argued that technology-based standards and other similar regulatory tools are suboptimal in a number of respects. Most prominently, these critics point out that such traditional "command and control" approaches—which, they argue, require every regulated source to apply identical pollution control equipment and measures—are inefficient. This is so because the costs of compliance may vary considerably among different industrial sectors (for example, it might be less costly for the printing sector to comply with a mandate to curb certain air pollutants than computer chip manufacturers) and among different sources within a particular industrial sector (for example, it might be less costly for pulp and paper facility that uses one bleaching process to control its dioxin emissions than for a pulp and paper facility that uses a different process). As a result, economists and other critics have called for greater reliance on economic incentives, or market-based tools, to achieve environmental objectives. Economic incentives comprise a range of tools that rely on business' economic self-interest, rather than direct regulation, to reduce pollution and that therefore allow businesses to reduce their pollution in the most cost-effective manner. Market-based tools can take numerous forms: pollution charges or "taxes," which impose a fixed dollar amount for each unit of pollution emitted or disposed; deposit-refund systems (such as bottle bills) in which purchasers receive a refund when an article is properly returned or disposed of; government subsidies or tax breaks for certain environmental behavior; or "cap-and-trade" regimes, which impose a ceiling or cap on total emissions for a given geographic area (which can be local, regional, national, or even global), allocate these total emissions among contributing sources in the form of allowances that entitle the holder to emit a certain quantity of emissions, and then permit these sources to buy and sell the allowances to each other. Within this market, the firms that can control emissions more cheaply will have the incentive to reduce their emissions to a greater degree because they can sell the excess allowances thereby generated to firms that have higher costs of control. As a result, overall emissions are reduced at a lower aggregate cost to industry. As explained in this section, however, market-based approaches, and in particular cap-and-trade regimes, can exacerbate environmental inequities.

Pathfinder on Economic Incentives

For general background about market-based approaches, see Robert Stavins, *In the Toolkit, Economic Incentives,* 18 EPA J. 21 (May/June 1992); Daniel Dudek & John Palmisano, *Emissions Trading: Why is this Thoroughbred Hobbled?,* 13 COLUM. J. ENVTL L. 217 (1988); Bruce Ackerman & Richard Stewart, *Reforming Environmental Law,* 37 STANFORD L. REV. 1333 (1985). For a more critical view of market-based programs, see David Driesen, *Is Emissions Trading an Economic Incentive Program?: Replacing the Command and Control/Economic Incentive Dichotomy,* 55 WASH. & LEE L. REV. 289 (1998), and David M. Driesen, *Trading and Its Limits,* 14 PENN. ST. ENVTL. L. REV. 169 (2006). In addition to the articles discussed in this chapter, other articles exploring the environmental justice implications of market approaches include; Thomas Lambert & Christopher Boerner, *Environmental Inequity: Economic Causes, Economic Solutions*, 14 YALE J. ON REGULATION 195 (1997); Lorna Jaynes, Comment, *Emissions Trading: Pollution Panacea or Environmental Injustice?*, 39 SANTA CLARA L. REV. 207 (1998); and Lily N. Chinn, Comment, *Can The Market Be Fair And Efficient? An Environmental Justice Critique of Emissions Trading*, 26 ECOLOGY L.Q. 80 (1999). (For critiques of emissions trading in connection with climate change initiatives, see Chapter 12.)

Market-based approaches have assumed greater importance in recent years, and are likely to be a key underpinning of regulatory efforts to reduce greenhouse gases. In an early article, Professor Stephen Johnson discussed the theory and history behind some of the most widely used market-based tools and their environmental justice implications.

Stephen M. Johnson, Economics vs. Equity: Do Market-Based Environmental Reforms Exacerbate Environmental Injustice?

56 Washington and Lee Law Review 111 (1999)

Inevitable Inequities in Market-Based Reforms

... Although the traditional [regulatory] approach clearly has not adequately addressed distributional inequities, market-based approaches will inevitably exacerbate those inequities. While the traditional command and control environmental laws and regulations do not explicitly require the government to avoid actions that disparately impact low-income or minority communities, those laws also do not affirmatively encourage unequal distribution of pollution. By contrast, as explained below, many market-based approaches to environmental protection affirmatively encourage polluters to shift pollution to lower-income communities....

Classical economic theory institutionalizes and exacerbates existing social disparities that are based on unequal distributions of income. As Judge Richard Posner suggested, in a free market economy, in which voluntary exchange is permitted, "resources are shifted to those uses in which the value to consumers, as measured by their willingness to pay, is highest. When resources are being used where their value is highest, we may say that they are being employed efficiently." Although Judge Posner defined "value" in terms of "willingness to pay," on closer reflection it is clear that Judge Posner and other economists incorporated "ability to pay" into the concept of "willingness to pay." Thus, under traditional economic theory, a pollutant trading program, tax program, or similar market-based reform that shifts pollution to low-income communities is operating efficiently and, therefore, desirably because resources, such as clean air and clean water, are shifted to the uses in which the value to consumers, as measured by their willingness (and ability) to pay, is highest. Because wealthy communities are "willing to pay" more for clean air and water than low-income communities, the market operates efficiently when it funnels those resources to those communities rather than to low-income communities. In a free market, low-income communities will never have sufficient financial resources to buy clean air, clean water, and similar environmental and public health resources from wealthy communities or polluters....

[E]conomists admit that economic theory does not make value judgments regarding the distribution of resources or regarding the moral or social implications of "efficient" allocations of resources. Economists admit that economic theory does not address the important underlying question regarding whether an efficient allocation of resources is socially or ethically desirable. . . .

However, environmental law developed and flourished precisely because economic theory, and the free market, did not address those social concerns. . . . While environmental laws should weigh economic issues, the laws should not substitute economic considerations for the important social considerations that motivated legislators to enact the laws in the first place. . . .

Pollutant Trading Systems and Potential Disparate Impacts

Most of the pollutant trading programs that have been implemented in the United States have focused on reducing air pollution. . . . [T]he EPA began experimenting with pollutant trading under the Clean Air Act in the 1970s. Those early experiments matured into EPA's 1986 Clean Air Act emissions trading policy for "criteria" pollutants, including sulfur dioxide, nitrogen dioxide, particulates, carbon monoxide, lead, and ozone. Under the policy, companies are allowed to build new major air pollution sources or make major modifications to major air pollution sources in areas of the country where national air pollution standards are not being met if the companies build the source to meet certain technology-based standards and enter into an agreement with an existing air pollution source in the area whereby the existing source reduces its pollution output by at least as much pollution as the new or modified source plans to discharge. The policy refers to the reductions as "emission reduction credits," which can be used to "offset" proposed pollution increases. Companies can obtain offsets by entering into agreements with other companies or by reducing the output of pollution from another source that they own in the polluted area where the new or modified source will be sited. . . .

While EPA's emission trading policy was the agency's first major foray into pollutant trading, the sulfur dioxide emission trading program created by the 1990 Clean Air Act Amendments often is cited as a model for future pollutant trading programs at the federal and state levels. The trading program is designed to reduce by half sulfur dioxide emissions from coal-fired electric power plants by early in the next century. During Phase I of the program, which began in 1995 and ends in 2000, 111 of the dirtiest power plants were given annual "allowances" to emit 2.5 pounds of sulfur dioxide for every million Btu consumed by the plant. During Phase II, which begins in 2000, all power plants that produce more than 25 megawatts will be given "allowances" to emit 1.2 pounds of sulfur dioxide for every million Btu consumed by the plant. Total emissions from all of the plants are capped at 8.90 million tons of sulfur dioxide at the end of the program. . . .

While the state and federal pollutant trading programs promise to reduce pollution in a "cost-effective" manner, these programs could disparately impact low-income communities. . . . First, while some trading programs limit trading to a specific air quality control region, many trading programs do not include any geographic limits on trades. As a result, while trading programs may decrease overall pollution levels, they may increase pollution in certain areas and create "toxic hot spots." Older, heavily polluting industries may find that it is more cost-effective to continue polluting and to buy pollution rights than to install new technologies to reduce pollution. Thus, communities surrounding those industries will be exposed to higher levels of pollution than other communities. Geographic limits on trades will not eliminate the "toxic hot spot" problem, especially if the geographic area in which trades are authorized is fairly large, but the limits could, at least, reduce the potential volume of pollution that will be imparted into a toxic hot spot. . . .

If the trading programs will create toxic hot spots, economic theory suggests that the hot spots will most likely occur in low-income communities. . . . First, heavily polluting industrial facilities (the facilities that may purchase pollution credits) will more likely be sited in low-income, urban areas than in middle-to upper-income, suburban areas. Second, low-income communities may be less likely than affluent communities to urge an outdated, heavily polluting industry to implement new pollution controls instead of buying pollution rights. Low-income communities may fear that if they urge the industry to adopt new pollution controls, then the industry will close, depriving the community of essential jobs and tax revenue. Finally, low-income communities often lack the political power to influence industries to adopt new pollution controls instead of buying pollution rights....

Pollution Taxes, Fees, and Charges and their Potential Disparate Impacts

Pollution taxes, fees, and charges promise to reduce pollution in cost-effective ways similar to pollutant trading programs.... Several states impose variable fees on polluters for water pollution permits or air pollution permits based on the volume or toxicity of the pollution authorized by the permit.... [M]any municipalities are implementing variable waste disposal fees ... [where] residents pay variable waste disposal fees, which depend on the amount of waste that they dispose, instead of paying uniform fees....

[P]ollution taxes, fees, and charges ... can also perpetuate environmental injustices. First, if governments impose uniform tax rates on pollution discharges based on the volume or toxicity of the discharge without regard to the location of the discharge, pollution taxes could create toxic hot spots in the same manner as pollutant trading systems. It may be more cost-effective for old, heavily polluting industries to pay pollution taxes than to reduce their pollution discharges, especially when the taxes are not set at rates that force polluters to reduce pollution. Unless governments tax pollution in heavily polluted areas at a higher rate than pollution in other areas, only newer, cleaner industries will have any incentive to reduce their pollution.

More significantly, though, pollution taxes could have regressive effects on low-income communities. For instance, low-income households would feel the impacts of an energy tax much more keenly than high-income households because low-income households spend a greater proportion of their income on heat, electricity, and gasoline than high-income households. Similarly, variable-rate waste disposal fees impose more significant financial burdens on low-income residents than high-income residents....

Addressing Environmental Justice in Market-Based Reforms

... Because Congress and EPA will continue to implement market-based environmental reforms, this Part examines some of the ways that laws could be reformed to empower low-income communities to participate more fully in the markets for environmental or public health benefits....

Theoretically, markets operate "efficiently" if consumers have perfect information. In practice, consumers almost never have perfect information.... One obvious way to address this market failure and to foster environmental justice is to improve consumers' access to information. Market-based reforms could include provisions that require participants or the government to provide detailed information to communities about the potential environmental and public health impacts of pollution trades, waivers, or modifications of regulatory requirements or similar market-based initiatives. Existing "information disclosure" laws should also be expanded and improved. Those information disclosure requirements would reduce, but not eliminate, the likelihood that the market would allocate resources inefficiently....

[Additionally,] to facilitate the participation of low-income communities in the market-based decisionmaking process ... technical assistance grants to review trades, waivers, and other market-based actions could be expanded and simplified and targeted at low-income communities or communities that have been disparately impacted by pollution....

While technical assistance grants and loans may increase the likelihood that a community can afford to participate in environmental decisionmaking in market-based programs, other obstacles have limited public participation by low-income and minority communities in environmental decisionmaking in the past....

Accordingly, broad and flexible public participation procedures should be included in all pollutant trading, regulatory waiver or variance programs, and other market-based environmental protection programs that enable low-income communities, and all citizens, to participate in the market for health and environmental amenities. In addition, broad and flexible public participation procedures should be incorporated into traditional command and control programs to ensure that baseline pollution levels in low-income communities are not disproportionately high before trading or other market-based programs are implemented....

* * *

Notes and Questions

1. Professor Johnson argues that providing environmental justice communities with more information about the environmental and public health impacts of pollution trades, and providing them with technical assistance grants to review market-based actions, will help them more effectively participate in market-based environmental programs. Do you agree that this is an effective approach? What limits are there to relying on information disclosure as a strategy for communities to safeguard their interests? Consider that information about environmental risks may be confusing, technical, and difficult to process for most individuals. Are these insurmountable obstacles?

2. Professor Johnson uses an illuminating example to identify what may be a fundamental theoretical problem with an efficiency oriented approach. In a footnote, he explains that:

> Judge Posner relates the following story to explain the economist's definition of "value":

> Suppose that pituitary extract is in very scarce supply relative to the demand and is therefore very expensive. A poor family has a child who will be a dwarf if he does not get some of the extract, but the family cannot afford the price.... A rich family has a child who will grow to normal height, but the extract will add a few inches more, and his parents decide to buy it for him. In the sense of value used in this book, the pituitary extract is more valuable to the rich than to the poor family, because value is measured by willingness to pay.... [citing RICHARD A. POSNER, ECONOMIC ANALYSIS OF LAW § 1.1, (4th ed. 1992), at 13]. While Posner suggests that the rich family is more "willing to pay" for the extract than the poor family, it seems that the rich family is more "able to pay" than the poor family, rather than more "willing to pay." Posner's definition of willingness to pay, therefore, seems to incorporate ability to pay.

Johnson, *supra,* at 118 n.43. If willingness to pay is dependent upon our ability to pay, at least at the lower end of the economic scale, then this standard economic metric does not accurately reflect true preferences. It would be hard to imagine that heavily impacted communities near refineries and other large facilities "value" clean air less than the rest of society. Is such a metric tantamount to a position that the preferences and values of the poor simply do not count? If so, is the movement to market-based environmental protection inconsistent with democratic values, including pluralistic ideals?

3. The acid rain trading program described by Professor Johnson is considered to be a major success in many respects. It has reduced SO2 emissions by 40 percent from 1990 levels, at a far lower cost than originally anticipated. EPA estimates that the health benefits from the program exceed its costs by a 40 to 1 ratio. U.S. ENVTL. PROT. AGENCY, ACID RAIN PROGRAM 2006 PROGRESS REPORT (2007). As economist Robert Stavins explains, however, the assumptions that underlie the acid rain trading program are different than trading for conventional air pollutants:

> [T]rades [in sulfur dioxide permits] switch the source of the pollution from one company to another, which is not important when any emissions equally affect the whole trading area. This "uniform mixing" assumption is certainly valid for global problems such as greenhouse gases or the effect of chlorofluorocarbons on the stratospheric ozone layer. It may also work reasonably well for a regional problem such as acid rain, because acid deposition in downwind states of New England is about equally affected by sulfur dioxide emissions traded among upwind sources in Ohio, Indiana, and Illinois. But it does not work perfectly, since acid rain in New England may increase if a plant there sells permits to a plant in the Midwest, for example.

> At the other extreme, some environmental problems might not be addressed appropriately by a simple, unconstrained tradeable emission permit system. A hazardous air pollutant such as benzene that does not mix in the airshed can cause localized hot spots. Because a company can buy permits and increase local emissions, permit trading does not ensure that each location will meet a specific standard. Moreover, the damages caused by local concentrations may increase nonlinearly. If so, then even a permit system that reduces total emissions might allow trades that move those emissions to a high-impact location and thus increase total damages.

Robert N. Stavins, *The Myth of Simple Market Solutions,* ENVTL. F. 12 (July/Aug. 2004). Keep these concerns in mind as you consider the excerpts in the next subsection discussing VOC trading under Rule 1610, the RECLAIM program, and mercury trading under the EPA's Clean Air Mercury Rule.

4. Some observers have argued that the concern for hot spots is overblown, at least in the context of the acid rain trading program. According to attorney Byron Swift:

> [A]n assessment of the actual performance of trading programs shows that the choice of regulatory method has little to no environmental impact on hot spots. In fact, because trading programs promote reductions at the largest plants, they outperform rate standards and tend to reduce instead of create hot spots.

> A regional analysis shows that neither major SO2 or NOx cap-and-trade program has resulted in regional shifts of emissions. The hot spot issue was an early concern in the Acid Rain Program, as it was feared that trading might exacerbate the high emissions levels in the Midwest. In fact, the opposite happened, and in both Phases I and II a *greater* proportion of reductions were made in the Midwest than in other major regions, as depicted in the following table:

SO₂ emissions reductions from 1980 baseline levels achieved in Phase II (2001 data):

Midwest	4,046,904 tons	(55% reduction)
Southeast	1,466,343 tons	(30% reduction)
Northeast	1,404,920 tons	(37% reduction)

U.S. ENVTL. PROT. AGENCY, ACID RAIN PROGRAM: 2001 EMISSIONS SCORECARD (2002).

... A more striking finding is made when the data is examined at the plant level. [C]ap-and-trade ... trading programs have resulted in disproportionately high emissions reductions at the largest plants. This is because the economics of installing capital equipment to reduce emissions provides the greatest financial rewards when installed at the largest sources, leading to disproportionate emissions reductions at these most polluting sources. Therefore, in the Acid Rain Program Phase II, the quartile of plants with the largest emissions reduced emissions by 73 percent, the next largest by 48 percent, the next by 41 percent, and the smallest quartile by 10 percent....

Byron Swift, *U.S. Emissions Trading: Myths, Realities, and Opportunities*, 20 NAT. RESOURCES & ENV'T. 3, 7–8 (Summer 2005). More specifically, another study determined that, based on the first three years of trading data, the acid rain program did not lead to greater hot spots in poor communities and communities of color. Jason Corburn, *Emissions Trading and Environmental Justice: Distributive Fairness and the USA's Acid Rain Programme*, 28 ENVTL. CONSERVATION 323 (2001).

5. Emissions trading is, of course, but one among several market-based approaches. It is perhaps the most prominent approach in current public policy debates, however, and is considered in greater depth in the next section.

2. Emissions Trading

During the 1990s, the most advanced local air pollution trading program in the country was established in the Los Angeles region. The program has been looked to as a test case for evaluating the effectiveness of emission trading strategies. The following excerpt critiques a central component of this program, which allowed stationary sources to satisfy their pollution control obligations by purchasing credits from mobile sources.

Richard Toshiyuki Drury, Michael E. Belliveau, J. Scott Kuhn & Shipra Bansal, Pollution Trading and Environmental Injustice: Los Angeles' Failed Experiment in Air Quality Policy
9 Duke Environmental Law and Policy Forum 231 (Spring 1999)

The Los Angeles, California, region provides an ideal testing ground for environmental policies. Los Angeles' environmental problems are severe, its regulatory agencies are sophisticated, its resources are relatively ample, and the region's population is multi-racial and economically diverse.... The South Coast Air Basin, which includes the metropolitan Los Angeles area, suffers the worst air quality in the nation....

... In 1993, SCAQMD [the South Coast Air Quality Management District] approved the first old vehicle pollution trading program in the country, known as Rule 1610 or the "car scrapping program." Rule 1610 allows stationary source polluters (such as factories and re-fineries) to avoid installing expensive pollution control equipment if they purchase pollu-tion credits generated by destroying old, high-polluting cars. Ideally, an equal or greater amount of pollution can be reduced at a much lower cost by purchasing and destroying old cars than by forcing stationary sources to install expensive pollution control equipment.

Under Rule 1610, "licensed car scrappers" can purchase and destroy old cars. SCAQMD then grants the scrapper emissions credits based on the projected emissions of the car had it not been destroyed, which may then be sold to stationary source polluters (e.g. factories). The stationary sources use the pollution credits to avoid on-site emission re-ductions that would be required under the technology-based regulatory regime. Rule 1610 requires polluters to purchase credits representing twenty percent more emission reductions than would be achieved through compliance with technology-based regulations for their plant. Although industrial plants avoid emission reductions, the scrapping of older, high polluting cars should result in greater air quality improvements at a lower cost than regulatory mandates.

SCAQMD then adopted the centerpiece of its pollution trading strategy, the Regional Clean Air Incentives Market (RECLAIM), the world's first urban smog trading program.... RECLAIM, a "declining cap and trade" program, mandates annual emission reductions for industry but provides them the flexibility to achieve that goal by either purchasing emission reduction credits or by reducing their own pollution.

SCAQMD's pollution trading programs have resulted in the creation of toxic hot-spots by concentrating pollution in communities surrounding major sources of pollution.... SCAQMD studies indicate that cars destroyed through the Rule 1610 program were reg-istered throughout the air quality management district, a four-county region. Air pollu-tion from these automobiles would have also been distributed throughout this region. By contrast, stationary sources in Los Angeles are densely clustered in only a few communities in this four-county region. As a result of these distribution patterns, Rule 1610 effectively takes pollution formerly distributed throughout the region by automobiles, and concen-trates that pollution in the communities surrounding stationary sources.

Most of the emissions credits purchased to avoid stationary source controls have been purchased by four oil companies: Unocal, Chevron, Ultramar and GATX. Of these four companies, three are located close together in the communities of Wilmington and San Pedro; the fourth facility, Chevron, is located nearby in El Segundo. These companies have used pollution credits to avoid installing pollution control equipment that captures toxic gases released during oil tanker loading at their marine terminals. When loading oil tankers, toxic gases are forced out of the tanker and into the air, exposing workers and nearby residents to toxic vapors, including benzene, a known human carcinogen. Thus, by using pollution credits, these companies are allowed to avoid reducing local emissions of haz-ardous chemicals in exchange for reducing regional auto emissions. As a result of Rule 1610, the four oil companies created a toxic chemical hot-spot around their marine terminals, exposing workers and nearby residents to elevated health risks....

... The demographics of this hot-spot area starkly contrast with that of the metro-politan Los Angeles region. The residents living in San Pedro and Wilmington, which host a majority of the oil companies emitting hazardous toxic chemicals, are overwhelmingly Latino. Furthermore, the racial composition of communities living near three of the ma-rine terminals ranges from 75 to 90 percent people of color, while the entire South Coast Air Basin has a population of only 36 percent people of color....

The hazards of trading extend beyond the shifting of pollution from a dispersed region to more concentrated localized areas; inter-pollutant trading can also create toxic hot-spots. Many trading programs allow facilities to trade pollution credits generated through reductions in a large variety of chemicals. For example, the Rule 1610 program allows pollution credits to be generated through reductions in [volatile organic compounds] VOCs. VOCs are a family of over 600 chemical compounds, some of which have high toxicity and some of which have low toxicity. VOC trading raises concerns about the difference in toxicity of VOC emissions from marine terminals compared to VOCs from automobiles. For example, benzene levels may be higher in VOC emissions from marine terminals than from cars, which leads to greater exposure and risks concentrated in the communities around the marine terminals.... Therefore, the Rule 1610 program may allow continued release of highly toxic chemicals into certain communities in exchange for small area-wide reductions in much less toxic chemicals....

In addition to concerns about variable toxicity, VOCs also exhibit different degrees of reactivity related to their ability to form photochemical smog. These differences in photochemical reactivity have long been recognized in air pollution regulation and have guided priority setting in the control of VOC sources for smog control. In pollution trading programs, however, if highly reactive VOCs are emitted by purchasing credits earned for reducing low reactivity VOCs, then downwind ozone (smog) formation may be increased rather than reduced....

The complex chemistry of air pollution leads to further problems with pollution trading. Emissions are composed of complex mixtures of chemicals, not the single pollutants often targeted for regulation or trading. We use the term "co-pollutants" to describe the secondary pollutants that inextricably accompany the emission of primary targeted pollutants.... Since pollution trading enables polluters to avoid emission reductions, or even increase emissions, at one location by purchasing credits earned elsewhere, the co-pollutants associated with that emission source may also persist and concentrate around that polluter....

Most states have permitting procedures through which affected community members can advocate for pollution control requirements on facilities. However, pollution trading allows facilities to avoid those permit requirements—usually without the knowledge or involvement of the affected community. Pollution trades made pursuant to Rule 1610 and RECLAIM are not subject to public review or comment. In fact, the public faces numerous difficulties finding out what companies are trading to avoid compliance with pollution control standards. For instance, RECLAIM credits can be purchased from independent brokers, without any environmental agency or public oversight.... In this way, the democratic will, as represented in permit and regulatory requirements imposed after full public review and comment, can be reversed by a simple economic transaction....

* * *

Notes and Questions

1. In addition to the points raised in the excerpt above, environmental attorney Richard Drury and his colleagues also pointed out that the car scrapping program had a substantial number of design flaws that potentially worsened the situation:

> Pollution trading programs primarily rely on industry self-reporting of emission reductions and increases. Based on these self-reports, regulatory agencies must allocate air pollution credits. In Los Angeles, widespread under-reporting, in-

accurate modeling, and potential financial windfalls for polluters plague the pollution trading program....

... The program creates an incentive to under-report actual emissions. By under-reporting their air pollution, the companies can reduce their purchase of emission reduction credits.

Rather than measure actual emissions released, companies estimate emissions using emission factors developed by the Western States Petroleum Association. Emissions factors are surrogate estimates of emissions based on activity level.... Emissions factors are poor surrogates for actual measurements. With margins of error ranging from fifty percent to one hundred percent, emissions factors are highly uncertain, making claimed emission reduction difficult to verify....

Information recently obtained through the Freedom of Information Act reveals that the oil companies did, in fact, measure their emissions. When the actual measurements were compared to reported emissions based on industry emissions factors, striking differences were revealed. Oil companies under-reported their oil tanker emissions by factors between 10 and 1000. As a result, the oil companies purchased between 10 and 1000 times too few credits from scrapping old, high-polluting cars to offset their tanker pollution. This persistent problem was completely overlooked by SCAQMD and was only detected through a time-consuming investigation by Communities for a Better Environment....

Several assumptions underlying the Rule 1610 program are also dubious. In order to quantify the credits generated by scrapping a vehicle, SCAQMD assumes that the old cars would have been driven approximately 4,000 to 5,000 miles annually for an additional three years and that the owner of the car would replace it with a "fleet average" automobile. Although these assumptions were based on studies of old car driving patterns, they have not been borne out in reality.

According to [SCAQMD's Chief] Inspector [Bruce] Lohmann and an audit conducted by SCAQMD, many of the cars scrapped through the Rule 1610 program were at the end of their useful life, and would have been destroyed through natural attrition.... Since less than 23,000 cars have been destroyed through the Rule 1610 program in its five-year life, most of these cars are probably among those that would have been destroyed even without the program.

Drury et al., *supra*, at 259–262. Can these design flaws be overcome or are flaws of this nature endemic to a market program? For example, in designing market programs, should reductions that would have occurred anyway, such as those that occur when a facility shuts down for economic reasons, count as offsets? Should emission reductions that occurred in years past be used for offsets years later? Why or why not? In switching from a traditional system to a market-based system, how should emission credits be allocated among facilities initially?

2. Mr. Drury and his colleagues call for broad reforms in trading programs, including prohibitions on the trading of any toxic substances, trading between mobile and stationary sources, and "cross-pollutant" trading (trading for credits generated by reduced emissions of less hazardous pollutants). They also argue that a demographic analysis of affected communities should be required before any trading program is approved, and that affected communities should be given the right to review and comment on any proposed trade that would increase or continue the release of toxic emissions in a given community. Agencies should retain the discretion to reject or amend the proposed trade based on community comments. Drury, *supra*, at 283–286.

3. Reforms that place geographic limits on trading or that increase the government's role in reviewing trades can be considered health-based "safety nets." *See, e.g.,* Richard L. Revesz & Jonathan R. Nash, *Markets and Geography: Designing Marketable Permit Schemes To Control Local and Regional Pollutants,* 28 Ecol'y. L. Q. 569 (2001). While designed to protect vulnerable communities, they also interfere with the unfettered functioning of the market and in part undermine the efficiency rationale of market-based tools. Professor Johnson notes, for example, that determining whether trades or other actions in market-based programs disparately impact certain communities may require the government to gather large amounts of data regarding community demographics and the cumulative and synergistic impacts of pollution on a community, a potentially time-consuming and expensive task. Likewise, advocates of tradable permits oppose giving the public notice and the right to comment on proposed trades, arguing that this would delay or chill trades. To what extent are limitations that undermine the efficient functioning of market-based reforms — and that may make businesses less likely to utilize market-based tools — justified?

3. Mercury

The following excerpt discusses the EPA's effort to address mercury emissions from coal-fired utilities by means of a cap-and-trade regime, known as the "Clean Air Mercury Rule" (CAMR).

Catherine A. O'Neill, Environmental Justice in the Tribal Context: A Madness to EPA's Method
38 Environmental Law 495 (2008)

Mercury has long been known to be highly toxic to humans.... The developing fetus and children are particularly sensitive to methylmercury's adverse neurological effects. Exposure to even small amounts of methylmercury during this developmental window can lead to irreversible neurological damage....

Once released into the environment, mercury's behavior is complex, and includes local, regional, and global components.... Anthropogenic emissions of mercury in the United States are currently dominated by coal-fired utilities. Mercury is emitted from utilities in three species, each of which is characterized by a different fate and transport in the environment. In every case, this mercury is deposited to surrounding land and water, although at varying distances and times. Mercury that enters water bodies becomes methylated.... Methylmercury is an extremely bioavailable form of mercury, readily taken up by fish in these waters; [it] bioaccumulates in fish tissue....

Many of the fish species on which humans rely for food are highly contaminated with methylmercury. In fact, humans are exposed to methylmercury primarily through the consumption of contaminated fish....

Based on studies of methylmercury's adverse human health effects, EPA has derived a reference dose (RfD) of 0.1 microgram per kilogram of body weight per day. This RfD represents a threshold for exposure, i.e., the amount that EPA believes can be ingested each day over the course of a lifetime without adverse health effects. According to a recent study, some 15.7% of women of childbearing age in the United States had blood mercury levels above EPA's RfD, thus posing a risk to a developing fetus. Importantly, this study also found marked differences among women in groups characterized by race/ethnicity. Whereas 15.3% of "white" women of childbearing age had mercury in their blood above the RfD, this number [nearly] doubles, to 31.5%, for women who identified themselves as "other," a category comprised primarily of Native Americans, Pacific Islanders, those of "Asian origin," or those of "mixed race." …

[In the 1990s,] EPA took steps to regulate the major sources of mercury emissions. [I]t issued standards for two of the top three categories of emitters—medical waste incinerators and municipal waste combustors—requiring that these sources reduce their mercury emissions on the order of 90%. In 2000, EPA listed the third of these major contributors—coal-fired utilities—among the source categories to be regulated under section 112 of the Clean Air Act, finding regulation of mercury from these sources to be "appropriate and necessary." As a consequence of this listing, it was widely expected that EPA would require similarly significant reductions in utilities' mercury emissions. Crucially, it was also widely expected that these reductions would be realized quickly.… Specifically, EPA is directed [under the CAA] to issue technology-based standards (known as "MACT" standards) for those source categories listed under section 112, and sources are given a tight, three-year timeline to comply with the resulting emissions limits (with the possibility of, at most, a one-year extension). EPA is further directed to issue additional standards, within eight years, if this MACT standard leaves unaddressed any residual risk to human or environmental health. Thus, up until the time that EPA announced its proposed rule for coal-fired utilities in December 2003, observers looked forward to a MACT standard that would require these sources to achieve roughly 90% reductions in their mercury emissions, and to do so by 2007.…

In its final rule, EPA abandoned any pretense of providing a MACT standard. Rather, EPA opted for a cap-and-trade program, promulgated under section 111 [the section of the Clean Air Act that imposes controls on new stationary sources of pollution]. The CAMR instates a cap on mercury emissions from utilities in two phases. The first-phase cap is set for 2010 to require no additional reductions beyond those already to be achieved as "co-benefits" of a companion rule, known as the "Clean Air Interstate Rule" (CAIR), governing criteria pollutants in the eastern portion of the country. Thus, the CAMR's first-phase cap is set to allow utilities to emit thirty eight tons of mercury per year—down from roughly 48 tons per year emitted by these sources at the outset of the program. The second-phase cap is set for 2018 to allow utilities to emit fifteen tons of mercury per year. However, given structural features of the cap-and-trade program, the 70% reduction in emissions that this second-phase cap promises will not actually be realized until well after the year 2020, and perhaps even as late as the 2030s. Note, too, that the cap-and-trade program, issued as it was under the auspices of Section 111, makes no provision for addressing any residual risk to human health or the environment, as would be required under section 112.…

State after state declined to participate in EPA's cap-and-trade program, calling instead for more meaningful and immediate reductions within their borders. Ultimately, several states, tribes, and environmental groups sued the EPA.

The harms of mercury contamination are visited overwhelmingly on various tribes and their members, particularly the fishing peoples of the Great Lakes, the Northeast, and the Pacific Northwest. EPA was aware of this fact as it embarked upon its efforts to regulate mercury.… While EPA purported to consider environmental justice in the CAMR rulemaking, EPA's account reveals a misunderstanding of what it would mean to evaluate and respond to the particular issues raised by the tribal context.…

EPA discussed the environmental justice issues relevant to tribes and their members in the portions of the Preamble to the final CAMR that explain EPA's compliance with Executive Orders 13,175 and 12,898, which address, respectively, consultation with tribal governments and environmental justice. This discussion is supported in turn by a host of technical documents, including the Effectiveness Technical Support Document (TSD) and the Regulatory Impact Analysis (RIA)....

The TSD described EPA's methods for estimating the effect of CAMR on human health. To this end, the TSD considered the portion of various populations that would be left exposed to unsafe levels of methylmercury under CAMR in 2020 (after accounting for the implementation of CAIR), due to utility-attributable emissions alone.... EPA assembled tables that permit one to determine the levels of utility-attributable methylmercury to which those in the general population and in Native American populations are exposed, assuming various degrees of contamination in the fish species consumed. These tables usefully reveal just how high a percentage of the Native American population would be left exposed at levels above EPA's RfD under CAMR in 2020, due to utility-attributable mercury emissions alone.... Assuming fish tissue methylmercury concentrations at the 99th percentile, an extraordinary portion—some 45 percent—of those consuming at contemporary tribal consumption rates would be left exposed to methylmercury levels above EPA's threshold. This remarkable number presents a grave picture, in absolute terms, of the potential impacts to tribal members' health left unaddressed by the CAMR. Moreover, in comparative terms, the picture is similarly stark. Whereas all those consuming fish at rates above the 55th percentile in the Native American population will be left exposed to utility-attributable methlymercury at levels above EPA's RfD, only those consuming fish at rates above the 99th percentile in the general population of recreational anglers will be similarly exposed to utility-attributable methlymercury at levels above EPA's RfD....

As bleak as these figures are, EPA's TSD likely fails to capture the true extent of the disproportionate burden. First, EPA's analysis employed a fish consumption rate that mischaracterizes actual, contemporary consumption practices.... Second, EPA's analysis glossed over the matter of real-world exposures for tribal people [by considering only incremental exposure from coal-fired utilities and not absolute levels of exposure].... Because it neglects other sources of exposure to mercury, EPA's statement ... to the effect that [reducing] mercury emissions from utilities [could be expected to result in] ... no real public health [benefits] was at the very least misleading....

EPA's only attempt to grapple with the implications of its TSD is crude and unavailing. As noted above, when faced with its data suggesting that some forty-five percent of the Native population will be left exposed to unsafe levels of methylmercury, EPA claimed that "[v]isual inspection [of maps correlating modeled deposition with tribal census tracts] shows very few locations where Native Americans live where there is also a high residual deposition due to utilities." ... EPA relied on a crude tool to dispose entirely of a central question for environmental justice. The large opportunities for error with so coarse a method were in fact borne out when ... it required EPA to maintain that Native Americans do not live in significant numbers in places such as Michigan. [Michigan is home to some 12 federally-recognized tribes and, according to the 2000 census, 58,479 American Indian people. Eds.] EPA's method here brings up a related point: if EPA had wanted to delve further into the complexities of Native people's actual exposures, it should have sought the expertise of those affected. That is, rather than making do with rough proxies and visual inspections, it should have consulted with the tribes, many of whom had long been gathering data regarding tribal demographics; tribal members' consumption practices (including unique seasonal and ceremonial consumption practices); local fish tissue methylmercury concentrations; and the like.

* * *

Notes and Questions

1. As the articles above recognize, the potential for "hot spots" is the Achilles' heel of cap-and-trade approaches. While cap-and-trade approaches promise an overall decrease in emissions, they make no guarantees about decreases from any one source. To the contrary, they permit emissions to be increased by sources that are net buyers of emissions allowances. In the case of mercury, a hot spot analysis is complex, given the complexities of mercury's behavior in the atmosphere once it is emitted from a source. As noted above, some mercury may be deposited in the immediate vicinity of the utility that emitted it; some may travel greater distances, and be deposited regionally, or even globally. Professor O'Neill considered EPA's projections at the time of the proposed CAMR about the likely effects of trading in the Great Lakes states:

> As of 2020, cap-and-trade is estimated to reduce emissions in the upper Great Lakes region by 26.59% from current levels. Importantly, in 2020, emissions actually *increase* under cap-and-trade as compared to present levels at 7 (out of 19) sources in Michigan; at 7 (out of 10) sources in Minnesota; and at 6 (out of 15) sources in Wisconsin.

Catherine A. O'Neill, *Mercury, Risk, and Justice*, 34 ENVTL L. REP. 11,070, 11,100 (Dec. 2004) Given that mercury—which has localized effects—is projected to increase at a substantial number of facilities, is a market-based regime for mercury likely to be protective of public health? Could attention to market design adequately address the potential for hot spots? By the time of the final rule, EPA took the position that hot spots would not be an issue under the CAMR. EPA claimed, among other things, that its models showed that the areas of high residual deposition of mercury due to utilities' emissions would not coincide with areas in which the fishing tribes resided. *See* U.S. ENVTL. PROT. AGENCY, METHODOLOGY TO GENERATE DEPOSITION, FISH TISSUE METHYLMERCURY CONCENTRATIONS, AND EXPOSURES FOR DETERMINING THE EFFECTIVENESS OF UTILITY EMISSIONS CONTROLS (2005). Do these complexities in and of themselves suggest reason for concern with a cap-and-trade approach? How, if you were representing one of the fishing tribes in the upper Great Lakes states, would you go about determining whether hot spots were likely to affect your clients?

2. Is the real problem with EPA's CAMR its lenient cap and generous deadline for compliance? Recall that the CAMR requires 70 percent reductions by the year 2018, rather than the 90 percent reductions by the year 2007 expected under a MACT-based approach. Byron Swift argues that whether a cap-and-trade approach is adequately protective depends more on the level at which the cap is set and less on the matter of hot spots:

> [A]t any equivalent level of stringency, the choice of regulatory method (trading, rates, or whatever) should have little to no effect on hot spots. This is because regulatory programs do not control plant size, siting, or utilization, which are the key determinants of hot spots. Therefore, even source-specific standards such as rates will actually lead to just as much variability as cap-and-trade or other standards as they allow pollution levels to vary greatly depending on plant size, utilization, and location. Instead, a concern about hot spots should focus on the stringency of a program, which determines the overall level of pollution, and not on regulatory method, which has little environmental consequence.

Swift, *supra*, at 8. What if the CAMR had permitted emissions trading but set the cap to require a 90% reduction in mercury emissions by 2007? Can you think of any advantages, from the perspective of environmental protection, of a cap-and-trade approach restructured to meet these more ambitious goals? Would there be any remaining environmental justice objections?

3. As in the case of its most recent revision to the ozone NAAQS, EPA conducted an environmental justice analysis of the CAMR. U.S. Envtl. Prot. Agency, Standards for Performance of New and Existing Sources: Electric Utility Steam Generating Units, 70 Fed. Reg. 28,606, 28,648 (May, 18, 2005). Professor O'Neill criticizes EPA's approach:

> EPA reframed the relevant inquiry to suggest that the real concern for environmental justice was whether Native people [as well as Southeast Asian Americans and other high-consuming subpopulations] were disproportionately *benefited* by the mercury rule. Thus, EPA flatly refused to consider whether a more stringent rule would better address the disproportionate burdens it had identified. Worse, EPA cavalierly expressed concern that its lenient rule might go too far to ameliorate the harms suffered by tribes and their members and so raise issues of distributional equity.

> In the Preamble to the final CAMR, EPA recognized that, in the absence of regulation, certain groups, including "low-income and minority populations" will disproportionately suffer adverse health effects, given their fish consumption practices. EPA further acknowledged that these practices may have "economic, cultural, and religious" dimensions. EPA noted that Executive Order 12,898 requires it to "assess whether minority or low-income populations face risks or a rate of exposure to hazards that are significant and that 'appreciably exceed or is likely to appreciably exceed the risk or rate to the general population....'" EPA then stated that, "[i]n accordance with EO 12,898, the Agency has considered whether the final rule may have disproportionate negative impacts on minority or low-income populations." EPA concluded that "[t]he Agency expects the final rule to lead to beneficial reductions in air pollution and exposures generally with a small negative impact through increased utility bills." Thus, EPA's first step was to reframe the question. Rather than consider whether the CAMR goes far enough to reduce minority and low-income populations' exposures to mercury that EPA concedes "appreciably exceed" those of the general population, EPA pointed out that the CAMR does *something*. By assuming an unregulated baseline, EPA was able to claim that these highly exposed populations are better off with the CAMR.

> EPA then turned the disproportionate impacts analysis inside-out. In fact, continued EPA, the real issue was whether the CAMR makes these populations too much better off. "To further examine whether high fish-consuming (subsistence) populations might be *disproportionately benefited* by the final rule (i.e., whether distributional equity is a consideration) ... EPA conducted a sensitivity analysis [using fish consumption rates for Ojibwe in the Great Lakes region] focusing specifically on the distributional equity issue." To its apparent relief, EPA's environmental justice analysis revealed that "although Native American subsistence populations (and other high fish consuming populations) might experience relatively larger health benefits from the final rule compared with general recreational anglers, the absolute degree of health benefits [in terms of IQ decrements] are [sic] relatively low."

O'Neill, *Environmental Justice in the Tribal Context, supra,* at 519–20. Again, how do you think agencies should frame an environmental justice analysis for their rules?

4. The Clean Air Mercury Rule stands out as one of the most controversial rulemaking efforts under the CAA. The checkered history leading up to the proposed rule is re-

counted in three articles: Lisa Heinzerling & Rena I. Steinzor, *A Perfect Storm: Mercury and the Bush Administration,* 34 ENVTL L. REP. 10,297 (Apr. 2004); Lisa Heinzerling & Rena I. Steinzor, *A Perfect Storm: Mercury and the Bush Administration, Part II,* 34 ENVTL L. REP. 10,485 (June 2004); and O'Neill, *Mercury, Risk, and Justice, supra.* In 2008, the Mercury Rule was overturned by the D.C. Circuit, which sternly rebuked EPA for adopting a rule divorced from the relevant statutory directives under the Clean Air Act. *New Jersey v. Environmental Protection Agency,* 517 F.3d 574 (D.C. Cir. 2008). A trade association for the coal-fired utilities, the Utility Air Regulatory Group (UARG), and the EPA both petitioned the U.S. Supreme Court for certiorari, seeking review of the D.C. Circuit's decision vacating the CAMR in *New Jersey v. EPA.* When the new Obama Administration entered the White House, the EPA withdrew its petition. Shortly thereafter, the Supreme Court denied the UARG petition for certiorari.

5. In addition to the disproportionate impact on higher-consuming fishing peoples, the CAMR raises other issues of environmental justice for tribes. Professor O'Neill observes:

> EPA's analysis of the CAMR appears oblivious to the fact that tribes' fishing rights are at stake. Indeed, it is unclear how or even whether EPA viewed its analysis as engaging the matter of the tribes' legally protected rights to fish. Notably, the word "treaty" appears nowhere in the Preamble to the final CAMR, nor in any of the technical documents supporting the final rule, including the TSD and RIA. Further, by the time it litigated *New Jersey v. EPA,* EPA showed itself to be openly hostile to tribes' treaty-secured rights, as it willfully mischaracterized their source and import....

> EPA thus made a fundamental error: it treated tribes and their members as if they were simply another highly-exposed subpopulation....

O'Neill, *Environmental Justice in the Tribal Context, supra,* at 515–16. This quote requires one to consider how EPA should go about ensuring that its decisions under the CAA or other environmental statutes also respect tribes' rights, including those secured by treaty. These and other issues presented by tribes' unique legal and political status are taken up in Chapter 4.

Chapter 8

Permits and Public Enforcement

A. Facility Permitting

1. Introduction

Although disparities in environmental protection have occurred in enforcement, cleanup, and standard-setting endeavors, most environmental justice challenges appear in the permitting context. There are good reasons why this occurs. First, consider the immediacy of the adverse impacts on a local level, such as toxic air emissions, chemicals that are discharged into waterways, dust, increased truck traffic through neighborhood streets, noise, odor, and at times increased vermin and rodents. Understandably, residents in overburdened communities often view a new facility or a facility expansion as the proverbial straw that breaks the camel's back. Permit proceedings also raise concerns about whether the facility operator will comply with the permit terms, thus injecting into permit proceedings issues such as subsequent enforcement and potential contamination. In a sense, the permit is the gateway to environmental inequity that may stem from inadequacies that may exist in enforcement, cleanup, and even standard-setting activities.

More often than not, community groups are first made aware of matters only when public notice requirements of permit proceedings have been triggered. At that point, the community is placed in a reactive position and must attempt either to challenge a plan for siting of a facility that is fairly far along, or to seek concessions in the form of marginally more protective permit terms or mitigation measures beyond those directly required by existing regulations. This mission often pits community groups against the facility sponsor and permitting officials—both of whom may have become committed to issuing the permit—and may unfairly cause community groups to be characterized as anti-development or "NIMBY" (Not In My Back Yard) oriented.

This section explores both the legal authority under environmental statutes to impose additional permit conditions (or to deny the permit altogether), as well as the difficulties encountered in attempting to change the permitting status quo to better respond to environmental inequities. For the most part, neither the federal government nor most states have legislation specifically addressing environmental justice in permit proceedings. To find legal authority to address these concerns, affected communities and their lawyers often ask regulatory officials and the courts to look to more broadly worded provisions in environmental statutes and regulations, such as provisions to "protect health and welfare." This section will examine how federal and state permitting officials have responded to environmental justice claims based on these provisions. Other sources of legal authority, such as provisions under planning statutes and constitutional provisions, are explored in Chapters 11 and 14, respectively.

2. The Legal Hook: Potential Federal Sources of Authority to Address Environmental Justice and the Decisions of the EPA's Environmental Appeals Board

As you read the following short excerpt which identifies sources of legal authority existing in federal environmental statutes, isolate the precise statutory language that you, as a lawyer, would use to argue that the permitting official may legally consider a community's claims that it is already unfairly overburdened with environmental pollution, risk, and nuisance impacts, and that the permit should contain additional requirements or be denied altogether.

Richard J. Lazarus & Stephanie Tai, ### Integrating Environmental Justice into EPA Permitting Authority
26 Ecology Law Quarterly 617 (1999)

Background: The Meaning of "Environmental Justice" in the EPA Permitting Context

... In the context of an EPA permitting decision, the core expression of environmental justice is that EPA should take into account the racial and/or socioeconomic makeup of the community most likely to be affected adversely by the environmental risks of a proposed activity. This involves two steps: the identification of the environmental justice community and the incorporation of that community's concerns into the permitting process. Taking into account the makeup of the community does not mean that EPA must automatically deny a permit solely because the affected area is a community of color or low-income. The Agency's inquiry into these characteristics of the community is, however, necessary to allow the Agency to make an informed permitting decision regarding the actual environmental and health effects of a permit applicant's proposed activity....

Some of the environmental justice concerns that can be addressed through permit conditions are discussed below. They include the enhancement of a community's capacity to participate in environmental enforcement and compliance assurance, assessment of risk aggregation or cumulative risk, and identification of disproportionality in risk imposition. The relevance of each of these concerns to the permitting process is fairly clear. What is less clear to those officials responsible for issuing the permits is whether they have the necessary authority to consider such concerns and to take actions, including the imposition of permit conditions, based upon those concerns....

Survey of Federal Statutory Provisions Authorizing Permit Conditions or Denials Based on Environmental Justice

The history of environmental law is replete with instances when broadly worded statutory language or regulations have been successfully enlisted in support of arguments that the federal government has authority or obligations beyond those initially contemplated by the regulated entities, environmentalists, affected communities, or even the government itself....

The [Clean Air] Act's nonattainment provisions provide [] potential environmental justice opportunities. [Nonattainment means an air shed that does not meet health-based air quality standards for certain pollutants. Eds.] Section 173 describes the requirements for a nonattainment permit. An explicit permit requirement in the Act mandates that [a permit cannot be granted unless] "an analysis of alternative sites, sizes, production processes, and environmental control techniques for such proposed source demonstrates that benefits of the proposed source significantly outweigh the environmental and social costs imposed as a result of its location, construction, or modification." The references to both "social costs" and "location" serve as strong bases for EPA's assertion of statutory authority to take environmental justice concerns into account in evaluating the "location" of a facility seeking a nonattainment permit....

In the context of permitting, the CAA provisions of greatest interest are those that may allow EPA (or a state permitting authority that has assumed permitting responsibility pursuant to CAA Section 502) greater discretion in using the permitting process to increase community participation and build community enforcement capacity. Section 504 would seem to confer on EPA just such authority. Subsection (a) provides that "[e]ach permit issued under this subchapter shall include ... such other conditions as are necessary to assure compliance with applicable requirements of this chapter...." A major component for achieving compliance assurance under the CAA is the citizen suit provision of that statute. Without that provision acting as a credible enforcement threat, there is no assurance of compliance. Therefore, Section 504(a) may authorize EPA to impose upon those receiving CAA permits the condition that they take certain steps to enhance the affected community's ability to ensure that the permitted facility complies with applicable environmental protection laws. Such conditions could range from simply providing more ready access to the information necessary to overseeing the permitted facility's operation and compliance to working to increase the resources of citizen groups participating in environmental oversight and compliance assurance.

To that same effect, Section 504(b) authorizes EPA to prescribe "procedures and methods for determining compliance," and Section 504(c) requires that each permit "set forth inspection, entry, monitoring, compliance certification, and reporting requirements to assure compliance with the permit terms and conditions." There is nothing on the face of the statute to preclude either Section 504(b)'s "procedures and methods" or Section 504(c)'s "requirements to assure compliance" from extending to permit conditions that enhance the community's own capacity to oversee the permitted facility's compliance....

Section 402 of the [Clean Water Act] ... is likely the most significant potential source of permit conditioning authority [under that statute]. Section 402 provides that the Administrator may issue a permit for the discharge of any pollutant: "upon condition that such discharge will meet either (A) all applicable requirements under [various sections of the CWA], or (B) prior to the taking of necessary implementing actions relating to all such requirements, such conditions as the Administrator determines are necessary to carry out the provisions of this chapter." A broad construction of clause (B) could confer on the Administrator wide ranging authority to impose permit conditions promoting environmental justice....

* * *

Notes and Questions

1. As early as 2000, EPA's Office of General Counsel (OGC) issued a memo that similarly found significant authority under numerous statutory provisions for addressing environmental justice issues in the permitting process, including some not discussed by

Professors Lazarus and Tai. *See* OFFICE OF GEN. COUNSEL, U.S. EPA, MEMORANDUM FROM GARY GUZY, GENERAL COUNSEL, TO THE ASSISTANT ADMINISTRATORS OF VARIOUS PROGRAM OFFICES WITHIN THE EPA (Dec. 1, 2000).

However, in the memo, the General Counsel cautioned that "[a]lthough the memorandum presents interpretations of EPA's statutory authority and regulations that we believe are legally permissible, it does not suggest that such actions would be uniformly practical or feasible given policy or resource considerations or that there are not important considerations of legal risk that would need to be evaluated." Why would the General Counsel specifically decline to endorse the use of legal authority as a matter of policy?

The OGC memo was not the first memorandum of this sort. An internal memo drafted by EPA's General Counsel in 1994 outlined authorities for incorporating environmental justice into a broad range of EPA activities other than permitting, including enforcement, standard-setting, cleanup actions, pesticide registration, authorization of state delegated programs, grants, procurement, and audits by EPA's Inspector General. This broader memo was never finalized, however, apparently because it was too politically controversial. *See* John Stanton, *Special Report, EPA "Buried" 1994 Plans for Major Environmental Justice Roadmap*, INSIDE EPA WEEKLY REP., 1–2, 24 (Mar. 3, 2000).

2. Several reports discuss facility permitting in the environmental justice context and similarly find considerable authority in existing law to address environmental justice. *See* ENVTL. LAW INST., OPPORTUNITIES FOR ADVANCING ENVIRONMENTAL JUSTICE: AN ANALYSIS OF U.S. EPA STATUTORY AUTHORITIES (2001); NAT'L ACAD. OF PUB. ADMIN., MODELS FOR CHANGE: EFFORTS BY FOUR STATES TO ADDRESS ENVIRONMENTAL JUSTICE (2002); NAT'L ACAD. OF PUB. ADMIN., ENVIRONMENTAL JUSTICE IN EPA PERMITTING: REDUCING POLLUTION IN HIGH-RISK COMMUNITIES IS INTEGRAL TO THE AGENCY'S MISSION (2001); *see also* NAT'L ACAD. OF PUB. ADMIN., A BREATH OF FRESH AIR: REVIVING THE NEW SOURCE REVIEW PROGRAM (2003) (concluding that the New Source Review program of the Clean Air Act performs poorly in reducing pollution from the nation's oldest and dirtiest factories and power plants).

3. Professors Lazarus and Tai also note the willingness of the Environmental Appeals Board (EAB) to endorse conditioning permits on environmental justice grounds:

> The evolving perspective of the Environmental Appeals Board on EPA's authority to base permits on environmental justice grounds can be seen in a series of decisions beginning in September 1993 and continuing to [1999]. Although the Executive Order on Environmental Justice expressly did not enlarge any agency's permitting power, the Order has had a marked effect on the Board's interpretation of the scope of authority available to permitting agencies. Prior to the Order, the Board rejected an environmental justice community's claim that environmental justice concerns should be considered in an air quality permitting process. The Board held instead that permitting agencies lacked environmental justice authority because they were limited to considering whether a facility would meet federal air quality requirements.

> After the Order was issued, the Board seemed to accord increasingly more acceptance to the contention that permitting agencies were able to condition permits on environmental justice grounds. Although none of these decisions required agencies to interject environmental justice considerations into their permitting processes, the opinions focused less on whether complainants were able to claim that agencies failed to consider environmental justice concerns and more on whether those agencies adequately considered environmental justice con-

cerns. The net effect of the Order may have been to draw attention to existing areas of authority that the Board had previously overlooked so that agencies had the means to actually comply with the Order.

Richard J. Lazarus & Stephanie Tai, *Integrating Environmental Justice Into EPA Permitting Authority*, 26 ECOLOGY L. Q. 617, 655–56 (1999).

4. Although it appears that broadly worded clauses in federal environmental statutes grant authority to condition or deny permits on environmental justice grounds, the willingness of permitting authorities to use their legal authority is critically important. In order to prompt federal agencies to take more aggressive action to address environmental inequities, in 1994 then President Clinton issued Executive Order 12,898, requiring federal agencies to "make achieving environmental justice part of [the agency's] mission by identifying and addressing, as appropriate, disproportionately high and adverse human health or environmental effects of its programs, policies and activities...." (See Chapter 10). As of mid-2009, this executive order had not been rescinded or modified. Ideally, this message from the highest level of the federal executive branch should prompt permitting authorities to further test the potential of existing sources of authority. However, if permitting officials decline to do so, the role of reviewing bodies becomes essential to the longer-range goal of a protective permitting system. Administrative judges and courts will be increasingly called upon to support these efforts in two respects. The first is to recognize the authorities in omnibus clauses (statutory clauses that provide general authority for agencies to take environmentally protective measures). Beyond that, however, reviewing bodies may prompt the development of substantive environmental justice criteria to be applied to permitting. As you read the following section, consider how the cases decided by the Environmental Appeals Board either support the permitting status quo or encourage the development of more protective permitting approaches.

In re Chemical Waste Management of Indiana, Inc.
United States Environmental Protection Agency
Environmental Appeals Board
1995 EPA App. LEXIS 25; 6 E.A.D. 66
June 29, 1995

Before Environmental Appeals Judges Nancy B. Firestone, Ronald L. McCallum, and Edward E. Reich; Opinion of the Board by Judge Reich

On March 1, 1995, U.S. EPA Region V issued a final permit decision approving the application of Chemical Waste Management of Indiana, Inc. ("CWMII") for the renewal of the federal portion of a Resource Conservation and Recovery Act ("RCRA") permit and a Class 3 modification of the same permit for its Adams Center Landfill Facility in Fort Wayne, Indiana. The Environmental Appeals Board has received three petitions challenging the Region's permit decision....

During the comment period on the draft permit and draft modification (collectively the "draft modified permit"), Petitioners and other commenters raised what the parties refer to as "environmental justice" concerns. More specifically, issues were raised as to whether the operation of CWMII's facility will have a disproportionately adverse impact on the health, environment, or economic well-being of minority or low-income populations in the area surrounding the facility. The gist of Petitioners' challenge is that the measures taken by the Region to address the environmental justice concerns failed to conform to the rules governing the permitting process, violated an Executive Order relating to environmental justice, resulted in factual and legal errors and an abuse of discretion, and raised an important policy issue warranting review. For the reasons set forth in this opinion, we conclude that Petitioners have failed to demonstrate that either the Region's permit decision or the procedures it used to reach that decision involved factual or legal errors, exercises of discretion, or policy issues that warrant review. Accordingly, we are denying review of the petitions.

Background

The Region issued the HSWA [Hazardous Solid Waste Amendments] portion of the draft modified permit on May 23, 1994. The public comment period began on that date and extended through July 13, 1994. On June 29, 1994, the Region held a public hearing in accordance with the procedures set out in [the applicable regulations]. On March 1, 1995, the Region issued a response to comments and its final permit decision....

During the pendency of CWMII's permit application, Executive Order 12898, relating to environmental justice, was issued. The Order mandates that:

> To the greatest extent practicable and permitted by law.... each Federal agency shall make achieving environmental justice part of its mission by identifying and addressing, as appropriate, disproportionately high and adverse human health or environmental effects of its programs, policies, or activities on minority populations and low-income populations in the United States....

Section 1-101. *59 Fed. Reg. 7629* (Feb. 16, 1994). The Order also requires that:

> Each Federal agency shall conduct its programs, policies, and activities that substantially affect human health and the environment, in a manner that ensures that such programs, policies, and activities do not have the effect of ... subjecting persons (including populations) to discrimination under, such programs, policies, and activities, because of their race, color, or national origin....

Section 2.2 *Id.* At 7630–31.

In response to the environmental justice concerns raised during the comment period on the draft modified permit, the Region held what was billed as an "informational" meeting in Fort Wayne, Indiana, on August 11, 1994. The meeting was attended by concerned citizens, and representatives of CWMII, the Indiana Department of Environmental Management, and the Region. The purpose of the meeting was to "allow representatives of all parties involved to freely discuss Environmental Justice and other key issues, answer questions and gain understanding of each party's concerns." The Region also performed a demographic analysis of census data on populations within a one-mile radius of the facility. The Region ultimately concluded that the operation of the facility would not have a disproportionately adverse health or environmental impact on minority or low-income populations living near the facility....

Under the rules governing this proceeding, the Regional Administrator's permit decision ordinarily will not be reviewed unless it is based on a clearly erroneous finding of fact or conclusion of law, or involves an important matter of policy or exercise of discretion that warrants review. The preamble to [the regulation] states that "this power of review should only be sparingly exercised," and that "most permit conditions should be finally determined at the Regional level...." The burden of demonstrating that review is warranted is on the petitioner. For the reasons set forth below, we conclude that Petitioners have not carried their burden in this case.

We believe it is useful to begin by considering the precise nature of Petitioners' environmental justice claim in the context of this RCRA proceeding and the effect, if any, the issuance of Executive Order 12898 should have on the way in which the Agency addresses such a claim.

"Environmental justice," at least as that term is used in the Executive Order, involves "identifying and addressing, as appropriate, disproportionately high and adverse human health or environmental effects of [Agency] programs, policies, and activities on minority populations and low-income populations...." Some of the commenters also believe that environmental justice is concerned with adverse effects on the *economic* well-being of such populations. Thus, when Petitioners couch their arguments in terms of environmental justice, they assert that the issuance of the permit and the concomitant operation of the facility will have a disproportionately adverse impact not only on the health and environment of minority or low-income people living near the facility but also on economic growth and property values. The main support in the record for this assertion is an environmental impacts study submitted by the City of New Haven. That study purports to "evaluate the potential for human exposure to toxic chemicals derived from the treatment and disposal of chemicals at the Adams Center." It identifies "exposure pathways" by which citizens living near the facility may be exposed to pollutants from the facility, but its central conclusion is that more risk assessment needs to be done before the extent and probability of such exposure can be determined accurately.

Although it is not made explicit in the petitions, it is nevertheless clear that Petitioners do not believe that the threats posed by the facility can be addressed through revision of the permit. Rather, it is apparent that Petitioners believe that their concerns can be addressed only by permanently halting operation of the facility at its present location or, at a minimum, preventing the Phase IV Expansion of the facility. Thus, Petitioners challenge the permit decision, including the modification, in its entirety, rather than any specific permit conditions.

At the outset, it is important to determine how (if at all) the Executive Order changes the way a Region processes a permit application under RCRA. For the reasons set forth below, we conclude that the Executive Order does not purport to, and does not have the effect of, changing the substantive requirements for issuance of a permit under RCRA and its implementing regulations. We conclude, nevertheless, that there are areas where the Region has discretion to act within the constraints of the RCRA regulations and, in such areas, as a matter of policy, the Region should exercise that discretion to implement the Executive Order to the greatest extent practicable....

While, as is discussed later, there are some important opportunities to implement the Executive Order in the RCRA permitting context, there are substantial limitations as well. As the Region notes in its brief, the Executive Order by its express terms is to be implemented in a manner that is consistent with existing law. The Region correctly points out that under the existing RCRA scheme, the Agency is *required* to issue a permit to any applicant who meets all the requirements of RCRA and its implementing regulations. The statute expressly provides that:

> Upon a determination by the Administrator (or a State, if applicable), of compliance by a facility for which a permit is applied for under this section with the requirements of this section and section 3004, the Administrator (or the State) *shall issue* a permit for such facilities.

RCRA § 3005(c)(1), 42 U.S.C. § 6925 (emphasis added). Thus, as the Region observes:

> Under federal law, public support or opposition to the permitting of a facility can affect a permitting decision if such support or opposition is based on issues relating to compliance with the requirements of RCRA or RCRA regulations or

such support or opposition otherwise relate to protection of human health or the environment. RCRA does not authorize permitting decisions to be based on public comment that is unrelated to RCRA's statutory or regulatory requirements or the protection of human health or the environment.

The Region correctly observes that under RCRA and its implementing regulations, "there is no legal basis for rejecting a RCRA permit application based solely upon alleged social or economic impacts upon the community." Accordingly, if a permit applicant meets the requirements of RCRA and its implementing regulations, the Agency *must* issue the permit, regardless of the racial or socio-economic composition of the surrounding community and regardless of the economic effect of the facility on the surrounding community....

Nevertheless, there are two areas in the RCRA permitting scheme in which the Region has significant discretion, within the constraints of RCRA, to implement the mandates of the Executive Order. The first of these areas is public participation. Part 124 already provides procedures for ensuring that the public is afforded an opportunity to participate in the processing of a permit application. The procedures required under part 124, however, do not preclude a Region from providing other opportunities for public involvement beyond those required under part 124. We hold, therefore, that when the Region has a basis to believe that operation of the facility may have a disproportionate impact on a minority or low-income segment of the affected community, the Region should, as a matter of policy, exercise its discretion to assure early and ongoing opportunities for public involvement in the permitting process.

A second area in which the Region has discretion to implement the Executive Order within the constraints of RCRA relates to the omnibus clause under section 3005(c)(3) of RCRA. The omnibus clause provides that:

> Each permit issued under this section shall contain such terms and conditions as the Administrator (or the State) determines necessary to protect human health and the environment.

Under the omnibus clause, if the operation of a facility would have an adverse impact on the health or environment of the surrounding community, the Agency would be required to include permit terms or conditions that would ensure that such impacts do not occur. Moreover, if the nature of the facility and its proximity to neighboring populations would make it impossible to craft a set of permit terms that would protect the health and environment of such populations, the Agency would have the authority to deny the permit. *See In re Marine Shale Processors, Inc.*, 5 E.A.D. 751, 796 n.64 (EAB 1995) ("The Agency has traditionally read [section 3005(c)(3)] as authorizing denials of permits where the Agency can craft no set of permit conditions or terms that will ensure protection of human health and the environment."). In that event, the facility would have to shut down entirely. Thus, under the omnibus clause, if the operation of a facility truly poses a threat to the health or environment of a low-income or minority community, the omnibus clause would require the Region to include in the permit whatever terms and conditions are necessary to prevent such impacts. This would be true even without a finding of disparate impact.

There is nothing in section 3005(c)(3) to prevent the Region from taking a more refined look at its health and environmental impacts assessment, in light of allegations that operation of the facility would have a disproportionately adverse effect on the health or environment of low-income or minority populations. Even under the omnibus clause some judgment is required as to what constitutes a threat to human health and the environment. It is certainly conceivable that, although analysis of a broad cross-section of the community may not suggest a threat to human health and the environment from the operation of a facility, such a broad analysis might mask the effects of the facility on a disparately affected minority or low-income segment of the community. (Moreover, such an analysis might have been based on assumptions that, though true for a broad cross-section of the community, are not true for the smaller minority or low-income segment of the community.) A Region should take this under consideration in defining the scope of its analysis for compliance with § 3005(c)(3).

Of course, an exercise of discretion under section 3005(c)(3) would be limited by the constraints that are inherent in the language of the omnibus clause. In other words, in response to an environmental justice claim, the Region would be limited to ensuring the protection of the health or environment of the minority or low-income populations. The Region would not have discretion to redress impacts that are unrelated or only tenuously related to human health and the environment, such as disproportionate impacts on the economic well-being of a minority or low-income community. With that qualification in mind, we hold that when a commenter submits at least a superficially plausible claim that operation of the facility will have a disproportionate impact on a minority or low-income segment of the affected community, the Region should, as a matter of policy, exercise its discretion under section 3005(c)(3) to include within its health and environmental impacts assessment an analysis focusing particularly on the minority or low-income community whose health or environment is alleged to be threatened by the facility. In this fashion, the Region may implement the Executive Order within the constraints of RCRA and its implementing regulations. . . .

Petitioners also question the Region's efforts to determine whether operation of the facility will have a disproportionate impact on a minority or low-income community. To assess whether there would indeed be a disproportionate impact on low-income or minority populations, the Region performed a demographic study, based on census figures, of the racial and socio-economic composition of the community surrounding the facility. The Region concluded that no minority or low-income communities will face a disproportionate impact from the facility. Petitioners argue that, in arriving at this conclusion, the Region erred by ignoring available census and other information submitted during the comment period that allegedly demonstrate a disproportionate impact of the facility on minority or low-income populations, particularly those at distances greater than one mile. Petitioners particularly criticize the Region's decision to restrict the focus of its study to the community living within a one-mile radius of the facility. Petitioners contend that the facility adversely affects citizens who live further than one mile away from the facility. In its response to the petitions, the Region defends its decision to focus on a one-mile radius for its demographic study, as follows:

> The Region 5 office of RCRA has chosen a one-mile radius for demographic evaluation of disproportionately high and adverse human health or environmental impacts of RCRA facilities upon minority populations and low-income populations, based upon a Comprehensive Environmental Response, Compensation and Liability Act, ... guidance (Hazard Ranking System Guidance Manual, November 1992, EPA 9345.1-07) developed for CERCLA sites without groundwater contamination; however, the demographic evaluation did not exclude the population located outside of the one-mile radius.

As explained above, the Region can and should consider a claim of disproportionate impact in the context of its health and environmental impacts assessment under the omnibus clause at section 3005(c)(3) of RCRA. The proper scope of a demographic study to consider such impacts is an issue calling for a highly technical judgment as to the probable dispersion of pollutants through various media into the surrounding community. This is precisely the kind of issue that the Region, with its technical expertise and experience, is best suited to decide.... In recognition of this reality, the procedural rules governing appeals of permitting decisions place a heavy burden on petitioners who seek Board review of such technical decisions. To carry that burden in this case, Petitioners would need to show either that the Region erred in concluding that the permit would be protective of populations within one mile of the facility, or that, even if it were protective of such close-in populations, it for some reason would not protect the health or environment of citizens who live at a greater distance from the facility. We believe that Petitioners have failed to demonstrate that the Region erred in either of these respects....

* * *

Notes and Questions

1. When broadly worded omnibus clauses such as RCRA section 3005(c)(3) are used to support an environmental justice claim, federal permitting authorities have tended to be fairly conservative in abiding by constraints plausibly inherent in the language of the clause. Accordingly, the outer bounds of regulatory discretion to condition or deny a permit based upon environmental justice considerations remain unclear from the EAB decisions.

As noted by one of the editors, as of 2001, there were ten cases adjudicating environmental justice claims. These claims generally involved challenges by environmental justice advocates who claimed that the permitting agency did not exercise its discretion in a sufficiently protective manner, instead of permit applicants claiming that the permit conditions were too onerous. In those cases, the Regions ultimately concluded that there was no disproportionate adverse impact on the basis of race or income, either due to the results of a demographic analysis or an impact analysis. However, in two cases additional conditions appear to have been placed on the permit in response to concerns of the affected communities. *See* Eileen Gauna, *EPA at 30: Fairness in Environmental Protection*, 31 Envtl. L. Rep. 10,528, 10,534 (2001) (discussing cases). The methodology the Regional officials used in the environmental justice analysis in those cases appears to follow a basic approach that uses (1) census data to determine demographics (mean income or ethnic minority), and (2) a one or two mile radius to determine the area of maximum impact. The methodology for identifying a potential environmental justice community and determining disparity is vulnerable to complicating factors, and is continually changing and evolving. *See id.* In a more recent case the Board noted that the claimant had offered no specific information to support a claim that it was disproportionately affected. *See* In Re: Phelps Dodge Corporation, Verde Valley Ranch Development, E.A.D. 460 (2002). In another, the Board denied review based upon the response to comments by the Illinois Environmental Protection Agency, the delegated permitting agency, which noted that the "[l]ow income communities are actually located many miles from the plant, at distances with which other, more affluent communities are interspersed." Prairie State Generating Co., PSD Appeal No. 05-05, slip op. at 164 (Aug. 24, 2006) (order denying review).

2. The Environmental Appeals Board permitting cases illustrate the tension, on appeal, between the principle of deference to agencies embodied in an abuse of discretion review standard and the counter-balancing policy, embodied in the federal executive order and recognized by the EAB, that discretion should be exercised in a more protective man-

ner where impacts affect vulnerable communities. The EAB's approach has been to resolve this tension by a more probing review of procedural matters, requiring a detailed environmental justice analysis and good evidentiary support for a claim of disparate impact. However, at this point, the EAB will not look too closely into how discretion was in fact exercised by the permitting official. As methodologies advance and more specific criteria are developed, by statute or rule, reviewing bodies may have a better basis to evaluate the adequacy of a permitting authority's response to environmental justice concerns. Given the need to substantially improve conditions in overburdened communities, while at the same time affording permit applicants fairness and certainty in the permitting process, how would you devise a more protective permitting scheme that accomplishes these goals?

3. Some state courts have turned to state constitutions and general welfare omnibus clauses that exist in relevant environmental statutes to find authority to address environmental justice concerns. The following cases illustrate this approach:

3. Environmental Justice Claims in State Permit Proceedings

NAACP—Flint Chapter v. Engler

Genesee (Michigan) County Circuit Court
(Transcript of Ruling, May 29, 1997)

Hayman, Circuit Judge:

[The case arose out of the Michigan Department of Environmental Quality's (DEQ's) decision to approve an application of the Genesee Power Station Unlimited Partnership for a permit to operate a wood waste incinerator in Genesee Township in 1992. The permit allowed the incinerator to emit lead in the amount of 2.2 tons per year, or 65 tons over its lifespan, which had the potential to increase the concentration of lead in the soil by ten to fifteen percent. The incinerator was located immediately adjacent to a predominantly African American (and heavily polluted) neighborhood near Flint. After the permit was unsuccessfully appealed to EPA's Environmental Appeals Board, the incinerator began operation in 1995. Plaintiffs then filed suit in state court alleging violations of federal and state civil rights and environmental statutes.

The trial judge found that the cumulative impact of multiple sources emitting multiple pollutants imposed a significant burden on the area near the facility, that soil in the area contained levels of lead substantially above statewide background levels, and that at least 50 percent of the children in the northern sector of Genesee County exceeded the maximum level of lead exposure as defined by the health community.]

... In analyzing this case the Court would first note that under Article IV, Section 51 of the Michigan Constitution, it provides: "The public health and general welfare of the people of the State are hereby declared to be matters of primary public concern. The Legislature shall pass suitable laws for protection and promotion of the public health."

Here the Constitution of Michigan has given the representatives of the people of Michigan the authority to pass laws for the protection and promotion of the public health and welfare.

Defendants contend that the Clean Air Act requires them to grant permits when zoning has been approved and the permit meets the NAAQ Standards [National Ambient

Air Quality Standards, also commonly referred to as NAAQS]. They argue that they have no authority to deny permits which meet the above stated standards.

This Court disagrees with Defendant's position on this issue. The Clean Air Act and its amendments to same recognize the states' ability to regulate emissions. The act encourages the enactment of uniform State and local laws relating to the prevention and control of air pollution on an interstate level. The act gives primary responsibility for implementation of these interstate standards to State governments, not to the Federal Government. The Federal domain in matters covered by the Clean Air Act has been held not to be exclusive or preemptive of State legislation....

Further, a state may impose pollution control requirements which are more strict than those specified by the Federal plan....

Under the facts of this case, the Court holds that the policies and regulations that are enforced by the State do not go far enough to carry out the duty the State has under the Constitution to protect the health, safety and welfare of its citizens, regardless of their race.

There are some facts in this case that need noting at this point. First, the plant that is at issue in this case was sited in Mt. Morris Township, right at the northeast border of Flint. The relevance of this fact to the decision in this case is that the zoning decision for this plant was made by Mt. Morris Township's local governmental authorities. The significant impacts of pollution fallout will be felt in the City of Flint, by approximately 3,000 white residents to the southeast of the plant and by as many as 50,000 or more African-Americans to the south of the plant. The Plaintiffs are all residents of the City of Flint. Therefore, they had little, if any, standing or political influence to prohibit the zoning approval for the plant in Mt. Morris Township. The elected officials in Mt. Morris did not represent, nor were they elected by City of Flint residents.

Second, the communities in Flint that will be hit by the two tons per year of increased pollution during the estimated 35 years span [sic] of this plant already suffer from significant pollution in the environment. Many of the major polluting facilities are located on the north side of Flint and have been there for many years polluting the environment. The soil in this area of Genesee County has an extremely high lead content. The housing stock is old and many have lead based paint, a major source of lead pollution in the environment. The experts have testified that as many as 50 percent of the children in these communities have lead levels that exceed the national maximum exposure to lead. This causes significant problems for developing children.

Third, since the State has taken the position that they are only concerned with meeting the NAAQ[S], there was no Risk Assessment Study required to determine the impact of introducing this additional two tons of pollution into an environment that already is beyond being safe due to pollution sources....

This Court also finds that Defendant violated the Michigan Air Act by failing to perform a Risk Assessment Analysis in this case. The Michigan Clean Air Act states in Section B: "The Michigan Department of Environmental Quality [M.D.E.Q.] may deny or revoke a permit if installation of the source presents or may present an imminent and substantial endangerment to human health, safety, or welfare, or the environment."

Unless the M.D.E.Q. performs a Risk Assessment to determine the impact of the plant in the surrounding area, at least within a five-mile radius, it cannot conclude that the plant does not violate this provision and must therefore refuse to grant a permit....

Another problem that exists in this case is with the Defendant's failure to provide a meaningful avenue for cities and other governmental units, who are in the situation that

Flint is in [here], to have a meaningful and knowledgeable opportunity to have it's [sic] concerns and those of its residents considered in the siting process involving plants that are located in another jurisdiction, but which pollute adjoining governmental units.

And I think that's a big problem in this case. The Department of Environmental Quality is saying, look, we have no authority to decide where the plants are going to be sited. That's a local issue. But in this particular case, you have a local governmental authority deciding to site a plant and it's polluting another community that has no authority to stop that local community from zoning that plant. And there has to be a procedure in place to give those communities an opportunity to be heard.

The State's position that zoning is a local issue is harmful to the health, safety and welfare of citizens who are situated like Flint who do not have a voice at zoning board meetings that are held outside of their communities. In these situations the State must have in place a procedure that gives adjoining communities a fair opportunity to be notified and heard concerning the siting of pollution facilities near their borders that pollute their communities.

There is little or no incentive for Mt. Morris Township to deny zoning to a facility that will pollute an adjoining community. Mt. Morris gets an increased tax base and the residents of the City of Flint will get pollution....

Given that this Court has concluded that the State has violated its constitutional duty to protect the health, safety and welfare of its citizens by failing to enact policies that protect cities like Flint and its residents and gives them a fair opportunity to be heard in a meaningful way, this Court concludes that there is no remedy at law and therefore it is appropriate to exercise its equitable power and to grant an injunction against the Michigan Department of Environmental Quality preventing it from granting permits to major pollution sources—and I use the term major pollution sources—until a Risk Assessment is performed and those interested parties and governmental units that will be impacted based upon the Risk Assessment Study are notified and given an opportunity to be heard before the Michigan Department of Environmental Quality....

And it has to also give interested parties and governmental units that [such] study shows will be impacted by the pollution an opportunity to be heard and an opportunity, a meaningful opportunity, not just an opportunity to come in front of the Commission and air their voices, but something meaningful, before zoning is granted for major polluting facilities and permits are granted....

* * *

Colonias Development Council v. Rhino Environmental Services Inc. & New Mexico Department of Environment
138 N.M. 133, 117 P.3d 939 (2005)

Background

On September 10, 2001, more than 250 people packed the middle school cafeteria in Chaparral, New Mexico, for a public hearing. The purpose of the meeting was to review an application by Rhino Environmental Services, Inc. (Rhino) for a permit to put a landfill in Chaparral pursuant to the [New Mexico] Solid Waste Act.

Even though the September 11 terrorist attack on the World Trade Center in New York City disrupted the public hearing, emptying chairs the day after the attack, more than 300 people eventually came forth between September 10 and 19, with about sixty actively testifying or conducting cross-examination. Some community members attended the sessions during the day. Others came at night, after driving home from jobs across the border in Mexico and El Paso, Texas. People brought their children and crying babies. They held press conferences. They tried to hang banners protesting the landfill. Some spoke in Spanish, through a translator provided by the Department.

Although a few community members supported the landfill during the hearing, the vast majority did not. Many testified that they did not understand why another landfill had to be placed just a couple of miles from Chaparral, an unincorporated community that lacks infrastructure, political representation, and medical facilities. As a border community consisting primarily of low-income, minority residents, Chaparral has been called New Mexico's largest *colonia* [*colonias* are rural settlements, usually along the United States-Mexico border, that lack safe housing, potable water, wastewater treatment, drainage, electricity, and paved roads. Eds.]....

Despite the overwhelming community opposition, the Secretary, acting through the Director of the Water and Waste Management Division, granted the permit for a period of ten years subject to a list of twenty conditions....

CDC [Colonias Development Council, a nonprofit dedicated to improving conditions in New Mexico *colonias*] appealed that decision to the Court of Appeals, which affirmed the Department's approval of the landfill permit. On certiorari to this Court, CDC acknowledges that community members were given an opportunity to speak but claims the hearing officer erred by interpreting the Department's role too narrowly. In CDC's view, the hearing officer perceived her duty as strictly confined to overseeing the technical requirements of the permit application. As a result, the Secretary approved the landfill permit based on an erroneous assumption that the Department was neither required nor allowed to consider the impact of the proliferation of landfills on a community's quality of life. This perception, CDC contends, ultimately undermined any influence the public's nontechnical testimony could have on the decision to grant a landfill permit....

CDC further contends that the hearing officer erred in refusing to consider testimony regarding the adverse cumulative effects caused by the proliferation of landfills and other industrial sites. CDC claims there are four waste disposal facilities and three industrial sites near Chaparral....

Discussion

CDC argues that the impact of the landfill on the community's quality of life, and the general concerns of community members opposed to the landfill, were not considered in determining whether to grant the solid waste permit. It contends that such considerations are required by the Environmental Improvement Act, the Solid Waste Act, and the regulations adopted pursuant to the acts. CDC does not challenge the technical issues addressed in the permitting process....

The Solid Waste Act directs "the establishment of a comprehensive solid waste management program." One purpose of the act is to "plan for and regulate, in the most economically feasible, cost-effective and environmentally safe manner, the reduction, storage, collection, transportation, separation, processing, recycling and disposal of solid waste." Another important purpose is to "enhance the beauty and quality of the environment; conserve, recover and recycle resources; and protect the public health, safety and welfare." ...

In issuing [regulations under the Solid Waste Act], the Board is required to "assure that the relative interests of the applicant, other owners of property likely to be affected and the general public will be considered prior to the issuance of a permit for a solid waste facility." In addition, the Board is required to adopt procedural regulations providing for notice and a public hearing on permit actions.

Pursuant to this statutory authority, the Board adopted regulations providing technical siting criteria. The Board also adopted regulations governing permitting procedures, which encourage public participation.

... [T]he regulations regarding permit issuance state: "The Secretary *shall* issue a permit if the applicant demonstrates that the other requirements of this Part are met *and* the solid waste facility application demonstrates that neither a hazard to public health, welfare, or the environment nor undue risk to property will result." ...

Pursuant to the authority delegated by the enabling statutes, and the regulations adopted to implement those statutes, CDC urges this Court to conclude that the Secretary is required to allow testimony regarding the impact of a proposed landfill on a community's quality of life. Such consideration is required, CDC argues, in order to realize the general purposes of the statutes to confer optimum social well-being, to protect public health, safety and welfare, and to assure that "relative interests" of all parties are considered.

In the view of Rhino and the Department, on the other hand, the purposes of the enabling statutes to promote public welfare and social well-being are addressed in the implementing regulations. Concerns such as landfill proliferation are not mentioned in the regulations, they assert, and cannot be an independent factor in considering whether to issue a solid waste facility permit. The Department sees its role as dictated by the technical regulations. If the siting criteria is met, they argue, the Department has no discretion to deny a permit or impose conditions on one. The Court of Appeals agreed, stating, "[The Department] cannot reasonably be expected to weigh sociological concerns, which it has no expertise in doing. Its role is to pass judgment on the technical aspects of a solid waste site, a subject within its expertise and which it was designed to do." Thus, the Court of Appeals determined that the hearing officer could properly limit evidence relating to "social impact" because the term is not mentioned in the statutes or regulations, and therefore is legally irrelevant.

We think the Court of Appeals' view of the Department's role is too narrow and has the potential to chill public participation in the permitting process contrary to legislative intent. The Solid Waste Act is replete with references to public input and education. The process of applying for a landfill permit attempts to facilitate public participation in several ways. First, the applicant submits an application for a permit, which includes all the technical information required to support the permit, and files notice to the public and affected parties. The Department solicits comments, and once the application is complete, conducts a public hearing, which provides the public and interested parties an opportunity to comment and present evidence. By directing the Department to adopt procedural regulations to provide all persons with a reasonable opportunity to be heard, the Legislature has clearly indicated its intent to ensure that the public plays a vital role in the hearing process....

In finding public participation and the hearing requirement central to the Solid Waste Act, our courts have protected and promoted the role of public input in the Department's decision to issue a permit. In our view, the Legislature did not limit the Department's role to reviewing technical regulations. Instead, our courts have acknowledged that the Secretary must use discretion in implementing the Solid Waste Act and its regulations in order to encourage public participation in the permitting process.

Given the Legislature's goal to involve the public in the permitting process to the fullest extent possible, we do not agree with the Court of Appeals that the Secretary was not allowed to consider testimony relating to the community's quality of life. The Legislature clearly believed public participation is vital to the success of the Solid Waste Act. Members of the public generally are not technical experts. The Legislature did not require scientific evidence in opposition to a landfill permit, but instead envisioned that ordinary concerns about a community's quality of life could influence the decision to issue a landfill permit. While testimony relating to something as broad as "social impact" may not require denial of a permit, the hearing officer must listen to concerns about adverse impacts on social well-being and quality of life, as well as report them accurately to the Secretary. In reviewing the hearing officer's report, the Secretary must consider whether lay concerns relate to violations of the Solid Waste Act and its regulations. Therefore, the Secretary should consider issues relating to public health and welfare not addressed by specific technical regulations....

Proliferation

Although we hold that the Department must allow testimony regarding the impact of a landfill on a community's quality of life, we agree with the Department that its authority to address such concerns requires a nexus to a regulation. Like the Court of Appeals, we are not persuaded that the general purposes of the Environmental Improvement Act and the Solid Waste Act, considered alone, provide authority for requiring the Secretary to deny a landfill permit based on public opposition. The purposes of the enabling acts, which include the goal of protecting the "public health, safety and welfare," are designed to invoke the general police power of the state. This general expression of legislative police power, without more, does not create a standard for protecting "public health, safety and welfare." Thus, the Court of Appeals was correct to reject CDC's reliance on the purposes of the acts as a statutory mandate to respond to issues that fit ever so loosely under the umbrella of "sociological concerns." Such a broad mandate would offer no guidance to the Department, and violate the well-settled principle that a legislative body may not vest unbridled or arbitrary power in an administrative agency.

Unlike the Court of Appeals, however, we do find that quality of life concerns expressed during the hearing bear a relationship to environmental regulations the Secretary is charged with administering. Although both parties refer to the issues on appeal in a wide variety of ways, including "social impact," "sociological concerns," "social well-being," and "environmental justice," we believe there are legitimate concerns at the core of CDC's claim that are within the purview of the Secretary's oversight role. Contrary to the Department's position, the impact on the community from a specific environmental act, the proliferation of landfills, appears highly relevant to the permit process.

As we have discussed, the regulations implementing the Solid Waste Act demand more from the Department than mere technical oversight. The regulations regarding permit issuance direct the Secretary to issue a permit if the applicant fulfills the technical requirements *and* "the solid waste facility application demonstrates that neither a hazard to public health, welfare, or the environment nor undue risk to property will result." The regulations also require all solid waste facilities to be *located* and operated "in a manner that does not cause a public nuisance or create a potential hazard to public health, welfare or the environment." The regulations do not limit the Secretary's review to technical regulations, but clearly extend to the impact on public health or welfare resulting from the environmental effects of a proposed permit.

Landfill opponents presented testimony that Chaparral is a residential, low income border community that is being overrun by industrial sites including numerous pre-existing landfills. If this is true, we think it is reasonable for the Department to consider whether the cumulative effects of pollution, exacerbated by the incidences of poverty, may rise to the level of a public nuisance or hazard to public health, welfare, or the environment. If proliferation has an identified effect on the community's development and social well-being, it is not an amorphous general welfare issue, but an environmental problem. The adverse impact of the proliferation of landfills on a community's quality of life is well within the boundaries of environmental protection. Thus, the testimony regarding the impact of the proliferation of landfills is relevant within the context of environmental protection promised in the Solid Waste Act and its regulations. For that reason, the Secretary must evaluate whether the impact of an additional landfill on a community's quality of life creates a public nuisance or hazard to public health, welfare, or the environment.

The Department concluded as a matter of law that granting the permit would not result in a public nuisance or a hazard to public health, welfare or the environment. These conclusions, however, were made only after the Department incorrectly found that lay testimony relating to living near multiple disposal facilities was beyond the scope of the Secretary's authority for granting or denying a landfill. In our view, the Department's own regulations not only allow, but require consideration of the cumulative effect of large-scale garbage dumps and industrial sites on a single community.

As the regulations indicate, the Department cannot ignore concerns that relate to environmental protection simply because they are not mentioned in a technical regulation. The Department has a duty to interpret its regulations liberally in order to realize the purposes of the Acts. Because the impact of the proliferation of landfills and industrial sites on a community is relevant to environmental protection, we conclude that the Solid Waste Act and its regulations require the Department to consider whether evidence of the harmful effects from the cumulative impact of industrial development rises to the level of a public nuisance or potential hazard to public health, welfare or the environment.

Remedy

Because of the potential chilling effect of the hearing officer's error, we direct the Secretary to afford CDC a reasonable opportunity at a limited public hearing to tender additional evidence regarding the impact of proliferation.... Rhino shall have a reasonable opportunity to respond. We further instruct the Secretary to reconsider the public testimony opposing the landfill and explain the rationale for rejecting it, if the Secretary decides to do so. We are not suggesting that the Secretary must reach a different result, but we do require, as the Act itself requires, that the community be given a voice, and the concerns of the community be considered in the final decision making....

* * *

Notes and Questions

1. The cases adjudicating environmental justice claims in permit and related proceedings under state laws by no means uniformly provide remedies to affected communities. Some state courts have been reluctant to find environmental justice requirements in statutes that do not expressly include them. *See, e.g.,* Pine Bluff for Safe Disposal v. Ark. Pollution Control & Ecology Comm'n, 354 Ark. 563, 127 S.W.3d 509, 521–22 (2003) (in connection with an air and hazardous waste permit, finding no adverse health effects to *any persons* will result from the Facility's emissions). On the other hand, where statutes specifically require consideration of environmental justice or environmental equity, state courts will enforce those requirements. *See, e.g.,* Hartford Park Tenants Ass'n v. R.I. Dep't of Envtl. Mgmt., No. C.A. 99-3748, 2005 WL 2436227 (R.I. Super. Ct. Oct. 3, 2005) (pro-

visions under the state's Industrial Property Remediation and Reuse Act, a cleanup statute). However, even in these instances, they will defer to agency interpretations of how extensive the considerations must be and will narrowly interpret statutory mandates. *See, e.g.,* Harrelson Materials Mgmt. v. La. Dept. of Envtl. Quality, No. 2006 CA 1822, 2007 WL 1765563 (La. Ct. App. June 20, 2007) (demolition, debris, and landfill permit); In re Gaeta Recycling Co., 2007 WL 609161 (N.J. Super. Ct. Mar. 1, 2007); Bronx Envtl. Health & Justice, Inc. v. N.Y. City Dept. of Envtl. Protection, No. 25754/04, 2005 WL 1389360 (N.Y. Sup. Ct. May 11, 2005) (solid waste facility permit). A hesitancy to aggressively enforce environmental justice requirements may be due in part to their relatively recent vintage. *See, e.g.,* Mayor of Lansing v. Pub. Serv. Comm'n, 666 N.W.2d 298, 309 n.7 (Mich. Ct. App. 2003) (in a proceeding requesting approval from the Public Service Commission, the court noted that the issue of environmental justice had not been addressed by the state's appellate court).

2. Note on *NAACP-Flint Chapter.* The trial court was troubled by the fact that the economic benefits of the plant flowed to persons who lived outside the neighborhood, while residents of the impacted area were unable to obtain jobs from the plant. What is the legal relevance of this finding? The court also found problematic the fact that the impacts of the projects would be felt largely by persons outside the permitting agency's jurisdiction, in the next town. If this is an inevitable consequence of the local nature of most permitting decisions, how should the permitting agency account for this complication? Are there mitigation requirements that it should consider, or should it deny the permit altogether if the impacts reach a particular magnitude?

Postscript: on appeal, the court of appeals reversed in an unpublished decision, ruling that the trial judge had improperly granted relief based on claims that plaintiffs had not pleaded or raised at trial. *See* NAACP — Flint Chapter v. Engler, No. 205264 (Mich. Ct. App. Nov. 24, 1998).

3. Note on *Rhino.* In the wake of the *Rhino* decision, the New Mexico Environment Department promulgated regulations enumerating factors to be considered if a community impact assessment is applicable to permit proceedings under the State's Solid Waste Act. *See* N.M. CODE R. §20.9.3.8 D(2)(a)-(j). For a discussion of this case, see Kristina G. Fisher, *The Rhino in the Colonia: How* Colonias Development Council v. Rhino Environmental Services, Inc. *Set a Substantive Standard for Environmental Justice,* 39 ENVTL. L. 397 (2009).

4. The Pennsylvania Environment Department has taken a different approach, requiring among other things, that the project proponent of a waste disposal facility demonstrate that the project's benefits, including social and economic benefits, clearly outweigh its burdens, including social and economic harms. In *Eagle Envtl. II, L.P. v. Commonwealth Dept. of Envtl. Protection,* 584 Pa. 494, 884 A.2d 867 (2005), a landfill permitting case, the court endorsed this "benefits and burdens" test and rejected the argument that Pennsylvania's police power was exceeded because police power only protects the public against harm and does not extend to providing public benefits. In that case, the benefits and burdens were described as follows:

> Eagle cited the following potential short term benefits: disposal of debris in the event of a disaster; payments for health and safety training courses for landfill operators; and use of coal excavated from the site. Eagle identified additional real short term economic benefits: jobs for local residents at the landfill; increased employment at businesses associated with or located near the landfill; increased local, state and federal income taxes as a result of increased employment; higher real estate taxes; a $2 dollar per ton host fee to the township (as specifi-

cally authorized by [Pennsylvania law]); and provision of a recycling drop-off center. Eagle further noted real long term benefits of the project: replacement of wetland acreage (although the project would disturb .17 acres of wetlands, the disturbed wetland would be replaced with .42 acres of wetlands); improvement of the roads leading to the landfill; benefit to wetlands in the form of landfill runoff and reduced erosion; reclamation of a strip mine, and the resulting visual enhancement and increased soil fertility.

In contrast, Eagle identified harms resulting from the landfill and described how those harms could or could not be mitigated. The potential harm of a malfunction of the leachate treatment plant could be mitigated by proper operation of the plant and utilization of a leachate storage tank [Leachate is a liquid that percolates through a landfill. Students have been known to refer to leachate as "garbage juice." Eds.]. Eagle recognized the potential negative impact on the residents of the area but concluded that any impact would largely be anticipatory and could be alleviated by working with the residents. Eagle acknowledged sediment-laden runoff as a harm but asserted that it could be mitigated by erosion and sedimentation control features, and various measures relating to sediment required by other regulations. Furthermore, the resulting sedimentary ponds would be beneficial to aquatic life and migratory birds. Eagle observed that an increased risk of fires, emergencies, and accidents that could result from the project would burden the local emergency services, but could be mitigated by contingency planning, fire protection measures, and payments to the local fire departments to cover the increased burden. Eagle further noted the short term harms caused by waste hauling trucks which include fumes, visual impact, noise, spills, and odors. Eagle offered to mitigate these harms by insuring that the trucks are well maintained and that other measures would be employed to reduce the dust, noise, and odors resulting from the site.

Eagle acknowledged the long term harms of the project. After closure of the landfill, the land, which is currently woodland, would be converted to grassland. Eagle argued that, although the conversion could be viewed as a harm, it could also be seen as a benefit because it would increase species diversity in the area. Another long term harm is the negative aesthetic aspect of the landfill, however, Eagle planned to mitigate this by planting vegetation around the perimeter of the landfill.

Id. at 501–02, 871–72. Based upon the foregoing, how would you decide whether the permit should be issued?

5. How would you assess the overall approach to environmental justice claims in the permitting context? Does it matter whether the claims are premised upon state law or federal law? Quite apart from the assessment of adequacy of legal authority, however, the overall dynamic among the various stakeholders in a permitting dispute can present significant challenges, as the next section illustrates.

4. The Permit Applicant's Perspective

Given the broad grants of legal authority under environmental laws and the then recent legal activity under Title VI of the Civil Rights Act (discussed in Chapter 14), consider the following comments and observations of Terry Bossert, who represents permit applicants and who served for four years as Chief General Counsel to the Pennsylvania Department of Environmental Protection.

Terry R. Bossert, The Permit Applicant's Perspective
18 Temple Environmental Law and Technology Journal 135 (2000)

... Let me start by answering the question that I posed in the title of my talk, "what does environmental justice mean to the permit applicant?" As we stand here today, what it means to the permit applicant is uncertainty, confusion, and delay with regard to your permit application. Which is not to say there is anything wrong with the environmental justice movement or the issues that are being raised. I am simply saying that things are in such a state of uncertainty that it is difficult for a businessperson who says "I want to create a facility and I want to get a permit."...

In fairness, [state environmental regulators] tend to look at technical and scientific solutions; they don't tend to look at social issues. Compound this with the fact that they have been told repeatedly by the court, by the legislatures, by their own lawyers, over the years, that they must act within the confines of the authority given to them by the Legislature.

What does that mean in the permitting context? That means that you get a permit application as the permit reviewer and you think it is a lousy permit, location, or facility, you think the owner is a lousy person, too bad. If they meet the laws, they get the permit. The other thing they have been told, in Pennsylvania particularly, land use and zoning belongs to the local municipality. Even though there are 2300 local municipalities, and trying to make any of their zoning laws match up and make any sense is difficult, it is their business. Years ago when DEP [Pennsylvania Department of Environmental Protection] tried to venture into that area and make decisions based on what they thought was wise land use, they were slapped down rather significantly by the Commonwealth Court....

Now, what happens next? Guess who brings the environmental justice issue to them? Their favorite agency in the federal government, the EPA. EPA says, "remember those [Title VI] regulations we have had around for all of those years that we never talked about and remember every year when we would give you those millions of dollars in your grant and you sign off on the form and say you are going to comply with those regulations, well, by the way, those regulations that we never mentioned and you never read and we never enforced, we just realized, that we should have been paying attention to those and you guys have to start paying attention to those too."...

What does that mean more realistically? Well, what it means is if I am thinking about raising an environmental justice claim, I am not going to go to EPA where there has been one environmental justice decision and it appears to say something environmental justice advocates do not like. I am going to go to court and seek my relief there.

So where does that all leave the permit applicant? You might understandably think that they are confused. Are you going to file an application and are you going to run the risk of making the state make a decision which will get it accused of being discriminatory or get it pressured by EPA and face a threat of loss of funds? Maybe ... you are going to get sued by citizens who are opposed to the facility. All right, that is one side. What is the other side of the equation[?] What is the state's authority to deny my permit on environmental justice grounds? I don't know. It has not been decided, there is nothing out there. You can't go to the DEP's regulations and find the environmental justice section. Okay, you want to do the right thing. What are the standards? How do you satisfy environmental justice concerns? Don't know the answer to that either. There aren't any standards. There is no guidance. There is EPA internal guidance, which may give you some help but a limited amount.

So, what do you do? What you do has been the biggest success to date of the environmental justice movement[.] That is that if you are a savvy applicant you recognize that all of these uncertainties make it difficult for the agency to act and your job is to make it easier for the agency to act. And how do you do that? You have more, not less, public outreach, public visibility, involvement with the community. You show up at DEP public meetings. You explain your application and your facility, not in acronyms and formulas and coefficients and calculations, but in ways that people can understand. You try to find out what are the real concerns of the community. Maybe their real concern is that they hate your facility and you are not going to be able to do anything about that. But maybe their real concern is that you are going to bring twenty trucks a day through their neighborhood and they don't like that. Maybe you have the ability to build another road a different way to get into your facility. Maybe their concerns are just more quality of life concerns and you have some ability to make some contribution to the community. Those aren't legal requirements, those aren't guidelines or rules, but they are a way to get around the uncertainty to try to get your permit to move forward....

What else are you seeing? Well, states are recognizing, as I indicated, that public participation has to be improved. Agencies, like DEP, have looked at public notice and public involvement very mechanistically and very rigidly. I used to say when I was at DEP that we could hold a public hearing, get three inflatable dolls, put them behind a podium, and the hearing could go on anyway because we never responded to everything. People got up and they railed about everything under the sun and we never said anything except for 'thank you for your comments.' It was the stupidest way to have a public hearing that there ever was. The [Southeast Regional Office of DEP] has pioneered efforts to have open house type public meetings where people can come and actually get answers and actually find out information and actually understand what these projects are all about. Again, the states are going to do that, the states are going to make applicants do that, applicants that have a brain are going to do it themselves....

I want to end on what I see as kind of the most significant potential impact down the road for the environmental justice movement, at least as it is played out in Pennsylvania. That is, I think, when the dust clears we are going to see that this was not a civil rights movement at all but an environmental movement. And the reason that I say that is because, and again at least as it is played out in Pennsylvania, environmental justice has focused on where facilities are located, how many of them are located there, what sorts of fringe environmental impacts have they had. If you applied the *Select Steel* logic [a high profile Title VI administrative claim rejected by EPA and excerpted in Chapter 14. Eds.] to the facilities in Chester [Pennsylvania, a community with a disproportionate concentration of polluting facilities], they would all pass. But the facilities in Chester had impacts on traffic, noise, light pollution, odors, stigma, quality of life issues. The question is, is that something that an environmental agency should look at? Frankly, DEP's authority and their enthusiasm for regulating nuisance type impacts is questionable. If you looked at some regional enforcement statistics, you would find that malodors are the biggest complaints that the agency responds to. Again, a nuisance type impact. What is possible is that this whole movement will cause a refocusing and a reexamination of how environmental controls and traditional land use controls should work together and what ... environmental agencies [sic] roles should be. Now, DEP is never going to get the authority to say "you have to put the facility right here." But maybe they will get the authority to say, maybe they already have the authority to say, "you can't put this facility here even though it complies with local zoning because it is going to have an inappropriate impact on the community." A lot of people talk about cumulative impacts. When they talk about that, they talk about air emissions, cancer risks and all that stuff we haven't gotten there yet scientifically. But how about cumulative nuisance impacts? They are a lot easier to analyze. Maybe more subjective but a lot easier to analyze....

* * *

Notes and Questions

1. Mr. Bossert's article describes responses that are often voiced by state permitting agencies to environmental justice issues—that siting decisions are local land use and zoning matters, and that cumulative impacts and non-environmental impacts are problems beyond their authority to address. What do you think of Bossert's advice to permitting applicants and permitting agencies? Does it make sense from a business perspective? Former developers' lawyer and now Professor Michael Gerrard stresses involvement of the community at an early (pre-application) stage:

> At this early stage, a little bit of community opposition can go a long way. If the sponsor has several different options for where to site the project, protests in one community and silence in another may point to the path of least resistance. If it is the type of project that a community might accept if it were modified in certain ways, at this preliminary stage modifications are often rather easy, before heavy investments have been made in design and engineering.

Michael B. Gerrard, *Stopping and Building New Facilities, in* THE LAW OF ENVIRONMENTAL JUSTICE 511 (Michael B. Gerrard & Sheila R. Foster eds., 2d ed. 2008).

2. Consider, as one example, a framework analogous to that used by the Army Corps of Engineers for protecting wetlands—environmentally sensitive areas that are rapidly declining. Under the Clean Water Act, the permitting authority determines if there is a practicable alternative to placing fill material in a wetland. If an alternative site is available, the permit is denied without further inquiry into the suitability of the proposed site. *See* 40 C.F.R. § 230.10. What do you think of this approach? Would this approach be workable in the context of environmentally stressed areas? What problem do you foresee in using such an approach?

3. As mentioned earlier in this chapter, community residents often base their opposition to a new or expanded facility in part upon a claim that the facility sponsor has a history of not complying with permit terms. In other words, from the community's perspective, permitting and enforcement are fundamentally connected and should be considered together. Permit officials often reply that in a permit proceeding they are obligated to assume that the permit applicant will comply with all the permit requirements. Is this assumption sound? As you read the following section on public enforce-

ment, consider whether public enforcement is adequate. If not, what enforcement approaches might be more effective?

B. Enforcement of Environmental Pollution Control Laws by Public Officials

1. Introduction

Enforcement is a sometimes overlooked aspect of environmental regulation, since it is carried out quietly by federal and state agencies, removed from the public spotlight. But adequate enforcement is critical to achieving the objectives of our environmental laws, particularly in environmental justice communities where so many polluting facilities are located.

As described more fully in Chapter 2, a 1992 study by the National Law Journal (NLJ) found that penalties imposed by EPA for violations of federal environmental laws were substantially lower in minority communities than in white communities. The effect of a community's income on penalties was more ambiguous. The NLJ study also found racial disparities in EPA's response to contaminated waste sites — abandoned waste sites took longer to be placed on the national priorities list than those in white areas and EPA chose less protective cleanup remedies more often at minority sites. The study found similar, but less pronounced, gaps between poor and wealthy communities.

The NLJ study had a powerful impact in environmental justice communities, as well as with policymakers. First, it reinforced widespread anecdotal evidence of unequal enforcement. *See* Robert Kuehn, *Remedying the Unequal Enforcement of Environmental Laws*, 9 St. John's J. Legal Comment. 625, 633–634 (1994). More fundamentally, the NLJ study resonated with deeply held beliefs in minority communities that laws are enforced unfairly against them, concerns highlighted by racial profiling, bias in the administration of the death penalty, and other law enforcement practices beyond the environmental law context.

Even assuming neutral criteria is applied even-handedly in enforcement decisions such as where to inspect, where to allocate resources, what level of fines to impose, and so forth, environmental justice communities are likely to bear greater burdens simply because more polluting facilities are located in their midst than elsewhere, which means they disproportionately experience the impacts of noncompliance. Considerable evidence exists showing that rates of noncompliance among regulated entities are quite substantial. For example, a 2003 nationwide analysis by EPA found that approximately 25% of major facilities were in significant noncompliance with their Clean Water Act permits at any given time. It noted that rates of significant noncompliance had effectively remained steady since 1994. U.S. EPA, Office of Enforcement & Compliance Assurance, A Pilot for Performance Analysis of Selected Components of the National Enforcement and Compliance Assurance Program (2003).

2. Sources of Disparate Enforcement

The excerpt below by Professor Robert Kuehn examines some factors that may contribute to disparate enforcement by environmental agencies.

Robert R. Kuehn, Remedying the Unequal Enforcement of Environmental Laws

9 St. John's Journal of Legal Commentary 625 (1994)

Noncompliance with environmental laws is widespread.... The effects of noncompliance can be serious. Unauthorized releases of toxic chemicals may pose acute health hazards to those living in the vicinity of the facility. Moreover, if permits and pollution standards are carefully set at levels that provide an adequate margin of safety, and if noncompliance results in greater amounts of pollution being emitted than calculated by the agency in making its determination, then the surrounding community may not, in fact, be provided the protection required by the law or assumed by the agency. In addition, the failure to enforce means that an accurate history of noncompliance, and an accurate portrayal of the status of the facility and its operator, will not be available to the agency or the public in subsequent permit or enforcement proceedings....

Even if the empirical data of unequal enforcement of environmental laws is scarce and open to criticism, the conditions that could give rise to discriminatory enforcement are present. The causes of unequal enforcement are likely to be the same structural causes that have been blamed for the general unequal distribution of environmental hazards among minorities and low income communities. Racist attitudes, lack of economic and political clout, and lack of participation in government decisionmaking all play a causal role. "To be sure, poor minority communities face some fairly high barriers to effective mobilization against toxic threats, such as limited time and money; lack of access to technical, medical or legal expertise; relatively weak influence in political or media circles; and cultural and ideological indifference or hostility to environmental issues."

In fact, the conditions that give rise to the discriminatory impact of environmental hazards may be even greater when the government acts as enforcer, since few areas of the law invest more discretion in agency employees or are more hidden from the public's view and oversight than an agency's enforcement actions. The initial decision about which facilities to inspect and how often to check for violations is generally left to the discretion of the agency, although some statutes do provide for annual or biannual inspections. Once the agency gets notice of a violation, it can choose to take an informal response, such as a phone call, site visit, warning letter or notice of violations; an administrative remedy, such as an administrative penalty assessment or compliance order; a judicial action for penalties or injunctive relief; or a criminal prosecution. The process for cleaning up waste sites, and the decisions regarding which, when, and how, provide similar opportunities for the exercise of discretion.

* * *

Notes and Questions

1. In addition to the discretionary nature of enforcement decisions, consider also that the EPA and the states lack sufficient staff to inspect more than a fraction of regulated

facilities or the resources to pursue more than a small percentage of violations (by one 1996 estimate, at least 700,000 facilities are subject to one or more federal environmental laws, while government agencies combined conduct fewer than 100,000 inspections per year). Under many environmental laws, EPA and the states have great latitude in choosing whether to prosecute a violation administratively, civilly, or criminally, or not at all. The Supreme Court has ruled that agency decisions about whether to initiate enforcement actions are generally not subject to judicial review. *See* Heckler v. Chaney, 470 U.S. 821 (1985). When determining penalties in the approximately 95 percent of civil and administrative cases that settle before trial, EPA staff are instructed to follow agency penalty policies, but these also leave substantial room for judgment calls, such as determining the potential harm from noncompliance, a company's good faith efforts to remedy the violation, a violator's culpability, its ability to pay, and other mitigating circumstances. *See, e.g.,* U.S. EPA, *Policy on Civil Penalties*, 17 ENVTL. L. REP. 35,083 (1984).

2. According to EPA, the purposes of imposing penalties are to recover the economic benefit derived by noncompliance, to specifically deter the violator, and to generally deter the larger regulated community from future noncompliance. As Professor Kuehn points out, a stated goal of EPA's penalty policies is the fair and equitable treatment of regulated entities. Do you agree with him that EPA should also include as a goal that enforcement policies should not discriminate against any communities? If so, what are the practical impediments in implementing such a policy?

3. The State Trend Away From Enforcement. The National Law Journal study described above focused on enforcement actions carried out by EPA. The states, however, rather than EPA, administer 75% of major federal environmental programs, and carry out 80–90% of inspections and enforcement actions in the country. As the following excerpt explains, the states have significantly changed their enforcement philosophy and practices in recent years.

Clifford Rechtschaffen, Competing Visions: EPA and the States Battle for the Future of Environmental Enforcement
30 Environmental Law Reporter 10,803 (2000)

Deterrence-Based Enforcement

Deterrence-based enforcement is the approach that Americans are most familiar with; it is the prevailing societal strategy for regulating unlawful conduct. The deterrence model is premised on the idea that regulated entities are rational economic actors that act to maximize profits. Decisions regarding compliance are based on self-interest; businesses comply where the costs of noncompliance outweigh the benefits of noncompliance. The benefits of noncompliance with environmental regulations consist of money saved by not purchasing pollution control equipment, training workers, abating contamination, or taking other required measures. The costs of noncompliance include the costs of coming into compliance once a violation is detected, plus any penalties imposed for being found in violation, multiplied (discounted) by the probability that the violations will be detected. These costs can also include damage to the business' reputation, potential tort liability, legal system expenses, and increased regulatory scrutiny.... Under a deterrence model, the essential task for enforcement agencies is to make penalties high enough and the probability of detection great enough that it becomes economically irrational for regulated entities to violate the law....

Cooperation-Based Enforcement

A cooperation-based system of enforcement is premised on a different set of assumptions about why individuals and corporations comply with the law. It views corporations not as economic actors solely interested in maximizing profits, but as influenced by a mix of civic and social motives, and generally inclined to comply with the law. Therefore, if corporations are found in violation of regulatory requirements, they should be treated like partners, and they will respond positively to suggestions and advice about how to achieve compliance.... Generally speaking, a cooperation-based system emphasizes securing compliance rather than punishing wrongdoing. It disfavors legalistic responses.... Penalties are seen as threats rather than sanctions, and are typically withdrawn if compliance is achieved....

The State Approach to Environmental Enforcement

While there are significant differences among individual states ... [g]enerally speaking, the states advocate a more cooperation-based enforcement strategy.... Many states argue that the appropriate response to noncompliance in almost all cases is working with violators to achieve compliance, rather than initiating enforcement actions....

States start from the premise that education and technical assistance is the preferred tool for achieving compliance.... Thus, over the past 5 to10 years the states have sought to develop and expand compliance assistance programs, particularly programs aimed at small businesses. These include workshops, newsletters, fact sheets, web page information, technical assistance visits, and "plain-English" guides explaining regulatory requirements....

At the same time that states have expanded compliance assistance programs, they have cut back on the use of deterrence-based tools—traditional inspections, administrative and civil enforcement actions, and penalties.... [A] series of audits by EPA's Inspector General and the [General Accounting Office, subsequently renamed the Government Accountability Office] in the late 1990s found that states were not carrying out the monitoring and inspection activities required by EPA policy.... [I]n many instances, actions taken by the states are not "timely and appropriate"—characteristics which, according to deterrence theory described above, are necessary to deter future violations....

Many states also have chosen to de-emphasize penalties as a means of securing compliance. Several have adopted amnesty programs that expressly prohibit sanctions for minor violations.... Beyond these initiatives, many states have stopped imposing penalties on violators, including significant violators, or now impose only very limited fines. (Some states never assessed large penalties in the first place.) ... When penalties are imposed, according to a host of studies, they frequently are inconsistent with EPA's penalty policies. Many states fail to recover economic benefit when assessing penalties—a core element of deterrence theory designed to ensure that companies do not gain from noncompliance and that there is a level playing field among regulated entities....

A central element of the states' enforcement approach is greater reliance on industry self-policing and self-regulation, particularly voluntary audits. An environmental audit is a systematic review of a facility's compliance with environmental requirements.... As companies began auditing more regularly [in the 1980s], they began lobbying the states for audit privilege and immunity provisions, arguing that without such protections firms would forego audits because of fear that the information discovered would be used against them in enforcement actions or tort lawsuits.... The privilege measures generally bar the use of audit documents as evidence in litigation over compliance with environmental laws, and otherwise allow them to be withheld from public or governmental disclosure.... The immunity laws protect companies from sanctions for environmental violations if the violations are discovered pursuant to the audit, voluntarily reported, and corrected within a certain time....

Research on Cooperative Strategies

... Despite the widespread calls for moving away from a deterrence-based enforcement, there is relatively little data to support the argument that cooperation works better to achieve compliance with environmental law....

A few studies indicate improvements in compliance rates after cooperative strategies were substituted for traditional practices.... We are also starting to see some data analyzing the effectiveness of compliance assistance programs being implemented by the states and EPA. For instance, in a 1998 survey of state hazardous waste officials, several states reported demonstrable improvements from various compliance assistance or other alternative enforcement activities....

There are only a handful of studies directly comparing the effectiveness of deterrence and cooperative-oriented strategies. A study by Kathryn Harrison of the pulp and paper industries in the United States and Canada, where enforcement has been more aligned with the cooperative school, found that rates of compliance with effluent limitations in Canada are significantly lower than in the United States.... Raymond Burby has conducted two studies comparing enforcement approaches. In his review of the nonpoint source control programs in 20 states, he found that the degree of coercion that programs apply to the private sector and to local governments is the critical element in explaining the program's effectiveness.... Cooperative approaches were less effective than deterrence, particularly those that relied on building capacity and public awareness without providing technical assistance to regulated entities....

We have considerably more research examining the impacts of traditional enforcement activities [although] this data is relatively limited.... Thus, a series of studies of the pulp and paper industry in both the United States and Canada show that increased levels of traditional enforcement activity — including inspections, the threat of inspections, timely and appropriate enforcement responses, or other enforcement actions — tends to increase the rate of industry compliance.... Conversely, we have considerable evidence showing that the absence of deterrence-based enforcement, that is, the absence of a threat of meaningful sanctions, often translates into noncompliance....

The Theoretical Bases for Rejecting Deterrence-Based Models

... Critics [of deterrence-based enforcement] dispute the view of corporations as driven only by economic factors, and contend that corporate actors are instead motivated by a variety of social, civic, and other considerations. Some argue that corporations conceive of themselves as political citizens, who are ordinarily inclined to comply with the law, partially because of their belief in the law, and partially as a matter of their long-term self-interest.

The critics of deterrence-based enforcement are correct to reject an economically deterministic model as the only explanation for voluntary compliance.... But bottom-line profitability still matters a great deal in industry choices about compliance, and often overcomes even good-faith efforts to comply.... Likewise, a number of observers have noted that environmental programs often hit a "green wall," a point at which an organization refuses to move forward with its strategic environmental management program. The lack of progress results from an uneasy fit of environmental management with traditional business functions and traditional business culture. Environmental management programs still are largely judged on their ability to make money for the company rather than their intrinsic merits.

Moreover, many critics understate the role that ideological resistance to regulation plays in undermining compliance. Absent deterrence, corporate actors are far more likely to adhere to laws that in their eyes are legitimate, particularly when compliance is expensive.... There is no question that many businesses remain philosophically opposed to some substantial portion of the current regime of environmental regulation, and indeed, consider it illegitimate....

Internal Regulatory Systems

Commentators also argue that traditional enforcement approaches should be modified because many corporations have adopted extensive internal regulatory programs and effectively police themselves. Self-regulation can take a number of forms, ranging from relatively simple procedures for regularly monitoring for compliance, to sophisticated internal programs [such as environmental management systems, or EMSs] or codes of conduct that some observers contend are more comprehensive and more effective than government enforcement efforts....

[T]here is little hard data demonstrating the degree to which these self-policing policies, in particular EMS and codes of conduct, have actually enhanced compliance.... At least a couple of studies have found that use of an EMS does not necessarily lead to better environmental performance. [Additionally], many firms—certainly the great majority of regulated entities—cannot afford environmental audits or management systems and do not have sophisticated internal regulatory programs.... Finally, and perhaps most fundamentally, the growth in self-policing by companies is directly linked to strong governmental enforcement; without such enforcement, the incentives for companies to spend money on internal compliance programs is greatly reduced. Thus, EPA has concluded that its strong enforcement efforts have played a major role in the growth of environmental auditing in recent years....

* * *

Notes and Questions

1. If you were a member of a low-income community or community of color concerned about disparate environmental impacts in your neighborhood, would you prefer to have environmental agencies use a "carrots" or a "sticks" approach to enforcement? Would you favor the use of sanctions in response to noncompliance or greater emphasis on counseling and providing technical assistance to facilities to achieve compliance?

2. Most federal environmental statutes allow states and tribes to implement federal statutes under EPA oversight. Most states have received authority to implement the bulk of the major federal programs; some tribes also have received such authority. In recent years, states in particular have been pushing for less stringent federal oversight in order to pursue their preferred approach to enforcement and other regulatory programs. States argue that, as compared with EPA, they are more flexible, more innovative, have more interaction with regulated entities, and are more responsive to local conditions and priorities. Environmental groups counter that states are more susceptible to industry capture and that absent federal controls states will engage in a "race to the bottom" to attract industry by lowering environmental standards. They also cite evidence in some states of significant rates of noncompliance with environmental requirements and cutbacks in state enforcement activity and spending. In your view, what degree of state autonomy/federal oversight is desirable? Are states more or less likely than the EPA to deal with concerns about inequitable enforcement and disparate impacts in environmental justice communities? Do we need a federal enforcement "gorilla in the closet" to ensure adequate state enforcement?

3. Perhaps the clearest difference between EPA and state enforcement practices is the level of penalties obtained. In one empirical study, Professor Mark Atlas found that state hazardous waste penalties were consistently lower than those imposed by the regional EPA office in which the state is located. For instance, controlling for various characteristics about the nature of enforcement actions, he found that state penalties are about half of what EPA would impose in similar circumstances. Professor Mark Atlas, Separate But Equal?: An Empirical Comparison of State Versus Federal Environmental Enforcement Stringency, Address Before the Association for Public Policy Analysis and Management Annual Research Conference (Nov. 2, 2000). Other studies have reached similar conclusions, and additionally have found that penalties vary widely among states (studies also have found wide variations in per capita spending by states on environmental protection). Whether these differences are problematic and whether significant penalties are necessary to deter violations and promote compliance depends upon one's perspective. Many states argue that significant penalties are unnecessary to prompt compliance by most businesses, which in their view are generally inclined to obey the law, while EPA maintains that adequate penalties play a key role in deterring violators. From the perspective of impacted communities, even more may be at stake from the penalty disparities. In recent years, environmental agencies increasingly have been willing to reduce penalties that they would otherwise assess in exchange for environmentally beneficial projects, including ones that decrease pollution and directly benefit impacted communities (such Supplemental Environmental Projects, or SEPs, are discussed below). Thus, lower state penalty assessments may in the end mean less money funneled to local communities for mitigation, community education, and pollution prevention.

3. Strengthening Public Enforcement in Environmental Justice Communities

The NLJ investigation and other similar evidence led EPA (and other federal agencies) to rethink aspects of their enforcement policies. As discussed in Chapter 10, President Clinton issued an executive order on environmental justice in 1994, requiring all federal agencies to promote enforcement of health and environmental statutes in areas with minority populations and low-income populations. In 1995 EPA issued its Environmental Justice Strategy, indicating that it would use its enforcement discretion to focus on environmental justice issues raised by violations in communities disproportionately harmed by environmental pollution. Other EPA enforcement policies discuss prioritizing efforts in impacted communities. *See, e.g.*, U.S. EPA, GUIDANCE ON USE OF SECTION 7003 OF RCRA (1997) ("When prioritizing actions to be taken under Section 7003 ... the Regions should give particular consideration to sites and facilities that pose environmental justice concerns, such as those involving risk aggregation."). But some observers have questioned whether EPA actually has increased its enforcement efforts in these areas. *See* Denis Binder et al., *A Survey of Federal Agency Response to President Clinton's Executive Order No. 12,898 on Environmental Justice*, 31 ENVTL. L. REP. 11,133, 11,142 (2001). More recently, EPA has developed a screening approach called "EJSEAT" for identifying disproportionately impacted communities in which its compliance and enforcement efforts, including inspections, can be targeted. This approach is more fully explained below.

Numerous state statutes and policies also seek to enhance enforcement in low-income and minority communities heavily impacted by pollution sources. The Massachusetts Environmental Justice Policy, for example, provides that the state environmental agency shall prioritize minority and low-income neighborhoods "when selecting facilities for inspection and monitoring, prosecuting noncompliance, providing compliance assistance, and allocating resources." MASSACHUSETTS ENVIRONMENTAL JUSTICE POLICY OF THE EXECUTIVE OFFICE OF ENVIRONMENTAL AFFAIRS 9 (Oct. 17, 2002). Likewise, the New Jersey Department of Environmental Protection has initiated a program of "enforcement strikes" in which multi-media enforcement teams are sent into heavily impacted neighborhoods to conduct broad-based inspections and force compliance and clean up. *See* PUB. LAW RESEARCH INST., UC HASTINGS COLLEGE OF THE LAW & AM. BAR ASS'N, ENVIRONMENTAL JUSTICE FOR ALL: A FIFTY-STATE SURVEY OF LEGISLATION, POLICIES AND CASES 65 (2007). California law more broadly requires the state Environmental Protection Agency to achieve the fair treatment of people of all races, cultures, and incomes with respect to the enforcement of environmental laws. *See* CAL. PUB. RES. CODE § 71110(b); CAL. GOV'T CODE § 65040.12(e).

What other ways might government enforcement efforts better address issues of noncompliance in low income communities and communities of color? The responses fall into three broad categories. The first involves using penalties, either enhanced penalties or penalty return (to the community). Another response involves using "supplemental environmental projects" in lieu of penalties to not only address noncompliance, but to effectuate broader more protective environmental justice goals. The third response involves ways to target enforcement resources to promote more strict enforcement in highly impacted communities.

a. Enhanced Penalties and Penalty Return

Most environmental statutes provide that in determining penalties, a court or EPA shall consider, in addition to specific factors, "such other factors as justice may require." *See, e.g.*, Clean Air Act § 113(e)(1), 42 U.S.C. § 7413. Should EPA and states seek enhanced penalties against facilities in environmental justice communities to deter future violations? Professors Richard Lazarus and Stephanie Tai suggest that such higher penalties may be justified because of inadequate past government enforcement in these areas and the lack of community resources to oversee facilities' ongoing compliance. *See* Richard J. Lazarus & Stephanie Tai, *Integrating Environmental Justice into EPA Permitting Authority*, 26 ECOLOGY L. Q. 617, 637 (1999). In addition to historically inadequate enforcement, are higher penalties also justified because of the enhanced cumulative risks facing community residents? Or do such increased fines unfairly penalize individual facilities for a problem caused by multiple entities? How do you evaluate this suggestion in light of the debate about the relative effectiveness of deterrence-oriented versus cooperation-oriented enforcement strategies discussed above? Another idea—that of penalty return—is discussed in the following excerpt.

Alex Geisinger, Rethinking Environmental Justice Regulation: A Modest Proposal for Penalty Return
55 Syracuse Law Review 33 (2004)

Numerous studies have shown that minorities disproportionately bear the burden of pollution. The redistribution of penalty money away from those who bear the risk is a further manifestation of this environmental injustice.

… Current environmental justice regulation focuses on decreasing the risks borne by such communities. These burden-reducing schemes are ineffective as a means of dealing with the problems of environmental injustice because of both political and economic ob-stacles to their implementation. A scheme of penalty return responds to a number of the major concerns of environmental justice while not falling prey to the economic and po-litical obstacles currently confronting burden-reducing schemes....

[T]he remedy of penalty return would require that all or a portion of penalties paid for violation of environmental standards be returned to a disparately impacted commu-nity affected by the fined facility's emissions ...

As a general rule, when a penalty for violating environmental laws is paid, the money collected is put into the general treasury of either the United States or the state under whose law the violation was prosecuted. Some states use the penalty money they receive to fund the state's environmental programs. Interestingly, the current distribution of penalty money is itself a further manifestation of environmental injustice. Take, for ex-ample, a minority community that is subject to high levels of environmental contamination from permitted sources. Assume that one of the sources exceeds its permitted standards and thus further increases the level of ambient contamination. The increased health risk from this source will be borne generally by the nearby community, yet the fine paid by the polluter will not be received in any proportional amount by the affected community. Instead, the money paid will go to a general fund where it will be distributed for the ben-efit of all communities within the state or federal government. Similarly, when penalty money is used to fund environmental protection, that money too is not directed back to the com-munity that bore the majority of the harm in any proportional amount. Instead, the money is used to support a program created to regulate pollution throughout the entire state. Indeed, to the extent minority communities do not receive the same amount of en-forcement resources, the benefit will not even be received in proportion to the rest of the state or country.

A scheme of penalty return would rectify this inequity. Under such a scheme the penalty money paid by a polluter would be returned to the community that bore the risk created by the violation to be used for the community's benefit. There are a number of analogs to a penalty return scheme that already exist in the law.... [For example, in] some cases parties can use a supplemental environmental project ("SEP") to return some benefit back to the area harmed by their violations. A SEP is a voluntary project created to rem-edy an environmental or public health problem related to the violation [SEPs are dis-cussed below. Eds]....

At least two states have also made provision for returning penalties to local commu-nities in certain circumstances. The North Carolina Constitution, for example, states that "... the clear proceeds of all penalties and forfeitures and of all fines collected in the sev-eral counties ... shall belong to and remain in the several counties, and shall be faithfully appropriated and used exclusively for maintaining free public schools." In California, half the penalties received for violation of certain non-vehicular air pollution controls are paid to the treasurer of the district on whose behalf judgment was entered, while the other half goes to the State Treasury.... Thus, at least two states ensure that some penalty money is returned to those who are harmed by the violation.

The two aforementioned schemes ... represent a choice for cheap administrative costs at the expense of ensuring that those harmed by a violation receive the penalty money paid. A simple scheme such as one that requires penalty money to be paid to a county trea-sury combines very low administrative costs with a scheme that does only rough justice. As a general matter, counties encompass many more communities than the minority communities that are being impacted by a polluter. Thus, return to the county will benefit a much larger number of individuals than those who have been most directly harmed by the pollution. In such cases, it is arguably better to return money to a municipality instead of the county, however, given the possibility that more than one municipality may bear a substantial portion of the risk, even this type of simple scheme might create too little "justice" in some cases.

Obviously, the more effort that is made to ensure that penalty money goes to those harmed, the more costs that will be borne by a system of penalty return. A system designed to ensure that penalty money is returned more directly to those who bear the harms caused by pollution will often encounter difficult and potentially resource-depleting decisions. The costs of determining who was harmed by pollution might be extremely high in some cases. For example, as compared to a plume of contamination in groundwater, where contamination boundaries are somewhat well-defined, it can be very difficult to determine who has been exposed to air pollution where no real boundary of contamination exists. In communities with many sources, it will be virtually impossible to determine exactly which permitted source a pollutant comes from....

Another factor that would have to be considered in designing such a penalty return scheme would be whether penalty money should be treated as an addition, or as an offset, to taxes. On the one hand, penalty payments are not regular and thus, efforts to plan municipal budgets based on potential penalty payments would be difficult. Similarly, to the extent that only certain individuals or parts of a community were harmed by a violation, offsetting the taxes of all community members would, again, sacrifice justice for administrative efficiency. Thus, offsetting taxes would be an imperfect scheme in a number of situations.

On the other hand, it could be argued that offsetting municipal taxes with penalty money is the best solution. First, assuming individuals are in the best position to determine what use of penalty money would most benefit them, returning money to the individual through a decrease in taxes would provide the most benefit from the penalty payment. Tax-offset schemes may also have certain less obvious effects. In particular, the direct benefit to individuals established by such a scheme would enable community members to overcome standing issues that bar a number of environmental citizen suits. [Standing and citizen suits are discussed in Chapter 13. Eds.] In cases where violations of environmental laws are wholly past and not continuing, it has been held that citizens lack standing to bring a citizen suit because there is no "present or threatened injury" and hence, none of the relief sought by the respondent would likely remedy its alleged injury in fact. The ability to recover monetary payments for the violation cures this defect. If individuals were entitled to monetary payment, such payment would provide the kind of personal interest in litigation that would overcome this problem. A scheme of penalty return conjoined with tax-offset could thus actually energize a community to police polluters by decreasing the traditional obstacles behind citizen enforcement of environmental laws....

A scheme of penalty return will also help counter the market conditions that may exacerbate problems of environmental injustice. As discussed previously, the current burden-reduction scheme does little to counter the market phenomenon that may play a role in the creation of some environmental injustice. The use of penalty money for community benefit, whether to create lower taxes, to add to school quality, or to add other municipal amenities, would counterbalance the existing forces that lead to dissatisfaction with the community and property devaluation. In sum, a scheme of penalty return would provide a useful compliment [sic] to efforts to decrease the burden of pollution borne by minorities. A penalty return regulatory scheme would at least provide some redress to those who disproportionately bear the risks of environmental toxins, while also helping to counter some of the broader causes of environmental injustice....

* * *

Notes and Questions

1. What do you think of the penalty return approach? By channeling penalty money to the local community rather than to the general state or federal fund, could it discourage government enforcers from bringing actions (consider that in some states environmental penalties are used to help directly fund environmental programs)? On the other hand, might it create an incentive for citizen enforcers (where they have authority to sue) to bring marginal actions in order to recover penalties that will be used to fund municipal programs?

b. Supplemental Environmental Projects

As noted by Professor Geisinger, penalties awarded under environmental statutes typically go into the U.S. Treasury or a state's general fund, not directly to individuals impacted by a facility's noncompliance. As an alternative, EPA's Supplemental Environmental Projects Policy allows violators to reduce penalties in exchange for undertaking environmentally beneficial projects such as pollution prevention or pollution reduction projects, or projects to remedy harms to health caused by a violation. Such projects can include establishment of community health centers, monitoring of environmental or health conditions, establishment of alternative water supply systems, reduction of emissions beyond required levels, and so forth. EPA's policy specifically encourages SEPs in communities where environmental justice may be an issue: "Emphasizing SEPs in communities where environmental justice concerns are present helps ensure that persons who spend significant portions of their time in areas, or depend on food and water sources located near, where the violations occur would be protected." Final Supplemental Environmental Projects Policy Notice, 63 Fed. Reg. 24,796, 24,797 (May 5, 1998).

Many states also have SEP policies. A report canvassing SEPs throughout the fifty states summarizes its findings, and also notes the potential promise and pitfalls of SEPs:

> The results of this fifty state survey show that twenty-eight states and the District of Columbia have instituted formal, published SEP policies in the form of legislation, executive agency regulation or guidelines. Nine states with formal policies also enjoy some form of statutory authorization for their use of SEPs. Only twenty-one states rely on internal, unpublished policies or informal practices, although within the past year two states have taken steps towards formalizing their SEP policies. The figure of twenty-eight states and the District of Columbia with formal policies and/or laws represents a significant increase over the past ten years, up from nineteen states with formal policies or statutes and thirteen others informally negotiating SEPs, as shown in the only prior survey of state SEP practices. Two states, North Carolina and South Carolina, have rejected the use of SEPs outright as a matter of policy or law....

> SEPs represent a real and practicable opportunity to provide significant benefits to all the stakeholders in the environment: the environment itself, affected communities, the regulated industry, and the regulators. By funding environmentally beneficial projects, violators can help improve and protect the envi-

ronment, whereas the traditional fine paid for environmental violations is simply absorbed into the federal or state treasury. Accordingly, SEPs benefit the environment directly, protecting the common interest in a clean and healthy environment beyond what may be achieved through penalties. In addition, violators and regulators can benefit from SEPs that carry patent environmental benefits by improving environmental quality and repairing public image and relationships that may have been damaged as a result of the environmental violation.

However, SEPs also present potential pitfalls. Foremost, this report argues against leaving the negotiation of SEPs to the unfettered discretion of enforcement personnel and suggests that states without formal guidelines look to other states as examples. SEPs uninformed by guidelines may be insufficiently transparent and open, leading to inequities for both violators and affected communities. Community groups may perceive unstructured negotiations as softening enforcement penalties, undermining the effectiveness of environmental regulation, and resulting in SEPs that fail to address environmental justice (that is, the fair distribution of environmental benefits and risks).

PUB. LAW RESEARCH INST., UC HASTINGS COLLEGE OF THE LAW & AM. BAR ASS'N, SUPPLEMENTAL ENVIRONMENTAL PROJECTS: A FIFTY STATE SURVEY WITH MODEL PRACTICES 14–15 (Steven Bonorris ed., 2007).

In 2007, the National Policy Consensus Center (NPCC) hosted a colloquium on SEPs that included representatives from environmental justice communities and other stakeholders to explore how collaborative approaches involving affected communities create economic, environmental and social benefits through leveraging SEPs with other investments and resources. Participants stressed that information is the key to a transparent and inclusive SEP process, particularly a collaborative SEP with the potential for community involvement and investment, and that increased public accessibility to SEP information—including project identification—is a prerequisite for a community-based collaborative SEP. The participants came up with five key conclusions and recommendations:

   • SEPs are underutilized generally; US EPA and states should examine how to expand opportunities for SEPs, especially where there may be enhanced benefits for the affected community.

   • Collaborative governance processes can lead to greater community benefits by leveraging SEPs with other investments, actions, and commitments.

   • US EPA and states should consider (1) undertaking pilot collaborative SEPs to determine violator and community interest and (2) developing appropriate "best practices" for each state based on a collaborative governance process such as the Public Solutions model developed by NPCC.

   • Agencies should consider developing publicly accessible SEP libraries, idea banks, and fund banks to expand the opportunities for SEPs and make the process more efficient, transparent, and accessible.

   • Agencies could benefit by examining SEP policies and practices, enhancing opportunities for collaborative SEPs and incorporating "best practices" for them.

NAT'L POLICY CONSENSUS CTR., ENVIRONMENTAL ENFORCEMENT SOLUTIONS: HOW COLLABORATIVE SEPs ENHANCE COMMUNITY BENEFITS (2007).

Notes and Questions

1. Is the SEP approach good or bad for environmental justice communities? Why? What would be some of the incentives and disincentives involved in pursuing SEPs for violations in heavily impacted communities? Some community groups have argued that they lack the expertise to meaningfully participate in the SEP approval and implementation process. Some also believe that prosecuting enforcement actions to their conclusion, rather than settling with violators in exchange for SEPs, may be desirable to guard against unduly favorable treatment for regulated entities. The NPCC report addresses in part the first concern. What about the second? In addition to SEPs, there are other more direct means of shifting resources to the benefit of communities impacted by the violations. But there are complications, discussed below.

c. Targeting Enforcement Resources

How should an agency's enforcement resources be targeted? Should agencies devote more resources to communities in which there is a disproportionate share of polluting facilities? Should community residents be given a role in suggesting sites or industries to target for inspection? One study found that the per-capita income of communities surrounding pulp and paper mills influenced the likelihood of an inspection, with plants in more affluent communities more likely to be inspected (the study also found that the level of pollution in the surrounding community, weighted by population, increased the probability of inspection). *See* Eric Helland, *The Enforcement of Pollution Control Laws: Inspections, Violations, and Self-Reporting*, 80 REV. ECON. & STAT. 141, 152 (1998). Some scholars have suggested that facilities in heavily impacted areas should be targeted for regular inspections to counteract the tendency of some regulators to inspect in response to complaints from affected parties. Are there disadvantages to limiting the scope of agency discretion in selecting targets for inspections?

As noted earlier, the EPA is currently experimenting with a screening approach used to target enforcement resources to communities that many consider to be environmental justice communities. But this approach, termed the Environmental Justice Strategic Enforcement Assessment Tool, or "EJSEAT" is in some respect problematic to all stakeholders concerned (albeit for different reasons). How would you evaluate EJSEAT, described by the EPA as follows:

> [EJSEAT] is a tool for the EPA Office of Enforcement and Compliance Assurance (OECA) to consistently identify areas with potentially disproportionately high and adverse environmental and public health burdens. EJSEAT uses 18 select federally-recognized or managed databases and a simple algorithm to identify such areas. EJSEAT data sets are divided into the following four indicator categories: 1) environmental; 2) human health; 3) compliance; and 4) social demographics to calculate EJSEAT Scores.
>
> Environmental indicators include data about: [a] National Air Toxics Assessment (NATA) cancer risk; [b] NATA noncancer neurological and respiratory hazard index; [c] NATA noncancer diesel particulate matter (PM); [d] Toxic chemical emissions and transfers from industrial facilities, as modeled using the Risk-Screening Environmental Indicators (RSEI) tool; [e] Population weighted ozone monitoring data; [and f] Population weighted PM 2.5 monitoring data.
>
> Human health indicators include data about: [a] Percent infant mortality [, and b] Percent low birth weight births.

Compliance indicators include data about: [a] Inspections of major facilities; [b] Violations at major facilities; [c] Formal actions at major facilities; [and d] Facility density based on all facilities in EPA's facility registry system.

Social demographic indicators include data about: [a] Percent of population living in poverty; [b] Percent of population counted as minority; [c] Percent of population 25 years old and over without a high school diploma; [c] Percent of population over 65 years of age; [d] Percent of population under 5 years of age; and [e] Percent of population of limited English proficiency.

Census tracts in each state are assigned an EJSEAT score. The scores are determined by a simple mathematical algorithm using the scaled data. Data within each indicator category are ranked and then summed and averaged for each Census tract located in a state.

The final EJSEAT score for a Census tract is calculated by summing and averaging the data across the four indicator categories. The top 10 and 20 percent scoring Census tracts in a state are considered potential EJ areas of concern. Facilities listed in EPA's On-line Tracking Information System (OTIS) which are located in top scoring Census tracts (i.e., potential EJ areas of concern) are flagged in OTIS with a "1" or "2," depending on whether the Census tract ranks in the top 10 or 20 percent, respectively.

U.S. EPA, ENVIRONMENTAL JUSTICE STRATEGIC ASSESSMENT TOOL (available on the EPA's Compliance and Enforcement website).

Notes and Questions

1. Do you think that this framework adequately captures all of the impacts that might affect a vulnerable community and that should be considered in targeting enforcement resources? If you were the lawyer for a permit holder, what further information might you want to know? What if you were the lawyer for a community-based group that considers itself to be comprised of residents of an environmental justice community?

2. The Department of Justice (which represents EPA in all court proceedings) instructs its attorneys to review each case to determine if it raises potential environmental justice issues. If the case does, attorneys are directed to consider alternative dispute resolution or remedial solutions intended to directly benefit affected communities, and also are encouraged to make special efforts to encourage public participation and solicit community input. What do you think of this approach?

3. As a responsible governmental official, what strategies would you adopt to remove existing disparities from public enforcement? Of the approaches described herein, which one would you prefer? Do you think that these various approaches, working together, are likely to adequately address this problem?

Chapter 9

Contaminated Properties

A. Introduction

In addition to standard setting, permitting, enforcement, and other matters, environmental laws also address the challenge of cleaning up or remediating sites at which contamination has already occurred. Cleanup for any given site may be technically complex and often requires considerable time and resources. Cleanup at the hundreds of thousands of sites in the United States that, at present, harbor toxic contamination is a daunting task. This chapter discusses some of the environmental justice issues that arise in the context of health and environmental agencies' efforts to undertake this cleanup. The first part of this chapter provides an overview of the federal statute that governs cleanup of contaminated lands and resources. This part also considers the possibility that contamination may be so severe and cleanup so problematic that those people living in the vicinity of a site seek relocation. The second part of this chapter is devoted to brownfields redevelopment — an area that presents important opportunities for revitalization in poor communities but that also has emerged as prominent among environmental justice advocates' concerns in the cleanup context.

1. An Introduction to CERCLA Cleanups

The Comprehensive Environmental Response, Compensation and Liability Act (CERCLA), enacted in 1980, is the primary federal statute governing the remediation of spills or releases of hazardous substances. A large part of CERCLA, its implementing regulations, and its case law concerns the questions of who is potentially liable for cleaning up existing contamination and what is the extent of that liability. However, this chapter leaves to the side these liability issues and focuses instead on the substantive issues involved in the cleanup of contaminated sites. A discussion of the principal provisions of CERCLA can be found in Robert V. Percival et al., Environmental Regulation: Law, Science and Policy 366–438 (5th ed. 2006) and John S. Applegate et al., The Regulation of Toxic Substances and Hazardous Wastes 867–1026 (2000). For an overview of CERCLA and environmental justice, see Veronica Eady Famira, *Cleaning Up Abandoned or Inactive Contaminated Sites, in* The Law of Environmental Justice: Theories and Procedures to Address Disproportionate Risks 569 (Michael B. Gerrard & Sheila R. Foster, eds., 2d. ed. 2008).

CERCLA is often called "Superfund," which is somewhat of a misnomer because although the statute established a trust fund designed to provide financing for cleanups in some circumstances, a signature component of CERCLA is its requirement that responsible parties contribute financially to site cleanups, either directly or by reimbursing the trust fund for monies expended by government agencies. CERCLA also originally provided for a tax on oil and chemical companies, with the revenues collected to go to the trust fund; this provision, however, has been allowed to expire, as elaborated below. The "Superfund" is thus but one part of the much broader CERCLA statute.

There are hundreds of thousands of contaminated sites where releases of hazardous substances occurred or are occurring. Some of these sites remain undiscovered. Most are less serious and are left to the attention of state, tribal, and local authorities. Some of the more seriously contaminated sites trigger response activities under CERCLA.

CERCLA authorizes EPA to investigate and clean up releases of hazardous substances (or to permit private parties to do so) in accordance with the National Contingency Plan (NCP). The NCP, which was adopted by EPA, sets forth guidelines and procedures for such responses, but does not itself specify what level of cleanup is appropriate at a given site. The NCP divides responses into two types: short-term "removal" actions, meant to minimize the immediate effects of a release, and longer-term "remedial" actions, designed to clean up contamination and permanently eliminate the resulting risk to public health. Remedial actions often consist of measures such as excavating contaminated soils, treating contaminated groundwater, and properly disposing of contaminated materials off-site.

Once a site has been identified, EPA undertakes a preliminary assessment, placing the data in an information system called CERCLIS, a database of all hazardous substance release sites. It then quantifies the potential risks considering such factors as the toxicity, quantity, and concentration of wastes present at the site, and gives the site a numerical score under the Hazard Ranking System (HRS). The higher scoring sites are placed on the National Priorities List (NPL). Priority for determining the order in which these sites will be cleaned up is based upon factors such as the size of the population at risk, the potential for contaminating water supplies, the potential for public contact, and the possibility that damage to natural resources might affect the human food chain.

After any short-term removals are conducted, the EPA undertakes a remedial investigation and feasibility study (RI/FS) to evaluate a range of remedial options. Whereas the RI is focused on a technical assessment of the contamination and the health risks it may pose, the FS is concerned with identifying and evaluating the various remedial alternatives that will satisfy EPA's cleanup goals.

As a general matter, CERCLA statutorily establishes a preference for a remedial action that "permanently and significantly reduces the volume, toxicity or mobility of the hazardous substances" at a site. 42 U.S.C. §9621. In terms of the degree of cleanup to be attained—the answer to the question "how clean is clean?"—CERCLA requires that the remedy selected both (a) protect human health and the environment and (b) provide a level of cleanup equivalent to that required by any legally applicable or relevant and appropriate federal or state standard (such standards are known as ARARs). What constitutes an ARAR entails the exercise of considerable discretion on the part of the relevant agency; ARARs are thus often contested. For example, an ARAR might involve the choice between cleaning contaminated groundwater to "potable water" standards under the Safe Drinking Water Act because of the presence of nearby drinking water wells and cleaning it to standards that would apply to industrial uses because the contaminated property is deemed an industrial site. The difference in cost may be considerable, as potable water standards are significantly more stringent.

The options for remedial actions are evaluated according to two sets of statutory factors, which the NCP combines into nine criteria, among them: overall protection of human health and the environment; compliance with ARARs; long-term effectiveness and permanence; reduction of toxicity, mobility, or volume through treatment; short-term effectiveness; implementability; cost; state government acceptance; and community acceptance. According to EPA, the first two of these (protection of health and environment and compliance with ARARs) operate as "threshold" criteria: only those alternatives that satisfy these criteria will be among those considered. The next five serve as "primary balancing" criteria, providing the technical bases for choosing among the alternatives remaining on the table. Finally, the last two (state and community acceptance) serve as "modifying" criteria, suggesting ways in which aspects of the preferred alternative might be modified. U.S. ENVTL. PROT. AGENCY, THE FEASIBILITY STUDY: DETAILED ANALYSIS OF REMEDIATION ALTERNATIVES 2 (1990). In practice, the first four of these criteria weigh most heavily in the selection of a remedy. *See* APPLEGATE ET AL., *supra*, at 905–06. Community acceptance, in particular, is often something of an afterthought. *See* Eady Famira, *Cleaning Up, supra,* at 576–77.

At bottom, environmental agencies have wide latitude in choosing a cleanup remedy from among the set of plausible options. As noted in Chapter 3, some research suggests that agencies routinely choose less protective cleanups for poor and minority communities, and notes that such sites generally take longer to achieve NPL listing.

It is also worth noting that, under CERCLA, the role for citizen suits is fairly limited. Citizens cannot initiate an enforcement action against potentially responsible parties to compel the cleanup of a contaminated site, and cannot challenge the cleanup remedies selected by the government before they are completed. While CERCLA also provides for technical assistance grants (TAGs) of up to $50,000 for affected citizen groups in order to enable the affected community to evaluate the risks posed by a site, these TAG monies cannot be used to underwrite citizen suits.

CERCLA's twenty-fifth anniversary in 2005 provided occasion for scholars to reflect upon whether its promise had been realized. Professor Rena Steinzor and Margaret Clune, in a report published by the Center for American Progress and the Center for Progressive Reform, concluded that cleanups were lagging as the funding source originally provided for in the statute had been allowed to lapse. To provide a sense of the impact of this "neglect," they profiled 50 NPL sites that still awaited cleanup, selecting five sites each from the ten most populous states: California, Texas, New York, Florida, Illinois, Pennsylvania, Ohio, Michigan, New Jersey and Georgia.

Rena Steinzor and Margaret Clune, The Toll of Superfund Neglect: Toxic Waste Dumps & Communities at Risk

(2006)

Many [sites] have languished on the [NPL] for well over a decade and some have awaited cleanup for almost a quarter century, as lack of resources, industry opposition, technical challenges and mismanagement plagued the program....

Over the last decade, cleanups have slowed to a crawl because the program lost its stable "polluter pays" funding base in 1995. A series of Republican-controlled Congresses allowed the industry taxes that support the program to expire and ignored yearly requests by the Clinton administration to reinstate them....

In the absence of political commitment and resources, the number of completed Superfund cleanups fell abruptly in 2001 to 50 percent of previous annual totals. Cleanups were completed at just 40 sites in each of the [years 2003, 2004, and 2005]....

In observing the 25th anniversary of the Superfund law in December 2005, EPA reminded the public that, "even today, 1 in 4 Americans live within 3 miles of a Superfund site." Approximately three to four million children live within one mile of a Superfund site, and due to their unique physical susceptibilities, are at greater risk to the effects of exposure from environmental contaminants. . . .

As of the 2000 Census (the most recent tabulation of data available at the census tract level), 234,524 people lived in the census tracts containing one of the 50 profiled sites. Of those, 34,127 are children aged nine and younger. . . . In 30 of the 50 census tracts (60 percent of tracts), the median household income for 1999 (again, the most recent tabulation of data available at the census tract level) was below that for the nation, that is, below $ 41,994. . . .

Thirteen of the profiled sites are located in census tracts where the population is at least 40 percent racial minority or Hispanic, including four sites where the percentage is greater than 70. . . .

Superfund sites come in many guises. . . . Some sites date back as far as the turn of the last century. They have been included on the NPL for long periods of time, with the oldest having been listed on the very first NPL in 1983 and the most recent listed in 2001, at the same time that annual construction completions dropped by half. . . . Inexplicably, some of the sites that have waited the longest for cleanup are owned by companies that remain viable, even profitable. For example:

> • Universal Oil Products (Chemical Division), a 75-acre site in Bergen County, New Jersey, was added to the NPL in 1983 and was used to manufacture a variety of toxic chemicals from 1932–79. Approximately 4.5 million gallons of liquid waste heavily laced with such volatile organic compounds as vinyl chloride, benzene and trichloroethylene were dumped in unlined lagoons, resulting in contamination of soil, surface water and groundwater. The runoff of waste polluted the nearby Hackensack River Basin, which is used by local residents for recreation. Allied Signal, now Honeywell, has been identified as a responsible party at the site and has been conducting cleanup activities. In 2005, Honeywell was ranked number 75 on the Fortune 500, with profits topping $1.2 billion.

> • The 85-acre Bofors-Nobel site in Muskegon County, Michigan, was first listed in 1988, and responsible parties include American Cyanamid, Akzo-Nobel, Bissell Corporation, DuPont, Eli Lilly, General Electric, IBM and Union Carbide, most of which either are or were listed on the Fortune 500. Unlined lagoons were used for disposal of the wastes generated by the production of alcohol-based detergents, saccharin, pesticides, herbicides and dye intermediaries. Final cleanup plans were completed in the early 1990s, but negotiations with the companies listed above, among others, slowed implementation until the late 1990s, and even then, federal funding was used to construct groundwater treatment facilities. The census tract in which the site is located has a median household income of about $38,000.

Several of the 50 sites were owned by companies that used extraordinarily toxic chemicals, some of which (e.g., creosote and lead) are now banned for most purposes. Over decades, excess chemicals and metals spilled or dropped onto the bare ground, where they seeped into underground aquifers or were washed by rain into adjacent storm sewers, rivers, or creeks. For example:

> • The American Creosote Works (Pensacola Pit) site in Escambia County, Florida, was used from 1902–1981 for wood preserving. Creosote was used until 1950,

when pentachlorophenol became the chemical of choice. Ponds set up to "percolate" these highly toxic liquids overflowed, spilling into Bayou Chico and the Pensacola Bay. The census tract encompassing the site is 48 percent minority, with a median household income of $23,000....

• The DePue/New Jersey Zinc/Mobil Chemical Company in Bureau County, Illinois, was used by a series of companies to smelt zinc for close to a century, creating waste piles, lagoons and cooling ponds filled with toxic wastes that now threaten a community with a median household income of $37,000, as well as the nearby DePue Lake, which houses a fishery, state wildlife refuge and numerous wetlands.

Other sites served as dumping grounds for multiple companies, many of which have changed their names, metamorphosing into other businesses or simply disappearing.

• One of the oldest and most notorious sites on the NPL, the 17-acre Stringfellow site, is located in a canyon near the southern California town of Glen Avon. It served as a hazardous waste disposal facility from 1956–1972, accepting over 34 million gallons of waste from metal refinishing, electroplating and pesticide manufacturing companies. This waste was dumped into surface evaporation ponds. Rainfall caused the ponds to overflow, sending streams of heavily polluted water into nearby neighborhoods. The population of the census tract around the site is 52 percent minority and has a median household income of $43,000....

• The 550-acre LCP Chemicals site in Glynn County, Georgia, was used for seven decades as an oil refinery, paint manufacturing plant, power plant and chlor-alkali factory. Five major companies have been identified as responsible parties at the site: ARCO, Georgia Power Company, Dixie Paints and Varnish Company (currently O'Brien Company), Allied Chemicals, Inc. (now Allied Signal, or Honeywell) and the Hanlin Group, a subsidiary of LCP Chemicals-Georgia, Inc. EPA estimates that more than 380,000 pounds of highly toxic mercury was "lost" in the area between 1955–1979 and, as a result, commercial fishing has been banned in the area. The census tract in which the site is located is 63 percent minority, with a median household income of $24,000.

* * *

Notes and Questions

1. Although the addition of a site to the NPL is meant to designate a site as among the "worst of the worst" and to ensure that ample resources are devoted to cleanup, relatively few sites have actually been cleaned up to the point where they can be deleted from the list. Professor Rena Steinzor and Margaret Clune explain:

Once a site requires no additional cleanup activities, it may be deleted from the NPL. Of the 1,553 sites that had been added to the NPL as of April 2006, only 309, or 20 percent, had been deleted. According to EPA, however, measuring success by simply looking at the ratio of deleted NPL sites to total sites on the NPL fails to "recognize the substantial construction and reduction of risk to human health and the environment that has occurred at NPL sites not yet eligible for deletion." So, in 1990, to "communicate more clearly to the public the status of cleanup progress" among NPL sites, EPA established the new category of "construction complete" as its main indicator of program success. Sites are considered "construction complete" when any necessary physical construction and engineering work is complete, even if final cleanup goals have not been achieved. In addition to the sites deleted from the NPL, another 600 or so have achieved the "construction complete" designation.

As of April 2006, none of the 50 sites profiled in [the report excerpted above] had progressed far enough in the cleanup process to be designated "construction complete." STEIN-ZOR & CLUNE, *supra*, at 11. In your view, does EPA's adoption of the term "construction complete" in fact communicate more clearly to the public the status of cleanup progress at sites about which they might be concerned?

2. CERCLA, as originally enacted, was widely heralded for embracing the "polluter pays" principle, a principle espoused by environmental justice advocates and others that seeks to place the burden of addressing contamination on the entities that caused it, rather than on the general public or on those communities that are left to host contaminated sites. CERCLA affirmed this principle via a two-pronged approach. First, it created a liability scheme that required "responsible parties" to pay for the cleanup of the sites to which they contributed contamination. Second, it established a trust fund that the federal government could use to pay for site cleanups where responsible parties could not be located, were insolvent, or otherwise would not pay for cleanup (sometimes called "orphan sites"). This trust fund was financed by a tax levied "on those industrial sectors most likely to have contributed to the hazardous waste sites." STEINZOR & CLUNE, *supra*, at 18. When, in 1995, Congress allowed this tax to expire, it began the shift to what Professor Steinzor and Ms. Clune call the "let the people pay" principle. *Id.* at 18. As they explain, moreover, the two original sources of funding worked in concert, and EPA was dependent on a robust trust fund to enable it to investigate sites, prosecute responsible parties, and, via enforcement actions, to replenish the trust fund. Thus, while the first of these sources of funding for cleanup remains intact, the loss of the second—a tax that generated $1.5 billion per year— has greatly hampered cleanup efforts under CERCLA. In fact, they observe, "from [fiscal year] FY 1993–1999, the share of the Superfund program funded by general taxpayers remained constant at $250 million, less than 20 percent of the overall appropriation[s], ... [but] from FY 2000–2003, [the taxpayers' contribution] rose to more than $600 million per year—around 50 percent of the total appropriations. By 2004, general revenues accounted for 100 percent of appropriations to EPA for the Superfund program." *Id.* at 20. Which do you think is a more appropriate source of funding for cleanups of orphan sites: general taxpayers or the industrial sectors formerly subject to the Superfund tax?

3. The EPA has offered an additional explanation for the recent decline in sites obtaining "construction complete" status. Because the EPA's regional offices focused on cleaning up less complex sites first, "EPA is now left with many of the sites that require more complex, lengthy, and expensive cleanups, which take more work overall and a longer amount of time to reach construction complete status." *Id.* at 13. While there is disagreement among observers over the extent to which this explanation holds true, it is fair to say that among the challenges facing EPA (and their governmental partners in the states and tribes) in the years ahead are the so-called "megasites"—sites at which contamination is serious and widespread and cleanup is expected to be complex and costly. For a recent study of ongoing cleanup effort at one such site, see NAT'L RESEARCH COUNCIL, SUPERFUND AND MINING MEGASITES—LESSONS FROM THE COEUR D'ALENE RIVER BASIN (2005). For an on-the-ground account of this effort from the perspective of an EPA attorney and law professor, see Clifford J. Villa, *Superfund vs. Mega-sites: The Coeur D'Alene River Basin Story*, 28 COLUM. J. ENVTL. L. 255 (2003). One of the issues raised by megasites and other sites at which contamination is serious and remediation likely to take

years—if indeed it is possible at all—is the potential that those living in the vicinity or affected by the contamination will seek relocation. This issue is considered in the next section.

2. A Note on Relocation

Remediation of contaminated sites may be so problematic that the surrounding community wants to relocate. Permanent relocations are governed by the Uniform Relocation Assistance and Real Property Acquisition Policies Act of 1970 and are considered by EPA only as a matter of last resort. 42 U.S.C. § 4601–4655. In general, relocation will be included in a site remedy only where the contamination poses a risk to human health that cannot be addressed by engineering solutions or by restrictions on the use of the property, or where the inhabited structures (i.e., peoples' homes) themselves present a physical impediment to cleanup activities. Relocations to date have been sparse, with EPA estimating as of 2000 that they had been included as part of the remedy at only approximately 17 sites. U.S. ENVTL. PROT. AGENCY, SUPERFUND NATIONAL POLICY DIALOGUE 3 (March 2–3, 2000). Environmental justice activists have questioned EPA's reluctance to provide for relocation, particularly in communities of color and low-income communities. These activists point to data suggesting that, of 14 sites at which relocation was included in the remedy, only two were in communities that were not "overwhelmingly white." *Id.* at 4.

One of the few instances in which relocation has been included in a site remedy occurred at the Escambia Treating Company (ETC) site, located in Pensacola, Florida, as part of a "pilot" project by EPA. This site is among those profiled by Professor Steinzor and Ms. Clune, above; as noted, decades of wood treatment activities left the site highly contaminated with creosote and pentachlorophenol. This contamination threatened a predominantly African American community, which formed Citizens Against Toxic Exposure (CATE) in response. Professor Veronica Eady Famira recounts CATE's efforts. "CATE received technical assistance grants, hired a technical advisor, and pushed for complete removal of on-site and off-site contamination in a direct challenge to EPA's draft proposed plan of excavation, solidification, and on-site burial. Ultimately, 358 households were relocated...." Eady Famira, *Cleaning Up, supra,* at 573. Although CATE counted among its successes the fact that community members were able to secure relocation, it should be noted that relocation itself can present a host of challenges for the affected community. Moving one's residence is a well-known source of stress, and this is particularly likely to be so where the move is not wholly voluntary. Moreover, where people have lived in a community for a long time, they may be especially distressed by having to leave. And, as environmental justice advocates have pointed out, the web of relationships that comprises an intact community is likely to be severed when community members are dispersed; this web provides an important—and perhaps irreplaceable—"asset" of many communities of color and low-income communities. These concerns can be exacerbated if the relocation is not properly handled by the relevant governmental agencies. In the case of the ETC relocation, for example, a follow-up study by EPA in 2002 found that community members had several concerns:

> Participants felt that little support was given for identifying the needs and preferences of the individuals displaced. A common complaint was that the government did not seem to take into consideration that some individuals were elderly or handicapped or had concerns about the travel distance to work. Additionally, many felt that the comparability of homes that the government of-

fered them was based more on square footage and cost than on these concerns.... [M]ost participants did not seem to fully understand how their homes were appraised, and felt that the end result did not accurately reflect the value of their house....

U.S. Envtl. Prot. Agency, Escambia Wood Treating Company (ETC) Superfund Site Permanent Relocation: Focus Groups Summary Report 3 (undated document).

Additionally, not every community member may wish to be relocated. Consider, for example, the perspectives raised by those affected by the Tar Creek Superfund site, located in northeast Oklahoma and placed on the NPL in 1983. After years of pressure from community members and their political allies, the EPA in 2008 announced plans for voluntary relocation. Press Release, U.S. Envtl. Prot. Agency, Cleanup Plan Finalized for Tar Creek Superfund Site (Feb. 22, 2008). The following excerpt describes the extent of the contamination and some community members' reactions:

> Tar Creek was once the location of extensive lead and zinc mining operations that ha[ve] left more than 50 million tons of mine tailings in hundreds of piles and ponds over a 40-square mile area. Some of these piles are hundreds of feet tall ... while others are as wide as several football fields. There are sinkholes and abandoned mineshafts everywhere. These mountains of lead and zinc waste completely surround the towns of Picher and Cardin located at the center of the site. The nearby towns of Commerce and Quapaw are also affected as are portions of the Quapaw tribal reservation. The Quapaw tribe owns most of the land which has been leased to people who have built homes on the site.

> Dust contaminated with lead, cadmium and other toxic metals blow[s] off these huge storage piles onto streets, homes and school yards throughout these communities. Not realizing that there was any danger, residents used this dust, known locally as "chat," to make driveways, foundations for their homes, or as fill for home improvement projects. Children innocently played on these piles often riding their bikes up and down them.

> According to the USEPA, approximately 25 percent of the children living on the site have elevated blood lead levels, compared to a state average of 2 percent; approximately 1,600 residential homes have been identified with unsafe soil lead levels (having more than 500 ppm lead in soil); and five public water supply wells have been impacted....

> [As of 2008, the option to relocate was] made available to families with children six years old or younger who live in the towns of Picher and Cardin located at the center of the Tar Creek Superfund site....

> Children under the age of six were targeted because they are especially vulnerable to the effects of exposure to lead and because there's strong scientific evidence linking chronic lead exposure to adverse health problems in children including permanent neurological damage and learning disabilities....

> What does this mean to the children who are now 8, 10 or 12 who lived in Tar Creek when they were six and younger? What does it mean to adults who have lived there all their lives and who now suffer from neurological problems linked to lead exposure? What does it mean to Quapaw tribal members who live on the site?

> [According to local resident Rebecca Jim], "we know that it's more than just the children and [it's] more than just the families in the epicenter [of the site]." There are, says Jim, "... four other whole towns, the Quapaw tribal headquar-

ters where tribal members have danced for 130 years, with two rivers that have fish advisories for metals that form Grand Lake which is a water source for another three counties of people." ...

Says Jim, "We'll continue to demand relocation for those who want to go and for clean up for those who want to stay. We need to find ways to make the area habitable for those who want to stay." Hopefully, in time, the people who live on the Tar Creek Superfund site will succeed in getting the state and federal governments to agree to relocate those in the entire affected community who want to leave, not just those who are most vulnerable.

Center for Health, Environment and Justice, *Echoes of Love Canal in Tar Creek Relocation,* 22 EVERYONE'S BACKYARD 4, 4, 10 (Summer 2004).

Notes and Questions

1. Community members relocated at the ETC site expressed a variety of concerns with the EPA's appraisal process. In theory, the affected properties are to be assessed at their fair market value in the absence of an adjacent Superfund site, i.e., at the price they would command but for the contamination. Assuming that an appraiser is in fact able to construct this number, are those who are relocated likely to be "made whole"—the ordinary goal of legal remedies—by the government's provision of a new home of equal value located elsewhere? If not, how would you calculate adequate compensation for the loss of stable community roots, and who should pay this additional cost?

2. How, in your view, should EPA go about determining whether relocation is appropriate in a given instance? To what extent should a community's perception of the relevant health risks govern? What if their "subjective" perception doesn't square with the EPA's "objective" calculation of those risks, e.g., what if the community appears to be more concerned than is warranted by the quantitative estimate of the risk from the site? How, if at all, should affronts like noise and odor factor into the overall determination?

3. Don't those who are responsible for the contamination (or, where the responsible parties no longer exist, the government) benefit from relocation, inasmuch as they do not have to clean up the site to residential use standards? Should this be viewed as a windfall?

4. As noted above, the NPL includes relatively few of the hundreds of thousands of contaminated sites. While NPL sites are eligible for federal funding under CERCLA, financing the necessary cleanup activities can be a challenge at the remaining sites. In fact, these sites are so numerous that observers, including those in affected communities, have questioned whether it is realistic to expect these sites ever to be cleaned up. Among these sites are those that have been characterized as "brownfields"—sites that have been abandoned or are underutilized, and that are unlikely to be redeveloped for use by private parties due to contamination (whether actual or perceived). These sites are ubiquitous, particularly in urban areas adjacent to people of color and low-income neighborhoods. Governmental responses to brownfields raise a host of environmental justice issues; these are considered in the next section.

B. Brownfields

From an environmental justice perspective, brownfield redevelopment leads to the potential for both good and bad consequences. On the positive side, brownfield redevelopment may result in cleaner urban environments and economic development. The abandoned industrial sites called "brownfields" often contain unremediated contamination and may contribute to urban blight, depress surrounding property values, become a magnet for drug activity, and generally become a source of community demoralization. With little or no prospect that these sites will ever be cleaned up and returned to use, the presence of brownfields sites may foment decay rather than revitalization. From this grim baseline, any degree of cleanup and added employment opportunities may be attractive, especially if the redevelopment project involves light industrial use or a non-polluting business. On the negative side, the less stringent "use-based" cleanup standards generally permitted at brownfields sites are problematic when considering the existing aggregate pollutants impacting many host communities. And, because firms often purchase these sites with plans to return the site to heavy industrial use, brownfield redevelopment can have the effect of locking in a legacy of past industrial development.

Although EPA has sponsored several brownfield pilot projects around the country, most brownfield cleanups are guided not by federal law, but by state cleanup statutes (virtually every state has some analogue to CERCLA). Like CERCLA, these state statutes typically do not prescribe in advance the level to which each individual site will be cleaned up. Moreover, as elaborated below, most states have enacted provisions specifically directed at brownfields sites. These provisions typically seek to incentivize cleanup of these sites, for example by establishing voluntary cleanup programs.

The issues involved in brownfield redevelopment are complicated and interrelated. The first issue is a familiar empirical issue of causation: what causes sites to remain undeveloped and underutilized? Although fear of liability is often touted as the primary disincentive, other reasons for the proliferation of these sites are apparent, making it questionable whether reducing liability and lowering cleanup standards will in fact result in successful redevelopment projects. In addition to the optimal mix of incentives that may be necessary, the host community's role is controversial. Some argue that public participation is indispensable while others are concerned that too much participation may be the kiss of death for a project. In the excerpts provided below, thoughtful commentators examine these issues in greater detail.

Pathfinder on Brownfields and Environmental Justice

For an overview of brownfields and the environmental justice issues raised in this context, see Veronica Eady Famira, *Recycling Brownfields Sites, in* THE LAW OF ENVIRONMENTAL JUSTICE: THEORIES AND PROCEDURES TO ADDRESS DISPROPORTIONATE RISKS 605 (Michael B. Gerrard & Sheila R. Foster, eds., 2d ed. 2008). For those wishing to research this area further, in addition to the articles excerpted below, see John S. Applegate, *Risk Assessment, Redevelopment, and Environmental Justice: Evaluating the Brownfields Bargain,* 13 J. NAT. RESOURCES & ENVTL. L. 243 (1997–1998); Lincoln L. Davies, *Working Toward a Common Goal? Three Case Studies of Brownfields Redevelopment in Environmental Justice Communities,* 18 STAN. ENVTL. L.J. 285 (1999); Joel B. Eisen, *Brownfields Policies for Sustainable Cities,* 9 DUKE ENVTL. L. & POL'Y F. 187 (1999); Gabriel A. Espinosa, *Building on Brownfields: A Catalyst For Neighborhood Revitalization,* 11 VILL.

ENVTL. L.J. 1 (2000); William T.D. Freeland, *Environmental Justice and the Brownfields Revitalization Act of 2001: Brownfields of Dreams or a Nightmare in the Making?*, 8 J. GENDER RACE & JUST. 183 (2004); Jennifer Felten, *Brownfield Redevelopment 1995–2005: An Environmental Justice Success Story?*, 40 REAL PROP. PROB. & TRUST. J. 679 (2006); and Joel B. Eisen, *Brownfieds at 20: A Critical Reevaluation*, 34 FORD. URB. L.J. 721 (2007).

1. Brownfields Background

Joel B. Eisen, Brownfields of Dreams?: Challenges and Limits of Voluntary Cleanup Programs and Incentives
1996 University of Illinois Law Review 883

The Challenge of Brownfield Redevelopment

... Brownfield sites include abandoned industrial facilities, warehouses, and other commercial properties such as former gas stations and dry cleaning establishments. Although brownfields exist in many areas, they are concentrated in aging, predominantly minority and lower-income neighborhoods of "Rust Belt" cities such as Newark and Chicago. For decades, manufacturers have been fleeing these cities and moving to "greenfields" locations in the suburbs. The abandonment of inner-city sites has left a 'witch's brew of contamination' at abandoned brownfield sites.

The number of brownfield sites, and the magnitude of contamination at them, is not known. Despite this uncertainty, brownfield sites have significant potential for redevelopment. Developers propose projects that range from industrial uses to retail uses, technology and office centers, airports, and even sports stadiums.

Although the costs of continued inactivity at brownfield sites are potentially immense, they are not well quantified. The types of costs, however, are well understood. Inner-city neighborhoods fail to benefit from jobs that redevelopment might provide. Cities receive lower property tax revenues from brownfield sites, which weakens their ability to provide basic services such as education. Brownfields are unsightly and threaten to contaminate drinking water and cause neighborhood health problems. Vacant properties contribute to high crime rates and deterioration of urban neighborhoods. They encourage further environmental abuse, such as "midnight dumping." Finally, brownfields are conspicuous symbols of the decline of lower-income and minority neighborhoods in which they are overwhelmingly located. They discourage urban investment and contribute to a pervasive sense of poverty and hopelessness.

Moreover, there are substantial environmental costs to locating new commercial or industrial activities at a greenfield site instead of a brownfield site. Greenfield development often devours previously unspoiled land. Development in suburbs and exurbs exacerbates their growing pollution problems. These developments will have adverse impacts for many years to come, even long after their useful lives have ended. Stormwater, groundwater, and air pollution from additional traffic will increase. Suburban and exurban jurisdictions will have to build or expand existing infrastructures such as highways and public water and sewer systems to serve new development. Officials in these jurisdictions are concerned about the financial burden this imposes on them, a burden that is often alleviated to some extent by wasteful subsidies (in the form of grants and other funding) from the federal and state governments.

By contrast, brownfield redevelopment can take advantage of existing urban infrastructures. A brownfield site often features excellent water and sewer systems, and rail and highway access to the metropolitan area, the region, and outlying areas. Densely concentrated urban areas offer better accessibility to workers and other advantages. Other potential benefits include aesthetic qualities such as waterfront access and views, proximity to downtown business districts, public tax and financing initiatives to support development, access to major universities and medical centers, and ancillary benefits of spending by rejuvenated industries and their workers on local goods and services.

Despite these potential advantages, brownfields remain abandoned or underutilized. In the eyes of many, this is due to widespread fears of brownfield developers … that the cost of cleaning brownfield sites to meet government standards is both so uncertain and so high that it might outweigh the sites' market value.… A developer must also be concerned about the uncertainties caused by state hazardous waste cleanup programs, because it cannot predict at the outset whether it will be subjected to state or federal regulation. The states have primary responsibility for sites that do not rise to the threshold for federal action and for sites that states have decided to regulate in the absence of federal requirements.…

… This uncertainty is attributable in part to the considerable vagueness and uncertainty associated with applicable cleanup standards. For example, it is nearly impossible to determine in advance the required level or cost of a cleanup under CERCLA. The cleanup standard embodied in Section 121 of CERCLA forces a detailed inquiry to be undertaken at each site. Establishing the appropriate level of cleanup requires a wealth of information about the remedies that might work at each site. This information is generated in a lengthy, multistep process that is expensive and has been called a "slow-motion Kabuki." Cleanups also must comply with the standards of other federal and state laws that are "applicable or relevant and appropriate" which introduces a maddening complexity to the process. Furthermore, there is no ability to learn from past experiences and develop predictability: under the statute, each site must be analyzed individually.

Proponents advance several justifications for promoting certainty in cleanup standards. First, they argue that predetermining (i.e., standardizing) the level of cleanup required can help make project decisions more efficient. Standardizing cleanup standards allows project developers to internalize project costs and, therefore, helps to ensure that only those projects that are efficient will be built. Owners and prospective investors presumably will be more motivated to invest in brownfield redevelopment if they can determine in advance whether they will recoup their expenditures on cleanups. Lenders, once wary of any involvement at brownfield sites, will open the money tap and provide the indispensable funding for brownfields. Insurers can even underwrite the cost of remediation, so that there will be a 'cap' on financial responsibility. Finally, the pace of cleanups can be more rapid with pre-set standards.

Brownfield redevelopment advocates also say Superfund's cleanup standards are too strict. They believe that cleanup standards are based on inaccurate and unrealistic assumptions about the risks posed by hazardous waste that overestimate the true risks posed by Superfund sites and produce overly stringent cleanups, particularly because cleanups are required to meet residential standards at all sites. If this view is correct, standards could be relaxed without increasing the actual threat to human health and the environment. This is particularly true in the brownfield context, many say, given the intended use of most property for industrial or commercial purposes.…

Uncertainty for Lending Institutions

Perhaps even more important than the disincentives for developers is the perception of lenders that they face risks for lending on contaminated property. As "the traditional sources of capital for factory rehabilitation and renovation for start-up companies," their participation at brownfield sites is crucial to the success of most projects. However, lenders often practice "greenlining," routinely refusing to extend loans to brownfield redevelopers....

There are other considerations besides liability. Lenders fear that the discovery of contamination at the site will decrease the market value of their collateral or compel borrowers to spend large sums on cleanups, forcing them to default on loans....

The Call for Reform

[However, w]e should be cautious about making generalizations about the impact of developers' fears of environmental laws and, for that matter, any other assertion that environmental laws prevent activity that would otherwise take place. The flight of businesses to greenfield sites began long before CERCLA's enactment in 1980. Researchers have yet to establish a causal link between businesses' location decisions and perceived environmental costs. Moreover, ... [a] study by the nonprofit group Resources for the Future concluded that there are many ... reasons ... why brownfield sites remain undeveloped. High urban crime rates, obsolescence of existing infrastructures and manufacturing facilities at brownfield sites, and access from greenfield sites to amenities and recreation are frequently cited as reasons for developers' flight to greenfield sites....

Features of Voluntary Cleanup Statutes

[The design and details of brownfield programs vary by state.] Most states require a developer to submit a work plan for cleanup actions that is typically accompanied by the site investigation report and other supporting documents. This plan may be part of, or submitted pursuant to, an agreement with the state to remediate the site. Indiana, for example, requires a developer to enter into a "voluntary remediation agreement" that sets forth the terms and conditions of a "work plan" for the site. In some states, the plan may be part of a consent decree entered in judgment to memorialize the agreement between the state and a developer who is a responsible party at the site. Under some approaches, the plan may provide for a partial cleanup either of certain contaminants or of a portion of the site....

Although some state programs do not change existing cleanup standards, many attempt to implement modified, risk-based standards as an incentive to developers. The Office of Technology Assessment has termed modifications to cleanup standards "perhaps the most significant feature in many voluntary programs." Most states aim to spur redevelopment by redefining cleanup standards in terms of actual risks posed to human health and the environment. There is widespread variation in the states' approaches to developing cleanup standards due to differing assumptions about the risk associated with contamination (e.g., toxicity, exposure pathways, and other factors), the importance of considering the proposed use of the site, and other considerations such as the effectiveness of engineering controls....

States are developing two general types of cleanup standards: (1) standardized state-approved generic statewide cleanup standards, based on assumptions about exposure to contamination; and (2) site-specific standards, requiring a risk assessment to be performed at every site, but often incorporating consideration of the future use of the site (i.e., industrial, commercial, or residential) and allowing some cleanups that result in a public health risk higher than that currently allowed under CERCLA....

The site-specific approach holds considerable promise for developers. A number of states provide explicitly for standards allowing levels of health risk higher than those permitted under CERCLA. The allowable level of risk for carcinogens can be higher than a 1 in 1 million (1×10-6) lifetime upper bound risk; as high as 1 in 10,000 (1×10-4) in some instances. Site-specific standards, like generic standards, also consider factors such as the intended use of the property. A number of states provide explicitly that the cleanup required at a site must be based on the public health risk that is expected in light of the site's proposed or reasonably anticipated future use....

Some states modify or reverse the usual statutory preference for permanent remedies such as destruction of hazardous substances. The preference for engineering controls (measures designed to entomb the contamination at the site, such as placement of a parking lot over contaminated soil) or institutional controls (managerial controls such as fences and warning signs, and land use restrictions), which reduce cleanup costs significantly, is perhaps the "ultimate relaxation of cleanup standards." States incorporate a variety of provisions regarding engineering or institutional controls....

A number of states do not mandate public participation in their voluntary cleanup programs. The reason for this is readily apparent: public involvement is often viewed as a "deterrent to undertaking a voluntary cleanup." ...

In states that require public participation at each site, some require that the affected community be notified of proposed cleanup activities. The most typical form of public participation is a brief notice and comment period (often less than thirty days) on the proposed remedial action plan. The form of notice to be used varies, with few states requiring direct notice to residents in the affected community. A minority of states provide for more participation than a notice and comment process allows by requiring that a public hearing be held on the remedial action plan; the hearing, however, is often available only upon a written request....

The incentives for brownfield redevelopment are based on a "Brownfields of Dreams" premise: "if you provide the appropriate climate, they [developers] will clean and invest." ... The transition away from the rigorous cleanup standards of the regulatory regime, however, is prompting the states to move too far to relax cleanup standards and requirements for contaminated sites, jeopardizing public health and safety....

* * *

Notes and Questions

1. Congress responded to claims that developers were likely to be hesitant to redevelop brownfields because of the uncertainties surrounding potential liability for cleanup costs. To this end, the Small Business Liability Relief and Brownfields Revitalization Act of 2002 creates a "bona fide prospective purchaser" (BFPP) exemption: a BFPP whose potential liability under CERCLA derives solely from the fact that it owns or operates a property or facility "shall not be liable as long as the [BFPP] does not impede the performance of a response action." 42 U.S.C. §9607(r)(1). The exemption applies to those who acquire ownership after Jan. 11, 2002 and who satisfy a list of criteria for obtaining status as a BFPP. Although this and other provisions of the Act were meant to address developers' concerns and so spur brownfield development, some commentators have questioned whether these really are the critical barriers in practice. Professor Heidi Gorovitz Robertson, for example, suggests that concern regarding potential environmental liability is only one of many factors in a business' decision to redevelop a "brownfield" rather than develop a "greenfield." Heidi Gorovitz Robertson, *One Piece of the Puzzle: Why State Brownfields Programs Can't Lure Businesses to the Urban Cores Without Finding the Missing Pieces,* 51 Rutgers L. Rev. 1075 (1995). Based on both a literature review and an original survey, she found other factors — including site location, size, and configuration; cost of

renovation; availability of skilled workforce; access to transportation; and presence of crime—to be as or more important than environmental costs. She concludes that "an offer of environmental immunity alone will not lure businesses to urban areas. Unless cities and states are able to meet businesses' other pressing needs, the urban renewal and job growth goals of their brownfields programs will remain unrealized." *Id.* at 1121. Professor Joel Eisen argues further that it is a mistake to think that all brownfields "stories" are the same or that all potential developers of brownfields sites face the same set of barriers. *See* Eisen, *Brownfields at 20, supra.*

2. When the brownfield agenda first surfaced in the mid-1990s, environmental justice advocates quickly recognized that the discussion was too narrowly focused on removing barriers to real estate transactions. In response, the Waste and Facility Siting Subcommittee of the National Environmental Justice Advisory Council (NEJAC) began a series of public dialogues to allow residents of impacted communities and environmental justice advocates to contribute to the public policy debate. Environmental justice advocates argued that potential liability was a relatively minor impediment to brownfield redevelopment. Redlining by investment and insurance companies, lack of training, and the poor quality of education, public safety, housing and transportation all led to deindustrialization of urban areas, along with the contribution of indirect subsidies for suburban development. Activists promoted the concept of "urban revitalization," a community-based approach focused on building capacity and mobilizing resources, as opposed to "urban redevelopment," a gentrification-driven policy that displaces existing communities. If multiple factors result in abandoned and contaminated properties, what revitalization strategies would be necessary to provide the necessary incentives for private sector investment and to insure meaningful community input?

3. Reflecting upon the ambivalence concerning brownfield redevelopment, Professor Kirsten Engel observes that the negative view stems from a right-based perspective while the more positive view stems from a market-based perspective. In the article excerpted below, she promotes a third "pragmatic" approach as a means to resolve the tensions in brownfield redevelopment.

Kirsten H. Engel, Brownfield Initiatives and Environmental Justice: Second-Class Cleanups or Market-Based Equity?

13 Journal of Natural Resources and Environmental Law 317 (1998)

State Voluntary Cleanup Laws

... Regulations implementing CERCLA, as well as state Superfund laws, limit CERCLA-quality cleanup and liability to only the most hazardous sites presenting the most extreme threats to human health and the environment. Thus, the theoretical eligibility of the site for CERCLA cleanup is irrelevant; the reality is that if not addressed under the brownfields program, such sites will probably never be cleaned up at all. Focusing on this real life constraint, however, obscures the equity issues underlying the unavailability of CERCLA-quality remedies at brownfield sites. Most importantly, it obscures the fact that the unavailability of CERCLA-quality remedies at brownfield sites is a policy choice by agency officials, and not a requirement of CERCLA itself....

The "Rights-Based" Critique of Brownfields Programs

The dominant thrust of environmental justice is that all persons and communities, without regard to race or socio-economic status, are entitled to equal treatment under the law concerning the distribution of the environmental benefits and burdens of modern society. The violation of this rights-based norm is the basis for the environmental justice movement which has galvanized around empirical studies demonstrating that minority and low-income communities are disproportionately exposed to environmental hazards, such as hazardous waste landfills. The rights-based approach demands that state and local government agencies alter their siting and other environmental policies so as to achieve substantive equity in the distribution of environmental hazards by race and class and procedural equity in environmental decision-making so as to include traditionally disenfranchised groups such as minorities and the poor.

According to the rights-based conception of environmental justice, brownfield programs that contemplate reduced cleanup standards and less comprehensive liability by affected parties are antithetical to the goal of substantive and procedural equality in the distribution of environmental hazards across the lines of race, class, and ethnicity. Under the rights-based conception, state voluntary cleanup programs force the victims of environmental discrimination to bear the costs of that discrimination. Due to the low land values prevailing in their communities together with their relative political powerlessness, poor and minority communities have been targeted historically as the sites for heavy industrial development and, as a result, are subject to a disproportionate share of the environmental hazards that frequently accompany such development. Rather than reverse this legacy, brownfield cleanups could actually perpetuate it. If, for example, the cleanup of a brownfield site is sufficient only for future industrial uses, the community will never escape this industrial legacy but will continue to be located near potentially environmentally hazardous industrial development. In this manner, the rights-based conception of environmental justice could see brownfield initiatives as betraying the promise of Superfund legislation which, at least for the sites that qualify for Superfund remedies, would normally require more expensive cleanups consistent with future residential and recreational uses of the property.

The benefits touted by brownfield initiatives would likely be discounted by the rights-based environmental justice approach. The increased economic opportunities that are to accompany brownfield initiatives might be considered a "bribe" that asks residents to trade health for dollars....

The "Market-Based" Approach to Achieving Environmental Justice

... According to the market-based approach to environmental justice, the pattern of disproportionate exposure to environmental hazards by poor minority and urban communities will only be broken when either the residents of such communities obtain the economic resources to leave contaminated urban neighborhoods or a rise in the value of urban land begins to attract less polluting businesses. The market-based approach holds that neither of these can take place, so long as urban neighborhoods are riddled with abandoned contaminated sites that operate as a net drag upon the already scarce resources of the community. Reforms of government industrial facility siting procedures, so as to prevent sitings that result in disproportionate impacts upon poor and minority communities, cannot achieve lasting gains in environmental equity unless the communities possess the infrastructure, skills, and political organization necessary to attract more desirable development. Given the economic and political empowerment of disadvantaged communities, the market-based view holds that environmental inequities will eventually disappear.

In contrast to the rights-based approach, the market-based approach to achieving environmental justice generally supports current state brownfield laws. To the extent compromises can be made concerning cleanup and environmental liability in exchange for the cleanup and redevelopment of such abandoned sites, the community will be better off.

With increased economic resources, the community will gradually break the pattern of disproportionate exposure to environmental hazards.

Finding a Middle Ground Between the Rights-Based and Market-Based Conceptions of Environmental Justice

... [A] third approach, labeled here as the "pragmatic" approach, supports departures from a strict rights-based approach to environmental justice where the probability of environmental harm is minimal and the potential economic benefits are large. Such departures, however, are only justifiable if mechanisms are in place to ensure that departures from the rights-based approach will result in concrete economic gains for disadvantaged communities. The pragmatic approach to environmental justice, in the context of brownfield programs, is suggested as a recommended approach to achieving environmental justice goals in the context of brownfield programs, and not as a replacement for either the rights-based or market-based approaches in other contexts where they may be more suitable to the achievement of environmental justice goals.

In the context of brownfields, the pragmatic approach would likely support the use of less extensive liability and use-based cleanup standards at contaminated urban sites because such departures from the CERCLA model may be necessary in order to attract new business opportunities and to obtain some remedial action at these sites. However, the pragmatic approach would insist that the government take more pro-active measures to ensure that brownfield redevelopment actually results in such opportunities. Accordingly, it is possible to sketch the requirements that might be necessary for brownfield-related laws and projects to meet the demands of a pragmatic approach to environmental justice: (1) completion of government or independent research studies demonstrating that environmental liability is responsible in substantial measure for the lack of development of brownfield sites; (2) that the local community be fully involved in all decisions made regarding brownfield redevelopment; and (3) that the local community be afforded real economic opportunities—jobs, job training, and opportunities for new or spin-off business start-ups—as part of any redevelopment proposal that reduces cleanup standards or immunizes any potentially responsible parties....

* * *

Notes and Questions

1. Does looking at the potential conflicts surrounding brownfield redevelopment from a rights-based versus market-based perspective help to understand the tensions involved? Notice that Professor Engel's "pragmatic" approach addresses causation, as well as public participation and incentive questions. What might be the potential problems involved in implementing her approach? For instance, what does it mean for the local community to be "fully involved" in all decisions regarding brownfield development? Should such decisions require a community consensus?

2. As noted by Professor Eisen, the substantive standards that guide voluntary cleanup of brownfields sites are often significantly relaxed from the usual preference for permanent remedies and for risk reduction to levels determined to be protective of humans who, at present or in the future, might live near and use the resources at a site. Instead, the standards are relaxed based on the premise that the future uses of a site can be constrained such that humans will not be exposed to any contaminants that remain untreated on-site. Future uses under this new paradigm are not unlimited, but restricted. This is, note, a fundamental alteration of the cleanup baseline. The resulting cleanups are termed

"use-restricted" or "risk-based" cleanups (and sometimes, more euphemistically, "flexible" or "differentiated" cleanups). In order to ensure that humans are not, in fact, exposed to the contaminants permitted to remain, environmental agencies must enlist appropriate mechanisms to advise or require that human contact with these contaminants be limited. These mechanisms go by the name of "activity and use limitations" or "institutional controls;" they are a subset of "risk avoidance" approaches to managing risk (risk avoidance is discussed at length in Chapter 6). The two excerpts that follow describe in greater detail the array of mechanisms employed in the brownfields context and raise a number of concerns with these mechanisms from the perspective of environmental justice.

Andrea Ruiz-Esquide, The Uniform Environmental Covenants Act — An Environmental Justice Perspective
31 Ecology Law Quarterly 1007 (2004)

... [T]here has been a general "paradigm shift" away from requiring cleanup to "background standards" towards adopting risk-based corrective actions (RBCAs), either in the form of generic state standards, or in the form of site-specific standards. In this new RBCA paradigm, remediation goals are achieved by limiting exposure to hazardous substances, instead of removing them or decreasing their toxicity. RBCA theory asserts that by limiting exposure, a partial cleanup can achieve the same amount of protection to human health and the environment as a complete cleanup, without incurring often prohibitive removal costs. Risk assessment methods determine the levels of contamination that are acceptable to leave on-site. These analyses take into account several factors, such as the nature and concentration of the contaminants at the site (e.g., the concentration of benzene, lead, arsenic, or PCBs); the existing pathways of exposure by which these contaminants can affect human health or the environment (e.g. inhalation, dermal exposure, ingestion by drinking, or through the food chain); and the potential for actual contact between people and the contaminants (e.g., by children, residents, construction workers, the elderly, etc).

The devices used to limit exposure to residual contamination and thus ensure the effectiveness of risk-based cleanups are a type of activity and use limitation (AUL) called institutional controls. AULs are "legal or physical restrictions or limitations on the use of, or access to, a site or facility to eliminate or minimize potential exposures to chemicals of concern or to prevent activities that would interfere with the effectiveness of a response action." They can take the form of easements, restrictive covenants, equitable servitudes, zoning, building permits, well-drilling prohibitions, contractual agreements (such as permits and consent decrees), informational devices, or other types of controls. AULs provide notice to property owners, lenders, tenants, potential purchasers, and other parties of the presence and location of residual chemicals of concern, and identify uses and activities that are either prohibited or consistent with maintaining a condition of "no significant risk" at the property. Finally, AULs specify ongoing monitoring and maintenance operations necessary to meet the goals of the response action.

These controls are expected to make the property safe for its intended use, despite the remaining contamination. The most common restrictions limit the future use of the land, since different uses of property result in different potential routes and duration of exposure to hazardous wastes. For example, petroleum or lead contamination remaining under a shopping center's parking lot would make that site, although suitable for its current commercial use, inappropriate and dangerous for residential use. With residential use, children may play in the soil over a prolonged period of time and be exposed to contaminants through dermal contact, inhalation, or ingestion. Similarly, agricultural use may result in significant exposure through dermal contact and inhalation when the soil is worked. Industrial use, on the other hand, is unlikely to give rise to the same level of exposure since any contamination will likely be covered, most of the work will be done inside a building, and exposure times would be shorter.

According to the EPA, institutional controls are "generally to be used in conjunction with, rather than in lieu of, engineering measures such as waste treatment or containment." They can be used "during all stages of the cleanup process to accomplish various cleanup-related objectives," and "should be 'layered' (i.e., use multiple [institutional controls]) or implemented in a series to provide overlapping assurances of protection from contamination." While in the past institutional controls served as merely interim measures to protect people from exposure until a cleanup was complete, they are now used as an end strategy to provide long-term protection from exposure when total site remediation is not contemplated.

Three types of institutional controls exist: proprietary controls, governmental controls, and informational devices. Proprietary controls rely on traditional common law property doctrines, including restrictive covenants, reversionary interests, easements, and equitable servitudes. Under a property-based restriction, a private party seeking to enter into a RBCA cleanup that leaves some contamination on-site would enter into an agreement with a third party (e.g., the state environmental agency, a prospective purchaser, or a neighbor) conveying a property right, usually of a non-possessory nature, to that third party. For example, a prospective purchaser may use a restrictive covenant to agree to use the property for industrial purposes only, or he may agree to refrain from using the groundwater. Governmental controls, such as zoning, local ordinances, building permits, and restrictions on well drilling or groundwater activities may also limit future uses of properties with residual contamination. Informational systems include signs, educational materials, site registries, databases, and warnings about the nature of the contamination and consumption of fish or wildlife....

Programs allowing less stringent cleanups at brownfield sites may disproportionately affect minority and low-income groups, since most brownfields are concentrated in predominantly minority and low-income inner city neighborhoods. Environmental justice advocates have voiced serious concerns, therefore, regarding brownfields redevelopment, risk-based cleanups, and institutional controls. While redevelopment does provide opportunities to clean up contaminated properties and to improve economic and environmental conditions in poor neighborhoods, these benefits implicate important trade-offs, such as the health risks that lower cleanup standards create for members of poor communities. Many scholars worry that streamlining regulatory processes and relaxing remediation liability standards also threaten community health and safety. Environmental equity advocates have argued that "[d]ifferential cleanup standards, if set at a level lower than some 'ideal' standard, can readily be characterized as continuing this discrimination against poor and minority communities, shifting to them part of the costs of cleaning up Brownfields (in the sense that a Brownfield does not get completely cleaned up)." As a result, these scholars have suggested that redevelopment of these sites leads minority inner-city communities to accept disproportionately higher health risks in exchange for the possibility of jobs and economic development.

* * *

Robert Hersh & Kris Wernstedt, Out of Site, Out of Mind: The Problem of Institutional Controls

8 Race Poverty & the Environment 15 (Winter 2001)

State voluntary cleanup programs are increasingly taking "risk-based" or "land-use based" approaches to brownfields redevelopment. The terms are shorthand for a decision-making process wherein—at least ideally—regulators, developers, site owners, and the local community determine a cleanup level in accordance with the site's probable future use. The premise is straightforward: instead of cleaning up a contaminated site to background levels for unrestricted use, prospective developers or site owners may be permitted to leave residual contamination on the site if its future use will be restricted to commercial or industrial activities. This requirement for less stringent cleanups may lead to less expensive remedies for developers, promote economic development in urban areas, and improve public involvement in cleanup and reuse deliberations.

The decision to base cleanup levels on restricted land uses typically requires the establishment of institutional controls to ensure that the use of a site remains consistent with its level of cleanup....

Institutional controls often are described rather bloodlessly as legal mechanisms, but they are better understood as a part of the political economy of brownfields. If institutional controls were to fail—exposing persons to hazardous chemicals, for example—one could argue that the benefits accruing to the brownfields developers and site operators from the less costly clean up has been borne by the local community in increased health risks, and that the municipality and regulatory agencies involved should shoulder the financial and administrative costs.

A number of factors limit the effectiveness of institutional controls. First, to be effective, institutional controls that rest on private property restrictions—such as easement—must bind both current and future users of the site. Although an easement between a site owner and a regulatory agency might bind the current owner to the stipulated restrictions, it is unclear to what extent subsequent owners will be bound by the agreement. The ability of third parties, such as community groups or local residents, to enforce a restriction at a site if the property owner fails to comply, and the holder of the easement fails to act promptly, is also uncertain.

Second, the efficacy of institutional controls based on zoning ordinances relies on the consistent application of those ordinances. Yet in no other area of American law are such frequent requests made for amendments to the law (i.e., requests for rezoning) or so many minor revisions made to the law under the guise of an administrative action (i.e., variances and special exemptions).

The most profound limitation to the reliability of institutional controls may be the incapacity of local government to track and enforce them. According to [] surveys of state and local administrators, budget cuts are eroding the capacity of local government to put inspectors in the field and coordinate data exchange among building, engineering, and public works departments. Perhaps even more disturbing, the results of a survey of members of the International City/Council Management Association suggest that only 26 percent of the local government respondents have experience implementing and enforcing institutional controls at hazardous waste sites. The survey results also indicate that citizen complaints and property sales, rather than regular inspections, are more likely to prompt enforcement of institutional controls. A survey of state hazardous waste officials conducted by the Association of State and Territorial Solid Waste Management Officials reinforces those findings, concluding, "The lack of funding and lack of authority, along with unclear jurisdictional issues," are the main obstacles to the effective implementation of institutional controls.

Clearly, additional funding for monitoring and enforcement and more effective coordination between government agencies is necessary. But the larger concern is to consider what kinds of institutional arrangements are needed to design and enforce land use restrictions in a regulatory context in which cleanups increasingly are initiated and implemented by the private sector, and in which voluntary cleanup provisions provide few entrance points for public input. A first step, running somewhat counter to the prevailing trend, would be to include members of the local community in the design, implementation, and enforcement of institutional controls. While the participation of the local community would not be sufficient to ensure the integrity of institutional controls, it is a necessary and badly needed safeguard.

* * *

Notes and Questions

1. Data have begun to be gathered on the use of institutional controls. The evidence to date suggests that advocates' concern regarding the effectiveness of institutional controls (ICs) is well-founded. Professor Catherine O'Neill discusses some of this evidence:

> There [is] evidence that restrictions on the use of contaminated sites and resources are often not implemented, monitored, or enforced. A [2005] study by the Government Accountability Office (GAO) of Superfund sites at which institutional controls were employed provides several examples. At one site, an institutional control prohibited any use of groundwater without prior written approval from EPA. However, in 2003, EPA discovered that over 25 million gallons of this water had been pumped for use as drinking water during 2002 and that this use may have been going on for some time during the previous five years as well. At another site, an institutional control required monitoring for worker safety precautions during any digging operations at the site. A GAO visit, however, revealed active digging about which the supervising EPA official for the site was unaware because he had not visited the site in four years. At a third site, the GAO found "significant evidence of trespassing at the site," but a steadfast refusal on the part of the responsible official to monitor the site. Other sources similarly relate accounts of broken fences and breached prohibitions. Advisories and warnings, too, may not be adequately maintained. Agency officials in New Jersey found that a sign advising against crabbing on the Hackensack River had fallen or been taken down and was being used, ironically, by a family who had placed it over a fire to support a cooking pot filled with river water and freshly caught crabs. An agency review of the Agriculture Street Landfill site in New Orleans ... revealed that there were no provisions for forwarding to new property owners the instructions designed to ensure the integrity of engineering controls ... (e.g., for handling and cultivating soils above the geotextile barrier). [The Agriculture Street Landfill is located in a neighborhood that is 98% African American. The cleanup plan for the "developed" portion of this site, on which residences and a school were located, called for replacing the top two feet of contaminated soils but leaving the remainder in place under a geotextile barrier. Eds.] And zoning restrictions or other proprietary controls may not be enforced.

Catherine A. O'Neill, *No Mud Pies: Risk Avoidance as Risk Regulation,* 31 Vт. L. Rev. 273, 313–14 (2007). In fact, one scholar has estimated that, over time, ICs can be expected to fail at as many as 100 percent of non-NPL sites that have not achieved unrestricted use standards. John Pendergrass, *Institutional Controls in the States: What Is and Can Be Done to Protect Public Health at Brownfields,* 35 Conn. L. Rev. 1303,1312 (2003).

2. Another problem that may arise at sites that undertake a use-restricted cleanup is the potential for recontamination. That is, because use-restricted cleanups allow some amount of contamination to remain untreated on-site, they leave open the possibility that these contaminants will migrate or otherwise behave in unpredictable ways. Again, Professor O'Neill recounts some disturbing examples:

> [R]ecent reviews of the Superfund cleanup at the Bunker Hill Mining and Metallurgical Site in the Coeur d'Alene River Basin have identified several instances in which lead has migrated to recontaminate areas that have already been cleaned up. Soils contaminated with lead are eroding from surrounding hillsides, are being tracked by vehicles from unpaved surfaces, or are otherwise migrating into relatively clean areas, including residential yards that have already been remediated.... In a similar vein, lead, arsenic, and [polyaromatic hydrocarbons or] PAHs left untreated in the "undeveloped" portion of the Agriculture Street Landfill Site in New Orleans remain a potential threat to human health. [T]he [Agency for Toxic Substances and Disease Registry] ATSDR and others have found evidence that humans continued to access the area, despite the presence of a fence. People use the area for storage of Mardi Gras floats and other vehicles—vehicles that potentially track contaminants into clean areas of the site. In addition, when Hurricane Katrina hit New Orleans, the entire site was inundated and remained under water for days. Although data are still being gathered, there is evidence that lead, arsenic, and other contaminants were carried by floodwaters and may now contaminate the soils at the site and across much of New Orleans.

O'Neill, *supra,* at 309–10. Can EPA or other agencies require that this recontamination be addressed? In its typical release of liability, the EPA may insert a "reopener clause" that provides that the EPA may revisit the issue of liability upon certain circumstances such as the subsequent discovery that past contamination is more extensive than previously thought, requiring additional cleanup. Agencies are often reluctant, however, to exercise this reopener authority. Can you think of reasons why this might be so? Note, too, that for some brownfields redevelopment activities, the new use contemplated at the site might be for industrial activities. Would a reopener clause be triggered if post-cleanup industrial processes resulted in contamination? If the new industrial activity is similar to past activity, how will the EPA or its state counterpart distinguish between pre- and post-development contamination for purposes of using the reopener clause to finance additional cleanup?

3. As noted above, a central component of the appeal of use-restricted cleanups is their promise that the same amount of human health protection can be provided at far less cost. *See, e.g.,* Philip E. Karmel, *Achieving Radical Reductions in Cleanup Costs,* 499 Prac. Law Inst./Real 371 (Nov. 2003). Professor O'Neill sounds a cautionary note about the potential cost savings from reliance on use restrictions as compared to a complete cleanup:

> Where cost data exist, they are especially incomplete. Efforts to estimate the costs of institutional controls, for example, have to date failed adequately to incorporate the costs of implementing, monitoring, reporting, and enforcing over

the entire life of the institutional control—a period that could last decades, if not in perpetuity. In fact, as EPA has itself acknowledged, "once the total life-cycle costs of implementing, monitoring and enforcing an [institutional control]—which may exceed 30 years—are fully calculated, it may actually be less costly in the long term to implement a remedy that requires treatment of the waste." Note, too that cost data here tend to be incomplete in asymmetric ways: the costs of engineering controls are more fully characterized and more readily quantified than the costs of institutional controls. As well, such tallies tend to neglect the economic benefits of prevention, reduction, or cleanup. At the Bunker Hill Mining and Metallurgical Site, for example, cleanup activities are estimated to have contributed $77.4 million to the state and local economy as of 2003.

O'Neill, *supra*, at 327. Professor O'Neill goes on to highlight some of the ways in which attempts to compare the costs of a use-restricted cleanup and a full-blown cleanup are likely to be incomplete or inaccurate. What might these be? What considerations would you recommend be included on each side of the ledger if you were trying to assess fully the relative costs of these two options at a site slated for potential brownfields redevelopment? How would you recommend that the temporal dimensions of these costs be considered; specifically, should future costs be "discounted"? (For an elaboration of cost-benefit analysis and the related practice of discounting, see Chapter 5.)

4. As noted above, observers have questioned agencies' ability accurately to predict future uses of a site at which they permit a use-restricted cleanup. Again, based on even a few years' experience, evidence suggests there is reason for concern. "[At numerous sites,] future land uses once thought highly unlikely may come to pass, as former industrial sites become desirable urban residential properties and former mining or agricultural wastelands become attractive rural retreats." O'Neill, *supra*, at 312. If agencies' predictions are incorrect, of course, their assumptions about human exposure at the site may be inaccurate—leading to inadequate protection of human health. Even if such predictions of future use are accurate, however, environmental justice advocates have pointed to the concern that such determinations can "lock in" particular future land uses, thus taking away from the community the ability to shape its future in terms of the uses to which it aspires. *See, e.g.,* Ruiz-Esquide, *supra*, at 1022. This concern can be ameliorated—in part—by ensuring that the community participates from the very earliest stages in planning a redevelopment effort. The role of public participation in ensuring the success of brownfields redevelopment is one of the issues taken up in the following section.

2. Evaluating Brownfields Redevelopment on the Ground

Given the potential promise and pitfalls of brownfields redevelopment, many environmental justice advocates have observed that, with regard to "success" on the ground, the devil is in the details. With some years of experience in brownfields redevelopment, observers are now better able to assess redevelopment efforts in practice, particularly efforts by state and local governments. By way of example, the following excerpt provides a close examination of such efforts by the City of Chicago.

Jessica Higgins, Evaluating the Chicago Brownfields Initiative: The Effects of City-Initiated Brownfield Redevelopment on Surrounding Communities

3 Northwestern Journal of Law & Social Policy 240 (2008)

The City of Chicago has taken an active role in such redevelopment projects by creating its own Chicago Brownfields Initiative. The Chicago Brownfields Initiative was established in 1993 and is based on the premise that in many cases, public resources are necessary to return brownfield sites to productive use. Through a process of acquiring, cleaning, and coordinating the redevelopment of brownfields, Chicago claims to have succeeded in reversing the urban blight associated with brownfields by transforming them into industrial facilities, green space, affordable housing, and technical and manufacturing centers in some of the City's most challenging areas and economically disadvantaged neighborhoods.

Chicago's Brownfields Initiative (the "Initiative") has completed or is in the process of completing over 40 site-remediation and redevelopment projects, and the general consensus appears to be that the Initiative has successfully spurred redevelopment and reuse of sites that otherwise would have sat vacant and unproductive. An examination of the program's results indicates that Chicago's Brownfields Initiative has created and retained jobs, objectively increased the quality of life in surrounding communities, provided housing stock, prompted some additional investment, increased nearby property values, improved environmental health and safety, and provided valuable services to communities.

However, enthusiasm regarding these successes must be tempered by a series of more critical questions. Do the jobs, services, and amenities created at brownfield sites actually benefit the communities in which they are placed? Is redevelopment causing gentrification and pushing out the original community? Is the community's reaction even being measured? Are the technical and institutional controls put in place to protect environmental and human health sufficient? Do lowered cleanup standards lock sites into one type of use that may not always serve the needs of the community? In sum, has the Chicago Brownfields Initiative made the leap from redevelopment to actually alleviating economic and social problems? ...

Illinois's brownfields program, created in 1995, includes versions of each of the typical components of state brownfields programs. The core of the Illinois brownfields scheme is the voluntary Site Remediation Program (SRP). Parties enter the program by allowing their site to be evaluated by the [Illinois Environmental Protection Agency] IEPA and preparing a site remediation plan to be approved by the IEPA. Upon approval of a site remediation plan, the site qualifies for a variety of financial assistance programs, including grants, loans, and tax credits, to cover the costs of assessment and remediation. Sites in the voluntary SRP are then remediated under the Tiered Approach to Corrective Action [Objectives] (TACO) which allows sites to be cleaned to differing degrees depending upon the intended future use. Once the cleanup is completed, the IEPA issues a No Further Remediation letter (NFR letter) for the property, which releases the program participant from future liability and contains the terms and conditions for the future use of the property. Illinois is able to provide such protection from CERCLA liability because the state has entered into the Superfund Memorandum of Agreement with the U.S. EPA stating that the U.S. EPA will not generally pursue legal action with respect to sites cleaned voluntarily under the Illinois SRP....

First, the Successes

The literature on brownfields redevelopment uses a number of measures to judge the success of a project or program. Though the potential rubrics are many, they can be distilled into a few basic measures which can be evaluated on a project by project basis: job creation and retention, housing development, improvements to quality of life/services and amenities provided to the community, encouragement of additional investment in the area, improvement in the environmental health and safety of the community, and benefits to local government due to increased tax revenues. Chicago has achieved success in each of these areas.

Job Creation and Retention

The original focus of the Chicago Brownfields Initiative was industrial and economic redevelopment with the purpose of job creation, and the City actively recruited employers and manufacturers to occupy former brownfields. While numbers vary greatly from project to project, brownfields in the Chicago area have created an average of 77 jobs and retained an average of 68 jobs per project, 76.2% of which reported higher wages than were paid under previous uses of the land.

Numerous examples demonstrate the success of the Initiative in this arena. At 445 North Sacramento Avenue, the City coordinated the transformation of the former Sacramento Crushing Company, which had deteriorated into a pile of debris, into the Chicago Center for Green Technology. The Center created 38 jobs, and the redevelopment also saved 450 jobs at a neighboring company that was planning to leave Chicago. The former International Amphitheater is now home to a new Aramark manufacturing and warehouse facility, which will retain 217 jobs and create an additional 90 jobs at the site. An abandoned parcel at 927 South California Avenue—a site that was targeted for redevelopment by the Initiative due to the high surrounding unemployment rate and consequential available labor force—became the California Avenue Business Park, creating between 400 and 600 new jobs. The list goes on … Even factoring in normal economic growth, the sheer number of jobs created by the Chicago Brownfields Initiative is impressive.

Residential Redevelopment

While brownfields redevelopment, across the country and in Chicago, initially focused on industrial projects, attention is now being paid to residential development on these sites. As of 2003, 25 publicly assisted residential brownfields projects had been undertaken in Chicago. These 25 projects produced a total of 4,853 units, around 2,000 of which were designated to be affordable.… Perhaps more importantly, Chicago's brownfield redevelopment has gone beyond "cherry picking" the best properties in the best locales. City government has successfully promoted development in areas where few developers would have otherwise ventured. Chicago's programs and incentives have also succeeded in causing developers to incorporate affordable units into new housing, even in higher-end projects.

Again, examples illustrate the City's success. At Columbia Pointe, located at 63rd and Woodlawn streets, 51 new homes replaced a vacant and abandoned commercial strip, and the addition of up to 209 more homes is under consideration. Twenty percent of these homes are designated to be affordable. In Bronzeville, at 705 East 40th Street, 33 new homes were constructed, 16 of which are now occupied by residents who had previously moved from the neighborhood due to its deterioration and lack of housing stock.…

Improvements to Quality of Life, Services & Amenities Provided

The City of Chicago seems to have recognized the importance of improving the quality of life in the areas surrounding brownfields and has responded by incorporating service-providers, amenities, and open spaces into many Chicago Brownfields Initiative projects. By providing such useful services and recreational facilities while at the same time eliminating vacant lots that harbor criminal activity, the Chicago Brownfields Initiative has contributed to improved quality of life near redeveloped sites.

At 3333 East 87th Street, the site of the new Solo factory, the City created two TIF [Tax Increment Fund] districts—one for Solo and one for "the betterment of the surrounding neighborhood." [TIFs facilitate redevelopment by utilizing future property tax revenues, generated within the district, to pay for necessary public improvements. Eds.] The Chicago Park District worked with the Department of Planning and Development to create a lakefront park at the site. The roads to and from the park were revamped into boulevard-style roadways to improve community access and aesthetics. The development of the Columbia Pointe Homes was similarly beneficial to the area. The new affordable housing provided a basic necessity for the community, and the development was accompanied by bike trails, new lighting in alleys, and neighborhood fruit and vegetable gardens. At the 76th and Parnell Street residential redevelopment, the north portion of the site was reserved for green space and a community center was built to provide after-school programming, education, and family-oriented activities. The California Avenue Business Park includes a job training facility and prompted the expansion of local transportation facilities....

In addition to providing services and amenities, brownfield redevelopment also improves the quality of life in a neighborhood by reducing the incidence of detrimental activities in the area. Redevelopments have been linked to a decrease in criminal behavior. Vacant lots and abandoned buildings provide out-of-sight venues for drug use, dealing, and other criminal activity. Such sites also invite illegal dumping that deepens the risk to human and environmental health in the area. By eliminating these vacant lots and structures, these illicit activities are pushed out as well.

Encouragement of Additional Investment

Brownfields legislation and programs are no longer just about remediation and reuse, but rather function as a means to increase the economic viability of an area. One new building does not an economic turnaround make, so to be deemed successful a brownfield redevelopment must bring with it additional investment, businesses, and development. Many of Chicago's brownfields projects are credited as the source of additional investment in the area. The ATA Airline Training Center came hand in hand with the modernization of Midway Airport. A company near the Chicago Center for Green Technology changed its plans to leave the community. On West Adams Street, the Scott Petersen Sausage Plant, located across the street from a City-initiated brownfield development, added a new smokehouse and hired locals to fill 100 new positions in the plant.... In many cases, it is difficult to directly attribute additional investment in an area to a brownfield redevelopment. However, the benefits that accompany brownfield redevelopment—such as increased population due to new housing stock, city investment in infrastructure, and improved aesthetics—all seem likely to encourage additional investment, and the instances above demonstrate that this is occurring in Chicago....

Environmental Health and Safety

One of the goals of the Brownfields Initiative, and of all brownfields programs and legislation, is to improve environmental health. The degree of both contamination and cleanup varies substantially from site to site within the City, so Chicago conducts site-specific assessment and remediation planning. This allows for cleanup to be matched to the current contamination and to the future use of the site.

At the California Business Park site, 964 tons of lead and chromium contaminated soil and eleven underground storage tanks were removed and backfilled with crushed stone. At the Gateway Park site, 600,000 cubic yards of concrete, asphalt, construction debris, rubbish, and hazardous automobile shredder residue were removed. The International Union of Operating Engineers (IUOE) site was freed of 2,990 tons of radioactive and contaminated soil as well as a number of underground storage tanks. The new Solo site was remediated to residential standards, returning the site to its pre-industrial condition....

Next, the Concerns

It is apparent that Chicago's Brownfields Initiative has been largely successful by conventional measures. These successes, however, are not unqualified....

Do the Jobs Generated Benefit Members of the Community?

... [B]rownfield redevelopment should reduce the high unemployment that plagues many of the inner city neighborhoods in which the redevelopment occurs. Chicago has made an effort to do so in many of its brownfield projects. Because many of the sites became home to industrial facilities, most of the jobs created are likely to be accessible to the less educated workforce that resides near brownfields. Furthermore, a number of the Chicago brownfield redevelopment projects incorporated job training programs aimed at bringing local residents up to speed with the skills needed to fill the jobs created by redevelopment.

Other redevelopments, however, seem less locally-oriented. The ATA Training Center includes a hotel, restaurant, and training facilities for airline pilots, attendants, and customer service personnel—jobs not likely to go to area residents. Likewise, the Chicago Center for Green Technology houses an environmental consulting firm and a solar panel company—creating positions largely foreclosed to those lacking higher education. The IUOE provides a new facility for union members, which may or may not include area residents. While not harmful to a community, these sites do not fully incorporate community members in the benefits of redevelopment.

Another deeper question accompanies the "job creation" goal of brownfield redevelopment: whether new industrial jobs really benefit a community in the long run. The Chicago Brownfields Initiative has focused on re-industrialization of abandoned or unused sites. Meanwhile, in the economy at large, there has been a systematic disinvestment in the nation's industrial capacity. Should this pattern of deindustrialization result in the loss of jobs in the manufacturing sector, the Chicago Brownfields strategy could end up contributing to central city unemployment in the future....

Do the New Services and Improvements Benefit Members of the Community?

Many of the Chicago Brownfields Initiative sites in which the provision of "services" was a focus were sites initiated by, or redeveloped in close collaboration with, an organized community group. Columbia Pointe, the Lawndale site, and the Bronzeville site provide prime examples of how brownfield redevelopment, prompted by community groups and facilitated by the active efforts of the City, can reflect and fulfill the needs of the community. It is encouraging that in cases where community groups have become involved, their participation has been welcomed and the results have been positive.... With local groups initiating projects, the needs of the community are likely to be addressed.

However, in many other cases, where community groups are less active, it is difficult to find any mention of efforts to provide services to a community; and unfortunately, it is often the communities least able to organize that are most in need of the services and improvements that brownfields redevelopment has the potential to offer....

Has Brownfield Redevelopment Led to Gentrification, Pushing out Original Residents?

According to some observers, redevelopment in Chicago has been synonymous with displacement. Critics allege that City Hall has followed the lead of downtown corporate interests and the real estate industry, and that the low-income and working class enclaves that stand in the way of redevelopment are simply removed and the community disbanded. Further, as affordable housing stock shrinks and the rental market tightens, the concern becomes even more urgent because gentrification may not only force residents out of their communities, but also might leave them without a place to go. While the Brownfields Initiative cannot be blamed for this alleged pattern of city-center gentrification pushing the poor to the west and inner suburbs, there is some indication that the brownfields program has perpetuated this problem.

Smaller Chicago Brownfields Initiative sites are unlikely to contribute to the gentrification of an area to any substantial degree. For example, at 76th and Parnell Streets, six single-family, eighteen two-flat homes, and twelve single-family foster care homes were constructed. The homes are "moderately-priced" and intended for community residents who are first-time home buyers.... Projects like these are not only geared towards current community residents, but their size also makes it unlikely that they will substantially change the character of the neighborhood and push area residents out.

Larger redevelopment projects, however, bear an increased risk of causing gentrification and displacement. Columbia Pointe, upon completion, created 260 new residential units, 20% of which are reserved as affordable housing. While the intent of the redevelopment was to expand area housing options for a mix of income levels and promote economic opportunity for the local community, concern arose early amongst neighborhood residents that there was a need for more affordable housing and that too many condominiums were replacing subsidized rental housing, pricing residents out of their own neighborhood. Though these concerns were discussed with community stakeholders, the percentage of designated affordable housing was never changed and the units, none of which were rental, sold for between $200,000 and $400,000 soon after completion. In a neighborhood such as Woodlawn, in which 39% of the residents live below the poverty level and only 28% of households have annual incomes of more than $35,000, housing in a large new-construction development like Columbia Pointe is inaccessible to a majority of the existing residents and is likely to contribute to gentrification that could eventually push these residents from their community.

At University Village, a similar situation resulted in a boycott of the project by a number of community groups. Hundreds of vendors who had operated in the area were displaced by the redevelopment, and locals feared that the new residents would alter the fabric of the surrounding neighborhood and cause exclusionary displacement of the original residents and businesses. The controversy eventually subsided, and 21% of the units were designated to be in the affordable range, but the 930 units (ranging in price from $165,900 to $1,299,900) were marketed as a planned community and were sold overwhelmingly to University of Illinois, Chicago faculty and staff, staff from nearby hospitals, city employees, and suburbanites moving back to the City. This large redevelopment, which also included restaurants, shops, academic buildings, and student housing, is inherently different from the mixture of immigrant culture, commerce, and enterprise that formerly occupied the space, and neighborhood residents do not consider the redeveloped area "part of the neighborhood anymore." ...

The issues of affordable housing and gentrification are much larger [in] scope ... [and] although brownfield projects are but a small part of the larger patterns, they are not exempt from scrutiny in this arena....

Is Site Remediation Sufficient to Protect Community Health and Safety?

... Because states often offer relaxed cleanup standards, streamlined administrative procedures, and releases from future liability to spur development and reuse, voluntary brownfield cleanups may involve trading increased health risks for the prospect of economic improvements. The environmental and human health concerns raised by the Chicago program are similar to those associated with most brownfields programs and legislation. Because the site-specific TACO approach is used in Illinois, there is significant flexibility with respect to cleanup standards depending upon the expected post-development use of a site. Under Illinois brownfield legislation, each site must be cleaned to a level that is considered safe enough for the developer's self-identified next use. At each site, the IEPA evaluates the consequences of leaving certain contaminants at the site with or without certain controls, and an engineer must certify that the selected cleanup methods are sufficient to protect human health and the environment. While the TACO cleanup standards for brownfields are fairly conservative, there remains concern that lowered standards may expose neighbors to contaminants.

Additionally, when a site is remediated with only the next use in mind, the future use of the property is restricted to that (or a similar) use.... At the Parnell Place site, [for example,] one section of contaminated soil was allowed to remain on the site but covered with a three foot barrier to eliminate exposure at the surface. The decision to cap, instead of remove, the contaminated soil was made because it was not necessary to put water or sewer lines in the parcel, and capping requires less time and resources than excavating the soil. Consequently, the insertion of underground utilities will never be an option at the site.... [R]emediators and redevelopers do not have to consider whether drinking water may be drawn from the site at any point in the future, and that the program allows developers to segment portions of a brownfield, remediate a "fenced off" section, and disregard the effects on neighbors still exposed to the contamination present in the unremediated sections.

While some flexibility is necessary in order to make projects fiscally approachable, allowing different remediation standards and control techniques presents questions of environmental justice, long-term community well-being, and sustainability.

* * *

Notes and Questions

1. Do the criteria employed by Ms. Higgins to assess the success of the various brownfields redevelopment projects in Chicago provide a useful gauge? Are there other considerations that, in your view, ought to come into play in evaluating the success of brownfields efforts on the ground?

2. As mentioned above, many environmental justice advocates, including Ms. Higgins, have suggested that meaningful community involvement is the key to the success of brownfields redevelopment efforts. In response to these concerns, the EPA reportedly revised its criteria for projects that it funds to require that community input be solicited and verified. *See* NAT'L ENVTL. JUSTICE ADVISORY COUNCIL, WASTE AND FACILITY SITING SUBCOMMITTEE, U.S. ENVTL. PROT. AGENCY REPORT NO. 500-R-96-002, ENVIRONMENTAL JUSTICE, URBAN REVITALIZATION, AND BROWNFIELDS: THE SEARCH FOR AUTHENTIC SIGNS OF HOPE (December 1996). Local officials were concerned that extensive public involvement would be a disincentive for industry stakeholders and would hinder brownfield redevelopment. In early 1999, in response to these concerns, the EPA conducted a study of seven EPA Assessment Pilot Projects. U.S. ENVTL. PROT. AGENCY, REPORT NO. 500-R-99-003, BROWNFIELDS TITLE VI CASE STUDIES: SUMMARY REPORT (June 1999). As expected, the case study disclosed that community residents were concerned about cleanup and reuse. However, community residents were generally supportive when the redevelopment was perceived to be an improvement over the existing blight and the project sponsor was willing to promote job creation for local residents. Of the three pilots that involved heavy industrial use, an important component of reducing conflict was that "involving the community allowed potential problems to be identified and solved from the beginning when stakes were lower and design changes could more easily be made." *Id.* at 8. For example, in a cement processing operation in Miami, a neutral toxicologist was hired to explain the emissions, and in Camden, the developer described the new, cleaner process and agreed to the community's request that an independent engineering firm conduct on-site monitoring.

Another important finding was that projects that provided tangible benefits for the community had greater community support. For example, a stamping press manufacturer in Chicago created 100 new jobs for local residents and a plastic rack manufacturer in Detroit created 30 new jobs with a potential for 70 more. As the case study report noted, what is striking is that the "community define[d] the problem [i.e., the abandoned site] from the vantage point of their aspirations," thus injecting more positive elements into an economic transaction formerly devoid of social responsibility or civic possibility. NAT'L ENVTL. JUSTICE ADVISORY COUNCIL, *supra*, at 23. In the Chicago Pilot, for example, stakeholders built upon the brownfield-inspired relationship between the City and local communities to subsequently institute a cooperative enforcement program that included brochures in several languages, a hotline for citizens to report illegal dumping in their communities, and heavier penalties for violators.

The case studies indicate that use-based cleanup standards and new industrial activity can be acceptable to the community if there is early and meaningful public input, independent technical review, a genuine attempt to mitigate the facility's adverse impacts on health, safety and quality of life in the host community, and tangible benefits to the host community. These projects arguably reflect a more comprehensive strategy of addressing brownfields in its complex social context.

3. EPA-sponsored brownfield pilot projects, however, may differ from some state initiatives in the degree to which public participation is required. Many states have been hesitant to provide robust public participation opportunities in their voluntary cleanup programs because of concern about public opposition. However, as noted in NEJAC's Authentic Signs of Hope report, "[t]hose who claim that the community will always require the maximum level of cleanup, ignore the fact that, far better than anyone else, the community recognizes the dangers of losing any cleanup by demanding a full cleanup." *See* NAT'L ENVTL. JUSTICE ADVISORY COUNCIL, *supra* at 41. Moreover, other studies con-

firm the value of public participation. As one author notes, "In almost every case study analyzed, carefully orchestrated public outreach and involvement plans were implemented from the outset. Without this critical community buy-in, many project participants note, their efforts easily could have fallen apart." *See* EDITH M. PEPPER, LESSONS FROM THE FIELD: UNLOCKING ECONOMIC POTENTIAL WITH AN ENVIRONMENTAL KEY 22 (1997). As noted in 1999, "[t]here is still a lag between reality and law, however, in that most state statutes still require little more than nominal public participation, and most public outreach efforts are done through ad hoc groups or task forces convened for particular projects. Where developers undertake public outreach efforts without a framework to constrain their activities, one person's 'carefully orchestrated' outreach can easily become another's 'illegitimate process.'" Joel B. Eisen, *Brownfields Policies for Sustainable Cities,* 9 DUKE ENVTL. L. & POL'Y F. 187, 224 (1999).

4. Professor Eisen and others argue that the federal government must maintain a strong role in brownfield redevelopment because of the lax oversight and lack of robust public participation that some state programs have exhibited:

> The primary brownfields incentives, of course, are those offered by the voluntary cleanup programs now available in all but one state that provide road maps for developers to approach state environmental agencies or brownfields revitalization agencies (if they exist) and deal directly with the states. The [Small Business Liability Relief and Brownfields Revitalization Act of 2002] provides some shelter for a developer that engages with the state, reducing the risk (claimed to exist well over a decade ago) that the Environmental Protection Agency ("EPA") will overfile and conclude that a cleanup completed successfully in a state program is not acceptable at the federal level ["Overfiling" is when the federal government sues a regulated entity for a violation that was the subject of a state enforcement action because the state action was inadequate. Eds.]....

> This brownfields story has led to certain basic trends in remediation and reuse. First and foremost, developers are treated as a monolithic group in most voluntary cleanup programs. Virtually anyone willing to tackle the remediation and reuse of a site can do so, with few exceptions. Because developers engage voluntarily with the state, they presumably lack culpability and, therefore, control the timing, sequencing, and even the comprehensiveness of remediation and reuse. The developer that takes the lead at a brownfield site dictates the terms of the cleanup and redevelopment strategy, otherwise it is assumed that it would not be worthwhile to proceed. The result is a level of trust unheard of in other contexts. The [Memorandum of Agreement] MOA or a similar document empowers the developer to clean up the site, and the state's role is limited to that of overseer. This means that the remediation outcome is only as good as the state's ability to verify the results. In states where remediation at a brownfield site can proceed without state involvement of any sort, the only verification is indirect through state-certified consultants who approve the cleanup results....

> Allowing developers to control their own cleanups also does not comport with a vision of community-wide real estate development, such that after a decade of experience, a "consensus is building among environmental and real estate professionals that the remediation and reuse of brownfields that were not addressed through 'first generation' brownfield programs will require new strategies."

Eisen, *Brownfields at 20, supra,* at 729–30, 755. The call for federal oversight raises federalism issues. *See* William W. Buzbee, *Brownfields, Environmental Federalism, and Institutional Determinism,* 21 WM. & MARY ENVTL. L. & POL'Y REV. 1 (1997), and more generally, Chapter 5. Is there a way for the federal government to assure adequate protection for brownfield communities, while simultaneously allowing states to experiment with redevelopment approaches and respond to local political and economic complexities?

5. Some observers have argued that the parcel-by-parcel approach to brownfield redevelopment fails to account for the potential cumulative and synergistic effects of several sites located close together in an inner-city neighborhood, a concern that arises in permitting generally (see Chapter 8). To better protect against this risk, some commentators advocate a city-wide approach to evaluating impacts and the use of traditional zoning classifications to create adequate buffer zones and other safeguards. Others have advanced the idea of a state certification program for brownfield redevelopment, with states reserving the authority to withdraw certification upon a failure of institutional controls or discovery of additional contamination. *See* U.S. ENVTL. PROT. AGENCY, Final Draft Guidance for Developing Superfund Memoranda of Agreement (SMOA) Language Concerning State Voluntary Cleanup Programs, 62 Fed. Reg. 47,495 (Sept. 9, 1997).

6. One consequence of brownfields redevelopment efforts that deserves attention is the potential for gentrification and, ultimately, the displacement of people of color and low-income people. As brownfields are returned to productive use and the surrounding blight is diminished, an area that was formerly unappealing to the white and affluent may become more desirable. Although in the run of cases, redevelopment of a single brownfield site will not unduly influence development patterns in an entire area, this is not always so. It is sometimes the case that brownfield redevelopment efforts are significant enough to have this effect. In either event, although other forces that contribute to land-use patterns may be at work as well, brownfields redevelopment activities can nonetheless play a significant role in bringing about gentrification. For a provocative exchange on the impact of gentrification, see J. Peter Byrne, *Two Cheers for Gentrification,* 46 How. L.J. 405 (2003) and john a. powell & Marguerite L. Spencer, *Giving Them the Old "One-Two": Gentrification and the K.O. of Impoverished Urban Dwellers,* 46 How. L.J. 433 (2003). For a revealing case study of gentrification in what was until recently a community of color in Seattle, see Henry W. McGee, Jr., *Seattle's Central District, 1990–2006: Integration or Displacement?,* 36 URB. LAW. 167 (2007).

7. Given that there is the potential for significant positive gain from brownfield redevelopment, how might you devise a framework that would give firms the incentive to invest in brownfields that provide substantial benefits to local communities, while at the same time minimizing the risk of inadequate cleanups and the host of other potential pitfalls raised by brownfields redevelopment?

Chapter 10

Governmental Initiatives to Address Environmental Justice

A. Introduction

In addition to considering environmental justice when environmental agencies perform core governmental functions such as standard-setting, enforcement, and cleanup, governmental agencies at all levels have attempted to address environmental inequities through a wide range of broader initiatives. In fact, a few states, notably California, have enacted specific environmental justice legislation. This chapter examines how environmental justice issues have been addressed at different levels of governance, including international, federal, state, and tribal. Moreover, because environmental justice is a crosscutting issue, some agencies have elected to address disparities through broad-based collaboration among public and private actors in many fields and at different levels of governance. This chapter concludes by discussing the emergence of this strategy and some of the interagency and collaborative initiatives that have been undertaken to date. Please note that this chapter contains many acronyms. For the reader's convenience, a glossary of these acronyms appears at chapter's end.

B. Environmental Justice at the International Level

What is an international environmental justice issue? Such issues are potentially far-ranging, from degraded environments that cannot support a healthy existence, to food security, to the disproportionate effects of climate instability. These situations may be directly linked to international activities or involve environmental problems that cross national borders and are not addressed by the domestic law of any nation involved. In other instances, the scale of the environmental problem may be so dire that it presents a logical relationship to human rights. Professor Dinah Shelton explains:

> The interrelationship of human rights and environmental protection is undeniable.... Without diverse and sustained living and non-living resources, human beings cannot survive. The problem can be demonstrated by the example of freshwater. Only 2 per cent of the water of the earth is accessible for human use. Any loss of water resources, especially pollution of underground aquifers, poses dangers for generations to come. According to the [United Nations] UN

317

Water Council between 5 million and 10 million people die each year as a result of polluted drinking water, most of them women and children in poverty. Severe water shortages exist in 26 countries and by 2050, two-thirds of the world's population could face water shortages. Sixty per cent of the world's drinking water is located in just 10 countries and much of it is polluted. Freshwater shortages are already raising tensions and threaten to be a cause of future interstate conflicts. Air pollution, contaminated soil and loss of food sources add to the problems of health and survival. Maintenance of the earth's cultural diversity, in particular the preservation of indigenous peoples and local communities, requires conserving the areas in which they live.

Dinah Shelton, *Environmental Rights*, in PEOPLES' RIGHTS 185, 189–90 (Philip Alston ed., 2001).

Given the absence of global regulatory authority for environmental protection, how can disparities and extreme degradation be addressed? Although concrete initiatives to address these issues in the international arena are rare, there have been a series of proclamations adopted in recent years concerning environmental harms in relation to human rights. From these statements, impacted peoples have attempted to utilize adjudicatory fora to press for remedies. The authors below discuss these emerging responses. One prevalent approach asserts that a basic level of environmental security is a human right. To some, this is an uneasy fit, as Professors Donald Anton and Dinah Shelton explain in the excerpt below.

Human Rights and Environment
(Donald K. Anton & Dinah Shelton eds., forthcoming 2009)

... Tension or Complementarity?

The assertions in the Stockholm Declaration sparked an early academic search for jurisprudential underpinnings for linkages between human rights and the environment. A number of texts and articles made their appearance in which the international legal case was made for "the human rights of individuals to be guaranteed a pure, healthful, and decent environment." Today, the protection of the environment and promotion of human rights are increasingly seen by many as intertwined, complementary goals. For Christopher Weeramantry, a former Vice-President of the International Court of Justice, this is self-evident. In his separate opinion in the *Case Concerning the Gabčikovo-Nagymaros Project* Judge Weeramantry wrote:

> The protection of the environment is ... a vital part of contemporary human rights doctrine, for it is a *sine qua non* for numerous human rights such as the right to health and the right to life itself. It is scarcely necessary to elaborate on this, as damage to the environment can impair and undermine all the human rights spoken of in the Universal Declaration and other human rights instruments.

Case Concerning the Gabčikovo-Nagymaros Project, [1997] ICJ Rep. 7, 91–92.

Yet, other scholars reject the connection between human rights and the environment and see incompatibility or even danger in their coupling. They see human rights and environmental protection based on fundamentally different and ultimately irreconcilable value systems. These differences are, to them, much more likely to lead to conflict than to be complementary. The arguments proceed, on the one hand, with some environmental lawyers maintaining that a human rights focus for environmental law ultimately reduces all other environmental values to an instrumental use for humanity so that the quality of human life can be enhanced. This human-centered, utilitarian view reduces the non-human and nonliving aspects of ecosystems to their economic value to humans and promotes unsustainable resource exploitation and environmental degradation as a human good. Furthermore, some human rights lawyers believe that linking human rights and the environment diminishes the importance and focus on protection of more immediate human rights concerns such as ending genocide, extra judicial killings, torture, and arbitrary detention.

Professor Dinah Shelton posits a third view which she says seems to best reflect the current state of play in law and policy.

> [This view] sees human rights and environmental protection as each representing different, but overlapping, societal values. The two fields share a core of common interests and objectives, although obviously not all human rights violations are necessarily linked to environmental degradation. Likewise, environmental issues cannot always be addressed effectively within the human rights framework, and any attempt to force all such issues into a human rights rubric may fundamentally distort the concept of human rights. This approach [thus] recognizes the potential conflicts between environmental protection and human rights, but also the contribution each field can make to achieving their common objectives.

Dinah Shelton, *Human Rights, Environmental Rights, and the Right to Environment,* 28 Stan. J. Int'l L. 103, 105 (1991). Perhaps these conflicting or differing views help explain why the relationship between human rights and the environment has had a slow, *ad hoc,* and uneven development. Disputes continue about how best to ensure human rights and environmental protection are mutually supportive. For instance, some favor approaches that deploy or reinterpret existing human rights in the cause of environmental protection. Others insist that the development of new substantive rights for the environment [*per se*] is necessary....

* * *

Notes and Questions

1. Do you view protection of the environment and human rights as complementary or incompatible? Professor Shelton has written that environmental justice might be thought of comprising three distributive justice aims: intra-generational equity, inter-generational equity, and inter-species equity. In a subsequent article Professor Shelton makes an explicit link between environmental justice and human rights. She writes:

> Recently, the concept of environmental justice has come to play an important role in international environmental law and policy as a means of integrating human rights and environmental law, even as the content and scope of the term remains under discussion. It is increasingly recognized that favorable natural conditions are essential to the fulfillment of human desires and goals. Preservation of these conditions is a basic need of individuals and societies. Environmental justice encompasses preserving environmental quality, sustaining the ecological well-being of present and future generations, and reconciling competing interests. There is also an element of distributional justice, as it has become clear that the poor and marginalized of societies, including the global society, disproportionately suffer from environmental harm.

Environmental justice emphasizes the environment as a social good rather than a commodity or purely economic asset. The focus is on the proper allocation of social benefits and burdens, both in the present and in the future. Thus, it requires the equitable distribution of environmental amenities and environmental risks, the redress and sanctioning of environmental abuses, the restoration and conservation of nature and the fair allocation of resource benefits. The "polluter-pays" principle itself is based on the concept of environmental justice, as it encompasses the notion that those who engage in and profit from activities that damage the environment should be liable for the harm caused. On the most fundamental level, environmental justice can be seen as a term that encompasses the twin aims of environmental protection and international protection of human rights.

Dinah Shelton, *The Environmental Jurisprudence of International Human Rights Tribunals, in* LINKING HUMAN RIGHTS AND THE ENVIRONMENT 23 (Romina Picolotti & Jorge Daniel Taillant eds., 2003).

2. Procedurally, international claims related to environmental justice concerns potentially may be brought in a variety of fora. The European and Inter-American Commissions and Courts of Human Rights, for example, allow claims by individuals as well as states. As the excerpts in this subsection illustrate, once individuals (or impacted communities) have access to pursue claims, there are various international law frameworks that might be fruitful. While the American and European Conventions on Human Rights have limited references to environmental rights, linkages can be made between environmental rights and the substantive provisions of the treaties, which predominantly relate to civil and political rights. The Human Rights Council of the United Nation's Economic and Social Council has mechanisms for states to be investigated for "pattern and practice" human rights abuses, which could potentially entail environmental injustices of various kinds. Certain treaties adopted under the auspices of the United Nations, such as the International Covenant on Civil and Political Rights, which the U.S. has ratified, have established Committees to which signatories must report. The International Covenant on Economic, Social and Cultural Rights provides for a Committee as well, but this treaty has not been ratified by the U.S. In addition, as with the regional human rights treaties, linkages can be made between environmental rights and general civil and political rights. States that have ratified the International Covenant on Economic, Social and Cultural Rights are required more explicitly to explain and justify their laws and policies that impact upon the environment and environmental health issues. International law is an area that is rich and nuanced—as well as massive—and this section only lightly touches upon the possible environmental justice related avenues that might be pursued.

3. In the following excerpts, the authors explore the potential redress for environmental harms through international and regional pronouncements, or in connection with multilateral agreements, such as the North American Free Trade Agreement's (NAFTA) environmental side agreement.

Barry E. Hill, Steve Wolfson & Nicholas Targ, Human Rights and the Environment: A Synopsis and Some Predictions
16 Georgetown International Environmental Law Review 359 (2004)

Over the last fifty years or so, our understanding and, indeed, definition of human rights has evolved and expanded. Human rights are basically understood to mean those inalienable rights that we possess by virtue of being human. Human rights, therefore, are not based on one's citizenship, race or color, creed, education, or income. Human rights are, in short, universal, and must be respected by all societies and governments....

As lawyers, we are trained to think in terms of rights, whether procedural or substantive, as being enforceable under law. And, conversely, if they are not enforceable, they do not qualify as rights as a practical matter. This is at the heart of the continuing debate in the international environmental law community regarding the distinction between "hard law" and "soft law." "Soft law" recognizes that there are certain norms that are not enforceable by an international court but are, nonetheless, presumed to have some validity. "Hard law," on the other hand, involves legal norms that are legally binding as a matter of international law and are often accompanied by mechanisms for enforcement by an international court or some other international organ/tribunal.

... [W]hile there appears to be a growing trend favoring a human right to a clean and healthy environment—involving the balancing of social, economic, health, and environmental factors—international bodies, nations, and states have yet to articulate a sufficiently clear legal test or framework so as to ensure consistent, protective application and enforcement of such a right....

Since the United Nations first expressly linked human rights to the environment in 1972, the international community has grappled with whether the relationship is best stated in terms of a right owed to individuals (i.e., "hard law"), and, if so, whether that right derives from an another [sic] already recognized right, and whether such a right should be considered hard law or soft law. The right to a healthy environment was first expressed as a right derivative of the "right to life," in the Stockholm Declaration. Since then, as the complexity of the link has become better understood, the international community has demonstrated a reluctance to establish the right as "hard law."

The evolution of the concept of a human right to a clean and healthy environment dates back to the United Nations Stockholm Declaration of 1972. Among other things, the Stockholm Declaration provides that: "Man has the fundamental right to freedom, equality and adequate conditions of life, in an environment of a quality that permits a life of dignity and well-being, and he bears a solemn responsibility to protect and improve the environment for present and future generations." ...

The Stockholm formulation, however, has been criticized as conceiving of an environmental human right narrowly in that in deriving the environmental right from "the right to life itself," the Stockholm formulation limits the right to only apply in life-threatening situations....

In 1992, the Rio Declaration placed the issue of a human right to a clean and healthy environment squarely within the context of sustainable development. Principle 1 of the Rio Declaration provides that "[h]uman beings are at the center of concerns for sustainable development. They are entitled to a healthy and productive life in harmony with nature." Although Rio Principle 1 recognizes the links between a clean and healthy environment, development, and the protection of human health, it has been criticized for avoiding the use of *rights* language. The Rio Declaration takes a softer approach than the Stockholm Declaration. The approach taken in the Rio Declaration can be viewed as reflecting growing recognition by governments of the complexity of political, social, and economic concerns that are involved in the quest for sustainable development.

After the Rio Declaration, the debate continued to evolve. The *rights* based formulation was expressed at a U.N. meeting of Experts on Human Rights and the Environment at the United Nations in 1994. That group of experts produced a U.N. Draft Declaration of Principles on Human Rights and the Environment, stating that "[a]ll persons have the right to a secure, healthy and ecologically sound environment." However, the members of the United Nations did not choose to enact this into a binding legal instrument, perhaps recognizing that a legislative/policy based approach is more appropriate than a court/adjudicative based approach.

Indeed, the evolution of a legally enforceable right to a clean and healthy environment, at the international level, continues to encounter obstacles, even as the issue gains greater prominence. The Plan of Action issued at the 2002 World Summit on Sustainable Development is notably non-committal with respect to a human right to a clean and healthy environment. It recommends that States "[a]cknowledge the consideration being given to the possible relationship between environment and human rights, including the right to development." The Plan of Action recognizes the complexity of sustainable development, containing discussion of the myriad challenges that need to be addressed for sustainable development to become a reality. At the same time, the Plan of Action recognizes the critical role of good governance both within countries and at the national level, including the importance of public participation and government responsiveness—thus converging in at least this respect with the process-focused thread in the evolution of a human right to a clean and healthy environment.

The United States Court of Appeals for the Second Circuit recently sounded a further note of caution, with respect to an internationally recognized right to a clean and healthy environment. In *Flores v. Southern Peru Copper Corporation*, the plaintiffs brought personal injury claims under the Alien Tort Claims Act against copper mining corporations doing business in Peru. Plaintiffs alleged that pollution from Southern Peru Copper Corporation's mining, refining, and smelting operations emitted large quantities of sulfur dioxide and heavy metals into the local air and water, resulting in adverse health impacts. Plaintiffs claimed that this violated customary international law by infringing upon their rights to life and health. The lower court rejected their claim, and the Court of Appeals affirmed the decision. The Court of Appeals noted, "as a practical matter, it is impossible for courts to discern or apply in any rigorous, systematic, or legal manner international pronouncements that promote amorphous, general principles." The Court of Appeals also noted that the rights to life and health as expressed in various international instruments cited by plaintiffs are "boundless and indeterminate. They express virtuous goals understandably expressed at a level of abstraction needed to secure the adherence of States that disagree on many of the particulars regarding how actually to achieve them." The Court of Appeals concluded that the asserted "right to life" and the "right to health" are insufficiently definite to constitute rules of customary international law.

Although the evolution of a legally enforceable human right to a clean and healthy environment continues to face obstacles, the concept endures and appears to have evolved in ways that can have a significant impact on environmental law and policy. Recent action at the United Nations highlights the central importance of access to safe drinking water to life and health. In November 2002, the U.N. Committee on Economic, Social and Cultural Rights adopted a comment on Article 11 of the International Covenant on Economic, Social, and Cultural Rights, stating that: "The human right to water is indispensable for leading a healthy life in human dignity. It is a pre-requisite to the realization of all other human rights." ...

Regional legal instruments have also contributed to the evolution of the concept of a human right to a clean and healthy environment. The link between human rights and environmental quality is more frequently couched in terms of rights in regional instruments than in instruments of a more global nature. The African Charter of Human and

People's Rights, the American Convention on Human Rights, and country reports of the Inter-American Commission on Human Rights have all made contributions to the evolution of the concept of a human right to a clean and healthy environment. Nonetheless, the evolution towards such a right as "hard law" is by no means complete or certain....

The monitoring activities of regional human rights bodies have also contributed to the evolution of the concept of a human right to a clean and healthy environment. The Inter-American Commission on Human Rights (IACHR) devoted particular attention to the environment, human health, and human rights in several of its recent studies on the human rights situations in various countries. The IACHR, in its report on the human rights situation in Ecuador, noted the threat environmental degradation poses to the realization of the right to life and physical security and integrity in the context of health impacts resulting from pollution caused by oil extraction activities. The IACHR linked such pollution to the denial of basic human dignity, noting that "[c]onditions of severe environmental pollution, which may cause serious physical illness, impairment and suffering on the part of the local populace, are inconsistent with the right to be respected as a human being...." Thus, in this report, the IACHR echoed the "derivative right" approach of the Stockholm Declaration. The IACHR also noted the link to development, expressing the view that the Convention does not prevent development, but requires that it take place in a manner that respects individual rights....

Efforts to derive an environmental right from other rights contained in the European Charter of Human Rights have yielded mixed results. In *Powell & Rayner v. U.K.*, for example, the European Commission on Human Rights rejected a claim based on adverse effects of airport noise under a balancing test that considered the positive impact of the airport to justify infringement on the right to privacy. In *Lopez Ostra v. Spain*, however, the European Court of Human Rights ruled in favor of a claim that the failure by the public authorities to take measures to control noxious fumes and effluents from a treatment plant near an apartment building infringed upon the right to private and family life. In both decisions, balancing of environment and economic concerns played a major role....

Similar to environmental justice and sustainable development, the right to a clean and healthy environment appears to be moving, slowly but surely, to a higher degree of relevance....

One thing that can be said for sure is that internationally, the right to a clean and healthy environment has not reached the enforceable "hard law" stage as yet. But every article, every court decision, every treaty negotiated, every pronouncement from an international body, whether pro or con, is potentially critically important to the emerging general acceptance of this human right to a clean and healthy environment. Whether or when a right to a clean and healthy environment will become recognized as a fundamental right under international law, treaty, or a particular constitution remains to be seen....

* * *

Notes and Questions

1. Do you anticipate that the right to a minimum level of environmental amenity will eventually become enforceable in international law?

2. The Alien Tort Claims Act (ATCA) allows federal district courts to take jurisdiction of any civil action by an alien for a tort committed in violation of the law of nations. In *Sosa v. Alvarez-Machain*, 542 U.S. 692 (2004), the Supreme Court held that ATCA would

allow courts to hear a limited number of claims recognized under federal common law. However, district courts were admonished to exercise caution in recognizing claims based on international norms that are non-specific and not defined with the specificity that existed for the three common law claims that existed in 1789, the year of the ATCA's enactment. These three claims were safe passage, infringement of the rights of ambassadors, and piracy. Plaintiff Alvarez's false arrest claim did not meet that exacting standard. Would claims alleging a human rights violation based upon environmental harm meet this high bar? In recent years, there has been substantial interest in pressing environment-related human rights claims in several arenas. From 2001 to the present, the public interest law firm Earthjustice has compiled annual reports on Human Rights and the Environment that discuss many of these claims. These reports can be downloaded from the Earthjustice website. *See also* Jennifer Cassell, *Enforcing Environmental Human Rights, Selected Strategies of U.S. NGOs*, 6 Nw. U. J. INT'L HUMAN RTS. 104 (2007).

3. The United Nations in September of 2007 added the Declaration on the Rights of Indigenous Peoples to the roster of legal instruments addressing issues of what may be considered international environmental justice. This Declaration was the culmination of two decades of negotiations between nation-states and indigenous peoples. While 143 nation-states voted in favor of the Declaration, the opposition of four countries with large indigenous populations—Australia, Canada, New Zealand, and the United States—was notable. Among the important features of the Declaration is that it recognizes both individual rights and group rights. Article 3, for example, recognizes indigenous peoples' right to "self-determination," which entails the right to "freely determine their political status and freely pursue their economic, social and cultural development." Article 4 enshrines indigenous peoples' right to "autonomy" and "self-government." Article 5 recognizes indigenous peoples' "right to maintain and strengthen their distinct political, legal, economic, social and cultural institutions, while retaining their right to participate fully, if they so choose, in the political, economic, social and cultural life of the State [within which they are located]."

A host of provisions speak to indigenous peoples' right to and relationship with their traditional homelands. Article 25 provides that "[i]ndigenous peoples have the right to maintain and strengthen their distinctive spiritual relationship with their traditionally owned or otherwise occupied and used lands, territories, waters and coastal seas and other resources and to uphold their responsibilities to future generations in this regard." Article 26 states that they "have the right to the lands, territories and resources which they have traditionally owned, occupied or otherwise used or acquired." Other provisions address traditional knowledge and cultural patrimony. Article 31, for example, provides that

> [i]ndigenous peoples have the right to maintain, control, protect and develop their cultural heritage, traditional knowledge and traditional cultural expressions, as well as the manifestations of their sciences, technologies and cultures, including human and genetic resources, seeds, medicines, knowledge of the properties of fauna and flora, oral traditions, literatures, designs, sports and traditional games and visual and performing arts. They also have the right to maintain, control, protect and develop their intellectual property over such cultural heritage, traditional knowledge, and traditional cultural expressions.

Other provisions, too, are relevant to considerations of environmental justice for indigenous peoples. *See* U.N. DECLARATION ON THE RIGHTS OF INDIGENOUS PEOPLES, A/61/L.67 (Sept. 14, 2007). Although the Declaration includes language directing nation-states to provide mechanisms to ensure realization of the various rights it recognizes, as with other international instruments, a critical question is how these rights are actually enforced.

4. As noted above, an alternative means of addressing international environmental justice issues is through multilateral institutions. For example, as part of the NAFTA agreement signed in 1993 by Mexico, the U.S., and Canada, the countries entered into an environmental "side agreement" which created a new body, the Commission for Environmental Cooperation (CEC). The CEC has the responsibility of conducting assessments of the environmental impacts of NAFTA. In addition, the side agreement establishes a process whereby both citizens and nation-states can assert claims:

> Under the side agreement, the parties are required to ensure high levels of environmental protection and to "effectively enforce" their environmental law. The agreement also contains a citizen submission process through which anybody, including private individuals, NGOs, and corporations, can complain about a NAFTA party's failure "to effectively enforce its environmental law." ... In broad outline, there are five basic steps:

> (1) a petition or submission to the Commission for Environmental Cooperation alleging a failure to effectively enforce environmental laws;

> (2) review and a decision by the secretariat that the submission is essentially nonfrivolous, and a request for a response from the target state;

> (3) a decision by the Council, made up of the environmental ministers of the NAFTA countries, on whether to develop a factual record;

> (4) Commission preparation of a factual record [under Article 14 of the side agreement], which may take from months to years;

> (5) Council vote on whether to release the final report to the public; a two-thirds majority vote is required for public release.

> At this point, the process has run its course. There is no substantive remedy at the end. The outcome is a report documenting the facts underlying the enforcement failure allegations.

> The side agreement, however, does contain a bilateral dispute settlement process in Part V. The standard for triggering that process is that a country must have engaged in "a persistent pattern of failure to ... to [sic] effectively enforce its environmental law." The standard is thus higher than for triggering of factual records. Theoretically, however, the Article 14 factual records could provide the factual predicates for such a dispute settlement proceeding.

> [As of April 2006], the Secretariat has received fifty-three submissions; eleven are pending, and another eleven have resulted in factual records. The rest never made it to the factual record stage. There have been no Part V proceedings.

Tseming Yang, *The Challenge of Treaty Structure: The Case of NAFTA and the Environment*, 100 Am. Soc'y Int'l L. Proc. 32 (2006).

5. As the excerpt below indicates, recent experience with NAFTA illustrates the difficulty in addressing environmental degradation through multilateral institutions, even when there is a clear duty and enforceable right (in this case under Mexican law) involved. The case involves a *colonia*. Recall from Chapter 8 that *colonias* are rural settlements, usually along the United States-Mexico border, that lack safe housing, potable water, wastewater treatment, drainage, electricity, and paved roads.

Tseming Yang, The International Significance of an Instance of Urban Environmental Inequity in Tijuana, Mexico

31 Fordham Urban Law Journal 1321 (2004)

... Metales had been operated by its San Diego based U.S. parent company, New Frontier Trading, and the shareholders, Jose Kahn and his family, in violation of various Mexican environmental regulations for a number of years. Many surrounding residents attributed respiratory problems, skin rashes, and even birth defects to the pollution emissions of Metales. Even years after the facility stopped operating, a study of area children found elevated blood lead levels. When Metales had failed to comply with a number of notices of violation, the Mexican government shut down the facility, filed criminal charges, and then issued a criminal arrest warrant for Jose Kahn. Kahn then abandoned the facility and returned, unscathed, to the United States....

Metales is one of the very scenarios that environmentalists feared when NAFTA was being negotiated and adopted. Environmentalists objected to NAFTA as potentially allowing not only for the subversion of American environmental standards but also for the exportation of pollution and toxics to the South. The assumption was that ever-present pressure for competitive businesses to lower the cost of production and operation would surely lead them to prefer operating in jurisdictions where environmental regulations were more lenient and standards lower. Reduced regulatory compliance expenses would contribute to lower overall operating costs, thus making it easier to profit.

To address some of these concerns, the Mexican government restructured its environmental regulatory system to raise standards to those of its NAFTA partners. Furthermore, the NAFTA parties adopted an environmental side agreement, the North American Agreement for Environmental Cooperation, designed to ensure that the parties would properly enforce and implement their environmental laws as written. To date, assessments of NAFTA's environmental consequences have yet to provide a clear picture. Many of the most dire predictions about NAFTA's potential large scale impact on the U.S. and Mexican environmental and regulatory systems appear to have been wrong. Metales, however, is a glimpse of the other side.

... Even though Metales is owned by a U.S. parent company and U.S. citizens, the U.S. government has taken no direct responsibility or accountability to the community just across the border. Colonia Chilpancingo has had little political influence over the actions of U.S. government agencies.

... Metales exposes the deficiencies of supra-national organizations in filling the gaps left by national failures. Organizations such as the North American Commission for Environmental Cooperation ("CEC"), which is tasked with supervising the NAFTA environmental side agreement, and institutions operating at the U.S.-Mexico border, such as the North American Development Bank ("NADBank") and the Border Environment Cooperation Commission ("BECC"), have provided little substantive assistance in spite of their interest in transnational environmental problems. With the exception of approximately $85,000 allocated by the EPA as seed money toward a study on future cleanup, funding or other substantive assistance to remediate the contamination at Metales remains outstanding.

... Metales suggests how poorly the design of international environmental institutions address [sic] issues of community justice. Their inability to provide substantive solutions to the contamination suggests that organizations operating at the inter-governmental level are not suited to address equity and justice issues at the community level. The fact that their structure makes them accountable to states alone, and not to communities directly, makes it likely that they will act only when and to the extent that member governments are interested in allowing it.

There is also another lesson that Metales teaches—process alone cannot protect marginalized communities. The contamination at Metales has existed for almost a decade since it was abandoned. Community activists have sought to utilize the political process and lobbied government agencies; yet no substantive government remedy has come forth. They filed a petition with the CEC, which resulted in a factual record that demonstrates not only the serious environmental problems of the site but also Mexico's enforcement failures. Nevertheless, no governmental agency has come forward with a substantive remedy for the Colonia Chilpancingo residents. Metales has been an open secret for years. Hence, regulatory failures cannot be attributed to inadvertence or lack of information. Instead, it is more likely the result of a lack of willingness to act....

* * *

Notes and Questions

1. As the development of a norm of conduct into international "hard law" takes many years, it is understandable that environmental justice issues are pressed in tribunals as derivative rights, under the banner of more broadly articulated norms. Another approach, as explained above, has been for environmental degradation issues to be brought to light in reports of commissions that monitor human rights on a regional level. What are the advantages and disadvantages of these two approaches?

2. More broadly, how should nation-states develop frameworks to address international environmental justice issues? How should these issues be defined, and by whom? What role should non-governmental organizations (NGOs) play in this endeavor? Professor Hari Osofsky notes that "the focus of environmental treaties is primarily on constraining environmentally deleterious behavior, rather than on preventing injuries to people." Hari M. Osofsky, *Learning from Environmental Justice: A New Model for International Environmental Rights*, 24 Stan. Envtl. L. J. 71, 78 (2005). In contrast, international human rights law and international laws seeking to prevent discrimination focus on human impact with little concern for the environment. *Id*. In your view, is it sensible to press environmental justice issues under the banner of human rights or environmental agreements, or is an alternative framework possible?

3. As for the aftermath at the Metales site, Professor Yang writes:

On June 24, 2004, the activists of Colonia Chilpancingo signed an agreement with the Mexican government to provide for a comprehensive four-stage, five-year cleanup of the Metales site. For the first stage of the cleanup ... the Mexican government has committed to spending about US$700,000, including an US$85,000 grant from the EPA. It calls for the removal of 2,500 tons of toxic materials from the site and was to be completed by November 2004. The initial US$700,000, however, will be inadequate to fully rehabilitate the site, and it is unclear where the funds to finish the job will come from. But the agreement and initial actions give cause to hope that this time the Mexican government will follow through on substantive remedial action....

The agreement is a milestone in the struggles of the communities. Yet ... [s]uccess came in spite of the obstacles in the way. It was the result of efforts outside of established and normal regulatory channels. Their success vindicates not the existing regulatory structures but the communities' and activists' conviction that alternatives had to be pursued. Maybe, if they can succeed against the odds, the prospect of reform of the submission process and the structure of environmental governance at the border stands a chance as well.

Tseming Yang, *The Effectiveness of the NAFTA Environmental Side Agreement's Citizen Submission Process: A Case Study of Metales y Derivados*, 76 U. Colo. L. Rev. 443, 502 (2005); *see also* Carmen Gonzales, *Beyond Eco-Imperialism, An Environmental Justice Critique of Free Trade*, 78 Denv. L. Rev. 981 (2001). Professor Yang notes that governmental initiatives came about only after decades of persistent pressure by the affected communities. The same is true of domestic governmental initiatives, whether at the federal, state, or local level. As you read the various approaches governments are taking to redress inequities, consider the role of private citizen actors both before and during the execution of these initiatives.

C. Federal Initiatives

As mentioned in Chapter 1, as early as 1971 the Council on Environmental Quality issued an annual report acknowledging that racial discrimination adversely affects the urban poor and the quality of their environment. However, it was not until the early 1990s that a concerted effort was undertaken to address this and other disparities in environmental protection. In 1992 (during the George H. W. Bush administration) the Environmental Protection Agency (EPA) released the first governmental report comprehensively examining environmental justice. Shortly thereafter it established what later became the Office of Environmental Justice and convened a 25-member National Environmental Justice Advisory Council (NEJAC) to the EPA. In 1994, the first formal policy directive was issued by the White House subjecting all agencies to the following executive order.

1. The Executive Order on Environmental Justice

Executive Order 12,898: Federal Actions to Address Environmental Justice in Minority Populations and Low-Income Populations
February 11, 1994

Section 1-1. Implementation.

1-101. Agency Responsibilities. To the greatest extent practicable and permitted by law, and consistent with the principles set forth in the report on the National Performance Review, each Federal agency shall make achieving environmental justice part of its mission by identifying and addressing, as appropriate, disproportionately high and adverse human health or environmental effects of its programs, policies, and activities on minority populations and low-income populations in the United States and its territories and possessions, the District of Columbia, the Commonwealth of Puerto Rico, and the Commonwealth of the Mariana Islands.

1-102. Creation of an Interagency Working Group on Environmental Justice.

(a) Within 3 months of the date of this order, the Administrator of the Environmental Protection Agency ("Administrator") or the Administrator's designee shall convene an interagency Federal Working Group on Environmental Justice ("Working Group"). The Working Group shall comprise the heads of the following executive agencies and offices, or their designees: (a) Department of Defense; (b) Department of Health and Human Services; (c) Department of Housing and Urban Development; (d) Department of Labor; (e) Department of Agriculture; (f) Department of Transportation; (g) Department of Justice; (h) Department of the Interior; (i) Department of Commerce; (j) Department of Energy; (k) Environmental Protection Agency; (l) Office of Management and Budget; (m) Office of Science and Technology Policy; (n) Office of the Deputy Assistant to the President for Environmental Policy; (o) Office of the Assistant to the President for Domestic Policy; (p) National Economic Council; (q) Council of Economic Advisers; and (r) such other Government officials as the President may designate. The Working Group shall report to the President through the Deputy Assistant to the President for Environmental Policy and the Assistant to the President for Domestic Policy....

1-103. Development of Agency Strategies.

(a) Except as provided in section 6-605 of this order, each Federal agency shall develop an agency-wide environmental justice strategy ... that identifies and addresses disproportionately high and adverse human health or environmental effects of its programs, policies, and activities on minority populations and low-income populations. The environmental justice strategy shall list programs, policies, planning and public participation processes, enforcement, and/or rulemakings related to human health or the environment that should be revised to, at a minimum:

(1) promote enforcement of all health and environmental statutes in areas with minority populations and low-income populations;

(2) ensure greater public participation;

(3) improve research and data collection relating to the health of and environment of minority populations and low-income populations; and

(4) identify differential patterns of consumption of natural resources among minority populations and low-income populations.... Federal agencies shall provide additional periodic reports to the Working Group as requested by the Working Group....

Sec. 2-2. Federal Agency Responsibilities for Federal Programs.

Each Federal agency shall conduct its programs, policies, and activities that substantially affect human health or the environment, in a manner that ensures that such programs, policies, and activities do not have the effect of excluding persons (including populations) from participation in, denying persons (including populations) the benefits of, or subjecting persons (including populations) to discrimination under, such programs, policies, and activities, because of their race, color, or national origin.

Sec. 3-3. Research, Data Collection, and Analysis.

... 3-302. Human Health and Environmental Data Collection and Analysis.... [E]ach Federal agency, whenever practicable and appropriate, shall collect, maintain, and analyze information assessing and comparing environmental and human health risks borne by populations identified by race, national origin, or income. To the extent practical and appropriate, Federal agencies shall use this information to determine whether their programs, policies, and activities have disproportionately high and adverse human health or environmental effects on minority populations and low-income populations; ...

Sec. 4-4. Subsistence Consumption of Fish and Wildlife.

4-401. Consumption Patterns. In order to assist in identifying the need for ensuring protection of populations with differential patterns of subsistence consumption of fish and wildlife, Federal agencies, whenever practicable and appropriate, shall collect, maintain, and analyze information on the consumption patterns of populations who principally rely on fish and/or wildlife for subsistence. Federal agencies shall communicate to the public the risks of those consumption patterns.

4-402. Guidance. Federal agencies, whenever practicable and appropriate, shall work in a coordinated manner to publish guidance reflecting the latest scientific information available concerning methods for evaluating the human health risks associated with the consumption of pollutant-bearing fish or wildlife. Agencies shall consider such guidance in developing their policies and rules.

Sec. 5-5. Public Participation and Access to Information.

... (b) Each Federal agency may, whenever practicable and appropriate, translate crucial public documents, notices, and hearings relating to human health or the environment for limited English speaking populations.

(c) Each Federal agency shall work to ensure that public documents, notices, and hearings relating to human health or the environment are concise, understandable, and readily accessible to the public....

Sec. 6-6. General Provisions.

6-601. Responsibility for Agency Implementation. The head of each Federal agency shall be responsible for ensuring compliance with this order. Each Federal agency shall conduct internal reviews and take such other steps as may be necessary to monitor compliance with this order....

6-606. Native American Programs. Each Federal agency responsibility set forth under this order shall apply equally to Native American programs. In addition, the Department of the Interior, in coordination with the Working Group, and, after consultation with tribal leaders, shall coordinate steps to be taken pursuant to this order that address Federally-recognized Indian Tribes....

6-608. General. Federal agencies shall implement this order consistent with, and to the extent permitted by, existing law.

6-609. Judicial Review. This order is intended only to improve the internal management of the executive branch and is not intended to, nor does it create any right, benefit, or trust responsibility, substantive or procedural, enforceable at law or equity by a party against the United States, its agencies, its officers, or any person. This order shall not be construed to create any right to judicial review involving the compliance or noncompliance of the United States, its agencies, its officers, or any other person with this order.

* * *

Notes and Questions

1. An important limitation of the Executive Order on Environmental Justice ("Executive Order" or "Order") is section 6-609, an express provision stating that the Order does not create any new rights enforceable at law or equity, a provision common to such executive orders. Of what practical value is the Order given this limitation? Assuming the Order is intended to signal administrative policy at the highest level, do you think it will accomplish its goal?

2. Several agencies subsequently submitted environmental justice strategies. In 1995 the EPA issued a strategy that listed specific objectives in several areas, including outreach and partnerships, technical assistance, training, management accountability, and public participation. The strategy also listed several specific projects, including initiatives in brownfields redevelopment and public health pilot activities, and described targeted initiatives in several geographic locations. U.S. EPA, ENVIRONMENTAL JUSTICE STRATEGY (1995).

3. President Clinton also issued a memorandum with the Executive Order. In it, he noted that "[t]he purpose of this separate memorandum is to underscore certain provisions of existing law that can help ensure that all communities and persons across this Nation live in a safe and healthful environment." Memorandum on Environmental Justice, 30 WEEKLY COMP. PRES. DOC. 279 (Feb. 11, 1994). The Memorandum explicitly referred to Title VI of the Civil Rights Act of 1964, and directed agencies to ensure that programs or activities receiving federal financial assistance "do not directly, or through contractual or other arrangements, use criteria, methods, or practices that discriminate on the basis of race, color or national origin." Id. As discussed in detail in Chapter 14, the Title VI initiative has a torturous and, some would argue, unfortunate history. The Memorandum also directed agencies to "analyze the environmental effects, including human health, economic and social effects, of Federal actions, including effects on minority communities and low-income communities, when such analysis is required by [the National Environmental Policy Act]." Id. Chapter 12 examines federal agency decision-making under the National Environmental Policy Act in light of the Executive Order.

4. At the end of the Clinton Administration, a group of law professors surveyed the actions of federal agencies in responding to the Executive Order through 2000. The survey provided interesting insights into the ways agencies sought to accomplish the goals of the Order. Ultimately, the authors concluded:

> All of the federal agencies surveyed pay homage to EJ [environmental justice] to some extent. A few have made major institutional investments in promoting and achieving EJ. Clearly, substantial federal environmental resources are now directed at minority and low-income communities, especially in brownfield development and lead-based paint remediation efforts.... [On the other hand] [m]eaningful community participation in decisionmaking is still lacking in some agencies.

> All agencies had an initial burst of energy upon issuance of the EO [Executive Order]. Carry through, though, has sometimes been problematic. Perhaps the most critical factor is the level of commitment at the highest levels of an agency. A Secretary or Administrator who makes EJ a priority, follows through with a commitment of resources and strong leadership, and requires accountability by agency employees, will see the agency respond accordingly. No agency has apparently been dragging its feet on the issue, but clearly some stand out in their level of success. EPA, HUD, DOT, and the NIEHS have consistently performed at a higher level. The record at the DOJ and at the DOI has been sporadic. DOE is somewhere in between....

> Every agency has considerable discretionary authority to implement measures that will reduce existing environmental disparities. Agency responses may be conceptualized as a continuum: On the one end we see "repackaging" of normal agency activities as "EJ programs." The next strategy is to undertake discrete environmental projects, such as pilot projects and initiatives that lie outside the

purview of broadly applicable requirements. The third and more advanced strategy is to design explicit EJ protections into the core design of major regulatory programs and activities. The fourth and last strategy on the continuum would be to undertake a comprehensive review of all agency EJ efforts to determine their effectiveness in impacted communities. The agencies vary in how far they have progressed. Repackaging and identifying existing programs was the norm, with a trend towards undertaking discrete new projects. Integrating EJ into program design has been relatively rare, and comprehensive assessment and analysis exceedingly uncommon. Based upon the agency responses, there appears to be only a few instances in which agencies have incorporated EJ principles and protections into programmatic design.... While all agency actions that reduce disparities are admirable and constitute an advance, clearly full integration is the strategy most likely to result in significant, long-term progress....

Denis Binder, et al., *A Survey of Federal Agency Responses to President Clinton's Executive Order 12898 on Environmental Justice*, 31 Envtl. L. Rep. 11,133 (2001). Other reports since have criticized, in particular, the adequacy of EPA's implementation of the Executive Order. *See* Nat'l Acad. of Pub. Admin., Environmental Justice in EPA Permitting: Reducing Pollution in High Risk Communities is Integral to the Agency's Mission (2001); U.S. Comm'n on Civil Rights, Not in My Backyard: Executive Order 12,898 and Title VI as Tools for Achieving Environmental Justice (2003) (reviewing programs of EPA, Department of Housing and Urban Development, Department of Transportation, and Department of Interior). For an in-depth and more recent discussion of the Executive Order compliance initiatives by several federal agencies, see Bradford C. Mank, *Executive Order 12,898*, *in* The Law of Environmental Justice: Theories and Procedures to Address Disproportionate Risks 101, 103 (Michael B. Gerrard & Sheila R. Foster eds., 2d ed. 2008).

5. With the change from the Clinton administration to the George W. Bush administration, the Executive Order was not rescinded. However, the administration appeared to take a different approach to environmental justice. Most striking was the shift in focus by EPA. In 2001, EPA redefined its interpretation of environmental justice to mean environmental protection for everyone, and de-emphasized the need to focus special attention on minority and low-income populations, including these populations along with all others. *See* Memorandum on EPA's Commitment to Environmental Justice from Administrator Christine Todd Whitman to Assistant Administrators (Aug. 9, 2001). EPA's shift was sharply criticized in a 2004 report by the agency's Inspector General. The report noted that:

> [The EPA] indicated it is attempting to provide environmental justice for everyone. While providing adequate environmental justice to the entire population is commendable, doing so had already been EPA's mission prior to implementation of the Executive Order; we do not believe the intent of the Executive Order was simply to reiterate that mission. We believe the Executive Order was specifically issued to provide environmental justice to minority and/or low-income populations due to concerns that those populations had been disproportionately impacted by environmental risk.

Office of Inspector Gen., U.S. EPA, Evaluation Report: EPA Needs to Consistently Implement the Intent of the Executive Order on Environmental Justice, Rep. No. 2004-P-00007 at ii (2004).

6. The Bush Administration's change in approach was likely influenced by a different philosophy of governance coupled with the evolving constitutional jurisprudence in the

area of equal protection law, including the 2003 Supreme Court decision in *Grutter v. Bollinger*. This case involved an Equal Protection challenge to the use of race in law school admissions for the purpose of promoting a diverse student body. Although the case was decided in a context different than environmental protection, in reading the following excerpt of the decision, consider how the case bears upon the actions of the EPA in devising a strategy to alleviate racial environmental disparities.

2. Limitations on Governmental Initiatives

Grutter v. Bollinger
539 U.S. 306 (2003)

... Enrolling a "critical mass" of minority students simply to assure some specified percentage of a particular group merely because of its race or ethnic origin would be patently unconstitutional....

To be narrowly tailored, a race-conscious admissions program cannot "insulat[e] each category of applicants with certain desired qualifications from competition with all other applicants." Instead, it may consider race or ethnicity only as a "'plus' in a particular applicant's file"; *i.e.,* it must be "flexible enough to consider all pertinent elements of diversity in light of the particular qualifications of each applicant ... and to place them on the same footing for consideration, although not necessarily according them the same weight." ... It follows that universities cannot establish quotas for members of certain racial or ethnic groups or put them on separate admissions tracks. The Law School's admissions program, like the Harvard plan approved by Justice Powell [in the *Regents of the University of California v. Bakke* decision, Eds.], satisfies these requirements. Moreover, the program is flexible enough to ensure that each applicant is evaluated as an individual and not in a way that makes race or ethnicity the defining feature of the application. The Law School engages in a highly individualized, holistic review of each applicant's file, giving serious consideration to all the ways an applicant might contribute to a diverse educational environment. There is no policy, either *de jure* or *de facto,* of automatic acceptance or rejection based on any single "soft" variable....

... [T]estimony indicated that when a critical mass of underrepresented minority students is present, racial stereotypes lose their force because nonminority students learn there is no "minority viewpoint" but rather a variety of viewpoints among minority students....

[Justice Powell's] holding for the Court in *Bakke* was that a "State has a substantial interest that legitimately may be served by a properly devised admissions program involving the competitive consideration of race and ethnic origin." ... In [his] view, when governmental decisions "touch upon an individual's race or ethnic background, [such individual] is entitled to a judicial determination that the burden he is asked to bear on that basis is precisely tailored to serve a compelling governmental interest." Under this exacting standard, only one of the interests asserted by the university survived Justice Powell's scrutiny....

First, Justice Powell rejected an interest in "'reducing the historic deficit of traditionally disfavored minorities in medical schools and in the medical profession'" as an unlawful interest in racial balancing. Second, Justice Powell rejected an interest in remedying societal discrimination because such measures would risk placing unnecessary burdens on innocent third parties "who bear no responsibility for whatever harm the beneficiaries of the special admissions program are thought to have suffered." Third, Justice Powell rejected an interest in "increasing the number of physicians who will practice in communities currently underserved," concluding that even if such an interest could be compelling in some circumstances the program under review was not "geared to promote that goal." Justice Powell approved the university's use of race to further only one interest: "the attainment of a diverse student body." ...

[N]othing less than the "'nation's future depends upon leaders trained through wide exposure' to the ideas and mores of students as diverse as this Nation of many peoples." ...

Justice Powell was, however, careful to emphasize that in his view race "is only one element in a range of factors a university properly may consider in attaining the goal of a heterogeneous student body." ...

Context matters when reviewing race-based governmental action under the Equal Protection Clause.... In *Adarand Constructors, Inc. v. Peña*, we made clear that strict scrutiny must take "relevant differences into account." Indeed, as we explained, that is its "fundamental purpose." Not every decision influenced by race is equally objectionable, and strict scrutiny is designed to provide a framework for carefully examining the importance and the sincerity of the reasons advanced by the governmental decisionmaker for the use of race in that particular context....

[The] benefits [of a diverse student body] are substantial. As the District Court emphasized, the Law School's admissions policy promotes "cross-racial understanding," helps to break down racial stereotypes, and "enables [students] to better understand persons of different races." These benefits are "important and laudable," because "classroom discussion is livelier, more spirited, and simply more enlightening and interesting" when the students have "the greatest possible variety of backgrounds." ...

[S]tudies show that student body diversity promotes learning outcomes, and "better prepares students for an increasingly diverse workforce and society, and better prepares them as professionals." These benefits are not theoretical but real, as major American businesses have made clear that the skills needed in today's increasingly global marketplace can only be developed through exposure to widely diverse people, cultures, ideas, and viewpoints....

For this reason, the diffusion of knowledge and opportunity through public institutions of higher education must be accessible to all individuals regardless of race or ethnicity. The United States, as *amicus curiae*, affirms that "[e]nsuring that public institutions are open and available to all segments of American society, including people of all races and ethnicities, represents a paramount government objective." And, "[n]owhere is the importance of such openness more acute than in the context of higher education." ...

Properly understood, a "quota" is a program in which a certain fixed number or proportion of opportunities are "reserved exclusively for certain minority groups." ...

In contrast, "a permissible goal ... require[s] only a good-faith effort ... to come within a range demarcated by the goal itself," and permits consideration of race as a "plus" factor in any given case while still ensuring that each candidate "compete[s] with all other qualified applicants ..."

... The Law School does not, however, limit in any way the broad range of qualities and experiences that may be considered valuable contributions to student body diversity. To the contrary, the 1992 policy makes clear "[t]here are many possible bases for diversity admissions," and provides examples of admittees who have lived or traveled widely abroad, are fluent in several languages, have overcome personal adversity and family hardship, have exceptional records of extensive community service, and have had successful careers in other fields....

Narrow tailoring does not require exhaustion of every conceivable race-neutral alternative. Nor does it require a university to choose between maintaining a reputation for excellence or fulfilling a commitment to provide educational opportunities to members of all racial groups....

Narrow tailoring does, however, require serious, good faith consideration of workable race-neutral alternatives that will achieve the diversity the university seeks....

Accordingly, race-conscious admissions policies must be limited in time.... In the context of higher education, the durational requirement can be met by sunset provisions in race-conscious admissions policies and periodic reviews to determine whether racial preferences are still necessary to achieve student body diversity.

* * *

Notes and Questions

1. In 2005, partially in response to the unfavorable Inspector General report noted above, the EPA released a new draft environmental justice framework and strategy for public comment. The framework listed twelve potential priorities: reducing asthma attacks; making fish/shellfish safe to eat; making drinking water safe; reducing exposure to water borne pathogens; revitalizing brownfields and contaminated sites; reducing the incidence of childhood lead poisoning; reducing exposure to mercury; reducing exposure to pesticides; reducing exposure to air toxics; assuring compliance; increasing environmental health along the U.S. borders; and promoting healthy schools. The agency then requested that commenters rank these goals. *See* U.S. EPA, WORKING DRAFT OF ENVIRONMENTAL JUSTICE STRATEGIC PLAN 3–4 (2005). EPA also reiterated its view that environmental justice means environmental protection for all, stating "[e]nvironmental justice is achieved when everyone, regardless of race, culture, or income, enjoys the same degree of protection from environmental and health hazards *and* equal access to the decision-making process to have a healthy environment in which to live, learn, and work." *Id.* at 2 (emphasis in original).

2. The draft framework and strategy provoked a storm of criticism from environmental justice organizations, members of Congress, and others. Illustrative of some of the criticism are the following comments submitted to EPA by community groups in the San Francisco area, who noted that:

> ... [T]he Plan ignores the mandate of [the] Executive Order, which, by its title, specifically requires "Federal Actions to Address Environmental Justice in Minority Populations and Low-Income Populations." ... [Moreover,] EPA is asking commenters to rank a list of twelve potential national environmental justice priorities on a scale of greatest to least importance. This ranking scheme creates an artificial and meaningless ordering of important priorities that are not comparable and fails to take into account the cumulative health and environmental effects experienced by minority and low-income populations that are frequently exposed to disproportionately high levels of multiple environmental hazards at the same time.... [N]either the Strategic Targets nor any of the twelve proposed national environmental justice priorities address the interests of minority and low-income populations as is required by Section 1-103 [of the Executive Order], and likewise, they do not address areas where EPA's policies and programming

are lacking with respect to those populations. Instead, by definition, EPA's Environmental Justice Strategic Plan applies to "all people regardless of race, color, national origin, or income." The Plan by omission fails to identify and then target low-income or minority communities facing multiple hazards and thereby defeats any focus upon these communities.

Letter to U.S. EPA commenting on the 2005 Draft Environmental Justice Strategic Plan submitted by the Golden Gate University Environmental Law and Justice Clinic on behalf of Bayview Hunters Point Community Advocates, the Chinese Progressive Association, People Organizing to Demand Environmental and Economic Rights, and Our Children's Earth Foundation (July 15, 2005).

3. EPA's rationale for its approach is explained in its response to comments on the draft strategy:

> EPA's use of racial classifications as a basis for making decisions would raise significant legal issues. Several Supreme Court decisions, such as Adarand Constructors, Inc. v. Pena, 515 U.S. 200, 227 (1995), and Grutter v. Bollinger, 539 U.S. 306, 326 (2003), provide that, whenever a racial classification is used as a basis for any federal, state, or local government decision, courts must apply a strict scrutiny standard of review. To survive strict scrutiny, the government must demonstrate that it uses the racial classification to achieve a compelling governmental interest and that the use of the racial classification is narrowly tailored to serve that interest.

> The compelling governmental interests for most EPA decisions are protecting human health and the environment and achieving the fair treatment and meaningful involvement of all people regardless of race, color, national origin, or income with respect to the development, implementation, and enforcement of environmental laws, regulations, and policies. To pass the narrow-tailoring test, the Agency would have to show that no race-neutral alternative is available to achieve those compelling interests. However, in general, EPA has race-neutral alternatives for achieving its compelling governmental interests.

U.S. EPA, Draft Environmental Justice Strategic Plan Thematic Response to Comments (2005).

4. The 2005 Draft Environmental Justice Strategy was not finalized. Instead, the EPA in its more general EPA strategic plan (a 184-page document governing overall agency priorities), made several references to "environmental justice," albeit, as noted earlier, environmental justice was re-defined to include protection of all people. The agency noted that:

> EPA is establishing measurable environmental justice commitments for eight national priorities: reducing asthma attacks, reducing exposure to air toxics, increasing compliance with regulations, reducing incidence of elevated blood lead levels, ensuring that fish and shellfish are safe to eat, ensuring that water is safe to drink, revitalizing brownfields and contaminated sites, and using collaborative problem-solving to address environmental and public health concerns. We will promote environmental justice in all aspects of our work by training staff; providing guidance, online tools, and other resources; sharing information about successful strategies; and enhancing staff skills in working with community-based organizations. We will continue to use dispute resolution, facilitation, listening sessions, and other consensus-building techniques and to convene stakeholders to address environmental and public health issues....

U.S. EPA, 2006–2011 EPA Strategic Plan: Charting Our Course 94, 114 (2006). The plan also directed the EPA to identify strategies to ensure that resources reach "disproportionately exposed" communities. *Id.* at 83.

5. Do you view the two approaches sketched above as fundamentally different? If so, in what respects might they result in different outcomes? Assuming that racial disparities do in fact exist, is it possible for a strategy that does not explicitly consider race to alleviate these disparities? Will attempts to improve measures related to environmental justice concerns for "all people regardless of race, color, national origin, or income" achieve parity? How is this different from the EPA's general mission to protect the environment? Alternatively, can the EPA use racial criteria to evaluate whether its general strategy is, in fact, alleviating racial disparities (even if not explicitly considered in the strategy itself)? Why might the use of race in the former context be problematic to the agency, but not the latter? In light of these considerations, what steps would you recommend that the Obama administration take to see that the goals of the Clinton-era Executive Order are fully realized? For example, would it be better to adopt a more conservative approach (and avoid litigation) or adopt a more aggressive approach and take the position that we need race-conscious strategies in order to alleviate racial disparities? Since income is not a suspect classification, can (and should) the agency take targeted initiatives in low-income communities? Will that likely alleviate racial disparities as well? Recall that in Chapter 2, studies indicated that race is a stronger predictor of exposure and proximity to environmental harms than income. Does this affect your answer?

6. At the end of the George W. Bush administration, the EPA signaled its intent to focus its agency activities on a limited number of target areas:

> ... [W]e believe new or significant changes in strategies or performance measurement are most critical in helping the Agency to better achieve and measure environmental and human health outcomes. These targeted areas include:
>
> • Reduction of Greenhouse Gas (GHG) Emissions
>
> • Sustainable Agriculture
>
> • Impacts of Global Climate Change
>
> • Contaminants
>
> • Import Safety
>
> • Improving Program Implementation in Indian Country
>
> • Enforcement/Compliance Measurement Approach
>
> • Research Strategic Directions and Targets
>
> • Environmental Indicators, Monitoring, and Related Information

U.S. EPA, 2009–2014 EPA Strategic Plan Change Document 3 (2008). The agency indicated its intent to retain the performance measures of the earlier 2006–2011 plan. The later document also listed several issues in Indian Country and noted its intent to improve compliance in all areas, including those with environmental justice concerns. *See id.* at 57. More specifically, the agency noted a special emphasis on disproportionately impacted populations in reducing exposure to asthma triggers, addressing blood lead levels in low-income children, and cleaning up abandoned waste sites in the US-Mexico border region. *See id.* at 26, 42, and 47, respectively. Does this approach, at least implicitly, consider race as a factor?

7. Many in the environmental justice community believed that the Bush administration lacked a genuine commitment to environmental justice, especially so in light of EPA's

record discussed above, the community's disappointing experiences with Title VI remedies (discussed in Chapter 14), and the reduction in funding to community-based organizations working on environmental justice projects that occurred during the Bush
Administration. Mank, *supra*, at 110. As a result, many organizations refocused their efforts towards prompting state and local governments to address environmental inequities.

D. State Initiatives

States have responded in a variety of ways to the challenges raised by the environmental justice movement. While a handful of states have not taken any action and others have
taken only modest steps, some have been fairly aggressive. California, for example, has
(with considerable sustained effort) enacted several environmental justice bills. California's
primary statute, SB 115, requires the California Environmental Protection Agency (Cal/EPA)
to follow principles that closely parallel the provisions of President Clinton's Executive
Order. SB 115 was passed in 1999 after five other environmental justice bills were vetoed by
former Governor Pete Wilson in the prior seven years. Under the bill, Cal/EPA is required
to promote enforcement of health and environmental statutes and conduct its programs
and policies "in a manner that ensures the fair treatment of people of all races, cultures,
and income levels." It is also required to develop a model environmental justice mission
statement for its constituent departments. *See* Cal. Gov't Code §65040.12 (1999); Cal. Pub.
Res. Code §§72000–01 (1999). Subsequent legislation also requires Cal/EPA to ensure that
environmental justice considerations are addressed in carrying out reviews by the agency
under the California Environmental Quality Act (the state's version of NEPA), and to make
recommendations for ensuring that public documents, notices, and hearings are understandable and accessible to the public, including translation for limited-English-speaking
populations. *See* Ellen M. Peter, *Implementing Environmental Justice: The New Agenda for
California State Agencies*, 31 Golden Gate U. L. Rev. 529 (2001). More recently, California's climate change legislation, AB 32, requires that environmental justice considerations
be incorporated into regulations adopted to reduce greenhouse gas emissions (see Chapter
12). Delaware, Hawaii, Illinois, Louisiana, Maryland, New York, and the District of Columbia have also enacted environmental justice statutes. Pub. Law Research Inst., UC
Hastings College of the Law & Am. Bar Ass'n, Environmental Justice for All: A Fifty
State Survey of Legislation, Policy and Cases 8–9 (3d ed. 2007).

More broadly, state responses are fairly diverse. Several states have statutes that seek
to limit the geographic concentration of waste facilities or that allow decision-makers to
consider "soft" criteria such as the socioeconomic status of the host community in permit decisions about waste facilities. A number of states have sought to increase public
participation in their programs, and others have convened environmental justice task
forces or advisory groups. The recommendations of these task forces generally include
increasing public participation in agency decisions, improving public education and outreach by agencies, heightening awareness among agency staff about environmental justice issues, collecting better data about environmental disparities, facilitating
community-industry dialogue, and targeting enforcement efforts in environmental justice communities. A smaller number of states have gone further and adopted formal environmental justice policies or established environmental justice positions within state
government. In several states the primary response has been to conduct research into the
extent of environmental disparities.

The following is a matrix of state initiatives compiled from the Fifty State Survey cited above, available on the Hastings Public Law Research Institute web page.

Environmental Justice (EJ) Program, Initiative, Policy, Statute, or Regulation	States Where Such Programs Exist
Executive Orders	AL, LA, MD, NJ, NM
Anti-concentration or Fair Share Regulations or Statutes	AL, AR, GA, MS, TX, WY
Research & Study	DE, HI, IN, KY, LA, NJ, NM, NY, RI, SC, VA
EJ Office	CA, NY, PA, TX, WV
EJ Strategic Plan	CA, HI, IN, MO, NH, TN
EJ Policy or Mission Statement	AZ, CA, CT, IL, IN, MA, MN, PA, RI, WV
EJ Staff Position	AL, AR, AZ, CA, CO, CT, DE, DC, GA, IL, LA, MD, MA, NC, NJ, SC, TN, UT, VA, WA
EJ Statewide Advisory Board	CA, DE, IL, MD, NJ, NY, OR, PA, TX
Community or Local Advisory Boards	AZ, CT, FL, LA, OH
Agency or Interagency Working Group	CA, MI, PA, WA
Performance Partnership Agreement	AR, CO, CT, IL, IN, MD, MA, MN, MT, NH, PA, RI, SD, UT, WA, VA
Agency EJ Personnel Training	IL, ME, TN, WA
Capacity Building and Citizen Tools to Enhance Public Participation	CA, CT, IL, IN, MA, NY, PA, TX
Accountability or Measurement of Success of EJ Programs	CA
Transportation initiatives	AL, AK, CA, FL, GA, HI, MD, WI
Small Grants Program	CA, MN, NY
Permit Criteria to Enhance Public Participation	AZ, CA, CT, DC, IL, NY, OH, PA, RI, SC, VA, WA
Permit Criteria for Demographic, Impact and/or Alternative Site Analysis	AL, CA, DC, KY, MD, MA, MT, NM, NY, NC
Cleanup initiatives	FL
EJ Program targeted to discrete EJ issues or concerns	AK, AR, CA, FL, MD, MA, MN, NJ, NC, PA, RI, WA, WI
Brownfield Program with EJ Criteria	FL, GA, IN, MA, NJ, NY, WI
Supplemental Environmental Projects with EJ Criteria	CO, CT, FL, MA, OR, VA
Enforcement Initiatives	CT, DE, MA, NJ, PA
No EJ Programs, Policies, or Statutes	ID, IA, KS, NE, NV, ND, OK, SD, UT, VT

Notes and Questions

1. The survey of state responses indicates that relatively few states have adopted comprehensive environmental justice legislation or changed their permitting, standard setting, or enforcement policies. The most popular responses seem to be creating environmental justice advisory committees or environmental justice policies, and enhancing public participation programs. Why do you think this is the case? Which ap-

proaches would you like to see adopted in your state? Can you think of other approaches that would help to alleviate environmental disparities?

2. Assume that you are counsel to Cal/EPA and have been asked to draft a model environmental justice mission statement. What would you recommend? How would you define "fair treatment" for purposes of implementing the policy?

3. If you were devising an environmental justice strategy for a state, would the Supreme Court decision in *Grutter* affect the way that you might decide to address environmental justice concerns? If so, how?

4. Are tribal governments in a relatively better position to help alleviate environmental disparities? Consider the material in the next section.

E. Tribal Initiatives

In managing tribal lands and resources, tribes today must contend with a legacy of colonialism and non-tribal management that presents a formidable set of challenges to tribal efforts to address environmental harms. Numerous aspects of United States policy have worked in concert to separate American Indian peoples from their aboriginal lands, to usurp these peoples' inherent authority to govern the use of their lands and resources, and to undermine their ability to make environmental management decisions as a practical matter through a host of actions that ensured conditions of economic poverty and social distress. Moreover, although tribes were legally recognized as sovereign nations within the United States in early decisions by the U.S. Supreme Court — "domestic dependant nations" — the federal government in fact has exercised broad decision-making authority over mineral and timber extraction; fishing, hunting, and wildlife management; and land and water use. As discussed in Chapter 4, these federal management decisions continue to have an enormous impact on tribes' resources and rights and, in turn, on the health of tribal people. Professor David Rich Lewis estimates that these decisions have "scarred thousands of acres with minimal protection for inhabitants":

> Beginning as early as 1900 with the discovery of oil on Osage land, nonrenewable resource development has unleashed some of the most environmentally destructive forms of exploitation. Today, mine and drilling sites, roads and machinery, tailing pipes and settling ponds threaten tribal land, water, air, health, and lifestyles. Inequitable leases and federal, state, and tribal government mismanagement have compounded these problems.

David Rich Lewis, *Native Americans and the Environment: A Survey of Twentieth-Century Issues*, 19 AM. INDIAN Q. 423, 431 (1995). The consequences of this mismanagement have been left for tribal governments to address today; in many cases, they present daunting challenges to tribal environmental regulatory efforts.

Against this backdrop, it is perhaps not an overstatement to suggest that every tribal effort to address depletion and contamination of tribal lands and resources — and the profound harms these visit on tribal members and other inhabitants of tribal lands — is, in effect, a tribal environmental justice initiative. As Mr. Dean Suagee, an attorney and longtime scholar of environmental justice in the tribal context, observes, "[i]f environmental justice problems are characterized by disproportionate impacts on communities of color or low-income, then almost every environmental issue in Indian country is an environmental justice issue. An observer with some understanding of federal Indian law and policy, and some appreciation for tribal cultures, can find disproportionate impacts." Dean B. Suagee, *Environmental Justice and Indian Country*, Hum. Rts., Fall 2003, at 16.

On this view, tribes' recent efforts to reinvigorate tribal management over tribal lands and resources comprise important steps toward ameliorating environmental injustice in Indian Country. Efforts to this end include tribes' exercise of their inherent authority to manage the lands and resources over which they have jurisdiction (the issue of tribal jurisdiction is itself often contested, with tribes having to defend their claims against surrounding states and others); tribes' efforts to obtain delegation of authority to administer programs under the Clean Water Act, the Clean Air Act, and other federal environmental statutes; and tribes' devotion of personnel and resources to a host of other environmental management endeavors. *See, e.g.*, William H. Rodgers, Jr., *Tribal Government Roles in Environmental Federalism*, Nat. Res. & Env't, Winter 2007, at 3; Timothy C. Seward, *Survival of Indian Tribes Through Repatriation of Homelands*, Nat. Res. & Env't, Winter 2007, at 32; Mary Christina Wood & Zachary Welcker, *Tribes as Trustees Again (Part I): The Emerging Tribal Role in the Conservation Trust Movement*, 32 Harv. Envtl. L. Rev. 373 (2008). An example of one such tribal effort by the Isleta Pueblo is discussed in Chapter 7.

Professor Charles Wilkinson notes that tribes generally devote a substantial proportion of their governmental resources to environmental protection — often far greater amounts, relatively, than their federal and state counterparts. *See* Charles Wilkinson, Messages from Frank's Landing: A Story of Salmon, Treaties, and the Indian Way 94 (2000). In absolute terms, however, tribal expenditures may still be modest. Many tribes are still working to address poverty and other pressing social issues, and many are still laboring to build the administrative infrastructure necessary to address the environmental problems they face. On the one hand, tribes and their members often possess a wealth of expertise as environmental managers — including traditional ecological knowledge born in many instances of generations of residency in place. On the other hand, funding is a perennial issue for many tribal governments. Professor Judith Royster elaborates:

> In environmental matters, Indian tribes acting as governments face both tremendous opportunities and enormous obstacles. Perhaps the most significant obstacle to tribes' assertions of their environmental rights is money. Despite the recent success of some tribal casinos, many Indian reservations remain among the poorest communities in the nation. Tribes have neither the economic base nor the monetary resources to undertake major environmental protection programs, generally from scratch, without substantial federal financial assistance. Although the federal government has offered limited funding for tribes, the lack of money has been identified as the "key problem" in a study of tribal actions to protect reservation water quality. As one scholar has noted, "[w]hatever else environmental justice means[] in Indian country," it must include sufficient funding for tribes to develop effective environmental programs designed to serve tribal needs and protect tribal values.

Judith V. Royster, *Native American Law*, *in* The Law of Environmental Justice: Theories and Procedures to Address Disproportionate Risks 199, 213–14 (Michael B. Gerrard & Sheila R. Foster eds., 2d ed. 2008) (quoting Dean Suagee). By comparison, scholars note, substantial federal financial assistance has been provided to state environmental programs for decades.

While advocates point to greater tribal control over traditional and culturally-important lands and resources as the solution to environmental injustice for American Indian people, some familiar issues may arise as tribal governments contemplate proposed economic development projects and otherwise regulate economic activities within their jurisdiction. Ms. Jana Walker, attorney and former member of the NEJAC Subcommittee on Indigenous Peoples, and her colleagues raise this point: "But what of potentially 'bad' development decisions made by Tribes? As pointed out by some scholars, recognition of tribal self-government 'does not mean that every decision of a Tribe is beyond scrutiny on environmental justice grounds' ...". Jana L. Walker, Jennifer L. Bradley & Timothy J. Humphrey, Sr., *A Closer Look at Environmental Injustice in Indian Country*, 1 Seattle J. for Soc. Just. 379, 391 (2002) (quoting Dean Suagee). At times, impacted communities within tribal lands are in open opposition to proposed developments supported by tribal authorities, and the alliances formed by these opposition campaigns sometimes include non-Indian advocacy organizations. Or, in other instances, non-Indian advocacy groups may challenge tribal developments that have spillover effects beyond the boundaries of tribal lands. This raises a host of sensitive issues for the tribes. Suffice it to say that when tribal governments act as regulators there are different issues, such as tribal self-determination, to be considered than when federal, state, or other governments act as regulators. Several of these issues are elaborated on in Chapter 4.

Nonetheless, tribal governments have undertaken what might be viewed as environmental justice initiatives that are roughly analogous to those undertaken by their federal and state counterparts. For example, tribes may undertake particular regulatory initiatives to address severe problems that affect discrete communities—for example, a more traditional subset of tribal members—within their jurisdiction. Or tribes may need to consider the interests of non-tribal members within their jurisdiction. Note that a tribe's governmental function may at times put tribal regulators in conflict with impacted tribal communities. Tribal approaches to environmental justice need to be considered against this politically complex backdrop and in light of each tribe's unique historical circumstances. As tribal governments have increasingly exercised regulatory authority, particularly in conjunction with delegated programs under the federal environmental laws, concerns respecting "due process" and public participation have emerged. These considerations are explored in the following excerpt.

Dean B. Suagee & John P. Lowndes, Due Process and Public Participation in Tribal Environmental Programs

13 Tulane Environmental Law Journal 1 (1999)

... The opposition to tribal regulatory authority features an argument that is unique to Indian country, one that does not seem to arise in any other environmental-federalism context. It is the argument made by non-Indians who live within reservation boundaries, and by states on behalf of such people, that, since they have no right to representation in tribal government, they should not be subject to tribal law. This argument has some resonance. More than just the fear of being treated unfairly by a government in which one has no voice, it is an argument that can be framed as a matter of human rights. The right to participate in government is enshrined in article 25 of the International Covenant on Civil and Political Rights....

The tension between the interests of tribal governments in protecting the environment of all lands within reservations and the rights of nonmembers of tribes need not be resolved by sanctioning the intrusion of state governmental power within reservation boundaries. We may instead find ways to resolve this tension by looking into some of the details of environmental federalism and the modern practice of tribal sovereignty. When tribes assume state-like roles for purposes of carrying out federal environmental laws, they take on these roles in the context of federal regulations that provide numerous opportunities for public participation as well as safeguards for ensuring that persons whose interests are regulated by tribal governments are afforded due process....

Rights and Interests of Tribal Members

Individual tribal members have rights under tribal constitutions and customary law, as well as under the Indian Civil Rights Act. The institutions of tribal government carry much weight in making these civil rights meaningful. In addition, individual tribal members share in the collective rights of their tribes: Tribes have the right to exercise self-government, and each tribal member is a part of the "self" of the tribe. Some of the rights that individual Indians have as tribal members depend upon a healthy environment, for example, hunting and fishing rights and rights to carry on other cultural practices that make use of the natural world. Within the framework of federal environmental laws, environmental protection is carried out through a partnership between the federal government and ... [n]ow ... tribes.... Building tribal programs within the context of environmental federalism requires tribes to abide by some minimum requirements for due process and public participation.

Rights and Interests of Non-Indians

Non-Indians and nonmember Indians have numerous rights and interests that can be affected by tribal governments. Owners of fee land and lessees of trust land have property rights.... [P]eople do not want to simply be reassured that everything is being taken care of, they want and expect opportunities to participate in the governmental decisions that affect them and to vote for at least some of the officials who make those decisions....

Tribal Variations on Due Process and Public Participation

... [T]ribal cultural values must be drawn upon in determining the form that due process and public participation will assume in any given tribal community.

When considering tribal legislation or rules for due process and public participation, tribal officials and legal counsel should consider fashioning procedures to ensure that culturally important interests are taken into consideration. Many tribal cultures treat certain kinds of interests as being very important, things such as the welfare of future generations, the final resting places of ancestors, the welfare of wildlife and other living things, sacred places, and spiritual beings. Procedural rules could be fashioned with these interests in mind. For example, culturally important kinds of wildlife or sacred places might be given standing in their own right to participate in administrative proceedings or to challenge decisions in tribal court. Tribal government agencies with relevant expertise or established groups within a tribal community might be authorized to act as guardian ad litem for such interests. Additionally, special procedures could be established to protect the confidentiality of certain kinds of information, such as simply deferring to the judgment of a tribal religious society on certain kinds of issues. Many different approaches can be imagined.

Tribal cultures often treat the rights of individuals somewhat differently than does the larger American society. In the dominant society, the rights of individuals are widely regarded as sacrosanct: Individuals have rights that the government cannot take away. The tension between the powers of government and rights of individuals is often seen as two-sided, but in tribal communities, a third side can be seen: the web of relationships with and responsibilities to other people in the community. Tribal procedures to provide for due process and public participation could be shaped with this web of relationships and responsibilities in mind....

If the decisions of tribal court judges regarding due process cases differ greatly from the way such cases would be resolved in the dominant society, the judges should articulate their reasoning clearly so that their opinions are respected in both the larger society and the tribal community. Legal scholars, as well as some tribal courts, have suggested that tribal courts draw on tribal cultural traditions rather than on Anglo-American law in fashioning due process jurisprudence. For example, Professor Frank Pommersheim, in his book *Braid of Feathers*, quotes the following passage from a decision by the Supreme Court of the Oglala Sioux Tribe:

> It should not have to be for the Congress of the United States or the Federal Court of Appeals to tell us when to give due process. Due process is a concept that has always been with us. Although it is a legal phrase and has legal meaning, due process means nothing more than being fair and honest in our dealings with each other. We are allowed to disagree.... What must be remembered is that we must allow the other side the opportunity to be heard.

* * *

Notes and Questions

1. In the excerpt above, Messrs. Suagee and Lowndes allow that the right to participate in governance is a human right. They continue, however, to observe that:

> [o]ne can also make a human rights counter argument. For example, since federal laws that opened reservations to settlement by non-Indians violated the collective right of tribes to self-determination, federal recognition of tribal authority over environmental protection for all lands within reservation boundaries is part of a contemporary remedy for the historical violation of self-determination.

Id. at 4. In your view, how should these competing claims be resolved in this context? Does this history mean we should think differently about issues of due process and public participation when tribal—as opposed to federal or state—governments are the decision-makers and, if so, how?

2. The Indigenous Peoples' Subcommittee of the NEJAC considered the issues of due process and public participation in the tribal context. *See* NAT'L ENVTL. JUSTICE ADVISORY COUNCIL, MEANINGFUL INVOLVEMENT AND FAIR TREATMENT BY TRIBAL ENVIRONMENTAL REGULATORY PROGRAMS (Nov. 2004). This report presents several examples of tribes that have, in the view of the NEJAC, "effectively provid[ed] meaningful public participation and fair treatment." For example:

> [A] "Minority Communications Board" ... was established [by the Shoshone-Bannock Tribes of Idaho] in 1979 for the following reasons:
>
> > "The Tribes have existed as a minority for more than a century, and thus are highly aware of the feelings of frustration and helplessness associated with minority status. To ensure a voice on land use matters for non-Indians who reside on the Reservation and who are ineligible to vote in Tribal elections by virtue of the Tribal Constitution and Bylaws, the [Land Use Policy] Commission shall appoint a board to be known as the "Minority Communication Board."
>
> The purpose of the three-member Board is to "provide a vehicle for communication and cooperation between the Tribes and non-Indians residing on the Reservation."

> The Land Use Policy Commission works "with the Board to ensure that the land use problems and needs of non-Indians are expressed, and that the legitimate land use rights of non-Indians are protected."
>
> The Board meets on a quarterly basis with the Commission to discuss issues, gather information about the status of various environmental matters, give input on pending matters, raise questions and voice concerns that they may have about tribal land use issues and environmental programs. The Board has proved useful in building non-Indian support for Tribal jurisdiction over non-Indians on a wide variety of issues beyond environmental regulation. The Board distributes information to other non-Indian landowners about the Tribal programs, permits, and other regulations that are required throughout the Reservation. Non-Indians routinely telephone or contact the Tribal Land Use and environmental programs about possible violators of Tribal law, for assistance with potential pollution discharges, to inquiry about permits and a myriad of other issues.

Id. at 25–26. In your view, are the measures taken by the Shoshone-Bannock Tribes likely to address adequately the legitimate due process and public participation concerns of non-members?

3. Suppose you represent a group of traditional tribal members that opposes an economic development project that is supported by the tribal government, on the grounds that it would permit contamination of a sacred spring. Assuming that your clients are committed to addressing the environmental injustices suffered by American Indian peoples as a general matter, how would you frame your clients' claims? Are there different considerations in play here given that a tribal government and its members are involved? For the observation that, within a modern tribe, the locus of spiritual authority and the locus of political authority may not be one and the same, see Robert A. Williams, Jr., *Large Binocular Telescopes, Red Squirrel Piñatas, and Apache Sacred Mountains: Decolonizing Environmental Law in a Multicultural World*, 96 W. Va. L. Rev. 1133 (1994) (exerpted in Chapter 4).

4. As is discussed in Chapter 5, for several decades now environmental regulation has been steadily moving in the direction of greater "stakeholder" participation by public institutions and private firms and individuals that are affected by environmental regulation. This trend appears as well in governmental initiatives to address environmental justice. Through these collaborative approaches, a lead agency, like the EPA, typically will convene a group of governmental officials from other federal agencies and from state and local governments, as well as business firms, environmental and environmental justice organizations, and community residents, to attempt to leverage resources and effectively address (usually localized) environmental justice issues. As you read the following section, consider how these collaborative approaches might incorporate different perspectives.

F. Collaborative Approaches

The concept of a collaborative process is deceptively simple and appealing. Although it makes eminent good sense, there are a variety of reasons why well-meaning collaborative processes may fail and end up doing more harm than good. Although collaborations can take various forms—from advisory groups to oversight groups—most in the environmental justice context involve public and private actors attempting to identify and address interrelated environmental problems on a local scale. These place-based efforts often require some devolution of authority in order to implement more innovative strategies, but at the same time must maintain accountability to traditional regulatory authorities. As explained by Professor Sheila Foster:

> There are at least two recognizable strands of devolved collaboration currently in practice. The first involves mostly ad hoc local groups that are concerned with diverse issues in natural resources planning and management. The second features more formalized, local working groups that focus on land use and pollution control decisions. Both strands expand the influence of, and demand deeper participation by, public and private local actors in environmental and natural resource decisions. Yet, neither strand requires a complete abdication of government authority and responsibility over those decisions. Accountability to central government decision-makers is preserved through a multilateral relationship whereby local actors supplement central regulatory authorities, which in turn support local efforts. In both strands, regulators (and sometimes legislators) expect to, and often do, use the proposals and recommendations of community-based participants to manage natural resources in accordance with local values, reformulate minimum performance standards, or impose additional conditions and monitoring requirements on regulated sources.

Sheila Foster, *Environmental Justice in an Era of Devolved Collaboration*, 26 HARV. ENVTL. L. REV. 459, 473 (2002).

One early collaborative effort was spearheaded at the federal level. In 1999 the Interagency Working Group on Environmental Justice (IWG) established an Integrated Federal Interagency Environmental Justice Action Agenda. The Action Agenda led to a number of interesting demonstration projects involving collaboration among government agencies, communities, and other private parties. Some of these projects, and the philosophy underlying the collaborative approach of the Action Agenda, are described by Charles Lee, presently a high-ranking official in EPA's Office of Environmental Justice and author of the landmark Toxic Waste and Race study (see Chapter 2).

Charles Lee, Submission to the National Environmental Policy Commission*
(May 15, 2001)

IWG Interagency Action Agenda

... Because of the enormous complexity and interrelated/multi-faceted nature of the issues that make up the concept of environmental justice, a primary challenge facing the IWG was to develop a mechanism which can leverage the benefits of many important federal initiatives and public-private partnerships....

... [T]he Action Agenda is spearheading the development of a distinctively new collaborative model for achieving environmental justice.... In order for this model to work, it requires not only cooperation and coordination among Federal agencies, but leadership and direction from place-based partnerships of all relevant stakeholder groups....

---

* These written comments were submitted in connection with a presentation made on December 15, 2000, at the Newark, New Jersey Listening Session of the National Environmental Policy Commission.

To test and develop the collaborative model of the Action Agenda, the IWG has sponsored 15 demonstration projects, almost all of which is [sic] geographically based and which embrace a plethora of environmental justice issues and stakeholder communities. Presently, the IWG is developing, with input from all stakeholders, criteria for evaluating these current projects and criteria for selecting possible future projects....

Background: IWG Collaborative Model

Collaborative processes requires [sic] the building of genuine partnerships among all relevant parties, and the process results in better understanding for all participants of the perspectives and concerns of each party. Constructive processes are geared toward local[ly] solving problems, which require proactive, pragmatic and innovative strategies. The resulting action must be solution-oriented and of benefit to impacted communities (who must be at the center of the decision making process) and relevant stakeholders.

... Environmental health and quality of life concerns which often spark environmental justice disputes more often than not include issues of environment, housing, transportation, urban sprawl, community infrastructure, economic development, capacity building and others. In addition, there are special concerns with respect to Tribes and indigenous populations.... No single agency can adequately address the multi-faceted dimensions of any environmental justice situation.... Without focused and concerted efforts on the part of multiple agencies, the singularly directed initiatives of a given agency, no matter how well intentioned, fall short in the face of the overwhelming challenges presented by the combined ills of environmental, social and economic distress on impacted communities.

A cautionary note: The collaborative model is not appropriate for all environmental justice situations. Some of the most intractable and difficult issues affecting impacted communities may in fact only be resolved in litigation....

On May 24, 2000, EPA formally announced the [Action Agenda] on behalf of the eleven participating federal departments and agencies, including the initial round of fifteen National Demonstration Projects [Below are selected examples of some of the projects. Note the diversity of the issues addressed. Eds.]....

Selected Demonstration Projects Protecting Children's Health & Reducing Lead Exposure through Collaborative Partnerships

Location: East St. Louis, Illinois

Population: African American

Issue: Lead Screening and Abatement

Partners: Involve 17 different organizations, including St. Mary's Hospital, East St. Louis, St. Clair County, EPA, HUD, USDA, USACE

Activities:

- Screening over 3,000 children for blood lead
- Conduct lead based paint assessments
- Conduct site assessments in abandoned lots where children play
- Participate in worker training program
- Initiated phytoremediation project
- Develop outreach and education, including video
- Leveraged over $4 million in federal funding

- Designated a National Brownfields Showcase Community ...

Metlakatla Indian Community Unified Interagency Environmental Management Task Force

Location: Annette Islands, Alaska

Population: Alaska Native

Issue: Environmental cleanup and restoration

Partners: Tlingit & Haida Indian Tribes, BIA, DOD, EPA, FAA-DOT, USCG-DOT; Metlakatla Indian Community Unified Interagency Environmental Management Task Force

Activities:

- Develop Master Plan for cleanup and restoration of Metlakatla Peninsula
- DOD anticipates commitment of $2.5 million for site assessment
- Protect traditional use of food resources
- Planning to promote economic development through tourism and commercial fishing
- Designated a National Brownfields Showcase Community ...

Addressing Asthma Coalition in Puerto Rico: A Multi-Faceted Partnership for Results

Location: Puerto Rico

Population: Children in Puerto Rico

Issue: Protect children's health

Partners: PR Dept of Health, Pediatric Pulmonary Program, PR Lung Association, others HRSA, ATSDR, CDC, EPA

Activities:

- Two strategic planning conferences involving over 1000 people in NYC and Puerto Rico
- Support development of the Asthma Coalition of Puerto Rico
- Increase public awareness and professional training
- Coordinate better between asthma care providers and insurance companies
- Institute asthma research and surveillance programs ...

Easing Troubled Waters: Farm Worker Safe Drinking Water Project

Location: State of Colorado

Population: Migrant Farm workers

Issue: Public Health

Partners: Plan de Salad del Valle, High Plains Center for Agricultural Health and Safety, National Center for Farmworker Health, CO DPH, CO DOL, CO DOA HRSA, EPA, DOL, USDA Colorado State Agricultural Extension

Activities:

- Develop GIS maps of migrant farm worker camps and drinking water sources
- Assess water quality data for camps

- Recommend changes to federal policy regarding testing of migrant worker water sources
- Develop interagency and community plan to address communication and education needs
- Build sustainable network to implement policy and communications changes …

* * *

Notes and Questions

1. As the demonstration pilot projects illustrate, there are a variety of agencies that can participate both "horizontally" and "vertically." Sister federal agencies often agree to participate initially because of the mandate of the Executive Order. However, because environmental hot spots implicate local land use decisions, the participation of municipal, county, regional, and state agencies is indispensable. The participation of the business sector is also a key component to the project. Yet, how do these various agencies and stakeholders get together in a collaborative effort, and what is the framework that is most likely to result in tangible results to the impacted area?

A May 2001 forum convened by the International City/County Management Association (ICMA), entitled Building Collaborative Models to Achieve Environmental Justice, provided interesting insights into the successes and failures of the IWG demonstration projects. At the conference, long-time environmental justice activists began by explaining why collaborative efforts were necessary, but extraordinarily difficult to implement in light of a skepticism that still exists in impacted communities — a view that stems from their experiences with governmental agencies that previously exhibited hostility to environmental justice claims. Government regulators noted that the task was difficult initially because the federal government operates on big issues and big policies, while communities work on a different scale; the "levers of decision-making" were necessarily different and not easily subject to coordination. The participants appeared to agree that certain components are critical to successful collaborative partnerships. Among them are:

- There must be a high level of community education and empowerment about the issues. Environmental justice advocates, in particular, argued that a well-organized community group was a critical component of the process;
- Early resident and community involvement and visioning is key. All other stakeholder participants should recognize that the community is different than all other stakeholder groups;
- There must be a development of a clear action plan;
- The partnership must include the community, businesses and government agencies;
- Collaborating must include "win-win" scenarios for many stakeholders;
- There must be a commitment to facilitate conflict resolution, where appropriate. Sometimes, parties engaged in a conflict cannot work their way through the conflict by themselves and may need to find a third person that has a sensitivity to the issues; and
- There must be sufficient resources to address the problem. One can better leverage available resources by interagency coordination.

INT'L CITY/COUNTY MGMT. ASS'N, REPORT: FORUM ON BUILDING COLLABORATIVE MODELS TO ACHIEVE ENVIRONMENTAL JUSTICE (2001).

Perspectives differed, however, concerning the interplay between collaborative partnerships and collateral, more adversarial proceedings, such as litigation. Environmental justice advocates were clear in their view that there must be recognition that the collaborative process has limitations. Thus, they maintained that there are some issues that require resolution by litigation or other methods. They saw no problem with these proceedings occurring simultaneously and collaterally to the collaborative processes. In fact, one activist noted that her organization had collaterally participated in proceedings that resulted in a $150,000 fine against one of the partners. Business stakeholders, on the other hand, viewed collateral litigation as disruptive of and counterproductive to the collaborative effort. Some questioned whether litigation might preclude potential partners from joining a collaborative project. What is your view about the interplay between these approaches? Should groups forego litigation where they are involved in collaborative projects such as those described above?

2. In an article examining a proposal by the Conservation Alliance (an environmental organization dedicated to preserving grassland ecosystems) to establish the Greater Black Hills Wildlife Protection Area, Professor John LaVelle, an Indian Law scholar and member of the Santee Sioux Nation, sounds a note of caution about the proposal. *See* John P. LaVelle, *Rescuing Paha Sapa: Achieving Environmental Justice by Restoring the Great Grasslands and Returning the Sacred Black Hills to the Great Sioux Nation*, 5 GREAT PLAINS NAT. RESOURCES J. 40 (2001). In its proposal, the Conservation Alliance specifically notes that "[o]ne group which must be consulted throughout the process would be those Native Americans whose traditional and current territory might be involved. Native American participation should be encouraged as a way to open the door to a broader discussion about the past and a common future on the Great Plains." *Id.* at 42–43. However, the sort of consultation envisioned by the Conservation Alliance—presumably a form of collaboration—cannot proceed in a way that does not consider the ongoing claims of the Sioux Nation. Professor LaVelle explains:

In contemplating the possibility of establishing a "Greater Black Hills Wildlife Protected Area," the "treacherous history" of the dispossession of *Paha Sapa* should give the Conservation Alliance pause to consider carefully the political, moral, and ethical implications of how it chooses to proceed with its proposal. The advocates of the proposal must be willing to clarify and deepen their commitment to achieving justice through the proposal's development beyond the mere avowal that Indian people "must be consulted" and that "Native American participation should be encouraged." As Professor [Frank] Pommersheim reminds us, "[j]ustice emanates from conversation rather than declaration," and with respect to *Paha Sapa* in particular there remains an urgent "need for enduring and honest dialogue." Hence, any "conversation" or "dialogue" about our "common future on the Great Plains" must begin by acknowledging that the dispossession of the Black Hills from the Great Sioux Nation is a *present and ongoing* injustice, and not simply a doleful moment in a "broader discussion about the past."

What the Conservation Alliance must conscientiously avoid—and what the Sioux tribes must vigilantly guard against—is the prospect of advancing a policy scheme that charts a course toward a "common future" in which the intolerable and continuing injustice of the dispossession of *Paha Sapa* is further "legitimized" under the guise of "protecting" or "restoring" or "renewing" the environment. If that were to happen—the Lakota, Dakota, and Nakota people's aspirations for the return of the sacred Black Hills were to be sacrificed once again under the edict that the invaders "simply need that country ... [as] part of the geography of hope"—then the plan for "[r]enewing the Great Plains" will have failed to help realize "the dream of dwelling on an earth made whole." Instead, the Conservation Alliance will have opened yet another "tragic[] chapter in the history of the Nation's West" by effectively deploying environmental colonialism to exacerbate the ethnocide manifested in the dispossession of *Paha Sapa*.

Id. at 69–71. How might a collaborative process to restore this area—unquestionably in the best interest of all—proceed?

3. Professor Sheila Foster also probes the collaborative process—one strongly oriented towards consensus—for potential bias. She too introduces a cautionary note:

Even with broad representation, however, devolved collaborative processes can be highly problematic from a substantive point of view. As critics of consensus aptly observe, the theory of consensus itself contains an inherent ideological bias. Its emphasis on securing unanimous agreement through the identification of common interests ("win-win") can be antithetical to achieving substantive justice. Such emphasis can skew the process in favor of the outcome which reflects the lowest common denominator acceptable to all parties. The problem with outcomes reflecting the lowest common denominator is that, while the process can be deemed "legitimate" in a democratic process sense, its outcome may reflect a type of "domination by means of leveling." In other words, it tends to leave out difficult, unpopular, or minority concerns, and may orient the process away from sorely needed innovative solutions that address these concerns.

The substantive bias also reveals itself in the very mechanisms upon which consensus depends. Consensus simultaneously stresses agreement and compromise while "veiling the increased potential for coercion by leaders" of collaborative groups. The primary mechanism through which this coercion is practiced is the veto power possessed by each participant. This veto power can force agreement by threatening complete failure of the process if it is exercised. Given current disparities in material resources and social capital, "those with greater power possess and [will] frequently use their prerogative to exert substantial influence over other members and, through them, the content of group decisions." In this way, by forcing agreement through coercion, more powerful and knowledgeable participants are able to co-opt dissident viewpoints that may be critical to seeking more creative, and just, decisions.

By ignoring, marginalizing, or co-opting difficult questions of distributional justice, or other pressing policy dilemmas, consensus processes at their most benign replicate the status quo. Communities disproportionately bearing the costs of current environmental policy and natural resources management may not be left any worse off by consensus solutions, but they will not likely be helped by them either. At their most dangerous, consensus solutions may change the status quo for the worse, exacerbating existing distributional disparities. In the final analysis, the outcomes from some consensus-based process will no more reflect the "public interest" than the problematic pluralistic processes they replace.

Foster, supra, at 493–94. Do you agree with Professor Foster that collaboration will simply replicate the problematic processes they replace and are unlikely to promote substantive justice? In light of these potential biases, is collaboration worth the effort? What are the potential gains?

4. Professor Mank notes that the EPA's fiscal year 2006 budget did not include any money for the demonstration projects. *See* Bradford C. Mank, *Executive Order 12,898, in* THE LAW OF ENVIRONMENTAL JUSTICE: THEORIES AND PROCEDURES TO ADDRESS DISPROPORTION-ATE RISKS, *supra,* at 102. Do you think that collaboration is a promising strategy and should be pursued more aggressively? How would you structure collaboration to avoid some of the pitfalls discussed above? Do you think enough is being done to redress environmental justice concerns, or should legislatures and agencies consider other approaches as well? What approaches would you recommend to avoid the pitfalls described above?

Glossary of Acronyms Used in this Chapter

ATCA   Alien Tort Claims Act

ATSDR   Agency for Toxic Substances and Disease Registry

BECC   Border Environmental Cooperation Commission

BIA   Bureau of Indian Affairs

CDC   Centers for Disease Control

CEC   North American Commission for Environmental Cooperation

DOA   Department of Agriculture

DOD   Department of Defense

DOE   Department of Energy

DOI   Department of Interior

DOJ   Department of Justice

DOL   Department of Labor

DOT   Department of Transportation

DPH   Department of Public Health

EO   Executive Order

EPA   Environmental Protection Agency

FAA   Federal Aviation Administration

GIS   Geographic Information Systems

GHG   Greenhouse Gas

HRSA   Health Resources and Services Administration

HUD   Department of Housing and Urban Development

IACHR   Inter-American Commission on Human Rights

ICMA   International City/County Management Association

IWG   Interagency Working Group

NAD   BankNorth American Development Bank

NAFTA   North American Free Trade Agreement

NEJAC   National Environmental Justice Advisory Council

NEPA   National Environmental Policy Act

NIEHS   National Institute of Environmental Health Sciences

NGO   Non-Governmental Organization

UN   United Nations

USACE   United States Army Corps of Engineers

USCG   United States Coast Guard

USDA   United States Department of Agriculture

Chapter 11

Land Use Planning, Environmental Review, and Information Disclosure Laws

A. Introduction

Overburdened communities potentially can rely on a range of legal and political tools to remedy disproportionate environmental harms. These include challenging permitting decisions and pressing for brownfields redevelopment (*see* Chapters 8 and 9), seeking to enforce the requirements of pollution control statutes or bringing common law actions (*see* Chapter 13) or utilizing civil rights remedies (*see* Chapter 14). Many of these approaches are reactive—they are employed by a community to stop a proposal for an unwanted facility, or to mitigate harm at an existing site. This chapter examines several approaches that are more proactive. Section B looks at traditional land use planning and zoning mechanisms, as well as one of the favored solutions offered by some academics: compensation for host communities. Sections C and D are applications of what Professor Zygmund Plater has characterized as "stop and think" statutes—they require information to be developed and disclosed about facilities or activities that cause environmental damage, but they do not prohibit such activities from going forward. Specifically, Section C looks at environmental review statutes such as the National Environmental Policy Act and state law equivalents, while Section D examines the federal "right to know" law. To some extent, all of these approaches provide communities, government agencies, or businesses with the opportunity to plan and prevent disparate siting or other environmental harms from occurring.

B. Planning, Land Use, and Compensated Siting Approaches

1. Planning and Zoning Changes

The excerpt below advocates greater reliance on planning and zoning mechanisms to address disparate siting patterns.

Craig Anthony Arnold, Planning Milagros: Environmental Justice and Land Use Regulation

76 Denver University Law Review 1 (1998)

The next frontier for both the movement and the focus of environmental justice scholarship ... is land use planning by communities of color and low-income communities. Local neighborhoods can use land use planning to articulate visions for what they want their communities to be, and negotiate land use regulations to implement these visions. In other words, they would not be merely late participants in using existing rules to stop (or attempt to stop) current proposals for unwanted land uses, but also pre-siting participants in developing the rules that will determine what will and will not go in their neighborhoods....

Land Use Planning & Regulation: Another Vision of Environmental Justice

Land use planning and regulation offer several advantages for achieving environmental justice goals. First, an owner or operator of a prospective [Locally Unwanted Land Use] LULU would have much more difficulty obtaining approval for siting the LULU in a minority or low-income neighborhood, if the comprehensive plan and zoning ordinances prohibited the LULU in that neighborhood than if they allowed the LULU, either by right or conditionally. Assume that a waste company wants to locate a hazardous waste incinerator in a low-income, Hispanic neighborhood. If the city zoning code prohibits hazardous waste incinerators in every zone except I-3, and the zoning map does not designate any land in the target neighborhood as I-3, the waste company will need a zoning amendment, as well as use-specific environmental permits. If the city's comprehensive plan provides for non-industrial uses only in the neighborhood or explicitly states that waste facilities are not appropriate for that neighborhood, the waste company also will need an amendment to the comprehensive plan. The waste company nonetheless might have enough political and economic power to obtain all the needed approvals, but it will face several obstacles.... Furthermore, the neighbors will have more government approvals to challenge in litigation....

Comprehensive Plan

The first land use regulatory mechanism is the comprehensive plan. Zoning regulations that implement low-income and minority neighborhoods' goals may be legally ineffective if they are not preceded by amendments to the city's comprehensive plan to reflect those goals....

Amendments to Zoning

[T]he crux of land use regulation for environmental justice will be the amendment of existing zoning codes. Most low-income and minority communities that suffer or risk exposure to environmental harms exist in areas with zoning classifications that currently permit intensive uses. Because people of color and the poor live near and among a higher proportion of industrial and commercial uses than do white, high-income people, an appropriate land use regulatory response for cities would be to change the permitted uses in those areas to correspond more closely to the residents' desired neighborhood environment, as well as their health and safety needs....

Zoning map amendments change the zoning district designation for a particular parcel, tract of land, or set of parcels. Although rezoning has been used to allow intensive uses in neighborhoods of color and low-income communities, grassroots environmental justice activists might seek zoning map amendments to change more intensive use designations in their neighborhoods to less intensive use designations, a technique known as "downzoning." For example, a low-income minority neighborhood might contain several parcels zoned for heavy industrial use in close proximity to residences, schools, churches, health care facilities, and the like. Residents might seek to rezone some or all of these parcels for less intensive, yet economically viable, commercial uses....

Low-income and minority neighborhood groups will be most successful in achieving valid rezoning of neighboring properties from more intensive to less intensive uses if they follow four guiding principles: (1) seek rezoning before controversial specific land use proposals arise; (2) carefully document the incompatibility of existing high-intensity use designations and their impact or potential impact on the health and safety of local residents, as well as community character; (3) seek rezoning for all neighboring parcels with similar use designations and similar impacts (do not leave a landowner the argument that only his or her property has been downzoned while neighboring parcels remain zoned for more intensive uses); and (4) do not downzone so greatly that the landowner suffers a substantial diminution in the property's value (leave the owner some economically viable use—for example, downzone from an industrial use to a commercial use, instead of all the way to a single family residential use).

Perhaps the most successful strategy of all includes a comprehensive set of amendments to the zoning text, the zoning map, and the comprehensive plan. These combined text and map amendments often create new zoning designations and apply them to existing parcels, and they often receive judicial approval because of their comprehensive nature....

Flexible Zoning Techniques

... Buffer zones, like performance zoning, both help and hurt low-income people and people of color. Buffer zones are use designations that create a buffer or transition between a less intensive use, such as single-family residential, and a nearby more intensive use, such as commercial or industrial. The buffer zone exists between the two areas to minimize the impact of the more intensive use on the less intensive, more sensitive use.

The most frequent type of buffer between single-family residential areas and industrial or commercial areas is medium-or high-density residential uses.... Buffer zones are perhaps one of the major reasons why low-income and minority neighborhoods have so much industrial and commercial zoning: the multi-family housing, where many low-income and minority people live, is purposefully placed near the industrial and commercial uses to create a buffer that protects high-income, white, single-family neighborhoods. Zoning practices place large numbers of poor and minority people near intensive uses because traditional zoning and planning theory values most the single-family residence, instead of the integrity and quality of all residential areas.

[L]ow-income and minority neighborhoods need buffers to protect them from intensive industrial and commercial activity. Buffer zones can also include physical screening, landscaping, significant set backs, open space, and even low-intensity commercial uses like offices, shops, churches, and medical care facilities. Environmental justice advocates can use the concept of buffer zoning but redefine it to protect low-income and minority residences....

Exactions

.... Exactions require the developer to provide the public either real property (land, facilities, or both) or monetary fees as a condition for permission to use land in ways subject to government regulation. These dedications and fees provide the public facilities necessitated by new development, including schools, parks, open space, roads, sidewalks, public utilities, fire and police stations, low-income housing, mass transit, day care services, and job training programs.... Already, various federal, state, and local environmental regulatory programs require developers to dedicate land or pay fees to mitigate the environmental impacts of development in ecologically sensitive areas. A comprehensive environmental justice land use program, though, might include environmental impact fees and dedications for inner-city industrial and commercial development. The exactions would be based on the various environmental and social impacts of intensive uses and LULUs on the surrounding neighborhood(s), not just the publicly funded local infrastructure, and would be earmarked for ameliorating amenities in the affected neighborhood(s)....

Limits to Land Use Regulations as Environmental Justice Tools

The land use regulatory model of environmental justice, while promising for many low-income communities of color, contains inherent limits. Among these limits are legal constraints on land use regulation that are largely designed to protect the private property rights of landowners. Courts, increasingly protective of private property rights and skeptical of local political processes, have eroded the well-established judicial presumption that zoning decisions are valid by imposing greater scrutiny on decisions about land use regulation.... The final limits to land use regulation as an environmental justice strategy are political and economic. How successful, as a practical matter, will grassroots neighborhood groups be in changing land use patterns in low-income communities and communities of color? There is reason for a mix of sober realism and thoughtful optimism.... Local government is likely to regard changes to existing industrial or commercial zoning as politically or fiscally inconvenient, especially when these uses cannot be relocated to higher-income, lower-minority areas without political conflict. Indeed, many local governments engage in "fiscal zoning," favoring industrial and commercial uses because these uses generate tax revenues without creating expensive demands for local services in the way that single-family residences do, particularly through public school costs....

* * *

Notes and Questions

1. What is your response to Professor Arnold's question about the political obstacles to changing land use patterns? How successful are community activists likely to be in getting their neighborhoods rezoned to exclude industrial uses? What kind of organizing strategy might accomplish these goals? Another approach suggested by attorney Michael Gerrard is for local governments to focus attention on prior noncomforming uses. He argues that municipalities "may wish to survey their noncomforming uses and determine whether any of them pose such health and environmental problems that they should be

targeted for closure, either immediately as public nuisances or later through an amorti-zation process." Michael B. Gerrard, *Environmental Justice and Local Land Use Decision-making, in* TRENDS IN LAND USE LAW FROM A TO Z 148 (Patricia Salkin ed. 2001). One example of this approach is an ordinance adopted by National City, California that establishes a process for the gradual phase-out of approximately 100 industrial businesses from res-identially zoned neighborhoods in the city's Old Town area. *See* NATIONAL CITY, CAL., ORDINANCE 2286, §§ 1–2.

2. Exactions often raise Fifth Amendment challenges if there is not a sufficient nexus between the exaction required of the developer and the activity regulated. What kinds of exactions could be imposed upon, for example, a manufacturing facility emitting toxic chemicals? A buffer zone, a park, a community center? How closely must the exaction mit-igate the effects of the regulated activity to survive a takings challenge? The leading tak-ings cases in the context of exactions are *Dolan v. City of Tigard,* 512 U.S. 374 (1994) and *Nollan v. California Coastal Comm'n*, 483 U.S. 825 (1987).

3. In another article, Professor Arnold identified eighteen principles for "planning for environmental justice, or equitable planning" that he argues can be incorporated into any local planning processs. What are the core principles that you would identify in such a list? Professor Arnold also notes that "effective planning for environmental and land use jus-tice requires good information about environmental conditions in communities with a relatively high percentage of low-income people or people of color." He suggests that agen-cies should gather this information by conducing "environmental justice audits" that pro-vide demographic, historical, cultural, environmental, land use, and economic information about a local community. Tony Arnold, *Planning for Environmental Justice,* PLAN. & ENVTL L., Mar. 2007 at 7–8 (2007).

4. Professor Patricia Salkin contends that planning agencies must use more proactive strategies to ensure meaningful participation by all citizen interest groups in the plan-ning process, and that decision-making bodies must become more representative of their communities. She notes:

> In most localities, environmental justice considerations will be factored into local land use planning, zoning and siting decisions only where the impacted com-munities are represented on the bodies empowered to make these critical deci-sions. A 1987 survey by the American Planning Association revealed that:
>
> - Nearly eight out of 10 members of planning boards were men;
> - More than nine out of 10 members were white, although in some larger cities the number was closer to seven out of 10;
> - Almost eight out of 10 were 40 years of age or older; and
> - Most board members were professionals such as business people, lawyers, engineers, educators and real estate agents....
>
> This arguable "elitism" in the composition of local boards is a major barrier to addressing environmental justice concerns and promoting effective citizen par-ticipation for all communities in local planning and zoning decision making. This data also explains and substantiates the fact that marginalized citizens are not sufficiently empowered to impact community development decisions. To address this situation, states could advocate or require that localities appoint board members who represent the diversity of the community as a whole....

Patricia E. Salkin, *Intersection Between Environmental Justice and Land Use Planning,* PLAN. & ENVTL L., May 2006 at 7–8.

5. In 2003, the National Academy of Public Administration profiled a number of innovative land use measures that had been adopted by local agencies, including the following:

• Huntington Park, CA, which revised its zoning ordinance for commercial mixed use areas to allow the city to impose conditions in building/operating permits that require mitigation and reduction of adverse environmental impacts on residential areas, including impacts from diesel emissions.

• Chester, PA, which adopted an ordinance that prohibits any new heavy industrial facility from producing a net increase in environmental pollution, and adopted a series of performance measures to mitigate impacts from new facilities, including noise, glare and air pollution.

• Austin, TX, which created an overlay district requiring that any new facility with operations more intense than a commercial use must obtain a special use permit. When current industrial owners close their facilities in the district, the zoning is then changed to a less intense use.

The report also recommends that the federal government condition federal funding for land use, transportation, or environmental programs on having state and local governments adopt policies that address environmental justice issues through local planning and zoning mechanisms. NAT'L ACAD. PUB. ADMIN., ADDRESSING COMMUNITY CONCERNS: HOW ENVIRONMENTAL JUSTICE RELATES TO LAND USE PLANNING AND ZONING (2003).

6. Some states have passed statutes seeking to control the distribution of waste and other unwanted facilities, i.e., by prohibiting the placement of a waste facility where others exist, requiring plans that provide for a reasonable geographic distribution of facilities, or creating a rebuttable presumption against placing a waste facility where others exist. For example, Alabama law prohibits more than one commercial hazardous waste treatment facility or disposal site within each county. ALA. CODE § 22–30-5.1. New York City's "Fair Share Ordinance" requires that the selection of sites for city facilities "further the fair distribution among communities of the burdens and benefits associated with [these] facilities." NEW YORK CITY CHARTER § 203. California adopted legislation in 2001 requiring that the state's general plan guidelines include provisions that encourage local agencies to adopt general plans that achieve an equitable distribution of beneficial public facilities and services and avoid over-concentrating industrial facilities near schools and residences. CAL. GOV'T CODE, § 65040.12. As Professor Sheila Foster notes, more commonly found statutes require decision-makers to consider "soft criteria" in permit decisions, such as "the socioeconomic status of the host community, community perceptions, psychic costs, the potential for change in property values, and the cumulative health risks presented from other environmental sources in the host community." Typically, however, there is no statutory guidance for the weight decision makers must give these factors in the permitting process. Sheila Foster, *Impact Assessment, in* THE LAW OF ENVIRONMENTAL JUSTICE: THEORIES AND PROCEDURES TO ADDRESS DISPROPORTIONATE RISKS 295, 323–24 (Michael Gerrard & Sheila Foster eds., 2d ed. 2008). Are geographic constraints such as the Alabama and New York City statutes desirable? Recall Professor Kuehn's taxonomy of the four kinds of justice embodied in environmental justice principles (*see* Chapter 1). Is the distributive justice embodied by these laws easier to achieve than procedural, corrective, or social justice?

7. As discussed in Chapter 12, dramatic shifts in our energy infrastructure are likely to occur in response to climate change. The siting of large scale wind and solar facilities, new nuclear and liquid natural gas facilities, new transmission lines, and so forth will

raise significant land use issues. This is an area where there could be a significant local-federal clash, perhaps resulting in preemption of local land use prerogatives.

2. Compensated Siting Proposals

As noted, one of the earliest proposed solutions for addressing the inequitable distribution of polluting facilities is the idea of compensating communities that "host" unwanted facilities. This reform is discussed below.

Vicki Been, Compensated Siting Proposals:
Is it Time to Pay Attention?
21 Fordham Urban Law Journal 787 (1994)

The Theories Underlying Compensation Proposals

The siting of LULUs ... has become an extraordinarily difficult public policy challenge.... A primary, although by no means the only, explanation for the vehemence with which communities protest proposed sites is that the benefits of LULUs are spread diffusely over an entire community, region, state, or nation, while their costs are concentrated upon the host neighborhood. Industry associations, academics, and public policy makers have responded with a seemingly simple solution: compensate host communities for the harms the LULU causes. Proponents advance several justifications for compensation programs. First, they argue that if a LULU's benefits to the community outweigh its costs, the community will have no reason to oppose the project, and indeed may welcome it.

Next, proponents justify compensation programs as an equitable solution to the siting problem.... Compensation schemes are advanced to redress that injustice in situations where it would be impractical to equitably distribute risks physically or spatially. It may be unwise, for example, to site a radioactive or hazardous waste facility in every community that produces such waste, because a few large centralized facilities generally are considered safer, more environmentally sound, and more efficient than many small facilities. Those communities that must serve as host to the larger centralized facilities should be compensated, however, for bearing the burden by those who enjoy the benefits.

A third major justification for compensation proposals is that compensation can help to make siting decisions more efficient. Compensation forces the facility's developer to internalize the costs of the facility, and therefore helps to ensure that only those facilities that are efficient will be built. In addition, liability for the costs of the facility gives the facility's developer a strong incentive to take precautions to avoid or reduce those costs. Moreover, a community's participation in negotiations over the facility may make the public more willing to accept the risks associated with its operation....

Differences in Compensation Proposals

While the basic theoretical justifications for compensation tend to be relatively constant among proponents, the details of the proposals vary in several significant ways. This section offers a rough typology of the different types of proposals....

Remedial Nature of the Compensation

As a remedy, compensation seeks to make a community whole for damages it will suffer as a result of the facility. Agreements to pay neighboring property owners for any decrease in the market value of their homes caused by the facility are an example of remedial compensation. Alternatively, compensation may seek to prevent or reduce the harm the facility will cause. Such compensation measures are often referred to as "mitigation." The provision of buffer zones between a facility and its residential neighbors is an example of mitigation. Finally, compensation may serve to reward the community for accepting the facility by providing funds or benefits in excess of those required to remedy any harms caused by the facility....

Method of Compensation Proposed

Compensation either may be *ex ante* (before the facility is constructed or causes any harm to the community), on-going, or *ex post* (after the facility causes some harm). *Ex ante* compensation often takes the form of grants, which allow the host community to hire its own experts to evaluate the proposed facility. *Ex ante* compensation also may involve community participation in the design of the facility, selection of alternative facility operating procedures, or selection of the facility operator. Finally, *ex ante* compensation may consist of "risk substitution" rather than money, amenities, or rights of participation. Several academics have proposed, for example, that developers of waste disposal facilities offer to clean up all or some of a community's existing toxic waste sites in exchange for approval of the new facility.

On-going compensation often takes the form of special taxes or fees the facility regularly pays to the community, or services the facility regularly provides the community.... In addition, on-going benefits may take the form of continuing opportunities for community participation in the management of the facility. Local community representatives may be guaranteed a role in site monitoring, or be allowed to have an independent third party serve as a monitor, or be given funds to buy monitoring equipment, for example. Moreover, the community may be given some role in decisions about whether to close a facility down in the event of an emergency, or ... given representation on the facility's governing board.

Ex post compensation may include commitments to pay for, or insure against, future damages. Such commitments take the form of property value guarantees, local product price guarantees, agreements to indemnify local governments, or funds to compensate victims in the event of an accident.

Determining the Compensation Package

Compensation proposals also differ in how the terms of the compensation package are determined. One approach is for the governing statute to establish the level of compensation applicable to all communities. Alternatively, the statute can authorize a regulatory agency to determine the compensation package on a case by case basis. Another technique is to allow the facility developer and the community to negotiate a mutually satisfactory package. A fourth approach is to auction the facility to the community willing to accept the least compensation....

Theoretical Tests on the Proposals

Several scholars have attempted to test the likelihood that compensation programs will succeed through surveys asking people whether they would be willing to accept a facility in their community in exchange for some form of compensation. The surveys' results show that a relatively small number of people are willing to change their mind about a facility in exchange for compensation.... [T]he studies provide substantial evidence that at least those compensation measures that guarantee local monitoring and control may sway a significant number of people to accept a facility. The studies also suggest that while compensation measures may not be sufficient to secure acceptance, they nevertheless may be necessary to gain sufficient support for the facility....

State Negotiated Compensating Siting Programs for Hazardous Waste Facilities

Several states have adopted compensated siting as part of their hazardous waste siting programs.... The Massachusetts program is highlighted because the Massachusetts Hazardous Waste Facility Siting Act ("the Massachusetts Act") was hailed as a major advance in siting policy by both industry and environmentalists....

Under the Massachusetts Act, any developer proposing to construct a hazardous waste facility must notify the chief executive officers of the proposed host community and of all adjoining communities of its plan. The developer is then prohibited from constructing the facility until the "local assessment committee" of the host community has accepted a "site agreement" for the facility.

Although the Massachusetts Act's siting agreement requirement affords potential host communities some protection against unwanted facilities, it also limits four significant tools that communities previously had used in excluding hazardous waste facilities from their neighborhoods. [These include imposing new permitting requirements on the facility or adopting zoning changes to exclude a proposed facility.] ...

The notice of intent that triggers the siting agreement negotiation process must include a description of the following: the proposed facility; the type of wastes it would accept; the processes that would be used for the treatment or disposal of the wastes; the developer's prior experience in the construction and operation of hazardous waste facilities; and the developer's plans for financing the project. In addition, the notice of intent may either name a specific proposed site, or describe the characteristics of a theoretically ideal site and ask for possible candidates.

[If the notice is deemed complete and feasible by the Hazardous Waste Facility Site Safety Council ("the Council")], the developer and the proposed host community's local assessment committee then begin negotiating the terms under which the proposed host community would agree to accept the facility. The local assessment committee consists of the chief executive officer and representatives of the proposed host community's board of health, conservation commission, planning board, and fire department. The committee members then elect four residents of the municipality to serve on the committee; three of the four must be residents of the area within the municipality most immediately affected by the proposed facility. In addition, the chief executive officer may appoint up to four additional members, whose appointments must be approved by the municipality's legislative body.

The local assessment committee is charged with representing the "best interests of the host community" by negotiating with the developer "to protect the public health, the public safety, and the environment of the host community, as well as to promote the fiscal welfare of said community through special benefits and compensation." The local assessment committee is authorized to negotiate over the facility's design, construction, maintenance, operating procedures, and monitoring practices. In addition, the committee may negotiate regarding the services the host community will provide the developer and the compensation, services, and special benefits that the developer will provide the host community....

If the negotiations fail the Council may declare an impasse and require the parties to submit the disputed issues to [binding] arbitration....

Since the Massachusetts Act was passed in 1980, [as of 1994] it has been unsuccessful in encouraging communities to accept hazardous waste facilities. Although six different developers have attempted to site facilities under the terms of the Massachusetts Act, no facility has been sited....

Solid Waste-Industry Compensation Programs

The solid waste industry also has turned to compensation in order to secure community acceptance of undesirable land uses such as solid waste landfills and incinerators. The programs have been successful in the sense that few communities now accept such facilities without bargaining for some form of compensation, and some communities do accept LULUs that they almost certainly would have rejected in the absence of compensation....

Conclusion

.... No compensated siting program has been a "success" in getting LULUs sited. But neither has any other siting program. The experience so far suggests that while compensation may not be sufficient to resolve siting impasses, it can't hurt, and indeed may be one of several necessary elements of a solution. Until some panacea for siting controversies comes along, the temptation to use compensation to reduce opposition to siting proposals will be too strong to resist without better evidence that it is ineffective or counter-productive....

Because the programs are here, and here to stay, the environmental justice movement should be prepared to meet them head on. It should begin to formulate a more thoughtful and comprehensive policy about compensated siting programs.

Several lines of questioning should be pursued. Initially, environmental justice advocates should seek to articulate the circumstances under which compensation schemes are morally objectionable, and why. There are at least four major moral questions that require further exploration. First, because the siting of noxious LULUs often involve risks to health and safety, the question arises whether compensation schemes commodify, or subject to the free market, matters that should not be bought and sold. Society has chosen not to allow people to sell their kidneys to the highest bidder; should a similar judgment be made about whether people can sell their freedom from the health risks posed by nearby LULUs?

Second, it is likely that the communities that accept LULUs under compensated siting programs will be our poorest communities, because those communities lack alternative sources of funds. The distributional consequences of compensated siting programs therefore raise fundamental questions about our treatment of the poor and about the voluntariness of any site accepted by the communities.

Third, compensated siting programs allow a community to trade away the rights of future generations, who aren't represented at the bargaining table.... Finally, compensation schemes are likely to be considered immoral unless the community voluntarily enters into the siting agreement. What are the essential elements of a voluntary agreement? Is an agreement voluntary, for example, if communities are, relative to site developers, ignorant about the risks and harms the facilities will impose?

[A]ssuming that at least some forms of compensation are moral in at least some circumstances, how do we structure compensation programs to be most fair? Those issues include, for example, the question of how to ensure that communities and siting officials have relatively equal bargaining power.... [C]ommunities are at a severe disadvantage in finding out about what other communities have bargained for. The industry sometimes imposes as a condition of the bargain that the community not reveal the terms of the agreement.... At the same time, there has been little research on how siting agreements have worked out in practice, so communities may find it hard to assess whether they should follow another community's example....

* * *

Notes and Questions

1. Professor Been raises a host of difficult and important questions about compensation schemes. Other tough issues include who gets to negotiate and make these decisions on behalf of a community, and whether we should give special weight to the interests of those community members most affected by the sitings. Professor Bradford Mank advocates a system in which "the relative say that nearby residents, residents in a municipality, and regional neighbors have on a siting negotiation committee would depend on the relative amount of risk to which individuals are potentially or actually exposed, as determined by the risk assessment process," even if affected individuals live outside the host community's political boundaries. Bradford C. Mank, *Environmental Justice and Discriminatory Siting: Risk-Based Representation and Equitable Compensation* 56 Ohio. St. L.J. 329, 401 (1995).

2. Compensated siting approaches have been attractive to states, at least in theory. As of 1994, thirteen states mandated compensation for hazardous waste facilities, twelve offered compensation for low level radioactive waste facilities, and nineteen had procedures for negotiation between facility developers and proposed host communities. Michael Gerrard, *Fear and Loathing in the Siting of Hazardous and Radioactive Waste Facilities: A Comprehensive Approach to a Misperceived Crisis*, 68 Tul. L. Rev 1047, 1154, 1156 (1994). But as Professor Been points out, most compensated siting schemes have been unsuccessful, at least with respect to hazardous waste facilities. Indeed, a more recent evaluation concluded that as of 2008, no hazardous facility had been successfully sited using the Massachusetts siting scheme. Joseph W. Dayall & Christopher B. Myhrum, *Hazardous Materials Law in* Massachusetts Environmental Law Vol. II §21.5.5 (Massachusetts Continuing Legal Education Handbook & Supp. 2008). Why do you think that is the case? Professor Joel Eisen argues that the negotiated schemes have failed largely because they have not provided opportunities for meaningful public participation. In Massachusetts, for example, many communities resisted proposed facilities because they had no input into the site selection process and because the negotiations process excluded discussion of the need for a facility, which to many communities is the central issue for negotiations. Joel B. Eisen, *Brownfields of Dreams?: Challenges and Limits of Voluntary Cleanup Programs and Incentives*, 1996 U. Ill. L. Rev. 883, 998, 1005–1006, 1008. Michael Gerrard argues that monetary compensation will rarely gain acceptance of hazardous or radioactive waste facilities in places that do not want them. He maintains that "[t]he reason is clear: the opposition to these facilities stems mainly from concern over their impact on health, particularly children's health, and people will not accept any amount of money that will allow others to endanger their children. Individuals that perceive these facilities as dangerous will not change these perceptions when offered money, and they view the offer itself as immoral, 'bribery,' or 'blood money.'" Gerrard, *Fear and Loathing, supra,* at 1154–55. He adds that compensation works when, and only when, the community does not believe the

proposed facility poses an undue hazard. Compensation has accordingly been quite successful in siting municipal solid waste and incinerators, which have much lower perceived risks than hazardous waste and radioactive waste facilities (a point also made by Professor Been in the above excerpt). *Id.* at 1155.

3. Professor Lynn Blais argues that "[r]ather than constituting an immoral buy-off of the residents of a host community, compensation can be understood as a mechanism for increasing the otherwise limited options faced by poor and minority communities and residents." She adds that "compensation can be used to finance the option most environmental racism scholars say is fatally lacking in siting decisions: the opportunity to leave the community if one does not agree with the risk/benefit analysis that led to the siting in the first place." Lynn E. Blais, *Environmental Racism Reconsidered,* 75 N.C. L. Rev. 75, 149 (1996). Does the latter argument overlook racial barriers in the housing market that constrain the mobility of nonwhite families? Is it likely that the compensation offered would be sufficient to relocate to comparable yet safer neighborhoods? Even if sufficient compensation is offered, does relocation-oriented compensation address the threats to community stability that result if residents relocate? Relocation issues are discussed in more detail in Chapter 9.

C. Environmental Review:
The National Environmental Policy Act and
State Environmental Policy Acts

1. An Introductory Note on NEPA And SEPAs

The National Environmental Policy Act (NEPA) is a cross-cutting statute that requires review of all environmentally significant decisions undertaken by federal agencies. NEPA requires that agencies prepare a detailed Environmental Impact Statement (EIS) discussing the environmental impacts of all federal projects that significantly affect the environment. Impacts are broadly defined to include ecological, aesthetic, historic, cultural, health, as well as cumulative effects. An EIS must also discuss alternatives to the proposed project and appropriate mitigation measures. In many cases an agency will prepare a less detailed Environmental Assessment (EA) to determine if an EIS is necessary. EAs are also prepared for projects with minor impacts, unless the projects are categorically excluded by agency regulation (i.e. minor maintenance operations). An EA is a "concise public document" that briefly discusses the need for the project, alternatives, and impacts of the project and alternatives. 40 C.F.R. § 1508.9.

While NEPA applies only to actions carried out by, funded by, or with some regulatory nexus to the federal government, fifteen states plus the District of Columbia have adopted similar statutes, known as state environmental policy acts (SEPAs), which govern projects approved by state or local agencies. Daniel R. Mandelker, NEPA Law and Litigation § 12:1 (2d ed. 1992 & Supp. 2008).

NEPA or its state analogues frequently will be implicated in environmental justice matters, particularly the siting of new facilities. Some of NEPA's provisions seem particularly well-suited for incorporating environmental justice concerns into the agency decision-making process. For example, unlike most pollution control statutes, NEPA requires that agencies evaluate the cumulative impacts of proposed projects. This logically would impose a duty on agencies to consider the pre-existing concentration of industrial facilities, health risks, and environmental exposures in a community.

Likewise, NEPA requires federal agencies to provide for meaningful public involvement in their environmental review process. Agencies must seek public input at various points in the NEPA process, such as when determining the scope of matters to be included in the EISs ("scoping"), after issuing a draft EIS, and after issuing a final EIS but before final decisions have been made about the project. Agencies also are required to hold public hearings when there is substantial controversy surrounding a project or substantial interest in a hearing. Additionally, agencies must respond to all public comments submitted on the draft EISs. To facilitate public review, NEPA's regulations require that EISs must be written in "plain language … so that decision makers and the public can readily understand them." 40 C.F.R. § 1502.8. Some courts have invalidated EISs that were too dense for average persons to understand.

The public participation requirements of NEPA & SEPAs also may require translation for communities that do not speak English. One prominent case raising this issue involved a hazardous waste incinerator proposed by Chemical Waste for Kettleman City, a tiny farmworker community in California's San Joaquin Valley, where at the time of the proposed project 95% of the residents were Latino, 70% spoke Spanish at home, and 40% were monolingual Spanish speakers. Despite repeated requests, the local county permitting agency failed to translate into Spanish hearing notices, public testimony, or three versions of the Environmental Impact Report (EIR) prepared for the incinerator pursuant to the California Environmental Quality Act (CEQA). At the only public hearing on the project, the county refused to provide simultaneous translation of the proceedings or allow private translators (and ordered Spanish-speaking residents to sit in the back of the huge auditorium where the hearing took place). Residents sued, alleging that the County violated CEQA's public participation provisions, and a superior court ruled in their favor:

> [T]he strong emphasis in CEQA on environmental decisionmaking by public officials which involves and informs members of the public would have justified the Spanish translation of an extended summary of the [EIR], public meeting notices, and public hearing testimony in this case. The residents of Kettleman City, almost 40 percent of whom were monolingual in Spanish, expressed continuous and strong interest in participating in the CEQA review process for the incinerator project at [Chemical Waste's] Kettleman Hills facility, just four miles from their homes. Their meaningful involvement in the CEQA review process was effectively precluded by the absence of the Spanish translation.

El Pueblo Para el Aire y Agua Limpio v. County of Kings, [1992] ENVTL L. REP. 20,357 (Super. Ct. Sacramento, Dec. 30, 1991).

While the *Kettlemen City* case illustrates the positive potential of this type of planning statute, NEPA has a number of important limitations. These limits include the following:

• NEPA's broad public participation requirements apply when an EIS is required, not when EAs are prepared—which is the level of review for approximately ninety-nine percent of projects subject to NEPA. Stephen Johnson, *NEPA and SEPA's In the Quest for Environmental Justice*, 30 LOY. L.A. L. REV. 565, 575 (1997). Agencies are required to notify the public only after the agency has completed the EA.

• NEPA only requires analysis of social and economic impacts in limited circumstances. This limitation is explored in more detail below.

• NEPA does not impose any substantive obligations on federal agencies, mandating only that agencies consider and fully disclose the environmental impacts of proposed projects. As the Supreme Court has explained, NEPA "merely prohibits uninformed—rather than unwise—agency action." Robertson v. Methow Valley, 490 U.S. 332, 351 (1989). Agencies are not obligated to choose less environmentally harmful alternatives, or to adopt mitigation measures to reduce the impacts of a project. SEPAs vary in this regard; while many are similarly procedural, several require state agencies to minimize or avoid significant adverse impacts (for example Minnesota, New York, and California).

• The courts have held that EPA does not have to comply with NEPA when the environmental assessment and public participation procedures required by an EPA regulatory action are "functionally equivalent" to those mandated by the NEPA process. EPA thus does not comply with NEPA, when, for example, it issues hazardous waste permits under the Resource Conservation and Recovery Act (RCRA). EPA also has been successful in arguing that it does not have to prepare EISs in connection with cleanup orders under Superfund. Congress has created express statutory exemptions from NEPA for a number of EPA programs, such as all actions under the Clean Air Act and many under the Clean Water Act. Professor Stephen Johnson argues that the "functionally equivalent" exemption improperly exempts from NEPA review many federal actions that have disparate impacts on low income and minority communities. He notes, for example, that when EPA issues a permit under RCRA, the agency does not have to consider socioeconomic impacts or project alternatives, as required by NEPA, and that the permitting process provides fewer opportunities for public participation than NEPA. Likewise, he argues, EPA's regulatory process for setting standards should not be considered the functional equivalent of NEPA when the agency is not required to consider the cumulative, indirect, or socioeconomic impacts of these standards. Johnson, *supra*, at 590–96.

• Most pollution control permits are issued not by EPA, but by states (or in some instances tribes) that have been granted authority to implement federal environmental programs in lieu of EPA. Since NEPA only applies to *federal actions*, the state permitting agency's actions are outside of NEPA's purview.

Pathfinder on NEPA

For general background about NEPA, *see* DANIEL R. MANDELKER, NEPA LAW AND LITIGATION (2d ed. 1992 & Supp. 2008). Regulations implementing NEPA that are binding on all federal agencies have been adopted by the Council on Environmental Quality ("CEQ Regulations"), and can be found at 40 C.F.R. §§ 1500–1518. For discussion of State Environmental Policy Acts (SEPAs), *see* DANIEL P. SELMI & KENNETH A. MANASTER, STATE ENVIRONMENTAL LAW § 10 (1999 & Supp. 2008). For a discussion of the extent to which NEPA and other environmental review statutes require consideration of environmental justice issues, *see* Sheila R. Foster, *Impact Assessment in* THE LAW OF ENVIRONMENTAL JUSTICE: THEORIES AND PROCEDURES TO ADDRESS DISPROPORTIONATE RISKS 295 (Michael Gerrard & Sheila Foster eds., 2d ed. 2008). NEPA and environmental justice also is discussed in Browne C. Lewis, *What You Don't Know Can Hurt You: The Importance of Information in the Battle Against Environmental Class and Racial Discrimination*, 29 WM. & MARY ENVTL. L. & POL'Y REV 327 (2005).

* * *

Notes and Questions

1. Although NEPA is often criticized as weak because it does not impose any substantive requirements on federal agencies, Professor Johnson contends that it can nonetheless be of considerable value to environmental justice communities as an information-gathering, educational, and organizational tool. For example, mandated disclosure of alternatives and mitigation measures can leave the agencies more vulnerable to criticism and result in pressure for them to take steps to mitigate adverse project impacts they might have otherwise overlooked. Likewise, the environmental review process can create important opportunities for organizing community opposition. Johnson, *supra*, at 572–80. How useful do you think NEPA's requirements are for communities engaged in environmental justice battles?

2. The impact assessment approach pioneered by NEPA is the most widely emulated form of environmental regulation in the world, having been adopted by dozens of countries as well as international institutions like the World Bank. What do you think accounts for the singular attractiveness of this approach?

2. Agency NEPA Guidance

Many commentators have argued for a broader reading of NEPA to address environmental justice issues. In addition, since the Executive Order on Environmental Justice was issued in 1994, federal agencies have sought to adapt the NEPA process to take into account environmental justice concerns.

The Executive Order and the accompanying Memorandum issued by President Clinton (discussed in Chapter 10) require agencies to identify "disproportionately high and adverse human health or environmental effects" of their programs. The Memorandum directs that agencies shall analyze environmental effects, including economic and social effects of federal actions, and including effects on minority and low-income communities, when such analysis is required by NEPA. The Executive Order also requires agencies, whenever feasible, to identify multiple and cumulative exposures in their environmental human health analyses and to identify mitigation measures that address significant and adverse environmental effects on minority and low income communities.

The Council on Environmental Quality (CEQ), the agency created by Congress for coordinating federal agencies' compliance with NEPA, responded to the Executive Order by promulgating NEPA environmental justice guidance, which applies to all federal agencies in their implementation of NEPA. COUNCIL ON ENVIRONMENTAL QUALITY, ENVIRONMENTAL JUSTICE: GUIDANCE UNDER THE NATIONAL ENVIRONMENTAL POLICY ACT (1997). NEPA documents traditionally analyzed impacts on broadly defined affected areas and populations without focusing on potential impacts to smaller subpopulations of minority or low income groups. CEQ's guidance, however, calls on agencies to determine whether an area impacted by a proposed project may include low-income populations, minority populations, or Indian tribes, and whether the proposed action is likely to have a disproportionately high and adverse human health or environmental impact on these populations. Agencies should also consider the potential for multiple or cumulative exposure, historical patterns of exposure to environmental hazards, and cultural differences which may lead certain communities to experience impacts more severely than the general population. For example, the Guidance notes, "data on different patterns of living, such as subsistence fish, vegetation, or wildlife consumption and the use of well water in rural communities may be relevant to the analysis." *Id.* at 14.

With respect to alternatives, the Guidance instructs that the distribution and magnitude of any disproportionate adverse effects should be a factor in the agency's identification of the "environmentally preferable alternative" for a project (which agencies are required to identify in record of decisions following preparation of an EIS). *Id.* at 15. Moreover, in developing mitigation measures, agencies should solicit the views of the affected populations throughout the public participation process, and mitigation measures should reflect the views of affected low-income populations, minority populations, or Indian tribes to the maximum extent practicable.

The Guidance points out that encouraging the participation of low-income populations, minority populations, or tribal populations in the NEPA process may require "adaptive or innovative approaches to overcome linguistic, cultural, economic, or other potential barriers." *Id.* at 13. The Guidance suggests that agencies enhance their customary practices for public outreach—practices that typically rely on publication in the *Federal Register* or notice in local newspapers—by contacting a wide array of community, social service, homeowner, religious, civic, tribal, and other organizations. Agencies should take other steps to encourage effective public participation, including translation of major documents, provision of opportunities to participate other than through written communications, such as interviews or oral or video recording devices, provision of translators at meetings and other efforts to ensure that limited English speakers potentially affected have an understanding of the proposed actions and its potential impact, and use of locations and facilities that are local, convenient and accessible.

Notably, the CEQ guidance makes clear that the Executive Order "does not change the prevailing legal thresholds and statutory interpretations under NEPA and existing case law." *Id.* at 9.

Other federal agencies have issued directives for how to address environmental justice concerns in their own NEPA documents. *See* Dennis Binder, et al., *A Survey of Federal Agency Response to President Clinton's Executive Order No. 12898 on Environmental Justice*, 31 ENVTL. L. REP. 11133, 11137–38, 11147 (2001). EPA's guidance is the most detailed and parallels the CEQ's emphasis on more focused analysis, careful attention to cumulative impacts, and the need to enhance the participation of affected communities. ENVIRONMENTAL PROTECTION AGENCY, FINAL GUIDANCE FOR INCORPORATING ENVIRONMENTAL JUSTICE CONCERNS IN EPA'S NEPA COMPLIANCE ANALYSES (1998). EPA also published guidance for its review of Environmental Impact Statements prepared by other agencies, carried out pursuant to section 309 of the Clean Air Act. ENVIRONMENTAL PROTECTION AGENCY, FINAL GUIDANCE FOR CONSIDERATION OF ENVIRONMENTAL JUSTICE IN CLEAN AIR ACT 309 REVIEWS (1999). The Department of Transportation (DOT) issued an order requiring that all programs and activities be evaluated to determine whether they would have disproportionately high adverse impacts on minority or low income populations, considering the "totality" of individual and cumulative effects. If a DOT activity would create such adverse effects, then it cannot go forward unless mitigation measures or alternatives that would avoid or reduce the effects are not practical. 62 FED. REG. 18377 (Apr. 15, 1997).

Notes and Questions

1. Are there other ideas that you think should be included in agency guidance to address environmental justice concerns?

2. Should EPA and other agencies be required to translate NEPA documents whenever a project will impact a community that has a significant percentage of members that do not speak English? How large a percentage should this be? What if there are numerous, monolingual subpopulations within the affected community—should agencies be required to translate documents into multiple languages? Should entire documents be translated, or only summaries and/or important documents? (EISs can sometimes be several hundred pages long.) What other approaches should be explored? Should technical assistance be provided to help communities participate in the NEPA review process?

3. Judicial Review of NEPA

What has been the impact of the Executive Order on Environmental Justice and other agency guidance on decisions under NEPA? Thus far, relatively few reported cases have reached this question. As an initial matter, since section 6-609 of the Executive Order provides that it does not create any private right of action to judicial review, some courts have held that they lack jurisdiction to consider challenges to environmental justice analyses carried out under the Order. *See Citizens Concerned About Jet Noise, Inc. v. Dalton*, 48 F. Supp. 2d 582, 604 (E.D. Va. 1999). In other cases, though, the courts have found that once federal agencies exercise their discretion to include an environmental justice analysis in its NEPA evaluation, this analysis is reviewable under NEPA and the Administrative Procedure Act. *See Communities Against Runway Expansion, Inc. v. Federal Aviation Administration*, 355 F.3d 678, 688–89 (D.C. Cir. 2004); *Senville v. Peters*, 327 F. Supp. 2d 335 (D. Vt. 2004). Most of the rulings that reach the question of whether the environmental justice analysis is adequate have, under principles of deference to the agency, been quick to uphold the EIS.

One case in which this issue was fully explored involves the Nuclear Regulatory Commission (NRC), an independent regulatory agency not technically covered by the Executive Order, but that nonetheless voluntarily agreed to be bound by it in 1994. In 1997, the Atomic Safety and Licensing Board (Board) of the NRC heard a challenge to a Final Environmental Impact Statement (FEIS) prepared for a proposal by Louisiana Energy Services (LES) to build an $855 million uranium-enrichment facility in the midst of two historically black communities in Claiborne Parish, Louisiana (the project was known as the Claiborne Enrichment Center, or CEC). The Board issued the following ruling.

In the Matter of Louisiana Energy Services, L.P.
45 N.R.C. 367 (1997)

This Final Initial Decision addresses the remaining contention—environmental justice contention J.9—filed by the Intervenor, Citizens Against Nuclear Trash ("CANT"), in this combined construction permit-operating license proceeding.... The Applicant plans to build the CEC on a 442-acre site in Claiborne Parish, Louisiana, that is immediately adjacent to and between the unincorporated African-American communities of Center Springs and Forest Grove, some 5 miles from the town of Homer, Louisiana.... The site, called the LeSage property ... is currently bisected by Parish Road 39 (also known as Forest Grove Road) running north and south through the property.... [Center Springs] lies along State Road 9 and Parish Road 39 and is located approximately [a third of a mile] to the north of the LeSage property.... [Forest Grove] lies approximately [two miles] south of the site along Parish Road 39.... The two community churches, which share a single minister, are approximately 1.1 miles apart, with the LeSage property lying between them.

The community of Forest Grove was founded by freed slaves at the close of the Civil War and has a population of about 150. Center Springs was founded around the turn of the century and has a population of about 100. The populations of Forest Grove and Center Springs are about 97% African American. Many of the residents are descendants of the original settlers and a large portion of the landholdings remain with the same families that founded the communities. Aside from Parish Road 39 and State Road 9, the roads in Center Springs or Forest Grove are either unpaved or poorly maintained. There are no stores, schools, medical clinics, or businesses in Center Springs or Forest Grove.... [F]rom kindergarten through high school the children of Center Springs and Forest Grove attend schools that are largely racially segregated. Many of the residents of the communities are not connected to the public water supply. Some of these residents rely on groundwater wells while others must actually carry their water because they have no potable water supply....

The Intervenor's environmental justice contention is grounded in the requirements of [NEPA].... Subsequent to ... the Staff's issuance of the draft EIS, on February 11, 1994, the President issued Executive Order [on Environmental Justice No.] 12,898.... Although Executive Order 12898 does not create any new rights that the Intervenor may seek to enforce before the agency or upon judicial review of the agency's actions, the President's directive is, in effect, a procedural directive to the head of each executive department and agency that, "to the greatest extent practicable and permitted by law," it should seek to achieve environmental justice in carrying out its mission by using such tools as [NEPA].... Thus, whether the Executive Order is viewed as calling for a more expansive interpretation of NEPA as the Applicant suggests or as merely clarifying NEPA's longstanding requirement for consideration of the impacts of major federal actions on the "human" environment as the Intervenor argues, it is clear the President's order directs all agencies in analyzing the environmental effects of a federal action in an EIS required by NEPA to include in the analysis, "to the greatest extent practicable," the human health, economic, and social effects on minority and low-income communities....

Impacts of Road Closing/Relocation

The Intervenor [asserts] that the FEIS is deficient because if [sic] fails to address the impacts of closing Parish Road 39, which currently bisects the LeSage site and joins the communities of Forest Grove and Center Springs. Dr. Robert Bullard [a sociologist and prominent environmental justice scholar] testified.... that if the road is not relocated it would impose upon the residents of Center Springs and Forest Grove an additional 8- or 9-mile trip by way of Homer to go from one community to the other.

Additionally, Dr. Bullard asserted that even if Parish Road 39 is relocated around the site, the Staff incorrectly concluded in the FEIS that the impacts would be very small and not pose unacceptable risks to the local community. According to Dr. Bullard, it is apparent that the Staff did not even consult with any of the residents of Forest Grove and Center Springs before reaching its conclusion for if it had, the Staff would have found that Forest Grove Road is a vital and frequently used link between the two communities, with regular pedestrian traffic....

[T]he FEIS indicates that the road relocation will add approximately 120 meters (0.075 mile) to the traveling distance between State Roads 2 and 9 and will add an additional 600 meters (0.38 mile) to the 1800 meter (1.1 mile) distance between the Forest Grove Church and the Center Springs Church, which are the approximate centers of the respective minority communities....

The Staff's FEIS treatment of the impacts of relocating Parish Road 39 does not discuss Forest Grove Road's status as a pedestrian link between Forest Grove and Center Springs and the impacts of relocation on those who must walk the distance between the communities on this road. In the FEIS, the Staff calculates how much additional gasoline it will take to drive between the communities when the road is relocated and the added travel time the road relocation will cause for various trips....

Dr. Bullard testified, however, that Forest Grove Road is a vital and frequently used link between the communities with regular pedestrian traffic. Neither the Staff nor the Applicant presented any evidence disputing Dr. Bullard's testimony in this regard. Further, the Bureau of Census statistics introduced by the Intervenor show that the African American population of Claiborne Parish is one of the poorest in the country and that over 31% of black households in the parish have no motor vehicles. Again this evidence is undisputed. It thus is obvious that a significant number of the residents of these communities have no motor vehicles and often must walk. Adding 0.38 mile to the distance between the Forest Grove and Center Springs communities may be a mere "inconvenience" to those who drive, as the Staff suggests. Yet, permanently adding that distance to the 1- or 2-mile walk between these communities for those who must regularly make the trip on foot may be more than a "very small" impact, especially if they are old, ill or otherwise infirm. The Staff in the FEIS has not considered the impacts the relocation of Forest Grove Road will have upon those residents who must walk. Accordingly, we find that the Staff's treatment in the FEIS of the impacts on the communities of Forest Grove and Center Springs from the relocation of Parish Road 39 is inadequate and must be revised.

Property Value Impacts

Intervenor [also] asserts that property values in the neighboring communities will be adversely affected by the facility and that this economic effect will be borne disproportionately by the minority communities that can least afford it....

In support of [this] assertion...., Dr. Bullard testified that the general "benefit streams" to counties with large industrial taxpayers do not have significant positive effects on low income minority communities, which are already receiving a disproportionately low share of the services offered by the county....

The Staff's treatment of the economic impacts of the CEC on property values in the FEIS does indeed recognize that the CEC will depress some property values while increasing others, but the Staff fails to identify the location, extent, or significance of impacts. Further, although, the FEIS generally indicates the CEC is likely to increase both housing and land prices because of increased demand and the benefits capture effect, the Staff makes no attempt to allocate the costs or benefits. Dr. Bullard directly challenges the Staff's failure to assess the impacts of the CEC on property values in the communities of Forest Grove and Center Springs asserting that when facilities like the CEC are placed in the midst of poor, minority communities, the facility has negative impacts on property values in the immediate area of the plant. For the reasons specified below, we find his testimony on the negative economic impact of the CEC on property values in these minority communities reasonable and persuasive....

Dr. Bullard explained that unlike white residents of the parish, the black residents of Forest Grove and Center Springs face substantial "housing barriers" that preclude them from leaving when a large industrial facility is sited in the midst of their residential area. As a consequence, these already economically depressed communities must fully absorb the further adverse impact of having a heavy industrial facility nearby making them even more undesirable. He testified that the beneficial effects on housing values from increased demand by new migrating employees and the benefit capture effect relied upon by the Staff in the FEIS will have no effect on these minority communities that currently receive almost no parish services, are virtually 100% African American, and are inhabited by some of the most economically disadvantaged people in the United States. As Dr. Bullard stated, it is "extremely unlikely" new workers to the area will seek to live in Forest Grove and Center Springs. Dr. Bullard concludes that these factors lead to an overall negative impact on property values in the minority communities that must host the CEC....

The Staff witnesses made no attempt to explain how or why Dr. Bullard might be mistaken.... Indeed, given the Staff's recognition in the FEIS that there will be some negative impacts on property values from the CEC, it is difficult to envision an economic rationale that would demonstrate those adverse impacts from the CEC are likely to occur to properties well removed from the facility, such as in Homer or Haynesville, as opposed to the Forest Grove and Center Springs areas next to the facility.... By the same token, the opinions of [two witnesses for the applicant that] the effect that industrial facilities often increase property values in the vicinity of a facility are far too general to draw any reasonable conclusions about the impacts on property values in the circumstances presented here. Likewise, Mr. LeRoy's [another witness for the applicant] testimony about the positive impact on lakefront vacation home values from the construction of nuclear power plants is neither useful nor reasonable in making a comparison with the economically disadvantaged minority communities of Forest Grove and Center Springs. Certainly, the reality of Forest Grove and Center Springs hardly seems comparable to the description of Lake Wylie in Applicant's Exhibit 19, which states that "the Catawba plant was built on a beautiful lake, dotted with hundreds of expensive homes and homesites." Nor do these communities resemble the description of Lake Keowee in Exhibit 19 as "one of the most prestigious resort/retirement communities in the United States [which] is less than a mile from Oconee Nuclear Station. At Keowee Key more than 1500 people golf, boat, fish, relax and retire next door to a nuclear plant."

On this basis, we find that the Staff's treatment in the FEIS of the impacts from the CEC on property values in the communities of Forest Grove and Center Springs is inadequate....

* * *

Notes and Questions

1. What is different about the NEPA analysis demanded by the Board and the type traditionally prepared by federal agencies? Is it the particularized focus on how the project will impact very small subpopulations of larger communities? Is it the Board's careful attention to the project's social and economic impacts? The Board seems to embrace Dr. Bullard's longstanding view that achieving environmental justice requires examination of "who pays and who benefits" from industrial development. Note also that, although the Board requires an environmental justice analysis, it specifically declines to decide whether the Executive Order calls for a more expansive interpretation of NEPA or merely

clarifies NEPA's existing requirement that impacts on the human environment be analyzed. Should it matter?

2. The Board's decision elsewhere quotes Dr. Bullard's testimony that the NRC Staff did not consult with any of the residents of Forest Grove and Center Springs before reaching its conclusion about the negative impacts of relocating the road, and that if it had "the Staff would have found that Forest Grove Road is a vital and frequently used link between the two communities, with regular pedestrian traffic." *See id.* at 403. Does this in effect impose a duty to implement special outreach and public participation efforts in NEPA cases raising environmental justice concerns?

3. Apart from its claims relating to the FEIS' failure to analyze the project's social and economic impacts, the citizens group alleged that the NRC's siting process was racially discriminatory. The group presented testimony from Professor Bullard showing that at each successive stage of the siting process, the communities under consideration became poorer and more predominantly African American, culminating in the selection of a site that was ninety-seven percent African American and extremely poor. Bullard also testified that the applicant's use of facially race-neutral siting criteria—such as eliminating sites close to sensitive receptors like hospitals, schools, and nursing homes—disadvantaged poor and minority communities by reinforcing the impacts of prior discrimination that had left them without such institutions. The Board found that this evidence raised a "reasonable inference that racial considerations played some part in the site selection process," and remanded for a more complete investigation. Responding to the agency's contention that its decision was based solely on technical and business criteria, and that there was no specific evidence that racial considerations motivated the decision, the Board wrote that racial discrimination "cannot be uncovered with only a cursory review of the description of the [site selection process]. If it were so easily detected, racial discrimination would not be such a persistent and enduring problem in American society. Racial discrimination is rarely, if ever, admitted." *See id.* at 391–92.

On appeal, a panel of the NRC reversed this part of the Board's order, holding that NEPA is not "a tool for addressing problems of racial discrimination." The panel noted that the CEQ's Guidance on Environmental Justice (discussed above) encourages agencies to consider impacts on low income and minority communities, but "neither states nor implies that if adverse impacts are found, an investigation into possible racial bias is the appropriate next step." *See In re La. Energy Services, L.P.*, 47 N.R.C. 77, 101 (1998). Is the NRC opinion sound? Should there be no recourse under NEPA against a decision that results from a racially biased decision-making process? Recall the emphasis that NEPA places on procedure and meaningful public involvement in agency decisions. Could this be a basis for arguing that further review of the NRC's decision is warranted?

4. The NRC panel upheld the part of the Board's NEPA decision that is reproduced above. In April, 1998, after this ruling, Louisiana Energy Services dropped its application to construct the CEC. In 2004, the NRC issued guidance providing that it will not be bound by the Executive Order in licensing proceedings and that NEPA is the only basis for considering environmental justice contentions in licensing proceedings. The guidance also reiterates that the NRC will not consider issues of racial bias as part of a NEPA claim. 69 Fed. Reg. 52,040, 52044–45 (Aug 24, 2004).

5. Other NEPA challenges to environmental justice analyses largely have been unsuccessful. Professor Sheila Foster argues that "courts assume a very limited role when assessing the adequacy of an agency's analysis of disproportionate social or economic impacts from a proposed action and are extremely deferential toward agencies' analysis (and choice) of

the geographic scope of impact assessment, the measurement of cumulative or indirect impacts, and the range of alternatives considered." Sheila F. Foster, *Impact Assessment, supra,* at 313. For example, in *Communities Against Runway Expansion,* the court reviewed a challenge to the Federal Aviation Administration's (FAA) approval of a runway expansion at Boston's Logan Airport. In its environmental justice analysis, the FAA compared the demographics of the area immediately surrounding the airport that it determined would have the most significant noise impacts from the project with the demographics of the county in which the airport was located. It concluded that there would be no disproportionate impacts borne by low-income or minority populations, because the immediately affected area had a lower minority population (34%) than the larger surrounding county (48%). The City of Boston argued unsuccessfully that the appropriate population for making a comparison was not the county but the entire Boston metropolitan area (with a smaller minority population), because this was the "core service area" for the airport. The court noted that the agency's "choice among reasonable analytical methodologies is entitled to deference from this court." *Communities Against Runway Expansion,* 355 F.3d at 688. *See also Senville v. Peters, supra,* (rejecting challenge that EIS failed to consider adequately the adverse employment effects of a highway project on minority and low-income neighborhoods).

6. In contrast to these deferential NEPA decisions, consider the following recent ruling by a California state superior court. In this case, the local air district in Los Angeles had a rule establishing a priority reserve of emission reduction credits that could be used by facilities for limited purposes—such as innovative technology, research, and essential services. (Emission reduction credits are an example of emissions trading, discussed in Chapter 7. In areas like Los Angeles that are out of compliance with clean air requirements, purchasing such credits is required before a significant new facility can be constructed.) The district proposed changing the rule so that the reserve credits also could be used for the construction of eleven new power plants, on the ground that these plants were needed to ensure electricity reliability and prevent blackouts. Plaintiffs challenged the district's environmental review under CEQA, arguing among other things that the district violated CEQA's requirement to adopt all feasible mitigation measures to minimize the environmental impacts of the rule change. The court upheld the challenge:

> [P]etioners contend that the mitigation measures adopted in this case, notably a flat mitigation fee that is not linked to the reduction of the environmental effects at a particular location ... [is] inadequate as a matter of law.
>
> > The District requires the power plant to pay a mitigation fee. These fees, however, have not been designed to mitigate the emissions that will result from the withdrawal of these new credits from the Priority Reserve. For instance, although the staff recommended that mitigation fees be higher for facilities that were to be constructed in poor air quality zones, the [Air] Board rejected the amendment.... And, the mitigation fee is not linked, through binding commitments, to the reduction of emissions at the same location where the new facilities will operate. Thus, the program will allow facilities to be built in already heavily impacted neighborhoods and then, in its unfettered discretion, allow the mitigation fees to be spent making the air cleaner in communities where air quality has not been compromised. If the intention of the fee is to mitigate the significant environmental effects to be imposed on those communities where new power plants are to be constructed, then it is inexplicable why the District did not require the mitigation fee to be spent reducing pollution in that locale. There is no rationale, much less substantial

evidence, given for the District's decision to de-link the expenditure of the mitigation fees from the area needed to have the increase in pollution mitigated.

Natural Res. Def. Council v. S. Coast Air Quality Mgmt. Dist., Case No. BS110792 (Super. Ct. L.A., July 28, 2008) at 25–26. How might you explain the court's unwillingness to defer to the agency's choice of where the mitigation fee is directed?

4. Analysis of Social and Economic Impacts

As discussed above, NEPA only requires analysis of social and economic impacts in limited circumstances. This result is not self-evident from the face of the statute, which lists in its declaration of purpose the profound impact of man's activity on, among other things, "population growth, high density urbanization, and industrial expansion," NEPA § 101(a), and which requires EISs for actions that significantly affect the "human environment." Some early cases held that NEPA requires agencies to evaluate urban environmental effects, including urban decay, crime and congestion. Subsequently, however, both case law and implementing guidelines adopted by CEQ have interpreted NEPA to focus primarily on impacts on the physical or natural environment; social and economic effects must be considered only to the extent that they are related to the physical effects of a proposed action. 40 C.F.R. § 1508.14. Thus, for example, when a project's physical environmental impacts lead to secondary socioeconomic impacts, these latter impacts must be evaluated. The Executive Order on Environmental Justice did not change the underlying trigger for such analysis, but some commentators suggest that it has prompted renewed agency attention to these socioeconomic effects.

State SEPAs are similar in scope, although a few are broader than NEPA and require agencies to review social and economic impacts regardless of their link to physical impacts. In *Chinese Staff & Workers Ass'n v. City of N.Y.*, 68 N.Y. 2d 359 (1986), for example, plaintiffs challenged the proposed construction of a luxury condominium in New York's Chinatown on the grounds that it would displace local low-income residents and businesses and alter the character of the community. The court held that under New York's environmental review statute, the city was required to evaluate these potential impacts from the luxury housing development, noting that "land development impacts not only on the actual property involved but on the community involved."

Professor Sheila Foster argues that because NEPA and its state counterparts tend to elevate physical impacts over all others, they can obscure the degree to which land use decisions affect the social capital of impacted communities. She cites, for example, a controversy in New York City concerning urban gardens. During the 1970s, the city became the owner, through tax foreclosure, of thousands of abandoned lots in economically depressed neighborhoods. Neighborhood groups cleared these lots and turned hundreds of them into vibrant community gardens and gathering points. In the late 1990s, the city decided to sell the lots so that new housing could be built. In rejecting challenges that the city was required to prepare an environmental impact assessment, the court focused on the physical changes that would result from the sale of the lots and largely ignored arguments that the gardens provided the community with valuable social resources that would be destroyed by the new development. Sheila R. Foster, *The City as An Ecological Space: Social Capital and Urban Land Use*, 82 NOTRE DAME L. REV. 527, 546, 551–53 (2006).

In a few recent decisions, California courts have required local land use agencies to consider whether decisions to approve big box retail stores could result in significant urban blight by drawing customers away from a city's downtown business area. The leading such case is excerpted below.

Bakersfield Citizens for Local Control v. City of Bakersfield
124 Cal. App. 4th 1184 (2004)

Bakersfield Citizens for Local Control (BCLC) challenged the development of two retail shopping centers by two separate developers in the city of Bakersfield, California, alleging violations of the California Environmental Quality Act (CEQA). Each shopping center was to contain a Wal-Mart Supercenter as well as large anchor stores and smaller retailers.

In early 2002, both developers applied for project approvals ... and a separate Environmental Impact Report (EIR) was prepared for each development. In 2003 ... the Bakersfield City Council approved both projects. BCLC filed two actions challenging the sufficiency of the EIR for each development.... In each action the trial court found the EIRs deficient and ordered them decertified because they did not consider the direct and cumulative potential of the projects to indirectly cause urban decay.... Both sides appealed.

In this case, the trial court recognized that the shopping centers posed a risk of triggering urban decay or deterioration and it concluded that CEQA required analysis of this potential impact. C & C [Castle and Cooke Commercial-CA, Inc, one of the developers] has challenged this determination. We find C & C's arguments unpersuasive and agree that CEQA requires analysis of the shopping centers' individual and cumulative potential to indirectly cause urban decay.

[California Environmental Quality Act implementing regulations, known as CEQA Guidelines] Guidelines section 15126.2 requires an EIR to identify and focus on the significant environmental impacts of the proposed project.... [T]he economic and social effects of proposed projects are outside CEQA's purview. Yet, if the forecasted economic or social effects of a proposed project directly or indirectly will lead to adverse physical changes in the environment, then CEQA requires disclosure and analysis of these resulting physical impacts. Subdivision (e) of Guidelines section 15064 provides that when the economic or social effects of a project cause a physical change, this change is to be regarded as a significant effect in the same manner as any other physical change resulting from the project. (*See, e.g., El Dorado Union High School Dist. v. City of Placerville* (1983) 144 Cal. App. 3d 123 [potential of increased student enrollment in an already overcrowded school resulting from construction of the proposed apartment complex was an environmental effect that required treatment in an EIR because it could lead to the necessity of constructing at least one new high school].) Conversely, where economic and social effects result from a physical change that was itself caused by a proposed project, then these economic and social effects may be used to determine that the physical change constitutes a significant effect on the environment. (*See, e.g., Christward Ministry v. Superior Court* (1986) 184 Cal. App. 3d 180, 197 [when a waste management facility was proposed next to a religious retreat center, CEQA required study whether the physical impacts associated with the new facility would disturb worship in the natural environment of the retreat center]....

Case law already has established that in appropriate circumstances CEQA requires urban decay or deterioration to be considered as an indirect environmental effect of a proposed project.... It is apparent from the case law ... that proposed new shopping centers do not trigger a conclusive presumption of urban decay. However, when there is evidence suggesting that the economic and social effects caused by the proposed shopping center ultimately could result in urban decay or deterioration, then the lead agency is obligated to assess this indirect impact. Many factors are relevant, including the size of the project, the type of retailers and their market areas and the proximity of other retail shopping opportunities. The lead agency cannot divest itself of its analytical and informational obligations by summarily dismissing the possibility of urban decay or deterioration as a "social or economic effect" of the project....

[T]he administrative records as a whole contain sufficient indication that addition of 1.1 million square feet of retail space in the shopping centers' overlapping market areas could start the chain reaction that ultimately results in urban decay to necessitate study of the issue with respect to the entirety of the shopping centers. First, BCLC retained a professor of economics at San Francisco State University, C. Daniel Vencill, to study the cumulative economic effects that will be caused by the two new Supercenters (the Vencill report).... The Vencill report finds: "It is reasonably probable [that] competition provided by the two proposed [Supercenters], ... individually and especially cumulatively, will have economic impacts on existing businesses triggering a chain of events that may lead to adverse effects on the physical environment in the southern part of Bakersfield. One of the ways this may occur is that smaller retailers in the area ... will be unable to compete and will have to go out of business. In turn, this may cause permanent or long-term vacancies of retail space in the area. The result is typically neglect of maintenance and repair of retail facilities, the deterioration of buildings, improvements, and facilities. This may then culminate in physical effects associated with blight-like conditions, which include visual and aesthetic impacts accompanying the physical deterioration."

BCLC also submitted numerous studies and articles analyzing the adverse effects other communities in California ... and elsewhere ... have experienced as a result of saturation of a market area with super-sized retailers.... These effects include, but are not limited to, physical decay and deterioration resulting from store closures in the same market area or in established areas of the community (i.e., the "traditional downtown area") due to competitive pressures, followed by an inability to easily release the vacated premises....

Accordingly, we hold that the omission of analysis on the issue of urban/suburban decay and deterioration rendered the EIR's defective as informational documents....

* * *

Notes and Questions

1. In *Anderson First Coalition v. City of Anderson*, 130 Cal. App. 4th 1173 (2005), a California court rejected a CEQA challenge to a shopping center located on the outskirts of town anchored by a Walmart Supercenter store. It found that the EIR had adequately addressed the possible impacts of the project on urban decay, finding that the project was more likely to compete with the city's existing outlying shopping areas rather than its downtown area, and that property tax revenues generated by the project could contribute funds to revitalize the downtown area.

2. The Washington Supreme Court likewise has ruled that a land use agency must consider the possibility that a suburban shopping center would lead to job losses and urban decay by attracting customers away from the city's existing business district. Barrie v. Kitsap County, 613 P.2d 1148 (Wash. 1980).

3. A new power plant, landfill, or factory may have social, psychological, economic or other impacts that are not directly related to physical effects from the facility. The facility may decrease the attractiveness of the neighborhood or lower property values. Community residents may worry about the threat of accidental releases or spills, or experience stress about harm to their families from exposure to a new source of pollution. Should agencies be required to evaluate these impacts under NEPA or state NEPA statutes, without regard to whether these impacts are related to physical impacts? For a discussion of the social psychological impacts that residents exposed to toxic chemicals experience, *see* MICHAEL EDELSTEIN, CONTAMINATED COMMUNITIES: THE SOCIAL PSYCHOLOGICAL IMPACTS OF RESIDENTIAL TOXIC EXPOSURE (1988).

4. Are there downsides to a definition of impacts that includes a broad range of socioeconomic and quality of life issues? In the 1970s, for example, community groups attempted to argue that actions causing changes in the racial, social and economic makeup of a community, such as a housing project planned for a middle class neighborhood, triggered NEPA analysis. They argued that NEPA required analysis of the impacts of new poor and minority residents on crime, property values, physical safety, aesthetics, and economic quality of life. The courts rejected these arguments, described by Professor Daniel Mandelker and others as "people as pollution cases." *See* DANIEL R. MANDELKER, NEPA LAW AND LITIGATION §§ 8:37–8:47.2 (2nd ed. 1992 & Supp. 2008).

5. New Approaches: Health Impact Assessments

A new idea for addressing environmental justice concerns in the environmental review process is the concept of health impact assessments (HIAs). The idea has gained currency because of the emerging awareness that land use, transportation, and other public planning decisions can have very significant impacts on public health. For example, childhood obesity can be influenced by factors such as how walkable a neighborhood is, its proximity to open space and parks, its accessibility to public transit, and the availability of local farmers markets and grocery stores selling healthy food. These and other community design characteristics are determined by land use and other planning decisions, yet typically such decisions do not evaluate potential health impacts. HIAs are designed to examine such effects, as detailed in the following excerpt.

**Brian L. Cole, Michelle Wilhelm, Peter V. Long,
Jonathan E. Fielding, Gerald Kominski, & Hal Morgenstern,
Prospects for Health Impact Assessment in The United States:
New and Improved Environmental Impact Assessment or
Something Different?**
29 Journal of Health Politics, Policy and Law 1153 (2004)

Health impact assessment is a formal, systematic analysis to prospectively assess the potential health impacts of proposed projects, programs, and policies and communicate this information to policy makers and stakeholders. Several different approaches have been taken in this nascent and rapidly evolving field. In many countries where HIA has been applied, most notably Britain and Sweden, it is seen as a means to increase community participation in decision making on issues that impact health.... In some countries it has been considered an analytic tool to help assess the scientific evidence from which population health impacts can be estimated, for example Germany and New Zealand. Primarily, but not exclusively, in countries taking this latter approach, HIA has been linked to environmental impact assessment....

As of yet there is no large-scale movement to bring HIA into widespread practice in the United States. Several nonprofit foundations have advocated its use ... but government representatives and agencies have been largely silent on the issue....

Several arguments support the adoption of HIA. First, there is a growing recognition that the health of a population is largely determined by broad determinants including social factors, the physical environment, and economic policies. Thus, it is necessary to address these underlying health determinants if health disparities, and overall disease burden, are to be reduced, as well as to improve health in communities. These determinants are affected by policies that are largely outside the health sector. They are not usually within the jurisdictions of government health agencies or legislative committees charged with a health agenda. Health impact assessment explicitly addresses these intersectoral issues.

Second, HIA is a flexible tool to bring health issues into policy deliberations in other sectors with strong influences on health. For example, the fastest-growing major epidemic in the United States is the rapid and continuing growth in the frequency of overweight [sic] and obesity. Effectively surmounting this public health challenge will require changes in multiple sectors that influence both physical activity and nutrition, including community planning, transportation, and agriculture at a minimum. HIA can help policy makers in those sectors understand the likely health effects of policies they are considering.

A third argument for the adoption of HIA is that it provides a systematic method to gather and assess evidence about possible health effects—effects that are of deep and apparently growing concern to Americans....

Finally, HIA is a process that can include formal mechanisms for structured input by key stakeholders, thus facilitating a more informed decision-making process. Those sponsoring HIA can agree to communicate its methods and findings at critical stages to interested parties for review and comment and then use this feedback to help guide the subsequent analysis and dissemination....

Limited Consideration of Human Health Effects in EIA

NEPA-mandated EIAs [Environmental Impact Assessments] generally include little, if any, explicit consideration of human health impacts, even though the stated purpose of the act is to protect the "human environment" and "stimulate the health and welfare of man." ... [The same is true for most state environmental policy acts.] The reasons for this restricted scope are practical, methodological, and legal. First, it is more difficult to predict health outcomes than to predict emissions. Analysis of outcomes adds more links to the putative causal chains, with each link requiring more assumptions and leading to increased levels of uncertainty in predictions. Moreover, some causal relations are simply unknown. Second, scientific uncertainty, coupled with a narrow reading of the law, has been the basis for courts restricting the scope of NEPA.... Third, there is a clear emphasis in EIAs on impacts governed by specific standards, but few regulatory standards mandate health outcomes. Although environmental health standards may be based on human health risk, the actual standards are expressed in levels of permissible levels of substances in the physical environment....

Arguments for Integrating HIA into Existing EIA

Incorporation of HIA into the existing EIA process is intuitively appealing for two reasons. First, human health is closely linked to the natural environment. NEPA acknowledges this by declaring the protection of human health as one of its main purposes. While to date there has been only limited consideration of health impacts in NEPA-mandated EIAs, HIA would seem a logical extension of the existing assessment process. Second, the EIA process is a well-established process that effectively cuts across bureaucratic and sectoral boundaries. If the goal is to promote the widespread use of HIA in planning, then incorporation into EIAs may be a path of least resistance....

Environmental justice presents an opportunity to bring a greater emphasis on assessing health impacts in EIA, since human health has been a central concern in the environmental justice movement. With its emphasis on distributional equity, environmental justice is an especially appropriate avenue for addressing issues of health inequality....

[T]hirty years of experience with EIA has shown that the rationale underlying EIA, and shared by HIA, is sound—that a systematic review of potential impacts during the planning process can focus the attention of decision makers on issues that they would otherwise deem to be outside their agency's mandate.... The question that will determine the extent to which HIA can garner greater interest and acceptance in the United States is, then, given what is known about the strengths and weaknesses of EIA, how can HIA maximize its potential value while minimizing the costs and limitations of the process?

* * *

Notes and Questions

1. In addition to the countries mentioned in the excerpt above, countries that have conducted HIAs include Canada, Australia, Thailand and Lithuania. Moreover, the European Union's strategic environmental impact assessment framework includes evaluation of health impacts of policies, legislation and programs (although in practice this requirement apparently has not been widely implemented, *see* Rebecca Salay & Paul Lincoln, National Heart Forum, The European Union and Health Impact Assessments: Are They An Unrecognised Statutory Obligation? 5 (2008)). What do you think explains the slower embrace of HIAs in the U.S. as compared to other countries?

2. The San Francisco Department of Public Health has pressed the city's planning department to expand its standard environmental assessment process and address health impacts not usually considered in land use decisions. In one case, the planning department concluded that the proposed demolition of 360 rent-controlled apartments and reconstruction of 1400 new condominiums in the city would not have any adverse housing impacts because the total number of housing units would increase. However, the health department's comments noted that the displaced tenants likely would not find adequate housing at the rent-controlled rate they had been paying and concluded that they would suffer adverse health effects as a result, including inadequate housing, mental stress associated with eviction, and loss of community due to displacement. The planning department required the project's environmental impact report to consider the indirect health impacts of residential displacement. The ensuing public criticism of the project and the risk of an adverse finding in the report convinced the developer to negotiate with

the organized tenants, and it agreed to revise the proposal to include 360 rent-controlled units with continued leases for existing tenants. *See* Rajiv Bhatia, *Protecting Health Using an Environmental Impact Assessment: A Case Study of San Francisco Land Use Decisionmaking*, 97 AM. J. PUB. HEALTH 406 (2007).

3. What do you think of the concept of HIAs? Does it expand impact assessment of land use decisions too broadly? Are the links between land use decisions and health impacts too imprecise to analyze, as suggested in the excerpt above? One commentary cautions that "[s]ome HIA predictions (e.g., the associations between sidewalks, walking, obesity, and heart disease) are insufficiently robust to withstand the litigious environment of EIA practice." Andrew L. Dannenberg, et al, *Growing the Field of Health Impact Assessment in the United States: An Agenda for Research and Practice*, 96 AM. J. PUB. HEALTH 262, 266 (2006). Some legislation would advance the use of HIAs. For example, the proposed Federal Healthy Places Act of 2007 would establish programs to provide guidance for assessing potential health effects of land use, housing, and transportation policy and plans, provide funding and technical assistance to state or local governments to prepare HIAs, and create a national HIA database. Healthy Places Act, H.R. 398, 110th Cong. 1st Sess. (2007).

D. Right to Know and Information Disclosure Laws

Over the past two decades, right to know and information disclosure statutes have become increasingly popular as an alternative to conventional regulation. These laws serve numerous objectives. One, they improve the efficient functioning of the market by remedying information gaps facing consumers and workers. Such laws also are premised on an entitlement rationale; the underlying notion is that members of the public have a "fundamental right to know" what chemicals are "out there," to which they are being exposed. These laws also promote citizen power and advance democratic decision-making. Armed with more information, citizens can make better-informed decisions and are thus in a better position to bargain with private corporations and government. Finally, such measures provide indirect incentives for industry to undertake self-regulation and thereby reduce risky activities, help avoid accidents and facilitate emergency planning, and add to the data base that helps government agencies determine the need for additional regulation.

The most prominent information disclosure law is the Emergency Planning and Community Right-to-Know Act (EPCRA). Congress adopted EPCRA in 1986, spurred by a tragic toxic release from a chemical plant in Bhopal, India that killed 3,000 people and a similar (but far less damaging) accident in West Virginia. In part to facilitate emergency planning, EPCRA requires companies to report annually to local emergency planning agencies information about the location, identity and amounts of hazardous chemicals used at their facilities. Since 1990, EPCRA also requires companies to report facility source-reduction practices, recycling activities, and projected chemical releases for future years.

EPCRA also established the Toxics Release Inventory (TRI) program, which requires manufacturing and certain other industrial facilities to annually disclose their releases and transfers of 654 specified toxic chemicals, subject to reporting thresholds. The information is provided on standardized reporting forms that are submitted to EPA and state officials. EPA is required to make the information available to the public through a national computerized database accessible through personal computers.

By most accounts, TRI has been a major success. From 1988 to 2006, reported toxic releases (for chemicals reported in all years) dropped by fifty-nine percent. EPA officials, as well as environmentalists and regulated entities, regularly tout TRI as one of the nation's most effective environmental laws. Professor Bradley Karkkainen characterizes TRI as a "watershed," and in the excerpt below, explains that multiple factors contribute to its success.

Bradley C. Karkkainen, Information as Environmental Regulation: TRI and Performance Benchmarking, Precursor to a New Paradigm?
89 Georgetown Law Journal 257 (2001)

TRI works by establishing an objective, quantifiable, standardized (and therefore comparable), and broadly accessible metric that transforms the firm's understanding of its own environmental performance, while facilitating unprecedented levels of transparency and accountability. Firms and facilities are compelled to self-monitor and, therefore, to "confront disagreeable realities" concerning their environmental performance "in detail and early on," even prior to the onset of market, community, or regulatory reactions to the information they are required to make public. Simultaneously, they are subjected to the scrutiny of a variety of external parties, including investors, community residents, and regulators, any of whom may desire improved environmental performance and exert powerful pressures on poor performers to upgrade their performance as measured by the TRI yardstick.

Self-Monitoring: "You Manage What You Measure"

TRI mandates a sharply focused form of environmental self-monitoring, compelling firms to produce a stream of periodic, quantified reports on releases of listed pollutants at each reporting facility. This information becomes available, inter alia, to the firm itself, which may use it to evaluate its own performance and production processes.... Many top corporate managers, previously unaware of the volumes of toxic pollutants their firms were generating, were indeed surprised by the information produced in the first rounds of TRI.... One chemical company official states that prior to TRI, his firm had never set internal pollution prevention goals because "we never had the information we needed to know if progress was being made." ... This kind of careful self-monitoring may well be a necessary step toward improving the environmental performance of facilities and firms. As the well-worn adage has it, "what you don't know about, you can't manage," or yet more precisely, "you manage what you measure."

TRI-generated performance data are readily available to regulators, as well as to environmentalists and other citizen-critics of regulatory policy.... Adverse facility-, firm-, or industry-level TRI data thus carry the implicit threat that regulatory action may follow, whether at the initiative of regulators themselves or in response to rising political demand for regulatory action. But precisely because forward-thinking firms and investors anticipate that additional regulatory requirements may prove burdensome and costly, firms may come under self-imposed and market-driven pressures to undertake cost-effective, voluntary, pollution prevention measures....

Environmental and community organizations are among the principal users of TRI data, employing it in conscious efforts to pressure firms to raise environmental standards. At the national level, environmental organizations use TRI data to generate reports and profiles of toxic pollution and leading polluters, and to direct reputation-damaging publicity campaigns against polluting firms. TRI data are also used by both national and local organizations to produce community-level reports and profiles, and to single out the leading local sources of toxic pollution. Community groups use this information to educate and recruit community residents into local anti-pollution efforts, and to organize local campaigns seeking "good neighbor agreements" and similar commitments from polluting firms to reduce releases. And even where community residents do not explicitly put forth such demands, firms may self-regulate to preempt potentially costly and damaging attempts at informal regulation....

TRI's sponsors emphasized that it would encourage pollution prevention and enable communities to engage in local self-help — central themes of the "right-to-know" movement. The statute itself identifies informing the local citizenry and facilitating local action among TRI's core purposes. TRI has fulfilled those expectations, facilitating local organizing aimed at improving the environmental performance of polluting facilities. In recent years, TRI has taken on an "environmental justice" flavor as low-income and minority communities add complaints of disparate impact, backed by TRI-derived inter-community comparisons, to underlying concerns about toxic exposures....

TRI and Capital Markets

Many investors use TRI data to monitor the environmental performance of firms.... Investors may interpret adverse TRI data as an indicator of a greater risk of future liability, remediation, or regulatory compliance costs; potential loss of consumer market share; or potentially costly and disruptive "informal regulation" by citizens. Alternatively, investors may simply conclude that poor TRI performance indicates that the firm is poorly managed, and thus may be likely to fare poorly in other critical performance areas such as product quality or cost control....

Reputation

Because TRI data allow easy comparisons among facilities, firms, and industries, a poor environmental performance record as reflected in TRI data can cause reputational damage, potentially affecting relations with customers, suppliers, employees, or investors. Unlike conventional regulations, which garner publicity for firms only in the breach, however, TRI may also generate opportunities for positive environmental image-building. No one credits a firm for being in compliance with mandatory environmental standards, but firms can use objective and comparable TRI data to document claims of "superior" performance or progress toward ambitious voluntary targets....

[Another advantage of TRI, according to Professor Karkkainen, is that it is very cost-effective.] TRI achieves all this at a relatively low cost to the agency. EPA's direct administrative costs are approximately $25 million, a modest fraction of its $7 billion annual budget. TRI does not require the agency to produce the extensive, costly, and time-consuming studies necessary to establish quantified exposure levels, dose-response curves, and threshold levels of "significant" or "unreasonable" risk that are often required under other environmental statutes. Under TRI, the agency normally only needs to make the (relatively) low-threshold determination that a pollutant "can reasonably be anticipated to cause" cancer or other chronic health effects at *some* level of exposure.... TRI is thus able to cast its regulatory net over a much larger number of pollutants and polluters in a much shorter period of time than conventional forms of regulation.... Direct compliance costs [with the reporting requirements] are also quite low. . . . [I]f TRI does induce real reductions in pollutant releases, then some firms must be incurring the costs of investing in new technologies or processes, even if these are not properly labeled "compliance costs." But since firms have absolute flexibility under TRI to determine how, when, and to what extent they will reduce emissions, they are generally free to adopt the improvement targets, timetables, and strategies that best suit their individual circumstances. This is almost certain to be cheaper than compliance with the costly "end-of-the-pipe" controls typically imposed by conventional regulation. . . .

* * *

Notes and Questions

1. Professor Clifford Rechtschaffen, while praising TRI as a highly effective program, argues that it nonetheless is too limited in its reach, for several reasons: the program currently covers only 654 toxic chemicals, which represent less than one percent of the more than 75,000 chemicals manufactured in the United States. Moreover, as a result of TRI's statutory exemptions (for nonmanufacturing facilities, small businesses, and facilities manufacturing or using chemicals below certain thresholds), releases from exempted sources are greater than releases from covered facilities. Additionally, TRI does not require facilities to report information about their chemical use or the amount of chemicals that remain in products. As a result, while TRI has prompted reductions in toxic *releases*, the quantity of toxic chemicals *generated and used* by facilities has declined far more slowly. Clifford Rechtschaffen, *Reforming the Emergency Planning and Community Right to Know Act in* CPR FOR THE ENVIRONMENT 32, 34–35 (Center for Progressive Reform 2007)

2. Kathryn E. Durham-Hammer suggests that TRI's success is overstated, and that "the assumption that companies will change their use and release of hazardous waste because they are ashamed of being flagrant polluters in comparison to their competitors. . . . is not based on convincing empirical evidence. . . . [and] is pure speculation." These reported reductions "could be related to numerous factors besides the TRI, including regulatory requirements, changes in estimation methods, and changes in industry composition, production levels, and process technologies." She contends that "[c]ommunities cannot safely rely on EPCRA and TRI data because EPCRA allows facilities to report their own data, and requires only an estimate if a true measurement is not feasible. EPCRA establishes no means for communities or the EPA to confirm facilities' self-made reports. . . . By giving discretion to reporting entities, the EPA also allows entities to change their estimation methods to achieve 'paper reductions.'" Ms. Durham-Hammer also faults EPCRA for not providing the public with important information about the risks associated with environmental releases, which "may lead communities to over- or underestimate risks to their health." She maintains that communities "have no way to evaluate the significance of the data without consulting scientists and expert risk analysts, something that few communities have the resources or foresight to do." Kathryn E. Durham-Hammer, *Left To Wonder: Reevaluating, Reforming, and Implementing the Emergency Planning and Community Right-to-Know Act of 1986*, 29 COLUM. J. ENVTL L. 323, 326, 337–38, 340, 347–48 (2004).

3. Is an information disclosure law like TRI likely to be useful in remedying disparate environmental burdens? Consider the following observations by Professor Karkkainen:

> TRI information is most likely to reach environmentalists, community activists, and other audiences that are already receptive to it. Arguably, it will also reach the relatively well-off and more highly educated citizens who are most likely to own

and use computers, belong to environmental organizations, read newspapers, and view or listen to news broadcasts. In addition, information may be a more effective regulatory tool in some locations than others.... Beyond inequalities in the distribution of information, we should expect that some demographic groups and communities are more likely to act on TRI information once they acquire it. Some of these differences may arise from local and demographic differences in preferences with regard to environmental insults and amenities. For example, it is often argued that more affluent citizens value environmental amenities more highly than other groups. They may also have greater political efficacy—a mutually reinforcing combination of capacity to effect change through political processes and confidence in their ability to do so. The expected result, then, would be that polluting firms in more affluent communities would come under greater pressure to reduce pollution levels, subjecting them to more stringent effective environmental standards. Empirical evidence indicates that this pattern is, in fact, emerging.... Consequently, there is a danger that TRI and similar information-based regulatory approaches, especially if played out through "NIMBY"-like efforts at "informal regulation" by the most informed, affluent, and politically empowered, may reinforce existing inequalities in the social distribution of environmental risk.

Karkkainen, *supra,* at 338–40. Ms. Durham-Hammer echoes some of Professor Karkkainen's concerns, noting that "[i]nformation alone cannot generate sufficient political activism.... Environmental justice communities are, almost by definition, less politically empowered than other communities. As a result, EPCRA provides a greater benefit to some communities than others." Durham-Hammer, *supra,* at 346. Do you agree? On the other hand, one benefit of information disclosure requirements is that the information generated can be used effectively by only a few, highly motivated individuals who are able to carry the torch for their communities. As Professor Karkkainen points out, "in recent years some environmental justice advocacy groups have successfully used TRI data for precisely the opposite end, relying on community-level, TRI-based comparative data to advance claims that their communities are recipients of a disproportionate share of toxic pollution." Karkkainen, *supra,* at 340. It is also perhaps worth noting that environmental justice activists generally are strong supporters of the TRI program (including expanding and strengthening its provisions). EPA has developed a web-based environmental justice mapping tool (known as the "Environmental Justice Geographic Assessment Tool") that allows users to access a range of demographic information about communities surrounding EPA-permitted facilities.

4. One study looked at community characteristics influencing the substantial drop in nationwide TRI emissions and exposure to air toxics that occurred from 1988 to 1992. It determined that communities with higher African American populations were less likely to experience decreases in exposures in this period. (The opposite was true in communities where the likelihood of local collective action was high.) The study concludes that "[w]hile national attention [to publication of TRI data] does lead some firms to reduce exposure, this public pressure does not appear to impact high exposure communities uniformly. In particular, communities with a higher proportion of people of color are not as likely to experience decreases in exposure as other communities which are comparable with regard to their initial exposure levels." Nancy Brooks & Rajiv Sethi, *The Distribution of Pollution: Community Characteristics and Exposure to Air Toxics,* 32 J. ENVTL. ECON. & MGMT. 233, 248 (1997).

5. As Chapter 13 describes in more detail, in 2002 EPA began spotlighting the compliance records of approximately 800,000 regulated facilities with its Enforcement and

Compliance History Online ("ECHO") web site. To motivate better performance, do you think EPA also should rank or evaluate the facilities, or publicize noncomplying or superior performing firms? Thus far, it has resisted such suggestions. Great Britain's Environmental Agency annually publishes a report highlighting good and bad performers and listing firms with the highest fines. *See* Environment Agency, Spotlight on Business: 10 Years of Improving the Environment (2008) http://publications.environment-agency.gov.uk/pdf/GEHO0708BOFX-E-E.pdf?lang=_e.

6. The most well-known state information disclosure law is California's Proposition 65, which requires businesses to warn the public prior to exposing them to listed carcinogens or reproductive toxins. In addition to covering the type of industrial emissions subject to TRI, the statute also extends to exposures from workplace hazards and consumer products, the latter being the area in which it has had its most significant impact. In particular, Proposition 65 has generated reformulations of dozens of consumer products containing toxic chemicals, including brass faucets, ceramic ware, calcium supplements, plastic clothing, wooden playground structures, and portable classrooms. Clifford Rechtschaffen and Patrick Williams, *The Continued Success of Proposition 65 in Reducing Toxic Exposures,* 35 Envtl. L. Rep. 10850 (2005). Given Proposition 65's success in the consumer marketplace, should warning statutes be used more broadly in place of direct regulation of toxic substances? What are the pros and cons of such an approach?

Chapter 12

Responding to the Challenge of Climate Change

A. Introduction

There is an overwhelming scientific consensus that the earth's temperature is warming, that humans largely are responsible for this increase, and that if the world continues on its current path of energy use and economic growth, we run the risk of severe and widespread impacts from climate change. Stopping such disruptive climate change is perhaps the most daunting environmental challenge that we have ever faced, for a number of reasons.

Greenhouse gas (GHG) emissions come from diverse and ubiquitous sources, including driving cars and trucks, heating and lighting our homes, powering electronics and household appliances, fueling factories, producing cement, and raising livestock. These energy-intensive uses have been central to our way of life and have quite literally fueled our economic growth and prosperity. Moreover, at least for carbon dioxide, the primary GHG, there currently are no commercially ready "end-of-pipe" technological solutions for controlling emissions. The major approaches to mitigating carbon dioxide emissions are to burn less fossil fuel—by using it more efficiently, using less of it through conservation, or substituting alternative energy sources that are less carbon intensive. Regardless, we will feel the consequences of today's global warming pollution for decades if not centuries to come. This is so for two reasons: first because most greenhouse gas emissions persist in the atmosphere for decades, and second, because there is a long lag time in the climate's response to the build up of GHGs.

Forging an international response to climate change is especially complex because of vast differences between developed and developing countries in emissions and levels of development and economic capability. In 2004, developed countries constituted twenty percent of the world's population, but were responsible for nearly half of global greenhouse gas emissions, and a larger share of historical emissions. Emissions from some developing countries, particularly India and China, have been growing quickly in recent years as these countries engage in rapid economic expansion that will lift millions of their citizens out of poverty. The Intergovernmental Panel on Climate Change estimates that between the years 2000 and 2030, two-thirds to three-quarters of the projected increase in global carbon dioxide emissions will occur in developing countries. These countries, however, have larger populations and far lower per capita emissions than developed countries.

Moreover, whatever steps we take to reduce GHG emissions will by themselves be insufficient to address the challenges of living in a warmer world. We also will have to spend vast sums of money adapting our physical infrastructure and social systems to a world altered by climate change (known as "adaptation" costs).

This chapter examines the problem of climate change and government efforts to combat it. Sections B and C provide background about the nature of the problem, and the disparate impacts that will result from climate change, respectively. Section D explores responses in the international context, first summarizing international responses to date, the centerpiece of which is the Kyoto Protocol, and then presenting varying perspectives on how responsibility for addressing climate change should be apportioned in a future international climate regime. Section E considers biofuels as a means to reduce greenhouse gas emissions and the "food vs. fuel" debate that surrounds expansion of their use. Section F examines the environmental justice implications of the major domestic approaches, the most important of which is a national cap-and-trade program. Section G explores international human rights-based efforts to address climate change.

B. Background on Climate Change

The summary below provides general background about climate change and is drawn largely from the 2007 assessment of the Intergovernmental Panel on Climate Change (IPCC), the world's most authoritative body on the science of climate change.

The primary cause of global warming is emissions of greenhouse gases stemming from human activities. The most widespread greenhouse gas is carbon dioxide, emitted as a result of combustion of fossil fuels, such as coal, natural gas, and oil. Other greenhouse gases include methane, primarily from agriculture and landfills, gases used in refrigerants, nitrous oxide, also stemming largely from agriculture and fuel burning, and black carbon, a form of particulate air pollution produced by biomass burning, diesel exhaust and other sources. Since the beginning of the industrial era, atmospheric concentrations of carbon dioxide have climbed to their highest point in the last half-million years, rising from 275 parts per million (ppm) in the year 1750 to about 385 ppm in 2008. They now are rising at about 2 ppm per year. Carbon dioxide annual emissions increased by about 80% between 1970 and 2004, and growth rates have accelerated even more in recent years; between 2000 and 2008, for example, the annual rate of increase was almost four times that in the 1990s, 3.5% versus 0.9% per year.

The impacts of climate change already are being felt. Global average temperatures have increased over the past 100 years by about 0.74 degrees Celsius (1.33 degrees Fahrenheit). Eleven of the most recent twelve years (1995–2006) rank among the twelve warmest years since we began keeping records 150 years ago. The current global climate is warmer than it has ever been during the past 500 years, and probably warmer than it has been for more than a thousand years. Moreover, the rate of temperature rise is unprecedented.

Due to melting land ice and rising sea temperatures, sea levels have risen and are rising at an increased rate, eroding beaches and threatening to displace people who live in low-lying areas and on islands. The decline in Arctic sea ice during the summer of 2006 was the largest ever recorded—an area the size of California and Texas combined. Mountain glaciers throughout the world are disappearing. Changes in winter temperatures are causing more precipitation to fall as rain rather than snow. Since snowpack can be a critical source of water supply, and feeds rivers and streams gradually, the result is less water available in the quantities and during the seasons necessary for human uses.

Moreover, over the past fifty years, cold days and nights have become less frequent, while hot days and nights and heat waves have increased. These changes affect crops, which can result in food shortages and higher food prices. Climate change also impacts human health. While no individual weather event can be conclusively attributed to global warming, warming may already have increased the risk of serious heat waves such as the one that struck Europe in 2003 and caused 35,000 excess deaths.

We also are seeing more extreme weather, including increases in the intensity of tropical cyclones. Increases in the destructive potential of hurricanes are strongly correlated with increases in tropical sea surface temperatures that result from global warming. Since 1970, the number of category four and five hurricanes increased by about 75%. This suggests that events like Hurricane Katrina, which devastated the Gulf Coast in 2005, may become the norm and not the exception.

Scientists predict that if we continue on our current path of greenhouse gas emissions, the impacts of climate change will become increasingly severe, and at some point, may spiral beyond our ability to control or reverse them. In the near term—through the year 2030—our actions will not have much impact on the rate of global warming because our past emissions and inertia in the climate system have already committed us to some degree of warming, probably on the order of an additional 0.6 degrees Celsius (1 degree Fahrenheit) from levels in 2000. However, actions we take now (or fail to take) will dramatically affect the rate of warming in the long term. The IPCC predicts that if we fail to reduce GHG emissions, temperatures are likely to rise by 1.8 to 4.0 degrees Celsius (3.2 to 7.2 degrees Fahrenheit) between the years 2000 and 2100. In higher emission scenarios, the IPCC estimates a possible increase of as much as 6.4 Celsius (11 degrees Fahrenheit). It is worth noting that even the IPCC's higher-end emission scenarios do not take into account the unexpectedly high growth rate in emissions during the 2000s noted above.

Experts have identified an increase of 2.0 degrees Celsius (3.6 degrees Fahrenheit) as a threshold beyond which the impacts of climate change are likely to be particularly grave. This benchmark is often cited as constituting "dangerous human interference" with the climate, a term that has legal significance under the United Nations Framework on Climate Change, discussed below. With temperature increases above this level, we risk setting in motion unstoppable "feedback loops" that will exacerbate global warming. For example, the disintegration of large areas of snow and ice will expose darker land surfaces that will in turn absorb more sunlight, raising temperatures and speeding up the further loss of snow and ice. Higher temperatures will thaw the arctic tundra, causing organic materials in the permafrost to decompose, thereby releasing large amounts of methane. Methane is a powerful greenhouse gas—twenty-one times more potent than carbon dioxide.

Climate change also may have profound implications for regional conflicts and global security, as millions of residents are displaced from their homes and conflicts develop over increasingly scarce food, water and other natural resources. One recent analysis concludes that "[c]limate change acts as a threat multiplier for instability in some of the most volatile regions of the world. Projected climate change will seriously exacerbate already marginal living standards in many Asian, African, and Middle Eastern nations, causing

widespread political instability and the likelihood of failed states." THE CNA CORPORA-
TION, NATIONAL SECURITY AND THE THREAT OF CLIMATE CHANGE (2007).

The chart below from the IPCC vividly summarizes projected future impacts from climate change:

KEY IMPACTS AS A FUNCTION OF INCREASING GLOBAL AVERAGE TEMPERATURE CHANGE

(Impacts will vary by extent of adaptation, rate of temperature change, and socio-economic pathway.)

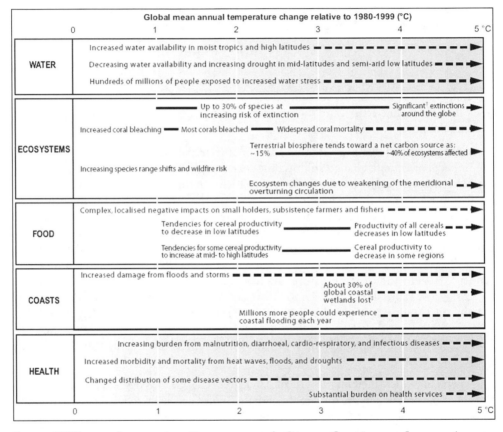

Source: IPCC, 2007: SUMMARY FOR POLICYMAKERS, *in* CLIMATE CHANGE 2007: IMPACTS, ADAPTA-
TION AND VULNERABILITY. CONTRIBUTION OF WORKING GROUP II TO THE FOURTH ASSESSMENT RE-
PORT OF THE INTERGOVERNMENTAL PANEL ON CLIMATE CHANGE 16 (M.L. Parry, et al. eds., 2007).

C. The Disproportionate Impacts of Climate Change

1. The International Context

Global warming's impacts, while widespread and severe, will not affect everyone equally.
As the Chair of the IPCC has stated, "[i]t is the poorest of the poor in the world, and this

includes poor people even in prosperous societies, who are going to be the worst hit." The adverse impacts often will fall hardest on people of color and poor people the world over because they are concentrated in areas that will bear the ecological brunt of climate change, and because they are often the least able financially to deal with its impacts.

The materials below explore in more detail how harm from climate change is likely to be most severe for poorer countries. The first excerpt summarizes some of the major impacts projected for developing regions of the world. The second describes some of the limitations in adaptive capacity faced by these countries and how climate change could dramatically impede development efforts.

M.L. Parry, O.F. Canziani, J.P. Palutikof, P.J. van der Linden & C.E. Hanson, eds, IPCC, 2007: Summary for Policymakers

Climate Change 2007: Impacts, Adaptation and Vulnerability.
Contribution of Working Group II to the Fourth Assessment Report of the
Intergovernmental Panel on Climate Change (2007)

Industry, settlement and society....

The most vulnerable industries, settlements and societies are generally those in coastal and river flood plains, those whose economies are closely linked with climate-sensitive resources, and those in areas prone to extreme weather events, especially where rapid urbanisation is occurring.

Poor communities can be especially vulnerable, in particular those concentrated in high-risk areas. They tend to have more limited adaptive capacities, and are more dependent on climate-sensitive resources such as local water and food supplies....

Africa

By 2020, between 75 million and 250 million people are projected to be exposed to increased water stress due to climate change. If coupled with increased demand, this will adversely affect livelihoods and exacerbate water-related problems.

Agricultural production, including access to food, in many African countries and regions is projected to be severely compromised by climate variability and change. The area suitable for agriculture, the length of growing seasons and yield potential, particularly along the margins of semi-arid and arid areas, are expected to decrease. This would further adversely affect food security and exacerbate malnutrition in the continent. In some countries, yields from rain-fed agriculture could be reduced by up to 50% by 2020.

Local food supplies are projected to be negatively affected by decreasing fisheries resources in large lakes due to rising water temperatures, which may be exacerbated by continued overfishing....

Asia....

Glacier melt in the Himalayas is projected to increase flooding, and rock avalanches from destabilised slopes, and to affect water resources within the next two to three decades. This will be followed by decreased river flows as the glaciers recede. Freshwater availability in Central, South, East and South-East Asia, particularly in large river basins, is projected to decrease due to climate change which, along with population growth and increasing demand arising from higher standards of living, could adversely affect more than a billion people by the 2050s.... Coastal areas, especially heavily-populated megadelta regions in South, East and South-East Asia, will be at greatest risk due to increased flooding from the sea and, in some megadeltas, flooding from the rivers.

Climate change is projected to impinge on the sustainable development of most developing countries of Asia, as it compounds the pressures on natural resources and the environment associated with rapid urbanisation, industrialisation, and economic development....

Endemic morbidity and mortality due to diarrhoeal disease primarily associated with floods and droughts are expected to rise in East, South and South-East Asia due to projected changes in the hydrological cycle associated with global warming. Increases in coastal water temperature would exacerbate the abundance and/or toxicity of cholera in South Asia....

Latin America....

By mid-century, increases in temperature and associated decreases in soil water are projected to lead to gradual replacement of tropical forest by savanna in eastern Amazonia. Semi-arid vegetation will tend to be replaced by arid-land vegetation.... In drier areas, climate change is expected to lead to salinisation and desertification of agricultural land. Productivity of some important crops is projected to decrease and livestock productivity to decline, with adverse consequences for food security.... Changes in precipitation patterns and the disappearance of glaciers are projected to significantly affect water availability for human consumption, agriculture and energy generation.

Polar Regions....

For human communities in the Arctic, impacts, particularly those resulting from changing snow and ice conditions, are projected to be mixed. Detrimental impacts would include those on infrastructure and traditional indigenous ways of life.... Arctic human communities are already adapting to climate change, but both external and internal stressors challenge their adaptive capacities. Despite the resilience shown historically by Arctic indigenous communities, some traditional ways of life are being threatened and substantial investments are needed to adapt or relocate physical structures and communities.

Small Islands

Small islands, whether located in the tropics or higher latitudes, have characteristics which make them especially vulnerable to the effects of climate change, sea-level rise and extreme events. Deterioration in coastal conditions, for example through erosion of beaches and coral bleaching, is expected to affect local resources, e.g., fisheries, and reduce the value of these destinations for tourism. Sea-level rise is expected to exacerbate inundation, storm surge, erosion and other coastal hazards, thus threatening vital infrastructure, settlements and facilities that support the livelihood of island communities....

* * *

Kevin Watkins, United Nations Development Programme
Human Development Report 2007/2008
Fighting Climate Change: Human Solidarity in a Divided World
(2007)

Across developing countries, millions of the world's poorest people are already being forced to cope with the impacts of climate change.... [I]ncreased exposure to drought, to more intense storms, to floods and environmental stress ... will undermine international efforts to combat poverty....

How the world deals with climate change today will have a direct bearing on the human development prospects of a large section of humanity. Failure will consign the poorest 40 percent of the world's population — some 2.6 billion people — to a future of diminished opportunity. It will exacerbate deep inequalities within countries. And it will undermine efforts to build a more inclusive pattern of globalization, reinforcing the vast disparities between the 'haves' and the 'have nots.' ...

While the world's poor walk the Earth with a light carbon footprint they are bearing the brunt of unsustainable management of our ecological interdependence. In rich countries, coping with climate change to date has largely been a matter of adjusting thermostats, dealing with longer, hotter summers, and observing seasonal shifts.... By contrast, when global warming changes weather patterns in the Horn of Africa, it means that crops fail and people go hungry, or that women and young girls spend more hours collecting water....

Climate shocks: risk and vulnerability in an unequal world....

Vulnerability to climate shocks is unequally distributed.... [C]limate disasters are heavily concentrated in poor countries. Some 262 million people were affected by climate disasters annually from 2000 to 2004, over 98 percent of them in the developing world. In the Organisation for Economic Co-operation and Development (OECD) countries one in 1,500 people was affected by climate disaster. The comparable figure for developing countries is one in 19 — a risk differential of 79.

High levels of poverty and low levels of human development limit the capacity of poor households to manage climate risks. With limited access to formal insurance, low incomes and meagre assets, poor households have to deal with climate-related shocks under highly constrained conditions....

In Ethiopia and Kenya, two of the world's most drought-prone countries, children aged five or less are respectively 36 and 50 percent more likely to be malnourished if they were born during a drought. For Ethiopia, that translates into some 2 million additional malnourished children in 2005. In Niger, children aged two or less born in a drought year were 72 percent more likely to be stunted. And Indian women born during a flood in the 1970s were 19 percent less likely to have attended primary school....

[C]limate change will steadily increase the exposure of poor and vulnerable households to climate-shocks and place increased pressure on coping strategies, which, over time, could steadily erode human capabilities. We identify [several] key transmission mechanisms through which climate change could stall and then reverse human development:

> • *Agricultural production and food security*. Climate change will affect rainfall, temperature and water availability for agriculture in vulnerable areas. For example, drought affected areas in sub-Saharan Africa could expand by 60–90 million hectares.... The additional number affected by malnutrition could rise to 600 million by 2080. [The impacts in agricultural output by region are depicted in the chart below from the report. Eds.]

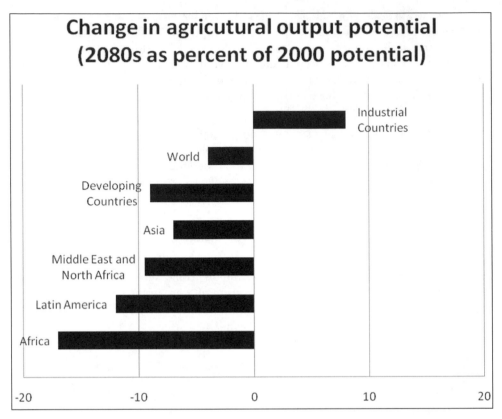

Source: WILLIAM R. CLINE, GLOBAL WARMING AND AGRICULTURE: IMPACT ESTIMATES BY COUNTRY (2007)

• *Water stress and water insecurity.* Changed run-off patterns and glacial melt will add to ecological stress, compromising flows of water for irrigation and human settlements in the process. An additional 1.8 billion people could be living in a water scarce environment by 2080. . . .

• *Rising sea levels and exposure to climate disasters.* Sea levels could rise rapidly with accelerated ice sheet disintegration. Global temperature increases of 3–4°C could result in 330 million people being permanently or temporarily displaced through flooding. Over 70 million people in Bangladesh, 6 million in Lower Egypt and 22 million in Viet Nam could be affected. . . . Warming seas will also fuel more intense tropical storms. With over 344 million people currently exposed to tropical cyclones, more intensive storms could have devastating consequences for a large group of countries. The 1 billion people currently living in urban slums on fragile hillsides or flood prone river banks face acute vulnerabilities. . . .

• *Human health.* Rich countries are already preparing public health systems to deal with future climate shocks, such as the 2003 European heat wave and more extreme summer and winter conditions. However, the greatest health impacts will be felt in developing countries because of high levels of poverty and the limited capacity of public health systems to respond. Major killer diseases [such as malaria] could expand their coverage. . . .

Adapting to the inevitable: national action and international cooperation

[E]ven the most stringent mitigation [action to prevent climate change, such as decreasing GHG emissions] will be insufficient to avoid major human development setbacks.... For the first half of the 21st Century there is no alternative to adaptation to climate change.

Rich countries.... are investing heavily in the development of climate [defense] infrastructures.... The United Kingdom is spending US $1.2 billion annually on flood [defenses]. In the Netherlands, people are investing in homes that can float on water. The Swiss alpine ski industry is investing in artificial snow-making machines.

Developing countries face far more severe adaptation challenges. Those challenges have to be met by governments operating under severe financing constraints, and by poor people themselves. In the Horn of Africa, 'adaptation' means that women and young girls walk further to collect water. In the Ganges Delta, people are erecting bamboo flood shelters on stilts. And in the Mekong Delta people are planting mangroves to protect themselves against storm surges, and women and children are being taught to swim....

Responding to climate change will require the integration of adaptation into all aspects of policy development and planning for poverty reduction. However, planning and implementation capacity is limited:

• *Information*. Many of the world's poorest countries lack the capacity and the resources to assess climate risks. In sub-Saharan Africa, high levels of rural poverty and dependence on rainfed agriculture makes meteorological information an imperative for adaptation. However, the region has the world's lowest density of meteorological stations. In France, the meteorological budget amounts to US $388 million annually, compared with just US $2 million in Ethiopia.

• *Infrastructure*. In climate change adaptation, as in other areas, prevention is better than cure. Every US $1 invested in pre-disaster risk management in developing countries can prevent losses of US $7. In Bangladesh, research among impoverished populations living on *char* islands shows that adaptation against flooding can strengthen livelihoods, even in extreme conditions. Many countries lack the financial resources required for infrastructural adaptation....

• *Insurance for social protection*.... Social protection programmes can help people cope with [climate change] risks while expanding opportunities for employment, nutrition and education.... While social protection figures only marginally in current climate adaptation strategies, it has the potential to create large human development returns....

[T]he international response on adaptation has fallen far short of what is required.... Total financing to date has amounted to around US $26 million.... For purposes of comparison, this is equivalent to one week's worth of spending under the United Kingdom flood [defense] programme....

It is not just the lives and the livelihoods of the poor that require protection through adaptation. Aid programmes are also under threat.... [C]limate change is contributing to a diversion of aid into disaster relief. This has been one of the fastest growing areas for aid flows, accounting for 7.5 percent of total commitments in 2005....

* * *

Notes and Questions

1. The disproportionate burdens that developing countries face seem particularly unjust because they are least responsible for climate change. From 1850 to 2004, the developed world—U.S., Europe, Canada, Australia and Russia, approximately 17% of the world's population—caused close to 70% of the world's cumulative greenhouse gas emissions. J. Andrew Hoerner & Nia Robinson, Envtl. Justice and Climate Change Initiative, A Climate of Change: African Americans, Global Warming, and a Just Climate Policy for the U.S. 7 (2008). What does this historical distribution suggest about how the responsibility for addressing climate change should be allocated? Should past contributions be more important than current capability (or weighted at all)? These questions are explored in more detail below.

2. Note that the anticipated severity of impacts from climate change are closely linked to the wealth and adaptive capabilities of nations. Does this mean that climate change efforts should only proceed in tandem with development efforts?

3. As the readings indicate, developing countries face a double, if not triple, whammy from climate change, stemming from geography, limits in adaptive capacity, and potential impacts on the stability of their political regimes. While the costs of adaptation are uncertain and vary dramatically based on emissions scenarios, under any circumstance they are likely to be very large, with estimates for developing countries ranging from $10 billion to $100 billion per year. Karoline Hægstad Flåm & Jon Birger SkjÆrseth, *Does Adequate Financing Exist for Adaptation in Developing Countries?*, 9 Climate Pol'y 109, 110 (2009). The IPCC estimates that for Africa, the cost of adaptation could amount to at least 5–10% of Gross Domestic Product (GDP). IPCC, 2007: Summary for Policymakers, Working Group II, *supra*, at 13. Does this suggest that massive aid from the developed to developing world to pay for adaptation programs is needed?

2. Impacts in the United States

The U.S. will experience many of the same devastating impacts from climate change as other regions of the world, although these impacts will be less severe than in some parts of the world due to geographic advantages and greater resources available for adaptation. As discussed below, however, these impacts will hit the poor and communities of color in the U.S. the hardest.

Congressional Black Caucus Foundation, African Americans and Climate Change: An Unequal Burden
(2004)

[T]here is a stark disparity in the United States between those who benefit from the causes of climate change and those who bear the costs of climate change....

Health Effects:

It is clear that African Americans will disproportionately bear the substantial public health burden caused by climate change. Health effects will include the degradation of air quality, deaths from heat waves and extreme weather events, and the spread of infectious diseases....

Air pollution is already divided down racial lines in this country, with over seventy percent of African Americans living in counties in violation of federal air pollution standards. The number of people affected will increase as the higher temperatures of global warming are expected to further degrade air quality through increased ozone formation. In every single one of the 44 major metropolitan areas in the U.S., Blacks are more likely than Whites to be exposed to higher air toxics concentrations....

Similarly, at present, African Americans are at a greater risk of [dying] during extreme heat events. The most direct health effect of climate change will be intensifying heat waves that selectively impact poor and urban populations. Future heat waves will be most lethal in the inner cities of the northern half of the country, such as New York City, Detroit, Chicago, and Philadelphia, where many African American communities are located.

African Americans may also be disproportionately impacted by the increased prevalence of extreme weather events and the spread of infectious diseases, such as malaria and dengue fever, primarily in Southern states.... All of these problems are compounded by the fact that Blacks are 50% more likely than non-Blacks to be uninsured.

Economic Effects

African American workers are likely to be laid off disproportionately due to the economic instability caused by climate change. In general, economic transitions strike hardest at those without resources or savings to adapt. In the United States, drought, sea level rise, and the higher temperatures associated with global warming may have sizeable impacts on several economic sectors including agriculture, insurance, and buildings and infrastructure....

In contrast to the burden of climate change, responsibility for the problem does not lie primarily with African Americans. African American households emit twenty percent less carbon dioxide than white households. Historically, this difference was even higher....

* * *

Notes and Questions

1. The report explains that heat-related deaths are more likely to be concentrated in urban areas because concrete and asphalt surfaces there help create the urban "heat island effect," and also because these areas often have worse air quality, and elevated pollution is often associated with heat waves. In addition, the authors note, "poverty is also an important factor in heat-related vulnerability. The poor are less likely to have adequate access to well-insulated housing or air-conditioning due to the combination of capital costs and utility bills. The [2000] National Assessment [of the U.S. Global Research Program] found that, 'High risk subpopulations include people who live in the top floors of apartment buildings in cities and who lack access to air-conditioned environment.' As of 1995, only a quarter of housing units in the Northeast were furnished with air-conditioning." UNEQUAL BURDEN, *supra*, at 20–21. Professor Maxine Burkett notes that "[h]eat stress has already been a public health nightmare for the poor and of-color. As an example, older black males living alone with poor health status suffered a disproportionate share of excess fatalities after the 1996 heat wave in Chicago." Maxine Burkett, *Just Solutions to Climate Change: A Climate Justice Proposal for a Domestic Clean Development Mechanism*, 56 BUFF. L. REV. 169, 177 (2008).

2. Recall the discussion in Chapter 2 that vulnerability to disasters is a function of both proximity to natural hazards and the social and economic characteristics of a community. As the readings above illustrate, the impacts of global warming experienced by minority and poor communities will be exacerbated because these groups are often the least able to

adapt. Poor people also typically have less access to home and renter's insurance and less money to move away from droughts, floods, and fires caused by global warming. Other impediments to adaptation include the following, discussed in this report about California:

> • *Lack of Health Insurance*: People without health insurance are vulnerable to ailments that timely and continual access to health care could minimize. These access disparities exist for different income, geographic and racial groups in California.... [For example,] Hispanics are three times more likely to lack health insurance than Whites. [Furthermore,] Californians in the lowest income category, below the federal poverty level, are five times more likely to be uninsured than those in the highest income category.

> • *Energy and Water Costs*: Climate change threatens to limit basic resources such as water and electricity. Supply reductions and demand increases together will increase water and energy prices.... Higher energy and water costs will hit low-income households the hardest because these costs make up a larger proportion of their expenditures—almost double the proportion of the highest income families.

ROBERT CORDOVA, ET AL., REDEFINING PROGRESS, *Executive Summary of* CLIMATE CHANGE IN CALIFORNIA: HEALTH, ECONOMIC AND EQUITY IMPACTS 3–6 (2006).

3. To what extent are the disproportionate impacts likely to result from climate change part of the larger pattern of disparate environmental harms seen in Chapter 2? What do the similarities/differences suggest about how domestic climate policies should be crafted?

4. The Congressional Black Caucus report notes that poor Americans, regardless of race, also are far less responsible for carbon dioxide emissions than wealthier Americans, "with the average household in the wealthiest decile emitting roughly seven times as much carbon dioxide as the average household in the bottom expenditure decile." UNEQUAL BURDEN, *supra*, at 70. What implications does this have for efforts to control carbon emissions, including the likely political support for such programs? Do you think that poor individuals will be less willing to accept higher costs for controlling GHG emissions because they contribute relatively less to the problem? Will rich citizens be willing to make greater sacrifices?

D. Climate Justice in the International Context

1. International Responses to Date

The international community first addressed climate change with the 1992 United Nations Framework Convention on Climate Change (UNFCCC). The parties to the treaty (which now has been ratified by 192 countries, including the United States), agreed to stabilize greenhouse gas concentrations in the atmosphere with the goal of "preventing dangerous anthropogenic interference with Earth's climate system," although no numerical targets for GHG emissions reductions were set. The Framework recognizes that nations have "common but differentiated responsibilities," reflecting the view that developed countries bear a greater historical responsibility for the problem of climate change and have a greater capacity to take action. In particular, Article 3(1) of the UNFCCC provides that

> The Parties should protect the climate for the benefit of present and future generations of humankind, on the basis of equity and in accordance with their common but differentiated responsibilities and respective capabilities. Accordingly,

the developed country Parties should take the lead in combating climate change and the adverse effects thereof.

In 1997, the Kyoto Protocol to the Framework Convention (Kyoto) was negotiated. The major industrialized countries (so called "annex I" countries) collectively committed to reducing their average annual greenhouse gas emissions between the years 2008 and 2012 to 5.2% below their 1990 levels. Developing countries (so called "non-annex I" countries) were not required to limit their emissions (and nearly all refused to consider such limits during the negotiations).

During the final negotiations period, the U.S. Senate by a 97–0 vote adopted a resolution directing that the president sign a treaty only if it included limits on emissions from developing countries within the same compliance period as for developed nations. In 2001, shortly after George W. Bush became president, the U.S. repudiated the treaty. Kyoto went into force in 2005 when it was ratified by Russia. (Kyoto required states representing fifty-five percent of developed countries emissions to ratify in order to go into force, meaning that it could not become effective without either the U.S. or Russia's participation. The U.S. still is not a party to Kyoto).

Kyoto provides for three flexible compliance mechanisms. First, it allows for trading of emission allowances among the industrialized countries that have reduction obligations under the treaty. Second, it allows industrialized countries or private parties to obtain emission credits by carrying out emission reduction projects in other industrialized countries (known as the "joint implementation" provision, and geared toward projects in Russia and other former communist countries in Europe). Third, its most significant (and controversial) trading provision is the "clean development mechanism" (CDM), which authorizes industrialized countries and private parties to obtain emission credits through mitigation projects undertaken in developing countries, which, as noted above, have no obligations under Kyoto. (The latter two programs often are referred to as offset programs.)

The CDM was designed to fund sustainable development efforts in developing countries, and also to provide a source of low-cost emission reductions for developed countries. CDM projects must result in emission reductions "additional to any that would otherwise occur." In other words, an applicant for funding must show that but for the funding provided by parties in developed countries wishing to "offset" their emissions, the mitigation project—such as developing new renewable power, capturing methane from animal waste, planting trees to serve as "sinks" that remove carbon from the atmosphere— would not have occurred. The CDM has grown rapidly since its inception in 2004. In 2007, the value of the CDM market was nearly $13 billion and as of October, 2008, included more than 3,800 projects either approved or awaiting approval. The CDM, however, has been sharply criticized on a number of grounds.

First, the CDM largely has failed to generate projects that promote cleaner energy production and sustainable development in the developing world. As Professor David Driesen notes, through mid-2007, the lion's share of emission credits (64%) were for projects that imposed end-of-the-pipe controls on non-carbon GHG emissions. Only 17% were for renewable energy, and 10% for energy efficiency. David M. Driesen, *Sustainable Development and Market Liberalism's Shotgun Wedding: Emissions Trading Under the Kyoto Protocol*, 83 IND. L.J. 21, 40–41 (2008).

Additionally, the very poorest developing nations—those in the greatest need—have received relatively little in CDM funding. China and India have received over half of all project investment; conversely, countries in Africa and the Middle East have received little investment, and only ten CDM projects have been registered in what the U.N. defines as "least developed countries." U.S. Gen. Accountability Office, International Climate Change Programs: Lessons Learned from the European Union's Emissions Trading Scheme and the Kyoto Protocol's Clean Development Mechanism 35–36 (2008).

Moreover, many emission reduction credits have been sold to parties for much more than the cost of achieving those reductions—the price having been set by the market for emission credits—and the CDM correspondingly has created perverse incentives to increase GHG-generating activity in order to generate profitable emission credits. Professors Michael Wara and David Victor illustrate this with an example. Much of the CDM's early activity involved controls of an extremely potent gas called HFC-23, produced mainly as a waste product during the manufacture of another gas that is used in some air conditioners and as a feedstock for plastics. However,

> the sale of credits generated from HFC-23 capture is far more valuable than production of the refrigerant gas that leads to its creation in the first place. Thus, refrigerant manufacturers were transformed overnight by the CDM into ventures that generated large volumes of CERs (Certified Emission Reductions), with a sideline in the manufacture of industrial gases.

Moreover, HFC-23 abatement was "a startlingly inefficient means for achieving emissions reductions in the developing world. Payments to refrigerant manufacturers, the Chinese government ... and to carbon market investors by governments and compliance buyers will in the end total approximately € 4.7 billion while estimated costs of abatement are likely less than € 100 million." Michael W. Wara & David G. Victor, *A Realistic Policy on International Carbon Offsets* 11–12 (Stan. U. Program on Energy & Sustainable Dev. Working Paper No. 74, 2008).

Finally, numerous reports have pointed out the potential for serious abuses in the CDM process, in considerable part because of the lack of adequate monitoring and the difficulty of determining whether projects truly are "additional." One U.N. official estimates that up to twenty percent of the emission credits generated by CDM did not represent actual reductions in GHGs; other commentators place the number much higher. *See* Jonathan Leake, *The Fool's Gold of Carbon Trading*, Sunday Times (U.K.), Nov. 30, 2008.

To implement their collective emission reduction targets, countries in the European Union (EU) created a cap-and-trade program for carbon dioxide emissions known as the European Union Emissions Trading Scheme ("EU ETS"). The program covers more than 10,000 energy intensive facilities in the twenty-seven countries comprising the EU, which collectively emit about forty-five percent of the EU's carbon dioxide emissions. The first trading period—phase I—ran from 2005 to 2007; the second phase runs from 2008 to 2012.

The EU system also has come under heavy criticism, particularly for its overallocation of emission allowances, and because of its decision to distribute allowances for free rather than to auction them. The overall emissions cap exceeded actual emissions by more than three percent in the first phase, contributing to a collapse in the price of allowances two years into the program. Investigators report that it is unclear to what degree the first phase of trading has achieved real emissions reductions, because of a lack of adequate baseline emissions data. Congr. Res. Service, Climate Change and the EU Emissions Trading Scheme (ETS): Kyoto and Beyond 5–6 (2008). A harsher assessment in 2008 contends that the plan "unleashed a lobbying free-for-all that led politicians to dole out favors to various industries, undermining its environmental goals. Four years later, it is becoming clear that the system has so far produced little noticeable benefit to the climate—but generated a multibillion-dollar windfall for some of the Continent's biggest polluters."

James Kanter & Jad Nouawad, *Pipe Dreams and Politics—Money and Lobbyists Hurt European Efforts to Curb Gases,* NY TIMES, Dec. 11, 2008 at B1.

In 2007, parties to the Kyoto Protocol and the UNFCCC met in Bali, Indonesia to discuss an agenda for negotiating a new agreement to succeed the Kyoto Protocol when it expires in 2012. After a contentious session and sharp disagreements, particularly between developing countries and the U.S. (as well as between the EU and the U.S.), the parties agreed to an "action plan" or "roadmap" to guide future negotiations, which the parties aim to conclude by the end of 2009. The roadmap did not include any firm targets for emission reductions, but the parties agreed that "deep cuts in global emissions" were needed (and referred, albeit in a footnote due to U.S. opposition, to cuts of 25–40% below 1990 levels by 2020). Future negotiations will proceed on four tracks, dealing with mitigation, adaptation, technology, and financing.

The Bali action plan made progress in that developing nations agreed to play a more significant role in addressing climate change, while developed countries committed to providing them with more resources to do so. Both groups agreed to take future steps that are "measurable, reportable and verifiable"—developing countries agreed to future "actions," supported by developed country assistance in technology financing and capacity-building, while developed countries agreed to future "commitments or actions." However, the hard decisions about how the nations actually would share the burden of cutting emissions were left for future talks. The action plan also strengthens an existing adaptation fund for developing countries that is financed by a two percent tax on CDM transactions. The fund is currently worth over $30 million and is expected to grow to an estimated $80–$300 million by 2012. (Recall that adaptation costs for developing countries are estimated to be from $10 to $100 billion annually.) The agreement includes commitments by developed nations for technology transfer to aid developing countries to grow sustainably, and to address for the first time the issue of deforestation (which is responsible for one-fifth of the world's greenhouse gases).

Notes and Questions

1. Critics have suggested numerous reforms for the CDM, including restricting projects eligible for generating credits to a small number of projects that promote energy and avoid deforestation and that would almost certainly be uneconomical without financial support from investors seeking to purchase credits. They also argue that instead of the CDM trading scheme, it would preferable to have a climate fund administered by an international institution that invests directly to help developing countries achieve low carbon development. Which is more preferable—direct assistance to developing nations or the CDM scheme, and why?

2. What do you think the principle of "common but differentiated responsibilities" articulated in the U.N. Framework Convention on Climate Change means in practice? As a general matter, do you think differentiated responsibility is a workable and desirable rule for addressing international environmental problems? Implementing this approach in the context of climate change is explored in the section below.

2. Designing an International Response

Determining the appropriate apportionment of responsibility in an international climate treaty raises very vexing questions, and the answers suggest a variety of approaches.

For example, should major emitters such as China and India face binding controls? On the one hand, their absolute emissions levels are high; China recently surpassed the U.S. as the top global emitter, and India is now number three in the world. On the other hand, their per capita emissions are much lower than those of developed countries, and emission limits may restrict developing countries' economic growth and keep them from lifting tens of millions of people out of desperate poverty. Should emission allowances be allocated based on the historical baseline of emissions, or does that just reward past wrongdoers? Alternatively, should they be allocated based on population? Allocating allowances based on population alone would create a system in which the United States would either have to reduce emissions dramatically or buy allowances from countries like China that are far more populous and therefore receive more allowances, and that are among the world's most rapidly growing economies. Is that appropriate? The following three excerpts grapple with these and other related questions.

Eric A. Posner and Cass R. Sunstein, Climate Change Justice
96 Georgetown Law Journal 1565 (2008)

The problem of climate change raises difficult issues of science, economics, and justice. Of course, the scientific and economic issues loom large in public debates, and they have been analyzed in great detail. By contrast, the question of justice, while also playing a significant role in such debates, has rarely received sustained attention. Several points are clear. Although the United States long led the world in greenhouse gas emissions, China is now the world's leading emitter. The two nations account for about 40% of the world's emissions, but to date, they have independently refused to accept binding emissions limitations, apparently because of a belief that the domestic costs of such limitations would exceed the benefits.

The emissions of the United States and China threaten to impose serious losses on other nations and regions, including Europe but above all India and Africa. For this reason, it is tempting to argue that both nations are, in a sense, engaging in tortious acts against those nations that are most vulnerable to climate change. This argument might seem to have special force as applied to the actions of the United States. While the emissions of the United States are growing relatively slowly, that nation remains by far the largest contributor to the existing "stock" of greenhouse gases. Because of its past contributions, does the United States owe remedial action or material compensation to those nations, or those citizens, most likely to be harmed by climate change? Principles of corrective justice might seem to require that the largest emitting nation pay damages to those who are hurt—and that they scale back their emissions as well.

Questions of corrective justice are entangled with questions of distributive justice. The United States has the highest Gross Domestic Product of any nation in the world, and its wealth might suggest that it has a special duty to help to reduce the damage associated with climate change. Are the obligations of the comparatively poor China, the leading emitter, equivalent to those of the comparatively rich United States, the second-leading emitter? Does it not matter that China's per capita emissions remain a mere fraction of that of the United States? Perhaps most important: Because of its wealth, should the United States be willing to sign an agreement that is optimal for the world as a whole—but not optimal for the United States? ...

[T]o put [the issues of justice] in their starkest form, we start with two admittedly controversial assumptions. First, the world, taken as a whole, would benefit from an agreement to reduce greenhouse gas emissions.... Second, some nations, above all the

United States (and China as well), might not benefit, on net, from the agreement that would be optimal from the world's point of view....

Climate Change and Distributive Justice

To separate issues of distributive justice from those of corrective justice, and to clarify intuitions, let us begin with a risk of natural calamity that does not involve human action at all.

The Asteroid

Imagine that India faces a serious new threat of some kind—say, a threat of a collision with a large asteroid. Imagine too that the threat will not materialize for a century. Imagine finally that the threat can be eliminated, today, at a cost. India would be devastated by having to bear that cost now; as a practical matter, it lacks the resources to do so. But if the world acts as a whole, it can begin to build technology that will allow it to divert the asteroid, thus ensuring that it does not collide with India a century hence. The cost is high, but it is lower than the discounted benefit of eliminating the threat....

The problem of the asteroid threat does have a significant difference from that of climate change, whose adverse effects are not limited to a single nation. To make the analogy closer, let us assume that all nations are threatened by the asteroid, in the sense that it is not possible to project where the collision will occur; scientists believe that each nation faces a risk. But the risk is not identical. Because of its adaptive capacity, its technology, and a range of other factors, assume that the United States is less vulnerable to serious damage than (for example) India and the nations of Africa and Europe. Otherwise the problem is the same. Under plausible assumptions, the world will certainly act to divert the asteroid, and it seems clear that the United States will contribute substantial resources for that purpose. Suppose that all nations favor an international agreement that requires contributions to a general fund, but, because it is less vulnerable, the United States believes that the fund should be smaller than the fund favored by the more vulnerable nations of Africa and Europe, and by India. From the standpoint of domestic self-interest, then, those nations with the most to lose will naturally seek a larger fund than those nations facing lower risks.

At first glance, it might seem intuitive to think that the United States should accept the proposal for the larger fund simply because it is so wealthy. If resources should be redistributed from rich to poor on the ground that redistribution would increase overall welfare or promote fairness, the intuition appears sound. But there is an immediate problem: If redistribution from rich nations to poor nations is *generally* desirable, it is not at all clear that it should take the particular form of a deal in which the United States joins an agreement that is not in its interest. Other things being equal, the more sensible kind of redistribution would be a cash transfer, so that poor nations can use the money as they see fit. Perhaps India would prefer to spend the money on education, or on AIDS prevention, or on health care generally.... If redistribution is desirable ... it remains puzzling why wealthy nations should be willing to protect poor nations from the risks of asteroid collisions (or climate change), while not being willing to give them resources with which they can set their own priorities....

There is a second difficulty. We have stipulated that the asteroid will not hit the earth for another 100 years. If the world takes action now, it will be spending current resources for the sake of future generations, which are likely to be much richer. The current poor citizens of poor nations are probably much poorer than will be the *future* poor citizens of those nations. If the goal is to help the poor, it is odd for the United States to spend significant resources to help posterity while neglecting the present....

Climate Change: From Whom to Whom?

In terms of distributive justice, the problem of climate change is closely analogous to the asteroid problem. From that problem, three general questions emerge. First, why should redistribution take the form of an in-kind benefit, rather than a general grant of money that poor nations could use as they wish? Second, why should rich nations help poor nations in the future, rather than poor nations now? Third, if redistribution is the goal, why should it take the form of action by rich nations that would hurt many poor people in those nations and benefit many rich people in rich nations? To sharpen these questions, suppose that an international agreement to cut greenhouse gas emissions would cost the United States $325 billion. If distributive justice is the goal, should the United States spend $325 billion on climate change, or instead on other imaginable steps to help people who are in need? If the goal is to assist poor people, perhaps there would be far better means than emissions reductions.

In fact, the argument from distributive justice runs into an additional problem in the context of climate change. No one would gain from an asteroid collision, but millions of people would benefit from climate change. Many people die from cold, and to the extent that warming reduces cold, it will save lives. Warming will also produce monetary benefits in many places, such as Russia, due to increases in agricultural productivity....

In addition, many millions of poor people would be hurt by the cost of emissions reductions. They would bear that cost in the form of higher energy bills, lost jobs, and increased poverty....

It follows that purely as an instrument of redistribution, emission reductions on the part of the United States are quite crude.... [T]here is a highly imperfect connection between distributive goals on the one hand and requiring wealthy countries to pay for emissions reductions on the other.

To see the problem more concretely, suppose that Americans (and the same could be said about citizens in other wealthy countries) are willing to devote a certain portion, X, of their national income to helping people living in poor countries. The question is, How is X best spent? If X is committed to emissions controls, then X is being spent to benefit wealthy Europeans as well as impoverished Indians, and, X is also being spent to harm some or many impoverished people living in China and Russia by denying them the benefit of increased agricultural productivity that warming will bring. And if all of X is spent on global emissions control, then none of X is being spent to purchase malaria nets or to distribute AIDS drugs — which are highly effective ways of helping poor people who are alive today rather than poor people who will be alive in 100 years....

Provisional Conclusions

.... [I]f the United States does spend a great deal on emissions reductions as part of an international agreement, and if the agreement does give particular help to disadvantaged people, considerations of distributive justice support its action even if better redistributive mechanisms are imaginable. As compared to the status quo, or to an agreement that requires all nations to freeze their emissions at existing levels, it is better, from the standpoint of distributive justice, for the United States to join an agreement in which it agrees to provide technological or financial assistance to poor nations, and it may even be better, from that standpoint, to scale back emissions more than domestic self-interest would dictate. We cannot exclude the possibility that desirable redistribution is more likely to occur through climate change policy than otherwise, or to be accomplished more effectively through climate policy than through direct foreign aid.

Our only claims are that the aggressive emissions reductions on the part of the United States are not an especially effective method for transferring resources from wealthy people to poor people, and that if this is the goal, many alternative policies would probably be better....

Corrective Justice

Climate change differs from our asteroid example in another way. In the asteroid example, no one can be blamed for the appearance of the asteroid and the threat that it poses to India (or the world). But many people believe that by virtue of its past actions and policies, the United States, along with other developed nations, is particularly to blame for the problem of climate change....

The Basic Argument

Corrective justice arguments are backward-looking, focused on wrongful behavior that occurred in the past. Corrective justice therefore requires us to look at stocks rather than flows. Even though China is now the world's leading greenhouse gas emitter, the United States has been the largest emitter historically, and thus has the greatest responsibility for the stock of greenhouse gases in the atmosphere.... The emphasis on the United States is warranted by the fact that the United States has contributed more to the existing stock than any other nation (nearly 30 percent)....

CUMULATIVE EMISSIONS (1850–2003)

	CO_2	Rank	Share
United States	318740	1	29%
China	85314	4	8%
European Union	286764	2	26%
Russia	88302	3	8%
Japan	45198	7	4%
India	24347	9	2%
Germany	78499	5	7%
United Kingdom	67348	6	6%
Canada	23378	11	2%
South Korea	8500	23	1%

[However,] the climate change problem poorly fits the corrective justice model, because the consequence of tort-like thinking would be to force many people who have not acted wrongfully to provide a remedy to many people who have not been victimized....

The Wrongdoer Identity Problem

The current stock of greenhouse gases in the atmosphere is a result of the behavior of people [many of whom are no longer alive]. The basic problem for corrective justice is that dead wrongdoers cannot be punished or held responsible for their behavior, or forced to compensate those they have harmed. At first glance, holding Americans today responsible for the activities of their ancestors is not fair or reasonable on corrective justice grounds, because current Americans are not the relevant wrongdoers....

The most natural and best response to this point is insist that all or most Americans today benefit from the greenhouse gas-emitting activities of Americans living in the past, and therefore it would not be wrong to require Americans today to pay for abatement measures.... To the extent that members of current generations have gained from past wrongdoing, it may well make sense to ask them to make compensation to those harmed as a result....

In the context of climate however, this argument runs into serious problems. The most obvious difficulty is empirical. It is true that many Americans benefit from past greenhouse-gas-emissions, but how many benefit, and how much do they benefit? Many Americans today are, of course, immigrants or children of immigrants, and so not the descendants of greenhouse-gas-emitting Americans of the past. Such people may nonetheless gain from past emissions, because they enjoy the kind of technological advance and material wealth that those emissions made possible. But have they actually benefited, and to what degree? Further, not all Americans inherit the wealth of their ancestors, and even those who do would not necessarily have inherited less if their ancestors' generations had not engaged in the greenhouse gas-emitting activities. The idea of corrective justice, building on the tort analogy, does not seem to fit the climate change situation.

Suppose that these various obstacles could be overcome and that we could trace, with sufficient accuracy, the extent to which current Americans have benefited from past emissions. As long as the costs are being toted up, the benefits should be as well, and used to offset the requirements of corrective justice.... [C]limate change is itself anticipated to produce benefits for many nations, both by increasing agricultural productivity and by reducing extremes of cold. And if past generations of Americans have imposed costs on the rest of the world, they have also conferred substantial benefits....

Rough Justice

However appealing, corrective justice intuitions turn out to be a poor fit with the climate change problem—where the dispute is between nations, and where an extremely long period of time must elapse before the activity in question generates a harm. This is not to deny that a corrective justice argument can be cobbled together and presented as the basis of a kind of rough justice in an imperfect world. Perhaps the argument, while crude, is good enough to provide a factor in allocating the burdens of emissions reductions. Unfortunately, even that conclusion would rely on notions of collective responsibility that are not easy to defend. Most of the attractiveness of the corrective justice argument derives, we suspect, from suppressed redistributive and welfarist assumptions, or from collectivist habits of thinking that do not survive scrutiny.

It is sometimes argued that because people take pride in the accomplishments of their nation, they should also take responsibility for its failures. Americans who take pride in their country's contributions to prosperity and freedom should also take responsibility for its contributions to global warming. This argument, however, is especially weak. Many people are proud that they are attractive or intelligent, or can trace their ancestry to the Mayflower, or live in a city with a winning baseball team, but nothing about these psychological facts implies moral obligations of any sort. A person who is proud to be American, and in this way derives welfare from her association with other Americans who have accomplished great things, perhaps should be (and is) less proud than she would be if she were not also associated with Americans who have done bad things. She does not have any moral obligation, deriving from her patriotic pride, to set aright what other Americans have done wrong....

* * *

Daniel A. Farber, The Case for Climate Compensation: Justice for Climate Change Victims in a Complex World
2008 Utah Law Review 377 (2008)

.... [T]wo of the nation's leading legal scholars, Eric Posner and Cass Sunstein, have recently questioned whether corrective justice or distributive justice have any relevance to climate change policy....

Collective Responsibility Versus Purely Individual Fault

Posner and Sunstein argue that "[h]olding Americans today responsible for the activities of their ancestors is not fair or reasonable on corrective justice grounds, at least not unless contemporary Americans can be said to have benefited from the actions of their ancestors." ...

Although many of the relevant actors may indeed be long dead, the contribution of living Americans to the problem should not be underestimated. Consider the following table:

U.S. CO2 EMISSIONS SUMMARY

Time Period of Emissions	Amount	Percentage of Total U.S. Emissions
Emitted After 1950 (1950–2004)	63,714,360	72.5%
Emitted After 1970 (1970–2004)	47,042,052	53.5%
Emitted After 1990 (1990–2004)	22,434,137	25.5%
Total Emissions (1800–2004)	87,855,374	100%

As the Table 2 indicates, seventy-six percent of all U.S. emissions took place after 1950, fifty-three percent after 1970, and twenty-five percent after 1990.

A large number of living Americans were alive during these time periods. Indeed ... about ten percent of all the emissions in U.S. history came from 2000–2004, a period when all current Americans above kindergarten age were alive....

Thus, to think of harmful emissions as only a historical phenomenon, unconnected with the lives of current-day Americans, is clearly mistaken. Roughly one-quarter of Americans were alive during the entire post-1950 period in which three-quarters of the emissions took place.... Eighty percent of Americans were alive during the more recent (post-1990) period in which the dangers of global warming were already acknowledged, when roughly a quarter of the emissions took place....

Posner and Sunstein contended that the corrective justice model is a poor fit for climate change "because the consequence of tort-like thinking would be to force many people who have not acted wrongfully to provide a remedy to many people who have not been victimized." ... In particular, those who are "currently injured would gain absolutely nothing from reduced American emissions," which would have an effect only in the future....

[T]he objection is overdrawn in two ways. First, it goes more to the form of compensation than its desirability.... And second, it greatly exaggerates both the need for precision in matching victims and compensators and the degree to which compensation would impose burdens on wholly innocent parties....

In a classic tort situation—say an automobile accident—the victim and injurer are clearly identified, and we can guarantee that compensation will flow only from the culpable party to the injured one. If this sort of precision in matching individual wrong doing with individual harm is necessary to support a moral case for compensatory measures, climate change is indeed a poor candidate for corrective justice. But we should hesitate before we accept the demands for such a high level of precision. We live in a much more complex world where harms lack the simplicity of [torts such as] automobile collisions [in which the victim and injurer are clearly identified]. If we demand a high level of precision to establish a moral claim, we also render morality irrelevant to the most serious harms created by modern society.

Perhaps a nineteenth century court would have required precise matching as a basis for finding liability. But there seems to be no reason why our concepts of justice should remain stuck in the nineteenth century. Nor is it clear why our sense of our own moral accountability should be subject to the same limitations as a court's finding of legal liability....

In moral terms, the more serious question seems to be the extent of responsibility for causing climate change. This requires an assessment of how Americans have contributed to climate change through excessive emissions of CO_2 and [how] they have benefited from their failure to address the issues.... [B]y excessive, I mean that the emissions causing activity resulted in greater harm than benefit to global social welfare....

The short-run benefits received by many Americans of ignoring climate change are clear. As consumers, millions of Americans have had the benefit of cheap gasoline and low mileage standards.... They obtain electrical power from cheap coal rather than more expensive renewable sources. In the meantime, major American corporations have profited ... [as have] Americans who own stock in these corporations.... [T]hese benefits were derived from actions that a reasonable person knew or should have known were harmful to others (at least since 1990).... This does not seem to be a difficult case in which to apply the concept of unjust enrichment.

It is also relevant that Americans had the capacity to limit these harms, not only as consumers but also as citizens. The United States government has stood virtually alone among industrialized countries in opposing serious action on climate change. In a democracy, voters must bear some of the responsibility for the actions of their governments.... Moreover, as citizens, they were engaged in a collective activity of governance from which they hoped to benefit and on average did receive substantial benefits such as protection from foreign threats. Holding citizens responsible for their pro rata share is not unreasonable....

In an ideal world, we could fashion a remedy that was responsive to differences in individual responsibility.... [However,] the mechanisms [for individualized remedies such as retroactive taxes for past owners of gas guzzlers] are probably outside the range of political possibility.... In the real world, we have to be content with a degree of mismatch.

In assessing the seriousness of the mismatch, we have to consider the magnitude of the burden that climate compensation would place on individual Americans.... A practical system of compensation ... is likely to translate into a [] modest per capita expenditure.... "Innocent" members of the group are included in the compensation scheme ... because the injustice to them (of having to pay a small amount of compensation that they do not really owe) is smaller than the injustice to victims if no compensation is paid....

[A]ccountability at the individual level is most relevant in terms of compensation. The question of individual accountability is less relevant to whether the United States has a moral duty to reduce its future emissions if doing so is in the interest of the rest of the world.... The burden of reducing future emissions falls in the first instance on those who are responsible for the emissions rather than potentially "innocent" third-parties. Thus, the collective responsibility issue is essentially irrelevant to the question of whether the United States has a duty to reduce future emissions. It is only relevant as a second-order consideration regarding whether the United States should bear a higher cost than it would otherwise for reducing future emissions because of its contribution to past emissions. Regardless of past emissions, however, if the United States is emitting excessive emissions now, it has a duty to reduce those emissions....

Is Wealth Relevant?

[Posner and Sunstein] treat[] the harms of climate change on poor countries as a problem for which the United States bears no moral responsibility. Rather, we would be acting as good Samaritans, trying to increase global welfare and along with it the welfare of poor countries.

One fundamental question is whether controlling greenhouse gases should be considered a "redistributive mechanism." It can only be considered redistributive if unrestricted emission—and therefore, unlimited climate change—is considered to be the baseline. Compared to this baseline of unrestricted emissions, restricting emissions makes poor countries better off and costs rich countries money, so it can be considered a redistribution of wealth. If, instead, we consider the baseline to be a world in which climate is stable, then the shoe is on the other foot. Starting with that baseline, we would say that the United States and other wealthy emitters are redistributing income to themselves at the expense of poor countries by their on-going damage to the planetary climate system. If we start with this baseline, reducing emissions is not a redistribution of income; it merely leaves the distribution of income where it would be in the baseline state. The question, in other words, is whether we should think of pollution as a right—so that limitations on polluters are seen a redistribution of wealth to their victims—or whether we should view freedom from pollution as a right, which would imply that the polluters are unjustly prospering at the expense of others.

Another weakness of the position taken by climate justice skeptics is that it compares emissions reductions with "imaginable" redistributive mechanisms without any real effort to specify these alternatives, except for large cash transfers to foreign governments. Climate justice skeptics have made no effort to establish the effectiveness of such large cash transfers in combating poverty, or for that matter, to show that they are politically feasible. The merits of this approach are certainly not obvious. It is not at all clear that the governments of the poorest countries have the institutional capacity to spend the unrestricted funds effectively....

It seems fairly clear ... that Americans—not just our ancestors but ourselves—are responsible for a disproportionate amount of greenhouse gases and that we have benefited, at least in the short run, from uncontrolled greenhouse emissions that have enabled our energy-intensive lifestyle and corporate profits; that these gases are causing harm, particularly to the poorest and most vulnerable segments of the global population; and that we have failed to take reasonable measures to limit our emissions.... [T]hese facts form an adequate basis to hold ourselves morally accountable for some share of the harm caused by climate change.... It is no excuse that such a system would be expensive or imperfect. Even more clearly ... we have a moral obligation to limit future emissions, not merely in our own benefit ... but also because of a moral duty to refrain from causing unreasonable harm to others.... Contrary to the views of commentators such as Posner and Sunstein, climate justice is an imperative, not a quixotic quest for a delusive quarry.

* * *

Notes and Questions

1. Wrongdoer identity. Professors Posner and Sunstein argue that it is unfair to hold current Americans responsible for the greenhouse gas emissions of prior generations. Professor Farber contests this supposition, showing that a large number of Americans were alive when a large share of U.S. emissions occurred. Which position do you find more persuasive? Even if they had not been alive during these periods, did individuals in industrialized countries personally gain from the past activities of their countries?

2. Professor Farber also maintains that the close matching of responsibility with liability that Professors Posner and Sunstein insist on is unduly narrow when fashioning international climate policy. What do you think of this response? How "rough" can rough justice be in this context? At some point, it there a case for a closer matching of responsibility and liability, and if so, what is that point?

3. Professors Posner and Sunstein suggest that some individuals and countries will realize ecological benefits from climate change. While true to some extent, these gains are likely to occur largely in northern, developed countries, and also only in the relatively near term future. Thus, while warmer winters could reduce the number of deaths from exposure to extreme cold, particularly in parts of Europe, "on balance it appears very probable that risks to human health will increase" from increased heat waves, increased flooding, the spread of infectious diseases and other climate-induced impacts. Michael E. Mann & Lee R. Kump, Dire Predictions: Understanding Global Warming — The Illustrated Guide to the Findings of the IPPC 137 (2008). Likewise, while in the short term agricultural productivity in the U.S., Canada, and Europe will result from moderate levels of global warming, many tropical and subtropical nations — already struggling to meet food demands — will see agricultural productivity decline. And the temperature increases predicted for the late 21st century will likely have negative agricultural impacts throughout the world. *Id.* at 130–31.

4. Professors Posner and Sunstein also assert that future generations are likely to be much richer than current ones. Do you agree with this assumption? If it is incorrect, how does it affect their argument?

An alternative approach for dividing up global responsibility is presented in the excerpt below.

Paul Baer, Tom Athanasiou, Sivan Kartha, & Eric Kemp-Benedict, The Greenhouse Rights Development Framework: The Right to Development in a Climate Constrained World

Published by the Heinrich Böll Foundation, Christian Aid, EcoEquity and the Stockholm Environment Institute (2d ed. Nov. 2008)

A warming of 2°C over pre-industrial temperatures has been widely endorsed as the maximum that can be tolerated or even managed.... [T]he 2°C line can indeed be held, but ... doing so demands a sharp break with politics as usual.... [S]ince carbon-based growth is no longer a viable option in either the North or the South, we set out to assess the problem of rapid decarbonization in a world sharply polarized between North and South and, on both sides, between rich and poor....

[E]ven if [northern countries] undertake bold efforts to virtually eliminate their emissions by 2050 ... [an] alarmingly small size of the carbon budget ... would remain to support the South's development.... In fact, developing-country emissions would ... have to peak ... before 2020 and then decline by nearly six percent annually through 2050. This would have to take place while most of the South's citizens were still struggling in poverty and desperately seeking a significant improvement in their living standards.

It is this last point that makes the climate challenge so daunting. For the only proven routes to development—to water and food security, improved health care and education, and secure livelihoods—involve expanding access to energy services, and, given today's inadequate, expensive, low-carbon energy systems, and the South's limited ability to afford them, these routes inevitably threaten an increase in fossil fuel use and thus carbon emissions. From the South's perspective, this pits development squarely against climate protection....

Despite progress at the margins, the climate negotiations are moving far, far too slowly. It is unlikely that we will be able to act, decisively and on the necessary scale, until we openly face the big question: What kind of a climate regime can allow us to bring global emissions rapidly under control, even while the developing world vastly scales up energy services in its ongoing fight against endemic poverty and for human development?

The Development Threshold

Development is more than freedom from poverty. The real issue is a path beyond poverty to dignified, sustainable ways of life, and the right to such development must be acknowledged and protected by any climate regime that hopes for even a chance of success. The bottom line in this very complicated tale is that the South is neither willing nor able to prioritize rapid emission reductions over development—not while it must also seek an acceptable level of improvement in the lives of its people—and that the key to climate protection is the establishment of a global climate policy framework in which it is not required to do so.

The Greenhouse Development Rights framework (GDRs) is, accordingly, designed to protect the right to sustainable human development, even as it drives rapid global emission reductions. It proceeds in the only possible way, by operationalizing the official principles of the UN's Framework Convention on Climate Change, according to which states commit themselves to "protect the climate system ... on the basis of equity and in accordance with their common but differentiated responsibilities and respective capabilities."

As a first step, the GDRs framework codifies the right to development as a "development threshold"—a level of welfare below which people are not expected to share the costs of the climate transition. This threshold ... is emphatically not an "extreme poverty" line, which is typically defined to be so low ($1 or $2 a day) as to be more properly called a "destitution line." Rather, it is set to be higher than the "global poverty line," to reflect a level of welfare that is beyond basic needs but well short of today's levels of "affluent" consumption.

People below this threshold are taken as having development as their proper priority. As they struggle for better lives, they are not similarly obligated to labor to keep society as a whole within its sharply limited global carbon budget. In any event, they have little responsibility for the climate problem (the approximately 70 percent of the population that lives below the development threshold is responsible for only about 15 percent of all cumulative emissions) and little capacity to invest in solving it. People above the threshold, on the other hand, are taken as having realized their right to development and as bearing the responsibility to preserve that right for others. They must, as their incomes rise, gradually assume a greater faction of the costs of curbing the emissions associated with their own consumption, as well as the costs of ensuring that, as those below the threshold rise toward and then above it, they are able to do so along sustainable, low-emission paths. Moreover, and critically, these obligations are taken to belong to all those above the development threshold, whether they happen to live in the North or in the South.

The level where a development threshold would best be set is clearly a matter for debate. We argue that it should be at least modestly higher than a global poverty line, which is itself about $16 per day per person (PPP [purchasing power parity] adjusted). This figure derives from an empirical analysis of the income levels at which the classic plagues of poverty—malnutrition, high infant mortality, low educational attainment, high relative food expenditures—begin to disappear, or at least become exceptions to the rule. So, taking a figure 25 percent above this global poverty line, we do our "indicative" calculations relative to a development threshold of $20 per person per day ($7,500 per person per year). This income also reflects the level at which the southern "middle class" begins to emerge.

National Obligations and the "Responsibility Capacity Index"

Once a development threshold has been defined, logical and usefully precise definitions of capacity and responsibility follow, and these can then be used to calculate the fraction of the global climate burden that should fall to any given country....

Capacity—by which we mean income not demanded by the necessities of daily life, and thus available to be "taxed" for investment in climate mitigation and adaptation—can be straight-forwardly interpreted as total income, excluding income below the development threshold. This is illustrated in figure ES2, which shows the development threshold (a horizontal line at $7,500) as it crosses the national income distribution lines and splits their populations into a poorer portion (to the left) and a wealthier portion (to the right). This crossing makes it easy to compare both the heights of wealth and the depths of poverty in different countries, and also graphically conveys each country's capacity [the darker shaded area], which we define as the income that the wealthier portion of the population has above the development threshold.

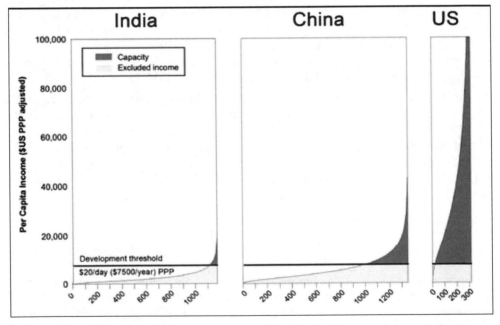

Figure ES2: Capacity: income above the development threshold. These curves approximate income distributions within India, China, and the United States. Thus, the [darker] areas represent national incomes above the ($20 per person per day, or PPP) development threshold—our definition of national capacity. Chart widths are scaled to population, so these capacity areas are correctly sized in relation to each other. Based on projected 2010 data.

A nation's aggregate capacity, then, is defined as the sum of all individual income, excluding income below the threshold. Responsibility, by which we mean contribution to the climate problem, is similarly defined as cumulative emissions since 1990, excluding emissions that correspond to consumption below the development threshold. Such emissions, like income below the development threshold, do not contribute to a country's obligation to act to address the climate problem.

Thus, both capacity and responsibility are defined in individual terms, and in a manner that takes explicit account of the unequal distribution of income within countries. This is a critical and long-overdue move, because the usual practice of relying on national per-capita averages fails to capture either the true depth of a country's developmental need or the actual extent of its wealth. If one looks only as far as a national average, then the richer, higher-emitting minority lies hidden behind the poorer, lower-emitting majority.

These measures of capacity and responsibility can then be straightforwardly combined into a single indicator of obligation, in a "Responsibility Capacity Index" (RCI). This calculation is done … based on country-specific income, income distribution, and emissions data. The precise numerical results depend, of course, on the particular values chosen for key parameters, such as the year in which national emissions begin to count toward responsibility (we use 1990, but a different starting date can certainly be defended) and, especially, the development threshold, which defines the overall "progressivity" of the system. The results also evolve over time—as the following table [see p. 416] shows, the global balance of obligation in 2020, or 2030, can be expected to differ considerably from that which exists today.…

Looking at just the 2010 numbers … the United States, with its exceptionally large share of the global population of people with incomes above—and generally far above—the $20-per-day development threshold (capacity), as well as the world's largest share of cumulative emissions since 1990 (responsibility), is the nation with the largest share (33.1 percent) of the global RCI. The European Union follows with a 25.7 percent share; China, despite being relatively poor, is large enough to have a rather significant 5.5 percent share, which puts it even with the much smaller but much richer country of Germany; India, also large but much poorer, falls far behind China with a mere 0.5 percent share of the global RCI.

As the table shows, the global balance of obligation changes over time, as differing rates of national growth change the global income structure. The results are most obvious, and startling, in the projected change in China's share of the total RCI, which—reflecting its extremely rapid growth and the increasing number of Chinese people who are projected to enjoy incomes above the development threshold—nearly triples (from 5.5 percent to 15.3 percent) in the two decades from 2010 to 2030.…

Note that in this indicative calculation, we have made the rather conservative assumption that all income (and all emissions) above the development threshold count equally toward the calculation of an individual's RCI. This amounts to a "flat tax" on capacity and responsibility. However, it might be more consistent with widely shared notions of fairness for RCI to be defined in a more "progressive" manner. That is, an individual's millionth dollar of income might contribute more to their RCI than their ten-thousandth dollar of income. A more progressive formulation of RCI would shift more of the global obligation to wealthy individuals and wealthy countries.…

GDRs results for representative countries and groups						
	2010					2020	2030
	Population (percent of global)	GDP per capita ($ US PPP)	Capacity (percent of global)	Responsibility (percent of global)	RCI (percent of global)	RCI (percent of global)	RCI (percent of global)
EU 27	7.3	30,472	28.8	22.6	25.7	22.9	19.6
EU 15	5.8	33,754	26.1	19.8	22.9	19.9	16.7
EU +12	1.5	17,708	2.7	2.8	2.7	3.0	3.0
United States	4.5	45,640	29.7	36.4	33.1	29.1	25.5
Japan	1.9	33,422	8.3	7.3	7.8	6.6	5.5
Russia	2.0	15,031	2.7	4.9	3.8	4.3	4.6
China	19.7	5,899	5.8	5.2	5.5	10.4	15.2
India	17.2	2,818	0.7	0.3	0.5	1.2	2.3
Brazil	2.9	9,442	2.3	1.1	1.7	1.7	1.7
South Africa	0.7	10,117	0.6	1.3	1.0	1.1	1.2
Mexico	1.6	12,408	1.8	1.4	1.6	1.5	1.5
LDCs	11.7	1,274	0.1	0.04	0.1	0.1	0.1
Annex I	18.7	30,924	75.8	78.0	77	69	61
Non-Annex I	81.3	5,096	24.2	22.0	23	31	39
High-income	15.5	36,488	76.9	77.9	77	69	61
Middle-income	63.3	6,226	22.9	21.9	22	30	38
Low-income	21.2	1,599	0.2	0.2	0.2	0.3	0.5
World	100	9,929	100%	100%	100%	100%	100%

Table ES1: Percentage shares of total global population, GDP, capacity, responsibility, and RCI for selected countries and groups of countries. Based on projected emissions and income for 2010, 2020, and 2030. (High-, Middle-, and Low-income Country categories are based on World Bank definitions as of 2006. Projections based on International Energy Agency World Energy Outlook 2007.)

[T]he GDRs framework ... would be a real game changer. For one thing, it would allow us to objectively and quantitatively estimate national obligations to bear the efforts of climate protection (obligations to support adaptation as well as obligations to mitigate) and to meaningfully compare obligations even between wealthy and developing countries....

Admittedly, this will be seen as a dangerous idea.... But it is also a liberating idea. It defines and quantifies national obligations in a way that explicitly safeguards a meaningful right to development....

Toward a New Political Realism

[T]he GDRs approach ... stresses the need for a system in which it is not "the North," but rather the affluent and consuming classes worldwide that bear the efforts of the climate transition.

This reframing is not merely ethical.... To be blunt, it is extremely unlikely that the working consensus needed in the North—a consensus to pay its "fair share" of the world's total mitigation and adaptation costs—could ever emerge if the wealthy minority in India and China and other developing nations are not also paying their fair shares. The GDRs framework is, above all else, an effort to transparently specify what those "fair shares" would be, and to do so in a manner that acknowledges and respects a meaningful right to development....

* * *

Notes and Questions

1. What do you think of the GDRs concept? Another proposed framework for reducing GHG emissions, developed by the Global Commons Institute, is that of "Contraction and Convergence." This approach calls for reducing worldwide GHG emissions to a safe level (contraction) and having this global GHG budget distributed so that over time per capita emissions for all countries are equalized (convergence). Is this a more desirable solution?

2. More generally, how would you devise an international climate change regime? What principles should govern? Do you agree with developing countries that they should not have the same CO_2 reduction burden, in part because historically their contribution to the CO_2 loading was not as great as developing countries? Or do you agree with developed countries that because of the existing imperative to reduce global warming, all countries should work to reduce CO_2 regardless of what happened historically? Historical contributions aside, should a country's relative financial capacity to reduce CO_2 emissions, in light of its level of development, be taken into consideration?

E. The Food vs. Fuels Debate

One suggested response to climate change that has received considerable attention is increasing the use of biofuels—fuels made from plant materials—as an alternative to fossil fuels. The argument for biofuels (also called agrofuels) is that they have the potential to reduce greenhouse gas emissions because the carbon dioxide released from burning them can, in theory, be offset by the carbon dioxide absorbed by the crops grown to make the fuel. (This is in contrast to fossil fuels, which release carbon that has been stored for millions of years under the earth's surface.) Both the U.S. and the European Union have sought especially to promote biofuels for transportation in recent years, spurred as much if not more by concerns about energy independence and rising fuel prices as a desire to reduce greenhouse gas emissions. In the U.S., the primary focus to date has been on promoting ethanol, particularly corn-based ethanol. Congress in the 2005 and 2007 energy laws set ambitious targets for the production of "renewable fuel": 4 billion gallons by 2006; 15.2 billion by 2012; and 36 billion gallons by 2022. In 2007, the European Union adopted a ten percent biofuels mandate for transportation fuels by 2020, although more recently the implementation schedule has been pushed back.

These mandates will require large-scale production of biofuels crops which cannot be wholly accomplished in the industrialized countries. For example, even "if 100 percent of the 2006 (record) corn crop of 10.5 billion bushels were used for ethanol, [the U.S.] would get a bit over 28 billion gallons of fuel (assuming conversion was at an efficient level), which is only about 75 percent of the 2022 mandate." Peter Z. Grossman, *If Ethanol Is The Answer, What Is The Question?* 13 Drake J. Agric. L. 149, 165 (2008). To meet a ten percent biofuels mandate, Europe would have to convert seventy percent of its arable land to biofuel crops.

The scale of proposed biofuel production has global environmental justice implications because of the potential impacts on food prices and land use in the developing world, as the report below explains.

The Right to Food,
Interim Report of the Special Rapporteur Jean Ziegler
United Nations General Assembly, Sixty-second session, Item 72(b)
of the provisional agenda A/62/289 (August 22, 2007)

[Although the world can produce enough food to feed twice the entire global population, an estimated] 854 million people ... do not get enough to eat every day. Every
year, more than six million children still die from hunger-related illness before their fifth
birthday.... Rushing to turn food crops—maize, wheat, sugar, palm oil—into fuel for
cars, without first examining the impact on global hunger is a recipe for disaster. It is estimated that to fill one car tank with biofuel (about 50 litres) would require about 200 kg
of maize—enough to feed one person for one year.

Agrofuel

The two main types of agrofuel are bioethanol and biodiesel. Both are produced from
a variety of food crops [which can be converted directly into energy and can be used as
transport fuel]. Bioethanol is produced from sweet and starchy crops, which can be fer-
mented to produce alcohol—mostly sugar cane and maize, but also sugar beet, pota-
toes, wheat or even manioc (the staple food of many African nations). Biodiesel is
produced from vegetable oils by reaction of the oil with methanol. The oils used are
mostly from soya, palm or rapeseed, but also from peanuts, coconuts and many other
oil-rich plants....

Global production of agrofuels is currently dominated by one continent (the Amer-
icas) and one type of fuel (bioethanol). This bioethanol is produced mostly from maize
(in the United States) or sugar cane (in Brazil). The United States has doubled its production of bioethanol over the past five years and has now overtaken Brazil as the dominant producer. Brazil, which produced over 12 million tons of ethanol in 2006, much
of it for the domestic market, plans to become a dominant producer for the global market by 2025. By contrast, Europe's production of ethanol, at 3.5 million tons, is still relatively low....

Global consumption of agrofuels is low, but will rise rapidly under targets set in the
European Union, the United States and Latin America.... [T]he industrialized countries
of the North are very interested in the production of the countries of the southern hemi-
sphere to meet these needs.

The Impact of Biofuels on the Right to Food

Increasing the production of biofuels could bring positive benefits for climate change
and for farmers in developing countries, including by improving food security, if the benefits trickle down. However, it is also important to examine the potential of biofuels to
threaten the realization of the right to food.... The greatest risk is that dependence on the
agro-industrial model of production will fail to benefit poor peasant farmers and will
generate violations of the right to food.

Increasing Food Prices

The prices of basic staple foods are likely to increase, threatening economic access to
sufficient food, particularly for the poorest who already spend a high proportion of their
incomes on food. It is estimated that there could be a rise of 20 per cent in the international price of maize between now and 2010, and 41 per cent by 2020. The prices of vegetable oil crops, especially soya and sunflower seeds could increase by 26 per cent by 2010
and 76 per cent by 2020, and wheat prices could increase by 11 per cent and then by 30

per cent. In the poorest regions of sub-Saharan Africa, Asia and Latin America, the price of manioc could rise by 33 per cent and up to 135 per cent by 2020.... [T]his will set up a battle of "food versus fuel", unless there are urgent investments in moving to the second generation of biofuels that will not depend so much on food products. The consequences of such a rapid increase in food prices would be grave.... [T]he number of people suffering from undernourishment would increase by 16 million people for each percentage point increase in the real price of staple food. This could mean that 1.2 billion people would be suffering from hunger by 2025....

Although increasing food prices should theoretically benefit millions of people working as peasant farmers in developing countries, this is not always the case. Many farming families are net buyers of staple foods, as they do not have enough land to be self-sufficient, and will therefore be affected by rising consumer prices. In addition, prices received by farmers at the farm gate are often exploitatively low, particularly for remote farmers with little choice of whom to sell their crops to, and often do not reflect global prices because of the greed of intermediaries. If increased agricultural production is to benefit poor peasant farmers, it will be essential to build mechanisms, such as cooperatives and non-exploitative out-grower schemes[] that would ensure a trickle-down to the poorest.

Increasing Competition Over Land and Forests, and Forced Evictions

A rapid increase in the prices of food crops will intensify competition over land and other natural resources, including forest reserves. This will pit peasant farmers and indigenous communities of forest dwellers against massive agribusiness corporations and large investors who are already buying up large swathes of land or forcing peasants off their land. The Belgian human rights organization Human Rights Everywhere (HREV) has already documented forced evictions, the appropriation of land and other violations of human rights in the palm oil plantations in Colombia, documenting responsibilities of all the actors along the production chain.... [T]he more recent expansion of soya production across Latin America ... has contributed to the deforestation of vast swathes of the Amazonian basin and has resulted in the forcible eviction of many peasants and indigenous peoples from their lands....

Although promises are being made that the production of biofuels will provide more jobs, there are risks that, given competition over land with peasant farmers, biofuel production may result in greater unemployment. In Brazil, it is estimated that 100 hectares dedicated to family farming generate at least 35 jobs, while 100 hectares dedicated to industrial farming of sugar cane and oil palm plantations provide only 10 jobs, and of soybeans half a job.... Biofuels can, however, be produced by non-industrial family farming that provides more employment: in Brazil, 30 per cent of sugar cane production is in the hands of 60,000 small producers.

Increasing Prices and Scarcity of Water

The production of biofuels will require substantial amounts of water, diverting water away from the production of food crops.... Rising prices of water would limit access to water for the poorest communities, in ways that would negatively affect the right to food.

* * *

Notes and Questions

1. The price increases forecast by the Special Rapporteur arguably already have started. Worldwide food prices increased sharply beginning in 2006 and lasted through most of 2008 (when they began declining). By February 2007, for example, the price of tortillas in Mexico had increased by over 400% from the previous year, causing tens

of thousands of people to march on Mexico City in protest. By June of that same year, protests over rising food prices had broken out in countries across the world. In 2008 the World Bank reported that food prices had risen 75% since 2000 and attributed 65% of the escalation to increased demand for biofuels. World Bank, Data & Research, High Food Prices—A Harsh New Reality, February 29, 2008. Others conclude that the impact of biofuels has been less significant and that other factors such as rising oil prices, increased worldwide demand for meat, and drought are more to blame.

2. As noted above, the growing biofuels market and higher agricultural prices could generate important economic benefits in poorer nations. "As such, biofuels may offer an opportunity for developing countries—where seventy-five percent of the world's poor depend on agriculture for their livelihoods—to harness agricultural growth for broader rural development and poverty reduction." UNITED NATIONS FOOD AND AGRICULTURE ORGANISATION, THE STATE OF FOOD AND AGRICULTURE 2008—BIOFUELS: PROSPECTS, RISKS AND OPPORTUNITIES 5–6 (2008). In your view, do these potential benefits compensate for the potentially adverse impacts of increased competition for food and land from biofuels production?

3. Criticism about biofuels has intensified as research suggests that biofuels may provide far less reduction in GHG emissions than initially believed, once emissions generated through the life cycle of the fuel, including growing, harvesting, and processing it, are factored into the equation. Corn-based ethanol produced in the U.S., for example, may rely on corn grown with energy-intensive methods and may be manufactured using coal (the most GHG-intensive fossil fuel) as an energy source. In 2008, two important studies concluded that biofuels production actually results in *greater* GHG emissions than manufacturing conventional fuels, once the indirect land use impacts of producing biofuels are considered. *See* Elisabeth Rosenthal, *Studies Call Biofuels a Greenhouse Threat*, N.Y. TIMES, Feb. 8, 2008 at A9. As explained by the late Professor Alex Farrell,

> The reason is that the way we make biofuels today increases the global demand for land and accelerates the clearance of wilderness for new farms. For example, if a farmer in the U.S. shifts from a corn/soybean rotation to continuous corn in order to supply a new ethanol facility, U.S. exports of soybeans go down. This causes the global price of soybeans to go up slightly, and farmers worldwide will find it profitable to clear a little more land to grow soybeans. Of course, population growth and greater meat consumption are also causing land clearance for new farmland, but increasing production of biofuels accelerates the process. Unfortunately, farmland expansion today often means clearing rainforest: burning the trees, releasing carbon dioxide from the soil into the atmosphere, and losing biodiversity.

Alexander E. Farrell, *Better Biofuels Before More Biofuels*, S.F. CHRONICLE, Feb. 13, 2008 at B9. For two critical assessments of biofuels, for both their limited impact on reducing greenhouse gases and their adverse effects on food prices, *see* UNITED NATIONS FOOD AND AGRICULTURE ORGANISATION, THE STATE OF FOOD AND AGRICULTURE 2008—BIOFUELS: PROSPECTS, RISKS AND OPPORTUNITIES (2008), and ORGANISATION FOR ECONOMIC CO-OPERATION AND DEVELOPMENT, BIOFUEL SUPPORT POLICIES: AN ECONOMIC ASSESSMENT (2008).

4. So called "second-generation" or cellulosic biofuels are produced from wood, grasses, or the leaves, stems, stalks, and other non-edible parts of plants. These biofuels can reduce competition for land and food because a much wider variety of feedstocks can be used as inputs, and because some of these crops can be grown on degraded soils where food crop production is not optimal. Cellulosic biofuels also can reduce life cycle GHG

emissions much more significantly than first generation biofuels because they generate higher energy yields (since the entire crop can be used), and because they can use left over parts of the plant as energy to process the fuels (as opposed to first generation biofuels which often use fossil fuels for processing). *See* BIOFUELS: PROSPECTS, RISKS AND OPPORTUNI-TIES, *supra*, at 18–19. While there are some demonstration plants making cellulosic bio-fuels, to date such biofuels only have been produced on a very small scale commercially. Should the U.S. proceed with expansion of first generation biofuels in order to create the necessary infrastructure—processing plants, distribution networks, etc.—for cellulosic-based fuels in the future? Or should we wait another five to ten years until cellulosic bio-fuels are more commercially viable to push forward? Overall, what do you think our policy toward biofuels should be?

5. As discussed above, biofuels expansion has been promoted as much for biofuels' other attributes, such as increasing energy independence and reducing fuel prices, as for their greenhouse gas benefits. In the next section, we turn to efforts by the U.S. to sys-tematically control GHG emissions.

F. Climate Justice in the Domestic Context

As of early 2009, efforts to adopt federal climate legislation had been unsuccessful, re-sisted by former President George W. Bush as well as majorities in Congress. This dy-namic is very likely to change in the near future, however, under an Obama Administration and with sizeable Democratic majorities in both the House and Senate. The centerpiece of virtually all federal climate bills has been, and is likely to continue to be, a cap-and-trade scheme for greenhouse gases, explored in the section below.

1. The Debate About Cap-and-Trade

As discussed in Chapter 7, the U.S. in the 1990s began adopting trading programs, es-pecially for air pollutants, most notably the acid rain program and the RECLAIM program in southern California. These programs addressed regional, or in the case of acid rain, national pollution problems. The underlying rationale is that the costs of controlling emis-sions vary among firms, and that a system allowing firms to reallocate emission allowances among themselves through trading will result in a more efficient overall outcome and, proponents claim, stimulate more innovation in control techniques. (*See* Chapter 7 for a critique of market based approaches to controlling pollutants that have a localized effect.) In the excerpt below, A. Denny Ellerman and his colleagues present the arguments in favor of using a similar type of emissions trading program to control greenhouse gases.

A. Denny Ellerman, Paul L. Joskow and David Harrison, Jr., Emissions Trading in the U.S.: Experience, Lessons, and Considerations for Greenhouse Gases
Pew Center on Global Climate Change (2003)

What special considerations might apply to the design of a program to address climate change? For climate change, the fundamental issue is the contribution that various emissions make to the greenhouse effect, which depends upon the atmospheric concentrations of the various greenhouse gases. Once emitted, greenhouse gases have long residence times in the atmosphere, usually measured in decades, centuries, and even millennia. Moreover, atmospheric currents ensure that emissions are dispersed quickly in the atmosphere, so that atmospheric concentrations of greenhouse gases are relatively uniform over the globe. In sum, emissions are uniformly mixed and long-lived, and the effects are cumulative and global.

Emissions trading seems especially well suited as part of a program to control greenhouse gas emissions.

The uniform mixing of GHG emissions in the atmosphere removes the chief concern limiting the scope of emissions trading in other applications and creates the opportunity to design trading programs without geographic limits defined by localized environmental impacts. Uniform mixing means that a ton of a given GHG will have the same effect on atmospheric concentration—and thus on climate change—regardless of whether the ton is emitted in California, New York, or elsewhere on the globe. Thus, trading can be national and international in scope, and the cost savings commensurately larger as the scope broadens. Moreover, the opportunities for cost savings through trading are greatest when the costs of control differ widely among sources. There is every reason to believe that the cost of reducing GHG emissions varies widely among sources and across countries. Accordingly, trading can provide the flexibility needed to allow GHG reductions to be achieved using the lowest-cost abatement options. Moreover, GHG emissions generally can be measured using relatively inexpensive methods (e.g., fuel consumption and emission factors), rather than the expensive continuous emissions monitoring required for some existing trading programs.

In addition, the cumulative effect of greenhouse gases and their long duration in the atmosphere means that the *timing* of emissions reductions within a control program will not have a significant effect on atmospheric concentrations and on climate. Thus, trading across time periods by banking offers still more potential for cost savings. [Banking allows sources to reduce emissions below their requirement in one year and bank the resulting "surplus" allowances for use or trade in future years. Eds.] And, as we have seen in other programs with phased-in emissions reduction requirements, which will almost certainly be the case for any GHG control program, banking can be a means of accelerating the required emission reductions.

A final feature that makes emissions trading particularly well-suited for a GHG control program, especially when it takes the form of a cap-and-trade program, is the incentive to take advantage of opportunities for less costly abatement that may lie outside the trading program. For a variety of reasons, ranging from concerns about measurement to varying political commitment, the least expensive abatement opportunities may lie outside the trading program. Examples would be domestic non-CO_2 GHG abatement possibilities (if the trading program initially focused on CO_2), the enhancement of forest and terrestrial sinks for CO_2, and reductions in developing countries that are not expected to accept GHG restrictions as soon or as demanding as those adopted by the relatively rich countries. Many issues must be dealt with in order to take advantage of these opportunities, but these difficulties can and should be addressed. The prerequisite, however, is an incentive to seek out opportunities for cheap abatement outside the cap. Although mechanisms could be devised to encourage cost-reducing abatement outside of the program under the emission tax or command-and-control approaches, these other approaches do not provide as exact and efficient an incentive for such abatement as does the emissions trading approach.

In sum, although the specific nature of domestic and global measures to address climate change will evolve over time, few environmental problems appear so well suited to emissions trading as GHG emissions control.

* * *

Professor Alice Kaswan acknowledges that a trading system could benefit environmental justice communities by lowering compliance costs to consumers and possibly facilitating greater GHG reduction goals than direct regulation. She also, however, raises a number of important concerns about such an approach.

Alice Kaswan, Environmental Justice and Domestic Climate Change Policy

38 Environmental Law Reporter News and Analysis 10287 (2008)

Carbon Trading and Distributive Justice

While CO[2] emissions do not raise direct distributive justice concerns, they implicate distributive justice because CO[2] emissions do not occur in a vacuum. The combustion that generates CO[2] also generates a range of harmful co-pollutants, including criteria pollutants like particulates, sulfur oxides, nitrogen oxides (NO[x]), ozone precursors, and carbon monoxide (CO), as well as a wide range of toxic pollutants, including many volatile organic compounds (VOC[s]), benzene, and other toxics.

The distribution of these co-pollutants in a trading system would, presumably, continue to be governed by the Clean Air Act's (CAA's) and the states' existing pollution control requirements. But, notwithstanding improvements in air quality, the existing regulatory structure has failed to achieve air quality goals. Climate change policy could have a significant environmental co-benefit: helping, to achieve the as-yet unattained goals of the CAA. Climate change policies will require changes to the same industrial processes that produce co-pollutants and, as a result, have the potential to not only reduce GHGs, but their more locally damaging co-pollutants as well. Depending upon their design, climate change policies could help prevent the creation of co-pollutant hot spots—hot spots that current law allows—as well as helping heavily polluted areas achieve air quality goals that have proven unattainable using current measures.

Policymakers have consistently emphasized the co-benefits of climate change regulation in justifying climate change policy, co-benefits that include not only co-pollutant reduction benefits, but greater energy security, benefits for local industries, and the potential economic benefits of new technology development. Given the centrality of carbon-emitting activities to almost every aspect of our industrial society, it is neither surprising nor inappropriate to implement climate change regulation so as to maximize its co-benefits, so long as GHG emission reductions are achieved.

The Hot Spots Problem

Market proponents and critics have talked past one another on the hot spot issue. Environmental justice advocates routinely critique market-based systems due to the risk of hot spots: the risk that, instead of reducing their emissions, one or more facilities could buy allowances that increase emissions above the existing status quo. In general, environmental justice advocates fear that the hot spots from trading could arise or be perpetuated in the poor communities of color which contain the nation's older, more polluting, facilities. Some market proponents dismiss the hot spot concern because CO[2] does not have adverse local effects. Environmental justice advocates then point to the risks presented by GHG co-pollutants and argue that if facilities can initiate or increase production by purchasing carbon allowances, then co-pollutant emissions are likely to increase. Market proponents respond that carbon trading would not lead to an increase in co-pollutants because existing co-pollutant permits would constrain them....

[A] cap-and-trade program would not, in most instances, directly cause co-pollutant hot spots. Nonetheless, because the existing regulatory system does not fully constrain hot spots, a GHG trading system would do less to control the existing risk than a regulatory approach that required all facilities to reduce GHGs. Even if the hot spot risk is generally caused by the existing regulatory system, not a GHG cap-and-trade system, a GHG-control program that can provide the co-benefit of reducing the existing hot spot risk is superior to one that does not.

Potential for Hot Spots of Regulated Co-Pollutants.

In a carbon trading system, many GHG co-pollutants would presumably continue to be controlled by existing permits and regulatory standards. Existing permits and standards do not, however, ensure that actual emissions will not increase. Existing permits will protect communities only to the extent that they are adequately enforced. If not adequately enforced, then allowance trading could lead to increases not authorized by existing permits.

Moreover, existing permits allow increases even if fully enforced. First, many facilities' actual emissions are much lower than their allowable emissions. Until actual emissions increase enough to trigger the rigorous pollution control requirements imposed on modified sources by the federal new source review (NSR) rules, facilities could increase their actual emissions and still remain within the terms of their permits.

Second, existing permits do not generally place absolute caps on the total quantity of actual emissions and thus allow emissions increases. Regulatory agencies analyze the technology available for the relevant industry or facility and then, most commonly, set performance standards. Performance standards are based on a selected pollution control technology's capacity, and are usually expressed in terms of a required emissions rate. Absolute quantities of actual emissions could generally increase under most of the different types of performance standards agencies might establish, so long as the rate of emissions did not exceed the permitted level. The primary constraint on co-pollutant emissions increases is the NSR program....

Moreover, not all significant emissions increases require NSR. Of relevance in this context, increases that result solely from an increase in the hours of operation, usually as a result of increased production, without an accompanying physical change in the plant, do not trigger NSR even if emissions increase more than the threshold amount. Thus, a facility that increased production without changing the physical plant would not be required to go through NSR and reduce co-pollutant emissions....

The risk of hot spots just described exists with or without a carbon trading system. A cap-and-trade system would not enable these increases, but it would allow them to continue. In some instances, however, a market-based mechanism could lead to increases that would not otherwise have occurred....

[W]hile reductions in GHGs are expected to generate reductions in co-pollutants, it is possible that some mechanisms for decreasing GHGs could, in fact, increase co-pollutants. For example, if an industry switched from gasoline to diesel due to diesel's greater efficiency, harmful co-pollutant emissions could increase. Moreover, power plants have been developing technologies that generate fewer GHGs, but that increase harmful particulate emissions. While these increases would presumably be controlled to some extent by existing permits, they nonetheless represent increases caused by the flexibility inherent in a market-based mechanism....

Trading from mobile to stationary sources could also cause distributional inequities. If carbon reductions from automobiles were used to facilitate increases from stationary sources, then widely distributed co-pollutants would become more concentrated.

Distribution of Co-Pollutant Reduction Benefits

The environmental justice community is concerned not only about the risk of co-pollutant increases, but about the distribution of co-pollutant reduction benefits. Communities near facilities that reduce CO_2 emissions and purchase fewer allowances are likely to benefit from the concurrent reduction in co-pollutant emissions, while communities near facilities that buy more allowances will not. Even if a facility only maintains, and does not increase, emissions, the neighboring community will not have obtained the potential pollution-reduction benefit of climate change regulation. To the extent that the facilities that choose to purchase allowances rather than reduce emissions are located in heavily polluted poor and minority communities, an unfettered market mechanism could deepen existing disparities....

In addition, the ability to use offsets, particularly biological carbon sequestration offsets, affects the extent of the pollution control co-benefits accompanying climate change regulation. Credits obtained from carbon sequestration would allow a facility to maintain co-pollutant emissions without a corresponding decrease in another facility's co-pollutant emissions. Carbon sequestration efforts may achieve other important environmental values, but it is worth noting that they do not provide a co-pollutant reduction benefit....

Mechanisms for Incorporating Environmental Justice

I present here some initial ideas for incorporating environmental justice into a cap-and-trade program....

Use a Market System to Supplement a Traditional Regulatory Approach for GHG Emissions

In the context of cap-and-trade programs more generally, a number of scholars have suggested that traditional regulatory mechanisms could provide a safety net. While existing regulations of co-pollutants already provide a partial safety net, they do not fully avoid the hot spot-risk and might not distribute co-pollutant reduction benefits equitably. To better distribute the benefits of climate change regulation, all facilities could be required to reduce GHGs to a certain extent using familiar regulatory mechanisms. These GHG reduction requirements would likely lead to incidental reductions in co-pollutants.

Once all facilities have reduced a certain amount, trading could be used to achieve greater reductions. As long as the reduced co-pollutant baseline became the baseline for determining the propriety of future increases in co-pollutants, future trades or allowance purchases would start from a lower baseline and be less likely to lead to increases in co-pollutants relative to current levels. In other words, since all spots would have been "cooled" to a certain extent, subsequent trading would be less likely to increase co-pollutants above their existing levels. To the extent that GHG reductions reduced co-pollutants, all communities would initially benefit from traditional climate change regulation....

In addition to addressing distributional concerns, coupling a market mechanism with traditional regulation could jumpstart essential emissions reductions. In light of the large-scale reductions that must be achieved to avert catastrophic climate change, most facilities are likely to have to reduce emissions to some extent. If the reductions are inevitable, then traditional regulation could be more effective and certain than the market at ensuring that existing mechanisms for reducing GHGs are in fact adopted....

Condition Trades

An alternative or additional approach, as scholars have noted, would be to place conditions on trades to achieve distributional fairness. Conditions could be imposed on a case-by-case basis or be determined according to preestablished geographic boundaries. Trades into disadvantaged areas could be discouraged and offset projects in disadvantaged areas could be encouraged....

Predetermined Geographic Restrictions

Restrictions based upon predetermined geographic restrictions could be ... compatible with a market system. Initially, regulatory agencies would have to identify disadvantaged areas. A regulatory agency would have to determine the level and type of emissions that would constitute disadvantage, as well as the size of the relevant area and whether it should be evaluated in broad terms, e.g., nonattainment area, or with reference to specific impacts experienced by local communities....

To avoid the creation of hot spots, trades or auction purchases that increased actual net co-pollutant emissions for the disadvantaged area could be prohibited or discouraged. To address equity in the distribution of benefits, trades into disadvantaged areas that simply maintained, rather than increased, emissions could also be limited or discouraged. The limitations could vary depending upon the degree of pollution in the affected area, with more stringent limitations on more polluted areas. Conditions could be placed on trades from non-disadvantaged areas to disadvantaged areas, so that less impacted areas would not reap the benefits of climate change reductions at the expense of disadvantaged areas....

Prohibitions or limitations based directly upon emissions increases would require detailed information on existing baseline emissions, a frequently controversial issue subject to gaming and dispute. To avoid baseline battles, trades or auction purchases could be indirectly controlled in disadvantaged regions by requiring a greater number of allowances per ton of emissions in disadvantaged areas. In an auction system, another option would be for the government to charge higher allowance prices for facilities in disadvantaged areas. A higher allowance ratio or higher fee would create a stronger incentive to reduce emissions rather than purchase allowances.

Finance Co-Pollutant Emission Reductions with Auction Revenues

The California Market Advisory Committee, charged with developing recommendations for a cap-and-trade program in California, has suggested that, if allowances are auctioned, some of the auction revenue could be used "to finance reductions of GHGs and criteria pollutants in communities that bear disproportionate environmental and public health burdens." That approach could address the potential negative environmental consequences of a cap-and-trade program without requiring such concerns to be integrated into trading mechanisms, and could thereby avoid some of the negative efficiency consequences that incorporating environmental justice might otherwise impose. It would delink the trading mechanism from its co-pollution reduction benefits.

Co-pollutants in impacted communities could be reduced in a variety of ways. The fund could be used to subsidize reductions at the facility purchasing the allowances or at other facilities in the area, finance mass transit, subsidize or finance less-polluting private vehicles, or for any other number of pollution-reducing activities. Subject to overarching state guidelines, community residents could participate in the selection of co-pollutant reducing activities, thus providing a role for public participation that ... is otherwise difficult to incorporate into autonomous trading regimes....

Allowance Distribution

Auctioning, rather than freely distributing, allowances would indirectly address some of the moral concerns raised by a trading system. By requiring facilities to purchase the right to pollute, the facilities would be forced to internalize the costs of pollution. It could also reduce the potential for windfall profits. In addition, auctioning would allow agencies to avoid the potential for gaming or fraud inherent in one of the most politically controversial steps in distributing allowances for free: determining preexisting baseline emissions....

* * *

Notes and Questions

1. What do you think of Professor Kaswan's suggestions for conditioning trading in emission allowances? She acknowledges that they conflict with the goal of maximizing the efficiency of a trading system. Is this tradeoff worthwhile? As Professor Kaswan notes, trading restrictions, such as paying more for credits used in impacted communities, and receiving more for reductions — credits generated — in impacted communities, have long been proposed to reform existing trading mechanisms, usually of pollutants that have more localized effect. These proposals have not been adopted. Why might they be considered seriously in a carbon market? As discussed below in note 7, California recently took some steps in this direction with its climate change legislation.

2. Should a greenhouse gas trading system focus solely on reducing greenhouse gases? Or should it also attempt to address problems that stem from the Clean Air Act's failure to adequately control co-pollutants?

3. Professor Kaswan goes on to discuss the impact that cap-and-trade systems have on public participation (an issue also explored in Chapters 5 and 7), noting that "[p]rivatized trading designed to maximize industry autonomy and flexibility does not provide opportunities for public participation in industry decisionmaking." She suggests that the public be allowed to participate in "allowance sales into the most polluted communities, where the stakes are highest and the need for public vigilance over the process is greatest" or in the event that this is not feasible, that "trading systems should seek to maximize the public transparency of all allowance trading and all monitoring results." *Id.* at 10302, 10306. For low-income communities that lack resources, is giving them an opportunity to participate in a trade likely to be an effective remedy? Could their participation ever take the form of a veto over the proposed trade?

4. Some critics have raised moral objections to trading, contending that pollution is a moral "bad," and that facilities should not be allowed to profit by selling what amounts to the right to pollute. What do you think of this argument? Is pollution different than other commodities that are bought and sold on financial exchanges? Does a trading program legitimize pollution and absolve sources of their responsibility to reduce the pollution they cause? If one accepts this view, then if a firm internalizes the cost of its polluting activities — by buying credits to pollute (via auction or another mechanism), instead of receiving them for free — does this dispense with the moral objection?

5. The major alternative to a cap-and-trade system is a tax on GHG emissions. In contrast to cap and trade, which caps emissions at a definite level but leaves the price of emission allowances to be determined by the market, a tax provides certainty in price for GHG emitters, but may not achieve the desired emissions-reduction level. Taxes often are favored by economists because they are simpler to administer and less prone to gaming or

manipulation than a trading system, but to date they have not gained much headway because they are politically unpopular. What do you think of the idea of taxes? Does your assessment change if it turns out that the costs of a tax on emitters are largely passed on to consumers? Is a tax likely to raise greater or lesser distributional concerns than a cap-and-trade system?

6. Addressing climate change will require the transition to a less fossil fuel-intensive economy. In addition to producing environmental gains, such a shift also presents great potential economic opportunities. As summed up by leading activist and author Van Jones, "If we are going to beat global warming, we are going to have to weatherize millions of buildings, install millions of solar panels, manufacture millions of wind turbine parts, plant and care for millions of trees, build millions of plug-in hybrid vehicles, and construct thousands of solar farms, wind farms and wave farms. That will require thousands of contracts and millions of jobs—producing billions of dollars in economic stimulus." Van Jones, The Green Collar Economy: How One Solution Can Fix Our Two Biggest Problems 10 (2008). Recognition of this fact (along with strong renewed interest in energy independence) has sparked a wave of interest in promoting green jobs and the "green-collar economy." Proponents point out that one of the many benefits of a green-collar economy is that it will give many people a more tangible stake in fighting global warming, and facilitate broader alliances among environmentalists and low-income workers and residents. Do you agree? Would it depend upon whether the green collar industries that feed local economies are themselves environmentally harmful?

7. In the absence of federal action, numerous states, local governments, and regional bodies have attempted to fill the void by enacting a wide variety of climate change measures. One measure in particular illustrates the increasing influence of environmental justice advocates. In 2006, California became the first state in the country to enact a mandatory emissions reduction law (the Global Warming Solutions Act of 2006, also known as AB 32 and codified at Cal Health & Safety. Code § 38500 et. seq.) requiring the state to reduce overall greenhouse gas emissions to 1990 levels by the year 2020, and mandating that in achieving this objective the state adhere to several environmental justice provisions. Specifically, the state must design control measures "in a manner that is equitable" and ensure that regulatory efforts do not disproportionately impact low-income communities. The statute also requires that prior to implementing any market-based mechanism, the California Air Resources Board (CARB) must consider the potential for localized impacts in communities that are already adversely impacted by air pollution and design any such mechanism to prevent any increase in the emissions of toxic air contaminants or criteria air pollutants. To what extent do you think these provisions might have been prompted by California's experience with the problematic "car scrapping trading program" described in Chapter 7?

In 2008, CARB issued a "scoping plan" outlining the main elements of its proposed strategy for implementing AB 32 that in part calls for the creation of a cap-and-trade system. Such a system is resolutely opposed by environmental justice groups in the state, who in 2008 issued a declaration arguing that trading is fundamentally undemocratic and that "it will not reduce greenhouse gas emissions at the pace called for by the international scientific community, it will not result in a shift to clean sustainable energy sources, it will support and enrich the state's worst polluters, it will fail to address the existing and future inequitable burden of pollution [and] it will deprive communities of the ability to protect and enhance their communities." The California Environmental Justice Movement's Declaration on Use of Carbon Trading Schemes to Address Climate Change (2008). In your view, is it possible to have a cap-and-trade system that satisfies the criteria of AB 32? How would you devise it? Although other states also have adopted mandatory greenhouse gas reduction measures, to date they have not incorporated environmental justice provisions like those in AB 32. Should they?

G. Human Rights Based Approach

A final avenue for addressing climate change employs claims based on violations of international human rights (human rights declarations that may be applicable to other environmental inequities are discussed in Chapter 10). As international climate expert Edward Cameron explains:

> Although a specific human right to the environment has not yet been elaborated in a binding international convention, the fundamental right to an environment capable of supporting human society and the full enjoyment of human rights is recognized, in varying formulations, in the constitutions of over 100 states and directly or indirectly in several international instruments. Moreover, the evolving body of work [of international institutions, governments, and non-governmental organizations] argues that associated climate impacts ... undermine the realization of human rights including *inter alia*: life; food; health; standard of living; means of subsistence; housing; culture; indigenous peoples rights; and gender rights. This position is now accepted by the bulk of the international community...."

Edwin Cameron, *The Human Dimension of Global Climate Change,* 15 HASTINGS W.-N.W. J. ENVTL. L. & POL'Y 1, 11 (2009).

A human rights based approach has been considered in most detail for indigenous communities in small island countries and the Arctic region that are particularly vulnerable to the impacts of climate change, as described below.

Sara C. Aminzadeh, A Moral Imperative: The Human Rights Implications of Climate Change

30 Hastings International and Comparative Law Review 231 (2007)

The Arctic region is warming twice as fast as any other region.... [T]he Inuit people living in the Arctic region have already borne witness to the problems caused by climate change. The problems currently affecting the Inuit include rising sea levels, melting sea ice and glaciers, thawing of permafrost, and increased precipitation in some areas and drought in others.... The thawing permafrost has damaged houses, roads, airports and pipelines, and caused erosion, slope instability, and landslides.

In the near future, scientists project climate change will wreak the same havoc on peoples living in SIDS [Small Island Developing States], jeopardizing their continued economic development. Small island countries such as the Maldives in the Indian Ocean, the Marshall Islands in the Pacific, and several Caribbean islands are particularly vulnerable.... Climate refugees from some Pacific island states are already seeking shelter in neighboring countries....

[Eds' Note: In 2005, the Inuit Circumpolar Conference, a non-government organization representing approximately 150,000 Inuit of Alaska, Canada, Greenland, and Chukotka

(Russia), filed a petition against the United States with the Inter-American Commission on Human Rights. The petition alleged that the United States' failure to reduce its greenhouse gas emissions and the resulting adverse global warming impacts violated numerous human rights embodied in the American Declaration of the Rights and Duties of Man. The legal basis of the petition is discussed below.]

The Impacts of Climate Change on Human Rights

There are arguably three viable strategies for constructing a human rights-based approach to climate change: 1) the application of procedural rights found in international human rights law to climate change litigation; 2) the recognition of a distinct right to environmental well-being; and 3) the re-interpretation of existing human rights in the environmental context. This note adopts the third approach, arguing that existing human rights law should be expanded to encompass climate change impacts when appropriate....

The following identifies some of the human rights that have been implicated by environmental issues in the past and suggests that the consequences of climate change for certain communities may similarly warrant consideration under human rights law.

Right to Privacy, and Family Life

.... Climate change has drastically undermined the Inuit people's rights to home, privacy, and family life. Thawing permafrost is causing rapid coastal erosion of Inuit territory. In one village, seven houses have already been relocated, three have fallen into the sea, and engineers predict that the entire village of 600 houses could fall into the sea within the next 20 years....

Right to Property

The UDHR [Universal Declaration of Human Rights] defines the right to property as follows: "1) Everyone has the right to own property alone as well as in association with others; 2) No one shall be arbitrarily deprived of his property." ...

[C]limate change has put Inuit communities in the Arctic in danger of losing their homes. These communities now face mass resettlement choices and destruction of culturally and historically significant lands and buildings. Thawing permafrost and coastal erosion has already forced several families to relocate. In the near future, small island nations may also face the loss of property as low-lying territories become inundated from sea level rise....

Right to Life

The right to life is increasingly understood to include the traditional protection against intentional or arbitrary deprivation of life, as well as the state's obligation to ensure that every individual within its boundaries has access to means of survival.... Past legal decisions have relied on the UDHR's "right to life" clause to vindicate environmental harms....

When a nation fails to take reasonable measures to prevent environmental damage, and the result of such non-action is climate change, those harmed may seek redress for violations of their right to life. For example, Alaskans affected by sea level rise or the melting of polar ice caps may assert a right to life claim against the United States for failing to take action....

Right to Health

As with other environmental problems, an examination of human health impacts provide the strongest link between climate change and human rights. Climate change poses serious health consequences, including premature death, serious illness, and the spread of disease....

The link between health and environment has long been recognized in both human rights and environmental jurisprudence.... As with the other climate change impacts, the Inuit and SIDS feel the brunt of health effects, which occur with greater frequency and severity....

A Response to Possible Criticisms Regarding a Human Rights-Based Approach to Climate Change

One theoretical problem to a human rights approach to climate change is that it may require subjective valuation of some rights over others. While climate change will seriously threaten the basic human rights of some individuals and groups, it may actually be beneficial for others. Climate change jeopardizes the lives and livelihoods of the Inuit and SIDS such as the Maldives and Tuvalu. However, the melting of sea ice could open up new sea routes for Russia, Iceland, and Canada, and parts of Russia might benefit from an increase in crop yields. In other words, if the Inuit have a human right to health and life, do not the people of Russia and Iceland have an equal right to development? ...

Others worry that emphasizing environmental aspects of human rights may divert attention from more important human rights objectives. Characterizing certain climate change impacts as human rights issues might weaken the protection of "real" human rights issues such as genocide and crimes against humanity. There are two responses to this point. First, the diversion of efforts to more so-called important objectives is not a legitimate concern because the consequences of climate change range from quite serious to catastrophic. Second, an approach that utilizes the human rights framework to address climate change would not undermine other environmental and human rights efforts. Instead, a human rights-based approach would aid the development of jurisprudence in both areas by encouraging debate and drawing new linkages between the two fields.

* * *

Notes and Questions

1. In 2006, the Inter-American Commission rejected the Inuit's petition, but without reviewing the merits of the claims. In 2007, the Commission granted petitioners a hearing in which they were allowed to appear and present testimony about the connection between global warming and human rights. Despite the Commission's refusal to review the petition, it has sparked considerable discussion about the viability of a human rights-based approach to climate change impacts.

2. Human rights claims offer some important advantages over claims brought under international environmental law. For one, international environmental law has a limited number of truly enforceable principles. By contrast, many of the obligations contained in human rights treaties have become norms of customary international law, and thus are more easily enforceable in appropriate tribunals. Also, international environmental treaties provide little recourse to individual victims of environmental harm, while human rights treaties potentially allow individuals, and not just states, to file claims for relief (recall the discussion of the environmental side agreement of the North American Free Trade Agreement in Chapter 10). Human rights treaties also provide a basis for intervention when harm occurs solely within one state, which environmental law treaties do not. Hari M. Osofsky, *Learning from Environmental Justice: A New Model for International Environmental Rights*, 24 STAN. ENVTL. L.J. 71, 82–83 (2005).

3. Professor Rebecca Tsosie notes that because the survival of indigenous peoples, such as those in the Arctic and Pacific Islands, is inextricably linked with their local environments, adaptation in response to climate change is not an effective solution:

> The appropriate framework for the justice or rights claims under current circumstances will require a change in global policy that considers the unique status of indigenous peoples in relation to their traditional lands and protects that relationship for future generations. Current international policy focuses on adaptation to climate change, including the potential need to relocate vulnerable communities.... A policy of relocation may make perfect sense in terms of an "equal citizenship" argument. Under such an argument, "global citizens" of underdeveloped nations must receive compensation for their harm at the hands of the developed nations. Presumably, if they are granted citizenship in the countries responsible for this harm and have equal access to the benefits of citizenship in the developed nation, then the appropriate redistribution of benefits can be achieved. This argument, however, is of little assistance to indigenous peoples. There is no other place that indigenous peoples can go and still continue to practice their unique lifeways and cultural practices. Geographical location is essential to indigenous identity.

Rebecca Tsosie, *Indigenous People and Environmental Justice: The Impact of Climate Change*, 78 U. COLO. L. REV. 1625, 1644–45 (2007). What does Professor Tsosie's argument suggest is the proper policy response to addressing climate change?

4. Rather than using international law, the Village of Kivalina, another indigenous Arctic community, filed suit under U.S. common law for damages for having to relocate its community as a result of climate change. The lawsuit is described in Chapter 13.

5. Considering the readings in this chapter, from an environmental justice perspective, where would you put your primary focus in combating climate change?

Chapter 13

Litigation, Citizen Enforcement, and Common Law Remedies

Part II of this book examined responses by governmental agencies to promote environmental justice in the regulatory context — setting standards, issuing permits, cleaning up waste sites, and so forth. We now turn, in Part III, to efforts by citizens and tribes to use the courts to achieve environmental justice goals. This chapter examines citizen enforcement of environmental laws and common law remedies; Chapter 14 discusses claims brought under the Free Exercise and Equal Protection Clauses of the Constitution, as well those brought under Title VI of the Civil Right Act. An excellent, practical guide to various legal theories that can be used to advance environmental justice is THE LAW OF ENVIRONMENTAL JUSTICE: THEORIES AND PROCEDURES TO ADDRESS DISPROPORTIONATE RISKS (Michael B. Gerrard & Sheila R. Foster eds., 2d ed. 2008).

Before we look at specific enforcement tools, however, we consider an important threshold set of issues that underlies environmental justice lawyering. Recall that as a political movement, environmental justice is premised on the principle that affected communities should speak for themselves and community empowerment is central. In light of this, to what extent should environmental justice activists rely on legal strategies at all? When is litigation appropriate, and what is the proper role of the lawyer in environmental justice disputes? These questions are perhaps highlighted most clearly in the context of enforcement actions, but they are applicable as well in many of the situations discussed in earlier chapters of the book.

A. The Role of the Lawyer and Litigation

Environmental justice activists have an ambivalent relationship with the legal system and with lawyers. On the one hand, legal representatives can play a powerful and essential role in advocating on behalf of communities. In addition, lawyers working with community groups are often activists in their own right and deeply committed to the principles and goals of environmental justice. On the other hand, many activists and community residents distrust lawyers and the legal process. In their view, past reliance on legal processes and procedures has resulted in the historic inequitable distribution of environmental harms. Lawyers may take over disputes from community leaders, and frame issues in narrow legal terms that do not seem to address the community's concerns. Moreover, communities will rarely, if ever, be able to match the legal resources of the government or private entities.

1. Environmental Justice Lawyering

The following article was written by Francis Calpotura, a long-time organizer with the Center for Third World Organizing in Oakland, California.

Francis Calpotura, Why the Law?
Third Force (May/June 1994)

I was once told by an organizer friend of mine that lawsuits are a tactic to be used during a fight when you want to (a) end the campaign and move on to another issue, (b) inspire your members by showing that you are not afraid to take on these bastards, or (c) force the hand of your opposition to react to your initiative during a stalemate.

In none of these instances, I remember, is a lawsuit a strategy for winning a fight. It is always a tactical move. So where does this penchant for legal strategies come from? Indigenous community organizations normally don't have lawyers (some don't even have paid staff) on their payroll; environmental organizations do. I would argue that the alliance of community organizations with the proliferating Environmental Law Centers around the country has resulted in legal strategies for winning environmental justice fights, to the detriment of direct-action, community-oriented strategies.

The political implications are serious. A legal strategy affects how the issues that confront a community are understood. For example, the fight by [activists in the Georgia Sea Islands against development] was framed as a "preservation" issue in order to employ a variety of zoning and endangered species laws to delay development. This cut on the issue fails to show the racial and class character of the developer's strategy, something organizing for community control and equitable development would do to a much greater extent.

In addition, a legal strategy takes the fight away from arenas in which people can have some direct influence — their politicians, local development company offices, residences of the CEO, bank offices, etc. — to a place where they don't, i.e. in some chamber controlled by a judge where only the lawyers are allowed to speak (and only in English). This strategy does not facilitate the building of a cohesive, imaginative and militant base of people willing to employ various tactics on the opposition. This has great implications on how deep our organizational base is, and how leaders get developed....

* * *

Notes and Questions

1. Do you agree with Mr. Calpotura's misgivings about relying on legal strategies? From the perspective of community groups, is it true that a lawsuit is never a strategy for winning a fight but is always a tactical move? Professors Gregg Macey and Lawrence Susskind explore the impact on the West Dallas Coalition for Environmental Justice of turning from an approach with community organizing at its center to one focused on litigation in *The Secondary Effects of Environmental Justice Litigation: The Case of West Dallas Coalition for Environmental Justice v. EPA,* 20 VA. ENVTL. L.J. 431 (2001). They note that the group's emphasis shifted from cumulative exposure stories that had prompted many residents to join the Coalition, to scientific testing and gathering evidence to support the litigation. As a result, "the perceived need for protests, meeting attendance, testimony at

hearings, and picketing around industrial land uses (as well as the use of stories of long-term exposure) diminished." *Id.* at 454. The authors also found that the coalition began to rely more heavily on lawyers to communicate with its members and to keep track of its internal operations, causing "[s]ocial networks, which accounted for the Coalition's initial growth in membership ... to erode." *Id.* at 456. Overall, their assessment of a litigation strategy is mixed; they conclude that "[w]hile the choice of litigation ... has yielded a number of positive outcomes for local residents [including cleanup and closure of some contaminated sites and increased blood lead testing of children], cumulative exposure and the need for resident relocation, two of the driving forces behind the initial building of social networks in 1989–90, remain unaddressed." *Id.* at 472–73.

2. In advising community groups about the pros and cons of a litigation strategy, Professor Helen Kang, Director of Golden Gate University's Environmental Law and Justice Clinic, notes that litigation can be very costly, time consuming, and psychologically draining; that most of the advocacy will be done by lawyers, not community members; and that the plaintiffs may not be able to share documents with the rest of the community or disclose to the community their discussions with lawyers because doing so could waive their attorney-client privileges. On the other hand, she explains that:

> [O]ur Clinic's experience is that legal analysis and strategies often support political and community organizing, and community groups have obtained the most desirable outcome in those situations.... [E]ven if your case may not bring about systemic change, filing a meritorious case may draw media attention to the problem and serve as an effective organizing tool. It may also be a catalyst for change. For example, if an agency is successfully sued multiple times, such events may trigger an internal review that results in management and policy changes. In some instances, litigation may be the only way for you to be at the table with government agencies and polluters who have shut the community out of discussions of issues that affect the community.... In other instances, meritorious litigation may be a way to have the polluter take your complaints seriously. The company may not have any incentives, even despite bad publicity, to sit down and negotiate, unless there are legal claims pending against it.

Helen Kang, Pre-Litigation Considerations for Grassroots Groups, Environmental Law Training Series for San Francisco Foundation's Environmental Health & Justice Initiative Grantees (Nov. 2003). Given this advice from Professor Kang, if you were a community activist, when would you choose to pursue a strategy of litigation?

3. What role should be played by lawyers who represent communities in environmental justice controversies? Do Professor Kang and attorney/activist Luke Cole, whose excerpt follows, differ from Francis Calpotura in their view of the role that a lawyer can take in an environmental justice battle?

Luke W. Cole, Empowerment as the Key to Environmental Protection: The Need for Environmental Poverty Law
19 Ecology Law Quarterly 619 (1992)

Client Empowerment

"Client empowerment" occurs when a lawyer's practice helps clients realize and assert greater control over decisions which affect their lives. Empowerment is also a process which enables individuals to participate effectively in collective efforts to solve common problems.... Client empowerment is about creating in the client community the dynamics of democratic decision making, accountability, and self-determination—ideals which one would like to create in society.

In the environmental poverty law context, empowerment means enabling those who will have to live with the results of environmental decisions to be those who actually make the decisions. "Community-based" and "community-led" are key descriptive and prescriptive phrases for the environmental poverty lawyer, who should seek to decentralize power away from herself and to her clients. The client empowerment model is thus the reverse of the legal-scientific mode of lawyering used by mainstream environmental groups. Rather than solving a problem *for* a community, the empowerment model calls upon attorneys to help community members solve their own problems.

"Empowerment law" is more a *method* than a *product*, a practice through which the lawyer helps the group learn empowering methods of operation. Empowerment of clients is the answer to the political organizers' eternal question: "What happens when we go away?" By helping people take control over the decisions which affect their lives, an attorney leaves the community stronger than when she arrived....

Law as a Means, Not an End....

While our first instinct as lawyers might be to use legal tactics, they may not achieve the results our clients desire. Other tactics may be more useful in generating public pressure on an unresponsive bureaucracy or polluting corporation: tactics such as community organizing, administrative advocacy, or media pressure. Because environmental problems are political problems—some government official is allowing one actor to pollute the neighborhood of another—non-legal tactics often offer the best approach. As is so often the case, there may not even *be* a legal solution to the problem faced by the community. Or, the legal approach may radically disempower a client community and thus should be avoided. Translating a community's problems into legal language may render them meaningless.... Finally, lawsuits take fights into the arena most controlled by the adversary and least controlled by the community....

Three Questions for Effective Advocacy

Activists for social change have long relied on [the following] three questions in evaluating prospective strategies and tactics. These three questions parallel the three tenets of environmental poverty law:....

Will the strategy educate people? This broad question fits the empowerment model of legal services because education is a key to empowerment. Environmental poverty lawyers must broadly construe their concept of "education"—it should encompass education of a client or client group by the lawyer, education of policymakers or decisionmakers, and education of the public. Further, the educational process should be two-way: a lawyer must not only educate her clients, but also be educated by them. By increasing the community's knowledge, and others' knowledge of the community's problems, the community's persuasive power is necessarily strengthened.

Will it build the movement? Group representation is a self-conscious strategy to build local movements by developing local community groups. Community groups and their lawyers should look for tactics that draw new members into a group, rather than alienate potential supporters. An environmental poverty law model which is based on community education and empowerment will necessarily "build the movement," while a narrow legal approach will almost certainly fail to build anything.

Does the strategy address the cause rather than the symptoms of a problem? Environmental issues—like most legal services issues such as housing, health care access and (un)employment—are systemic. The disproportionate burden borne by poor people is a direct result of the system of economic organization in the United States and the corresponding inequities in the distribution of political power. Legal solutions to the environmental problems faced by poor people most often treat only the symptom, the environmental hazard itself. Embracing non-legal approaches, and legal approaches which treat the law as a means rather than an end, can help environmental poverty lawyers attack the root cause of the environmental problems faced by their clients, political and economic powerlessness....

What Does it Look Like? Public Participation in Kettleman City

Kettleman City is a small, farmworker community located in California's San Joaquin Valley. The community is ninety-five percent Latino, and seventy percent of its 1,100 residents speak Spanish in the home. Most residents work in the agricultural fields that stretch out in three directions from the town. Many of Kettleman City's residents have lived there for years and own their own homes, purchased with low-interest loans from the Farmers Home Administration.

Kettleman City also hosts the largest toxic waste dump west of Louisiana. Established without the community's knowledge or consent in the late 1970's, Chemical Waste Management's (CWM) Kettleman Hills Facility is a Class I toxic waste landfill. Just four miles from town, it may legally accept just about any toxic substance produced.

In 1988, CWM proposed to build a toxic waste incinerator at the dump. A Greenpeace organizer tipped off the Kettleman City community about the proposal and gave residents information on toxic waste incinerators. Feeling that the incinerator would threaten their health, homes, and livelihoods, Kettleman City residents organized a community group, *El Pueblo para el Aire y Agua Limpio* (People for Clean Air and Water), held demonstrations, and pressured their local officials. In 1989, they also secured the legal representation of the California Rural Legal Assistance Foundation (CRLAF).

The young lawyer handling the case—his first—was faced with a dilemma [the lawyer was in fact the author, Luke Cole. Eds.]. The Kings County Planning Department, the local agency responsible for granting permits for the project, had issued a dense, tedious, more than 1,000-page Environmental Impact Report (EIR) on the proposed incinerator. The County had refused to translate the EIR into Spanish, despite repeated requests from Kettleman City residents. Kettleman City residents wanted to take part in the EIR process. The lawyer needed comment on the EIR, so that the administrative record would reflect the deficiencies of the document and the process. The lawyer faced a choice: the traditional mode of environmental lawyering or a new environmental poverty law approach.

Traditional approach. In the traditional model of environmental advocacy, the lawyer reads and analyzes the EIR document, shares parts of it with selected experts, and then writes extensive, technical comments on the EIR on behalf of a client group. These comments are submitted to the agency and form the basis of later lawsuits if the agency does not respond adequately.

Lawyering for social change model. The lawyer attempts to involve and educate the community while addressing the root of the problem: that the County is ignoring and dismissing the needs of Kettleman City residents without fear of repercussions because the residents are not organized.

Environmental poverty law in Kettleman City: How it worked. The lawyer chose the latter strategy. Working with several key leaders in the community, he and a CRLAF community worker held an initial series of three house meetings in Kettleman City. Each meeting was held in a different home, and all were held on the same day.

At a typical meeting, the community leaders would explain the incinerator proposal to eight to ten residents. The lawyer would then describe parts of the EIR and the County's response to the community's requests. The residents would ask questions, which the leaders and the attorney would answer to the best of their abilities. Discussions among the residents would ensue about the incinerator and why it was to be located in Kettleman City. The conversations were not limited simply to the incinerator, however. Residents would tell stories of health symptoms they had experienced (which they blamed on the existing toxic waste dump), of past dealings with County officials, and of other incidents they felt were important. Since the meetings involved almost entirely monolingual Spanish-speakers, the meetings were held in Spanish, with the community worker translating for the lawyer.

At the end of each meeting, the leaders and the attorney would ask each person present to write a letter of comment on the EIR to the Planning Commission. The letters—almost all in Spanish—questioned the Planning Commission about the incinerator, and also asked to have the EIR documents translated so that Kettleman residents could take part in the process. The meetings were as inclusive as possible: if a person was not literate, he or she would dictate a letter to a more educated Kettleman resident; children were encouraged to write as well. Out of the first three meetings, the community group generated twenty-five letters of comment on the EIR.

At the first meetings, people were asked to hold future meetings in their own homes, with five to eight of their neighbors. The community worker followed up with community leaders to ensure that the meetings continued. Over the course of the following three weeks more house meetings were held, and many more letters were written. When the EIR's public comment period closed, the record contained 162 comments from individuals—126 of them from Kettleman City residents. More importantly, 119 of the comments—seventy-five percent of all comments by individuals on the EIR—were in Spanish.

Although the results of such organizing are difficult to quantify—except, of course, for the large volume of letters—the letter-writing campaign served several important purposes. It brought Kettleman City residents together to learn about and discuss the incinerator. It allowed community leaders to bring Kettleman City residents up to date on the project. It informed the community of upcoming opportunities for participation, including a hearing before the Planning Commission. It encouraged individuals to take action—writing a letter—and to express themselves both in the house meetings and on paper. It validated residents' experiences with and concerns about the incinerator and the siting process by creating an opportunity to discuss and affirm them. People could collectively share other individual problems, tell their stories, and, through that process, see the commonality of their experiences. Lastly, the letter-writing campaign allowed residents to tell their stories to the Planning Commission, to act as "experts" in their own case.

Rather than gathering the residents' stories and translating them into narrow legal points (or even into English), the lawyer sought to facilitate the people of Kettleman City speaking for themselves. By asking others to hold meetings in their homes, the attorney and the community leaders fostered a sense of ownership of the campaign among members of the community. And finally, the letters created a stunning administrative record. The County could no longer claim that Kettleman residents and Spanish-speakers were not interested in the project: more than ten percent of the community had written letters to the Planning Commission. The attorney had helped create what he needed—the administrative record—in a way which fostered community action rather than shifting it.

The letter-writing campaign was an instance of empowering the client using group representation and non-litigation avenues. Ironically, by using tactics other than litigation, the campaign facilitated the litigation that ultimately resulted. The Kings County Board of Supervisors ultimately approved the incinerator proposal, and the environmental poverty lawyer was forced to take the County to Court. The Court overturned the County's approval, in part because of the County's exclusion of Spanish-speakers. [This case is discussed in Chapter 11. Eds.]

The letter-writing campaign also provided solid answers to the three questions environmental poverty lawyers must ask themselves. It educated people both in the community and in the County government. The campaign built the movement by bringing house meetings into new homes and involving residents who had not participated in the group to that point. Finally, it addressed the root of the problem, by using the EIR public comment process as an organizing focus and forcing the County decision makers to listen to the people of Kettleman City.

By contrast, a traditional approach would have educated Kettleman City residents that they were not intelligent or able enough to take part in the process. It would have reinforced, rather than challenged, what Joel Handler calls the "psychological adaptions of the powerless—fatalism, self-deprecation, apathy, and the internalization of dominant values and beliefs." The traditional approach would not have built the movement and would have perpetuated, rather than confronted, the problem of the people of Kettleman City not being heard. A traditional approach would not have highlighted the need for Spanish translation of the EIR, which was so apparent after the campaign. As Señor Auscencio Avila wrote, in Spanish, demanding a Spanish translation of the EIR, "To not do this is to keep the community ignorant of what is going to happen, and to keep the community without any political power, and to suppose that we do not have the mental ability to deal with our own problems." ...

* * *

Notes and Questions

1. Should empowerment of communities be the primary goal of attorneys? Or is this a task better performed by community organizers, activists, and others? What happens when a specific dispute is resolved and the lawyer's involvement with the community ends?

2. As the above excerpt makes clear, lawyers following an empowerment model have to adjust to a nontraditional role, since community lawyering often entails a combination of political, organizing, and legal strategies. Three community lawyers who worked on a successful effort to preserve open space in Boston's Chinatown offer the following advice about building relationships between lawyers and the communities they represent:

Do not assume "trust" exists simply because of shared ethnicity, race, or language ability.... Regardless of the similarities between lawyer and client, the client sees the lawyer first as a "lawyer." For many, the legal profession represents the hostile, inaccessible, and insensitive legal system that permeates and complicates their lives....

Build trust by learning about the community.... We mean learning about its history, its geography, and the various players, institutions, and organizations that constitute the community.... Such in-depth knowledge enabled us to identify what sorts of strategies, both legal and non-legal, might be viable and appropriate during the ... struggle.

> *Build trust by establishing a permanent presence within the community....* Besides
> serving on boards of community-based organizations, [community lawyers]
> need to volunteer their time and skills and use their legal training to further the
> best interests of the community on myriad issues. Examples include conduct-
> ing community legal education on relevant topics such as immigration, work-
> ers' rights and American government structure; mentoring community youth; and
> assisting community functions.

Zenobia Lai, Andrew Leong & Chi Chi Wu, *The Lessons of the Parcel C Struggle: Reflections on Community Lawyering*, 6 Asian Pac. Am. L.J. 1, 27–28 (2000). Can lawyers realistically undertake all of these various activities?

3. Lawyers engaged in community activism must keep in mind the roles they are playing and be cognizant about issues of legal ethics. For instance, before an attorney has
been retained by a community group, does the duty of confidentiality apply? Suppose
the lawyer is privy to discussions about a planned illegal protest outside a facility? Likewise, could a lawyer who goes door to door organizing neighbors to oppose a power plant
be accused of improperly soliciting clients? In short, how does a lawyer separate her role
as an activist from her role as an "officer of the court?" For more discussion of these issues, *see* Irma Russell & Joanne Sum-Ping, *Issues of Legal Ethics in Environmental Justice
Matters, in* The Law of Environmental Justice: Theories and Procedures to Address Disproportionate Risks 471 (Michael B. Gerrard & Sheila R. Foster eds., 2d ed.
2008).

4. Virtually all environmental laws provide the opportunity for public participation
in the decision-making process. Luke Cole describes two approaches that community
groups can follow in utilizing these public participation provisions in the context of a
land use permitting decision. Under the first approach, which he terms the "participatory" model, groups take part in every stage of the administrative process that provides
an opportunity for public input — commenting on draft documents, attending scoping
meetings and public hearings, and so forth. The second or "power" model is premised on
the assumption that participation by community groups in the administrative process almost never helps them change undesirable outcomes and that their sole focus should be
on the decision point and in actively trying to reach the actual decision makers. Luke W.
Cole, *Legal Services, Public Participation and Environmental Justice*, 29 Clearinghouse
Rev. 449 (Special Issue 1995). If you were representing a community group, which approach would you advise your client to follow? Are the two approaches mutually exclusive? Is participation in the administrative process largely a futile and co-optive exercise?
Does it provide an opportunity for educating and organizing community groups? Or is
it likely to lead to a slightly improved project that is more resistant to later legal challenge?

One distinct disadvantage of not participating in the administrative process is that a
party may be denied the right to pursue an issue that was not raised in earlier administrative proceedings, and in some instances, may not be able to file a claim for failure to
exhaust administrative remedies. *See, e.g.,* Cal. Pub. Res. Code § 21177 (California Environmental Quality Act).

5. For an interesting discussion of how the dispute over siting a polychlorinated biphenyl
(PCB) disposal site in Warren County, North Carolina (discussed in Chapter 1) led community members to successfully seek political office, and how their resulting political
power prevented additional PCB facilities from being sited in the county and led to detoxification of the landfill, *see* Dollie Burwell and Luke W. Cole, *Environmental Justice Comes
Full Circle: Warren County Before and After*, 1 Golden Gate U. Envtl. L.J. 9 (2007).

2. A Note on Environmental Law Clinics

There are approximately thirty-five environmental law clinics at law schools through-out the country, and some of them have been at the forefront of representing community groups in environmental justice matters. Law students are permitted to practice law under attorney supervision prior to their admission to the bar under state student practice rules, established by state bar associations or, in some instances, by state supreme courts.

With aggressive advocacy on behalf of environmental justice clients, however, the clinics themselves also have come under attack. The most prominent example occurred in the late 1990s in Louisiana, where complaints by business organizations and then-Louisiana Governor Mike Foster against the Tulane Environmental Law Clinic led the Louisiana Supreme Court to greatly restrict the state's student practice rules. The business organizations charged, among other things, that "the individual faculty and students' legal views [at Tulane] are in direct conflict with business positions." These complaints arose from the clinic's representation of citizens living in the low-income, eighty-four percent African American industrial corridor town of Convent, in St. James Parish, Louisiana. The residents opposed a plan by Shintech, a multinational petrochemical firm, to build a polyvinyl chloride plant that would result in emissions of over three million pounds of air pollutants per year, including close to 700,000 pounds of toxic air pollutants. (The project is discussed in more detail in Chapter 1.) As a result of administrative appeals filed by the clinic, EPA vetoed the state's proposed air permit for the facility and accepted the citizens' Title VI civil rights complaint for investigation. As the controversy over the plant grew, Shintech eventually dropped its plans to site the facility in St. James Parish and opted to build a smaller facility elsewhere in the state. *Environmental Law Clinic Raises Environmental Justice ... And a Hostile Reaction from the Governor and the Louisiana Supreme Court*, TULANE ENVTL. L. NEWS, Winter 1999 at 1, 1.

It appears that the revised Louisiana student practice rules adopted in 1999 were designed to preclude representation of virtually all of the community and environmental organizations served by the Tulane clinic in the prior ten years. For example, the rules prohibit student clinicians from representing any group unless an organization certifies that at least fifty-one percent of its members are considered indigent under federal Legal Services Corporations guidelines, and prohibit clinicians from representing individuals or organizations if any supervising attorney or clinician contacted them for the purpose of representation. LA. SUP. CT. R. xx. By contrast, in other states, eligibility for clinic representation is based on whether an organization itself can afford to hire an attorney. The story of the attack on Tulane's clinic is vividly recounted in Robert R. Kuehn, *Denying Access to Legal Representation: The Attack on the Tulane Environmental Law Clinic*, 4 WASH. U. J. L. & POL'Y 33 (2000). Professor Kuehn's account is replete with details of conflicts of interest; corrupt political practices, Louisiana style; business intimidation; and unequal justice.

Notes and Questions

1. What concerns are raised by requiring members of organizations to disclose personal financial information in order to obtain legal representation?

2. Business pressure on the Tulane clinic and on the law school was intense—some alumni withdrew their contributions to the law school, and others threatened to refuse to hire students who had participated in the clinic. If you had been a student in the clinic, would

you have risked a possible future job in Louisiana in order to represent the clients of the clinic?

3. Law clinics at other schools likewise have come under pressure to drop their representation of community groups in controversial environmental disputes; this has included pressure from other practicing attorneys. Is it ethical for attorneys to attack law clinics for representing community groups on environmental matters? For discussion of this issue, *see* Robert R. Kuehn, *Shooting the Messenger: The Ethics of Attacks on Environmental Representation,* 26 HARV. ENVTL. L. REV. 417 (2002).

4. Community groups may encounter similar pressures in the form of a Strategic Lawsuit Against Public Participation (SLAPP). SLAPPs are retaliatory actions filed by private developers or project applicants against organizations or individuals who oppose a project through litigation or other forms of advocacy. At their core, SLAPPs are a reaction to some political action; i.e., some effort to influence a government decision. Because they seek damages that easily can bankrupt a community or public interest group if successful, SLAPPs can chill public participation. As Professor Sheila Foster points out, however, most SLAPPs are successfully defended, particularly on grounds that the underlying activity is protected by the First Amendment's right to petition the government. She also notes that "the landscape of SLAPP litigation has become increasingly unfavorable to plaintiffs who bring SLAPPs, due to recent legislation that recognizes the antidemocratic nature of such lawsuits." Sheila Foster, *Public Participation, in* THE LAW OF ENVIRONMENTAL JUSTICE: THEORIES AND PROCEDURES TO ADDRESS DISPROPORTIONATE RISKS 225, 248–49 (Michael B. Gerrard & Sheila R. Foster eds., 2d ed. 2008).

B. Private Enforcement — Citizen Suits

When community groups turn to the courts, one set of enforcement tools available to them is found in the major federal environmental laws. These statutes authorize suits by private parties for violations of federal law, and allow citizens to sue in the absence of any economic injury and without demonstrating that harm to the environment has occurred. Citizen plaintiffs in these cases can obtain penalties or injunctive relief directing a polluter to comply with the law, but not damages for any harm suffered or punitive damages to punish the violator. These laws also provide for the recovery of attorney fees and costs. Some state environmental statutes also have citizen suit provisions, but they are far less common than under federal law.

Citizen suits have been used to supplement traditional enforcement when government agencies fail to act, either because of lack of resources or political will. Citizen suits also can prod agencies to target resources or press for stronger sanctions against certain facilities. For example, the National Law Journal study discussed in Chapter 2 found that cases in which citizen groups were involved resulted in higher penalties; it is not clear from the study, however, whether this refers to cases triggered by citizen suit notices or where citizens intervened in a pending case.

1. Legal Requirements for Filing Suit

In order to bring an action alleging a violation of federal environmental law, plaintiffs must satisfy various threshold procedural requirements. For a more detailed discussion *see* Ellen P. Chapnick, *Access to the Courts, in* THE LAW OF ENVIRONMENTAL JUSTICE: THE-ORIES AND PROCEDURES TO ADDRESS DISPROPORTIONATE RISKS 395 (Michael B. Gerrard & Sheila R. Foster eds., 2d ed. 2008).

Plaintiffs must first demonstrate that they have a right to sue under the statute that they are seeking to enforce. Virtually all of the major federal pollution-control and waste statutes contain a citizen suit provision authorizing suits by "any person" (or "any citizen" in the case of the Clean Water Act) in two circumstances: in suits against a regulated entity for a violation of any standard or requirement of the act's substantive provisions (enforcement actions); and in suits against an agency for failure to perform a nondiscretionary duty, such as meeting a statutory deadline (sometimes called "action-forcing suits"). Virtually all of the citizen suit provisions require that, at least sixty days before filing an enforcement action, plaintiffs must provide notice to government enforcement agencies and the alleged violator of their intent to sue. Suits are generally authorized after sixty days, provided that no government agency has commenced and "is diligently prosecuting" a civil or criminal action for the same violation.

For those environmental laws, such as the National Environmental Policy Act (NEPA), that do not have citizen suit provisions, citizens may bring claims under the general review provision of the Administrative Procedure Act (APA), which authorizes suits for persons "adversely affected" by a final agency action. *See* 5 U.S.C. §§ 702–04. In addition, in the absence of an express statutory authorization to sue for violations, plaintiffs can argue that a private right of action is "implied" in the statute. However, in recent years the Supreme Court has constricted considerably the circumstances under which implied rights of action will be found. *See, e.g.,* Alexander v. Sandoval, 532 U.S. 275 (2001), discussed in Chapter 14.

The Supreme Court also significantly limited the reach of citizen enforcement actions in Gwaltney of Smithfield Ltd. v. Chesapeake Bay Foundation, 484 U.S. 49 (1987), in which it held that because of the way the citizen suit provision of the Clean Water Act is worded, citizens cannot sue defendants for wholly past violations of that law. The *Gwaltney* decision had far-reaching implications because the great majority of environmental citizen suits are filed under the Clean Water Act and because several other federal statutes have similarly worded citizen suit provisions (although not the Clean Air Act, which authorizes citizen suits for repeated past violations). In addition, citizen suits against states for damages under environmental statutes are barred as a result of several Eleventh Amendment decisions. *See* Seminole Tribe v. Florida, 517 U.S. 44 (1996) (Congress lacks authority under Article I of the Constitution to abrogate states' Eleventh Amendment immunity from private suits in federal court); Alden v. Maine, 527 U.S. 706 (1999) (Congress lacks authority to abrogate states' immunity from private suits in state courts).

Apart from enforcement actions against violators and action-forcing suits, citizens can also challenge actions taken by administrative agencies, such as the adoption of regulations and the issuance of permits. Such actions are generally subject to judicial review provided certain preconditions are met, including that the agency actions be "final," that they are "ripe for review," and that plaintiffs have exhausted administrative remedies or otherwise raised their objections in earlier proceedings before the agency. Agencies' decisions about whether or not to initiate an enforcement action are generally not reviewable by the courts. Heckler v. Chaney, 470 U.S. 821 (1985).

In addition to establishing a statutory right to sue and meeting other procedural preconditions, plaintiffs suing in federal court must demonstrate constitutional standing to sue. Several Supreme Court decisions in the 1990s made it considerably more difficult for environmental plaintiffs to prove standing, although this trend was slowed down with the Court's decision in Friends of the Earth v. Laidlaw, 528 U.S. 167 (2000), excerpted below.

Standing derives from Article III, section 2 of the Constitution, which limits the jurisdiction of federal courts to "cases" and "controversies." To establish constitutional standing, a plaintiff must prove (1) an injury in fact that is concrete, affects the plaintiff in a personal and individual way, and is actual or imminent; (2) that the injury complained of is fairly traceable to the actions of the defendant (causation); and (3) that an order in the plaintiff's favor will redress the injuries complained of (redressability). Lujan v. Defenders of Wildlife, 504 U.S. 555, 560–61 (1992). The Court has also imposed a "prudential limitation," one that can be altered by Congress, which requires that the plaintiff's injury arguably falls within the zone of interests that the statute the plaintiff is enforcing is designed to protect. In Bennett v. Spear, 520 U.S. 154 (1997), the Supreme Court held that citizen suit provisions authorizing "any person" to sue—the language typically used in federal environmental statutes—establish the broadest possible zone of interests, authorizing any party with constitutional standing to sue. An association has standing to bring suit on behalf of its members when one or more of its members would otherwise have standing to sue in their own right, when the interests at stake are germane to the organization's purpose, and if neither the claim asserted nor the relief requested requires the participation of individual members in the lawsuit. See Hunt v. Wash. State Apple Adver. Comm'n, 432 U.S. 333 (1977).

In its seminal decision in Sierra Club v. Morton, 405 U.S. 727 (1972), the Supreme Court held that injury to aesthetic and environmental values may be sufficient to establish standing, provided that the plaintiffs are among those personally injured. In the 1990s, the Supreme Court issued three additional decisions on environmental standing. In the first case, Lujan v. National Wildlife Federation, 497 U.S. 871 (1990) (sometimes referred to as "Lujan I"), plaintiffs challenged a decision of the Bureau of Land Management to open 180 million acres of federal land to possible mining and oil and gas claims. A plaintiff organization filed affidavits from two of its members alleging that they used and enjoyed federal lands in the vicinity of about two million acres, approximately 4,500 acres of which were impacted by the BLM's action. The Court held that these allegations were insufficient to establish injury and that to prove standing, a plaintiff had to demonstrate that they actually use or visited the specific parcels of land affected by the BLM decision. Two years later, the Court issued the following opinion (sometimes referred to as "Lujan II").

Lujan v. Defenders of Wildlife
504 U.S. 555 (1992)

Justice Scalia delivered the opinion of the Court:

[This case involves a challenge to a rule promulgated by the federal government interpreting Section 7 of the Endangered Species Act (ESA). The ESA requires each federal agency to insure that any action authorized, funded, or carried out by such agency will not jeopardize the continued existence of any endangered species or threatened species or result in the destruction or adverse modification of habitat of such species. In 1986, the Interior Department promulgated a regulation stating that Section 7 is not applicable to actions taken in foreign nations. Respondents filed suit seeking to invalidate the regulation.]

The party invoking federal jurisdiction bears the burden of establishing [the elements necessary to demonstrate standing].... When the suit is one challenging the legality of government action or inaction, the nature and extent of facts that must be averred (at the summary judgment stage) or proved (at the trial stage) in order to establish standing depends considerably upon whether the plaintiff is himself an object of the action (or forgone action) at issue. If he is, there is ordinarily little question that the action or inaction has caused him injury, and that a judgment preventing or requiring the action will redress it. When, however, as in this case, a plaintiff's asserted injury arises from the government's allegedly unlawful regulation (or lack of regulation) of *someone else*, much more is needed. In that circumstance, causation and redressability ordinarily hinge on the response of the regulated (or regulable) third party to the government action or inaction—and perhaps on the response of others as well. The existence of one or more of the essential elements of standing "depends on the unfettered choices made by independent actors not before the courts and whose exercise of broad and legitimate discretion the courts cannot presume either to control or to predict," and it becomes the burden of the plaintiff to adduce facts showing that those choices have been or will be made in such manner as to produce causation and permit redressability of injury. Thus, when the plaintiff is not himself the object of the government action or inaction he challenges, standing is not precluded, but it is ordinarily "substantially more difficult" to establish....

Respondents' claim to injury is that the lack of consultation with respect to certain [federal agency-] funded activities abroad "increas[es] the rate of extinction of endangered and threatened species." Of course, the desire to use or observe an animal species, even for purely esthetic purposes, is undeniably a cognizable interest for purpose of standing. *See, e. g.*, Sierra Club v. Morton, 405 U.S. [727], 734 [1972]. "But the 'injury in fact' test requires more than an injury to a cognizable interest. It requires that the party seeking review be himself among the injured." To survive the Secretary's summary judgment motion, respondents had to submit affidavits or other evidence showing, through specific facts, not only that listed species were in fact being threatened by funded activities abroad, but also that one or more of respondents' members would thereby be "directly" affected apart from their "'special interest' in the subject."

With respect to this aspect of the case, the Court of Appeals focused on the affidavits of two Defenders' members—Joyce Kelly and Amy Skilbred. Ms. Kelly stated that she traveled to Egypt in 1986 and "observed the traditional habitat of the endangered Nile crocodile there and intend[s] to do so again, and hope[s] to observe the crocodile directly," and that she "will suffer harm in fact as the result of [the] American ... role ... in overseeing the rehabilitation of the Aswan High Dam on the Nile ... and [in] developing ... Egypt's ... Master Water Plan." Ms. Skilbred averred that she traveled to Sri Lanka in 1981 and "observed the habitat" of "endangered species such as the Asian elephant and the leopard" at what is now the site of the Mahaweli project funded by the Agency for International Development (AID), although she "was unable to see any of the endangered species"; "this development project," she continued, "will seriously reduce endangered, threatened, and endemic species habitat including areas that I visited ... [, which] may severely shorten the future of these species"; that threat, she concluded, harmed her because she "intend[s] to return to Sri Lanka in the future and hope[s] to be more fortunate in spotting at least the endangered elephant and leopard." When Ms. Skilbred was asked at a subsequent deposition if and when she had any plans to return to Sri Lanka, she reiterated that "I intend to go back to Sri Lanka," but confessed that she had no current plans: "I don't know [when]. There is a civil war going on right now. I don't know. Not next year, I will say. In the future."

We shall assume for the sake of argument that these affidavits contain facts showing that certain agency-funded projects threaten listed species—though that is questionable.

They plainly contain no facts, however, showing how damage to the species will produce "imminent" injury to Mses. Kelly and Skilbred. That the women "had visited" the areas of the projects before the projects commenced proves nothing. As we have said in a related context, "'Past exposure to illegal conduct does not in itself show a present case or controversy regarding injunctive relief ... if unaccompanied by any continuing, present adverse effects.'" And the affiants' profession of an "intent" to return to the places they had visited before—where they will presumably, this time, be deprived of the opportunity to observe animals of the endangered species—is simply not enough. Such "some day" intentions—without any description of concrete plans, or indeed even any specification of *when* the some day will be—do not support a finding of the "actual or imminent" injury that our cases require.

Besides relying upon the Kelly and Skilbred affidavits, respondents propose a series of novel standing theories. The first, inelegantly styled "ecosystem nexus," proposes that any person who uses *any part* of a "contiguous ecosystem" adversely affected by a funded activity has standing even if the activity is located a great distance away. This approach, as the Court of Appeals correctly observed, is inconsistent with our opinion in *Lujan v. National Wildlife Federation*, which held that a plaintiff claiming injury from environmental damage must use the area affected by the challenged activity and not an area roughly "in the vicinity" of it....

Respondents' other theories are called, alas, the "animal nexus" approach, whereby anyone who has an interest in studying or seeing the endangered animals anywhere on the globe has standing; and the "vocational nexus" approach, under which anyone with a professional interest in such animals can sue. Under these theories, anyone who goes to see Asian elephants in the Bronx Zoo, and anyone who is a keeper of Asian elephants in the Bronx Zoo, has standing to sue because the Director of [AID] did not consult with the Secretary regarding the AID-funded project in Sri Lanka. This is beyond all reason. Standing is not "an ingenious academic exercise in the conceivable," *United States v. Students Challenging Regulatory Agency Procedures*, 412 U.S. 669, 688 (1973), but as we have said requires, at the summary judgment stage, a factual showing of perceptible harm. It is clear that the person who observes or works with a particular animal threatened by a federal decision is facing perceptible harm, since the very subject of his interest will no longer exist. It is even plausible—though it goes to the outermost limit of plausibility—to think that a person who observes or works with animals of a particular species in the very area of the world where that species is threatened by a federal decision is facing such harm, since some animals that might have been the subject of his interest will no longer exist. *See Japan Whaling Assn. v. American Cetacean Society*, 478 U.S. 221, 231 n. 4 (1986). It goes beyond the limit, however, and into pure speculation and fantasy, to say that anyone who observes or works with an endangered species, anywhere in the world, is appreciably harmed by a single project affecting some portion of that species with which he has no more specific connection.

Besides failing to show injury, respondents failed to demonstrate redressability. Instead of attacking the separate decisions to fund particular projects allegedly causing them harm, respondents chose to challenge a more generalized level of Government action (rules regarding consultation), the invalidation of which would affect all overseas projects. This programmatic approach has obvious practical advantages, but also obvious difficulties insofar as proof of causation or redressability is concerned. As we have said in another context, "suits challenging, not specifically identifiable Government violations of law, but the particular programs agencies establish to carry out their legal obligations ... [are], even when premised on allegations of several instances of violations of law, ... rarely if ever appropriate for federal-court adjudication."

The most obvious problem in the present case is redressability. Since the agencies funding the projects were not parties to the case, the District Court could accord relief only against the [Secretary of Interior]: He could be ordered to revise his regulation to require consultation for foreign projects. But this would not remedy respondents' alleged injury unless the funding agencies were bound by the Secretary's regulation, which is very much an open question....

A further impediment to redressability is the fact that the [U.S. federal] agencies generally supply only a fraction of the funding for a foreign project. AID, for example, has provided less than 10% of the funding for the Mahaweli project. Respondents have produced nothing to indicate that the projects they have named will either be suspended, or do less harm to listed species, if that fraction is eliminated. As in Simon [v. Eastern Kentucky Welfare Rights Organization], 426 U.S. [26], 43–44 [1976], it is entirely conjectural whether the non-agency activity that affects respondents will be altered or affected by the agency activity they seek to achieve....

The Court of Appeals found that respondents had standing for an additional reason: because they had suffered a "procedural injury." The so-called "citizen-suit" provision of the ESA provides, in pertinent part, that "any person may commence a civil suit on his own behalf (A) to enjoin any person, including the United States and any other governmental instrumentality or agency ... who is alleged to be in violation of any provision of this chapter." 16 U.S.C. § 1540(g). The court held that, because § 7(a)(2) requires interagency consultation, the citizen-suit provision creates a "procedural right" to consultation in all "persons" — so that anyone can file suit in federal court to challenge the Secretary's (or presumably any other official's) failure to follow the assertedly correct consultative procedure, notwithstanding his or her inability to allege any discrete injury flowing from that failure. To understand the remarkable nature of this holding one must be clear about what it does *not* rest upon: This is not a case where plaintiffs are seeking to enforce a procedural requirement the disregard of which could impair a separate concrete interest of theirs (e.g., the procedural requirement for a hearing prior to denial of their license application, or the procedural requirement for an environmental impact statement before a federal facility is constructed next door to them).[7] Nor is it simply a case where concrete injury has been suffered by many persons, as in mass fraud or mass tort situations. Nor, finally, is it the unusual case in which Congress has created a concrete private interest in the outcome of a suit against a private party for the Government's benefit, by providing a cash bounty for the victorious plaintiff. Rather, the court held that the injury-in-fact requirement had been satisfied by congressional conferral upon *all* persons of an abstract, self-contained, noninstrumental "right" to have the Executive observe the procedures required by law. We reject this view.

---

7. There is this much truth to the assertion that "procedural rights" are special: The person who has been accorded a procedural right to protect his concrete interests can assert that right without meeting all the normal standards for redressability and immediacy. Thus, under our case law, one living adjacent to the site for proposed construction of a federally licensed dam has standing to challenge the licensing agency's failure to prepare an environmental impact statement, even though he cannot establish with any certainty that the statement will cause the license to be withheld or altered, and even though the dam will not be completed for many years. (That is why we do not rely, in the present case, upon the Government's argument that, *even if* the other agencies were obliged to consult with the Secretary, they might not have followed his advice.) What respondents' "procedural rights" argument seeks, however, is quite different from this: standing for persons who have no concrete interests affected — persons who live (and propose to live) at the other end of the country from the dam.

We have consistently held that a plaintiff raising only a generally available grievance about government—claiming only harm to his and every citizen's interest in proper application of the Constitution and laws, and seeking relief that no more directly and tangibly benefits him than it does the public at large—does not state an Article III case or controversy....

We hold that respondents lack standing to bring this action and that the Court of Appeals erred in denying the summary judgment motion filed by the United States....

* * *

Notes and Questions

1. A number of scholars have argued that the Supreme Court's current standing doctrine (as reflected in the above *Lujan* decision) is not supported by the text or history of Article III of the Constitution, and that the concept of standing itself was not even discussed in Court decisions until the 1940s. Rather, the courts traditionally focused on whether or not plaintiff had a right to sue under federal statute or federal common law. These scholars contend, moreover, that Congress has the power to confer standing on plaintiffs by authorizing them to bring suit. Professor Cass Sunstein, for example, argues that "[w]hen Congress creates a cause of action enabling people to complain against racial discrimination, consumer fraud, or destruction of environmental assets, it is really giving people a kind of property right in a certain state of affairs. Invasion of that property right is the relevant injury." Cass Sunstein, *What's Standing after Lujan? Of Citizen Suits, "Injuries," and Article III,* 91 MICH. L. REV. 163, 191 (1992).

2. Professor Sunstein's approach enjoys some support in Justice Kennedy's concurring opinion in *Lujan.* Justice Kennedy (joined by Justice Souter) suggested that Congress might be able to define the violation of a statute as creating an injury in fact sufficient for Constitutional standing. He wrote that "[a]s government programs and policies become more complex and far reaching, we must be sensitive to the articulation of new rights of action that do not have clear analogs in our common-law tradition.... In my view, Congress has the power to define injuries and articulate chains of causation that will give rise to a case or controversy where none existed before, and I do not read the Court's opinion to suggest a contrary view." *Id.* at 580.

3. In the third major standing case of the 1990s, Steel Company v. Citizens for a Better Environment, 523 U.S. 83 (1998), plaintiffs sued a manufacturing company for its failure to file reporting forms required under the federal right-to-know law (the Emergency Planning and Community Right-to-Know Act, or EPCRA) from 1988 to 1995. The defendant had filed the overdue forms after receiving plaintiffs' sixty-day notice of intent to sue and before the litigation was initiated. The Supreme Court ruled that where a defendant has come into compliance at the time the complaint is filed, plaintiffs lack standing to bring a claim for civil penalties, at least where the penalties are awarded to the federal treasury, because such penalties could not redress plaintiffs' injuries. The Court held that in these circumstances plaintiffs (even those directly injured by defendant's noncompliance) share only an "undifferentiated public interest" in seeing the law complied with.

In Friends of the Earth v. Laidlaw Environmental Services, 149 F.3d 303 (4th Cir. 1998), the Fourth Circuit decided an issue not addressed by *Steel Company.* If a defendant is in violation at the time a plaintiff files a complaint but comes into compliance at some other point during the litigation, does the plaintiff still have standing to sue for penalties? In *Laidlaw,* environmental groups sued the operator of a hazardous waste incinerator for violating its Clean Water Act permit. The trial court found that Laidlaw had committed hundreds of violations, including thirty-six violations after plaintiffs filed their complaint, and imposed a penalty of over $400,000. The trial court also found that Laidlaw had been in substantial compliance with its permit for several years by the time of the final order in the case, and denied plaintiffs' request for injunctive relief. The Fourth Circuit, relying on *Steel Company*, held that plaintiffs lacked standing to proceed because their only remaining relief requested was civil penalties paid to the federal treasury, and such penalties could not redress any injuries that plaintiffs had suffered. To the surprise of many, the Supreme Court reversed in the following decision.

Friends of the Earth v. Laidlaw Environmental Services
528 U.S. 167 (2000)

Justice Ginsburg delivered the opinion of the Court:

This case presents an important question concerning the operation of the citizen-suit provisions of the Clean Water Act. Congress authorized the federal district courts to entertain Clean Water Act suits initiated by "a person or persons having an interest which is or may be adversely affected." 33 U.S.C. §§ 1365(a), (g). To impel future compliance with the Act, a district court may prescribe injunctive relief in such a suit; additionally or alternatively, the court may impose civil penalties payable to the United States Treasury....

[The Act] provides for the issuance, by the Administrator of the Environmental Protection Agency (EPA) or by authorized States, of National Pollutant Discharge Elimination System (NPDES) permits. NPDES permits impose limitations on the discharge of pollutants, and establish related monitoring and reporting requirements, in order to improve the cleanliness and safety of the Nation's waters. Noncompliance with a permit constitutes a violation of the Act.

In 1986, defendant-respondent Laidlaw Environmental Services (TOC), Inc., bought a hazardous waste incinerator facility in Roebuck, South Carolina, that included a wastewater treatment plant.... Shortly after Laidlaw acquired the facility, the South Carolina Department of Health and Environmental Control (DHEC) ... granted Laidlaw an NPDES permit authorizing the company to discharge treated water into the North Tyger River. The permit, which became effective on January 1, 1987, placed limits on Laidlaw's discharge of several pollutants into the river, including—of particular relevance to this case—mercury, an extremely toxic pollutant.... Once it received its permit, Laidlaw began to discharge various pollutants into the waterway; repeatedly, Laidlaw's discharges exceeded the limits set by the permit.... The District Court later found that Laidlaw had violated the mercury limits on 489 occasions between 1987 and 1995.

[After filing a sixty-day notice of their intent to sue], plaintiffs (collectively referred to as Friends of the Earth, or FOE) filed suit against Laidlaw in June, 1992. The District Court found that FOE had standing to bring suit, and in a judgment issued in January, 1997, assessed a civil penalty of $405,800. The court denied plaintiffs' request for injunctive relief, finding that Laidlaw had been in substantial compliance with its permit since August, 1992. The Court of Appeals reversed.]

According to Laidlaw, after the Court of Appeals issued its decision but before this Court granted certiorari, the entire incinerator facility in Roebuck was permanently closed, dismantled, and put up for sale, and all discharges from the facility permanently ceased....

Laidlaw contends first that FOE lacked standing from the outset even to seek injunctive relief, because the plaintiff organizations failed to show that any of their members had sustained or faced the threat of any "injury in fact" from Laidlaw's activities. In support of this contention Laidlaw points to the District Court's finding, made in the course of setting the penalty amount, that there had been "no demonstrated proof of harm to the environment" from Laidlaw's mercury discharge violations.

The relevant showing for purposes of Article III standing, however, is not injury to the environment but injury to the plaintiff. To insist upon the former rather than the latter as part of the standing inquiry (as the dissent in essence does) is to raise the standing hurdle higher than the necessary showing for success on the merits in an action alleging noncompliance with an NPDES permit. Focusing properly on injury to the plaintiff, the District Court found that FOE had demonstrated sufficient injury to establish standing. For example, FOE member Kenneth Lee Curtis averred in affidavits that he lived a half-mile from Laidlaw's facility; that he occasionally drove over the North Tyger River, and that it looked and smelled polluted; and that he would like to fish, camp, swim, and picnic in and near the river between 3 and 15 miles downstream from the facility, as he did when he was a teenager, but would not do so because he was concerned that the water was polluted by Laidlaw's discharges.... Other members presented evidence to similar effect....

These sworn statements, as the District Court determined, adequately documented injury in fact. We have held that environmental plaintiffs adequately allege injury in fact when they aver that they use the affected area and are persons "for whom the aesthetic and recreational values of the area will be lessened" by the challenged activity. Sierra Club v. Morton, 405 U.S. 727, 735 (1972)....

Our decision in [Lujan] v. National Wildlife Federation, 497 U.S. 871 (1990) ["Lujan I" or "*National Wildlife Federation*"], is not to the contrary. In that case an environmental organization assailed the Bureau of Land Management's "land withdrawal review program," a program covering millions of acres, alleging that the program illegally opened up public lands to mining activities. The defendants moved for summary judgment, challenging the plaintiff organization's standing to initiate the action under the Administrative Procedure Act. We held that the plaintiff could not survive the summary judgment motion merely by offering "averments which state only that one of [the organization's] members uses unspecified portions of an immense tract of territory on some portions of which mining activity has occurred or probably will occur by virtue of the governmental action."

In contrast, the affidavits and testimony presented by FOE in this case assert that Laidlaw's discharges, and the affiant members' reasonable concerns about the effects of those discharges, directly affected those affiants' recreational, aesthetic, and economic interests. These submissions present dispositively more than the mere "general averments" and "conclusory allegations" found inadequate in *National Wildlife Federation*. Nor can the affiants' conditional statements—that they would use the nearby North Tyger River for recreation if Laidlaw were not discharging pollutants into it—be equated with the speculative "'some day' intentions" to visit endangered species halfway around the world that we held insufficient to show injury in fact in *Defenders of Wildlife* ["Lujan II"]....

Laidlaw argues next that even if FOE had standing to seek injunctive relief, it lacked standing to seek civil penalties. Here the asserted defect is not injury but redressability. Civil penalties offer no redress to private plaintiffs, Laidlaw argues, because they are paid to the government, and therefore a citizen plaintiff can never have standing to seek them....

We have recognized on numerous occasions that "all civil penalties have some deterrent effect." More specifically, Congress has found that civil penalties in Clean Water Act cases do more than promote immediate compliance by limiting the defendant's economic incentive to delay its attainment of permit limits; they also deter future violations. This congressional determination warrants judicial attention and respect....

It can scarcely be doubted that, for a plaintiff who is injured or faces the threat of future injury due to illegal conduct ongoing at the time of suit, a sanction that effectively abates that conduct and prevents its recurrence provides a form of redress. Civil penalties can fit that description. To the extent that they encourage defendants to discontinue current violations and deter them from committing future ones, they afford redress to citizen plaintiffs who are injured or threatened with injury as a consequence of ongoing unlawful conduct.

The dissent argues that it is the *availability* rather than the *imposition* of civil penalties that deters any particular polluter from continuing to pollute. This argument misses the mark in two ways. First, it overlooks the interdependence of the availability and the imposition; a threat has no deterrent value unless it is credible that it will be carried out. Second, it is reasonable for Congress to conclude that an actual award of civil penalties does in fact bring with it a significant quantum of deterrence over and above what is achieved by the mere prospect of such penalties. A would-be polluter may or may not be dissuaded by the existence of a remedy on the books, but a defendant once hit in its pocketbook will surely think twice before polluting again....

We recognize that there may be a point at which the deterrent effect of a claim for civil penalties becomes so insubstantial or so remote that it cannot support citizen standing. The fact that this vanishing point is not easy to ascertain does not detract from the deterrent power of such penalties in the ordinary case.... In this case we need not explore the outer limits of the principle that civil penalties provide sufficient deterrence to support redressability. Here, the civil penalties sought by FOE carried with them a deterrent effect that made it likely, as opposed to merely speculative, that the penalties would redress FOE's injuries by abating current violations and preventing future ones—as the District Court reasonably found when it assessed a penalty of $405,800.

Laidlaw contends that the reasoning of our decision in [*Steel Company*] directs the conclusion that citizen plaintiffs have no standing to seek civil penalties under the Act. We disagree. [*Steel Company*] established that citizen suitors lack standing to seek civil penalties for violations that have abated by the time of suit. We specifically noted in that case that there was no allegation in the complaint of any continuing or imminent violation, and that no basis for such an allegation appeared to exist.... In short, [*Steel Company*] held that private plaintiffs, unlike the Federal Government, may not sue to assess penalties for wholly past violations, but our decision in that case did not reach the issue of standing to seek penalties for violations that are ongoing at the time of the complaint and that could continue into the future if undeterred....

* * *

Notes and Questions

1. In an important subsequent portion of its opinion, the Court addressed the related question of mootness. Defendant argued that plaintiffs' claim for penalties was moot because it had voluntarily come into substantial compliance with its permit after the complaint was filed, and later permanently closed the facility at which the violations had

occurred. The Court ruled that a case "might become moot if subsequent events made it absolutely clear that the allegedly wrongful behavior could not reasonably be expected to recur," but that the "heavy burden" of demonstrating this rested with the party asserting mootness. The Court found that the effects of Laidlaw's voluntary compliance and facility closure were disputed facts that had not been litigated at the trial court, and remanded this question to the lower courts. *Id.* at 189, 193–94.

2. *Laidlaw* did not overrule *Steel Company,* distinguishing it on the grounds that *Steel Company* involved violations that had stopped by the time the complaint was filed, while *Laidlaw* concerned violations that stopped after the lawsuit was filed but before trial. But the logic underlying the *Steel Company* decision — that penalties awarded to the federal treasury as opposed to the plaintiffs themselves cannot redress the injuries of plaintiffs alleging statutory violations — is clearly undermined by *Laidlaw*'s conclusion that plaintiffs' injuries could be redressed by the imposition of civil penalties (which likewise go the federal treasury) and that "all penalties have some deterrent effect."

3. *Laidlaw* reversed what had been a pronounced judicial trend toward more restrictive standing requirements. In a 2009 decision, while not calling *Laidlaw* into question, the Court underscored that the *Lujan* precedents have continued strong vitality. In *Summers v. Earth Island Institute,* ___ U.S. ___, 129 S.Ct. 1142 (2009), plaintiffs challenged a salvage sale of timber on national forest land and alleged that, pursuant to a Forest Service regulation governing small salvage sales, the Service had improperly exempted the sale from the agency's notice and comment and appeals processes. The plaintiffs submitted an affidavit from one member alleging that he had repeatedly used the site on which the sale was planned and had imminent plans to do so again. The government conceded that these allegations were adequate to establish standing for that site. After the trial court granted a preliminary injunction enjoining the sale, plaintiffs settled their challenge to the specific salvage sale, but continued with their challenge to the Forest Service regulation. To demonstrate standing to challenge the regulation, plaintiffs relied in part on the affidavit of another member who alleged that he had visited seventy national forests in the past and planned to visit them in the future, although he did not name any specific forests. The member also alleged that there were a series of projects in the Allegheny National Forest that were subject to the challenged regulations, and that he had visited the forest in the past and "wants to go there" in the future, without specifying exactly when.

The Court found these allegations insufficient to show injury in fact. As to the first, the Court said there was no indication that the forests affected by the rule were the ones that the member would actually visit in the future. As to the second, the Court characterized it as only a "vague desire to return" to the forest, and that "such 'some day' intentions — without any description of concrete plans," is not an actual or imminent injury (citing *Lujan II).* In dissent, Justice Breyer argued that plaintiffs had shown a "realistic threat" that they would be harmed by the regulation, even if they did not specify the exact salvage sales that would be affected by it, given that the Forest Service admitted that it intended to conduct thousands of sales under the challenged regulation in the near future.

At the very least, *Summers* means that environmental plaintiffs only have standing to challenge programmatic decisions by the government in the context of a specific project. Whether it will be read by the lower courts to otherwise tighten standing doctrine remains to be seen.

4. In light of the above cases, do you believe that standing doctrine is a significant impediment for would be environmental justice plaintiffs? Recall that under the "injury in

fact" prong of the analysis, the courts focus upon injury to the plaintiff, not necessarily injury to the environment. Because environmental justice claims are often centered upon disproportionate burdens, cumulative impacts, and synergistic effects, how would you assess the ability of such plaintiffs to prove injury in fact sufficient for constitutional standing?

2. The Practicalities of Private Enforcement

Apart from the legal hurdles discussed above, there are important practical concerns with bringing citizen suits. The following excerpt describes the potential promises and limits of using such suits to achieve environmental justice.

Eileen Gauna, Federal Environmental Citizen Provisions: Obstacles and Incentives on the Road to Environmental Justice
22 Ecology Law Quarterly 1 (1995)

EPA, charged with enforcement of most federal environmental laws, lacks the ability to enforce all environmental laws to the maximum extent possible. Understanding that there would be undesirable underenforcement of environmental laws because of limited regulatory resources, Congress equipped many federal environmental laws with citizen suit provisions, which essentially confer "private attorney general status" on the citizenry.... After sufficient notice, and if a government agency is not already diligently prosecuting an action against the violator, any person may bring a private citizen enforcement action against a member of the regulated community to enforce requirements of the applicable law. Requirements are often, but not always, found in the permits required under the act in question. Some permit violations are easily proven, but other enforcement actions involve matters outside the ambit of clear violations of unambiguous permit requirements and standards. Sometimes requirements are found in administrative or court orders issued under the act in question.

Regardless of whether the enforceable requirement is easy to isolate or more difficult, the community must first become aware of a risk to the public and associate the risk with a suspected violation. A community group with limited resources will find it difficult to obtain information about public risks that may not be readily apparent, and secondly, will find it difficult to mobilize to influence agency response or initiate court proceedings....

Clean Water Act Enforcement Suits

Under the Clean Water Act, the detection and prosecution of permit violations are easy relative to other enforcement actions. As such, they constitute a disproportionately large percentage of citizen enforcement actions. Any facility discharging regulated pollutants into a body of water from a discrete conveyance must first obtain a Clean Water Act permit under the National Pollutant Discharge Elimination System (NPDES) program. In addition to limiting the amount of pollutant discharged with a facility's effluent, an NPDES permit requires its holder to test regularly its effluent and to submit reports with the recorded actual pollutant concentration. The reports are generally available to the public. It is relatively easy, with minimum training, for a citizen to check and compare the facility permits with the discharge reports if the citizen (or community group) suspects that violations may be causing undue pollution. If there is a violation, the citizen should be able to establish liability at the summary judgment phase of a case simply by submitting the permit and the discharge monitoring reports indicating a discharge beyond permit limitations. It would be relatively easy to train citizens in poor and minority communities to detect and prosecute Clean Water Act violations. . . .

Citizen Suits Under the Existing Clean Air Act Programs

Under the Clean Air Act, a private citizen can sue a person alleged to be in violation of an emission standard or limitation. . . . [A]lthough one might think that an "emission standard or limitation" refers to a quantifiable, permitted concentration of a regulated pollutant emitted into the air at a particular rate, this is not always the case. The general definition of "emission standard or limitation" under the Clean Air Act also includes requirements that are not easily subject to measurement, such as requirements relating to operation or maintenance, design and equipment, work practices, and operational standards. As a result, identifying the enforceable requirements for a particular business operation is often difficult. . . .

The regulation of small existing stationary sources emitting certain air pollutants will depend primarily upon how each state decides to achieve or maintain compliance with national ambient air quality standards (NAAQS), [pursuant to State Implementation Plans (SIP) processs]. . . . Each state may have an assortment of strategies designed to control pollutants. . . . [S]tandards are often expressed in general terms, and emission monitoring requirements may be equally general or nonexistent. . . .

[E]ven where SIP standards are specific and monitoring is required, the problem of obtaining reliable data to detect and prove the violation remains. . . .

An additional disincentive to identifying and prosecuting violations, not applicable to national environmental groups prosecuting like cases, is that the facility in question might employ community residents. If this is the case, compliance monitoring might place some community residents in fear of losing their jobs and a citizens group might be reluctant to challenge the practices of local emitters. . . .

It is fair to conclude that the highly technical nature of air pollution regulation, coupled with the decentralized nature of SIP's and permit decisions, systematically discourages citizen enforcement. . . . Citizens in poor and minority communities are likely to remain at a disadvantage as they generally have fewer resources and [less] access to the expertise needed to determine compliance and prosecute enforcement actions.

Comprehensive Environmental Response, Compensation and Liability Act Enforcement Suits

The primary focus of the Comprehensive Environmental Response, Compensation and Liability Act (CERCLA), commonly known as Superfund, is to clean up contaminated sites. Enforcement actions under CERCLA do not involve violations of permit requirements as is common under environmental laws regulating the release of pollutants, like the Clean Air Act and Clean Water Act. Until EPA initiates an action to clean up a contaminated site, there are no "requirements" for the persons responsible for the contamination (potentially responsible parties) to violate. Citizen suit provisions under CERCLA, termed "one of the crueler farces of contemporary environmental lawmaking," limit enforcement actions to circumstances where the regulatory agency (EPA) first obtains an order against a potentially responsible party to abate an imminent and substantial endangerment, and the potentially responsible party subsequently violates the requirements stated in the order. As a practical result, citizens on or near contaminated areas can obtain relief under CERCLA citizen suit provisions only after EPA elects to take action. . . .

Resource Conservation and Recovery Act Enforcement Suits and Imminent Hazard Suits

For communities located near solid waste and hazardous waste facilities, a citizen suit under the authority of the Resource Conservation and Recovery Act (RCRA) could provide a remedy in the event of regulatory inaction under CERCLA. RCRA is the federal statute that regulates the disposal, storage, and treatment of solid and hazardous wastes. Under RCRA citizen suit provisions, the citizen group may enforce any RCRA "permit, standard, regulation, condition, requirement, prohibition or order." In addition to enforcement suits, RCRA citizen suit provisions authorize private citizens to prosecute an action against any person who is contributing (or has contributed) to the handling of a solid or hazardous waste in a manner that presents an imminent and substantial endangerment to health or to the environment.

Each existing hazardous waste facility must have a RCRA permit to operate. A citizen group in a community located near a hazardous waste facility might choose to investigate the facility's compliance with RCRA and prosecute an enforcement action if the facility is violating its permit conditions....

A more promising avenue lies in the RCRA citizen suit imminent hazard authority. The standards to be applied under RCRA citizen suit imminent hazard provisions should be the same as the standards under the EPA Administrator's authority to address imminent hazards. EPA has taken the position that its authority under RCRA's imminent hazard provision may remedy hazards brought on by releases to land, water, or air. In this respect, RCRA's imminent hazard authority is "essentially a codification of common law public nuisance remedies." Unlike common law nuisance doctrine, however, RCRA's imminent hazard provisions may reach a broader range of defendants, specifically government agencies waiving sovereign immunity, and *past or present* generators, transporters, owners, or operators of waste facilities. Therefore, the advantage of RCRA citizen suit imminent hazard actions is that citizen groups may reach a wide range of defendants for dangerous conditions emanating from both operating and *abandoned* waste facilities....

Attorney's Fees and Costs Under Citizen Suit Provisions

The citizen suit provisions of the Clean Air Act allow an award of attorney's fees and costs where appropriate. Citizen suit provisions of the Clean Water Act, RCRA, and CERCLA provide for an award of attorney's fees and costs to prevailing parties or substantially prevailing parties. Environmental "fee shifting" provisions are a necessary incentive to environmental enforcement because few private plaintiffs can afford to finance expensive environmental litigation that typically results in nonmonetary benefits to the public at large (rather than damage awards to the individual plaintiffs)....

The citizens group must find an environmental lawyer who is willing to take the case without any guarantee that the plaintiffs will prevail. Few private attorneys are willing to undertake expensive lawsuits on behalf of underfinanced citizens groups, especially without the incentive of a contingent fee arrangement or an hourly rate agreement backed by a retainer....

Underfinanced citizens groups face other practical problems. Recovery of legal costs occurs, if at all, at the end of the lawsuit. Meanwhile, the citizens group must be able to finance the lawsuit, which may require significant discovery costs, expert witness fees, and transportation costs (if the suit is not local). Although compensation for the delay factor may be subsumed in the lodestar amount [The lodestar is the product of a reasonable number of hours times a reasonable hourly rate. Eds.] if attorney's fees are awarded, the problem of up-front financing is still a significant obstacle for underfunded community groups.

Clearly, fee shifting is an incentive to private enforcement generally, although arguably not enough of an incentive considering the expense involved in undertaking complex environmental litigation. The Supreme Court has further limited the incentive structure by prohibiting contingency adjustments. The practical difficulty of financing complex environmental citizen suits, combined with substantive and procedural limitations of enforcement suits generally, presents substantial impediments to court access for community-based environmental justice groups in low income and minority communities....

* * *

Notes and Questions

1. When Congress amended the Clean Air Act in 1990, one of its goals was to make the statute easier to enforce, including by authorizing citizens to obtain penalties for violations (as opposed to just injunctive relief), requiring additional emissions monitoring and reporting, and creating a new permit program modeled after the Clean Water Act's permit program (known as the Title V program). Environmental groups contend that EPA in part has thwarted Congress' intent by failing to require adequate monitoring from emitting sources, and many argue that the Clean Air Act remains much more difficult to enforce than the Clean Water Act. Attorney Jim Hecker cites several reasons for this, including that more defenses are available to defendants in Clean Air Act than Clean Water Act enforcement actions, particularly those based on data quality and operational malfunctions, and that the determination of what is the "best available control technology" for an individual source under the Clean Air Act often is not straightforward, inviting expert disputes over what the proper permit standard is for a facility. Jim Hecker, *The Difficulty of Citizen Enforcement of the Clean Air Act*, 10 WIDENER L. REV. 303 (2004). In *Romoland School District, et al. v. Inland Empire Energy Center, et al*, 548 F.3d 738 (9th Cir. 2008), the Ninth Circuit imposed another barrier to some Clean Air Act citizen suit cases, holding that where an air district has integrated the requirements of the new source review program (which imposes controls for major new or modified air pollution sources) into the Title V permitting process, plaintiffs cannot challenge violations of new source review directly under the Act's citizen suit provisions, but must first administratively challenge the Title V permit. This effectively imposes an administrative exhaustion requirement for plaintiffs in these situations.

2. One tool that should prove helpful to communities in detecting noncompliance is a website established by EPA in 2002 that provides enforcement and compliance information to the public on more than 800,000 regulated facilities. The site contains data about a facility's inspection history, penalties assessed, and compliance status under the Clean Air Act, Clean Water Act, and RCRA. The website, Enforcement and Compliance History Online (ECHO), may be visited at http://www.gov.epa/echo/.

3. As noted by Professor Gauna, many environmental statutes provide for an award of attorney's fees to "prevailing parties," or in some cases, "substantially prevailing parties." In Buckhannon Board & Home Care v. West Virginia, 532 U.S. 598 (2001), the Supreme Court held that a party is only "prevailing" when it obtains judicial relief from the court, either through a judgment on the merits or a court-ordered consent decree. The Court rejected the view, which had been widely followed by the lower courts, that a plaintiff is entitled to fees where it achieves its desired result because the lawsuit brought about a voluntary change in the defendant's conduct (the so-called "catalyst theory"). The impact of the ruling may be to discourage a significant number of citizen actions from being

brought, since defendants will be able to foreclose an award of fees by voluntarily agreeing to the relief requested by the plaintiffs and rendering the case moot.

Other environmental statutes, including the Clean Air Act, the Endangered Species Act, the Safe Drinking Water Act, and the Toxic Substances Control Act, contain a different fee-shifting provision than the "prevailing party" standard at issue in *Buckhannon*. Instead, they authorize fees "whenever the court determines that an award is appropriate" (or similar language). Post-*Buckhannon* cases under these statutes have continued to allow fee recoveries under the catalyst theory. *See* Sierra Club v. EPA, 322 F.3d 718 (D.C. Cir. 2003) (Clean Air Act); Loggerhead Turtle v. County Council of Volusia, 307 F.3d 1318 (11th Cir. 2002) (Endangered Species Act). In your view, does the different wording suggest that Congress intended attorney fee recovery to be more difficult under some environmental statutes?

4. As Professor Gauna points out, citizen suits are precluded when the government is "diligently prosecuting" an action against the violator. Not infrequently, citizens will file suit where the government has taken some enforcement action, but citizens contend it is too weak or ineffectual to constitute "diligent prosecution." Court decisions on the issue of "diligent prosecution" are fairly well divided between those finding "diligent prosecution" and precluding citizen enforcement and those rejecting it and allowing citizen suits to proceed. Attorneys Thomas Mullikin and Nancy Smith argue that the "diligent prosecution" bar should be interpreted broadly to preclude citizen suits where the government has acted:

> Diligence is the act of remedying the violations in any manner that the state decides. The mere fact that the state does not take the precise action that plaintiffs would prefer does not constitute lack of diligence.... [C]ollaborative and innovative environmental protection efforts between a state agency and regulated industry may be thwarted by the threat of potential citizen suits. In essence, these suits would second-guess an agency's discretion after the settlement.... If industry is subject to additional enforcement action, namely the prospect of penalties in excess of those already imposed by the agency, then they are less likely to negotiate the resolution of their violations. Clearly, this would result in the unnecessary proliferation of litigation.

Thomas S. Mullikin & Nancy S. Smith, *Community Participation in Environmental Protection*, 21 UCLA J. ENVTL. L. & POL'Y 75, 78, 80–81 (2002–03).

Professor Jeffrey Miller offers a contrary perspective, arguing that the courts frequently accord more deference to government prosecutions than Congress intended, and notes that it is the violators rather than federal and state prosecutors who argue that the prosecutorial choices should be accorded great deference. He contends that "while some degree of deference is due to prosecutorial decisions, blind deference ignores the fact that Congress authorized citizen suits precisely because government enforcers were not always diligent." Jeffrey G. Miller, *Theme and Variations in Statutory Preclusions Against Successive Environmental Enforcement Actions by EPA and Citizens: Part One: Statutory Bars in Citizen Suit Provisions*, 28 HARV. ENVTL. L. REV. 401, 466 (2004). Which approach do you find more desirable?

5. As noted in Chapter 8, public agencies in recent years have been settling some enforcement cases by agreeing to have defendants undertake environmental mitigation projects that benefit the local community ("supplemental environmental projects" or "SEPs"). Private parties also have been making greater use of SEPs in settling citizen suit enforcement actions. Community groups also sometimes have negotiated "good neighbor" agree-

ments in which industry commits to ongoing environmental improvements such as pollution prevention, emergency preparedness measures, or broader access to information for the public in exchange for the community settling ongoing challenges and ending protests or negative publicity. *See* Sanford Lewis, *Good Neighbor Agreements: A Tool for Environmental and Social Justice,* Social Justice (Winter 1996). A related approach that has become popular in recent years is a Community Benefits Agreement ("CBA"), discussed in Chapter 3. A CBA is a contract negotiated between a developer and community detailing the benefits that the developer will provide in exchange for community support for a proposed project.

> Because the agreements are negotiated between community coalitions and interested developers, the benefits can be tailored to meet specific community needs, such as the need for parks, daycare centers, or job training facilities. The parties involved in creating the LAX [Los Angeles International] airport CBA, for example, agreed that LAX would fund sound-proofing in nearby schools and residences.... Additionally, the CBA requires LAX to implement a number of environmental controls, including the electrification of passenger gates and cargo areas (to reduce the need for engine idling), emissions reductions, and the conversion of airport vehicles to alternative fuels.

Patricia E. Salkin & Amy Lavine, *Understanding Community Benefits Agreements,* The Practical Real Estate Lawyer, July 2008 at 19–20, 24.

6. As noted in Chapter 4, tribes can enact their own environmental protection programs on Indian land, although there are considerable challenges in doing so. Professor James Grijalva argues that tribes also can protect their health and environmental interests by bringing citizen enforcement actions under federal environmental laws. He notes that while some tribes have started exercising direct regulatory authority over activities occurring in Indian country, such programs require time and resources to develop, and in many areas there currently are no effective federal or Indian programs. Additionally, tribal regulatory programs are constrained by limits on the authority of tribes over non-Indian actors in Indian country or over activities occurring or resources located outside Indian country. He points out that non-Indian land can contain sites and resources of ongoing cultural and religious significance to tribes, where the tribes' use often is protected by treaty, but because the sites are outside Indian country, tribes cannot regulate activities of non-Indians adversely affecting these important areas. By contrast, a tribe suing under a citizen suit provision need not show that it has authority to directly regulate the defendant causing environmental harm, since the basis of the citizen suit is the defendant's violation of federal environmental statutes. Professor Grijalva also notes that SEPs resulting from private enforcement cases can have important benefits for tribes, including restoration of damaged areas, pollution reduction, and development of infrastructure and capacity for tribal regulatory programs. James M. Grijalva, *The Tribal Sovereign as Citizen: Protecting Indian Country Health and Welfare Through Federal Environmental Citizen Suits,* 12 Mich. J. Race & L. 33 (2006).

7. As the excerpt from Professor Gauna's article indicates, private enforcement actions against noncomplying facilities may be financially infeasible for many groups. Professor Gauna also notes that action-forcing suits, such as suits against agencies for failure to adopt required regulations, "are often luxuries that underfunded citizen groups cannot afford to undertake ... [since] they are often preoccupied attempting to remedy exigent local conditions." Gauna, *supra,* at 71. Can you think of ways that underfinanced citizen groups can fund lawsuits, or alternatively, use their limited resources in other ways to achieve results similar to those obtainable through lawsuits?

3. Building Community Enforcement Capacity

What approaches can be used to strengthen private enforcement in low-income communities and communities of color? Consider the following suggestions:

a. Upwardly Adjusting Attorney's Fees

Most environmental statutes allow prevailing parties in enforcement actions to recover attorney's fees. As noted above, the appropriate amount of fees is calculated as the product of a reasonable number of hours times a reasonable hourly rate, the so-called "lodestar" amount. Professor Gauna argues that courts should augment fees awarded to attorneys successfully prosecuting environmental justice enforcement cases:

> [J]udges could allow an upward lodestar adjustment, not as a contingency adjustment, but specifically to encourage and reward private attorneys who undertake enforcement actions in low income and minority neighborhoods (i.e., an "equity adjustment").... Fee shifting in the private attorney general context serves several important purposes, not the least of which is the incentive for citizens to bring suits that provide a recognized social benefit. In the case of environmental citizens suits, the recognized social benefit is the enforcement of environmental laws. One can assume that Congress (and the courts) had this general purpose in mind in developing the present fee shifting system based on a market rate lodestar calculation. However, in allowing attorney's fees based on the lodestar for environmental citizen suits across the board, Congress did not specifically address environmental justice concerns: that minority and low income communities suffer disparate environmental hazards due in part to a relative lack of resources as a class. Therefore, an upward adjustment is necessary to further another important policy objective that is not already subsumed in the lodestar calculation.

Gauna, *supra*, at 81. What do you think of this approach? Would it be consistent with the Supreme Court's decision in Grutter v. Bollinger, 539 U.S. 982 (2003), discussed in Chapter 10, which limits the use of racial considerations in government decisions?

b. Technical Assistance to Communities

Environmental justice activists often advocate the idea of providing technical assistance to communities. Such assistance could take a variety of forms, as described below.

i. Superfund's Technical Assistance Provisions

Superfund mandates that EPA provide opportunities for public participation before it adopts final cleanup plans. As early as 1986, the Superfund amendments authorized EPA to make Technical Assistance Grants (TAGs) of up to $50,000 to citizens affected by sites listed on the National Priorities List. Communities can use the grants to hire independent technical advisors to help them understand and comment on technical aspects of the cleanup process. The TAG program has been criticized as unduly complex and imposing administrative barriers to participation. Observers have called for the grant process to be simplified and expedited, and the range of allowable expenditures by community groups broadened. Attorney Deeohn Ferris additionally argues "[t]o ensure effective public participation and to improve the pace and quality of the cleanup process, EPA should be required to work with communities to create Community Working Groups (CWGs) at each Superfund site. CWGs would consist of community leaders, community representatives, and, if desired by the community, other appropriate organizations.... [The] CWGs would assume a key decision making role concerning health assessments, responses to hot-spots, remediation alternatives, cleanup schedules, and relocation decisions." Deeohn Ferris, *Communities of Color and Hazardous Waste Cleanup: Expanding Public Participation in the Federal Superfund Program,* 21 FORDHAM URB. L.J. 671, 682 (1994).

ii. Community Outreach and Education

Commentators also have argued that expanded government education and outreach can help environmental justice communities more effectively participate in the enforcement process:

> EPA is aware that low income and minority communities are less likely to be aware of the agency's activities and responsibilities and are, therefore, less likely to participate in the agency's decisionmaking process. The degree of attention paid by an agency to a violating facility or waste site can be strongly influenced by the amount of attention drawn to the site by the local community. The ability of an affected community to influence enforcement decisions takes both knowledge of the enforcement process and resources. Little information is provided by EPA, and probably less by states, identifying particular violations that have been detected and what enforcement responses the agency intends to pursue. Although EPA publishes its administrative penalties and proposed settlements in the Federal Register, this notice would not likely reach affected communities, particularly communities whose members lack knowledge of and access to the Federal Register.... A requirement that agencies publish notice, in a timely and accessible manner, of all violations detected by inspectors and of the enforcement actions pending and concluded would foster greater community involvement.

Robert R. Kuehn, *Remedying the Unequal Enforcement of Environmental Laws,* 9 ST. JOHN'S J. LEGAL COMMENT. 625, 659–61 (1994). As noted above, EPA in 2002 started the ECHO website that contains enforcement and compliance information about regulated facilities. Other environmental justice advocates have suggested that local residents be allowed to independently inspect facilities or to accompany agency staff on government inspections and that agencies provide local groups with enforcement information, such as inspection notices, notices of violations, and levels of pollutants being emitted, as they become available. (These and other recommendations can be found in the Report of the Environmental Justice Enforcement and Compliance Assurance Roundtable, available at http://es.epa.gov/oeca/oej/nejac/pdf/1096.pdf.)

iii. Training Communities to Detect Noncompliance

Should state and federal agencies provide local community groups with funding, training and equipment to independently monitor the environment? Or is it inappropriate for government agencies to promote such capacity since it could lead to enforcement actions against regulated entities? Professor Gauna suggests that "EPA [and the states] could greatly enhance [private] enforcement in poor and minority neighborhoods by training community residents in sampling and monitoring techniques," enabling them to determine whether facilities are in compliance. Gauna, *supra,* at 80. As Professors Robert Collin and Robin Morris Collin point out, citizen monitoring of environmental conditions has a well-respected tradition in this country (dating back to 1890 when the National Weather Service began training volunteers to report daily measurements of air temperatures and rainfall), and there are now hundreds of formal, volunteer water quality monitoring programs at the grassroots level. Many states rely upon volunteer citizen monitoring to meet the biennial water quality reporting requirements of section 305(b) of the Clean Water Act. Robert W. Collin & Robin M. Collin, *The Role of Communities in Environmental Decisions: Communities Speaking for Themselves*, 13 U. Or. J. Envtl. L. & Litig. 37, 82–84 (1998).

Notes and Questions

1. Some state and federal governmental officials believe that training communities to detect noncompliance is not wise policy because it encourages litigation. Do you agree? What are the pros and cons of this approach? What do you think are the most effective ways to strengthen enforcement in environmental justice communities? Which are most feasible? Are there additional tools that you would recommend?

C. Common Law Remedies

Before the start of the modern environmental movement, common law actions were the primary tool for protecting the environment. Although such actions largely receded into the background with the adoption of the major federal environmental laws beginning in the 1970s, they continued to be used at the local level, and have enjoyed a resurgence of interest among practitioners in recent years. This trend arguably is a response to some of the hurdles imposed on citizen enforcement discussed in Section B, and other weaknesses in agency enforcement of environmental laws, discussed in Chapter 8.

As Dr. Melissa Toffolon-Weiss and Professor J. Timmons Roberts explain:

> [f]or community groups fighting for environmental justice, the choice to pursue a toxic tort (a class action lawsuit brought with the help of a private personal injury lawyer) versus a public interest lawsuit is closely related to whether the environmental threat is an existing facility or a proposed use—yet to be constructed. Toxic torts may only be used when some form of injury has occurred. In environmental justice personal injury suits, a plaintiff presents with one or several of the following: a personal injury; fear of a future personal injury due to the latent effects of pollution; loss of property value; and loss of quality of life (e.g., nuisance, pain and suffering, or economic distress); invasion of property rights; and an intent to punish the perpetrator.

Melissa Tofflon-Weiss & J. Timmons Roberts, *Toxic Torts, Public Interest Law, and Environmental Justice: Evidence from Louisiana*, 26 Law & Pol'y 259, 260–61 (2004).

Environmental plaintiffs have achieved some important successes in actions seeking damages from catastrophic spills or accidents. However, tort actions alleging harm from routine, ongoing environmental releases are much more difficult to win, as Ms. Toffolon-Weiss and Mr. Roberts detail:

The plaintiff's case is often hindered by a lack of baseline health data in order to compare the health of the victims before and after an exposure. Poor people usually have limited access to medical care, and thus lack good medical records. Additionally, they may have been exposed to dangerous work and lifestyle factors that are often presented by the defense as alternative casual factors. Government and corporate officials often do not take the symptoms of these people seriously. They attribute the poor health of these communities to unhealthy lifestyles (e.g., eating fatty foods, smoking, drinking alcohol, and taking drugs). Carrying out comprehensive health assessments is expensive and lengthy, and state and federal health departments may not be willing or able to provide funding for such projects. Further, middle-class jurors' own prejudices may affect their judgments when viewing poorer individuals with different life experiences.

Lastly, a major hurdle that the environmental justice plaintiff faces is the lack of scientific evidence on the casual connection between certain exposures and health problems. It has taken years for scientists to draw a causal connection between lung cancer and smoking. In these environmental cases, we are talking about toxins that have received much less scientific attention. Additionally, it is often difficult for public health professionals to find specific information on the level and frequency of exposure. Some health studies conducted by firms producing the chemicals are never made public. Plaintiffs may also be exposed to multiple sources of industrial pollution and little may be known about their interactive effects. Technical assistance with medical and scientific evidence can be costly....

Id. at 261–62; *see also* Allan Kanner, *Tort Remedies and Litigation Strategies, in* THE LAW OF ENVIRONMENTAL JUSTICE: THEORIES AND PROCEDURES TO ADDRESS DISPROPORTIONATE RISKS 667 (Michael B. Gerrard & Sheila R. Foster eds., 2d ed. 2008).

Notes and Questions

1. Professor Tseming Yang notes that tort law could have advantages over statutory remedies for communities suffering disparate environmental harms. One, its focus on individual parties rather than the public at-large, "promotes outcomes that are more sensitive to the particular interests, including corrective justice claims, of these communities." For example, tort law can provide compensatory remedies to communities, but citizen suits under environmental laws against polluters provide only injunctions, not damages. Two, tort law could be more likely than environmental regulation to address the incommensurable harms that environmental justice activists complain of—destruction of community, quality of life concerns, etc.—since it recognizes harms such as claims for pain and suffering and emotional distress damages. Tseming Yang, *Environmental Regulation, Tort Law and Environmental Justice: What Could Have Been*, 41 WASHBURN L.J. 607, 617–18 (2002).

2. Common law claims alleging harm from pesticide exposure have been difficult to maintain because until recently, most appellate courts had found that the federal law governing pesticide registration (the Federal Insecticide, Fungicide and Rodenticide Act or "FIFRA") preempts state tort law claims related to pesticide warning and use labels. In Bates v. Dow Agrosciences, 544 U.S. 431 (2005), however, the Supreme Court reversed this jurisprudence, holding that common law claims for strict or negligent product liability, breach of warranty, and others were not preempted by FIFRA. It also ruled that plaintiffs' fraud and negligent failure to warn claims would not be preempted if state requirements were "equivalent to and fully consistent with" FIFRA's labeling requirements. After *Bates*,

common law claims stemming from pesticide exposures may become more prevalent. Professor Alexendra Klass notes that "[e]very year, hundreds of thousands of children are exposed to harmful pesticides, resulting in acute injury and even death" and contends that the Bates decision "creates a significant opportunity for [common law tort] claims to play an increasing role in pesticide policy with regard to children's health.... by spurring manufacturers to gather scientific data and provide additional protections for children." She explains that the desire to avoid tort claims such as negligent testing and design could prompt manufacturers to engage in more testing and create better and safer products. Alexandra B. Klass, *Pesticides, Children's Health Policy, and Common Law Tort Claims*, 7 MINN. J.L. SCI. & TECH. 89, 90, 92 (2005).

3. Common law claims against paint manufacturers on behalf of children injured by lead-based paint likewise have largely been unsuccessful, because of the difficulty of linking an individual's injuries to a specific company's paint, and more generally because of the reluctance of courts to apply theories of collective liability, such as market share, alternative liability or enterprise liability. Katie J. Zoglin, *Getting the Lead Out: The Potential of Public Nuisance in Lead-Based Paint Litigation in* CREATIVE COMMON LAW STRATEGIES FOR PROTECTING THE ENVIRONMENT 339, 343 (Clifford Rechtschaffen & Denise Antolini eds. 2007). More recently, cases in which public entities have alleged common law claims, particularly public nuisance, have shown some success—although the record is mixed. In these cases the plaintiffs have argued that the relevant inquiry is not whether individual housing units constitute a nuisance, but whether the overall impact of lead-based paint in the community housing stock is a nuisance. In County of Santa Clara v. Altantic-Richfield Co., 40 Cal. Rptr. 3d 313 (Ct. App. 2006), for example, the court agreed with plaintiffs' characterization of the issue and allowed several counties to proceed with their public nuisance claims on behalf of the public. *See* Zoglin, at 347–65.

In another case brought by the Rhode Island Attorney General, a jury in 2006 found three lead paint manufacturers liable under public nuisance law for the contamination of over 300,000 homes in that state, and ordered the companies to abate the nuisance. On appeal, however, the Rhode Island Supreme Court vacated the judgment, ruling that the injuries alleged by the state were not of a right common to the general public and that there was no allegation that the paint companies were in control of the lead pigment they manufactured at the time it caused harm to Rhode Island children. The court noted: "[W]e do not mean to minimize the severity of the harm that thousands of children in Rhode Island have suffered as a result of lead poisoning. Our hearts go out to those children whose lives forever have been changed by the poisonous presence of lead. But, however grave the problem of lead poisoning is in Rhode Island, public nuisance law simply does not provide a remedy for this harm." State of R.I. v. Lead Indus. Ass'n, Inc., et al., 951 A.2d 428, 435 (R.I. 2008).

4. As noted, the common law also can be used to obtain injunctive relief against polluting facilities. In the excerpt below, attorney Richard Drury chronicles how the residents of Huntington Park, a low-income, largely Latino community in southeastern Los Angeles, successfully used a public nuisance theory against a concrete crushing and recycling facility.

Richard T. Drury, Moving a Mountain: The Struggle for Environmental Justice in Southeast Los Angeles

CREATIVE COMMON LAW STRATEGIES FOR PROTECTING THE ENVIRONMENT 173
(Clifford Rechtschaffen & Denise Antolini eds. 2007)

In November 1993, ... [Aggregate Recycling Systems, Inc (ARS)] approached the city of Huntington Park [California] with a proposal for a concrete recycling facility for a long-vacant lot.... ARS' owner, Sam Chew, proposed to take concrete debris and crush it for reuse as aggregate for roadbeds and for mixing with cement for new roads and structures. The city issued a permit for the facility and it opened for business....

Two months later, the Northridge earthquake [destroyed portions of the Santa Monica Freeway, just west of Huntington Park].... In its haste to [reconstruct the freeway], CalTrans [the California Department of Transportation] had left itself little time to consider how to dispose of the huge amount of debris that used to be the Santa Monica Freeway. As low bidder on the disposal contract, ARS took in much of the debris, and its formerly small recycling operation quickly became the massive La Montaña, an 80-foot-tall mountain containing 600,000 tons of concrete debris.... ARS moved its crushing equipment to the top of the mountain, and began operating the crushers around the clock in a futile attempt to keep up with the incoming loads.

The continuous crushing operations from the top of the mountain created a massive plume of particulate matter (PM) that blanketed streets up to an inch deep, and covered nearby homes, cars, furniture, food, dishes, and lawns, particularly on the downwind Cottage Street side of the facility, with a layer of sticky concrete dust. Residents of the low-income community, many without air conditioning, were forced to keep their doors and windows closed even in the squelching heat of the Los Angeles summer, and many had to abandon outdoor activities entirely. The highly caustic concrete dust caused many residents to suffer from respiratory problems, including bloody noses, sinus headaches and irritated noses, eyes, and throats. Many area children suffered increased asthma episodes, frequent bloody noses, and breathing difficulty. Some nearby businesses also experienced problems....

To remove La Montaña from Huntington Park and shut down the ARS facility, [Communities for a Better Environment (CBE), a local environmental group] undertook to organize the community, to marshal scientific evidence of the deleterious health effects of the pollution from ARS, and ultimately to take legal action....

[First, Carlos Porras, CBE's Southern California Director] hire[d] veteran community organizer Alicia Rivera, ... [who] went door to door through the Cottage Street neighborhood to hear complaints directly from the people who were affected, and to encourage the neighbors to band together. In a short time, the neighbors were holding weekly house meetings.... The residents, now known as the Los Angeles Comunidades Asambleadas y Unidas para un Sostenible Ambiente, or Los Angeles Communities Assembled and United for a Sustainable Environment (LA CAUSA), decided to begin attending meetings of the Huntington Park City Council to raise their concerns [and].... conducted pre-meeting rallies outside of City Hall.... Word of the popular uprising spread quickly, and soon local newspapers, radio, and television were covering the demonstrations outside the formerly sleepy Huntington Park City Council chambers.... [T]he community was now organized, and the issue of La Montaña had been injected into the politics of Huntington Park.

[Second,] [t]he scientists of CBE … compiled a compelling mountain of evidence.…
CBE retained an independent test lab to gather dust samples upwind and downwind of
ARS. The company conducted polarized light microscopy on the samples, finding that 70%
of the downwind samples were composed of concrete dust, while only 16% of the upwind
samples were concrete.

[Huntington Park's] Mayor Loya obtained support from local doctors and the American
Lung Association to test Cottage Street residents for respiratory problems. The study revealed
that over one-half of the residents suffered from chronic obstructive pulmonary disease.

LA CAUSA members, supported by CBE staff, demonstrated at the South Coast Air
Quality Management District (SCAQMD) to demand air testing by the agency. After
meeting initial resistance, the SCAQMD agreed to conduct some tests. Despite giving
ARS advance notice of the test dates, the results of the downwind test revealed levels of
total suspended particulates (TSP) higher than any ever recorded in central Los Angeles
during the entire calendar year.

CBE also retained Los Angeles Unified School District atmospheric scientist Bill Pi-
azza, who conducted sophisticated air quality modeling to demonstrate that PM levels
generated by ARS were even higher than those measured by the SCAQMD.…

[Third,] recognizing that the options for legal action under environmental statutes
were limited, CBE's attorneys turned to the common law. The California Civil Code
§§ 3479 and 3480 contain an expansive public nuisance provision. Section 3479 defines
a nuisance as:

> Anything which is injurious to health … or is indecent or offensive to the senses,
> or an obstruction to the free use of property, so as to interfere with the com-
> fortable enjoyment of life or property, or unlawfully obstructs the free passage
> or use, in the customary manner, of any navigable lake, or river, bay, stream,
> canal, or basin, or any public park, square, street, or highway, is a nuisance.

Section 3480 defines a "public nuisance" to be one "which affects at the same time an entire community or neighborhood, or any considerable number of persons, although the
extent of the annoyance or damage inflicted upon individuals may be unequal."

CBE was aware of a long line of older California cases finding operations very similar
to ARS' to be nuisances.… The common law approach was also advantageous because of
the breadth and vagueness of the definition of nuisance under California law: if a nuisance
action were brought in trial court, the judge would have broad discretion to determine
whether the ARS facility was creating a nuisance and, if so, to balance the equities in determining the appropriate remedy.…

In assessing ARS' potential defenses, CBE again saw some advantages to a common
law approach. The California courts had held that a company may not claim a "permit
defense." That is, a company may not create a nuisance even if it is operating its business
under valid governmental permits. The courts had reasoned that a permit does not tac-
itly allow the company to create a nuisance even though the government has granted it a
permit to operate.…

The CBE legal team then discovered an interesting twist that offered the advantages of
the common law of nuisance but eliminated many of the uncertainties of a nuisance lawsuit. Rather than sue ARS in California Superior Court, the residents and CBE could
bring an administrative complaint for public nuisance before the city of Huntington Park.
If the city could be persuaded to declare ARS to be a public nuisance, then ARS, not the
residents, would have the burden of suing the city in the Superior Court to attempt to re-

verse the decision. But the result had some risks — the court would apply a highly deferential standard of review and likely support the city's determination either way, as long as it was supported by "substantial evidence." ...

Under [Huntington Park's] nuisance ordinance, any resident could petition to have a facility deemed a public nuisance. The matter would be assigned to an administrative law judge assigned by the city manager, and a decision could be appealed to the city council.... LA CAUSA launched a new organizing campaign to convince the city to institute a quasi-judicial administrative proceeding to determine whether ARS was creating a public nuisance pursuant to the city's nuisance ordinance.... [Thereafter] the city's attorney ... recommended that the city invoke its nuisance ordinance and commence a quasi-judicial public nuisance proceeding, as recommended by CBE and LA CAUSA.... [T]he city council agreed and retained the respected environmental lawyer Colin Lennard to preside as its hearing officer.

Lennard conducted five days of administrative hearings.... CBE's strategy was to combine real-life community experiences with scientific evidence and legal authority. CBE began the proceedings with almost a dozen area residents who testified to their personal experiences living near ARS — breathing problems, nosebleeds, asthma attacks, and hospitalizations. This testimony was supported by an atmospheric scientist, a respiratory health expert, an environmental scientist, and others, who testified that ARS was the likely source of the residents' health problems and that the health problems were consistent with high-level exposure to concrete PM....

In defense, Chew primarily argued that the dust was created by Saroyan Lumber [a facility located on the other side of ARS]. His legal argument hinged almost entirely on the partial SCAQMD tests results, which found ARS not to be in violation of Air District regulations.... [H]earing officer Lennard found the SCAQMD's test results largely unpersuasive for a variety of reasons and rejected ARS' arguments.... Lennard found ARS to be creating a nuisance per se because it was violating several provisions of the Huntington Park municipal code.... He also found ARS' operations to constitute a public nuisance within the definitions of California Civil Code §§ 3479 and 3480 because its operations were injurious to the health of its neighbors, were offensive to the senses, and interfered with the comfortable enjoyment of property.

[Lennard issued an order abating the nuisance] requir[ing] ARS to render all of its equipment inoperable immediately and to cease all deliveries of new material to the site. ARS was required to hire an independent consultant to develop a plan to remove all debris from the site in an environmentally responsible manner that included controls for dust, noise, and vibrations, and which would eventually decrease the pile's height to a maximum of eight feet. ARS was to remove the debris within 60 days....

[In subsequent reviews, the city council affirmed Lennard's order and a superior court found that the city had substantial evidence to support its nuisance determination.] ARS still refused to clean up the concrete mountain, even though it had lost all of its legal challenges. The city then brought a criminal enforcement action against ARS, but the company pled poverty. ARS claimed that without any revenues from the receipt of new aggregate debris or from the sale of crushed material, it did not have funding to comply with the cleanup order....

La Montaña, now idle, loomed over the community for the next seven years....

Then in 2004,.... [the city] secure[d] $2 million in state funding to clean up La Montaña.... At the urging of local community members, the city has since purchased the property and will turn it into a park....

The story of Huntington Park's struggle to remove La Montaña suggests that hybrid legal-political strategies are often most effective for achieving environmental justice. It is possible to achieve results by combining sound legal strategies with direct community organizing that might not be possible through either approach alone....

By bringing the legal strategy into the political arena of a quasi-judicial proceeding before the city council, it was possible to bring political pressure on elected officials to declare what had been obvious for so long—that the ARS facility was a public nuisance and had to close immediately. Elected officials can be swayed by media attention, direct pleas from their constituents, pickets, and other forms of organizing. Such pressures rarely come into play in a judicial proceeding....

* * *

Notes and Questions

1. Mr. Drury explains that his clients turned to nuisance law because of the weaknesses of applicable statutory remedies. Its options under the Clean Air Act were limited because the local air district had granted ARS a mobile source air permit, based on the fact that ARS used movable crushing equipment. The district's mobile source permitting rules were far more lenient than stationary source rules (on the assumption, inaccurate in the case of ARS, that a mobile source would not remain in one location for more than a few weeks). Likewise, the city had initially exempted ARS from review under California's environmental review statute, the California Environmental Quality Act, based on the company's representations that the project would have minimal impacts. In addition, the statute's very short (thirty-five-day) statute of limitations for challenging that determination had long since passed. *See id.* at 182–83. What does the experience of this case suggest about the relative usefulness of common law approaches?

2. In the Huntington Park case described above, the harm to residents stemmed from concrete dust. Another problem that traditional environmental laws do not address—but that the common law can—is odor. Although odor problems may not seem that bad, they can severely and adversely affect health and quality of life.

In another novel use of common law remedies, Native Alaskans living near the Arctic Circle filed a complaint in 2008 seeking to recover damages due to global warming that has forced them to relocate their village. An excerpt of the complaint follows:

United States District Court, Northern District of California, Native Village of Kivalina & City of Kivalina, Plaintiffs v. ExxonMobil Corporation, et al, Defendants
2008 WL 594713 (N.D.Cal.)

1. This is a suit to recover damages from global warming caused by defendants' actions. Plaintiffs, the Native Village of Kivalina and the City of Kivalina (collectively "Kivalina"), are the governing bodies of an Inupiat village of approximately 400 people. Kivalina is located on the tip of a six-mile barrier reef located between the Chukchi Sea

and the Kivalina and Wulik Rivers on the Northwest coast of Alaska, some seventy miles north of the Arctic Circle.... Kivalina residents are Inupiat Eskimo whose ancestors occupied the area since time immemorial. Global warming is destroying Kivalina and the village thus must be relocated soon or be abandoned and cease to exist. Relocating will cost hundreds of millions of dollars and is an urgent matter. The U.S. Army Corps of Engineers and the U.S. Government Accountability Office have both concluded that Kivalina must be relocated due to global warming and have estimated the cost to be from $95 million to $400 million....

3. Defendants contribute to global warming through their emissions of large quantities of greenhouse gases. Defendants in this action include many of the largest emitters of greenhouse gases in the United States....

5. Each of the defendants knew or should have known of the impacts of their emissions on global warming and on particularly vulnerable communities such as coastal Alaskan villages....

III. PARTIES....

13. The Native Village of Kivalina owns property and structures in Kivalina that are imminently threatened by global warming....

16. Global warming has severely harmed Kivalina by reducing the sea ice commonly present in the fall, winter and spring at Kivalina. The sea ice—particularly land-fast sea ice—acts as a protective barrier to the coastal storms that batter the coast of the Chukchi Sea. Due to global warming, the sea ice forms later in the year, attaches to the coast later, breaks up earlier, and is less extensive and thinner, thus subjecting Kivalina to coastal storm waves and surges. These storms and waves are destroying the land upon which Kivalina is located....

B. Defendants

[Defendants include five oil companies and their subsidiaries (BP, Chevron, Conoco-Phillips, Exxon Mobil Corp., and Royal Dutch Shell); and fifteen energy companies and their subsidiaries that generate and/or distribute energy in its various forms.]

IV. GLOBAL WARMING....

134. The science of global warming is not new. The heating of the planet from emissions of carbon dioxide and other greenhouse gases has long been forecast....

A. Defendants' Carbon Dioxide Emissions....

173. Carbon dioxide emissions from the U.S. electric power sector increased by more than 28 percent from 1990 to 2006, compared to an 18 percent increase in carbon dioxide emissions for the economy as a whole. Carbon dioxide emissions from the electric power sector are projected by the U.S. Department of Energy to increase by an additional 30 percent by the year 2030 if no action is taken to restrain such emissions....

[The complaint includes allegations about the actions of each of the individual defendants that contribute to global warming.]

D. Civil Conspiracy Allegations....

189. There has been a long campaign by power, coal, and oil companies to mislead the public about the science of global warming.... Initially, the campaign attempted to show that global warming was not occurring. Later, and continuing to the present, it attempts to demonstrate that global warming is good for the planet and its inhabitants or that even if there may be ill effects, there is not enough scientific certainty to warrant action....

First Claim for Relief

Federal Common Law: Public Nuisance....

250. Defendants' emissions of carbon dioxide and other greenhouse gases, by contributing to global warming, constitute a substantial and unreasonable interference with public rights, including, inter alia, the rights to use and enjoy public and private property in Kivalina....

Third Claim for Relief

Civil Conspiracy....

269. Defendants ExxonMobil, AEP, BP America Inc., Chevron Corporation, ConocoPhillips Company, Duke Energy, Peabody, and Southern ("Conspiracy Defendants") have engaged in agreements to participate in an unlawful act or a lawful act in an unlawful means. The Conspiracy Defendants have engaged in agreements to participate in the intentional creation, contribution to and/or maintenance of a public nuisance, global warming....

* * *

Notes and Questions

1. Why did the Village of Kivalina turn to common law theories of public nuisance and civil conspiracy to recover for the damages they have suffered due to global warming? What do you think of the merits of their case? Why do you think they selected the particular defendants they sued and not others? Can they (should they) be allowed to recover without the presence of other major contributors to global warming?

2. Do you think environmental groups should rely more on tort cases as opposed to citizen enforcement actions to deter corporate noncompliance? On the one hand, damages in large tort cases (both actual and punitive damages) can sometimes far exceed the penalties imposed (or even theoretically available) in enforcement actions. On the other hand, establishing liability in a citizen enforcement case typically only requires establishing that a defendant violated a permit requirement, and avoids complex and often insurmountable issues of causation. Which approach is preferable, and under what circumstances? For an example of a legally successful toxic tort lawsuit that failed to make the affected community feel whole, *see* DENNIS LOVE, MY CITY WAS GONE: ONE AMERICAN TOWN'S TOXIC SECRET, ITS ANGRY BAND OF LOCALS, AND A $700 MILLION DAY IN COURT (2006) (describing lawsuit against Monsanto for dumping polychlorinated biphenyls (PCBs) into Anniston, Alabama's local environment over a 40 year period which resulted in $700 million settlement).

3. If you were an attorney for community groups, what would you convey to your clients about the strengths and limitations of citizen suits and common law theories compared to regulation, governmental initiatives and multi-party collaboration as a means of achieving environmental justice?

Chapter 14

Constitutional and Civil Rights Claims

This chapter reviews efforts by impacted communities to use constitutional and civil rights remedies to address environmental harms. The first section deals with claims arising under the U.S. Constitution. We start first with cases attempting to use the Free Exercise Clause of the Constitution to protect sacred sites, and then turn to use of the Equal Protection Clause to attempt redress for a larger set of environmental justice concerns. Section B examines actions under Title VI of the Civil Rights Act of 1964.

A. Environmental Justice Framed as Constitutional Claims

1. The Free Exercise/Establishment Clause Cases

Many sites of great religious and cultural importance are found on public lands managed by the federal government. Approximately 29% of all the land in the United States is owned by the federal government. Federal public land laws establish different governing regimes depending on how the lands are classified (i.e., as a wilderness area, national park, national forest, etc.), but most vest significant discretion in agency land managers. Many public lands must accommodate multiple and sometimes competing uses, including timber harvesting and mineral development, recreation, wildlife protection, preservationist interests, and others. Inevitably, some of these uses occur on sites that have historical, religious, and cultural significance to some groups.

Bear in mind (as discussed in earlier chapters) that in addition to public lands management, other governmental actions affecting lands have enormous significance to particular communities, such as the acequia communities of the southwest, the Chinatowns of metropolitan areas, the coal field towns of Appalachia, southern towns originally settled by freed slaves, and sites that are sacred to Indians (and potentially others with land-based religious practices). Because of the significance of these places, environmental destruction, incompatible land uses, and relocation from these areas generate a special harm to certain communities.

While other constitutional claims to protect the sites of these communities are possible, to date, the most well-developed case law involves sites sacred to Native Americans. These cases involve challenges under the Free Exercise and Establishment Clauses of the U.S. Constitution, which raise two types of important and interrelated constitutional questions: do agency activities that interfere with Indian religious practices violate their free exercise of religion ("free exercise claims"), and do governmental efforts to protect Indian religious practices violate the establishment clause? The cases below reveal how the courts have attempted to resolve these conflicts, starting with the leading Supreme Court decision on the issue of First Amendment-based protection for Indian sacred sites located on federal land.

Lyng v. Northwest Indian Cemetery Protective Association
485 U.S. 439 (1988)

Justice O'Connor delivered the opinion of the Court:

This case requires us to consider whether the First Amendment's Free Exercise Clause prohibits the Government from permitting timber harvesting in, or constructing a road through, a portion of a National Forest that has traditionally been used for religious purposes by members of three American Indian tribes in northwestern California....

As part of a project to create a paved 75-mile road linking two California towns, Gasquet and Orleans, the United States Forest Service has upgraded 49 miles of previously unpaved roads on federal land. In order to complete this project (the G-O road), the Forest Service must build a 6-mile paved segment through the Chimney Rock section of the Six Rivers National Forest....

[T]he Forest Service commissioned a study of American Indian cultural and religious sites in the area. The Hoopa Valley Indian reservation adjoins the Six Rivers National Forest, and the Chimney Rock area has historically been used for religious purposes by Yurok, Karok, and Tolowa Indians. The commissioned study, which was completed in 1979, found that the entire area "is significant as an integral and indispensible [sic] part of Indian religious conceptualization and practice." Specific sites are used for certain rituals, and "successful use of the [area] is dependent upon and facilitated by certain qualities of the physical environment, the most important of which are privacy, silence, and an undisturbed natural setting." The study concluded that constructing a road along any of the available routes "would cause serious and irreparable damage to the sacred areas which are an integral and necessary part of the belief systems and lifeway of Northwest California Indian peoples." Accordingly, the report recommended that the G-O road not be completed.

In 1982, the Forest Service decided not to adopt this recommendation, and it prepared a final environmental impact statement for construction of the road....

[Plaintiffs then filed suit in federal court challenging this decision]

The Free Exercise Clause of the First Amendment provides that "Congress shall make no law ... prohibiting the free exercise [of religion]." It is undisputed that the Indian respondents' beliefs are sincere and that the Government's proposed actions will have severe adverse effects on the practice of their religion. Those respondents contend that the burden on their religious practices is heavy enough to violate the Free Exercise Clause unless the Government can demonstrate a compelling need to complete the G-O road or to engage in timber harvesting in the Chimney Rock area. We disagree.

In *Bowen v. Roy*, 476 U. S. 693 (1986), we considered a challenge to a federal statute that required the States to use Social Security numbers in administering certain welfare programs. Two applicants for benefits under these programs contended that their religious beliefs prevented them from acceding to the use of a Social Security number for their 2-year-old daughter because the use of a numerical identifier would "'rob the spirit' of [their] daughter and prevent her from attaining greater spiritual power." ... The Court rejected [this challenge]:

> "The Free Exercise Clause simply cannot be understood to require the Government to conduct its own internal affairs in ways that comport with the religious beliefs of particular citizens. Just as the Government may not insist that [the Roys] engage in any set form of religious observance, so [they] may not demand that the Government join in their chosen religious practices by refraining from using a number to identify their daughter." ...

The building of a road or the harvesting of timber on publicly owned land cannot meaningfully be distinguished from the use of a Social Security number in *Roy*. In both cases, the challenged government action would interfere significantly with private persons' ability to pursue spiritual fulfillment according to their own religious beliefs. In neither case, however, would the affected individuals be coerced by the Government's action into violating their religious beliefs; nor would either governmental action penalize religious activity by denying any person an equal share of the rights, benefits, and privileges enjoyed by other citizens....

Whatever may be the exact line between unconstitutional prohibitions on the free exercise of religion and the legitimate conduct by government of its own affairs, the location of the line cannot depend on measuring the effects of a governmental action on a religious objector's spiritual development. The Government does not dispute, and we have no reason to doubt, that the logging and road-building projects at issue in this case could have devastating effects on traditional Indian religious practices. Those practices are intimately and inextricably bound up with the unique features of the Chimney Rock area, which is known to the Indians as the "high country." ...

One need not look far beyond the present case to see why the analysis in *Roy* ... offers a sound reading of the Constitution. Respondents attempt to stress the limits of the religious servitude that they are now seeking to impose on the Chimney Rock area of the Six Rivers National Forest. While defending an injunction against logging operations and the construction of a road, they apparently do not *at present* object to the area's being used by recreational visitors, other Indians, or forest rangers. Nothing in the principle for which they contend, however, would distinguish this case from another lawsuit in which they (or similarly situated religious objectors) might seek to exclude all human activity but their own from sacred areas of the public lands.... No disrespect for these practices is implied when one notes that such beliefs could easily require *de facto* beneficial ownership of some rather spacious tracts of public property....

The Constitution does not permit government to discriminate against religions that treat particular physical sites as sacred, and a law forbidding the Indian respondents from visiting the Chimney Rock area would raise a different set of constitutional questions. Whatever rights the Indians may have to the use of the area, however, those rights do not divest the Government of its right to use what is, after all, *its* land.

Nothing in our opinion should be read to encourage governmental insensitivity to the religious needs of any citizen. The Government's rights to the use of its own land, for example, need not and should not discourage it from accommodating religious practices like those engaged in by the Indian respondents....

Although the Forest Service did not in the end adopt the report's recommendation that the project be abandoned, many other ameliorative measures were planned. No sites where specific rituals take place were to be disturbed....

Except for abandoning its project entirely, and thereby leaving the two existing segments of road to dead-end in the middle of a National Forest, it is difficult to see how the Government could have been more solicitous....

* * *

Notes and Questions

1. In dissent, Justice Brennan, joined by Justices Marshall and Blackmun, argues that:

> In the final analysis, the Court's refusal to recognize the constitutional dimension of respondents' injuries stems from its concern that acceptance of respondents' claim could potentially strip the Government of its ability to manage and use vast tracts of federal property. In addition, the nature of respondents' site-specific religious practices raises the specter of future suits in which Native Americans seek to exclude all human activity from such areas. These concededly legitimate concerns lie at the very heart of this case, which represents yet another stress point in the longstanding conflict between two disparate cultures — the dominant western culture, which views land in terms of ownership and use, and that of Native Americans, in which concepts of private property are not only alien, but contrary to a belief system that holds land sacred. Rather than address this conflict in any meaningful fashion, however, the Court disclaims all responsibility for balancing these competing and potentially irreconcilable interests, choosing instead to turn this difficult task over to the Federal Legislature.

Id. at 473. In your view, is the majority's fear of the potential for a vast "religious servitude" on public lands a legitimate concern? How might the Court have addressed the conflicts highlighted by the dissent in a more "meaningful fashion?"

2. *Lyng* clearly upheld the ability of federal agencies to factor tribal religious practices into land use decision-making, if at their discretion they choose to do so. Such protective steps by the government, however, may be challenged as violating the Establishment Clause. In *Badoni v. Higginson,* 638 F.2d 172 (10th Cir. 1980), which was decided before the Supreme Court's decision in *Lyng,* Navajo Indians alleged that the government's management of the Rainbow Bridge Reservoir and Glen Canyon Dam and Reservoir violated their freedom to practice religion. As the court recounted, the Navajo "plaintiffs believe that if humans alter the earth in the area of the Bridge, plaintiffs' prayers will not be heard by the gods and their ceremonies will be ineffective to prevent evil and disease.... Tourists visiting the sacred area have desecrated it by noise, litter and defacement of the Bridge itself." *Id.* at 177. After rejecting the claim that the government had impermissibly burdened plaintiffs' religious practices (i.e., the free exercise claim), the court discussed whether the affirmative steps in the nature of "measured accommodation to their religious interest" requested by plaintiffs (e.g., prohibiting consumption of beer at the Monument and closing the Monument on reasonable notice when certain religious ceremonies are to be held there) violated the Establishment Clause (which prohibits government actions that aid religion or prefer one religion over another, and which is discussed in more detail in the case below). The court held:

> Issuance of regulations to exclude tourists completely from the Monument for the avowed purpose of aiding plaintiffs' conduct of religious ceremonies would seem a clear violation of the Establishment Clause....
>
> We must also deny relief insofar as plaintiffs seek to have the government police the actions of tourists lawfully visiting the Monument. Although Congress

has authorized the Park Service to regulate the conduct of tourists in order to promote and preserve the Monument, we do not believe plaintiffs have a constitutional right to have tourists visiting the Bridge act "in a respectful and appreciative manner." ... Were it otherwise, the Monument would become a government-managed religious shrine.

The Park Service already has issued regulations applicable to the Monument prohibiting disorderly conduct, intoxication and possession of alcoholic beverages by minors, defacement, littering, and tampering with personal property. These regulations no doubt would be justified as authorized under its charge to conserve and protect the scenery, natural and historic objects for the enjoyment of the public. These regulations also provide the relief plaintiffs request as to control of tourist behavior, except perhaps for a total ban on beer drinking.

Id. at 179–80. Do you agree with the court that to grant plaintiffs their requested relief would turn Rainbow Bridge Monument into a "government-managed religious shrine?" Or alternatively is Rainbow Lodge—much like the 16th century Spanish missions on federal lands—a shrine that the government presumes to manage?

3. Although plaintiffs lost their legal challenge in *Badoni*, the Park Service has taken more steps in recent years to protect Rainbow Bridge and other sacred Indian sites. For example, in 1995, the agency built a shin-high rock wall to discourage visitors from leaving the viewing area of Rainbow Bridge and walking directly under the arch. Likewise, Park Service signs now explain that the area is sacred to some American Indians and ask visitors not to walk any farther. In 1996, park officials closed the "great kiva" at Chaco Culture National Historical Park after Navajos and Pueblo Indians complained it had been defiled by tourists leaving everything from crystals to cremated human remains. And at New Mexico's Bandelier National Monument, park rangers now do not publicize the existence of Stone Lions, two volcanic rocks carved into the shape of lions. The shrine is sacred to members of nearby Pueblos. *See* Chris Smith & Elizabeth Manning, *The Sacred and Profane Collide in the West,* HIGH COUNTRY NEWS, May 26, 1997. Such protective measures have led to challenges by non-Indian users, who want access to these same spectacular sites for recreational and other uses, as seen in the case below.

Bear Lodge Multiple Use Association v. Babbitt

2 F. Supp. 2d 1448 (D. Wyo. 1998),
affirmed 175 F.3d 814 (10th Cir. 1999)

Downes, District Judge:

[Devils Tower is a National Monument located in northeast Wyoming. Indian tribes have long viewed Devils Tower as a sacred site of special religious and cultural significance. At Devils Tower, Indians partake in Sun Dances and individual Vision Quests. The Sun Dance is a group ceremony of fasting and sacrifice performed around the summer solstice that leads to spiritual renewal of the individual and group as a whole. Vision Quests are intense periods of prayer, fasting, sweat lodge purification, and solitude designed to connect with the spiritual world and gain insight. These and other ceremonies require solemnity and solitude. Devils Tower is also world famous for its rock climbing. Over the past thirty years the number of climbers has increased dramatically. June is the most popular month for climbing Devils Tower. Recognizing that increasing climbing activity affects the environment as well as "the ability of American Indians to engage in their ceremonial activities in peace," the National Park Service (NPS) began preparing a draft climbing management plan in 1992. In 1995, it issued a Final Climbing Management Plan (FCMP). Eds.]

[T]he FCMP provides that no new bolts or fixed pitons will be permitted on the tower, and new face routes requiring new bolt installation will not be permitted. The FCMP does allow individuals to replace already existing bolts and fixed pitons.... The FCMP further provides that "[i]n respect for the reverence many American Indians hold for Devils Tower as a *sacred* site, rock climbers will be asked to *voluntarily* refrain from climbing on Devils Tower during the culturally significant month of June [when American Indians engage in the Sun Dance and other ceremonies]." ...

The NPS represents that it will not enforce the voluntary closure, but will instead rely on climbers' self-regulation and a new "cross-cultural educational program" "to motivate climbers and other park visitors to comply." The NPS has also placed a sign at the base of the Tower in order to encourage visitors to stay on the trail surrounding the Tower. Despite the FCMP's reliance on self-regulation, it also provides that if the voluntary closure proves to be "unsuccessful," the NPS will consider taking several actions including: (a) revising the climbing management plan; (b) reconvening a climbing management plan work group; (c) instituting additional measures to further encourage compliance; (d) change the duration and nature of the voluntary closure; (e) *converting the June closure to mandatory*; and (f) writing a new definition of success for the voluntary closure. Factors indicating an unsuccessful voluntary closure include, little to no decrease in the number of climbers, an increase in the number of unregistered climbers and increased conflict between user groups in the park. The NPS, however, states that the voluntary closure will be "fully successful" only "when every climber personally chooses not to climb at Devils Tower during June out of respect for American Indian cultural values."

The NPS plans to fully comply with its own June closure by not allowing NPS staff to climb on the tower in June except to enforce laws and regulations or to perform emergency operations. Originally the plan also contained a provision stating that commercial use licenses for June climbing guide activities would not be issued by the NPS for the month of June. Plaintiffs filed a Motion for Preliminary Injunction seeking to enjoin Defendants from the commercial climbing ban during the month of June. This Court granted that motion in June of 1996. In December of that year, Defendant issued a decision revoking the commercial climbing ban....

[P]laintiffs [Bear Lodge Municipal Use Association and several climbers] contend that the NPS has stepped outside of the bounds imposed by law.... [T]hey allege that the NPS's plan wrongfully promotes religion in violation of the establishment clause of the first amendment....

Voluntary Climbing Ban

The Establishment Clause of the First Amendment states that "Congress shall make no law respecting an establishment of religion...." The Courts of this country have long struggled with the type and extent of limitations on government action which these ten words impose. At its most fundamental level, the United States Supreme Court has concluded that this provision prohibits laws "which aid one religion, aid all religions, or prefer one religion over another." ... In *Lemon v. Kurtzman*, 403 U.S. 602 (1971), the court established a three part test for delineating between proper and improper government actions. According to this test a governmental action does not offend the Establishment Clause if it (1) has a secular purpose, (2) does not have the principal or primary effect of advancing or inhibiting religion, and (3) does not foster an excessive entanglement with religion.... The Supreme Court "has long recognized that the government may (and sometimes must) accommodate religious practices and that it may do so without violating the Establishment Clause." The Constitution actually "mandates accommodation, not merely tolerance, of all religions, and forbids hostility toward any." ...

Purpose

... The Plaintiffs can succeed on this prong only if they show that the action has no clear secular purpose or that despite a secular purpose the actual purpose is to endorse religion....

... The purposes underlying the ban are really to remove barriers to religious worship occasioned by public ownership of the Tower. This is in the nature of accommodation, not promotion, and consequently is a legitimate secular purpose.

Effect

Accommodation also plays a role in considering whether the principal effect of a policy is to advance religion....

If the NPS is, in effect, depriving individuals of their legitimate use of the monument in order to enforce the tribes' rights to worship, it has stepped beyond permissible accommodation and into the realm of promoting religion. The gravamen of the issue then becomes whether climbers are allowed meaningful access to the monument. Stated another way, is the climbing ban voluntary or is it actually an improper exercise of government coercion?

Plaintiffs argue that the "voluntary" ban is voluntary in name only. In support of their argument Plaintiffs note that the NPS has established a goal of having every climber personally choose not to climb at the Tower during June. Plaintiffs also cite to possible modifications to the FCMP if the NPS deems the voluntary ban unsuccessful. Specifically, ... the NPS may convert the closure to a mandatory closure.

Neither of these factors is sufficient to transform the voluntary ban into a coerced ban.... The goal of reducing the number of climbers to zero may or may not be a desirable one, but coercion only manifests itself in the NPS's actions, not in its aspirations....

Although the NPS has stated that an unsuccessful voluntary ban may lead it to make the ban mandatory, that is far from an inevitable result....

Excessive Entanglement

The Court concludes that the voluntary climbing ban also passes muster when measured against the excessive entanglement test.... The organizations benefitted [sic] by the voluntary climbing ban, namely Native American tribes, are not solely religious organizations, but also represent a common heritage and culture. As a result, there is much less danger that the Government's actions will inordinately advance solely religious activities.... [T]he Park Service has no involvement in the manner of worship that takes place, but only provides an atmosphere more conducive to worship. This type of custodial function does not implicate the dangerously close relationship between state and religion which offends the excessive entanglement prong....

* * *

Notes and Questions

1. On appeal, the Tenth Circuit affirmed on the grounds that plaintiffs lacked standing to sue, since they remained free to climb Devils Tower and thus had not demonstrated harm from the Park Service's voluntary ban.

2. What explains the different outcome in this case compared to that of the Rainbow Bridge Monument case? Is it the voluntary nature of the ban on climbing Devils Tower?

3. Does the Park Service's management plan violate the Establishment Clause by establishing religion? Or it is an appropriate plan to eliminate barriers to Indians' free practice of religion on federal public lands? Consider the following comments:

> [L]awyers from the Cheyenne River Sioux tribe, an intervenor on behalf of the Park Service, [argue] that if the Park Service has established religion at Devils Tower, it has also done so at other national monuments and parks. The [tribal] lawyers point out that twice a year at Tumacacori National Historical Park in Arizona, the Park Service sponsors a Catholic mass reenacting 18th-century religious traditions. And in Texas, at San Antonio Missions, the park's official brochure states the following: "Please be considerate. The historic structures are fragile resources. Help us preserve them for future generations. Remember also that these are places of worship. Parish priests and parishioners deserve your respect; please do not disrupt their services." The question, then, is why should a butte that is sacred to Native Americans be treated differently than a mission or a church managed by the Park Service? Because the butte is a natural feature and Native American religions are harder to understand than Western ones? Or because hundreds of thousands of tourists come to Devils Tower each summer to see the nation's first monument—and the place where spaceships landed in Steven Spielberg's Close Encounters of the Third Kind?

Smith & Manning, *supra.* Where do you come out in this debate?

4. Part of the rationale of the district court's opinion was that religious values were not the only values at stake, but that the spiritual significance of Devils Tower was inextricably bound to the cultural and social life of the affected tribes. From a tribe's perspective, are there likely to be any drawbacks to such a characterization and strategy?

5. As noted in Chapter 4, federal authority over Native Americans is subject to the federal government's trust responsibility to manage Indian lands, funds, and resources for the benefit of Indians. Before the court issued the ruling excerpted above, it had issued a preliminary injunction barring the National Park Service from implementing a temporary commercial climbing moratorium on Devils Tower during the month of June (subsequently dropped by the Forest Service). The court's preliminary injunction order makes no mention of the federal trust responsibility to the affected tribes, an omission criticized in the following commentary:

> The significance of this choice is that applying an exclusively Establishment Clause frame of reference operates by trying to demonstrate similarities in law between tribal spiritualism and Anglo-American religious denominations, while the trust responsibility approach instead emphasizes the uniqueness of the federal government relationship to the tribes as semi-sovereign peoples rather than religious practitioners. As applied in the Devils Tower trial court decision, pure Establishment Clause analysis seeks to accommodate pluralism by focusing on perceived sameness, while trust responsibility doctrine seeks the same objective by focusing on difference.
>
> The distinction between the two is more than strictly academic. Confining the analysis solely to Establishment Clause discourse denies both the NPS and the affected tribes the moral authority to seek any accommodation beyond that allowed by the decision (such as the temporary mandatory commercial climbing ban the superintendent first tried to impose at the Tower). Following this ap-

proach, the superintendent may have potent discretionary authority to prohibit all commercial and recreational activity in order to protect the physical integrity of the monument or the well-being of its wildlife, but not to assure the unimpeded replication of spiritual aspects of tribal culture.

Lloyd Burton & David Ruppert, *Bear's Lodge or Devils Tower: Inter-Cultural Relations, Legal Pluralism, and the Management of Sacred Sites on Public Lands,* 8 CORNELL J. L. & PUB. POL'Y 201, 231 (1999).

6. There are legal avenues other than constitutional challenges potentially available for protecting sacred sites. Professor Judith Royster describes a few of these:

[T]he American Indian Religious Freedom Act (AIRFA) asserts that it is "the policy of the United States to protect and preserve" tribal freedom of religion, specifically including access to sacred sites. Nonetheless, the Court in *Lyng* determined that the AIRFA was nothing more than a general statement of policy without "so much as a hint" that it created a cause of action. In 1996, President Clinton issued Executive Order 13,007, Indian Sacred Sites, which mandated federal land agencies to accommodate tribal access to and use of sacred sites, and to avoid adverse impacts on the physical integrity of sacred sites. Executive Order, 13,007, however, like all executive orders, does not create a cause of action and is not enforceable by the tribes.

Judith V. Royster, *Native American* Law, *in* THE LAW OF ENVIRONMENTAL JUSTICE: THEORIES AND PROCEDURES TO ADDRESS DISPROPORTIONATE RISKS 199, 211 (Michael Gerrard & Sheila R. Foster eds., 2d ed. 2008). Professor Royster notes that three other statutes offer some protection for places and objects of religious, cultural, or historical importance to Indian tribes: the National Historic Preservation Act, the Archaeological Resources Protection Act, and the Native American Graves Protection and Repatriation Act. *See id.* at 212–13.

A more recent statute, the Religious Freedom Restoration Act of 1993 ("RFRA"), may provide greater protections than afforded by current interpretations of the Free Exercise Clause of the U.S. Constitution. Under RFRA, the federal government may not "substantially burden a person's exercise of religion even if the burden results from a rule of general applicability, except as provided in subsection (b)." Subsection (b) provides, "Government may substantially burden a person's exercise of religion only if it demonstrates that application of the burden to the person (1) is in furtherance of a compelling governmental interest; and (2) is the least restrictive means of furthering that compelling governmental interest." "Exercise of religion" is further defined broadly to include "any exercise of religion, whether or not compelled by, or central to, a system of religious belief." *See* Religious Freedom Restoration Act, 42 U.S.C. § 2000bb-1. RFRA formed the basis of a challenge by the Navajo Nation, the Hopi Tribe, and several other tribes to protect the San Francisco Peaks. They challenged the U.S. Forest Service's decision to allow a ski area—one located on the highest and most religiously significant of the Peaks—to spread artificial snow made from recycled sewage effluent on the mountain. While a panel of the Ninth Circuit found a violation of RFRA, the court, rehearing the case en banc, instead affirmed the district court's finding that the proposed use did not violate RFRA. *See* Navajo Nation v. U.S. Forest Service, 479 F.3d 1024 (9th Cir. 2007), *vacated,* 506 F.3d 717 (9th Cir. 2008), *reheard en banc,* 535 F.3d 1058 (9th Cir. 2008) (affirming district court). A petition for certiorari is pending before the U.S. Supreme Court as this book goes to press.

Several states also have similar, and in some cases more protective, statutes. More generally, historic preservation laws may be used to protect other culturally significant places as well.

2. The Equal Protection Cases

Some of the earliest legal challenges to the siting of undesirable land uses in communities of color were based on violations of the Equal Protection Clause of the Fourteenth Amendment, which provides in part that "[n]o State shall ... deny to any person within its jurisdiction the equal protection of the laws." Professor Alice Kaswan provides background on this standard:

> Facially discriminatory laws and actions have become rare in today's race-conscious society. It is inconceivable that a government body would declare that all landfills shall be sited in minority neighborhoods. Instead, equal protection claims in the environmental justice context are likely to allege that a governmental decision that is facially neutral is nonetheless discriminatory. The current understanding of when a facially neutral decision or action can be considered discriminatory was established in 1975 in *Washington v. Davis* [426 U.S. 229 (1976)]. Stating that the "central purpose of the Equal Protection Clause ... is the prevention of official conduct discriminating on the basis of race," the Court held that a plaintiff must prove that the defendant acted with discriminatory intent.... The Court observed that a "racially disproportionate impact," standing alone, is generally insufficient to demonstrate a violation.... The Supreme Court did, however, recognize that since government actors rarely announce their intent to discriminate, discriminatory intent may not be explicit. The justifications presented by government actors may, in some instances, be pretexts for discriminatory conduct.... The Supreme Court addressed the question of what types of facts are relevant to inferring discriminatory intent in the 1976 case of *Village of Arlington Heights v. Metropolitan Housing Development Corp.* [429 U.S. 252 (1977)].... [T]he Court identified the following five factors as potentially probative of intentional discrimination: (1) disparate impact; (2) historical background to the decision; (3) history of the decision-making process; (4) departures from normal substantive factors or procedures; and (5) legislative or administrative history. The Court made clear that its five-factor test was not "exhaustive." Nevertheless, courts have continued to use the five-factor test to determine whether direct and circumstantial evidence reveal that a facially neutral decision is discriminatory.

Alice Kaswan, *Environmental Laws: Grist for the Equal Protection Mill*, 70 U. COLO. L. REV. 387, 408–412 (1999).

Pathfinder on Equal Protection and Environmental Justice

In addition to the articles discussed in this chapter, the following is a selected group of materials that discuss the equal protection doctrine in the environmental justice context: Philip Weinberg, *Equal Protection*, in THE LAW OF ENVIRONMENTAL JUSTICE: THEORIES AND PROCEDURES TO ADDRESS DISPROPORTIONATE RISKS (Michael B. Gerrard & Sheila R. Foster eds., 2d ed. 2008); Sten-Erik Hoidal, *Returning to the Roots of Environmental Justice: Lessons From the Inequitable Distribution of Municipal Services*, 88 MINN. L. REV. 193 (2003); Robert W. Collin, *Environmental Equity: A Law and Planning Approach to Environmental Racism*, 11 VA. ENVTL. L. J. 495 (1992); Peter L. Reich, *Greening the Ghetto: A Theory of Environmental Race Discrimination*, 41 U. KAN. L. REV. 271 (1992); Rodolfo Mata, Comment, *Inequitable Siting of Undesirable Facilities and the Myth of Equal*

Protection, 13 B.C. Third World L.J. 233 (1993); and Jill E. Evans, *Challenging the Racism in Environmental Racism: Redefining the Concept of Intent*, 40 Ariz. L. Rev. 1219 (1998).

In several cases in the mid 1980s, courts inferred discriminatory intent and found violations of the Equal Protection Clause based on the disparate provision of municipal services such as water hookups, street paving, and storm-sewer capacity to minority residents. One example is the case below:

Dowdell v. City of Apopka
698 F.2d 1181 (11th Cir. 1983)

Vance, Senior Circuit Judge:

The situs of this case is the small city of Apopka, Florida located in the fern and foliage growing region north of Orlando. More specifically, it is the poor, geographically separate, black community of that city. The plaintiffs (appellees and cross-appellants here) are a Fed. R. Civ. P. 23(b)(2) class comprising the black residents of Apopka "who are, or have been, subjected to the discriminatory provision of municipal services." ... Plaintiffs charged the City of Apopka, its mayor, and four council members with discrimination in the provision of seven municipal services: street paving and maintenance, storm water drainage, street lighting, fire protection, water distribution, sewerage facilities, and park and recreation facilities....

The district court found intentional discrimination in the provision of street paving, the water distribution system, and storm drainage facilities in violation of the fourteenth amendment; Title VI of the Civil Rights Act of 1964, 42 U.S.C. § 2000d and the State and Local Fiscal Assistance Act of 1972, 31 U.S.C. § 1242 (Revenue Sharing Act)....

To trigger strict scrutiny analysis under the fourteenth amendment, preliminary findings of both disparate impact and discriminatory intent are required. Appellants contend that the facts adduced in evidence do not support a finding of discriminatory intent....

We can reach no such conclusion. Substantial evidence, including video tapes, photographs, charts, and the testimony of community residents and of qualified experts who made on-site surveys revealed a disparity in the provision of street paving, water distribution, and storm water drainage.[3] Appellants do not question the accuracy of these statistical findings. Rather, they assert an absence of responsibility for them, claiming them, variously, to be beyond municipal jurisdiction or the result of historical and environmental forces. Their arguments are insubstantial and were properly rejected by the trial court.

Refutation of Apopka's attempt to deny municipal responsibility for these services one by one does not conclude our inquiry into discriminatory intent. The gravamen of plaintiffs' claim is that Apopka has intentionally maintained a racially and geographically segregated system of municipal services as a result of which the disparities in the provision of street paving, water distribution, and storm drainage facilities have reached constitu-

---

3. The district court found that 42% of the street footage in the black community was unpaved as compared to 9% in the white community and that 33% of the black community residences fronted on such unpaved streets while only 7% of the residences in the white community did so. As regards storm drainage, the court found that while 60% of the residential streets in the white community had curbs and gutters, no streets in the black community had curbs and gutters. Additionally, it found that water service in many homes in the black community was so inadequate that at many times of the day there was insufficient water for such normal purposes as bathing.

tional proportions. Discriminatory intent is not synonymous with a racially discriminatory motive. Neither does it require proof that racial discrimination is the sole purpose behind each failure to equalize these services. It is, rather, the cumulative evidence of action and inaction which objectively manifests discriminatory intent.

Although the fluid concept of discriminatory intent is sometimes subtle and difficult to apply, there is ample evidence in this case of the correlation between municipal service disparities and racially tainted purposiveness to mandate a finding of discriminatory intent. Nearly every factor which has been held to be highly probative of discriminatory intent is present.

First, the magnitude of the disparity, evidencing a systematic pattern of municipal expenditures in all areas of town except the black community, is explicable only on racial grounds. Second, the legislative and administrative pattern of decision-making, extending from nearly half a century in the past to Apopka's plans for future development, indicates a deliberate deprivation of services to the black community. A municipal ordinance restricting blacks to living only on the south side of the railroad tracks remained in force in Apopka until 1968. The ordinance contributed to the ghetto-like qualities of the black residential area. Blacks continue to be significantly under-represented in administrative and elective positions, and their requests for improved municipal services continue to be ignored while substantial funds are expended to annex and develop the new predominantly white sections of town. Third, the continued and systematic relative deprivation of the black community was the obviously foreseeable outcome of spending nearly all revenue sharing monies received on the white community in preference to the visibly underserviced black community. While voluntary acts and "awareness of consequences" alone do not necessitate a finding of discriminatory intent, "actions having foreseeable and anticipated disparate impact are relevant evidence to prove the ultimate fact, forbidden purpose."

Although none of these factors is necessarily independently conclusive, "the totality of the relevant facts," Washington v. Davis amply supports the finding that the City of Apopka has engaged in a systematic pattern of cognitive acts and omissions, selecting and reaffirming a particular course of municipal services expenditures that inescapably evidences discriminatory intent....

* * *

Plaintiffs have had far less success using the Equal Protection Clause in the siting context. In the following decisions, lower courts rejected Equal Protection challenges to siting decisions.

Bean v. Southwestern Waste Management Corporation

482 F. Supp. 673 (S.D. Texas 1979)
affirmed without opinion, 780 F.2d 1038 (5th Cir. 1986)

McDonald, District Judge:

[Plaintiffs filed suit seeking to invalidate a decision by the Texas Department of Health (TDH) to grant a permit to Southwestern Waste Management to operate a Type I solid waste facility in the East Houston-Dyersdale Road area in Harris County, Texas. They sought a preliminary injunction to restrain the project from going forward.]

Before getting to the merits, the Court must address one other procedural matter. The plaintiffs did not name the Texas Department of Water Resources (TDWR) as a defendant in this case. That, of course, is not particularly surprising. That agency did not participate in the decision to grant Permit No. 1193 and nothing it did with respect to the issuance of that permit is being challenged here. The plaintiffs have, however, submitted a large quantity of data related to solid waste sites in Houston operating under the auspices of TDWR and a dispute has arisen as to the relevance of this data. The Court is of the opinion that the evidence as to TDWR's actions is entirely irrelevant to the question of whether it was an historical policy or practice of TDH to discriminate, since TDH should not be held responsible for the commission of acts, e.g., issuance of permits by TDWR, over which it had no control. Evidence as to TDWR's action is relevant, however, to the question of whether TDH, being aware of the placement of solid waste sites throughout the city of Houston, if it was so aware, discriminated by approving the permit for the East Houston-Dyersdale Road site, since a state agency must not put its stamp of approval on a discriminatory practice or policy even if it did not initiate the practice or policy....

The burden on [plaintiffs] is to prove discriminatory purpose. That is, the plaintiffs must show not just that the decision to grant the permit is objectionable or even wrong, but that it is attributable to an intent to discriminate on the basis of race. Statistical proof can rise to the level that it, alone, proves discriminatory intent, as in Yick Wo v. Hopkins, 118 U.S. 356 (1886), and Gomillion v. Lightfoot, 364 U.S. 339 (1960), or, this Court would conclude, even in situations less extreme than in those two cases, but the data shown here does not rise to that level. Similarly, statistical proof can be sufficiently supplemented by the types of proof outlined in *Arlington Heights* to establish purposeful discrimination, but the supplemental proof offered here is not sufficient to do that.

Two different theories of liability have been advanced in this case. The first is that TDH's approval of the permit was part of a pattern or practice by it of discriminating in the placement of solid waste sites. In order to test that theory, one must focus on the sites which TDH has approved and determine the minority population of the areas in which the sites were located on the day that the sites opened. The available statistical data, both city-wide and in the target area, fails to establish a pattern or practice of discrimination by TDH. Citywide, data was produced for the seventeen (17) sites operating with TDH permits as of July 1, 1978. That data shows that 58.8% of the sites granted permits by TDH were located in census tracts with 25% or less minority population at the time of their opening and that 82.4% of the sites granted permits by TDH were located in census tracts with 50% or less minority population at the time of their opening. In the target area, an area which roughly conforms to the North Forest Independent School District and the newly-created City Council District B and is 70% minority in population, two (2) sites were approved by TDH. One, the McCarty Road site, was in a census tract with less than 10% minority population at the time of its opening. The other, the site being challenged here, is in a census tract with close to 60% minority population. Even if we also consider the sites approved by TDWR in the target area, which, as discussed earlier, are not really relevant to TDH's intent to discriminate, no pattern or practice of discrimination is revealed. Of all the solid waste sites opened in the target area, 46.2 to 50% were located in census tracts with less than 25% minority population at the time they opened. It may be that more particularized data would show that even those sites approved in predominantly Anglo census tracts were actually located in minority neighborhoods, but the data available here does not show that. In addition, there was no supplemental evidence, such as that suggested by *Arlington Heights*, *supra*, which established a pattern or practice of discrimination on the part of TDH.

The plaintiffs' second theory of liability is that TDH's approval of the permit, in the context of the historical placement of solid waste sites and the events surrounding the application, constituted discrimination. Three sets of data were offered to support this theory. Each set, at first blush, looks compelling. On further analysis, however, each set breaks down. Each fails to approach the standard established by *Yick Wo, supra*, and *Gomillion, supra*, and, even when considered with supplementary proof, *Arlington Heights, supra*, fails to establish a likelihood of success in proving discriminatory intent.

The first set of data focuses on the two (2) solid waste sites to be used by the City of Houston. Both of these sites are located in the target area. This proves discrimination, the plaintiffs argue, because "the target area has the dubious distinction of containing 100% of the type I municipal land fills that Houston utilizes or will utilize, although it contains only 6.9% of the entire population of Houston." There are two problems with this argument. First, there are only two sites involved here. That is not a statistically significant number. Second, an examination of the census tracts in the target area in which the sites are located reveals that the East Houston-Dyersdale Road proposed site is in a tract with a 58.4% minority population, but that the McCarty Road site is in a tract with only an 18.4% minority population. Thus, the evidence shows that, of the two sites to be used by the City of Houston, one is in a primarily Anglo census tract and one is in a primarily minority census tract. No inference of discrimination can be made from this data.

The second set of data focuses on the total number of solid waste sites located in the target area. The statistical disparity which the plaintiffs point to is that the target area contains 15% of Houston's solid waste sites, but only 6.9% of its population. Since the target area has a 70% minority population, the plaintiffs argue, this statistical disparity must be attributable to race discrimination. To begin with, in the absence of the data on population by race, the statistical disparity is not all that shocking. One would expect solid waste sites to be placed near each other and away from concentrated population areas. Even considering the 70% minority population of the target area, when one looks at where in the target area these particular sites are located, the inference of racial discrimination dissolves. Half of the solid waste sites in the target area are in census tracts with more than 70% Anglo population. Without some proof that the sites affect an area much larger than the census tract in which they are in, it is very hard to conclude that the placing of a site in the target area evidences purposeful racial discrimination.

The third set of data offered by the plaintiffs focuses on the city as a whole. This data is the most compelling on its surface. It shows that only 17.1% of the city's solid waste sites are located in the southwest quadrant, where 53.3% of the Anglos live. Only 15.3% of the sites are located in the northwest quadrant, where 20.1% of the Anglos live. Thus, only 32.4% of the sites are located in the western half of the city, where 73.4% of the Anglos live. Furthermore, the plaintiffs argue, 67.6% of the sites are located in the eastern half of the city, where 61.6% of the minority population lives. This, according to the plaintiffs, shows racial discrimination.

The problem is that, once again, these statistics break down under closer scrutiny. To begin with, the inclusion of TDWR's sites skew[s] the data. A large number of TDWR sites are located around Houston's ship channel, which is in the eastern half of the city. But those sites, the Assistant Attorney General argues persuasively, are located in the eastern half of the city because that is where Houston's industry is, not because that is where Houston's minority population is. Furthermore, closer examination of the data shows that the city's solid waste sites are not so disparately located as they first appear. If we focus on census tracts, rather than on halves or quadrants of the city, we can see with more particularity where the solid waste sites are located. Houston's population is 39.3% minority and 60.7% Anglo. The plaintiffs argue, and this Court finds persuasive, a definition of "minority census tracts" as those with more than 39.3% minority population and

Anglo census tracts as those with more than 60.7% Anglo population. Using those definitions, Houston consists of 42.5% minority tracts and 57.5% Anglo tracts. Again using those definitions, 42.3% of the solid waste sites in the City of Houston are located in minority tracts and 57.7% are located in Anglo tracts. In addition, if we look at tracts with one or more sites per tract, to account for the fact that some tracts contain more than one solid waste site, 42.2% are minority tracts and 57.8% are Anglo tracts. The difference between the racial composition of census tracts in general and the racial composition of census tracts with solid waste sites is, according to the statistics available to the Court, at best, only 0.3%. That is simply not a statistically significant difference. More surprisingly, from the plaintiffs' point of view, to the extent that it is viewed as significant, it tends to indicate that minority census tracts have a tiny bit smaller percentage of solid waste sites than one would proportionately expect.

In support of the proposition that there is a city-wide discrimination against minorities in the placement of solid waste sites, the plaintiffs also argue that the data reveals that, in 1975, eleven solid waste sites were located in census tracts with 100% minority population and none were located in census tracts with 100% Anglo population. There are problems with this argument, too, however. To begin with, the 1975 data is not entirely reliable. Compared with both the 1970 and the 1979 data, the 1975 data appears to overcount minority population. For example, of the eleven sites mentioned by the plaintiffs, only one had a 100% minority population in 1979. More importantly, there were, in fact, two sites located in 100% Anglo tracts in 1975. In addition, 18 other sites were located in tracts with a 90% or greater Anglo population in 1975. Thus, even according to the 1975 data, a large number of sites were located in census tracts with high Anglo populations.

Arlington Heights, supra, suggested various types of non-statistical proof which can be used to establish purposeful discrimination. The supplementary non-statistical evidence provided by the plaintiffs in the present case raises a number of questions as to why this permit was granted. To begin with, a site proposed for the almost identical location was denied a permit in 1971 by the County Commissioners, who were then responsible for the issuance of such permits. One wonders what happened since that time. The plaintiffs argue that Smiley High School has changed from an Anglo school to one whose student body is predominantly minority. Furthermore, the site is being placed within 1700 feet of Smiley High School, a predominantly black school with no air conditioning, and only somewhat farther from a residential neighborhood. Land use considerations alone would seem to militate against granting this permit. Such evidence seemingly did not dissuade TDH.

If this Court were TDH, it might very well have denied this permit. It simply does not make sense to put a solid waste site so close to a high school, particularly one with no air conditioning. Nor does it make sense to put the land site so close to a residential neighborhood. But I am not TDH and for all I know, TDH may regularly approve of solid waste sites located near schools and residential areas, as illogical as that may seem.

It is not my responsibility to decide whether to grant this site a permit. It is my responsibility to decide whether to grant the plaintiffs a preliminary injunction. From the evidence before me, I can say that the plaintiffs have established that the decision to grant the permit was both unfortunate and insensitive. I cannot say that the plaintiffs have established a substantial likelihood of proving that the decision to grant the permit was motivated by purposeful racial discrimination in violation of 42 U.S.C. § 1983....

Permanent Relief

The failure of the plaintiffs to obtain a preliminary injunction does not, of course, mean that they are foreclosed from obtaining permanent relief. Because of the time pressures involved, extensive pre-trial discovery was impossible in this case. Assuming the case goes forward, discovery could lead to much more solid and persuasive evidence for either side. Ideally, it would resolve a number of the questions which the Court considers unanswered.

Where, for instance, are the solid waste sites located in each census tract? The plaintiffs produced evidence that in census tract 434, a predominantly Anglo tract, the site was located next to a black community named Riceville. If that was true of most sites in predominantly Anglo census tracts, the outcome of this case would be quite different.

How large an area does a solid waste site affect? If it affects an area a great deal smaller than that of a census tract, it becomes particularly important to know where in each census tract the site is located. If it affects an area larger than that of a census tract, then a target area analysis becomes much more persuasive.

How are solid waste site locations selected? It may be that private contractors consider a number of alternative locations and then select one in consultation with city or county officials. If that is so, it has tremendous implications for the search for discriminatory intent. It may be that a relatively limited number of areas can adequately serve as a Type I solid waste site. If that is so, the placement of sites in those areas becomes a lot less suspicious, even if large numbers of minorities live there. Either way, this is information which should be adduced. At this point, the Court still does not know how, why, and by whom the East Houston-Dyersdale Road location was selected.

What factors entered into TDH's decision to grant the permit? The proximity of the site to Smiley High School and a residential neighborhood and the lack of air conditioning facilities at the former were emphasized to the Court. It is still unknown how much, if any, consideration TDH gave to these factors. The racial composition of the neighborhood and the racial distribution of solid waste sites in Houston were primary concerns of the plaintiffs. It remains unclear to what degree TDH was informed of these concerns....

[P]laintiffs' Motion for a Preliminary Injunction ... [is] DENIED.

* * *

Notes and Questions

1. Consider the evidence analyzed by the *Bean* court in denying the preliminary injunction. Which of the *Arlington Heights* factors does this evidence relate to? Consider also the additional evidence that the court suggests might have been persuasive to it, including where the solid waste sites were located in each census tract, how large an area a solid waste site affects, how solid waste sites are selected, and what factors entered into the Texas Department of Health's decision to grant the permit. How do each of the requested pieces of evidence relate to the *Arlington Heights* factors?

2. To what extent does the court find the actions of the Texas Department of Water Resources relevant to its analysis of the Texas Department of Health's discriminatory intent? In your view, should the decisions of agencies *other* than the immediate permitting agency be considered relevant in an analysis of the permitting agency? If not, what factors would you consider pertinent to determining the relevance of other agencies' actions? How far back in time should a court look — 5 years, 20 years, or longer?

3. How should discriminatory impact be measured? This threshold question, which also arises in the context of claims brought under Title VI of the Civil Rights Act, raises

a host of difficult methodological questions. What is the definition of a "minority" community? Is it a community that is more than 50% minority? A community that has a higher percentage of minority residents than in the permitting jurisdiction generally? Than in the relevant city or state? Likewise, for purposes of determining whether a community has suffered a disparate burden, what should be the geographic scope of the impacted community? Should it be defined by city blocks, neighborhoods, zip codes, census tracts, city quadrants, county lines? Or by a geographic radius extending from the unwanted land use? Should it vary depending on type of facility? As *Bean* demonstrates, the units chosen can have a huge impact on the outcome of a given case.

4. In another equal protection siting case, the plaintiffs challenged a decision by the Macon-Bibb County Planning & Zoning Commission to allow a landfill located in a census tract that was 60% black. The only other private landfill approved by the Commission was situated in a census tract that was 76% white. In that case, the court noted that the existence of the other landfill in a predominantly white census tract tended to undermine the plaintiffs' claim of a pattern, unexplainable on grounds other than race. The court also noted:

> [T]he Commission did not and indeed may not actively solicit this or any other landfill application. The Commission reacts to applications from private landowners for permission to use their property in a particular manner. The Commissioners observed during the course of these proceedings the necessity for a comprehensive scheme for the management of waste and for the location of landfills. In that such a scheme has yet to be introduced, the Commission is left to consider each request on its individual merits. In such a situation, this court finds it difficult to understand plaintiffs' contentions that this Commission's decision to approve a landowner's application for a private landfill is part of any pattern to place "undesirable uses" in black neighborhoods. Second, a considerable portion of plaintiffs' evidence focused upon governmental decisions made by agencies other than the planning and zoning commission, evidence which sheds little if any light upon the alleged discriminatory intent of the Commission.

East Bibb Twiggs Neighborhood Ass'n v. Macon-Bibb County Planning & Zoning Comm'n, 706 F. Supp. 880, 885 (M.D. Ga. 1989). How significant is it that the Commission did not actively solicit the landfill application? Do you agree that it is irrelevant to assessing discriminatory intent? The court concludes that decisions made by agencies other than the planning and zoning commission shed little light on the intent of the Commission. Is this consistent with *Bean*'s treatment of decisions by other regulatory agencies? This issue remains unsettled in equal protection case law. For further discussion, see Kaswan, *supra*, at 448–49, 453–454.

R.I.S.E. v. Kay

768 F. Supp. 1144 (E.D. Va. 1991)

Richard L. Williams, District Judge:

[This case involved a regional landfill in King & Queen County, Virginia, proposed in a predominantly black area. The County initially sought to negotiate a joint venture landfill with the Chesapeake Corporation, which identified the "Piedmont Tract" as a potential site and determined based on soil studies that it was suitable. Subsequently the County decided to develop the landfill on its own by purchasing the Piedmont Tract. In response to community opposition, the County reviewed at least one alternative site, in an area that was 85% black, which was determined to be environmentally unsuitable. It is unclear if the County considered any other alternatives. The Piedmont Tract is located close to the Second Mt. Olive Baptist Church, founded in 1860 by recently freed slaves, and re- quired rezoning from an agricultural to industrial area. The population of the county was approximately 50% black and 50% white. There were three existing landfills in the county. Plaintiffs brought suit under the Equal Protection Clause challenging the County's approval of the landfill. Eds.]

Demographic Analysis of County Landfill Sites

... 2. Thirty-nine blacks (64% of total) and twenty-two whites (36% of total) live within a half-mile radius of the proposed regional landfill site....

3. The Mascot landfill was sited in 1969. None of the present Board members were serving on the Board at that time. At the time the landfill was developed, the estimated racial composition of the population living within a one mile radius of the site was 100% black. The Escobrook Baptist Church, a black church, was located within two miles of the landfill.

4. The Dahlgren landfill was sited in 1971. None of the current Board members were on the Board at that time. An estimated 95% of the population living in the immediate area at the time the landfill was built [was] black. Presently, an estimated 90–95% of the residents living within a two-mile radius are black.

5. The Owenton landfill was sited in 1977. Supervisors Kay and Bourne were serving on the Board when the landfill was developed. In 1977, an estimated 100% of the resi- dents living within a half-mile radius of the landfill were black. The area population is still predominantly black. The First Mount Olive Baptist Church, a black church, is located one mile from the landfill.

[The Court then discussed a controversy surrounding a private landfill opened in 1986 by King Land Corporation. Since the county did not have a zoning ordinance in 1986, the landfill did not require county approval. In response, the county implemented a zoning ordinance and successfully sued to bar the landfill from operating. The County subse- quently denied King Land's application for a variance to use the property as a landfill, finding that the operation would result in a significant decline in property values of the adjacent properties, and that King Land had ignored environmental, health, safety, and welfare concerns. The racial composition of the residential area surrounding the King Land landfill is predominantly white.]

Conclusions of Law

... 2. The placement of landfills in King and Queen County from 1969 to the present has had a disproportionate impact on black residents.

3. However, official action will not be held unconstitutional solely because it results in a racially disproportionate impact....

4. The impact of an official action—in this case, the historical placement of landfills in predominantly black communities—provides "an important starting point" for the determination of whether official action was motivated by discriminatory intent.

5. However, the plaintiffs have not provided any evidence that satisfies the remainder of the discriminatory purpose equation set forth in *Arlington Heights*. Careful examina- tion of the administrative steps taken by the Board of Supervisors to negotiate the pur- chase of the Piedmont Tract and authorize its use as a landfill site reveals nothing unusual

or suspicious. To the contrary, the Board appears to have balanced the economic, environmental, and cultural needs of the County in a responsible and conscientious manner.

6. The Board's decision to undertake private negotiations with the Chesapeake Corporation in the hope of reaching an agreement to operate a joint venture landfill was perfectly reasonable in light of the County's financial constraints.

7. Once this deal fell through, the Board was understandably drawn to the Piedmont Tract because the site had already been tested and found environmentally suitable for the purpose of landfill development.

8. The Board responded to the concerns and suggestions of citizens opposed to the proposed regional landfill by establishing a citizens' advisory group, evaluating the suitability of the alternative site recommended by the Concerned Citizens' Steering Committee, and discussing with landfill contractor BFI such means of minimizing the impact of the landfill on the Second Mt. Olive Church as vegetative buffers and improving access roads.

9. Both the King Land landfill and the proposed landfill spawned "Not In My Backyard" movements. The Board's opposition to the King Land landfill and its approval of the proposed landfill was based not on the racial composition of the respective neighborhoods in which the landfills are located but on the relative environmental suitability of the sites.

10. At worst, the Supervisors appear to have been more concerned about the economic and legal plight of the County as a whole than the sentiments of residents who opposed the placement of the landfill in their neighborhood. However, the Equal Protection Clause does not impose an affirmative duty to equalize the impact of official decisions on different racial groups. Rather, it merely prohibits government officials from intentionally discriminating on the basis of race. The plaintiffs have not provided sufficient evidence to meet this legal standard. Judgment is therefore entered for the defendants.

* * *

Notes and Questions

1. Professor Alice Kaswan contends that the court's conclusion in *R.I.S.E.* that there were no procedural irregularities in the siting process is "somewhat glib" since the court failed to discuss the need to rezone the property from agricultural to industrial use, a factor considered relevant under *Arlington Heights. See* Kaswan, *supra*, at 444–45. Professor Robert Collin also points to other evidence in the record suggesting that the rezoning was legally suspect. *See* Robert Collin, *Environmental Equity: A Law and Planning Approach to Environmental Racism,* 11 VA. ENVTL. L. J. 495, 533 (1992). The *R.I.S.E.* court also did not discuss the project's legislative history, the fifth *Arlington Heights* factor, despite apparent evidence in the record suggesting some decision-makers' discriminatory views. According to plaintiffs' appellate brief, for example, the County Administrator, after hearing the concerns about the landfill expressed by two African American ministers, told another party that the ministers "should be given a one-way ticket back to Africa." Another white member of the supervisors referred to the "niggers'" opposition to the landfill. *Id.* at 532.

2. Did the courts in the cases discussed above find discriminatory impact? Could reasonable people have inferred discriminatory intent from the facts of the cases? As a judge, how would you decide these matters?

3. Why are the courts (such as in *Dowdell*, excerpted at the start of this section) seemingly more willing to infer discriminatory intent on the part of government actors and find an equal protection violation when the issue is the inequitable provision of services, rather than when it is the inequitable siting of locally unwanted land uses? For example, in a case alleging racial discrimination in providing municipal services to single family homeowners and residents of an area of town that was 98.5% minority and 46% low-income, the court applied the *Arlington Heights* factors and denied summary judgment to the city, finding that a genuine issue of material fact of discrimination existed despite an absence of direct evidence of discriminatory intent. *See* Miller v. City of Dallas, 2002 WL 230834 (N.D. Tex.). Consider the consequences that might follow from a successful equal protection claim under, respectively, the municipal services and the siting dispute cases.

4. Professor Michael Selmi has argued that the Supreme Court's reluctance to infer discrimination in equal protection cases is not a function of the *Arlington Heights* test itself, but is a consequence of the Court's underlying beliefs about the prevalence of racial discrimination. Professor Selmi argues that the Court has been hesitant to infer discrimination in the absence of direct evidence because it is unwilling to accept that discrimination remains a vital explanation for social and political decisions—an unspoken explanation for facially neutral decisions. *See* Michael Selmi, *Proving Intentional Discrimination: The Reality of Supreme Court Rhetoric*, 86 Geo. L. J. 279, 284–85, 332 (1997). Does this explain the results of the three lower court decisions discussed above?

5. Are equal protection challenges a dead end for environmental justice plaintiffs? Professor Kaswan argues that "a wholesale abandonment of the equal protection approach is premature." Kaswan, *supra*, at 456. She contends that "[a]lthough the environmental [equal protection] cases confirm that the evidentiary burden for proving intentional discrimination is high and the willingness of the courts to infer discrimination is low, the constitutional remedy should not be dismissed out of hand." She argues that the inquiry is highly fact-specific, and that while most cases may not be amenable to an equal protection claim, the facts of each case should be evaluated to determine whether they present the kind of evidence that would be considered probative under the demanding *Arlington Heights* test. *See id.* at 433–34, 456.

6. Equal protection clauses in some state constitutions have been interpreted to prohibit disparate impacts, not only actions that are intentionally discriminatory. For a discussion of these constitutional provisions, see Peter Reich, *Greening the Ghetto: A Theory of Environmental Race Discrimination*, 41 U. Kan. L. Rev. 271, 301–304 (1992).

7. Rethinking the Intent Standard. Some commentators have advocated for an intermediate level of scrutiny in disparate impact situations:

> Under an intermediate-level scrutiny approach, plaintiffs first would have to demonstrate that the government act had a significant disparate impact on a suspect class. Plaintiffs could meet this burden by showing that the act disadvantaged an inordinately large number or percentage of class members. A putative defendant could rebut plaintiffs' argument by showing that a substantial number or percentage of nonsuspect class members also were affected. In evaluating the persuasiveness of the defendant's proof, a court should be aware that institutionalized discriminatory acts are almost necessarily overinclusive because overt discrimination is no longer legal; thus, acts motivated by institutional discrimination often will affect a sizeable number of whites as well. Furthermore, when the evidence of impact is not conclusive, the court should examine past sim-

ilar decisions by the government body to see whether other decisions had disparate racial impacts. If the plaintiffs failed to meet their burden on the disparate impact issue, the defendants would win.

If the plaintiffs can demonstrate disparate impact, the defendants then would bear the burden of proving that the affected group's interests were represented adequately in the decisionmaking process. They may make a prima facie showing by demonstrating that representative members of the minority group were part of the decisionmaking process and that these representatives were fully informed about the detriments and risks the decision would bring to bear on class members. The burden then would shift to plaintiffs to show that the representation was inadequate or that some other substantial process defect existed which could have undermined the effectiveness of the group's representation....

The court's finding on the representation issue would not dispose of the case, but it would determine how carefully the court should scrutinize the defendants' decision. If the court finds that the affected group had adequate representation and was not hampered by process defects, the state merely must demonstrate that a rational basis for its decision exists. On the other hand, if the court found that the process did not adequately include participation by suspect class representatives, it should carefully scrutinize the decision to see whether defendants had considered sufficiently the interests of those affected....

Edward Patrick Boyle, *It's Not Easy Bein' Green: The Psychology of Racism, Environmental Discrimination, and the Argument for Modernizing Equal Protection Analysis*, 46 VAND. L. REV. 937, 980–82 (1993).

8. Professor Tseming Yang argues that the law and policy in civil rights and environmental protection are based on fundamentally different paradigms:

Environmental protection relies in large part on a conception of environmental degradation identified by Garrett Hardin in his seminal article *Tragedy of the Commons*, well as by Rachel Carson in her book Silent Spring. In contrast, civil rights laws and cases have in large part responded to issues of discrimination which are implicit in the Supreme Court's opinion in Brown v. Board of Education.... Under ... "the tragedy of the commons," the quintessential focus of environmental regulation is on actions by individuals that, while advantageous and beneficial to that particular individual, are harmful for the community overall. The result is that environmental regulation, like many other forms of government regulations, is primarily directed at protecting the collective from the irresponsible or selfish actions of individuals or small groups.

That perspective is entirely reversed in anti-discrimination law. The underlying premise of *Brown v. Board of Education* is that prejudice and minority oppression requires the law to focus its protections on minority groups against the majority. Because it was necessary to protect African Americans against continuing discrimination and oppression by whites following the Civil War, the Fourteenth Amendment's Equal Protection Clause was specifically designed to be counter-majoritarian in character.

Tseming Yang, *Melding Civil Rights And Environmentalism: Finding Environmental Justice's Place In Environmental Regulation*, 26 HARV. ENVTL. L. REV. 1 (2002). What does this suggest about relying on civil rights arguments to remedy environmental disparities at the judicial or regulatory levels? Consider this inherent tension as you consider the following civil rights cases.

B. Enforcement of the Civil Rights Act

1. Introduction

Because of lack of success of equal protection claims and the apparent reticence of environmental agencies—at local, state, and federal levels—to condition or deny permits on environmental justice grounds, in the 1990s activists and community residents turned to Title VI of the Civil Rights Act of 1964, a non-environmental statute, as a potential redress for environmental disparities. Title VI has two major provisions, section 601, a general prohibition of discriminatory conduct in programs or activities that receive federal funding, and section 602 which gives federal agencies authority to issue regulations to effectuate the purposes of the Act. Like the equal protection cases discussed above, section 601 has been interpreted to require proof of discriminatory intent to be actionable. Accordingly, this statutory section is generally not helpful to impacted communities because of the extraordinary difficulty in proving that a state environmental agency specifically intends to discriminate on the basis of race in issuing a permit or taking other actions while administering federal environmental programs (for which it receives funding).

However, section 602 has been interpreted by the U.S. Supreme Court to give federal agencies the authority to issue regulations precluding recipients of federal funds from engaging in activities that have a discriminatory "effect," i.e., regulations that prohibit disparate impacts rather than regulations prohibiting only intentional discrimination. Following the practice of many federal agencies, in 1973 EPA promulgated regulations aimed at discriminatory effects. The most recent iteration specifically provides that "[a] recipient shall not use criteria or methods of administering its program which have the effect of subjecting individuals to discrimination because of their race." 40 C.F.R. 7.35(b). This standard is easier to satisfy than the intentional discrimination standard applicable to claims brought under the Equal Protection Clause or to section 601 of Title VI. Typically, the remedy for a Title VI violation is for the federal agency to withdraw federal funds to the recipient in violation, or alternatively, the federal agency may refer the matter to the Department of Justice, which has the option to file suit to enjoin the discriminatory activity.

In September of 1993, community groups began submitting Title VI complaints to the EPA's Office of Civil Rights alleging that the actions of state and local environmental agencies receiving federal funds from the EPA to administer environmental programs were resulting in disparate impacts. Most of the complaints received by EPA involved the permitting process. The gravamen of these complaints is that state agencies, by continuing to issue permits in heavily impacted minority communities, are using criteria or methods that have the effect of causing or exacerbating existing racial disparities despite any lack of specific intent to discriminate. Initially, EPA had neither the resources nor the analytical framework to begin the task of investigating and administratively adjudicating these claims. In February of 1998, the Agency issued an 11-page document titled "Interim Guidance for Investigating Title VI Administrative Complaints Challenging Permits" (*Interim Guidance*). The *Interim Guidance* sparked a firestorm of criticism from the industry/business sector and state/local regulatory agencies, who argued that key terms were left undefined and that the framework was so burdensome that it would discourage economic development.

Partly in response to the strong criticism, in April of 1998 the EPA established the multi-stakeholder "Title VI Implementation Advisory Committee," which in March of 1999 submitted its report to the EPA. The Title VI FACA (so named because it was convened under the authority of the Federal Advisory Committee Act) identified eight crucial substantive issues that the EPA needed to address in adjudicating a disparate impact administrative claim, as well as several important procedural issues. In June of 2000 the EPA replaced the controversial *Interim Guidance* with two lengthy draft guidances; one of these guidances covered the EPA's process for investigating Title VI complaints (*Draft Investigation Guidance*) 65 Fed. Reg. 39,650 (2000).

As an alternative to filing an administrative complaint, community groups also tried to prosecute private lawsuits to enforce section 602 of Title VI. With a private lawsuit, the community group can bypass the administrative process and ask the court directly for the appropriate relief. In short order, however, the Supreme Court in *Alexander v. Sandoval* (excerpted below) ruled that there was no private right of action to enforce the disparate impact regulations. A private right of action (i.e., a lawsuit) could only be instituted for acts of intentional discrimination under section 601. However, Justice Stevens's dissent in *Sandoval* prompted scholars to examine the possibility of using another provision, § 1983 of the Civil Rights Act, to enforce Title VI disparate impact regulations. Under this legal theory, a disparate impact Title VI violation is a breach of federal law that is actionable under § 1983 of the Civil Rights Act, a provision that does allow a private right of action, even though there is no direct cause of action under section 602.

In this section we first discuss in greater detail the administrative avenues for redress under the disparate impact regulations EPA issued pursuant to section 602. We then examine the history of private rights of action under Title VI in the environmental justice context, the resulting legal impediments to pursuing a lawsuit alleging a disparate impact under section 602, and the potential of pursuing a Title VI claim through § 1983.

Pathfinder on Title VI and Environmental Justice

For those wishing to research this complex area in greater depth, an excellent resource on Title VI is Bradford C. Mank, *Title VI, in* THE LAW OF ENVIRONMENTAL JUSTICE (Michael B. Gerrard & Sheila R. Foster eds., 2d ed. 2008). In addition to the articles discussed in this chapter, the following is a select list of other articles on Title VI: Kyle W. La Londe, *Who Wants to Be an Environmental Justice Advocate?: Options for Bringing an Environmental Justice Complaint in the Wake of* Alexander v. Sandoval, 31 B.C. ENVTL. AFF. L. REV. 27 (2004); Avi Brisman, Note, *EPA's Disproportionate Impact Methodologies—RBA & COATCEM—and the Draft Recipient Guidance and Draft Revised Investigation Guidance in Light of* Alexander v. Sandoval, 34 CONN. L. REV. 1065 (2002); Bradford C. Mank, South Camden Citizens in Action v. New Jersey Department of Environmental Protection: *Will Section 1983 Save Title VI Disparate Impact Suits?*, 32 ENVTL. L. REP. 10,454 (2002); and Alice M. Shanahan, *Permitting Justice: EPA's Revised Guidance for Investigating Title VI Administrative Complaints*, 7 ENVTL. LAW. 403 (2001). *See also* NAT'L ADVISORY COUNCIL FOR ENVTL. POL'Y & TECH., REPORT OF THE TITLE VI IMPLEMENTATION ADVISORY COMMITTEE: NEXT STEPS FOR EPA, STATE, AND LOCAL ENVIRONMENTAL JUSTICE PROGRAMS (1999).

2. Administrative Complaints Grounded upon Disparate Impact Regulations

Before discussing the standard that the EPA uses when administratively determining a "disparate impact" under section 602, consider the following summary of procedural steps that may be involved:

- A complaint letter is sent to the EPA Office of Civil Rights (OCR), ideally within 180 days of the violation but this limit can be waived for good cause.

- OCR undertakes a preliminary review to determine if there is a valid claim (e.g., should the complaint be dismissed, investigated, or referred to another agency).

- If the OCR accepts the complaint for factual investigation (to determine if the recipient agency's actions cause or contribute to an existing disparate impact), it will notify the recipient and give it the opportunity to respond to, rebut, or deny the allegations. The OCR will generally attempt to resolve the matter informally.

- If the matter cannot be resolved, OCR may make a finding of noncompliance. At this point, the recipient may request a hearing before an administrative law judge, and will follow a new set of adjudicative procedures.

- The EPA Administrator can then review the OCR's decision or the Administrative Law Judge's decision. The recipient has another opportunity to file statements to the Administrator. If the Administrator decides to withdraw funding, s/he sends a report to the House and Senate Committee having jurisdiction over the program funded (as of December 2008, the EPA has yet to terminate funding).

- Alternatively, the EPA may elect to send the matter to the Department of Justice, but has not done so in any case.

- If at any point the case is dismissed, the complainant has no right to appeal the dismissal.

Note that the triggering document is not a complaint that must be proven by the complainant (the community group). Instead, the OCR initially investigates the matter and determines if there is a disparate impact that could give rise to a section 602 violation. Within this procedural context, we will closely consider the *Select Steel* decision, one of the few cases resolved on the merits after an investigation. This complaint was decided based upon the *Interim Guidance*, which was subsequently replaced by the two draft guidances mentioned above. Because EPA concluded that there was no adverse impact from the proposed facility in a technically complex permit proceeding, the first stage of the inquiry, it did not proceed through the remaining steps of the process.

The *Select Steel* Administrative Decision
As discussed in Letter from Ann E. Goode, Director, EPA
Office of Civil Rights to Father Phil Schmitter & Sister Joanne Chiaverini,
Co-Directors, St. Francis Prayer Center, & Russell Harding, Director,
Michigan Department of Environmental Quality

Alleged Discriminatory Effect Resulting from Air Quality Impacts

As outlined in EPA's *Interim Guidance*, EPA follows five basic steps in its analysis of allegations of discriminatory effects from a permit decision. "The first step is to identify the population affected by the permit that triggered the complaint." ... If there is no adverse effect from the permitted activity, there can be no finding of a discriminatory effect which would violate Title VI and EPA's implementing regulations. In order to address the allegation that MDEQ's [Michigan Department of Environmental Quality] issuance of a PSD [Prevention of Significant Deterioration] permit for the proposed Select Steel facility would result in a discriminatory effect, EPA first considered the potential adverse effect from the permitted facility using a number of analytical tools consistent with EPA's *Interim Guidance*....

VOCs [Volatile Organic Compounds]

To evaluate the impact of VOCs, EPA examined the permit application submitted by Select Steel and a variety of analyses conducted by MDEQ.... In examining VOCs as ozone precursors, EPA studied the additional contribution of VOCs from the proposed Select Steel facility and has determined those emissions will not affect the area's compliance with the national ambient air quality standards (NAAQS) [under the Clean Air Act] for ozone.

The NAAQS for ozone is a health-based standard which has been set at a level that is presumptively sufficient to protect public health and allows for an adequate margin of safety for the population within the area; therefore, there is no affected population which suffers "adverse" impacts within the meaning of Title VI resulting from the incremental VOC emissions from the proposed Select Steel facility....

The Complainants also have alleged that failure to require immediate VOC monitoring for the proposed Select Steel facility will result in a discriminatory effect. Select Steel's permit condition regarding VOC monitoring allows Select Steel one year from plant start-up to implement a continuous emissions monitoring system ("CEMS") for VOCs.... As discussed above, there would be no affected population that suffers "adverse" impacts within the meaning of Title VI resulting from the incremental VOC emissions from the proposed Select Steel facility. For this reason, EPA finds that, with regard to VOC monitoring, MDEQ did not violate Title VI or EPA's implementing regulations.

Lead

Similarly, to evaluate potential lead emissions from the facility, EPA studied the additional contribution of airborne lead emissions from the proposed Select Steel facility and has determined those emissions will not affect the area's compliance with the NAAQS for lead. As with ozone, there is a NAAQS for lead that has been set at a level presumptively sufficient to protect public health and allows for an adequate margin of safety for the population within the attainment area. Therefore, there would be no affected population which suffers "adverse" impacts within the meaning of Title VI resulting from the incremental lead emissions from the proposed Select Steel facility....

In this case, MDEQ also appropriately considered information concerning the effect of the proposed facility's lead emissions on blood lead levels in children in response to community concerns. EPA reviewed this information along with other available data on the incidence and likelihood of elevated blood lead levels in Genesee County, particularly in the vicinity of the site of the proposed facility. EPA considered this additional information in response to the Complainants' concerns that the existing incidence of elevated blood lead levels in children in the vicinity of the proposed facility were already high. Overall, EPA found no clear evidence of a prevalence of pre-existing lead levels of concern in the area most likely to be affected by emissions from the proposed facility....

Air Toxics

For airborne toxics, EPA conducted its review based on information presented in the permit application, existing TRI [Toxic Release Inventory] data, and MDEQ documents.

EPA reviewed MDEQ's analysis of Select Steel's potential air toxic emissions for evidence of adverse impacts based on whether resulting airborne concentrations exceeded thresholds of concern under State air toxics regulations. EPA also considered the potential Select Steel air toxic emissions together with air toxic emissions from [TRI] facilities, the Genesee Power Station, and other major sources in the surrounding area. EPA's review of air toxic emissions from both the proposed site alone, as well as in combination with other sources, found no "adverse" impact in the immediate vicinity of the proposed facility....

Dioxin

The information gathered from the investigation concerning the monitoring of dioxin emissions is consistent with EAB's [EPA's Environmental Appeals Board's] analysis of the issue. No performance specifications for continuous emissions monitoring systems have been promulgated by EPA to monitor dioxins. Without a proven monitor, MDEQ was unable to impose a monitoring requirement on the source....

Alleged Discriminatory Public Participation Process

To assess the allegations of discrimination concerning public process, EPA evaluated the information from interviews with Complainants and MDEQ, and from documents gathered from the parties. The first allegation was that the permit was "hastily sped through" by MDEQ to avoid permitting requirements (*i.e.*, conduct a risk assessment; provide opportunity for public comment on risk assessment; provide meaningful opportunity for all affected parties to participate in the permit process) imposed by a State trial court that are under appeal. The five months between receipt of the complete permit application and permit approval is actually slower than the average time of one and a half months for the past twenty-six PSD permits approved by MDEQ. EPA's review found that the public participation process for the permit was not compromised by the pace of the permitting process. MDEQ satisfied EPA's regulatory requirements concerning the issuance of PSD permits....

The Complainants alleged that the manner of publication of the notice of the permit hearing also contributed to the alleged discriminatory process. The Complainants allege that publication in newspapers was insufficient to inform the predominantly minority community because few community members have access to newspapers—something the Complainants allege was brought to MDEQ's attention during the permitting process for another facility in Genesee Township. EPA's regulations for PSD permitting require that notice of a public hearing must be published in a weekly or daily newspaper within the affected area. In this case, MDEQ went beyond the requirements of the regulation and published notices about the hearing in three local newspapers.

Complainants also state that MDEQ's failure to provide individual notice of the hearing to more members of the community also contributed to the alleged discriminatory process. In addition to newspaper notice, EPA's regulations require that notice be mailed to certain interested community members. MDEQ mailed hearing notification letters a month in advance to Fr. Schmitter, Sr. Chiaverini, and nine other individuals in the community who had expressed interest in the Select Steel permit—an action which is consistent with the requirements of EPA's regulations. The mailing list that MDEQ developed was adequate to inform the community about the public hearing, in part, because the Complainants took it upon themselves to contact other members of the community.

The Complainants also alleged that the location of the public hearing (Mount Morris High School) made it difficult for minority members of the community to attend. Complainants felt that the hearing should have been held at Carpenter Road Elementary School. Both schools are approximately two miles from the proposed Select Steel site; however, the elementary school is located in a predominantly minority area, while the high school is in a predominantly white area. MDEQ explored other possible locations and chose the high school, among other reasons, because of its ability to accommodate the expected number of citizens and its close proximity to the proposed site. The high school also is accessible by the general public via Genesee County public transportation.

For all of these reasons, EPA finds that the public participation process for the Select Steel facility was not discriminatory or in violation of Title VI or EPA's implementing regulations....

* * *

Notes and Questions

1. In this investigation, the EPA's Office of Civil Rights (OCR) noted that the county hosting the facility had been formally designated nonattainment for ozone in 1978, but that it had demonstrated compliance with the one-hour standard based upon three years of air quality data prior to 1998. Thus, reasoned the EPA's Office of Civil Rights, "[i]n practical terms, this means that the old classification of 'nonattainment' has been superseded by a determination that Genesee County was meeting the old ozone standard." *See* Investigative Report, at 14 (a report that accompanied the decision). In other words, OCR did not feel bound by the legal designation of the area. This is critical because the crux of the EPA's decision is that since the area in question is not violating a health-based standard, then by definition the impact (even assuming a disparity exists) is not "adverse." Environmental attorney Luke Cole criticized this approach and argued that, despite the EPA's contentions, as a legal *and* a factual matter Genesee County was not in attainment in 1998, the time of the permit proceeding in the Select Steel Title VI investigation:

> When the MDEQ made the decision to grant the permit to Select Steel on May 27, 1998, the area was not in attainment for the "old" one-hour ozone standard. In fact, less than two weeks earlier, on May 15, 1998, Flint hit a one-hour ozone level of 130 parts per billion (ppb)—a full 60 percent above EPA's health-based NAAQS of 80 ppb. On July 22, 1998—after Michigan issued the permit and after the Title VI complaint had been filed—EPA revoked the one-hour NAAQS for the Flint area, and the area was then covered by the eight-hour ozone NAAQS. On both of these dates—May 27, 1998, for the permit decision and June 9, 1998, for the filing of the complaint—Flint was not in attainment with either the one-hour ozone standard or the eight-hour ozone standard.... Thus, the central underpinning of EPA's decision and theory of no adverse impact—that Flint was in attainment for ozone—is demonstrably false.

Luke W. Cole, *"Wrong on the Facts, Wrong on the Law": Civil Rights Advocates Excoriate EPA's Most Recent Title VI Misstep*, 29 Envtl. L. Rep. 10,775, 10,777–78 (1999).

2. Should a facility's compliance with existing regulatory requirements be sufficient to establish "no adverse impact" and defeat a Title VI claim? How effective would Title VI be under this view?

3. Postscript: the EPA denied a joint petition by environmental justice activists to reconsider the case based, in part, upon Mr. Cole's argument that the area was not in attainment as a factual or legal matter at the time of the permit. The company subsequently decided to locate in Lansing, Michigan.

4. At the time that the *Select Steel* case was under investigation, the EPA had convened an advisory committee, the Title VI FACA referred to above, to provide advice on how states could better comply with Title VI in environmental permitting. The Title VI FACA found that determining whether a disparate impact exists is a particularly tricky endeavor. What follows is a partial list of the questions raised by this important inquiry, as summarized by Professor Eileen Gauna, who was a member of the Title VI FACA:

> At its most narrow, an adverse effect could be construed to mean adverse health effects directly caused by the permitted releases only. A more expansive interpretation of adverse effect would include not only the newly permitted releases, but those changes to the community's well being that are related to the permit at issue, in light of the aggregate sources of pollutants and other adverse impacts existing at the time the permit is under consideration.... Also included would be all foreseeable adverse impacts that may befall the community as a result of the permitted operations. These facility-related (rather than solely emission-related) impacts could include increased traffic, odors, and noise.... A question related to evaluating an adverse impact is the type of proof that may be required to establish a violation....
>
> [T]he reference area would be the recipient's jurisdiction under the relevant environmental statute.... Determining the "affected" population rather than the comparison population was more problematic to some [Title VI FACA] committee members. Some favored the use of monitoring data and computer modeling to determine the communities within the facility's exposure pathway. Environmental justice advocates were a bit more skeptical of this method because of their view that monitor placement is generally inadequate or nonexistent in many environmental justice communities....
>
> [In determining the degree of disparity that would support a claim, the] committee discussed alternative descriptive measurements, such as "significant disparity," "substantial disparity," "above generally accepted norms," "appreciably exceeding the risk to (or the rate in) the general population," or "any measurable disparity." ... Some objected [to a statistical approach] because of a perceived lack of connection between the statistical correlation and the actions of the facility at issue, others because the approach failed to account for communities that may be particularly vulnerable, for example, a community experiencing abnormally high rates of asthma....
>
> Industry representatives and some state regulators are strong adherents of the view that if a permit applicant complies with all applicable requirements under the relevant environmental standards, there can be no violation of Title VI. The logic supporting this position is that environmental laws are designed to—and in fact do—accomplish an adequate level of protection for all members of society.... Environmental justice representatives were adamantly opposed to using health-based standards in this manner.... Such standards, they argued, were often insufficiently protective to begin with, had not been fully implemented, and did not take into account the particular vulnerabilities of a community. Moreover, the health-based ambient standards tended to cover large geographical regions (like an airshed); thus, while the geographical area might comply with the standards overall, toxic hot spots could well occur within those areas [an airshed is usually a fairly large geographical region, one that shares a common flow of air which may become uniformly polluted by a particular pollutant. Eds]

... [In deciding whether permit renewals should be treated differently than new facilities, the Committee considered that when] a project sponsor initially commits substantial capital to build a facility, it likely anticipates a useful life of the facility of at least 30 years. But a permit typically expires in five years.... It would be unfair to tell [a] facility owner, who expected routine permit renewals, that her multimillion dollar facility can no longer operate because a permit renewal would violate the regulator's Title VI duty by continuing to subject the host community to a racially disparate impact.... At the other end of the spectrum is the perspective of environmental justice advocates. They point out that ... permit applicants expect new requirements upon renewal as standards often change over time. Presenting their own fairness claims, they point out that a ton of pollution resulting from a permit renewal is just as harmful as a ton of pollution resulting from an initially granted permit.

... In terms of how much mitigation should be required, the possibilities include mitigation sufficient to (a) eliminate the disparity, (b) reduce risk to acceptable levels, or (c) make reasonable progress in eliminating the disparity.... [And in determining what might justify a disparate impact, the committee discussed] proposed justification tests [that] ranged from strict necessity with benefits flowing directly—and perhaps exclusively—to the impacted community, to less stringent tests justifying disparate impacts that would be too costly to mitigate or involve facilities that provide some public benefit.

Eileen Gauna, *EPA at Thirty: Fairness in Environmental Protection*, 31 ENVTL. L. REP. 10,528, 10,540 (2001). In answering the deceptively simple question—does a disparity exist?—what would your investigative framework look like? How would you define and determine key concepts, such as "actionable disparity," "reference population," "reference area," "sufficient mitigation," and "justification"?

5. Subsequent to the Select Steel decision, the EPA under the Bush administration established a task force to address Title VI complaints. As of December 22, 2008 a request by the authors under the Freedom of Information Act revealed that the EPA had processed a total of 211 complaints since 1993. Of those, 40 (19%) were still pending, and 171 (81%) had been closed. Of the closed cases, 127 (60%) had been rejected and 44 (21%) had been dismissed. Reasons for dismissal may include informal resolution or voluntary withdrawal of the complaint. Some of the reasons for a rejection of a complaint include a lack of federal funding to the relevant state agency, failure to file within a certain time frame, and insufficient allegations. Similarly, in 2005, citing an unpublished table compiled by Michael Gerrard and Kristina Alexander, Professor Mank observes that:

First, only in a small minority of cases does the EPA actually decide whether there are adverse or disparate impacts. Second, in two cases, a case from Arizona the EPA dismissed in 2003 and a case from Mississippi the agency dismissed in 2002, the EPA applied a standard of whether the recipient had committed "*intentional discrimination.*" In a Georgia complaint, however, the EPA dismissed the case in 2002 because the agency found no disparity, and in the *Romulus* case from Michigan, the EPA dismissed the complaint in 2002 because there was no adversity or disparity. An intentional discrimination standard is clearly contrary to the agency's Title VI regulations.

Mank, *Title VI, supra*, at 29. In your view, what might account for the inconsistent treatment of Title VI claims? Notice that in no instance has the EPA made a formal finding of a Title VI violation. Does the inherent difficulty in factually determining what constitutes a disparate impact partly explain this history of administrative adjudications? The U.S. Commission on Civil Rights criticized the EPA's record of Title VI adjudications, along with the Title VI programs at the Department of Transportation, the Department of Interior, and the Department of Housing and Urban Development in a 2003 report. U.S. COMM'N ON CIV. RTS., NOT IN MY BACKYARD: EXECUTIVE ORDER 12,898 AND TITLE VI AS TOOLS FOR ACHIEVING ENVIRONMENTAL JUSTICE (2003). Do you anticipate that the final disposition of administrative investigations of Title VI complaints under the Obama administration might yield a slightly different pattern, perhaps with some cases resulting in a formal finding of a Title VI violation? If you predict this might be the case, how would you assess the relative advantages and disadvantages of proceeding in court instead of through an agency investigation? Consider the following:

3. Private Right of Action for Claims Grounded upon "Disparate Impact"

Some community based organizations and others asserting environmental justice claims prefer to sue in court instead of filing an administrative complaint with the funding agency (usually the EPA). Although the administrative complaint procedure is far less expensive than litigation, a lawsuit is perceived to have advantages that outweigh the relative costs. Consider that through discovery procedures, the plaintiff (community group) would have better control over the investigation. For example, the plaintiff can call witnesses, give evidence, and cross-examine defendant's witnesses. In addition, attorney fees may be recoverable by the prevailing plaintiff and a plaintiff who loses may appeal the decision. And most importantly, the court can issue an injunction. This is significant because, as explained above, the remedy in an administrative proceeding is the withdrawal of federal funds by the funding agency, a drastic remedy that is unlikely ever to be imposed.

As an initial matter, if we assume that courts would allow private actions—under § 1983 or otherwise—alleging that recipient state environmental agencies failed to comply with section 602 of Title VI, are courts more likely than the EPA to find violations of these regulations? If a state recipient agency is found in violation, do you think a court will be inclined to issue injunctive relief? In the following *South Camden* case (decided shortly before the U.S. Supreme Court *Sandoval* decision), plaintiffs sued alleging a violation of Title VI's regulations. Federal district court Judge Orlofsky found that the plaintiffs had a private right of action to enforce the regulations, and then decided the case on the merits. He applied the EPA's *Draft Investigation Guidance*, mentioned above, which had been recently issued. The *Investigation Guidance* gives much more detail about the investigatory framework than does the *Interim Guidance*, but at the same time it gives the EPA significant discretion to choose, on a case by case basis, the methodology it will use to determine whether a disparate impact exists. For example, when determining the degree of disparity needed to show a violation, the *Investigation Guidance* cautions that there is no fixed formula or analysis to be applied and that no single factor is applicable in all cases. *See* Gauna, *supra*, at 10,539–50. The EPA also gave itself substantial leeway in determining the applicable impacted area, reference area or reference population, and what impacts it would consider. *See id*. As you read and consider the *South Camden* decision, can you discern what methodology the judge used in determining whether a disparity in fact existed?

South Camden Citizens in Action v.
New Jersey Department of Environmental Protection
145 F. Supp. 2d 446 (2001)

Orlofsky, District Court Judge

[The case involves an application by St. Lawrence Cement Company (SLC), defendant-intervener, for an air permit to operate a facility in the Waterfront South neighborhood of South Camden, New Jersey, that would grind and process granulated blast furnace slug (GBFS). Plaintiffs had already constructed the facility when the lawsuit was filed.]

Introduction

... SLC's proposed facility will emit certain pollutants into the air. These pollutants will include particulate matter (dust), mercury, lead, manganese, nitrogen oxides, carbon monoxide, sulphur oxides and volatile organic compounds.... Outbound truck departures from the SLC facility will occur on approximately 225 days per year, with about 200 trucks departing per day. The contemplated truck routes pass through the Waterfront South Community.

The population of Waterfront South is 2,132, forty-one percent of whom are children. Ninety-one percent of the residents of Waterfront South are persons of color. Specifically, sixty-three percent are African-American, twenty-eight percent are Hispanic, and nine percent are non-Hispanic white. The residents of Waterfront South suffer from a disproportionately high rate of asthma and other respiratory ailments.

The Waterfront South neighborhood is already a popular location for the siting of industrial facilities. It contains the Camden County Municipal Utilities Authority, a sewage treatment plant, the Camden County Resource Recovery facility, a trash-to-steam plant, the Camden Cogen Power Plant, a co-generation plant, and two United States Environmental Protection Agency ("EPA") designated Superfund sites. Four sites within one-half mile of SLC's propos[ed] facility are currently being investigated by the EPA for the possible release of hazardous substances. The NJDEP [New Jersey Department of Environmental Protection] has also identified fifteen known contaminated sites in the Waterfront South neighborhood.

... [T]he NJDEP granted the necessary air permits to SLC to allow its proposed facility to begin operations. In doing so, the NJDEP considered only whether the facility's emissions would exceed technical emissions standards for specific pollutants, especially dust. Indeed, much of what this case is about is what the NJDEP failed to consider. It did not consider the level of ozone generated by the truck traffic to and from the SLC facility, notwithstanding the fact that the Waterfront South community is not currently in compliance with the National Ambient Air Quality Standard ("NAAQS") established by the EPA for ozone levels, nor did it consider the presence of many other pollutants in Waterfront South. It did not consider the pre-existing poor health of the residents of Waterfront South, nor did it consider the cumulative environmental burden already borne by this impoverished community. Finally, and perhaps most importantly, the NJDEP failed to consider the racial and ethnic composition of the population of Waterfront South....

For the reasons which follow ... I conclude that: (1) The NJDEP's failure to consider any evidence beyond SLC's compliance with technical emissions standards, and specifically its failure to consider the totality of the circumstances surrounding the operation of SLC's proposed facility, violates the EPA's regulations promulgated to implement Title VI of the Civil Rights Act of 1964; and (2) Plaintiffs have established a prima facie case of disparate impact discrimination based on race and national origin in violation of the EPA's regulations promulgated pursuant to section 602 of the Civil Rights Act of 1964....

Findings of Fact and Conclusions of Law

[The following are selected findings of fact and conclusions of law from the court's 257 findings and conclusions. Eds.]

Air contaminant emissions will be generated at the following stages of GBFS processing: (1) fugitive dust emissions will be generated from the handling and movement of GBFS when it is offloaded from trucks, piled, and then placed in the hopper; (2) GBFS particles may be blown into the ambient air once on the conveyor belt; (3) various air pollutants will be produced during the heating and grinding processes; and (4) [GBFS] emission may occur when the GBFS is stored and offloaded for delivery off-site.

In his deposition testimony, Dr. [Irwin] Berlin [a health expert] testified that he had been asked by Morris Smith, Esq., consultant for SLC, on behalf of the CAP [Community Advisory Panel created by SLC], to evaluate the overall SLC facility design and emission protections, with specific attention to particulate emissions. In the letter he submitted to Mr. Smith documenting his findings, Dr. Berlin identifies Camden County as a "Community of Concern" ("COC") based on initial findings of a study Dr. Berlin is currently performing regarding the bronchial and lung cancer and asthma rates of residents of New Jersey. The initial findings of Dr. Berlin's study, which are not challenged, indicate that in Camden County: [the age-adjusted cancer rate for black females is higher than 90% of the rest of the state; for black males is higher than 70% of the rest of the state; the rate of cancer is significantly higher for black males than for white males; the age-adjusted rate of death of black females in Camden County from asthma is over three times the rate of death for white females from asthma in Camden County; and the age-adjusted rate of death for black males in Camden County from asthma is over six times the rate of death for white males from asthma in Camden County.]

It is undisputed that, with all proposed emissions controls in place as stated in the permit applications, the SLC facility will emit 59.1 tons of particulate matter size PM-10 or smaller per year. The SLC facility will therefore be in compliance with the current NAAQ standard for PM-10 emissions.

Plaintiffs contend, however, that mere compliance with the NAAQ standard for PM-10 does not result in the avoidance of adverse health consequences for the residents of Waterfront South who will be exposed to the particulate emissions of the proposed SLC facility....

With respect to PM-10 emissions, [Plaintiff's Expert, Associate Professor] Dr. [Mark] Lavietes testified that there is a statistically significant relationship between PM-10 emissions and mortality, even where PM-10 emissions are *well below* the level set by NAAQS....

In his certification, Dr. Lavietes testified that PM-2.5, because it is smaller, can lodge more deeply in the lungs than coarser components of PM-10. Dr. Lavietes also testified that it is the most dangerous component of PM-10, and is likely responsible for most of the negative health consequences associated with PM-10.

The NJDEP responds to Plaintiffs' concerns regarding the SLC facility's potential PM-2.5 emissions by emphasizing that there is currently no NAAQ standard for PM-2.5. Essentially, the NJDEP argues that unless and until the EPA issues a NAAQ standard for PM-2.5, the NJDEP cannot be held responsible for failing to consider whatever adverse health consequences might result from PM-2.5 exposure....

The EPA specifically noted that "[s]ensitive subpopulations [] appear to be at greater risk to such effects, specifically individuals with respiratory disease and cardiovascular disease and the elderly (premature mortality and hospitalization), children (increased respiratory symptoms and decreased lung function), and asthmatic children and adults (aggravation of symptoms)."

SLC, through the CAP TAG, commissioned a study of existing and carbon monoxide emissions along the truck route to be used by the SLC delivery trucks. The study found that the SLC truck traffic would not cause an exceedence of the carbon monoxide NAAQS in the area. The study did not analyze the impact of the SLC facility or the SLC truck traffic on ozone.

Given the large volume of truck traffic which will be traveling to and from the SLC facility, NJDEP's failure to give any consideration whatsoever to the potential increase in ozone levels in an area which is in non-attainment with the existing [o]zone NAAQS, I find NJDEP's argument to be disingenuous. In these circumstances, it is clear that ozone levels will only get worse, not better.

[The] NJDEP's insistence that its obligation to Plaintiffs under Title VI does not go beyond ensuring compliance with the NAAQS is completely undermined by the NJDEP's own recognition, in numerous fora, that it has precisely such an obligation under Title VI. On October 22, 1998, NJDEP Commissioner Shinn issued the first of several Administrative Orders acknowledging the NJDEP's obligation under Title VI. In this Administrative Order, Commissioner Shinn established the NJDEP's "Advisory Council on Environmental Equity" ("Advisory Council"). The NJDEP defined "environmental equity" as "the fair and equitable treatment in environmental decision-making of the citizens of all New Jersey communities regardless of race, color, income, or national origin. Fair and equitable treatment means that no population should bear disproportionate amounts of adverse health and environmental effects." ...

It is the Court's understanding that none of the policies or procedures referred to in the Administrative Orders have been implemented....

It is uncontested that the NJDEP's permitting policy is facially neutral. The NJDEP uses a complicated system, including air dispersion modeling, to predict the level and pattern of pollutant emissions from a proposed facility such as the SLC facility. The NJDEP then compares these results to the federally established NAAQS, set by the EPA, for the particular pollutants which will be produced by the facility. As counsel for the NJDEP explained at oral argument, once the NJDEP reaches the conclusion that a proposed facility will be in compliance with the NAAQS, the NJDEP's inquiry into the environmental impacts of the facility stops, and the NJDEP will issue a permit to operate the proposed facility.

Plaintiffs contend that the operation of the proposed facility will adversely impact them in several ways. After reviewing the record, I have determined that the primary adverse impacts of which Plaintiffs complain are impacts to the health of the residents who live in the Waterfront South neighborhood where the proposed SLC facility is located. While Plaintiffs also complain of adverse effects to their quality of life, caused by the noise, vibrations and dirt associated with the truck traffic which will traverse the neighborhood if the facility becomes operational, I have concluded that the record in this case is insufficient to support such a claim. Accordingly, I shall deny Plaintiffs' request for a preliminary injunction to the extent that it is based on the alleged adverse impact of the operation of the SLC facility on Plaintiffs' quality of life.

While the EPA's method of analysis in *Select Steel* is instructive here, the circumstances of *Select Steel*, which led the EPA to conclude there was no adversity, are entirely distinguishable from the present case. First, the area of concern in *Select Steel* was in compliance for all relevant NAAQS; in contrast, it is undisputed that Camden County is in "severe nonattainment" of the established ozone NAAQS. Second, both MDEQ and the EPA OCR [Office of Civil Rights], in investigating the complainants' Title VI concerns, looked beyond mere compliance with the NAAQS and considered community-specific health data before determining that the facility would not adversely affect the residents' health. Third, the EPA examined the cumulative environmental burdens on the community, based on data from the TRI, before concluding that the aggregate effect of these pollutants would not adversely effect [sic] the residents' health. Only after this comprehensive review of community-specific data did the EPA OCR reach its conclusion that the MDEQ's decision to permit the facility did not violate Title VI.

.... SLC contends that based on [Plaintiff's Expert] Dr. [Michael] Gelobter's analysis, Plaintiffs make an "unsubstantiated leap" to the conclusion that the NJDEP's permitting process is causally linked to the admitted disparity in the distribution of industrial facilities in the State of New Jersey. According to SLC, this Court must reject Dr. Gelobter's data on causation because he failed to consider all of the factors that could account for the siting of industrial facilities in particular areas, such as access to transportation, existing infrastructure, and available labor force. Thus, SLC asserts that "even assuming the statistical evidence that Plaintiffs have produced is accurate, those statistics are not the result of some defect in NJDEP's permitting process, but are rather the result of hundreds, if not thousands, of individual siting decisions made by private entities searching on the basis of sound business principles for the most appropriate locations for their industrial facilities."

I reject SLC's argument for several reasons. First, this Court has already concluded that there is in fact a severe "defect" in the NJDEP's permitting process, namely, that the NJDEP relies exclusively on compliance with environmental regulations such as the NAAQS, without considering its obligations under Title VI, in issuing permits such as those it issued for the proposed SLC facility.

[A] review of the applicable regulations promulgated by the EPA clearly indicates that the EPA has determined that there is a causal connection between recipients' permitting practices and the distribution of polluting facilities, and ... has acknowledged that because recipients are responsible for permitting, they are also responsible for considering the distribution of the facilities which they permit with respect to the classes protected by the Civil Rights Act of 1964. The regulations therefore support the conclusion that a recipient's permitting decisions are causally linked to the distribution of facilities as a matter of law.

Plaintiffs contend that the NJDEP will not be harmed by the issuance of an injunction, because the injunction which Plaintiffs request only requires the NJDEP to meet its existing obligations under Title VI. Plaintiffs concede that SLC will suffer economic injury if an injunction issues, but argue that SLC assumed this risk by beginning construction of the proposed facility over a year before the NJDEP issued the permits.... Furthermore, Plaintiffs argue that SLC was aware, due to Plaintiffs' frequent protests, that Plaintiffs believed the NJDEP had not complied with the requirements of Title VI.... [T]he NJDEP advised SLC, by letter dated September 2, 1999, well before SLC began construction, that "[d]ue to the fact that St. Lawrence will be operating in an economically depressed area which has a substantial minority population, the Department will evaluate the need to conduct a Environmental Justice analysis."

... The harm alleged by SLC is entirely economic. Specifically, SLC argues that it has expended more than $50 million to construct the facility, and will lose $200,000 for each week that the facility does not operate. The Third Circuit has held, however, that purely economic injury is not irreparable harm.

... SLC's argument misconstrues the relief which Plaintiffs have requested and which I am granting. I am not "revoking" SLC's permits, but rather enjoining SLC from operating under the permits until the NJDEP performs an appropriate adverse disparate impact analysis in compliance with Title VI. While I have concluded, based on the evidence in the record before me, that Plaintiffs have established a likelihood of success on the merits that the permitting of the SLC facility will have an adverse, disparate impact in violation of Title VI, I have done so only in the context of issuing a preliminary injunction. It is now up to the NJDEP in the first instance to reevaluate its permitting decision with respect to the SLC facility after conducting the requisite adverse, disparate impact analysis.

* * *

Notes and Questions

1. What factors are most significant in the court's holding that the defendant likely violated Title VI? The court at one point notes that it is undisputed that the NJDEP's permitting policy is facially neutral, yet it later finds that NJDEP's permitting activities have contributed to the racially disparate distribution of industrial facilities in New Jersey. How could the court reach both of these conclusions?

2. *South Camden* is the most important Title VI environmental justice case decided by the courts and the only one that specifically applies EPA's *Draft Investigation Guidance* to the facts at issue. Two other Title VI decisions are *Goshen Road v. USDA*, 1999 U.S. App. Lexis 6135 (an unpublished Fourth Circuit decision), in which the court rejected a Title VI challenge to a wastewater treatment siting because plaintiffs failed to identify equally effective alternatives, and *New York City Environmental Justice Alliance v. Giuliani*, 214 F.3d 65 (2d Cir. 2000), in which the court rejected a Title VI challenge to New York City's sale of city-owned lots containing community gardens because plaintiffs failed to show adequately measured adverse impacts from the City's actions, or the existence of less discriminatory alternatives.

3. Shortly after the District Court decision in *South Camden*, the *Sandoval* case (below) was decided by the U.S. Supreme Court. The Court ruled that there is no private right of action available to enforce the section 602 discriminatory effect regulations, but left open the possibility that § 1983 could provide a remedy. In light of the *Sandoval* decision, NJDEP appealed. Before turning to the outcome of the *South Camden* appeal, consider the Court's analysis in *Sandoval*.

Alexander v. Sandoval

532 U.S. 275 (2001)

Justice Scalia delivered the opinion of the Court:

This case presents the question whether private individuals may sue to enforce disparate-impact regulations promulgated under Title VI of the Civil Rights Act of 1964.

The Alabama Department of Public Safety (Department), of which petitioner James Alexander is the Director, accepted grants of financial assistance from the United States Department of Justice (DOJ) and Department of Transportation (DOT) and so subjected itself to the restrictions of Title VI of the Civil Rights Act of 1964.... Section 602 authorizes federal agencies "to effectuate the provisions of [§ 601] ... by issuing rules, regulations, or orders of general applicability," and the DOJ in an exercise of this authority promulgated a regulation forbidding funding recipients to "utilize criteria or methods of administration which have the effect of subjecting individuals to discrimination because of their race, color, or national origin...."

The State of Alabama amended its Constitution in 1990 to declare English "the official language of the state of Alabama." Pursuant to this provision and, petitioners have argued, to advance public safety, the Department decided to administer state driver's license examinations only in English. Respondent Sandoval, as representative of a class, brought suit in the United States District Court for the Middle District of Alabama to enjoin the English-only policy, arguing that it violated the DOJ regulation because it had the effect of subjecting non-English speakers to discrimination based on their national origin....

[W]e must assume for purposes of deciding this case that regulations promulgated under § 602 of Title VI may validly proscribe activities that have a disparate impact on racial groups, even though such activities are permissible under § 601. Though no opinion of this Court has held that, five Justices in *Guardians* [Ass'n v. Civil Service Comm'n of New York City, 463 U.S. 582 (1983)] voiced that view of the law at least as alternative grounds for their decisions.... We therefore assume for the purposes of deciding this case that the DOJ and DOT regulations proscribing activities that have a disparate impact on the basis of race are valid....

It is clear now that the disparate-impact regulations do not simply apply § 601 — since they indeed forbid conduct that § 601 permits — and therefore clear that the private right of action to enforce § 601 does not include a private right to enforce these regulations. That right must come, if at all, from the independent force of § 602....

Implicit in our discussion thus far has been a particular understanding of the genesis of private causes of action. Like substantive federal law itself, private rights of action to enforce federal law must be created by Congress. The judicial task is to interpret the statute Congress has passed to determine whether it displays an intent to create not just a private right but also a private remedy. Statutory intent on this latter point is determinative. Without it, a cause of action does not exist and courts may not create one, no matter how desirable that might be as a policy matter, or how compatible with the statute....

We therefore begin (and find that we can end) our search for Congress's intent with the text and structure of Title VI. Section 602 authorizes federal agencies "to effectuate the provisions of [§ 601] ... by issuing rules, regulations, or orders of general applicability." It is immediately clear that the "rights creating" language so critical to the Court's analysis in *Cannon* [v. University of Chicago, 441 U.S. 677 (1979)] of § 601, is completely absent from § 602. Whereas § 601 decrees that "[n]o person ... shall ... be subjected to discrimination," the text of § 602 provides that "[e]ach Federal department and agency ... is authorized and directed to effectuate the provisions of [§ 601]." Far from displaying congressional intent to create new rights, § 602 limits agencies to "effectuating" rights already created by § 601. And the focus of § 602 is twice removed from the individuals who will ultimately benefit from Title VI' s protection. Statutes that focus on the person regulated rather than the individuals protected create "no implication of an intent to confer rights on a particular class of persons." Section 602 is yet a step further removed: it focuses neither on the individuals protected nor even on the funding recipients being regulated, but on the agencies that will do the regulating. Like the statute found not to create a right of action in *Universities Research Assn., Inc. v. Coutu*, 450 U.S. 754 (1981), § 602 is "phrased as a directive to federal agencies engaged in the distribution of public funds." When this is true, "[t]here [is] far less reason to infer a private remedy in favor of individual persons." So far as we can tell, this authorizing portion of § 602 reveals no congressional intent to create a private right of action.

Nor do the methods that § 602 goes on to provide for enforcing its authorized regulations manifest an intent to create a private remedy; if anything, they suggest the opposite. Section 602 empowers agencies to enforce their regulations either by terminating funding to the "particular program, or part thereof," that has violated the regulation or "by any other means authorized by law." No enforcement action may be taken, however, "until the department or agency concerned has advised the appropriate person or persons of the failure to comply with the requirement and has determined that compliance cannot be secured by voluntary means." And every agency enforcement action is subject to judicial review. If an agency attempts to terminate program funding, still more restrictions apply. The agency head must "file with the committees of the House and Senate having legislative jurisdiction over the program or activity involved a full written report of the circumstances and the grounds for such action." And the termination of funding does not "become effective until thirty days have elapsed after the filing of such report." Whatever these elaborate restrictions on agency enforcement may imply for the private enforcement of rights created *outside* of § 602 ... they tend to contradict a congressional intent to create privately enforceable rights through § 602 itself. The express provision of one method of enforcing a substantive rule suggests that Congress intended to preclude others. Sometimes the suggestion is so strong that it precludes a finding of congressional intent to create a private right of action, even though other aspects of the statute (such as language making the would be plaintiff "a member of the class for whose benefit the statute was enacted") suggest the contrary....

Both the Government and respondents argue that the *regulations* contain rights-creating language and so must be privately enforceable, but that argument skips an analytical step. Language in a regulation may invoke a private right of action that Congress through statutory text created, but it may not create a right that Congress has not. Thus, when a statute has provided a general authorization for private enforcement of regulations, it may perhaps be correct that the intent displayed in each regulation can determine whether or not it is privately enforceable. But it is most certainly incorrect to say that language in a regulation can conjure up a private cause of action that has not been authorized by Congress. Agencies may play the sorcerer's apprentice but not the sorcerer himself....

Justice Stevens, with whom Justices Souter, Ginsburg and Breyer, join, dissenting:

... At the time of the promulgation of [disparate impact] regulations, prevailing principles of statutory construction assumed that Congress intended a private right of action whenever such a cause of action was necessary to protect individual rights granted by valid federal law. Relying both on this presumption and on independent analysis of Title VI, this Court has repeatedly and consistently affirmed the right of private individuals to bring civil suits to enforce rights guaranteed by Title VI. A fair reading of those cases, and coherent implementation of the statutory scheme, requires the same result under Title VI's implementing regulations.

In separate lawsuits spanning several decades, we have endorsed an action identical in substance to the one brought in this case, *see* Lau v. Nichols, 414 U.S. 563 (1974); demonstrated that Congress intended a private right of action to protect the rights guaranteed by Title VI, *see* [*Cannon*]; and concluded that private individuals may seek declaratory and injunctive relief against state officials for violations of regulations promulgated pursuant to Title VI, *see* [*Guardians*]. Giving fair import to our language and our holdings, every Court of Appeals to address the question has concluded that a private right of action exists to enforce the rights guaranteed both by the text of Title VI and by any regulations validly promulgated pursuant to that Title, and Congress has adopted several statutes that appear to ratify the status quo....

The majority acknowledges that *Cannon* is binding precedent with regard to both Title VI and Title IX, but seeks to limit the scope of its holding to cases involving allegations of intentional discrimination. The distinction the majority attempts to impose is wholly foreign to *Cannon*'s text and reasoning. The opinion in *Cannon* consistently treats the question presented in that case as whether a private right of action exists to enforce "Title IX" (and by extension "Title VI"), and does not draw any distinctions between the various types of discrimination outlawed by the operation of those statutes. Though the opinion did not reach out to affirmatively preclude the drawing of every conceivable distinction, it could hardly have been more clear as to the scope of its holding: A private right of action exists for "victims of *the* prohibited discrimination." 441 U.S. at 703 (emphasis added). Not some of the prohibited discrimination, but all of it.... Moreover, *Cannon* was itself a disparate impact case....

As I read today's opinion, the majority declines to accord precedential value to *Guardians* because the five Justices in the majority were arguably divided over the mechanism through which private parties might seek such injunctive relief. This argument inspires two responses. First, to the extent that the majority denies relief to the respondents merely because they neglected to mention 42 U.S.C. § 1983 in framing their Title VI claim, this case is something of a sport. Litigants who in the future wish to enforce the Title VI regulations against state actors in all likelihood must only reference § 1983 to obtain relief; indeed, the plaintiffs in this case (or other similarly situated individuals) presumably retain the option of rechallenging Alabama's English-only policy in a complaint that invokes § 1983 even after today's decision....

Beyond its flawed structural analysis of Title VI and an evident antipathy toward implied rights of action, the majority offers little affirmative support for its conclusion that Congress did not intend to create a private remedy for violations of the Title VI regulations. The Court offers essentially two reasons for its position. First, it attaches significance to the fact that the "rights-creating" language in § 601 that defines the classes protected by the statute is not repeated in § 602. But, of course, there was no reason to put that language in § 602 because it is perfectly obvious that the regulations authorized by § 602 must be designed to protect precisely the same people protected by § 601. Moreover, it is self evident that, linguistic niceties notwithstanding, any statutory provision whose stated purpose is to "effectuate" the eradication of racial and ethnic discrimination has as its "focus" those individuals who, absent such legislation, would be subject to discrimination.

Second, the Court repeats the argument advanced and rejected in *Cannon* that the express provision of a fund cut-off remedy "suggests that Congress intended to preclude others." In *Cannon*, we carefully explained why the presence of an explicit mechanism to achieve one of the statute's objectives (ensuring that federal funds are not used "to support discriminatory practices") does not preclude a conclusion that a private right of action was intended to achieve the statute's other principal objective ("to provide individual citizens effective protection against those practices"). In support of our analysis, we offered policy arguments, cited evidence from the legislative history, and noted the active support of the relevant agencies. In today's decision, the Court does not grapple with — indeed, barely acknowledges — our rejection of this argument in *Cannon*.

Like much else in its opinion, the present majority's unwillingness to explain its refusal to find the reasoning in *Cannon* persuasive suggests that today's decision is the unconscious product of the majority's profound distaste for implied causes of action rather than an attempt to discern the intent of the Congress that enacted Title VI of the Civil Rights Act of 1964. Its colorful disclaimer of any interest in "venturing beyond Congress's intent" has a hollow ring.

* * *

Notes and Questions

1. Left undecided by the Supreme Court, for the moment at least, is the validity of the underlying Title VI discriminatory impact regulations. Some hints of the Court's position on this issue appear in *Sandoval*. Justice Scalia seems to suggest that it is inconsistent to allow regulations under section 602 to prohibit conduct having a discriminatory impact when that same conduct is permitted by section 601, which bars only intentional discrimination. *See Sandoval*, 532 U.S. at 286. It is likely that this issue will eventually be resolved by the Supreme Court as well.

2. Does the *Sandoval* case absolutely preclude lawsuits based upon Title VI's disparate impact regulations? As discussed above, an alternative theory is that recipients of federal funds acting under color of state law may be subject to a § 1983 action for failure to comply with section 602 of Title VI, a possibility raised, and arguably encouraged, by Justice Stevens's dissent. Section 1983, which originated in the Civil Rights Act of 1871, allows suits for violations of the Constitution and other federal laws against persons acting under color of law. *See* 42 U.S.C. § 1983. After the *Sandoval* ruling, the plaintiffs in *South Camden* pressed this approach, and Judge Orlofsky ruled that Title VI's regulations could be enforced under § 1983. 145 F. Supp. 2d 505 (D.N.J.). On appeal, the Third Circuit reversed. It held that an administrative regulation cannot create an interest enforceable under § 1983 unless the interest already is implicit in the statute authorizing the regulation, and that since Title VI (i.e., the statute itself) proscribes only intentional discrimination, the plaintiffs could not enforce the disparate impact discrimination regulations. *See* S. Camden Citizens in Action v. N. J. Dep't of Envtl. Prot., 274 F.3d 771 (2001), *cert. denied* 122 S. Ct. 2621 (2002).

In the excerpt below, Professor Brad Mank examines whether a right of action should exist under § 1983. As you will see from Professor Mank's argument, the issue is a complicated one involving a tension between separation of powers principles and agency deference principles, as well as the interpretation of sometimes conflicting Supreme Court precedent. This leaves the circuits in substantial disagreement and uncertainty.

Bradford C. Mank, Can Administrative Regulations Interpret Rights Enforceable under Section 1983?: Why *Chevron* Deference Survives *Sandoval* and *Gonzaga*

32 Florida State University Law Review 843 (2005)

... In 2001, in *Alexander v. Sandoval*, the Court indirectly cast doubt on the use of regulations to create enforceable rights by holding that there is no private right of action to enforce disparate impact regulations promulgated under Title VI of the 1964 Civil Rights Act....

In his dissenting opinion in *Sandoval*, Justice Stevens contended that Section 602 regulations could be enforced indirectly under § 1983 even if they could not create an implied right of action directly because regulations are "laws" within the statute's meaning....

In 2002, in *Gonzaga University v. Doe* [533 U.S. 273 (2002)], the Supreme Court held that the Family Educational Rights and Privacy Act's non-disclosure provisions were not privately enforceable through § 1983. The Court concluded that individual rights enforceable through § 1983 are similar to implied rights of action because courts are required to "determine whether Congress *intended to create a federal right.*" Because the Court held in *Sandoval* that only Congress can create implied rights of action, the *Gonzaga* decision suggests that only Congress can create rights enforceable through § 1983 and that regulations alone may not. The *Gonzaga* decision did not directly resolve, however, whether and to what extent regulations may interpret rights implicit in a statute....

It is not clear whether the *Chevron* [v. NRDC, 467 U.S. 837 (1984)] decision or similar deference principles apply to the interpretation of individual rights enforceable under § 1983. If a regulation goes beyond the explicit language of a statute to clarify or establish a right that is generally compatible with the statute's goals, should courts treat that right as enforceable under § 1983? ...

[T]his Article argues that courts should defer to agency regulations that clarify or further define individual rights reasonably implicit in a statute without contradicting the central underlying principle in *Sandoval* and *Gonzaga* that Congress alone possesses the legislative authority necessary to create individual rights in a statute.... [T]he current 42 U.S.C. § 1983 [] provides, in relevant part, as follows:

> Every person who, under color of any statute, ordinance, regulation, custom, or usage, of any State or Territory or the District of Columbia, subjects, or causes to be subjected, any citizen of the United States or other person within the jurisdiction thereof to the deprivation of any rights, privileges, or immunities secured by the Constitution *and laws*, shall be liable to the party injured in an action at law, suit in equity, or other proper proceeding for redress....

... Before 1961, there were relatively few § 1983 cases. From the nineteenth century until 1961, courts narrowly construed § 1983 claims, limiting them to civil rights cases alleging violations of federal constitutional rights, especially deprivation of the right to make contracts or purchase property.... During the 1960s and 1970s, the Supreme Court allowed a broad range of suits pursuant to § 1983 and declared that courts should construe § 1983 "generously" to advance its broad remedial goals. During the 1960s and 1970s, a few Supreme Court decisions suggested that a § 1983 suit might be based on a statutory right violation, but none of these cases clearly resolved the question because they focused on constitutional claims....

It was not until 1980, when the Supreme Court held, for the first time, in *Maine v. Thiboutot*, that the term "and laws" in § 1983 included a broad range of federal statutory violations.... Thus, the Court held that plaintiffs may use § 1983 to enforce both constitutional and federal statutory rights, but it did not specifically address whether regulations are enforceable.

Because the growth of [welfare benefits] programs led to an increasing number of beneficiaries and various social movements during the 1960s and 1970s, poor people became more willing to challenge the government and many beneficiaries began filing suits against states.... The fear that § 1983 suits often intrude on state governments and thus interfere with federalist concerns likely explains recent decisions, such as *Sandoval* and *Gonzaga*, that have restricted such suits.... In *Cort v. Ash*, a case involving an implied right of action and not a § 1983 suit, the Court stated that the existence of a federal substantive right depended upon whether the person claiming the right was "one of the class for whose *especial* benefit the statute was enacted." ... Under *Cort's* especial-benefit-of-a-particular-class test, a large number of regulations arguably could create individual federal rights.... For example, Congress and agencies intended Title VI regulations to especially benefit racial and ethnic minorities....

[T]he Court eventually began to define enforceable rights under § 1983 as mandatory obligations to provide specific benefits to a special class of persons.... To determine whether a federal statute establishes specific and individually enforceable federal rights, the Supreme Court in *Blessing v. Freestone* used a three-part test:

> First, Congress must have intended that the provision in question benefit the plaintiff. Second, the plaintiff must demonstrate that the right assertedly protected by the statute is not so "vague and amorphous" that its enforcement would strain judicial competence. Third, the statute must unambiguously impose a binding obligation on the States. In other words, the provision giving rise to the asserted right must be couched in mandatory, rather than precatory, terms....

Even when the plaintiff had asserted a federal right, however, the Supreme Court, in *Middlesex County Sewerage Authority v. National Sea Clammers Ass'n*, created an exception to *Thiboutot* by holding that a § 1983 suit based on a statutory right may not proceed if a defendant shows that Congress intentionally denied a remedy under § 1983, either expressly or impliedly, by providing a thorough enforcement scheme for the purpose of protecting a federal right.... The *Blessing* standard does not specifically address the role that regulations may play in defining statutory rights....

A key issue is whether the term "and laws" in § 1983 includes not only federal statutory rights but also "rights" contained in federal agency regulations.... *Chrysler Corp. v. Brown*, a 1979 decision that did not involve § 1983 ... held that

> regulations may have "the force and effect of law" if: (1) they are substantive rules affecting individual rights and obligations, and not merely interpretive rules or general policy statements; (2) Congress has granted "quasi-legislative" power to the agency; and (3) the agency has complied with applicable procedures such as the Administrative Procedure Act.

... Unfortunately the Court has never directly addressed whether Justice Stevens's analysis, that regulations having the force of law may establish rights enforceable through § 1983, is correct....

In *Wright v. City of Roanoke Redevelopment and Housing Authority*, the Supreme Court considered both specific Department of Housing and Urban Redevelopment (HUD) regulations and more general statutory language in holding that low-income tenants in a municipal housing project could bring a § 1983 action against Roanoke's public housing authority.... The plaintiffs argued that the Roanoke Housing Authority violated the Brooke Amendment by failing to include a reasonable amount for utility use in determining a tenant's rent, despite relevant HUD regulations defining the statutory term "rent" to include reasonable utility payments. Justice White's majority opinion ... agreed with the plaintiffs that courts should defer to HUD's interpretation of the definition of rent in the statute. The Court stated that the Brooke Amendment and relevant HUD regulations established enforceable rights under § 1983 ...

It is not clear whether the Court used the HUD regulations to just interpret the statutory language in the Brooke Amendment or relied on the regulations as providing additional rights beyond the statutory rights. To some extent, the Court may have viewed the regulations as helping to explicate the statutory rights Congress intended to provide to tenants such as the plaintiffs. The Court stated:

> The regulations ... defining the statutory concept of "rent" as including utilities, have the force of law.... In our view, the benefits Congress intended to confer on tenants are sufficiently specific and definite to qualify as enforceable rights under *Pennhurst* and § 1983, rights that are not, as respondent suggests, beyond the competence of the judiciary to enforce.

Additionally, in a footnote, the majority arguably implied that regulations alone may create rights enforceable through § 1983 provided that the governing statute delegates broad authority to the implementing agency to define rights implicit in the statute: "The dissent may have a different view, but to us it is clear that the regulations gave low-income tenants an enforceable right to a reasonable utility allowance and that the regulations were fully authorized by the statute." ...

There has been controversy over the meaning of *Wright* and especially over whether the Supreme Court indicated that a regulation alone could be enforceable through § 1983. Lower courts have disagreed over whether *Wright* implied that a regulation alone could be enforceable through § 1983. Based on a broad reading of *Thiboutot*'s reference to "laws" and of *Wright*'s use of HUD regulations to find a right to fair rent, both the Sixth and the District of Columbia Circuits have held that an agency regulation can create an individual federal right....

The Fourth Circuit, the Eleventh Circuit, the Third Circuit, and now the Ninth Circuit have narrowly interpreted *Wright* as enforcing only statutory rights and relying on the HUD regulations only to interpret statutory rights....

The Impact of Sandoval and Gonzaga: Congress Must Establish Enforceable Rights

Before the Supreme Court's *Gonzaga* decision, several decisions had allowed suits under § 1983 to vindicate federal statutory rights even when the underlying statute creating the right was not enforceable as a private right of action. The *Gonzaga* Court, however, concluded that individual rights enforceable through § 1983 and implied private rights of action are similar. "[W]e ... reject the notion that our implied right of action cases are separate and distinct from our § 1983 cases. To the contrary, our implied right of action cases should guide the determination of whether a statute confers rights enforceable under § 1983." ...

Although the *Gonzaga* decision has made the congressional intent test for implied rights of action the initial inquiry in § 1983 cases, it is still possible to enforce a federal statutory right through § 1983 even if that right cannot be enforced as a direct private right of action. Under the *Gonzaga* decision, for both suits asserting a private right of action and those proceeding under § 1983, a court first examines whether Congress intended, either expressly or by implication, to establish an individual federal right on behalf of a class including the plaintiff. After the initial *Gonzaga* inquiry about whether Congress intended to establish a federal right, however, there is a difference in determining whether the remedies are available under a private right of action and a § 1983 suit. Under a private right of action, a plaintiff must demonstrate not only that Congress intended to create a right on behalf of the plaintiff but also that Congress intended that plaintiffs have the right to sue to enforce that right. By contrast, in § 1983 cases, under the Supreme Court's three-part *Blessing* test, once a plaintiff shows that Congress intended to establish a right in favor of the plaintiff, there is a strong presumption that the plaintiff may enforce that right because § 1983 itself provides the remedy, unless the narrow *Sea Clammers* exception applies....

Because the Court held in *Sandoval* that only Congress can create implied rights of action, the *Gonzaga* decision's conclusion that only Congress may establish federal rights enforceable through § 1983 implies that a regulation alone may not create a right enforceable through § 1983. The *Gonzaga* Court stated that rights are enforceable by individuals through § 1983 only where there is "clear" and "unambiguous" evidence that Congress intended to establish an individual right. If an agency seeks to create a right in a regulation alone that is not at all in the underlying statute, then that right could not meet *Gonzaga*'s requirement that there must be "clear" and "unambiguous" evidence that Congress intended to establish an individual right.

Yet even after *Gonzaga*, a court might examine agency regulations that interpret statutory language or legislative history to understand whether Congress intended to create a statutory right. Because agencies are often involved in Congress's drafting of a statute that delegates authority to that agency, a court may find agency regulations useful in providing understanding of congressional intent. Although it demanded "clear" and "unambiguous" evidence in a statute that Congress intended to establish individually enforceable rights, the *Gonzaga* Court did not purport to overrule the Court's earlier *Wright* decision, which examined agency regulations in conjunction with a statute to help determine whether an enforceable right existed under § 1983, or the *Chevron* deference principle.

After Sandoval and Gonzaga: The First and Ninth Circuits Disagree About Whether Regulations Can Help Interpret Rights Enforceable Under § 1983

Because neither *Sandoval* nor *Gonzaga* clearly addressed the extent to which an agency's interpretation of statutory rights in regulations is entitled to deference, the lower courts have disagreed about that issue....

In *Save Our Valley*, the Ninth Circuit affirmed the district court's conclusion that the DOT regulations could not establish a right enforceable under § 1983 and, therefore, that the defendants were entitled to summary judgment. In light of both *Sandoval* and *Gonzaga*, the majority concluded that "agency regulations cannot independently create rights enforceable through § 1983." ... The Ninth Circuit concluded that *Sandoval*'s emphasis on the statute's text implied that "only Congress by statute can create a private right of action." ... Similarly, the majority concluded that *Gonzaga* "confirmed that individual rights enforceable through § 1983 and implied private rights of action are similar in respects relevant to this appeal." Quoting *Gonzaga*, the Ninth Circuit observed that in both private right of action cases and § 1983 cases, "courts are required to 'determine whether Congress intended to create a federal right.'" "Since only Congress can create implied rights of action" under *Sandoval*, the Ninth Circuit concluded that *Gonzaga* "suggests that only Congress can create rights enforceable through § 1983" because "rights enforceable through § 1983, no less than implied rights of action, are creatures of substantive federal law." The majority concluded that the *Gonzaga* decision strongly implied that "the Court's reasoning [in *Sandoval*] applie[d] equally to both kinds of rights" and that, "[l]ike substantive federal law itself, private rights of action to enforce federal law must be created by Congress." Accordingly, the Ninth Circuit held that enforceable rights "cannot be created by executive agencies." ...

Most recently, after the Supreme Court decided *Gonzaga*, the First Circuit, in *Rolland v. Romney*, relied on regulations in interpreting the scope of statutory rights. A class of developmentally disabled and mentally retarded residents living in Massachusetts nursing homes filed suit against the Commonwealth of Massachusetts in federal district court in 1998 ... alleging violations of a variety of federal statutes, including 42 U.S.C. § 1396r, a part of the Nursing Home Reform Amendments ("NHRA") to the Medicaid law. ... The First Circuit concluded that developmentally disabled and mentally retarded nursing home residents who were entitled to specialized services under the NHRA of the Medicaid law had a private right of action to enforce those rights in an action under § 1983, although federal Medicaid funding is not specifically conditioned upon the provision of specialized services, because the term "specialized services" is a specific right suitable to judicial enforcement and the NHRA unambiguously binds the states.

... The court concluded that the statute, when read as a whole and in light of the [Department of Health and Human Services] HHS regulations, demonstrated an intent to create rights on behalf of dual need patients ...

Examining the statute's structure, the First Circuit initially concluded that "although the NHRA does not specify states' obligations to provide specialized services to dual need residents, it does explicitly require states to provide specialized services to residents who do need them but who do *not* require nursing facility care." In light of the statute's overall structure, the First Circuit determined "[i]t is clear that the statute's intent in this regard was not to elevate those individuals with only the need for specialized services above those with dual needs, but rather to bring them up to par with the dual needs group." ...

The First Circuit next addressed whether the right to specialized services that both it and the HHS regulations found in the NHRA is enforceable under § 1983. In light of *Sandoval* and *Gonzaga*, the First Circuit observed that the crucial issue is whether Congress intended to create a private right for nursing home residents to receive specialized services. The First Circuit echoed the Supreme Court's statement in *Cannon v. University of Chicago* [441 U.S. 677 (1979)] by maintaining that the most crucial factor in determining whether Congress intended to create a cause of action is whether the statute contains "'right-or duty-creating language.'"

In determining whether the NHRA contains "right-or-duty-creating language," the First Circuit considered the HHS regulations. Quoting *Sandoval*, the First Circuit acknowledged that a regulation "'may not create a right that Congress has not.'" Even after *Sandoval*, however, the Eleventh Circuit had concluded that "regulations that merely interpret a statute may provide evidence of what private rights Congress intended to create." Citing *Wright*, which had in turn cited *Chevron*, the *Romney* court concluded that regulations that interpret what rights Congress intended to create in a statute are "entitled to some deference."

Reviewing the statute's language, its legislative history, and its interpretation by HHS, the First Circuit concluded that the NHRA contained "rights-creating" language that established an enforceable right under § 1983. The *Romney* court applied the three-part *Blessing* test to decide whether the statute's provision for "specialized services" created an enforceable right under § 1983. The Commonwealth had conceded that Congress intended the statute to benefit especially persons such as the residents and, therefore, that the NHRA met the first part of the *Blessing* test for an enforceable right.

Relying on *Gonzaga*, the Commonwealth contended, however, that the statute's reference to "specialized services" was too vague and amorphous to be judicially enforceable and, accordingly, did not meet the second *Blessing* prong. The First Circuit relied on the HHS definition of specialized services in determining that the NHRA's reference to "specialized services" was clear enough to be enforced under the second *Blessing* standard because Congress had expressly delegated authority to the HHS Secretary to define the term and the HHS regulations provided the necessary clarity.

> In the instant case, the NHRA expressly delegates authority to define "specialized services" and the Secretary has complied. The agency's definition, consistent with rights affirmed in prior case law, provides contextual guidance, and it is sufficient to allow residents to understand their rights to services, states to understand their obligations, and courts to review states' conduct in fulfilling those obligations. In complex areas such as this, more cannot reasonably be expected.

Finally, the First Circuit concluded that the NHRA unambiguously requires states to provide specialized services and, therefore, meets the third *Blessing* test.... The *Romney* court determined that the mandatory language in the NHRA made it enforceable under § 1983 and distinguished it from the discretionary right against disparate impact discrimination in the Title VI agency regulations that the *Sandoval* Court had found did not create a private right of action....

The First Circuit concluded that "[b]ecause we find that the right at issue is not vague and amorphous and that the NHRA unambiguously binds the states, we hold that the residents are endowed with a private right of action, which they may enforce via section 1983." The First Circuit had found that the statute and its legislative history at least implicitly indicated that Congress intended to establish a right to specialized services. Thus, the court found the right to these services in the statute itself and not the regulations. Where there were gaps in the statute regarding the definition of such services, however, the *Romney* court relied upon and deferred to the HHS regulations.

> In the complex field of care for mentally retarded individuals and the related regulation of nursing homes and states, however, Congress has made it clear that the Secretary is to fill in gaps and provide definition. The products of that delegation of authority, responding to widespread documented problems, provide an effective manner for care of mentally retarded nursing home residents and are entitled to deference.

Accordingly, the First Circuit, in *Romney*, used the agency's interpretation to help define the details of a right it had first found that Congress had intended to create in the statute itself....

The First Circuit in *Romney* appropriately considered the agency's interpretation in defining the scope of a statutory right.... The *Romney* decision illustrates the realities of modern administrative statutes in which Congress creates a general right and then delegates to an agency the task of filling in the often highly technical details of that right. If there is sufficient evidence in a statute and its legislative history that Congress intended to create a mandatory right on behalf of a defined group of beneficiaries, courts should enforce that right through § 1983 even if an agency has filled some gaps in the details of that right. That is ... consistent with the Supreme Court's approach in both *Sandoval* and *Gonzaga*.

* * *

Notes and Questions

1. Consider that advocates also may be able to press civil rights claims under state law. For example, California has a state law analogue to Title VI that prohibits discrimination in any "program or activity" that receives state funding, as well as by state agencies themselves (the latter provision is broader than Title VI, which does not directly apply to federal agencies). *See* CAL. GOV'T CODE § 11135. Implementing state regulations prohibit the carrying out of programs or activities that have a racially discriminatory impact, *see* CAL. CODE REGS. tit. 22, § 98101, and these regulations are enforceable in a private right of action. *See* CAL. GOV'T CODE § 11139; *see also* Blumhorst v. Jewish Family Servs. of Los Angeles, 126 Cal. App. 4th 993, 1002 (2005). In one recent case, a federal magistrate judge ruled that plaintiffs had a private right of action to enforce section 11135 in a case alleging that the Metropolitan Transportation Commission (in the San Francisco Bay Area) was allocating transportation funding among local agencies in a racially discriminatory manner. *See* Darensburg v. Metropolitan Transp. Comm'n (C-05-01597 EDL, N.D. Cal, Order dated Aug. 21, 2008).

2. One difficult set of questions concerns the application of Title VI of the Civil Rights Act of 1964 to American Indians. EPA has been wrestling with the related questions of whether tribes that receive financial assistance from EPA are subject to the requirements of Title VI, and whether individual members of tribes in Indian country are within the class of minority groups that are protected classes under Title VI. Professor Richard Monette argues that:

> These two questions illustrate the impossibly difficult, sometimes ironic, position of Indians in America. To put it bluntly, if Tribes answer "no" to the first question, their arguments will inevitably mirror the federalism arguments of Mississippi or Alabama fighting against federal civil rights for minorities within their borders. In other words, "Tribes' rights" will sound like "states' rights." The irony is that, in the larger scheme of things, tribal members are also minorities in America. Thus, if Tribes answer "yes" to the second question, their arguments will sound like those of the civil rights leaders who rose against Mississippi and Alabama. The irony here is, as sovereign entities, Tribes have civil rights complaints leveled against them, like any other government.... [These] questions force Tribes to choose between identifying as their own autonomous government, on the one hand, or as an aggregate racial group under another government's rule on the other.

Richard Monette, *Environmental Justice and Indian Tribes: The Double-Edged Tomahawk of Applying Civil Rights Laws in Indian Country*, 76 U. DET. MERCY L. REV. 721, 724–25 (1999). EPA's Draft Title VI Guidance issued in 2000 does not address the first question. As to the second issue, since EPA's Title VI implementing regulations define a "racial classification" to include an American Indian or Alaskan native, see 40 C.F.R. § 7.25, it appears that Native Americans may file Title VI complaints against states or off-reservation entities. How should Title VI be interpreted with respect to American Indians? For example, should a white citizen living in Indian country be able to assert a Title VI claim against a tribe as regulator for allegedly causing a disparate impact to white residents living within the reservation boundaries? Of what relevance is the fact that, historically, whites have not been subject to discrimination?

3. All things considered, if you had a situation that you thought might involve discrimination in environmental permitting, or other environmental disparities, would you

prefer to file an equal protection claim, a § 1983 claim, or an administrative complaint? What are the pros and cons of each legal strategy? Would you forego a federal claim altogether and attempt to find a redress under state antidiscrimination laws?

Index

AB 32 (California Global Warming Solutions Act of 2006), 428
abandoned waste facilities, 455
acequia, 471
adaptation to climate change, 390, 397, 432
Administrative Procedure Act, 142, 151, 371, 443, 450, 511
agency capture, 141, 142, 146
Agency for Toxic Substances Disease Registry (ATSDR), 306, 353
agriculture, 47, 80, 83, 305, 306, 329, 337, 353, 381, 390, 393–397, 399, 420
agrofuels (see biofuels), 417, 418
AIRFA, (see American Indian Religious Freedom Act), 479
air toxics exposures, 52, 53
Alien Tort Claims Act (ATCA), 323, 353
allowances, 232, 234, 245, 401, 402, 404, 421–427
alternatives analysis, 153, 370
American Indian Religious Freedom Act (AIRFA), 479
American Indians, (see Native Americans)
Anderson, Andy, 38, 39
Anderton, Douglas, 38, 39
Anton, Donald, 318
APA, (see Administrative Procedure Act), 151, 443
Appalachia, 471
apportionment, 17, 403
Arctic, 26, 390, 391, 394, 429, 430, 432, 467, 468
Army Corps of Engineers, 136, 270, 353, 468
Arnold, Craig (Tony), 77, 79, 93, 356, 358, 359

Arquette, Mary, 195
Ash, Michael, 52
asthma, 35, 64, 196, 197, 201–203, 217, 218, 220–222, 335–337, 348, 464, 466, 498, 501, 502
Atlas, Mark, 67, 277
Atomic Safety and Licensing Board, 84, 371
ATSDR, (see Agency for Toxic Substances Disease Registry), 306, 348, 353
aversive racist, 103

BACT, (see Best Available Control Technology under the Clean Air Act)
Bailey, Conner, 89
Baldwin Hills (Los Angeles), 64
Bali action plan, 403
Bandelier National Monument, 475
BAT, (see Clean Water Act), 223
Bear's Lodge, 479
Been, Vicki, 13, 17, 36, 40, 42, 89, 90, 91, 92, 93, 361, 365, 366
Bernard, Susan M., 46
Best Available Control Technology, (see Clean Air Act), 456
Best Available Technology, (see Clean Water Act)
Bhatia, Rajiv, 383
Binder, Denis, 6, 277, 332, 370
biofuels, 390, 417–421
    cellulosic biofuel, 420, 421
Blais, Lynn, 85, 88, 89, 366
Blumm, Michael, 131
Boerner, Christopher, 36, 45, 46, 233
Boyle, Edward Patrick, 491
Bradley, Jennifer L., 342, 384

Breyer, Stephen, 20, 186, 187, 208–210, 452, 507

Brisman, Avi, 493

Brooks, Nancy, 387

brownfields redevelopment, 285, 294, 303, 304, 306, 307, 309, 312–314, 316, 331, 355
  NEJAC subcommittee, 299, 342, 344
  Title VI challenges to brownfield redevelopment, 4, 314

Bryant, Bunyan, 5, 7, 36, 46, 47

buffer zone, 357, 359

Bullard, Robert, 5, 6, 8, 12, 19, 37, 45, 56, 58, 68, 70, 76, 84, 85, 87, 89, 91, 92, 95, 183, 372–375

Bureau of Indian Affairs (BIA), 110, 353

Burkett, Maxine, 399

Burton, Lloyd, 479

Bush, George W., 4 , 22, 25, 27, 165, 208, 221, 247, 328, 332, 337, 338, 401, 421, 499

Buzbee, William, 166, 316

Byrne, J. Peter, 316

California Air Resources Board (CARB), 428

California Environmental Justice Movement's Declaration on Use of Carbon Trading Schemes to Address Climate Change, 428

California Environmental Protection Agency (CAL/EPA), 338

California Environmental Quality Act (CEQA), 338, 367, 378, 440, 467

California Waste Management Board, 83

Callahan, Michael, 200

Camacho, Alejandro Esteban, 150

Cameron, Edwin, 429

cancer alley, 18, 26, 196

cap-and-trade, 232, 242, 243, 245, 246, 390, 402, 421, 422, 424–428

Cassell, Jennifer, 324

catalyst theory, 456

CBE, (see Communities for a Better Environment), 464–466

census tracts, 38, 40–45, 77, 78, 244, 284, 288, 483–487

CEQ, (see Council on Environmental Quality), 368–370, 375, 377

CEQA, (see California Environmental Quality Act), 367, 376, 378, 379

CERCLA, (see Comprehensive Environmental Response, Compensation, and Liability Act), 65, 66, 188, 257, 285–287, 290, 293, 294, 296–299, 301, 308, 454, 455

Cerrell Associates, 83

Cerrell Report, (see Cerrell Associates), 83, 84

Chaco Culture National Historical Park, 475

Chavis, Rev. Dr. Benjamin A., 29, 105, 106

Chemical Waste Management, 23, 87, 253, 437

Chicago (IL), 160, 295, 307–314, 399, 506, 514

children and risk assessment, 176

China, 389, 401, 404–407, 414–416

Chinatown, 79, 80, 377, 439

Chippewa, 132, 231

Chu, Flora, 49

Citizen suits, 100, 280, 287, 442, 443, 448, 453–459, 462, 469

City Project, 64, 75, 379, 438

civic republicanism, 146, 150

Clean Air Act, 53, 66, 99, 123, 126, 127, 158, 159, 168, 170, 177, 213, 215, 217, 219, 222, 223, 234, 243, 247, 250, 252, 259, 260, 278, 341, 368, 370, 423, 427, 443, 454–457, 467, 495
  BACT, (see Best Available Control Technology)
  Best Available Control Technology (BACT), 456
  Clean Air Mercury Rule (CAMR), 242
  hazardous air pollutants, 46, 53, 177, 215, 217
  LAER, (see Lowest Achievable Emissions Rate under Clean Air Act), 214
  Lowest Achievable Emissions Rate, 214
  NAAQS, (see national ambient air quality standards under Clean Air Act), 100, 215, 217, 220, 223, 454, 495
  national ambient air quality standards, 100, 214, 215, 217, 220, 223, 454, 495

new source review, 252, 424, 456
nonattainment, 201, 214, 219, 223, 250, 251, 426, 497, 504
prevention of significant deterioration, 100, 126, 495
State Implementation Plan (SIP), 217, 219, 454
Title V permit program, 456
Clean Air Mercury Rule (CAMR), (see Clean Air Act), 242
Clean development mechanism (CDM), 401
Clean Water Act, 66, 126, 128, 129, 132, 170–172, 213, 215, 223–225, 228–231, 251, 270, 271, 341, 368, 443, 449, 451, 453–457, 461
BAT (see Best Available Technology under Clean Water Act)
Best Available Technology (BAT), 223, 456
National Pollution Elimination Discharge System (NPDES), 228
total maximum daily load (TMDL), 224
water quality standards, 50, 119, 128, 129, 131, 132, 134, 171, 192, 194, 215, 216, 224–232
cleanup process, (see Comprehensive Environmental Response, Compensation, and Liability Act), 290, 303, 459, 460
climate change, 5, 25–27, 58, 165, 233, 337, 338, 360, 389–432
co-pollutants, 240, 423–427
dangerous human interference, 391
disproportionate impacts of climate change, 58, 392, 400
Clinton, Bill, 4, 7, 20, 190, 253, 277, 287, 331, 332, 338, 369, 370, 479
Cole, Brian, 380
Cole, Luke, 3, 5, 36, 82, 84, 88, 97, 101, 102, 435, 437, 440, 497
collaborative governance, 139, 146, 147, 149, 150, 282
collaborative process, 149, 282, 345, 350, 351
Collin, Robert, 75, 79, 460, 461, 480, 489
Collin, Robin Morris, 75, 79, 460, 461, 480, 489

colonias, 261, 262, 266
Columbia River Inter-Tribal Fish Commission, 50, 194, 206
command and control, 140, 232, 233, 236
Commission for Racial Justice, (see United Church of Christ Commission for Racial Justice), 3, 37
common law claims, 4, 324, 433, 462, 463
public nuisance, 264, 265, 455, 463, 465–467, 469
Communities for a Better Environment (CBE), 241, 464
community-based participatory research (CBPR), 200
Community Benefits Agreement, 96, 97, 458
community involvement, 17, 150, 240, 269, 270, 282, 314, 315, 349, 439, 460
commutative justice, 11
comparative risk assessment, 176, 208–210
compensated siting, 15, 356, 361, 363–365
compensatory justice, 11, 15
Comprehensive Environmental Response, Compensation, and Liability Act, 65, 188, 257, 285, 454
cleanup process, 290, 303, 459, 460
institutional controls, (see clean-up under Comprehensive Environmental Response, Compensation, and Liability Act), 204, 205, 298, 302–308, 316
risk-based cleanups, 187, 302, 303
use-restricted cleanups, 204, 302, 306
hazard ranking, 257, 286
National Contingency Plan, 286
National Priorities List, 271, 286, 335, 459
Superfund, 4, 18, 20, 65–67, 167, 187, 188, 285–288, 290–293, 296, 299, 300, 305, 306, 308, 316, 368, 454, 459, 460, 501
Treatment, Storage and Disposal Facility (TSDF), 87
TSDF, (see Treatment, Storage and Disposal Facility under Comprehensive Environmental Response Compensation and Liability Act), 37–45, 94

comprehensive plan, 356, 357
Congressional Black Caucus Foundation, 398
Congressional oversight of EPA, 142
contaminated fish, 49, 136, 179, 225
continuous emissions monitoring, 422, 495, 496
Contraction and Convergence, 417
cooperation-based enforcement, 273, 274
cooperative federalism model, 126, 165, 170
Corburn, Jason, 203, 238
Cordova, Robert, 400
Cornfield (Los Angeles), 64
corrective justice, 6, 11, 12, 22, 360, 404, 405, 407–410, 462
cost-benefit, 57, 113, 152–159, 161, 163, 177, 186, 192, 210, 218, 307
Council on Environmental Quality (CEQ), 328, 368, 369
Covello, Vincent, 210
Coyle, Marcia, 65
Cranor, Carl, 176, 191
critical race theory, 31, 33
CRJ, (see United Church of Christ Commission for Racial Justice), 3, 37
cumulative impact, 9, 259, 265, 270, 376
cumulative risk assessment, 53, 176, 181, 189, 195, 197, 199, 200, 250
    multiple stressors, 175, 196, 197, 199
Cusick, Daniel, 223
Cutter, Susan L., 58, 92

Dannenberg, Andrew L., 383
Dayall, Joseph W., 365
deterrence-based enforcement, 273–275
Detroit (MI), 49, 75, 201–203, 207, 314, 399
Development threshold, 413–415
Devil's Tower, 475–479
devolution, 165, 170–173, 346
Diaz, Antonio, 79
disaster vulnerability, 56, 58
discounting lives, 156–157, 307
discriminatory siting, 87, 94, 365, 375
disproportionate siting, 13, 16, 41, 42, 81, 82, 90–94, 300
distance-based methods, 44, 45, 55

distributive justice, 6, 8, 9, 11, 12, 22, 29, 158, 238, 319, 360, 404–406, 409, 423
dominative racist, 103
Driesen, David, 159, 232, 401
Durham-Hammer, Kathryn, 386, 387

EAB, (see Environmental Appeals Board), 250, 252, 253, 258, 259, 496
East Bay Regional Park District, 64
ECHO, (see Enforcement and Compliance History Online), 456
economic incentive programs, 232
Edelstein, Michael, 380
EIR, (see Environmental Impact Report), 367, 378, 382, 437
EIS, (see Environmental Impact Statement), 112, 151, 366, 370, 371, 447, 472
Eisen, Joel, 294, 295, 299, 301, 315, 316, 365
EJSEAT, (see Environmental Justice Smart Enforcement Assessment Tool), 277, 283, 284
El Pueblo para el Aire y Agua Limpio, 10, 367
Emelle (AL), 39, 87, 88
Emergency Planning and Community Right-to-Know Act (EPCRA), 383, 386, 448
emission reduction credits, 234, 239, 241, 376, 401, 402
emission standard, 454
empirical evidence, 35, 36, 47, 69, 70, 85, 92, 148, 386, 387
EMS, (see environmental management systems), 276
Endangered Species Act (ESA), 112, 113, 117, 136, 444, 457
enforcement, 4, 5, 7, 24, 25, 35, 65–67, 74, 75, 86, 90, 99, 100, 126, 130, 148, 167, 170, 173, 193, 249–285, 287, 290, 304, 305, 314, 315, 317, 321, 325, 327, 329, 336–339, 387, 433–469, 492, 507, 511, 514
Enforcement and Compliance History Online (ECHO), 456
Environmental Appeals Board (EAB), 250, 252, 253, 258, 259, 496

environmental assessment, 366, 368, 369, 376, 382

Environmental Defense (formerly Environmental Defense Fund), 22

Environmental Defense Fund, (see Environmental Defense), 22

Environmental Equity: Reducing Risk for All Communities (report), 46

environmental federalism, 126, 127, 129, 165, 167, 170, 316, 341–343

Environmental Impact Report (EIR), 367, 378, 382, 437

Environmental Impact Statement (EIS), 112, 151, 366, 371, 447, 472

Environmental Justice Mapper, 387

Environmental Justice Resource Center, 6

Environmental Justice Smart Enforcement Assessment Tool (EJSEAT), 277, 283, 284

Environmental Justice Strategic Plan, 336, 337

environmental justice strategy, 94, 277, 329, 331, 335, 336, 340, 358

environmental management systems, 276

Environmental Protection Agency
 Final Guidance for Consideration of Environmental Justice in Clean Air Act 309 Reviews, 370
 Final Guidance for Incorporating Environmental Justice Concerns in EPA's NEPA Compliance Analyses, 370
 Office of Civil Rights, 497
 Office of Enforcement and Compliance Assurance (OECA), 283
 Office of Environmental Justice, 4, 6, 7, 95, 328, 346

environmental racism, 3, 7, 20, 21, 23, 29, 30, 32, 62, 85–87, 105, 366

EPCRA, (see Emergency Planning and Community Right-to-Know Act), 383, 386, 387, 448

Equal Protection Clause, 4, 16, 30, 334, 471, 480–482, 488, 489, 491, 492

equity assessment, 12

ESA, (see Endangered Species Act), 112, 113, 117, 136, 444, 457

Establishment Clause, 230, 471, 472, 474, 476–478

ethanol, 417, 418, 420

European Union, 382, 402, 407, 415, 417, 418

European Union Emissions Trading Scheme (EU ETS), 402

Evans, Jill E., 481

exaction, 359

exclusionary zoning, 73, 75–77, 79

Executive Order 12,898, (see Executive Order on Environmental Justice), 4, 9, 252, 277, 328, 330, 332, 369, 371, 377

Executive Order 13,007, 108, 479

Executive Order 13,045, 190

Executive Order 13,175, 134

Executive Order on Environmental Justice (Executive Order 12,898), 4, 9, 222, 252, 277, 328, 330, 332, 369–372, 377
 interpretation of, 252, 258

expulsive zoning, 73–79, 83, 93

FACA, (see Federal Advisory Committee Act), 493

Fair Environmental Protection Act, 19

fair share ordinance, 360

fairness as process theory, 16

farmworker exposure to pesticides, 47

Faroes Statement, The, 190, 191

Farrell, Alexander, 420

Faupel, Charles E., 89

Federal Advisory Committee Act (FACA), 184, 493

Federal Insecticide, Fungicide and Rodenticide Act (FIFRA), 216, 462

feedback loop, 391

Feldman, David, 21

Ferris, Deeohn, 459, 460

Fetter, T. Robert, 52

FIFRA, (see Federal Insecticide, Fungicide and Rodenticide Act), 216, 462

Fifty State Survey, 282, 338, 339

First National People of Color Environmental Leadership Summit, 4, 24

fish consumption, 49, 185, 193–195, 204, 207, 208, 225, 228, 330, 370
 advisories, 50, 193, 194, 204–208, 224, 225, 293, 305
 suppression effects, 192, 193

Flåm, Karoline HÆgstad, 398

Fleder, Anna, 231
Fletcher, Matthew, 119, 137
Flint (MI), 259–261, 266, 497
Flynn, James, 210
FOE, (see Friends of the Earth), 22, 27, 444, 448, 449
Food Quality Protection Act, 190, 197
food security, 317, 393, 395, 413, 418
Foreman, Christopher, 5, 17, 21
Fort, Denise, 231
Foster, Sheila, 3, 12, 29, 82, 88, 102, 172, 346, 351, 360, 375–377, 442
Freedom Riders, 58
Freeman, Jody, 146, 149, 150
Friedman-Jiménez, George, 48
Friends of the Earth (FOE), 22, 27, 444, 448, 449
functional equivalence doctrine, (see National Environmental Policy Act)

Garcia, Robert, 64, 224
Gauna, Eileen, 144, 149, 150, 258, 453, 456–460, 498, 499
General Accounting Office (see Government Accountability Office), 3, 37, 91, 274
Genesee Power Station, 89, 259, 496
gentrification, 79, 81, 299, 308, 312, 313, 316
geographic concentric rings, 67
Gerrard, Michael, 6, 108, 109, 176, 270, 285, 294, 332, 341, 358–360, 365, 368, 433, 440, 442, 443, 462, 479, 480, 493, 499
global warming, 26, 27, 209, 389–392, 394–396, 398–400, 408, 409, 412, 417, 428, 430, 431, 467–469
Golden Gate University Environmental Law and Justice Clinic, 336, 435
Goldtooth, Tom, 27
Gonzales, Carmen, 328
good neighbor agreement, 385, 458
Gorovitz Robinson, Heidi, 298
Government Accountability Office (formerly General Accounting Office), 37, 132, 223, 274, 305, 468
Grant, Jill Elise, 132
green collar, 428

Greenhouse Rights Development (GDR), 412
Grijalva, James, 108, 118–120, 126, 131, 132, 458
Grodsky, Jamie, 184
Grossman, Peter Z., 417
Group of Ten, 23, 24
Gundlach, James H., 89
Guzy, Gary, 252

Hamilton, James, 67, 81, 188, 189, 200
Harper, Barbara, 193–195, 227
Harris, Stuart, 195, 227, 482
Hastings Public Law Research Institute, 339
hazard ranking, (see Comprehensive Environmental Response, Compensation, and Liability Act), 257, 286
hazardous air pollutants, (see Clean Air Act), 46, 53, 177, 215, 217
hazardous waste facilities, 3, 35–40, 42, 44, 46, 52, 79, 94, 168, 170, 363–366, 455
hazardous waste siting process, 76
health-based standard, 224, 495, 497
health impact assessment (HIAs), 380–382
Healthy Places Act, 383
Hecker, Jim, 456
Heinzerling, Lisa, 155, 157, 158, 247
Helland, Eric, 283
HIA, (see health impact assessment), 380, 381, 382
Hill, Kathleen, 125, 36, 64, 125, 142, 306, 307, 320
Hoerner, J. Andrew, 398
Hoidal, Sten-Erik, 480
Hornstein, Donald, 209
hot spots, 100, 213, 234, 235, 237, 238, 245, 349, 423, 424, 426, 498
Hsu, Shi-Ling, 158, 159
Huang, Peter, 210
Humphrey, Timothy J., Sr., 342
Huntington Park (Los Angeles), 463
Hurricane Katrina, 56–58, 68–70, 306, 391

ICMA, (see International City/County Management Association), 349, 353
IEN, (see Indigenous Environmental Network), 27, 108

India, 27, 383, 389, 401, 404, 405, 407, 414–416
Indigenous Environmental Network (IEN), 27, 108
information disclosure, 147, 235, 236, 355, 383, 386–388
injury in fact, 280, 444, 445, 448, 450, 452, 453
institutional controls, (see clean-up under Comprehensive Environmental Response, Compensation, and Liability Act), 204, 205, 298, 302–308, 316
institutional racism, 48, 102
Integrated Federal Interagency Environmental Justice Action Agenda, 346
intentional discrimination theory, 16
Interagency Working Group on Environmental Justice, 328, 329, 346
interest representation, 145–147, 152, 164
Intergovernmental Panel on Climate Change (IPCC), 26, 390
International City/County Management Association (ICMA), 349, 353
Inuit, 429–431
Inuit Circumpolar Conference, (see Inuit), 429
Isleta Pueblo, 129–132, 228–231, 341
Izaak Walton League, 22

Jesdale, Bill M., 54
Johnson, Stephen, 233, 236, 237, 367–369

Kahan, Dan, 210
Kang, Helen, 435
Karkkainen, Bradley, 384–387
Karmel, Philip, 306
Kaswan, Alice, 423, 427, 480, 487, 489, 490
Kettleman City (CA), 10, 367, 437–439
Kibel, Paul, 64
Klass, Alexandra B., 463
Kuehn, Robert R., 6, 21, 67, 89, 180, 181, 184, 195, 210, 271–273, 360, 441, 442, 460
Kump, Lee R., 412
Kyoto Protocol, 26, 27, 390, 401–403

LA CAUSA (Los Angeles Comunidades Asembleadas y Unidas para un Sostenible Ambiente), 464–466

La Londe, Kyle W., 493
LAER, (see Clean Air Act), 214
Lai, Zenobia, 80, 440, 80, 440
Lambert, Thomas, 45, 46, 233
land use regulation, 75, 77, 165, 356, 358
LaVelle, John P., 110, 350
Lavelle, Marianne, 65
Lavine, Amy, 97, 458
Lazarus, Richard, 99, 101, 106, 140, 143, 215, 217, 250, 252, 253, 278
leachate, 267
lead poisoning, 35, 46, 157, 197, 335, 463
Lee, Charles, 35, 346
Leong, Andrew, 80, 440
less developed countries, 84
Lewis, David Rich, 340
Lewis, Sanford, 458
Lincoln, Paul, 294, 382
locally unwanted land use (LULU), 99, 356
longitudinal analysis, 36, 40
Los Angeles Communities Assembled and United for a Sustainable Environment (see LA CAUSA), 464–466
Love, Dennis, 469
Lowest Achievable Emissions Rate, (see Clean Air Act)
LULU, (see locally unwanted land use), 13, 40, 44, 76, 81, 99, 356, 490

Macey, Gregg, 434
Macon-Bibb County Planning and Zoning Commission, 59, 487
Mandelker, Daniel, 366, 368, 380
Mank, Bradford, 332, 338, 352, 365, 493, 499, 509, 510
Mann, Michael E., 412
Manning, Elizabeth, 475, 478
market forces, 73, 81, 82, 85, 88, 91, 92, 106
Massachusetts Hazardous Waste Siting Facility Act, 363
McGeehin, Michael A, 46
McGinley, Patrick C., 101
Mennis, Jeremy L., 67
meta analysis, 55
methodological questions, 487
Miller, Jeffrey, 27, 457
Mission District (San Francisco), 79

Mohai, Paul, 5, 36, 39, 42, 43, 45–47, 81, 93
Monette, Richard, 516
Moore, Curtis, 217, 218
Moore, Richard, 27
mootness, 451, 452
Morello-Frosch, Rachel, 52–54, 56, 68
Moses, Robert, 65
Mother Earth, 24, 25, 118, 192, 218, 219
Mullikin, Thomas, 457
multivariate analysis, 41
Myhrum, Christopher B., 365

Nash, Jonathan, 242
National Academy of Public Administration (NAPA), 360
National Academy of Sciences (NAS), 178, 181, 182
national ambient air quality standards (NAAQS), (see Clean Air Act), 100, 214, 215, 217, 220, 223, 454, 495
National Audubon Society, 22
National Conference of Black Mayors, 223
National Contingency Plan, (see Comprehensive Environmental Response, Compensation, and Liability Act), 286
National Environmental Justice Advisory Council (NEJAC), 4, 17, 49, 184, 185, 197, 207, 299, 328, 353
National Environmental Policy Act (NEPA), 135, 150, 331, 353, 355, 366, 369, 443
    functional equivalence doctrine, 368
    Guidance under the National Environmental Policy Act, 369
    social and economic impacts, 367, 372, 374, 375, 377, 378
National Historic Preservation Act, 135, 479
National Institute of Environmental Health Sciences (NIEHS), 353
National Law Journal, 4, 65, 271, 273, 442
National Policy Consensus Center (NPCC), 282
National Pollution Elimination Discharge System (NPDES), (see Clean Water Act), 228
National Priorities List, (see Comprehensive Environmental Response, Com-

pensation, and Liability Act), 271, 286, 459
National Research Council, 176–178, 180, 189
National Wildlife Federation, 22, 23, 444, 450
Native American Graves Protection and Repatriation Act (NAGPRA), 479
Native Americans, 3, 12, 32, 35, 50, 95, 110, 129, 187, 198, 213, 226, 243, 244, 246, 340, 350, 471, 474, 478, 516
    Establishment Clause, 230, 471, 472, 474, 476–478
    Free Exercise Clause, 471–473, 479
    sacred sites, 108, 134, 138, 471–473, 475, 479
    self-determination, 9, 24, 25, 28, 31, 32, 109, 110, 120, 121, 124–126, 128, 129, 132, 185, 192, 324, 342, 344, 436
    treaties with the United States, 109
    treatment in the same manner as a state (TAS), 126, 128
    tribal sovereignty, 80, 109, 110, 118, 120, 124, 125, 127–130, 132, 133, 136, 231, 342
    trust doctrine, 109, 120, 478
Natural Resources Defense Council (NRDC), 22, 148
Negotiated Rulemaking Act, 151
negotiation, 96, 97, 140, 150–152, 219, 282, 363, 365
NEJAC, (see National Environmental Justice Advisory Council), 4, 17, 49, 184, 185, 197, 207, 299, 328, 353
NEPA, (see National Environmental Policy Act), 135, 150, 331, 353, 355, 366, 369, 443
New Orleans, 56–58, 69, 196, 305, 306
NIMBY, (see not in my back yard)
noncompliance with environmental laws, 272
North American Free Trade Agreement (NAFTA), 320, 353
Northridge, Mary, 201, 464
not in my back yard (NIMBY), 20, 42, 76, 77, 98, 99, 124, 167, 168, 169, 249, 332, 387, 489, 500

NPDES (National Pollution Elimination Discharge System), (see Clean Water Act), 228

NRDC, (see Natural Resources Defense Council), 22

Nuclear Regulatory Commission (NRC), 84, 371

O'Brien, Mary, 189, 190

O'Neill, Catherine A., 136, 137, 179, 187, 204, 207, 208, 225–227, 242, 245–247, 305–307

Obama Administration, 247, 337, 421, 500

Occupational Safety and Health Act (OSHA), 47

Office of Civil Rights, (see Environmental Protection Agency), 492, 494, 497, 504

Office of Enforcement and Compliance Assurance, (see Environmental Protection Agency)

Office of Environmental Justice, (see Environmental Protection Agency), 4, 6, 7, 95, 328, 346

Office of Inspector General (OIG), 172

Office of Management and Budget (OMB), 140, 153, 189, 329

OMB, (see Office of Management and Budget)

Oregon Department of Environmental Quality (ODEQ), 227

Osofsky, Hari M., 327, 431

Pace, David, 54

parathion, 48

parkland (see parks), 61, 62, 64

parks, 8, 22, 35, 58, 61–64, 100, 358, 380, 458, 478

particulate matter, 196, 201, 217, 219, 221, 283, 464, 501, 502

Pastor, Manuel, 36, 52, 56, 68, 92, 94

Pathfinders

American Indians and Environmental Justice, 108

Brownfields and Environmental Justice, 294

Economic Incentives, 232

Environmental Justice Generally, 5

Equal Protection and Environmental Justice, 480

NEPA, 368

Race and Income Disparities, 36

Risk Assessment, 176

Title VI and Environmental Justice, 493

Pendergrass, John, 306

People of Color Environmental Groups Directory, 6

Pepper, Edith, 315

performance standard, 346, 424

pesticides, 46–48, 126, 127, 140, 141, 185, 196, 205, 216, 288, 335, 463

Peter, Ellen M., 338

PIBBY, (see place in Blacks' back yards), 76

place in Blacks' back yards (PIBBY), 76

planning laws, 355

Plater, Zigmund, 355

pluralism, 145, 150, 478, 479

Poirier, Marc R., 65

Poisner, Jonathan, 150

pollution credits, 234, 235, 238–241, 425

population risk indices, 53

positivism, 161

Posner, Richard, 233, 236, 404, 409, 411, 412

post siting changes, 89

potentially responsible party, 454

powell, john a., 316

pragmatism, 161, 163

Prakesh, Swati, 201

preemption, 76, 81, 165–170, 361

prevention of significant deterioration, (see Clean Air Act), 100, 126, 495

Principles of Environmental Justice, 4, 8, 9, 11, 22, 24, 25, 32, 183, 322, 360, 371, 433

private preferences, 86, 145

private rights of action, 493, 506, 508, 510, 512–514

procedural justice, 6, 9–11, 21, 22, 133, 136, 259, 360

progressive siting, 15, 17

Proposition 65, 388

Proposition K (Los Angeles), 63

Pulido, Laura, 36

quantitative risk assessment, 175–181, 183, 186, 192, 200, 208, 227

uncertainty, 5, 143, 147, 155, 161,
    179, 180, 186, 187, 189, 218, 268,
    269, 295, 296, 381, 509
variability, 179, 180, 182, 184, 186,
    187, 202, 226, 245, 393

Rabin, Yale, 73, 77, 83, 93
race neutral, 83, 88
race-to-the-bottom, 168
racial discrimination, 29, 41, 73, 84, 88,
    90, 92, 102, 103, 328, 368, 375, 448,
    482, 484, 485, 490, 508
racializing environmental justice, 28, 31
Ramo, Alan, 21
Ranco, Darren, 127, 132, 133, 231
Rascoff, Samuel, 159, 160
RCRA, (see Resource Conservation and Re-
    covery Act), 11, 76, 170, 253, 368, 455
Rechtschaffen, Clifford, 386, 388, 463, 464
RECLAIM, (see Regional Clean Air In-
    centives Market), 239
Regional Clean Air Incentives Market
    (RECLAIM), 239
regulatory impact analysis, 153, 162, 163,
    244
Reich, Peter, 253, 480, 490
Religious Freedom Restoration Act, 479
republicanism, 146, 150
Resource Conservation and Recovery Act
    (RCRA), 11, 76, 170, 253, 368, 455
Responsibility Capacity Index (RCI), 415
restorative justice, 11
retributive justice, 11
Revesz, Richard, 159, 160, 242
Rhode Island Attorney General, 463
Right to Environment, 25, 319, 321–323,
    429
Right to Food, 24, 418, 419
Ringquist, Evan J., 51, 52, 55, 66, 67
risk avoidance, 7, 176, 204–208, 222, 302,
    306
risk-based cleanups, (see clean-up under
    Comprehensive Environmental Re-
    sponse, Compensation, and Liability
    Act), 187, 302, 303
risk management, 20, 176, 177, 181, 183,
    185, 189, 192, 199, 211, 397
risk-risk analysis (also risk-tradeoff analy-
    sis or health-health analysis), 159

Risk-Screening Environmental Indicators
    (RSEI), 283
Roberts, J. Timmons, 461
Robinson, Nia, 398
Rodgers, William H., Jr., 108, 125, 132, 341
Rodríguez, Sylvia, 80
Royster, Judith, 108, 109, 131, 341, 479
Ruppert, David, 479
Russell, Irma, 440, 494

sacred sites, (see Native Americans), 108,
    134, 138, 471, 472, 479
Sadd, James, 52, 92, 94, 95
SADRI, (see Social and Demographic Re-
    search Institute of the University of
    Massachusetts), 37, 39, 40, 44
Safe Drinking Water Act (SDWA), 66,
    229, 286, 457
Safe Drinking Water and Toxic Enforce-
    ment Act of 1986, (see Proposition
    65), 388
Sagoff, Mark, 158
Saha, Robin, 36, 42, 43, 45, 55, 81, 93
Salay, Rebecca, 382
Salkin, Patricia, 97, 359, 458
San Francisco Department of Public
    Health, 382
SCAQMD, (see South Coast Air Quality
    Management District), 238, 239, 241,
    465, 466
Sechena, Ruth, 50
second generation environmental law, 172
Section 1983 (42 U.S.C. § 1983), 485, 493,
    500, 505, 508–515, 517
Select Steel case, 495
Selmi, Michael, 368, 490
SEP, (see supplemental environmental
    project), 277–279, 281, 282, 339, 457
SEPAs, (see State Environmental Policy
    Acts), 366–368, 377
Sethi, Rajiv, 387
Seward, Timothy C., 341
Sexton, Ken, 197, 200
Shanahan, Alice M., 493
Shapiro, Sidney, 161, 164, 189
Shelton, Dinah, 317–320
Shepard, Peggy, 200, 201
Sierra Club, 22, 118, 444, 445, 450
Singel, Winona, 137

SIP, (see State Implementation Plan), 217, 219, 454
SkjÆrseth, Jon Birger, 398
Slovic, Paul, 210
Small Island Developing States (SIDs), 429
small islands, 394
Smith, Nancy, 443, 457, 475, 478, 502
Social and Demographic Research Institute of the University of Massachusetts (SADRI), 37
social capital, 43, 73, 89, 93–97, 196, 198, 351, 377
social justice, 6, 12, 13, 18, 22, 27, 31, 82, 88, 94–97, 101, 183, 196, 221, 264, 314, 320, 360, 458
social vulnerability, 57, 58, 94, 199
South Central Los Angeles, 83, 95
South Coast Air Quality Management District (SCAQMD), 206, 238, 465
Southwest Network for Environmental and Economic Justice (SNEEJ), 27
Spencer, Marguerite, 316
Standard Metropolitan Statistical Areas, 38
standing to sue, 443, 444, 446, 448, 477
state and local governments, 5, 144, 167, 170, 307, 338, 345, 360, 383
state environmental justice laws, 101, 265, 300
State Environmental Policy Acts (SEPA), 366, 368, 381
State Implementation Plan (SIP), (see Clean Air Act), 217, 219, 454
Stavins, Robert, 232, 237
Steinzor, Rena, 150, 170, 172, 192, 218, 219, 221, 222, 247, 287, 289–291
Stover, Gabriel, 201
Strategic Lawsuit Against Public Participation (SLAPP), 442
Suagee, Dean, 107, 108, 118–120, 133, 231, 340–342, 344
Subra, Wilma, 196
Summers, Lawrence, 84, 85, 395, 452
Sum-Ping, Joanne, 440
Sunstein, Cass, 153, 158, 186, 210, 404, 409, 411, 412, 448
Superfund, (see Comprehensive Environmental Response, Compensation, and Liability Act), 4, 18, 20, 65–67, 167, 187, 188, 285–288, 290–293, 296, 299, 300, 305, 306, 308, 316, 368, 454, 459, 460, 501
supplemental environmental project (SEP), 277–279, 281, 282, 339, 457
Susskind, Lawrence, 434
Swanston, Samara, 64, 65
Swift, Byron, 237, 238, 245
synergistic environmental risk, 181, 182, 195, 216, 242, 316, 453

TAG, (see Technical Assistance Grant), 148, 235, 236, 287, 291, 459
Takings Clause, 359
Tal, Alon, 196
Targ, Nicholas, 95, 96, 320
Technical Assistance Grant (TAG), 148, 235, 236, 287, 291, 459
technology based standards, 424
technology forcing, 214, 232
Tierney, Kathleen, 69, 70
TIP, (see Tribal Implementation Plan), 132, 217
Title VI of the Civil Rights Act of 1964, 4, 331, 471, 481, 492, 506, 509, 510, 516
    administrative complaint procedure, 500
    administrative complaints under, 500
    enforcement of Title VI, 4, 11, 61, 267, 268, 269, 331, 338, 433, 441, 481, 486, 492, 493, 495, 497–501, 503–509, 511, 516
    Implementation Advisory Committee, 493
    Interim Guidance for Investigating Title VI Administrative Complaints challenging permits, 492
    private rights of action, 493, 506, 508, 510, 512–514
    Section 601, 492, 493, 506, 509
    Section 602, 492–494, 500, 502, 505–507, 509, 510
Toffolon-Weiss, Melissa, 461
total maximum daily load (TMDL), (see Clean Water Act), 224
toxic tort, 353, 461, 469
Toxic Wastes and Race in the United States, 37
Toxics Release Inventory (TRI), 51, 383
    distribution of TRI facilities, 51

Treatment, Storage and Disposal Facility (TSDF), (see Comprehensive Environmental Response, Compensation, and Liability Act), 87

Tribal Implementation Plan (TIP), 132, 217

tribal sovereignty, (see Native Americans), 80, 109, 110, 118, 120, 124, 125, 127–130, 132, 133, 136, 231, 342

TSDF, (see Treatment, Storage and Disposal Facility), 37–45, 94

Tsosie, Rebecca, 118, 120, 125, 126, 137, 432

Tulane Environmental Law Clinic, 441

unconscious racism, 48, 102–105

unit of analysis, 35, 36, 39, 40, 43

unit-hazard coincidence method, 43–45

United Church of Christ Commission for Racial Justice, 3, 37

United Nations Convention on Genocide, 25

United Nations Declaration on the Rights of Indigenous Peoples, 324

United Nations Development Programme, 394

United Nations Food and Agriculture Organisation, 420

United Nations Framework Convention on Climate Change (UNFCCC), 400

United Nations Intergovernmental Panel on Climate Change (IPCC), 26

United States
  Department of Agriculture, 329, 353
  Department of Defense, 329, 353
  Department of Energy, 329, 353, 468
  Department of Health and Human Services, 329, 514
  Department of Housing and Urban Development, 329, 332, 353, 500
  Department of Interior, 139, 329, 330, 332, 353, 444, 500
  Department of Transportation, 136, 139, 329, 332, 353, 370, 464, 500, 506

Universal Declaration on Human Rights, 25, 318, 430

urban decay, 377–379

urban renewal, 73–75, 79, 80, 299

use-restricted cleanups, (see clean-ups under Comprehensive Environmental Response, Compensation, and Liability Act), 204, 302, 306

utilitarianism, 144, 150

Verchick, Robert, 33

Victor, David, 402

Villa, Clifford, 290

Village of Kivalina, 432, 467–469

Viscusi, Kip, 67, 188, 189, 200

voluntary programs, 294, 295, 297, 298, 300, 304, 314–316, 365

Wagner, Wendy, 178

Walker, Jana, 108, 342

Wara, Michael, 402

Warren County (NC), 37, 64, 440

water quality standards, (see Clean Water Act), 128, 129, 131, 132, 171, 215, 216, 224–231

Waye, Andrea, 64

Weinberg, Philip, 480

Welcker, Zachary, 341

West Dallas Coalition for Environmental Justice, 434

wetlands, 185, 231, 267, 270, 289

White, Aubrey, 64,

Wilderness Act, 116, 117

Wilkinson, Charles, 110, 341

Williams, Edith M., 65

Williams, Patrick, 388

Williams, Robert A., Jr., 111, 117, 118, 120, 132, 345

willingness to pay, 92, 156, 233, 236

Wood, Mary Christina, 120, 341

workplace exposures, 388

workplace risks, 48

World Bank, 84, 85, 369, 416, 420

Wright, Beverly, 56, 68, 223

wrongdoer identity, 407, 412

Wu, Chi Chi, 80, 440

Yang, Tseming, 5, 325–328, 462, 491

Yupiks of Gambell, 49

Zoglin, Katie J., 463

zoning, 29, 73–81, 83, 84, 90, 93, 102, 259–261, 268, 270, 302–305, 316, 355–360, 363, 434, 487, 488